Date	Chapter
	2
	4
	3
	5
15	7
22	6
29	8
NOV 5	9
12	10
19	11
DEC 3	12

ANTHOLOGY OF WORLD SCRIPTURES

SIXTH EDITION

ANTHOLOGY OF WORLD SCRIPTURES

ROBERT E. VAN VOORST

Western Theological Seminary
Holland, Michigan

THOMSON
WADSWORTH

AUSTRALIA • BRAZIL • CANADA • MEXICO • SINGAPORE
SPAIN • UNITED KINGDOM • UNITED STATES

THOMSON
✦
WADSWORTH

Anthology of World Scriptures, **Sixth Edition**
Robert E. Van Voorst

Acquisitions Editor: *Worth Hawes*
Assistant Editor: *Patrick Stockstill*
Editorial Assistant: *Kamilah Lee*
Technology Project Manager: *Julie Aguilar*
Marketing Manager: *Christina Shea*
Marketing Assistant: *Mary Anne Payumo*
Marketing Communications Manager:
  Darlene Amidon-Brent
Project Manager, Editorial Production: *Samen Iqbal*
Creative Director: *Rob Hugel*
Art Director: *Maria Epes*
Print Buyer: *Linda Hsu*
Permissions Editor: *Bob Kauser*

Production Service: *Aaron Downey, Matrix Productions Inc.*
Text Designer: *Lisa Henry*
Photo Researcher: *Don Schlotman*
Copy Editor: *Frank Hubert*
Cover Designer: *Yvo Riezebos Design*
Cover Image: *Top to bottom, left to right: Laura Watilo Blake/iStockphoto; Ben Mercer/ iStockphoto; Pascal Deloche/Godong/Corbis; Philippe Lissac/Godong/Corbis; Arjen Briene/ iStockphoto*
Compositor: *International Typesetting and Composition*

Thomson Higher Education
10 Davis Drive
Belmont, CA 94002-3098
USA

Library of Congress Control Number: 2007928270

ISBN-13: 978-0-495-50387-3
ISBN-10: 0-495-50387-8

For more information about our products,
contact us at:
Thomson Learning Academic Resource Center
1-800-423-0563
For permission to use material from this text or
product, submit a request online at
http://www.thomsonrights.com.
Any additional questions about permissions
can be submitted by e-mail to
thomsonrights@thomson.com.

To James and Genevieve Bos
My parents-in-law
In gratitude for your friendship

CONTENTS

PREFACE

The major living religions of the world have all expressed their teachings and practices in writing. Over the course of time, some of these writings gained unique standing in their traditions and became scriptures. As scriptures, they continue to influence the course of their religions. To read the scriptures of the world, therefore, is to encounter world religions in a direct and meaningful way.

This book is designed to facilitate this encounter for the general reader and especially for the student of religion. Its pages contain the most notable and instructive sacred texts of Hinduism, Buddhism, Jainism, Sikhism, Confucianism, Taoism, Shinto, Zoroastrianism, Judaism, Christianity, Islam, and four new religious movements: Baha'i, the Christian Science Church, the Church of Jesus Christ of Latter-day Saints, and the Unification Church.

This anthology not only presents scripture readings but also sets them in the context of their application in the traditions themselves, taking into account recent scholarship on the role of scriptures in religion. Moreover, it does this in one volume and in one format. Designed to be used as a secondary textbook, the anthology has an organization that is easily adaptable to a range of primary textbooks and most of the current methods of teaching comparative religion.

This sixth edition incorporates, in addition to dozens of smaller changes, the following significant revisions:

- Many opening vignettes and the closing sections on "Scriptures in Film" have been revised and updated to keep them fully contemporary. A new section on film has been added to the chapter on Taoism.
- About a dozen new scripture readings have been added on the recommendation of adopters and peer reviewers. Included in these new readings, for example, are treatments of "outcastes" in Hinduism; Buddhist teachings on the Pure Land, Zen, and Falun Gong; a Confucian critique of Buddhism; Taoist teachings on feng shui; Zoroastrian views of the last judgment; and the early noncanonical Jesus tradition in the *Gospel of Thomas*.

- The organization of the scripture readings has been made more consistent. Each chapter now follows as fully as possible the same order of history, teaching, ethics, organization, and ritual.
- All scholarship is updated throughout.

Anthology of World Scriptures is organized as follows: The first chapter examines the general phenomenon of scripture in the world's religions, its nature, use, and place in modern scholarship. Chapter 1 also introduces the reader to the art of reading scripture with practical suggestions.

Chapters 2 through 12 present the scripture of a single religion and are organized as follows: Vignettes about scripture and its usage draw the reader's interest and imagination. Then an introduction sets the context by explaining the overall structure, use, origin, and development of the scripture in its religion. (If the name of the scripture poses a problem for students, this is given a brief treatment before Overall Structure.) The first grouping of scripture passages concerns the history of the religion, especially the founder (if any) and early history of the tradition. The second grouping covers main doctrinal teachings, including divine or ultimate reality, creation and the environment, human nature, and human fulfillment. The third grouping deals with ethical systems, both personal and social; topics such as war and peace, justice, and the role of women are anthologized as fully as possible here. The fourth grouping focuses on organization, both the ways that religion orders itself and seeks to order its wider culture. The fifth grouping includes worship, devotion, ritual, and meditation. Chapters 8 (Shinto) and 13 (New Religious Movements) have a different internal order that is explained at the beginning of these chapters. As stated earlier, the final grouping deals with later, postscriptural developments of scriptural themes. Each chapter has full pedagogical aids, such as concise introductions to each passage, tables listing scripture canons, full annotations in footnotes to explain difficult items in the readings, questions for study and discussion, a glossary with pronunciations, a brief treatment of recent films that deal with scriptures, and suggestions for further reading. On the website for this book, students and professors will find interactive resources for learning and teaching, such as glossary lists, flashcards of glossary terms, tutorial quizzes, Internet exercises, and Microsoft PowerPoint® slides for lecture and review.

The translations used here have been selected for their accuracy and readability. I have been fortunate to receive permission to reprint many of the finest and most current English translations of many world scriptures. Where recent English translations are incomplete or too technical for undergraduate students, I have relied on a few older translations that have proven their worth over time. I have edited these to update vocabulary, spelling, and occasionally, syntax.

The scriptures presented here come from the religions commonly understood to be the major living world religions, both old and new. By "world religion," scholars generally mean those religions that have had an impact on the world's leading cultures, not necessarily religions that are spread throughout the world. But why not include here the writings of other important contemporary religions, such as those of Africa or North America or the ancient religions of Egypt, Greece, or Central America? The main reason is that, with a few possible exceptions (e.g., the Mayan *Popol Vuh*), *these religions do not have scriptures as this term is commonly defined today.* Ancient religions had comparatively little writing, and this writing was not used in religious practice in a way that qualifies it as scriptural. The tribal/primal religions of Africa and North America rely on oral traditions, which, though powerful and important, are not written scriptural traditions. Those that are written down have been compiled and used as texts mainly by anthropologists, not by the believers themselves. That these religions do not have scriptures does not, of course, imply that they are any the less religious.

I am very grateful for the strong reception this book has received. I trust that this edition will continue to stimulate its readers to explore the world of religion more deeply.

Acknowledgments

The editorial staff at Wadsworth continues to be a fine partner in developing and producing this book. I especially want to thank religion editor Worth Hawes and assistant editor Patrick Stockstill, as well as Aaron Downey of Matrix Productions and my copyeditor, Frank Hubert.

Scholars at numerous institutions offered detailed, insightful critiques at many points along the way. I thank those who reviewed the content of these chapters in earlier editions of this book: David W. Aiken, Ferris State University; Vivodh J. Z. Anand, Montclair State University; Paul Bernadicou, University of San Francisco; Anne Birdwhistell, Richard Stockton College of New Jersey; James Cook, Oakland Community College, Orchard Ridge; Dell deChant, University of South Florida; Marianne Ferguson, Buffalo State College; Roger Keller, Brigham Young University; Richard Mahon, Riverside Community College; William K. Mahony, Davidson College; Michael McKale, Saint Francis College; Anne Monius, University of Virginia; Vivian-Lee Nyitray, University of California at Riverside; Patrick S. O'Donnell, Santa Barbara City College; Richard Penaskovic, Auburn University; Christopher Queen, Harvard University; Stephen J. Reno, Southern Oregon State College; Philip Riley, Santa Clara University; Roger L. Schmidt, San Bernardino Valley College; Philip Schmitz, Eastern Michigan University; Daniel Sheridan, Loyola University of New Orleans; Robert Smith, Trenton State College; Gail Hinich Sutherland, Louisiana State University; Donald Swearer, Swarthmore College; James Whitehill, Stephens College; Boyd Wilson, Hope College; and Glenn Yocum, Whittier College. For their careful review for this new edition, I thank William Harman, University of Tennessee at Chattanooga; Harry Hight, Virginia Highlands Community College; Keith Kendall, Northern Michigan University; Frank Klapak, Seton Hall University; Tori Lockler, University of South Florida; Richard Mahon, Riverside Community College; Rebecca Norris, Merrimack College; Bryan Polk, Pennsylvania State University at Abington; and Alban Urbanas, Wesley College.

All those people made this a better book, but any errors that remain are mine alone. I would be most grateful if users of this book and its Wadsworth website resources would send me comments and suggestions for improvements. You can reach me at my postal address (Western Theological Seminary, 101 East 13th Street, Holland, MI 49423-3622) or by e-mail (bob.vanvoorst@westernsem.edu).

Finally, this sixth edition gives me the happy opportunity to renew my expression of gratitude to my family: to my wonderfully supportive wife, Mary; to our son Nicholas; and to our son Richard and the newest member of our family, his wife, Bonnie.

ANTHOLOGY OF WORLD SCRIPTURES

CHAPTER ONE

Scripture Among the World's Religions

- In North Carolina, a controversy brews over a book about Muslim scripture selected for the freshman orientation seminar at The University of North Carolina at Chapel Hill—Michael Sells's *Approaching the Qur'an: The Early Revelations*. In the shadow of September 11, 2001, some North Carolina citizens charge that "impressionable freshmen" will think that Islam is a harmless faith and perhaps be drawn to it. Even the American Civil Liberties Union enters the controversy, warning that teaching this book might be a violation of the constitutional separation of church and state.

- In an Indian city, Hindu priests and Sanskrit-language scholars call a news conference to criticize a song, "Shanti," by American pop singer Madonna. The criticism focuses on Madonna's pronunciation of that ancient divine name. Reflecting Hindu spoken use of scripture, the priests and scholars state that the spiritual power of this name is not effective unless it is pronounced correctly.

- Near the federal prison in Terre Haute, Indiana, demonstrators gather at the execution of Timothy McVeigh. He is being punished for the 1995 bombing of the federal office building in Oklahoma City in which 169 people died. Some people protest his execution by carrying signs with words from the *Bible* of both Judaism and Christianity: "You shall not kill." Counterprotesters also carry signs with biblical words: "You shall not allow a murderer to live." In 2004, similar scenes played out at the state trial of Terry McNichols, who was convicted of participating with McVeigh in this crime but did not receive the death penalty.

- Outside a movie theater in Utah, crowds gather, waiting for the director, producers, and actors of a film to arrive for the premiere. Although the scene is similar to most premieres, this film is not like most movies. It is a feature-film adaptation of the *Book of Mormon*, officially sanctioned by the Church of Jesus Christ of Latter-day Saints. Besides its general release to theaters and then to video-rental outlets, it will be used in the missionary activities of the church.

The influence of world scripture is felt throughout the world in ways both extraordinary and commonplace. Not all contemporary examples of scripture usage are as dramatic or controversial as these vignettes suggest. They do indicate, though, that the scriptures of world religions have a continuing profound impact on life and culture. This anthology introduces these scriptures and encourages a deep encounter with them in all their variety. Scriptures of the world are so vast in size that some sort of sampling is necessary for all but the most expert specialist. This anthology thus offers excerpts from each tradition that faithfully reflect the history and continuing life of the tradition.

A BRIEF HISTORY OF SCRIPTURE SCHOLARSHIP

In the last 150 years, the scholarly study of world scriptures has passed through three distinct stages that have strongly influenced how we read scriptures.[1] In the first stage, at the middle of the nineteenth century, European scholars began a vast enterprise of making critically reliable translations. They focused on the little-translated sacred literature of Asia and the scriptures of Islam and Zoroastrianism. Their concern was to translate individual texts, not to examine the general religious features of scripture. They treated scripture as a mine out of which to dig the history and doctrine of religions, with little regard for the different ways scripture functioned in religious communities.[2]

The academic movement known as the "History of Religions school" dominated religious studies in the second stage but led to neglect of scriptures. This school, which continues to exert a strong influence today, analyzes the development of each religion using historical and social-scientific methods.[3] Perhaps in reaction to the earlier methodological reliance on world scriptures, scholars like Joachim Wach and Mircea Eliade relied on the study of ritual, myth, symbols, and other nontextual elements of religion. Scripture, both Eastern and Western, was largely neglected at this stage. Such a respected treatment of comparative religion as Gerardus van der Leeuw's *Religion in Essence and Manifestation* contains only a brief discussion of

---

[1] For an excellent comprehensive discussion of the history of the academic study of world religions, with some detailed comments on scripture study, see E. Sharpe, *Comparative Religion: A History,* 2d ed. (LaSalle, IL: Open Court Press, 1987). The best succinct presentation of this topic is by S. Cain, "History of the Study of Religion," in M. Eliade, ed., *Encyclopedia of Religion* (New York: Macmillan, 1987), vol. 14, pp. 64–83.

[2] A continuing feature of this first stage is a number of popular anthologies of world scriptures that use world scriptures as a mine for enlightenment and pay little or no attention to how scripture functions in world religious communities. For example, Robert Ballou's *The Bible of the World* (New York: Viking, 1939) and its abridgment in *World Bible* (New York: Viking, 1944) have remained in print continually, although never revised. Selwyn Gurney Champion and Dorothy Short compiled *Readings from World Religions* (Boston: Beacon, 1952; reprinted most recently as *The World's Great Religions: An Anthology of Sacred Texts* (Mineola, NY: Dover, 2003). The Unification Church has published *World Scripture: A Comparative Anthology of Sacred Texts,* ed. Andrew Wilson (New York: Paragon House, 1991). Philip Novak has edited *The World's Wisdom: Sacred Texts of the World's Religions* (San Francisco: Harper-SanFrancisco, 1994).

[3] The German name of this movement, "Religionswissenschaft," means "science/scholarship of religion," indicating a wider method of study than simply historical scholarship.

scripture as a feature of world religions.[4] Also, as social-scientific methods increasingly entered the field of religious scholarship in this second stage, researchers turned away from studying literary sources from the past in favor of the study of present-day living communities of faith.[5]

Although this second stage is still very influential, a third stage has emerged in which scholars have rediscovered the value of scripture. The overreliance on scripture characteristic of the first stage and the neglect of scripture in the second stage are now being corrected as scholars increasingly view scripture as an important feature among the religions of the world. Now scripture is correctly seen as one religious facet among many and therefore not to be isolated from the others. Another new element is an emphasis on the actual ways in which scripture is viewed and used in world religions. To understand scripture, according to this view, we must know not just the scriptural text but also how it comes alive in the total life of the religion.

Recent research gives evidence of this emerging third stage. Large-scale studies such as Geo Widengren's *Phenomenology of Religion* and Friedrich Heiler's *Manifestations and Essence of Religion* deal extensively with the nature and use of scripture among the world's religions.[6] Ninian Smart's *Sacred Texts of the World* uses scripture to approach several different religious phenomena in each world religion.[7] Five recent books deal with scripture and its role in religion: *The Holy Book in Comparative Perspective,* by Frederick Denny and Roderick Taylor; *Sacred Word and Sacred Text,* by Harold Coward; *Rethinking Scripture: Essays from a Comparative Perspective,* by Miriam Levering; *Sacred Texts and Authority,* by Jacob Neusner; and *What Is Scripture? A Comparative Approach,* by Wilfred Cantwell Smith.[8] As a result of the research in this stage, the comparative study of scripture is today one of the leading features in the study of world religions. Smith, of Harvard University, and some of his students have had a strong influence on current scripture study. They argue for scripture study centered on the actual reception and use of scriptures. The work of William Graham on the oral dimensions of scripture has been especially influential.[9] A measure of the strength of this stage is that it is now appearing in textbooks, and several works are notable.[10] As a representative of this third stage of

---

[4]Gerardus van der Leeuw, *Religion in Essence and Manifestation* (London: Allen & Unwin, 1938; German original, 1933). One short chapter, 64, deals almost exclusively with scripture.

[5]For example, the widely used *Reader in Comparative Religion: An Anthropological Approach,* ed. W. A. Lessa and E. Z. Vogt, 4th ed. (New York: Harper & Row, 1997), has excellent readings in all the basic topics in the cultural-anthropological study of religion—symbol, myth, ritual, shamanism, magic—but not one essay on scripture and its uses.

[6]Geo Widengren, *Religionsphänomenologie* (Berlin: de Gruyter, 1969); Friedrich Heiler, *Erscheinungsformen und Wesen der Religion,* 2d ed. (Stuttgart: Kohlhammer, 1979).

[7]Ninian Smart, *Sacred Texts of the World* (London: Macmillan, 1982).

[8]F. M. Denny and R. L. Taylor, eds., *The Holy Book in Comparative Perspective* (Charleston: University of South Carolina Press, 1985); Harold Coward, *Sacred Word and Sacred Text* (Maryknoll, NY: Orbis, 1988); Miriam Levering, ed., *Rethinking Scripture* (Albany: State University of New York Press, 1989); Jacob Neusner, ed., *Sacred Texts and Authority* (Cleveland: Pilgrim, 1998); Wilfred Cantwell Smith, *What Is Scripture? A Comparative Approach* (Philadelphia: Augsburg Fortress, 1993).

[9]See especially William Graham's *Beyond the Written Word: Oral Aspects of Scripture in the History of Religion* (Cambridge: Cambridge University Press, 1983).

[10]T. W. Hall, R. B. Pilgrim, and R. R. Cavanagh, *Religion: An Introduction* (San Francisco: Harper & Row, 1985); Kenneth Kramer, *World Scriptures: An Introduction to Comparative Religion* (New York: Paulist, 1986); Roger Schmidt, *Exploring Religion,* 2d ed. (Belmont, CA: Wadsworth, 1988); Jean Holm and John Bower, *Sacred Writings* (London: Pinter, 1994); Richard Viladesau and Mark Massa, *World Religions: A Sourcebook for the Student of Christian Theology* (New York: Paulist,

scripture study, this text offers a wide range of scripture selections from the religions of the world, with introductions and annotations to set the readings in the context of their actual usage.

THE NATURE AND DEFINITION OF SCRIPTURE

At first glance, defining scripture seems easy enough. We think of scripture as the holy writing, the sacred text of a religion. All religions seem to have scriptures, and all appear to use them in the same way. As a phenomenon among religions, scripture seems on the surface to be a constant. On closer examination, however, these simple notions vanish.

Books that are traditionally regarded as scriptures vary in several important aspects. The first variation among scriptures is in literary form. People who come from religious traditions that include scriptures tend naturally to assume that the sacred texts of other religions look and function exactly like theirs. Scriptures, however, are as varied as the religions and cultures from which they come.

- Some scriptures, especially those of Judaism, Christianity, and Islam, prominently feature historical **narratives.** They tell an event in story form. Scriptures from other religions, especially Asian faiths, have few narratives or none at all.
- Some scriptures enshrine their religion's vision of a moral life in law codes, some feature more loosely bound moral precepts, and still others do not seem concerned about ethics.
- Poetry is the leading literary form of some scriptures; others feature prose.
- Some scriptural books have metaphysical philosophy (for example, the Hindu *Upanishads*), some have moral philosophy (for example, the Confucian *Analects,* the wisdom literature of the Jewish and Christian *Bible*), but many have no explicit philosophy at all.
- Some scriptures contain directions and songs for sacrifice (the Hindu *Vedas,* the Jewish *Bible*), whereas others have no developed prescriptions for rites and ceremonies (the *Qur'an*).
- Also present in scriptures are myth, legend, prophecy, sermons, love poems, divination, and magic, among many other **genres,** or literary forms.

Even this brief overview shows that world scriptures do not take a fixed literary form. Therefore, we cannot open a book, browse through it, and pronounce it scriptural. Scripturalness is primarily a relational, not a literary, quality. As William Graham has written, the holiness of a book is not automatically accepted when the text is first written, but it is "realized historically in the life of communities who respond to it as something sacred or holy."[11] Communities shape and receive scripture, and scripture shapes the life of faith. The relation between scripture and religion is reciprocal and dynamic.

The second variation among scriptures has to do with their *number.* Within any one religion, they can range from one book to an entire library. Like the *Qur'an,* scriptures can be one unified text of moderate size between two covers. Like the

---

1994); Ian S. Markham, ed., *A World Religions Reader* (Oxford: Blackwell, 1996); Terry D. Bilhartz, *Sacred Words* (New York: McGraw-Hill, 2006).
[11]W. A. Graham, "Scripture," *Encyclopedia of Religion,* vol. 13, p. 134.

Jewish and Christian scriptures, they can be collections of many short books between two covers. In Asian religions, they range in number from one book (the *Adi Granth* of Sikhism), to the dozen or so texts of Confucianism, to the hundred or more texts of Hinduism, to the more than a thousand texts of Taoism and some forms of Buddhism.

The third variation in scriptures lies in *function*. In some religions, scripture is so central—or appears so to outsiders—that the lives of believers seem almost dictated by scripture. Zoroastrianism, Judaism, Christianity, Islam, and Sikhism are all properly called "religions of the book" because of the high place and powerful function of their scriptures. New religious movements that originate from some of these religions are also scripture-centered. In contrast, most Asian religions often have a more informal relationship to their scriptures, which lay devotees consult mainly for general guidance and inspiration. (Monks and nuns, however, have a more formal and developed relationship to their scriptures.)

The varying oral and textual dimensions of scripture also lead to differences in function. Some religions view the spoken word of scripture as primary. In other religions, especially in the Western world, the power and function of the book seem to depend on its written, textual nature. Muslims, for example, believe the *Qur'an* is a transcription of a book already written in heaven. Like most Western scripture, it originated in a process of oral tradition, but its use and authority in its religion come from its written, textual nature. A later section of this chapter deals more fully with the uses of scriptures, but enough has been said here to suggest that they function in significantly different ways.

Given all this variety, is it possible to define the word *scripture* in a way that takes variety into account yet applies to all world religions? Although some scholars answer in the negative,[12] most argue that a comprehensive definition is possible and necessary. The definition we use here is this: **Scripture** *is writing that is accepted and used in a religious community as especially sacred and authoritative.* By looking closely at the key words and implications of this definition, we can discuss formal and functional aspects of scriptures—what they are and how people use them.

First, every scripture is a *writing*. Scriptures exercise much of their authority as books, and we encounter them as books. Some scholars argue that **oral tradition,** the passing down of material by word of mouth only, can be "scriptural."[13] Although oral and written traditions do have some similar characteristics and functions, strictly speaking "oral scripture" is a contradiction because scripture is by definition written. (The word *scripture* comes from the Latin *scriptura*, "writing.") The scriptures of all religions, however, do have continuing, significant oral and aural (hearing) dimensions.[14] Most scriptures originated in oral tradition, so the "imprint" of orality can be found in them. For example, David Carr has recently argued that

---

[12]In *Rethinking Scripture,* for example, the essays by Coburn and Folkert reject the term *scripture* for *the Word* and *canon.* The other authors in this book keep "scripture" as a conceptual category, and it is the dominant category in the volume as a whole, as the title implies.

[13]See, for example, Schmidt, *Exploring Religion,* p. 208: "Broadly conceived, *scripture* refers to oral as well as written traditions that a people regard as sacred. Each religious community has a scripture, a body of sacred oral or written traditions."

[14]See especially Graham, *Beyond the Written Word.* For a general treatment of orality, see W. Ong, *Orality and Literacy* (New York: Routledge, Chapman and Hall, 1982), and J. Goody, *The Interface Between the Written and the Oral* (Cambridge: Cambridge University Press, 1982).

Jewish scripture emerged as a support for an educational process in which written and oral dimensions were integrally intertwined, in particular as an aid to memorizing and reciting key traditions.[15] The same is probably true for other religions. Although the writing of scripture can obscure (especially for us moderns, for whom the written word predominates), the orality of the text is still embedded in the writing and waits to be drawn out by faithful vocalizing of the words. Scripture comes most fully alive when believers read it aloud and hear it in worship. Most believers, even those in highly literate cultures, hear scripture in worship more often and more meaningfully than they read it privately. In this book, as in any book, we encounter scriptures as texts, but these texts are meant to be spoken and heard.

According to our definition, scriptures are *especially sacred.* They have special religious significance in pointing to ultimate reality and truth. Sacredness should not be seen simply as of divine origin or even as the "wholly other," Rudolf Otto's influential conception of sacredness that suits Western religions but not many Eastern faiths. For example, the sacred Tao ("Way") witnessed by the *Tao Te Ching* is not wholly other but is hidden in the universe and the self, waiting to be discovered and "tuned in to." Moreover, only a few books among world scriptures explicitly claim sacredness for themselves; the *Qur'an* is the most notable example in Western religions. Most scriptures receive their sacred status only after they have been written, circulated, and widely accepted as reflecting the faith in some special sense. The relational aspect of all scripture comes to the fore in a religious community.

Notice that scriptures are books held to be *especially* sacred. Most religions have a secondary religious literature that is also viewed as holy, instructive, or authoritative. For example, Judaism has its *Talmud,* books of religious law, and Islam has its *hadith,* traditions about Muhammad. This may seem to complicate the matter of defining the idea of scripture. On what basis can we say that a certain holy book in a religious tradition is scripture but another holy book is not? The answer lies in the special reception and usage that believers give to works that they see as especially sacred. Most religions explicitly or implicitly hold some works to be secondary to scripture. *Talmud* is not the Hebrew *Bible; hadith* is not the *Qur'an.* Almost every religion has commentarial, devotional, or legal literature that follows up on scripture, and believers typically make a careful distinction between scripture and these works.

Another mark of special holiness is use in ritual. When believers read books aloud in worship, when they speak their words to carry out sacrifice, and especially when they venerate (pay formal, careful respect to) books during worship, we have a sure indication that these books are especially sacred. Secondary religious literature rarely makes its way into worship. Different types of veneration are practiced in every world religion and in the new religious movements. Even in everyday life, scriptures enjoy special respect: The Christian *Bible* is the only book in the West still often bound in leather; Buddhist monks still copy scriptures onto treated palm leaves. In the new religious movements, the key writings of the founders that function as scriptures are often printed and bound to resemble more traditional holy books.

The third element of our definition of scripture is the authority of the text. Just as sacredness is an aspect of every scripture, scriptures are also *especially authoritative* in

---

[15]D. M. Carr, *Writing on the Tablet of the Heart: Origins of Scripture and Literature* (New York: Oxford University Press, 2005).

their communities. Among all written texts in a community, a scripture is always the most authoritative and is often the court of final appeal in religious matters. The range of this authority and the way it is exercised vary depending on the nature of the religion and the content of its scriptures. In the Western "religions of the book," scriptures are comprehensive in content and regulate much of life. In the Eastern religions, scriptures are often not authoritative in the same way as in the Abrahamic traditions. Yet Asian scriptures often express the heart of their faith, the way of salvation. Moreover, "at least four of the six South Asian or Far Eastern fundamentalist-like movements...do in fact privilege a sacred text and presume to draw certain fundamentals—beliefs and behaviors—from it."[16] The authority of scripture for most followers of a given religion is paradoxically acknowledged even when some occasionally reject it. Typically among Western religions, to receive one religion's texts as scripture is automatically to exclude the texts of other religions. For example, the presentation of Jewish *Bible* material in the *Qur'an* means that Muslims should not look directly to the Jewish *Bible* and read it. An exception to this is the Christian *Bible,* which contains the entire Jewish *Bible* renamed as the "Old Testament."

The authority of scripture in both East and West is established by a special class of scholars who are the guardians of scripture and recognized experts in its intrepretation. In Buddhism, monks with special training and ability teach the sacred writings to other monks and inquiring laypeople. The Jewish rabbi, the Christian pastor, and the Muslim mullah, all leaders of local congregations, are experts in interpreting and teaching their scriptures. The authority of scripture in nearly every faith, including new religious movements, is therefore mediated largely by individuals considered to be its official interpreters. **Commentary,** a book written to explain another book, has a large role in the history of many religions and regulates how scriptures are received and used, especially at the official level. As John Henderson states, "Commentaries and commentarial modes of thinking dominated the intellectual history of most premodern civilizations.... Until the seventeenth century in Europe, and even later in China, India, and the Near East, thought, especially within high intellectual traditions, was primarily exegetical [text-interpretive] in character and expression."[17] We must also remember that only quite recently in the sweep of human history have mass-produced books appeared and mass literacy become possible. This is another reason for the existence of a special class to read, comment on, and relate sacred books to a religious community. Of course, the uses of scriptures by ordinary followers of a religion are at times quite different from the official prescribed use.

Two features of scripture not directly related to our definition should be stated here. First, scriptures of every religion are often heterogeneous but are nonetheless *seen as a unity* by their communities. Modern scholarship has shown that the *Qur'an* has passed through different phases of development during and since the life of Muhammad. But neither the conclusions of scholars nor the acknowledged difficulties of the *Qur'an* call its unity into question for a Muslim. Judaism's *Bible* went through a long period of development and has dozens of books in it, but it is seen as one distinct, unified book; indeed, *Bible* means "the Book."

---

[16]M. E. Marty and R. S. Appleby, eds., *Fundamentalisms Observed* (Chicago: University of Chicago Press, 1991), p. 820.

[17]J. B. Henderson, *Scripture, Canon, Commentary: A Comparison of Confucian and Western Exegesis* (Princeton, NJ: Princeton University Press, 1991), p. 3.

A second important feature of scripture is that it has *a degree of closure*. This closure is often called a **canon,** a list or collection of books recognized as scriptural. The canon is absolutely fixed in the three **Abrahamic monotheisms**—Judaism, Christianity, and Islam—and in Zoroastrianism. All the scriptures of these religions were long ago officially identified, and nothing can now be added or subtracted from their canons. In Hinduism, Buddhism, Jainism, Confucianism, and Taoism, however, the situation is quite different for two reasons. First, their sacred literature is vast. The problems in defining a canon for a religion like Taoism, for example, which has 1,200 sacred texts, are enormous. Second, the process of producing scripture has not officially ended. Where new scriptural revelations can be added—as Taoists added one in the twentieth century—a closed canon cannot exist.

How can believers relate to their religion's scriptures when they are so vast that no one person or group can know them all, let alone be expert in them all? In traditions with large canons, certain books are basic for almost everyone. Also, different groups in a religion attach themselves to a few select scriptures that reflect their particular interests. This tendency to choose specific books from among the total corpus of scripture results in a "canon within the canon." Most commonly, it occurs in religions with very large numbers of books, but it also can be found in religions with smaller canons. In sum, scripture canons can be either completely closed or open to development and change. No matter how readily they can be altered, canonical texts are still viewed and treated as scripture.

THE USES OF SCRIPTURE

When scripture is set in the full context of the everyday life of believers, its uses become plain. How believers use scripture shows its status and role in a religion. The following chapters of this book outline the varied uses of scripture in each religion. In this section, we discuss some basic dimensions of the comparative study of scripture usage.

We begin with three uses that are primarily *cognitive,* understanding and thinking in some way about the words and their meaning. First, scripture is a source for establishing and defending key doctrines. Scriptures can be used doctrinally because they typically contain the key teachings of the faith and because believers usually see them as continuing the voice of the founders. They have primary importance as statements of the deep truths of the universe and the right way to live in it. These teachings can assume different forms: God(s) and humanity; human imperfections and salvation; beginnings and ends of the individual and the cosmos; the moral life and how to achieve it. When scripture is used to establish doctrine, its official interpreters—monks, priests, scholars, and the like—most often do this. Sometimes, formal debate in councils or assemblies sets down doctrines, often within the confines of a monastery or temple. Defending doctrine occurs less often at the popular level, but even here scripture can function authoritatively. An appeal to a passage of holy writ is often the final word in any argument about religion.

Second, scripture is also prominently used in public worship. Worshippers often display and read it aloud. Although this practice is characteristic especially of the Abrahamic "religions of the book," it is also significant in religions such as Hinduism and Buddhism that are not so book oriented. The worship that goes on in a

Buddhist monastery, for example, prominently features scriptures. Monks read them, chant them, meditate on them, and walk around them in solemn procession. Even when the book is not prominent in worship, its content often permeates the ceremonies of most scripturalizing religions. Prayers, sacrifices, and hymns come from and echo the language of scripture. Many lyrics of the music of worship are drawn from the scriptural text. Hymns and chants, with their emotional power, are significant vehicles for the use of scripture in most religious traditions in both East and West.

Perhaps the place and function of scripture are never as prominent as when worshippers formally venerate it. Almost every religion with scripture pays it ritual respect in some way. Hindus speak the words of a *Veda* with great care. In certain Taoist and Confucian temples, the location of the scripture collection is itself holy. In Judaism, the scrolls are removed from their ark at the front center of the synagogue with great solemnity and on certain festival days are paraded around the synagogue. In many Christian churches, everyone stands for the oral reading of the gospels. **Bibliolatry** [bib-lee-AHL-ah-tree], literally, "worship of a book," results when believers give excessive veneration to their scriptures or become absolutely dependent on them.

A third typical cognitive use of scripture is in meditation and devotion. This is usually private and individual, but it can also occur in group settings, as when Buddhist monks meditate in session on sutra passages or on mantras drawn from scripture. In Western religions, the scripture books are often marked into sections for devotional reading; it is the duty of believers to read, ponder, and often memorize the words. In meditation and devotion, the scriptures teach the truth of the religion and promote the growth of the reader into the fullness of the faith.

Another important dimension of scripture use—one often overlooked—is *noncognitive,* using the words in a variety of ways without any mental attempt to understand their meaning.

• In decorative and iconic uses, the text itself is revered as a holy object. (An **icon** is a holy picture, usually of a saint.) One cannot live or travel in any Muslim area without encountering Qur'anic verses everywhere. They are displayed on private houses and public buildings, often in a stylized calligraphy that is a mainstay of art in Muslim lands. In these and other iconic usages of scripture, the appeal is typically more to the imagination and emotion than to the mind.

• A second noncognitive application stresses the objective spiritual power of a holy book. The power of scripture is such that it can bring blessing and keep away evil. Scripture can be used in charms or talismans, a manifestation of the supernatural power of scripture. The mere possession of a holy book also has power to bless and to ward off evil. For example, putting a certain Taoist text in the hands of a woman undergoing a perilous childbirth is said to cause the immediate safe birth of her child. In many religions, individuals who can afford to do so will often buy a holy book for possession in the home.

• **Bibliomancy** [BIB-lee-oh-man-see] is the use of holy books to foresee the future and guide one's response to it. Many religions feature the informal practice of opening a scripture book at random and reading the first passage that meets the eye. This passage is thought to have special power to direct the believer through an uncertain or difficult situation in life or through the difficulties of the new day.

One of the most famous ancient conversions to Christianity, that of Saint Augustine, featured bibliomancy of this sort. Some printed editions of the *Qur'an* have symbols at the top of the page by which a reader opening the book at random can discern whether a planned action is advisable, inadvisable, or neutral. All these forms of bibliomancy assume that supernatural guidance is exercised in and through the book for the blessing of the believer.

Scholars of religion have categorized scripture uses in other ways beyond cognitive and noncognitive. Perhaps the most helpful is that of Sam D. Gill, who proposed that uses of scripture are informative and performative. *Informative* means imparting information in various ways, such as in doctrine and history. *Performative,* in contrast, means doing something, as for example when scripture is used to make sacrifice, to make the laws of a religious or civil community, or to bless and curse.[18] In both its informative and performative aspects, scripture is also used for transformation. This transformative power is a result of its sacredness and authority. Scriptures come from a sacred source and are themselves sacred. This sacred quality generally entails some power to make holy those who read or listen to them.

The transformative power of scripture occurs in both individual and communal ways—for example, to gain insight about personal or group problems and find the resources to solve them. Not all religions consider their scriptures to be divinely inspired, but all hold them to be inspiring and transformative in some way. This transformative power can be based on cognition, in which believers directly encounter the scriptures and experience their life-changing meaning. It can also happen just as often in the noncognitive ways described earlier.

ADVANTAGES AND DISADVANTAGES OF STUDYING RELIGIONS THROUGH THEIR SCRIPTURES

The study of world religions through their sacred scriptures has both advantages and disadvantages. We need to be aware of the limitations of this method and work from strengths to overcome the weaknesses as much as possible.

The first disadvantage, as we saw earlier, is that the reception and use of scripture are *not uniform* across religions. Believers regard their scriptures in different ways, and scriptures function differently in each religion. As a student of world religions, you must take note of these variations and learn to look at each religion's scriptures in a fresh way. Readers of scripture who come from a "religion of the book" must especially try to lay aside their preconceptions. Protestant Christians, for example, must beware of assuming that certain qualities of scripture and its function to which they are accustomed (for example, the belief that scripture is best absorbed by individual silent reading and meditation) are true of every religion's scripture. Moreover, the use of new scriptures in new religious movements in both Asia and North America often differs from usage in older, classical religious movements. The more we genuinely encounter world scriptures in their

---

[18]Sam D. Gill, "Nonliterate Traditions and Holy Books: Toward a New Model," in Denny and Taylor, *Holy Book,* p. 234.

full range of reception and use, the less likely we will be to inject our own biases into the scriptures of others. Then "scripture" itself will become a fuller, more useful category.

A second disadvantage is that we must *read translations,* which cannot fully capture the literary characteristics or meaning of the original. We can describe four aspects of this disadvantage.

• Some of the original meaning and resonance of the words is lost or distorted in translation. For example, among Muslims, the identity and power of the *Qur'an* in its Arabic language are such that it would be unthinkable to translate it into another language and still consider it the true *Qur'an;* instead, it is often called an "interpretation."

• Some languages and styles are hard to translate into English. For example, the formal Chinese style used by several Confucian and Taoist scriptures is often elusive or even cryptic. Moreover, to cross the borders of language families in translation (to go from Semitic languages of the Jewish *Bible* and the *Qur'an* into English, for example) is more difficult than staying inside a language family (to go from the Greek *New Testament* into English). These difficulties result in translations that vary widely.

• Bias creeps in. Translators inevitably cannot be fully objective and sometimes distort meaning. A leading example today is the translation of the Arabic word *jihad* in the *Qur'an.* It has a variety of meanings, but many translators (some of them Muslim) render it only as "war," "holy war," or "fighting." It can also mean "struggle" or "striving."

• Updating is needed because languages change. Some scripture translations are updated regularly; others are not, for a variety of reasons, and become more and more outmoded as time goes on.

A third main disadvantage is that scriptures tend to *reflect only the patriarchal and elite perspectives* of their traditions. They come from times and cultures that are patriarchal, where the voices of women—if they come through at all—are muted and filtered.[19] Scriptures strongly tend to embody official and elite ideas, the mainstream that feminist scholars call "malestream." Comparatively little of popular religion can be found in them. Although the contents of scripture are patriarchal and elitist, feminist scholars today in many religions are working to make contemporary understanding and use of these scriptures more egalitarian. This book offers some coverage of social justice and the role of women, but the perspective through which these scriptures are filtered is necessarily that of the elite male.[20]

Finally, and perhaps most seriously, we *lack the living context* of scripture when we encounter only its textual form. Scripture, which for most traditions (except new religious movements, of course) comes from ancient times, comes alive as it is used in the life of religious communities. Despite growing religious pluralism, many North American readers of world scripture do not have access to these communities.

---

[19]See the introductory section of Serinity Young, ed., *An Anthology of Sacred Texts By and About Women* (New York: Crossroad, 1993), for good treatment of this issue.
[20]An excellent current series of books edited by Donald S. Lopez Jr., Princeton Readings in Religions, seeks to rectify this male-elite perspective with anthologies on nearly all religions of the world, drawing on more popular writings and anthropological field reports.

They cannot easily visit a mosque or see the ritual of a Jewish synagogue or a Buddhist monastery. They cannot directly see the broad ways that scripture is reflected in religious life or the more specific ways it is used in worship, devotion, or law. What can be reproduced in a book like this is primarily the written text itself. The uses of scripture can be outlined here, but a printed book inevitably emphasizes the written, textual aspects of scripture over the oral and living.

These disadvantages might seem strong enough to cause you to give up the encounter with world scriptures. The advantages of studying religions through their scriptures are compelling, however. By working from the strengths of this approach, you can overcome the weaknesses to some extent and use scripture appropriately to enter the world of other religions.

The first advantage of this approach is that scripture is *widespread* among religions. Even though it is not fully universal, each "major" (to use a traditional but rather prejudicial term) living religion has a scripture. Scriptures naturally vary in form, content, and usage, but they are usually present in a religion. As we have seen, recent researchers emphasize that they form a distinct and important element in the life of most religions. The tendency to *scripturalize,* to make and use scriptures, is strong among religions. Indeed, almost every contemporary religion that is based in a literate culture produces and uses scriptures of some sort.[21] New religious movements also express themselves in writings that have a scriptural status.

Second, scriptures tend to be *comprehensive* for their faiths. Matters that a religion considers of great importance for its life are generally written down for the continuing community. "The sacred writings provide not only the essence of each particular religious tradition, but also the archetypal experiences which stir in the depths of all human lives: death, trust, anxiety, wonder, loyalty to a cause greater than oneself, fascination, healing, fulfillment, peace."[22] Of course, what religions view as important does vary, and scriptures reflect this variety. For example, the Jewish scriptures regulate a multitude of aspects of life considered significant, from worship to ethics to diet. What each religion considers of supreme importance is strongly reflected in its scriptures. Scriptures offer broad insight into the key characteristics of their faiths.

Third, scriptures are *authoritative* for their religions. Because they are believed to come from God or the gods, an enlightened teacher, or a wise sage, and because they bear witness to an ultimate reality, the truth contained in scriptures is recognized and lived out by believers. To read a scripture is to discover what is of primary value in the world's religions. And because scriptures are authoritative, they typically reflect the distinctive main aspects of each tradition. "Despite the variety of attitudes to scriptural works [in the world's religions], there is a continuing tendency to find in a sacred text . . . the primary source for true doctrine, correct ritual, [and] appropriate conduct."[23]

The fourth advantage of studying scriptures lies in their *ancient* or *foundational* character. They or the oral traditions on which they are based arise soon after the beginning of a religion and often signal important stages in its early development. Chinese religions call their oldest scriptures "Classics," and in a sense, all world

---

[21]Only Shinto does not treat its holy books as scripture in the full sense. Thus, Shinto is the exception that proves the rule that religions based in literate cultures produce and use scriptures.
[22]Leonard J. Biallas, "Teaching World Religions Through Their Scriptures," *Horizons* 17 (1990): 80.
[23]Richard C. Bush et al., *The Religious World: Communities of Faith,* 2d ed. (New York: Macmillan, 1988), p. 3.

scriptures are classic treatments of their religious tradition. Where a religion has a founder or founders, scriptures usually give deep insight into the life of the founder(s) from the perspective of later followers. The foundational character of scriptures thus makes them valuable as a primary source for the history of religions. In the new religious movements that we examine in Chapter 13, scriptural books were completed and published by the founder himself or herself, at the very beginning of the movement.

Furthermore, because the traditional religions of the world have so richly influenced and been influenced by their cultures, scriptures are among the most important literary sources for the understanding of world cultures. Even though scriptures are indeed ancient and important, it is usually erroneous to argue, as does Charles Braden, that religion is somehow "founded on" scriptures.[24] This is a common misconception, especially in "religions of the book." Rather, as T. W. Hall puts it so well, "Historical investigations show that the religious communities existed prior to the writing of their scripture . . . religions produced scripture and scripture did not produce religion."[25] However, this conclusion is not as accurate when applied to new religious movements, because among them scriptures often do coincide with the beginnings of the movement.

Fifth, scriptures are *accessible* in translation to English-language readers. Most of the important religious books of the world have been translated into English, and many of those that have not are now being translated. Sometimes, the translations of a certain scripture are few, but others can boast a near riot of English versions. The *Tao Te Ching*, for example, had more than twenty English versions in print in 2006; and even though the *Qur'an* cannot be translated and still retain its holiest status, new English translations are produced regularly. Although no translation can convey the full meaning and feeling of the original, a good translation can suggest it. Students of world scripture who want a closer, more accurate look at a given passage should consult at least two or three different contemporary translations of it and compare them closely.

Finally, scriptures as literary texts are *open to analysis.* Both the specialist scholar and the beginning reader can analyze them directly or, better yet, enter a conversation with them. Although most religious texts range from mildly strange to completely baffling for those who come from other cultures and religious traditions, the same intellectual and scholarly skills that you use to read any other text can be put to use on world scriptures. With some effort, you can understand scriptures and use them as a pathway into other faiths.

WORLD SCRIPTURES AND MODERN SCHOLARSHIP

The earlier discussion of critical analysis of scripture leads us to an important but often neglected topic. How does the modern academic study of scripture influence how religions use scriptures and how we read them?

Historical and critical literary scholarship is largely Western and European in origin, stemming from various methods of interpreting literature developed in

---

[24]Charles Braden, *The Scriptures of Mankind: An Introduction* (New York: Macmillan, 1952), p. 8.
[25]Hall, Pilgrim, and Cavanagh, *Religion*, p. 109.

the Renaissance and the Enlightenment. Textual criticism methodically judges manuscripts to find the likely original reading; grammatical criticism analyzes the content and style of the wording of a work in its original language; literary criticism studies genres. Most important is historical criticism, in particular the **historical-critical method,** which probes the developmental genesis of works from the past, their original meaning as understood by their first audience. In the early nineteenth century, this approach began to be applied to the *Bible*. Critical study of the Christian scripture has uncovered development, diversity, and even some disagreement within it. Christianity's effort to understand the *Bible* critically has suffered reversals from time to time. Yet many Protestant groups accept this critical study and perceive that it offers a fuller understanding of scripture that is compatible with faith.

In the early twentieth century, biblical criticism spread to Judaism, and today Conservative and Reform Jews widely accept it; only Orthodox Jews still oppose it. Since the Second Vatican Council (1962–1965), Roman Catholics have also embraced the historical-critical method.[26] Today, the basic methods of literary study are still largely European academic methods. Scholars and students read sacred texts through Western eyes and by Western methods.

The effort to collect, edit, and publish the literature of world religions is also a Western academic enterprise. It had its roots in the eighteenth century, when the first copies of Chinese and Indian scripture made their way to Europe and were greeted with great interest, even enthusiasm, in some circles. One reason for this enthusiasm was an Enlightenment hope that these scriptures might be a religious or philosophical alternative to what some saw as the hidebound clericalism of Christianity. The Hindu *Vedas*, for example, were first viewed as religious expressions from near the dawn of time, pristine and unspoiled by priestcraft. Gradually, Europeans realized that the *Vedas* reflect a priestly system as traditional as that of Christianity. By the middle of the nineteenth century, as we saw, a more mature scholarly interest in world scriptures blossomed into a systematic effort to publish reliable translations. The editing and publishing of sacred texts continues today, especially in religions that have large canons. The methods used to edit, translate, publish, and interpret these scriptures draw generally from the Western tradition.

Scholarship in comparative religion came from a background that was largely Protestant in orientation. Thus, over the last century, an inevitable "Protestant bias" has crept into the way scholarship has looked at the scriptures of other faiths. Certain mainstream Protestant ideas about the nature of scripture colored the study of the scriptures of other religions and only today are being identified and corrected. These include

- A concern with textuality to the exclusion of orality, from the Protestant emphasis on the scripture as *written*.
- An orientation that assumes that scriptures are to be read mainly by the individual, from Protestant ideas of the "priesthood of all believers" and universal literacy.

---

[26]See G. P. Fogarty, *American Catholic Biblical Scholarship* (San Francisco: HarperCollins, 1989), and R. B. Robinson, *Roman Catholic Exegesis Since Divino Afflante Spiritu* (Atlanta: Scholars Press, 1988).

- The notion that scriptures are widely authoritative over every aspect of religious life, from the Protestant assertion that the scriptures are the sole authority in the Christian faith.
- The assumption that scriptures are best understood by objective, academically recognized methods of study, from mainstream Protestant attachment to sound academic procedures.[27]

Of course, believers of the other religions of the world do not share this bias, as we can see when we reflect comparatively on each of these assumptions. In some religions, such as Hinduism, the oral dimension dominates the written. In others, such as Islam, written and oral traditions are more in balance. Next, most religions do not share the Protestant notion that scriptures should be read by the individual; rather, their adherents speak and hear their scriptures in groups, usually in worship and ritual. Indeed, it comes as a striking realization for modern North Americans that most followers of many religions throughout history (and even today!) cannot read and therefore cannot read their sacred texts. For the typical follower of most faiths, texts must be *spoken* (often from memory) and *heard*.

We examined earlier the next Protestant assumption, that scriptures seek to regulate every aspect of religious life, and we concluded that they seek to regulate the center of religious life as their religion conceives that center. For most religions of the world, the Western academic approach to scripture goes against the grain of faith and is consequently viewed as alien. To study scripture historically and objectively is to question its sacredness because such study employs the same methods used to study other, nonsacred literature. For example, Islam discourages going behind the present edition of the Arabic text to inquire about earlier versions. Traditional, conservative Islam also forbids Muslims to study or use the *Qur'an* in such a way to question its unity or divine origin, as the Muslim writer Salman Rushdie discovered. His controversial novel, *The Satanic Verses,* allegedly committed blasphemy against the *Qur'an*. In 1989, Iranian officials put a $2 million price on his head, and he only recently—and tentatively—came out of hiding when the death threat was lifted. Each religion has some systematic study of its sacred texts, but such study usually remains devotional, meditative, and interpretive. Noncritical and unthreatening, it does not question the received beliefs about the origin and standing of the text.

When we read scriptures, then, we must always remember that the way we read is fully conditioned by our cultural backgrounds and academic enterprises. Those who read from a religious background must always try to keep their own viewpoints identified and in check. Those with no religious commitments must try to suspend any doubts they may have about religion and scriptures. We read scriptures as outsiders in an objective, scholarly, noncommittal way. This is altogether necessary as a first step in coming to grips with scriptures. A second step, more difficult than the first but equally necessary, is to read them as much as possible as *insiders,* with the eyes, minds, and hearts of those for whom these texts are much more than the object of scholarship.[28]

---

[27]See Levering, *Rethinking Scripture,* pp. 3–5, for more on this Protestant bias.
[28]See the excellent remarks by Eric Sharpe in *Encyclopedia of Religion,* vol. 14, p. 85, on "imaginative sympathy" in reading scripture as "insiders." See also Ross N. Reat, "Insiders and Outsiders in the Study of Religious Traditions," *Journal of the American Academy of Religion* 51 (1983): 459–475.

SCRIPTURES AND THE WORLD WIDE WEB

The last ten years have seen an explosive growth in the World Wide Web. Much information about religion can be found on the web; it seems to be one of the leading topics of discussion and inquiry. As a part of this interest in religion, many websites feature scriptures in translation or sometimes in the original.

Many positive features of this new opportunity to encounter world scriptures are obvious. The access is almost always free. The amount of scripture on the web is growing rapidly and may someday encompass most world scriptures. The Internet is an appealing way for most young, computer-oriented students (but not always their professors!) to encounter scriptures. It presents different ways of studying and learning—for example, the ability to search a text electronically. The Internet by its structure encourages exploration. Some sites are fully interactive, allowing students to ask questions and participate in online discussion groups. Finally, but not least, when students explore a religion site sponsored by its followers, the perspective provided there is likely to be a bit more that of an "insider" than classroom or textbook descriptions.

The drawbacks of studying scriptures on the web are also obvious. Some sites are not constructed well; they may have poor layout, little eye appeal, out-of-date links, or other technical deficiencies. The translations used are too often public domain works that are not edited for today's readers. When representatives of a religion post that religion's writings for religious conversion or public relations purposes, the interpretations they provide may not agree with the current academic consensus about that religion. Most significantly, these electronic publications are subject to little or no scholarly control, such as editorial or peer review before publication, so their quality varies greatly. Some sites are excellent, some average, and some poor.

This mixed situation means that many students need help in finding, using, and especially analyzing critically these web-based scripture sites. Readers of this anthology may access a special website to further their use of the web in religious studies. It has links to short, helpful essays on using the Internet in an academically appropriate way. It also has links to sites useful in the study of scriptures. The listing is not comprehensive, but it does offer a starting place to surf and learn. The address is: http://religion.wadsworth.com; search by *Anthology of World Scriptures,* and bookmark this book's site when you reach it.

THE PLAN OF THIS BOOK

This book contains excerpts of world scriptures in the following order of religions: Hinduism, Buddhism, Jainism, Sikhism, Confucianism, Taoism, Shinto, Zoroastrianism, Judaism, Christianity, Islam, and selected new religious movements. This progression keeps these religions together in their family groups and goes in order of historical development. Moreover, the reader can see the relationships among religions and scriptures more easily when related bodies of texts are dealt with in succession. For example, when the Christian scriptures and then the Islamic follow the Jewish scriptures, the deep relationship among them becomes apparent. The final chapter gives excerpts from the scriptures of Western new religious movements treated in order of their time of origin: Baha'i, the Church of Jesus Christ of Latter-day Saints, Christian Science, and the Unification Church.

Each chapter except the last (where each new religious movement is treated in a separate section) is structured as follows: An introduction outlines the scriptures included, setting them in the context of the whole religion by examining briefly their name(s), overall structure, contemporary use, and their historical origins and development. The first grouping of scripture passages deals with the history of the religion. If the faith has a founder, special attention is given to him or her; any subsequent history of the religion that scripture reflects is also excerpted. Second are passages covering the main doctrinal teaching of the religion. These topics include divine or ultimate reality, creation and the environment, the nature of humanity, and achieving human fulfillment (salvation, release, harmony, etc.). Third are passages about the moral/ethical structure of the scriptures: good, evil, and the authentic human life. Personal morality is probably more widely treated in world scriptures, but social ethics are also prominent. Such topics as war and peace, violence and nonviolence, tolerance and intolerance of people of other faiths, the status of women, and a just society are represented as fully as possible. Fourth are passages about the organization of the religion, either in its internal organization (for example, monks and laity in Buddhism) or in its attempts to organize its wider culture (such as the Hindu caste system in India). Last are passages about religious worship, ritual, devotion, and meditation. Of course, some religions have more in some of these categories than in others, but most religions do fit into them without significant distortion. Where they do not fully fit, this format is adapted to do justice to the particular nature of the texts.

The predominant rationale for this organization is *pedagogical*. It is meant to further the learning of students encountering world religions. North American readers are familiar with the categories used here, and both teachers and students of world religions will recognize them as a standard paradigm for research and teaching in religion. Moreover, they are categories that seem to fit world scriptures themselves. Why not discard any attempt to use categories of organization and simply provide one or two longer excerpts from each religion's body of scripture? A rather uniform scripture like the *Qur'an* may be possible to encompass in a few long readings. Even Islamic tradition says that the whole message of the *Qur'an* is contained in each of its chapters, so to read one is in a sense to read them all. However, what Paul Muller-Ortega says about Hinduism is true of most world religions, including the new religious movements: "It is not possible to put a single sacred text in the hands of students and expect the reading of that one text to allow students to encompass the tradition. . . . Thus, the preferred method of exposing students to the enormity of the Hindu sacred literature has been by means of anthologies."[29]

SUGGESTIONS ON HOW TO READ SCRIPTURES

Individuals reading world scriptures for the first time often feel they are entering a strange new world. Sometimes, preconceived notions of what reading a given scripture will be like turn out to be quite wrong. Students of world religion are especially

---

[29]Paul Muller-Ortega, "Exploring Textbooks: Introductions to Hinduism," in B. R. Gaventa, ed., *Critical Review of Books in Religion, 1988* (Atlanta: Scholars Press, 1989), p. 71.

susceptible to the difficulties of reading scripture. Their textbooks usually try to make scriptures easier to encounter by simplifying and summarizing the content. To encounter scriptures more directly and in their original form is a harder process. As Mortimer Adler and Charles Van Doren once wrote, "The problem of reading the Holy Book...is the most difficult problem in the field of reading."[30] In the end, however, it is more profitable for readers to wrestle as directly as possible with the texts. Of course, an anthology such as this does not present world scriptures in their totality but serves as a bridge to the full scripture text.

Each reader must ultimately find an individually suitable method for reading world scriptures. But these ten suggestions drawn from my experience and the experience of others may be helpful.

1. *Use your knowledge of religion to set these readings in a fuller context.* Try to relate scriptures as fully as possible to the life of the religions from which they come. For example, when you are reading a passage about ritual, visualize how the ritual is carried out.

2. *Read the introductions to each chapter before you turn to the passages.* They will provide an important background for understanding the passages.

3. *Skim the selections first.* Having a general feel for the "lay of the land" will help you when you begin to read in detail.

4. *Read the scripture passages objectively.* Use the same intellectual skills that you bring to any other text, religious or nonreligious. Remember their holy status in their religions, but don't be intimidated by it.

5. *Mark the text as you read.* Research shows that readers who mark the text, underlining or highlighting as few as three or four items per page, understand and remember more than readers who do not mark their text. Marking helps to make the text your own.

6. *Pay attention to literary genre.* The form and content of any literary passage reflect its genre. Read with a feeling for the differences among myth, poetry, narrative, law, and other literary forms.

7. *Make a personal glossary of unfamiliar terms and names as you go along.* You can do this easily by circling them in the text and writing them in the bottom margin. (Use circles or some other type of marking that will distinguish them from your other marked material.) Then you can go back later to make a short note of their meaning, also in the margin. The unfamiliarity and difficulty of so many words, both technical terms and personal names, are large obstacles for many students of world religions. With a little extra effort, you can minimize this difficulty.

8. *Read each selection repeatedly until you are familiar with it.* Familiarity enables you to identify any problems you have in understanding it. View these problems as opportunities for achieving greater understanding, not as roadblocks.

9. *Read the selections aloud as much as possible.* This may feel embarrassing at first because you are not accustomed to it. Listen to the sounds of the words, and try to get a sense of the oral dimensions of the text. You cannot reproduce the feeling of

---

[30]Mortimer Adler and Charles Van Doren, *How to Read a Book* (New York: Simon & Schuster, 1940), p. 288.

the original language, but reading aloud will at least remind you that the text does have an oral dimension.

10. *Put yourself, as well as you can, inside the faith of the scripture.* What could these writings mean to you if you were among those who first heard them? What could they mean to you today if you were a typical follower of that faith? By using your knowledge and imagination, you can participate in the unique use of scripture in each religion and become—partially and temporarily—an insider.[31]

---

[31]"By an act of historical imagination we can actually participate up to a certain point in the aspirations and devotions of other times and places. Yet this truly is only up to a certain point, for the curtain is suddenly lowered and we realize with a shock just how far away those places and times really are. That experience has been called 'the paradox of understanding.'" Jaroslav Pelikan, *On Searching the Scriptures—Your Own or Someone Else's* (New York: Quality Paperback Book Club, 1992), p. 7.

❧ GLOSSARY

Abrahamic monotheisms   Judaism, Christianity, and Islam.

bibliolatry   [bib-lee-AHL-ah-tree] excessive veneration of a scripture book.

bibliomancy   [BIB-lee-oh-man-see] the use of scripture to foresee future events and guide one's response to them.

canon   a more or less fixed collection of books regarded as scriptural.

commentary   a book written to explain another book, often passage by passage. Many religions possess commentaries on their scriptures.

genre   a literary form, such as poetry, myth, proverb, narrative history, and philosophical meditation.

historical-critical method   the scholarly study of a text that derives meaning from the text's earliest phases and traces the text's historical development.

icon   a holy picture. Metaphorically, scripture is an icon when it is revered as a sacred object apart from its content.

narrative   the telling of an event or series of events in story form.

oral tradition   the passing down, usually through many generations, of myths, narratives, poems, and the like by word of mouth.

scripture   text that a religious community holds to be especially sacred and authoritative.

❧ QUESTIONS FOR STUDY AND DISCUSSION

1. What does the word *scripture* mean to you?
2. "Scripture is more a Western concept than an Asian concept." To what extent do you agree or disagree with this common statement?
3. Suppose that a new potential scripture—a new gospel book about Jesus, for example—is discovered and shown to be authentic. Would such a potential scripture actually get into the scripture canon of Christianity? Why or why not?
4. What uses of scripture seem most important or interesting to you? Why?

5. What disadvantages are posed by the ancient character of scriptures? Can these be overcome? If so, how?
6. Reflect on this description of Mohandas Gandhi's teachings about studying others' scriptures: "One should read others' scriptures with respect and reverence even to be enriched in one's own religious convictions."
7. What other advantages and disadvantages of using the Internet in religious studies occur to you besides the ones given here?

✒ SUGGESTIONS FOR FURTHER READING

L. J. Biallas, "Teaching World Religions Through Their Scriptures." *Horizons* (Villanova University) 17 (1990): 76–91. Especially useful to teachers, but students can profit from it as well; focuses on narrative forms.

H. Coward, *Sacred Word and Sacred Text: Scripture in World Religions.* Maryknoll, NY: Orbis, 1988. Sound chapter-length treatments (especially of orality) of scripture in Christianity, Islam, and also Hinduism, Sikhism, and Buddhism.

H. Coward, ed., *Experiencing Scripture in World Religions.* Maryknoll, NY: Orbis, 2000. Brief, lively essays by various scholars who are also believers on the use of scripture in Judaism, Christianity, Islam, Hinduism, Sikhism, and Buddhism.

F. M. Denny and R. L. Taylor, eds., *The Holy Book in Comparative Perspective.* Columbia: University of South Carolina Press, 1985. After an introduction by the editors, this volume features up-to-date treatments of the scriptures of nine major religions, including the Church of Jesus Christ of Latter-day Saints.

W. A. Graham, "Scripture." In M. Eliade, ed., *The Encyclopedia of Religion,* vol. 13, pp. 133–145. New York: Macmillan, 1987. This lucid article is the best short survey of its topic.

P.-L. Kwok and E. Schüssler Fiorenza, eds., *Women's Sacred Scriptures.* London: SCM Press/Maryknoll, NY: Orbis, 1998. A treatment of the scriptures of several world religions with a view to a feminist reclaiming of scripture.

M. Levering, ed., *Rethinking Scripture: Essays from a Comparative Perspective.* Albany: State University of New York Press, 1989. Has an excellent essay by W. C. Smith, "Scripture as Form and Concept: Their Emergence in the Western World." W. A. Graham also has an essay, "Scripture as Spoken Word."

W. C. Smith, *What Is Scripture? A Comparative Approach.* Minneapolis: Fortress, 1993. An influential survey of its topic by the most influential researcher on world scriptures.

S. Young, *Anthology of Sacred Texts by and about Women.* New York: Crossroad, 1993. A comprehensive selection of scriptures and other important religious writings from, among others, Judaism, Christianity, Islam, Hinduism, Buddhism, Confucianism, Taoism, and select new religious movements.

✒ COMPANION WEBSITE

Visit the *Anthology of World Scriptures* companion website at **www.thomsonedu.com** for learning tools such as map explorations, flashcards of glossary terms, learning objectives, chapter practice quizzes, links to other websites for learning and research, and chapter summaries in PowerPoint® format.

CHAPTER TWO

Hinduism

Reading Hindu Scripture

A Hindu woman in Varanasi, India, reads the *Bhagavad Gita* devotionally. (*Photo by Diana Eck from the Image Bank of the Center for the Study of World Religions, Harvard University. Photo courtesy Diana Eck.*)

- In northern India, filmmaker Deepa Mehta and her cast and crew are driven out of the holy city of Varanasi by angry mobs stirred up by fundamentalist Hindu authorities. Her sets for the film *Water,* a story set in the 1930s of the confinement of widows to a life of self-denial in an ashram in an effort to follow the *Laws of Manu* scripture, are destroyed. Undeterred, she moves the filming to Sri Lanka and completes her controversial, powerful film.

- Just before dawn breaks in India, a householder rises and purifies himself with water. He then stirs back to life the embers of the sacred household fire while chanting sacred verses. Raising his arms to the rising sun, he recites a prayer to the sun-god from the most ancient scripture, the *Rig-Veda.* This ritual, the Agnihotra, has been performed continually in India for more than 3,000 years.

- In Hardwar, India, people gather in the "world's largest religious festival." Ten million people came to this site on the upper Ganges River. According to Hindu scriptures, bathing during this festival is the supreme act of worship. Much of the other activity focuses on scripture: Holy men read scripture aloud, chant their mantras, and teach mantras to the pilgrims.

- In Bangalore, twenty-three-year-old Lakshmi works in a call center, answering inquiries from customers of a prominent American corporation. She dropped out of college to work in the center, and she is paid enough to live a middle-class life and be independent of her parents. She and thousands of others like her have provoked a growing social crisis in India. According to Indian cultural norms grounded in ancient scripture called the *Laws of Manu,* young people live with their parents and are under their direction until they get married. "I want to live on my own," Lakshmi says.

INTRODUCTION

Hinduism is one of the oldest of world religions and certainly the most internally diverse. It encompasses many gods and offers many paths to salvation. The scriptures of Hinduism mirror this diversity. Vast in size, varied in usage, and profound in influence, many scriptures have been chanted, heard, taught, and repeated for 3,000 years. Generalizations about Hindu scriptures are thus especially difficult to make; almost every statement has exceptions. Still, the main lines of these scriptures can be reliably traced, and they provide good doors into the many-roomed mansion of Hinduism.

Overview of Structure

Hindus have not given any single comprehensive name to their scripture. They divide their scriptures into two classes: *Shruti* and *Smriti* (see Table 2.1). *Shruti* [SHROO-tee], "what is heard," is the primary revelation. It has no human or divine author but captures the cosmic sounds of truth first heard by **rishis** [REE-shees], ancient seers. Later seers began a process of oral transmission and practice through priestly families that continues today. *Shruti* consists of four *Vedas* (Books of Knowledge), the *Brahmanas* (Brahmin Books), the *Aranyakas* (Forest Books), and the *Upanishads* (Sittings near a Teacher). Taken together, they are "Vedic" scripture. The canon of *Shruti* has been basically fixed for almost 2,000 years, and all of Hinduism is in some sense based on it.

TABLE 2.1 Hindu Scriptures

Division	Name	Translation/Content	Size
Shruti (Vedic scripture)	*Vedas*		
	Rig-Veda	Hymn *Veda*	1,028 hymns in 10 books
	Yajur-Veda	Formula *Veda*	
	Sama-Veda	Song *Veda*	1,549 mantras
	Atharva-Veda	Spell *Veda*	731 hymns in 20 books
	Brahmanas	Brahmin Books	Correspond to each *Veda*
	Aranyakas	Forest Books	
	Upanishads	Sittings near a Teacher	123 total; 13 principal
Smriti (Post-Vedic scripture)	*Puranas*	Legends	18 books
	Mahabharata	Great Story of the Bharatas	18 books
	Ramayana	Story of Rama	50,000 lines in 7 books
	Manusmriti	Laws of Manu	12 books
	Vishnusmriti	Institutes of Vishnu	100 chapters
	Tantras	Weavings	Uncertain number of books

Smriti [SMRIH-tee], "what is remembered," designates all other scripture. It is all post-Vedic. The role of *Smriti* is to bring out the meaning of *Shruti* and apply it to later ages. Hindus consider *Smriti* revelatory only to the extent that it is grounded in *Shruti*. The *Smriti* literature is vast in size and scope. It ranges from myths and legends of the *Puranas*, epics like the *Mahabharata* and the *Ramayana*, and law codes like the *Laws of Manu* and the *Institutes of Vishnu*. These scriptures have been widely translated from their original Sanskrit into the other languages of the Indian subcontinent, and the canon of *Smriti* is still open. Because of its more popular and ever-developing nature, *Smriti* scripture has had, despite its officially secondary status to *Shruti*, a strong influence on Hindu religion and Indian culture.

In the *Shruti* category, the four *Vedas* [VAY-duhs] are the foundation of Hindu scripture. They are **samhitas** [SAHM-hee-tuhs], "collections" of hymns, formulas, songs, and spells.

- The *Rig-Veda* samhita has 1,028 hymns divided into ten books. Each hymn (*Rig*) is addressed to a single god or goddess. When a god is extolled in a hymn, the hymn praises that god above other deities, a form of worship called *henotheism*. Each hymn of the *Rig-Veda* has a fairly common sequence: It begins with the invocation of a deity; it then makes requests of that deity and offers praises by recounting her or his deeds in myth; it finishes with a brief restatement of the worshippers' request.
- The *Yajur-Veda* samhita consists mostly of prose sacrificial formulas (*yajus*) used by the presiding priest in a sacrifice.
- The *Sama-Veda* is a collection of songs and melodies (*saman*) used in sacrifice; most of the words are taken from the *Rig-Veda*. The *Rig, Yajur,* and *Sama Vedas* together are known in Hinduism as the "threefold *Veda*."

- The *Atharva-Veda* differs remarkably from the other three, containing mostly spells, curses, and charms in 731 hymns divided into twenty books. It reflects the everyday religious life of ordinary people just as the threefold *Veda* reflects the religious life of the priestly group.

The next part of *Shruti* to emerge was the **Brahmanas** [BRAH-muh-nuhs], which are manuals for sacrifice. They describe ancient Vedic sacrifice in great and fascinating detail and are organized to correspond to the four *Veda* samhitas. They present sacrifice—and especially ritual utterance, the powerful sacrificial word correctly spoken—as the power that strengthens the gods, keeps the universe intact, and brings blessing to the sacrificer. Brahmin priests sacrificed meat and other offerings to all the gods. The soma sacrifice is the most prominent. The **Aranyakas** [ah-RUN-yah-kuhs], which contain philosophical thoughts on sacrifice, especially the sacrificial fire, are a development of the *Brahmanas.* Reflections on the New Year festival are also prominent. These speculations were considered unsuitable for open knowledge and so were made in the privacy of the forest. Some *Aranyakas* have been incorporated into the *Upanishads.*

The **Upanishads** [oo-PAH-nee-shahds] form the final part of *Shruti.* One hundred twenty-three *Upanishads* have survived, but only thirteen have been influential in Hindu history. The *Upanishads* are philosophical treatments on cosmic reality and sometimes feature debates between opposing teachers. Their emphasis is on self-denial as a way to find religious truth—the way of asceticism. The ritualism of the four *Vedas* and especially of the *Brahmanas* is downplayed and even attacked in the *Upanishads.* The *Upanishads* are concerned to find the One, the absolute spiritual reality that lies in and behind all the visible elements and beings of this physical world. As the conclusion of *Shruti* and the Vedic scripture collection, the *Upanishads* are also known as the *Vedanta* (End of the *Veda*).

We begin describing the *Smriti* with the two main epics: the *Mahabharata* and the *Ramayana.* The *Ramayana* (Story of Rama) is traditionally attributed to the poet Valkimi. It was written in the third century B.C.E. Prince Rama was exiled from his kingdom and his wife, Sita, was kidnapped by the demon Ravana, but Rama was restored to his kingdom and his wife with the help of the monkey-god. The *Mahabharata* (Great Story of the Bharatas) is the longest epic in the world—four times longer than the Christian *Bible.* Its basic story involves the feud and eventual war between two sides of King Bharata's family. The *Mahabharata* is a vast repository of Indian myths and legends, and the **Bhagavad Gita** [BAH-gav-vahd GEE-tuh] (Song of the Lord) is a small part of this larger epic. The *Mahabharata* and the *Ramayana* share a common body of myth and folklore.

The *Puranas,* traditionally eighteen in number, are also concerned with myth, lore, and legend. Like the epics (and like *Smriti* in general), they are addressed to the ordinary person. Emerging about 400 to 1000 C.E., they stress devotion to a specific divinity as the way to release. Thus, some speak of Shiva, some of Vishnu, and some of Shakti, the three main devotional movements of Hinduism. By far the most popular, and influential for medieval and early modern Indian popular literature and painting, is the *Bhagavata-Purana.* This tenth-century work provides background on the Krishna of the *Bhagavad Gita,* especially his youth among the cowherders of his village and his romantic adventures with the cowherd women.

Tantras ("looms, weavings") mirror the Hinduism of medieval India. Books of mystical teachings, spells, and rituals, they deal with beliefs and yogic meditation in a popular way. Each of the three main devotional movements—Shiva, Vishnu, and Shakti—has its own official collections of tantras, which tell the exploits of the movement's gods and bring their powers to devotees by means of ritual and yoga.

The final type of *Smriti* to consider is manuals of dharma, or law codes. Law here is broadly conceived in its social and personal dimensions; it encompasses caste, life stages, diet, government, and other matters. The most important dharma manual is the *Laws of Manu,* composed around 200 C.E. in twelve books. The main concern of *Manu* is the codification and operation of the four-caste system, and *Manu*'s influence on Hindu life has been profound. Indeed, the two things that are most often said to define a practicing Hindu are acceptance of the *Vedas* and following caste duty.

Contemporary Use

Hindu scriptures have a wide variety of uses today, some of which have already been mentioned. In what follows, we trace these uses briefly, with a special focus on orality.

The four *Vedas* were orally composed and were handed down orally for thousands of years. To put them in a book would have seemed absurd, even sacrilegious, because they were in essence a spoken and heard revelation (*Shruti*), and their power resided in their spokenness.

Brahmin priests use the *Vedas* for ritual. The threefold *Veda* has always been the text of this religious aristocracy, never of the people as a whole. From the first, the sound of these scriptures was more important than their content. Traditionalist Hindus believe that the sounds of the *Veda* were the sounds that the sages heard reverberating from the creation of the universe and that the same sounds will be used again at the next cycle of re-creation. These sounds have been passed on orally from guru to student for thousands of years. Gurus teach their students every element of correct oral usage of the *Veda,* including correct enunciation, poetic meter, volume, and pitch. Brahmins who excel in *Veda* memorization and ritual enactment are known as **pandits** (compare with the English word *pundit*). As a student, each young Brahmin is educated in one of the four *Vedas* and becomes an expert in the use of that *Veda* in sacrifice. Hymns in the *Rig-Veda* often end with a request to the deity that the sacrificers might "speak as men of power" during the rites.

Hindus do not study the content of the *Vedas* in, for example, meditation or doctrinal instruction. Much of the ancient Vedic form of the Sanskrit language has been lost, and much of its meaning is not recoverable. For the past 2,000 years, accordingly, Brahmins often have not understood what they were saying as they chanted the *Vedas* in the rituals. This is not important; only the correct sounds matter. Today, only a few Brahmin families keep up a ritually correct form of the ancient Vedic sacrifices. However, all domestic rituals are done with Vedic formulas. Speaking and concentrating on the **mantra** [MAHN-truh] allow the believer to tap into the cosmic power of creative speech.

The *Upanishads* became the texts of the philosophers, especially of the Vedanta school of Hindu philosophy. Reflecting on the meaning of this scripture in a life of strict renunciation allows the sage to be set free from desire and rebirth. In the last hundred years, a neo-Vedantic school has arisen, mainly drawing on ancient Hindu themes and also influenced by Western religious ideas such as theism and interreligious tolerance.

Law codes are used for the ordering of society. They especially reflect the Brahmin caste and its view of Hindu life. How closely these books were followed and enforced in ancient times cannot now be determined, but their broadest aspects have certainly retained much authority.

Of all Hindu scripture, the epics have been the best known and most loved. The *Bhagavad Gita,* because of the way it affirms and integrates many main aspects of Hinduism, has been acceptable and influential among most Hindus. For its promotion of one way as the best, however, it remains the special text of the Vishnu-Krishna devotional movement.

For most of Hindu history, the primacy of these works has been in their oral, not their written, form. For example, the four *Veda* samhitas probably were composed and collected before writing was known in India. The *Upanishads* were not fully written down until 1656 C.E., and then only at the command of the non-Hindu Sultan Dara Shakoh, who ordered a translation of these oral works into Persian. Since then, the *Upanishads* have been translated by Hindus into the other main Indian languages; the original Sanskrit was written down as well. The Hindu tradition has regarded writing itself as polluting compared with the sanctity of the spoken word. Now, however, orality is fading, and it is common to see even holy men reading aloud from books instead of "reading" from memory. Still, the "sound" of the scriptures continues to be important, for sound is their very essence.

Comparing a typical Hindu attitude toward scripture with Western attitudes, Daniel Gold remarks, "The idea of Vedic authority known to traditional Hindus is much more diffuse and abstract than the idea of a closed biblical canon known to the West. Christians, for example, variously interpret a revealed text to which most people have access and of which they can make some literal sense. For Hindus, by contrast, a reverence for scriptural authority can often mean simply that they think that what they do somehow comes from the Vedas, texts which in their antiquity are very rarely used or understood anymore.... They exist now primarily as words of power incorporated into newer rites."[1]

To sum up, Hindus' use of scripture depends on their class and occupation and on the particular type of Hinduism (philosophical, devotional, etc.) they follow. All Hindus have a strong, if vague, reverence for the threefold *Veda,* a feeling for the structure of society as reflected in the law codes, and in devotional Hinduism, a strong feeling for the literature of one's single chosen god or goddess.

Historical Origin and Development

The long history of Hindu scripture parallels the history of Hinduism as a whole. We here briefly survey how Hindu scripture began, the process of its growth, and how it took its present form. Keep in mind this general principle of Hindu scripture as we begin this section: The literature grows by association. Earlier works, no matter how sacred, invite and attract later works with related themes and styles, which in turn attract still more sacred literature.

The four *Vedas* have their origin in ritual. Sacrifice itself seems to have come first, for even the earliest *Vedas* presuppose an established sacrifice. The songs, melodies, and formal directions for their performance were drawn up later, soon after the Aryan

---

[1]D. Gold, "Organized Hinduisms," in M. E. Marty and R. S. Appleby, *Fundamentalisms Observed* (Chicago: University of Chicago Press, 1991), pp. 542–543.

invasion of India around 1500 B.C.E. The *Rig-Veda* contains songs for sacrifice. The oldest hymns deal with the gods of the Indo-Aryans: the sky-god Dyaus Pitar, whom the Greeks knew as Zeus, and the earth-goddess Prithivi Mater. In the next stage, these old gods receded and new gods arose: Indra the new sky-god, Agni the god of fire, Soma the god of drugged sacrifice. The final hymns written down are found in the present *Rig-Veda* Books 1 and 10, which move from polytheistic nature gods to the kind of cosmic speculations that search for the oneness of all being. The final form of the *Rig-Veda* was reached about 1200 B.C.E.

The *Sama-Veda* was composed after the *Rig-Veda* was complete. It has lines from the *Rig-Veda*, which are chanted to fixed melodies. The melodies are not captured in the written text but are passed on from singing priest to his disciples. The proper lyrics and music were essential to the success of the rite. The *Yajur-Veda* contains directions for sacrifice and also was written down after the *Rig-Veda* was established. The *Atharva-Veda* with its magical spells gives a glimpse into the more popular levels of ancient Hinduism. The spells are addressed not to the great gods but to the gods and spirits that control everyday life, its cycles, and its challenges. The first seven books are the earliest; Books 8 through 12 are more recent and contain cosmological speculations similar to Book 10 of the *Rig-Veda* and the later *Upanishads*.

The *Brahmanas* mark the high point of Hindu ritualism. The power of the priesthood steadily grew in Vedic times (2000–1000 B.C.E.), and the focus of the *Brahmanas* is on sacrifice itself, not on the gods. Sacrifice is the power that generates the cosmos and keeps it going. The main group of the *Brahmanas* deals with the *Yajur-Veda* and the ritual process. Sacrifices using soma are prominent, as is the horse sacrifice, which took great expense and an entire year to enact.

The *Aranyakas* mark the beginning of a departure from Vedic ritualism. Mixed and disjointed in content, these reflections may have been developed by marginalized Brahmins or by members of the warrior caste.

The *Upanishads,* the last of the Vedic scriptures, are close in style to the *Aranyakas.* Most were written from the eighth to the fourth centuries B.C.E. The so-called principal *Upanishads* number about thirteen and are the only *Upanishads* accepted by all Hindus. Some with special devotion to a particular deity date from the beginnings of the Common Era all the way to the sixteenth century C.E. and are accepted only by certain Hindu sects as interest in ritual fades and philosophy/renunciation advances. The oldest of these are the *Chandogya* and *Brihad-Aranyaka Upanishads.*

The *Upanishads,* like most *Shruti,* are not uniform or systematic; they are diverse collections of philosophical materials from different teachers over the centuries. The "world-affirming" Vedic religion that originally sought blessing in this world has also become a "world-negating" religion that seeks release from continually reincarnated existence in this world. These *Upanishads* present the way of knowledge, the search for the eternal One called **Brahman** [BRAH-muhn] as it relates to **Atman** [AHT-muhn], the eternal Self at the hidden center of every human. They are the beginnings of Hindu philosophy, which has been and remains influential, although it has been an option for only a tiny minority of Hindus of any period.

Unlike the *Shruti,* the epics of *Smriti* display very little interest in ritual and instead deal with broad religious and cultural topics. The *Mahabharata* was finished by 400 C.E., the *Ramayana* by 200 B.C.E. Evident in both are three layers of development: (1) myths of the gods, from earliest Hinduism; (2) the central plot of each epic; and (3) discussions of religious duty and law. The insertion of this last layer into the epic is a typically Indian practice: to pause at key points in the narrative for a religious discussion. The most famous of these insertions, the *Bhagavad Gita*, section 6 of the *Mahabharata*, today is reckoned a book in itself. These discussions are precursors of the law books, to which we now turn.

The law codes are called **Dharma-Shastras** [DAHR-muh SHAS-truhs], "Writings on Duty." Books on duty began to be compiled in the schools in which the *Vedas* and *Brahmanas* were studied. They developed into comprehensive and systematic books that eventually formed the basis of Hindu law. *Manu* was written perhaps about 200 C.E. as a full code for all Hindu society, for every caste, occupation, and stage of life. Like the law books of most religions and civilizations, *Manu* and the other law codes were developed by commentary as the centuries passed, and thus, their influence was perpetuated. How deep this influence may have been is unknown because *Manu* (again like most law codes) gives prescriptions for an ideal society. Real Hindu life, like the life of all religions, no doubt fell short of its ideals.

Eighteen of the ancient stories of the *Puranas* are especially important. Their themes are creation, re-creation, origins of the gods and sages, eras of common history, and dynastic histories. Some, like the *Upanishads*, are sectarian, appealing to devotees of only one god. The *Puranas* fall into three main categories, as they promote the gods Vishnu, Shiva, and others. The most important *Purana* is the *Bhagavata-Purana*, composed about 400–1000 C.E. It is based on and furthers the book for which it is named, the *Bhagavad Gita*.

Tantras—books of mystical teachings, spells, and directions for rituals—arose as a popular supplement to Vedic religion. While acknowledging the truth and authority of the *Vedas,* the tantras go beyond them to provide updated rituals. They perfect the use of specific techniques for the body and the mind. Tantrism is widespread in Hindu religion, but the devotional cult of the goddess Shakti has a special attachment to it. The Shaktic tantras occasionally feature "left-handed" tantrism, which most Westerners wrongly associate with tantrism as a whole: esoteric practices, magic, and exotic sexual practices. The tantras were written in the period 500–1800 C.E.

TEACHING

Aditi and the Birth of the Gods

This hymn presents several different and seemingly contradictory explanations of the creation of the world: It was spoken by the lord of sacred speech; it came from nonexistence; the mother-goddess gave birth to it; it was formed from the mutual births of Aditi and Daksa; it was formed from Martanda. These and other explanations still exist among Hindus today.[2]

---

[2]All selections from the *Rig-Veda* are reprinted from *The Rig Veda, An Anthology,* by Wendy Doniger O'Flaherty (London: Penguin, 1981). Copyright © 1981 Wendy Doniger O'Flaherty. Used by permission.

Rig-Veda 10.72.

Let us now speak with wonder of the births of the gods, so that someone may see them when the hymns are chanted in this later age. The lord of sacred speech, like a smith, fanned them together. In the earliest age of the gods, existence was born from nonexistence. In the first age of the gods, existence was born from nonexistence. After this the quarters of the sky were born from her who crouched with legs spread. The earth was born from her who crouched with legs spread, and from the earth the quarters of the sky were born. From Aditi, Daksa was born, and from Daksa Aditi was born. [5] For Aditi was born as your daughter, O Daksa, and after her were born the blessed gods, the kinsmen of immortality. When you gods took your places there in the water with your hands joined,[3] a thick cloud of mist arose from you like dust from dancers. When you gods like magicians caused the worlds to swell, you drew forth the sun that was hidden in the ocean. Eight sons are there of Aditi, who were born of her body. With seven she went forth among the gods, but she threw Martanda, the sun, aside. With seven sons Aditi went forth into the earliest age. But she bore Martanda so that he would in turn beget offspring[4] and then soon die.

_____

[3]_hands joined:_ the typical Indian posture of greeting and respect.
[4]_offspring:_ humanity, which begets its offspring and dies.

Two Philosophical Views of Creation

Many accounts of the origin of the universe are philosophical rather than mythological. Questioning and puzzling, they stir the listener to reflection. In the first selection, "that one" is the impersonal creator by whom the gods themselves are created. This hymn has been most influential among Hindus. The second selection, from an important _Upanishad,_ presents a philosophical reflection on the origin of the world. It traces creation to Brahman, the world-soul that is the All in and behind the world. The cosmic Person _(purusha)_ identified with the world-soul is neither male nor female, despite the references to the Person as "he."[5]

[_Rig-Veda_ 10.129] There was neither nonexistence nor existence then; there was neither the realm of space nor the sky which is beyond. What stirred? Where? In whose protection? Was there water, bottomlessly deep? There was neither death nor immortality then. There was no distinguishing sign of night or of day. That one breathed, windless, by its own impulse. Other than that there was nothing beyond. Darkness was hidden by darkness in the beginning; with no distinguishing sign, all this was water. The life force that was covered with emptiness one arose through the power of heat. Desire came upon that one in the beginning; that was the first seed of mind. Poets seeking in their heart with wisdom found the bond of existence in nonexistence. [5] Their cord[6] was extended across. Was there below? Was there above? There were seed-placers; there were powers. There was impulse beneath; there was giving-forth above. Who really knows? Who here will proclaim it? Where was it produced? Where did this creation come from? The gods came afterwards, with the creation of this universe. Who then knows where it has arisen? Where this creation has arisen—perhaps it

_____

[5]This and all other selections from the _Upanishads_ are taken, with editing, from F. Max Müller, trans., _The Upanishads, Sacred Books of the East,_ vols. 1 and 15 (Oxford: Oxford University Press, 1878, 1884).

[6]_cord:_ the bond of existence, extending across the universe.

Rig-Veda 10.129; _Brihad-Aranyaka Upanishad_ 1.4.1–7.

formed itself, or perhaps it did not—the one[7] who looks down on it, in the highest heaven, only he knows—or perhaps he does not know.

[*Brihad-Aranyaka Upanishad* 1.4.1–7] In the beginning this world was Soul alone, in the shape of a Person. He looked around and saw nothing but himself. He first said, "This is I." Therefore, he became "I" by name. Therefore even now, if a man is asked he first says, "This is I," and then pronounces his other name. Before [*purva*] all this he burnt down [*ush*] all evils; therefore he was a Person [*purusha*]. Truly he who knows this burns down everyone who tries to be before him.

He feared, and therefore anyone who is lonely fears. He thought, "As there is nothing but myself, why should I fear?" Then his fear passed away. For what should he have feared? But he felt no delight. Therefore a man who is lonely feels no delight. He longed for a second person. As he was as large as a man and woman together, he made his Self to fall in two, and there came husband and wife. Therefore Yajnavalkya said: "We two are thus like half a shell." Therefore the void that was there [in the male] is filled by the wife. He had sexual intercourse with her, and humans were born.

She thought, "How can he have sexual intercourse with me, after having produced me from himself? I shall hide myself." She then became a cow. But he became a bull and had sex with her, and therefore cows were born. Then she became a mare, and he a stallion; then he a male ass, and she a female ass. He had sex with her [in both forms], and therefore one-hoofed animals were born. He became a she-goat, she a he-goat; he became a ewe, she a ram. He had sex with her, and therefore goats and sheep were born. In this way he created everything that exists in pairs, down to the ants. [5] He knew this: "I indeed am this creation, for I created all this." Therefore he became the creation, and he who knows this lives in this his creation.

Next he thus produced fire by rubbing. From the mouth, as from the fire-hole,[8] and from the hands he created fire. Therefore both the mouth and the hands are hairless inside, for the fire-hole is without hair inside.

People say, "Sacrifice to this god or that god." But each god is his manifestation, for he is all gods.

Whatever is moist he created from semen; this is Soma. So this universe is really either food or eaters of food. Soma is food, Agni the eater. This is the highest creation of Brahman, when he created the gods from his better part, and when he who was then mortal created the immortals. Therefore it was the highest creation. He who knows this lives in this highest creation....

He cannot be seen, for when breathing he is called breath. When speaking, he is called speech; when seeing, eye; when hearing, ear; when thinking, mind. All these are only the names of his acts. He who worships him as the one or the other, does not know him.... Let men worship him as Soul [Atman], for in the Soul all these are one. This Soul is the footprint of everything, for through it one knows everything. As one can find again by footprints what was lost, he who knows this finds glory and praise.

---

[7] *the one:* Prajapati, the high god.

[8] *fire-hole:* Sanskrit *yoni*, the circular religious image of the human vagina symbolizing the female cosmic creative power.

The God Indra

Indra is the sky-god, the king of the gods. This hymn extols Indra's accomplishments over several opposing gods and for promoting the welfare of the people. It seeks to defend the importance of Indra against those who ignore him or even deny his existence (verse 5). This defense evidently did not succeed, because in post-Vedic Hinduism, Indra has largely disappeared.

Rig-Veda 2.12.

The god who had insight the moment he was born, the first who protected the gods with his power of thought, before whose hot breath the two world-halves tremble at the greatness of his manly powers—he, my people, is Indra. He who made fast the tottering earth, who made still the quaking mountains, who measured out and extended the expanse of the air, who propped up the sky—he, my people, is Indra. He who killed the serpent and loosed the seven rivers, who drove out the cows that had been pent up by Vala,[9] who gave birth to fire between two stones, the winner of booty in combats—he, my people, is Indra. He by whom all these changes were rung, who drove the race of Dasas[10] down into obscurity, who took away the flourishing wealth of the enemy as a winning gambler takes the stake—he, my people, is Indra.

[5] He about whom they ask, "Where is he?," or they say of him, the terrible one, "He does not exist," he who diminishes the flourishing wealth of the enemy as gambling does—believe in him! He, my people, is Indra. He who encourages the weary and the sick, and the poor priest who is in need, who helps the man who harnesses the stones to press Soma, he who has lips fine for drinking—he, my people, is Indra.

He under whose command are horses and cows and villages and all chariots, who gave birth to the sun and the dawn and led out the waters, he, my people, is Indra. He who is invoked by both of two armies, enemies locked in combat, on this side and that side, he who is even invoked separately by each of two men standing on the very same chariot, he, my people, is Indra. He without whom people do not conquer, he whom they call on for help when they are fighting, who became the image of everything, who shakes the unshakable—he, my people, is Indra.

[10] He who killed with his weapon all those who had committed a great sin, even when they did not know it, he who does not pardon the arrogant man for his arrogance, who is the slayer of the Dasas, he, my people, is Indra. He who in the fortieth autumn discovered Sambara living in the mountains, who killed the violent serpent, the Danu, as he lay there, he, my people, is Indra. He, the mighty bull who with his seven reins let loose the seven rivers to flow, who with his thunderbolt in his hand hurled down Rauhina as he was climbing up to the sky, he, my people, is Indra. Even the sky and the earth bow low before him, and the mountains are terrified of his hot breath.

He who is known as the Soma-drinker, with the thunderbolt in his hand, with the thunderbolt in his palm, he, my people, is Indra. He who helps with his favor the one who presses and the one who cooks,[11] the praiser and the preparer, he for whom prayer is nourishment, for whom Soma is the special gift, he, my people, is Indra. [15] You who furiously grasp the prize for the one who presses and the one who cooks, you are truly real. Let us be dear to you, Indra, all our days, and let us speak as men of power in the sacrificial gathering.

---

[9] *Vala:* Indra's demonic enemy, who penned up the cows.
[10] *Dasas:* literally, "slaves," enemies of the Aryans whom they subjugated.

---

[11] *presses . . . cooks:* in preparation of the soma.

Rudra and Shiva

Although one of the main branches of devotional Hinduism is Shaivism, Shiva does not have a well-known text to celebrate him as Krishna does in the *Bhagavad Gita*. This late Upanishadic hymn identifies the Vedic god Rudra and the Cosmic Person with Shiva. It is used today by the worshippers of Shiva to express his praise. This hymn shows how the worship of one god characteristic of devotional Hinduism is related to the wider Hindu traditions with many gods.

Shvetashvatara Upanishad 3.1–13.

The snarer rules alone by his powers, rules all the worlds by his powers. He is the same, while things arise and exist. They who know this are immortal. There is only one Rudra. They do not allow a second; he rules all the worlds by his powers. He stands behind all persons. Having created all worlds, he, the protector, rolls it up at the end of time. This god has his eyes, his face, his arms, and his feet in every place. When producing heaven and earth, he forges them together with his arms and his wings. He is the creator and supporter of the gods. Rudra is the great seer, the lord of all, who formerly gave birth to Hiranyagarbha. May he endow us with good thoughts.

[5] O Rudra, dweller in the mountains, look upon us with your most blessed form that is auspicious, not terrible, and reveals no evil! O lord of the mountains, make lucky that arrow that you hold in your hand to shoot. Do not hurt man or beast! Beyond this is the High Brahman, the vast, hidden in the bodies of all creatures. He alone envelops everything, as the Lord. Those who know this become immortal. I know that great Person [*purusha*] of sunlike luster beyond the darkness. A man who truly knows him passes over death; there is no other path to go.

This whole universe is filled by this Person, to whom there is nothing superior, from whom there is nothing different, than whom there is nothing smaller or larger. This Person stands alone, fixed like a tree in the sky. [10] That which is beyond this world is without form and without suffering. They who know this become immortal, but others suffer pain.

The Blessed One exists in the faces, the heads, the necks of all. He dwells in the cave of the heart of all beings. He is all-pervading, and therefore he is the omnipresent Shiva. That Person is the great lord. He is the mover of existence. He possesses the purest power reaching everything. He is light; he is undecaying. The Person, not larger than a thumb, always dwelling in the heart of man, is perceived by the heart, the thought, and the mind. Those who know this become immortal.

"That You Are"

In this reading, the Oneness that exists in and beyond the world is developed in a dialogue between a son and his father. Popularly known as "The Education of Svetaketu," this story points to the cosmic Self as the inner essence of all that is.

Om.[12] There lived once Svetaketu Aruneya, the grandson of Aruna. To him his father, Uddalaka, the son of Aruna, said: "Svetaketu, go to school. For there is none belonging to our race, who, not having studied the *Veda*, is, so to speak, a Brahmana by birth only."

Having begun his apprenticeship with a teacher when he was twelve years of age, Svetaketu returned to his father when he was twenty-four, having then studied all the *Vedas*. But he was conceited, considering himself well read and stern. His father said to him: "Svetaketu, you are so conceited, considering yourself so well read, and so stern. My dear son, have you ever asked for that instruction by which we hear what cannot be heard? Have you asked for that by which we perceive what cannot be perceived, by which we know what cannot be known?"

"What is that instruction, sir?" he asked.

The father replied: "My dear, as by one clod of clay all that is made of clay is known, the difference being only a name, arising from speech, but the truth being that all is clay. As, my dear, by one

---

[12]*Om:* A lesson is often begun with this cosmic sound [OHM].

Chandogya Upanishad 6.1–2, 9–11.

nugget of gold all that is made of gold is known, the difference being only a name, arising from speech, but the truth being that all is gold. As, my dear, by one pair of nail scissors all that is made of iron is known, the difference being only a name, arising from speech, but the truth being that all is iron—thus, my dear, is that instruction."

The son said: "Surely those venerable men, my teachers, did not know that. For if they had known it, why should they not have told it me? Sir, tell me that."

"In the beginning, my dear, there was one thing only, without a second. It thought, May I be many, may I grow forth. It sent forth fire. That fire thought, May I be many, may I grow forth. It sent forth water. Therefore whenever anybody anywhere is hot and perspires, water is produced on him from fire alone. Water thought, May I be many, may I grow forth. It sent forth earth (food). Therefore whenever it rains anywhere, most food is then produced. From water alone is eatable food produced. . . .

[9] "As the bees, my son, make honey by collecting the juices of distant trees, and reduce the juice into one form, and as these juices have no discrimination, so that they might say, I am the juice of this tree or that, in the same manner, my son, all these creatures, when they have become merged in the True (either in deep sleep or in death), know not that they are merged in the True. Whatever these creatures are here, whether a lion, or a wolf, or a boar, or a worm, or a midge, or a gnat, or a mosquito, that they become again and again. Now that which is that subtle essence, in it all that exists has its self. It is the True. It is the Self, and that, Svetaketu, you are."

"Please, Sir, inform me still more," said the son.

"These rivers, my son, run, the eastern like the Ganges, toward the east, the western like the Sindhu, toward the west. They go from sea to sea, that is, the clouds lift up the water from the sea to the sky, and send it back as rain to the sea. They become indeed sea. And as those rivers, when they are in the sea, do not know I am this or that river, in the same manner, my son, all these creatures, when they have come back from the True, know not that they have come back from the True. Whatever these creatures are here, whether a lion, or a wolf, or a boar, or a worm, or a midge, or a gnat, or a mosquito, that they become again and again. That which is that subtle essence, in it all that exists has its self. It is the True. It is the Self, and that, Svetaketu, you are."

"Please, Sir, inform me still more," said the son.

"If someone were to strike at the root of this large tree here, it would bleed, but live. If he were to strike at its stem, it would bleed, but live. If he were to strike at its top, it would bleed, but live. Pervaded by the living Self that tree stands firm, drinking in its nourishment and rejoicing; but if the life (the living Self) leaves one of its branches, that branch withers; if it leaves a second, that branch withers; if it leaves a third, that branch withers. If it leaves the whole tree, the whole tree withers. In exactly the same manner, my son, know this. This body indeed withers and dies when the living Self has left it; the living Self dies not. That subtle essence is the self of all that exists. It is the True. It is the Self, and that, Svetaketu, you are."

ETHICS

Sin and Forgiveness

The god Varuna protects the cosmic order and punishes those humans who violate it by misdeeds. This passage presents the heartfelt pleas of the worshipper to Varuna to reveal his unknown sin to him and pardon it.

The generations have become wise by the power of [Varuna], who has propped apart the two world-halves even though they are so vast. He has pushed away the dome of the sky to make it high and wide; he has set the sun on its double journey and spread out the earth. I ask my own heart, "When shall I be close to Varuna? Will he enjoy my offering and not be provoked to anger? When shall I see his mercy and rejoice?" I ask myself what that transgression was, Varuna, for I wish to understand. I turn to the wise to ask them. The poets have told me the very same thing: "Varuna has been provoked to anger against you."

O Varuna, what was the terrible crime for which you wish to destroy your friend who praises you? Proclaim it to me so that I may hasten to prostrate myself before you and be free from sin, for you are hard to deceive and are ruled by yourself alone. [5] Free us from the harmful deeds of our fathers, and from those that we have committed with our own bodies. O king, free Vasistha[13] like a thief who has stolen cattle, like a calf set free from a rope. The mischief was not done by my own free will, Varuna; wine, anger, dice, or carelessness led me astray. The older shares in the mistake of the younger. Even sleep does not avert evil. As a slave serves a generous master, so would I serve the furious god and be free from sin. The noble god[14] gave understanding to those who did not understand; being yet wiser, he speeds the clever man to wealth. O Varuna, you who are ruled by yourself alone, let this praise lodge in your very heart. Let it go well for us always with your blessings.

---

[13]*Vasistha:* a wise man who, according to myth, broke into Varuna's house; he was tied up but then freed when he praised Varuna.
[14]*the noble god:* Varuna.

Rig-Veda 7.86.

The Three *Da's*

The main virtues of Hinduism are often put in their most elemental form as the three *da's: damyata,* restraint and self-control; *datta,* generosity; and *dayadhvam,* compassion. These are said to be commanded from the beginning.

The threefold offspring of Prajapati—gods, men, and demons—lived as students of sacred knowledge with their father Prajapati. Having lived the life of a student of sacred knowledge, the gods said: "Speak to us, sir."

Brihadaranyaka Upanishad 5.2.

Prajapati spoke to them this syllable, "*Da*. Do you understand this?"

They said to him, "We did understand. You said to us, 'Control yourselves (*damyata*).'"

"*Om!*" he replied. "You did understand."

Then they said to him again, "Speak to us, sir."

He spoke to them this syllable, "*Da*. Do you understand this?"

They said to him: "We do understand. You said to us, 'Give *(datta)*.'"

"*Om!*" he said. "You did understand."

So then the spiritual beings said to him, "Speak to us, sir."

He said this syllable to them, "*Da*. Do you understand?"

They said, "We understand. You said to us, 'Be compassionate (*dayadhvam*).'"

"*Om!*" he said. "You did understand."

The divine voice of the thunder repeats, "Da! Da! Da! Control yourself, give, and be compassionate." One should practice this same triad: self-control, giving, and compassion.

The Way of Asceticism

This reading presents all the ancient practices of Hinduism as necessary. But they are "unsafe boats," and those who trust in them to accomplish release are "fools" and "ignorant." The only effective way of release is the way of knowledge based on renunciation and asceticism. This belief has been a guiding principle for ascetics and holy men from Upanishadic times until today.

This is the truth: the sacrificial works that the poets saw in the hymns [of the *Veda*] have been performed in many ways in the Vedic age. Practice them diligently, you lovers of truth! This is your path that leads to the world of good works!

When the fire is lighted and the flame flickers, let a man offer his oblations between the two portions of melted butter, as an offering with faith. A man's Agnihotra sacrifice destroys his seven worlds if it is not followed by the new-moon and full-moon sacrifices, by the four-months' sacrifices, and by the harvest sacrifice. It destroys his seven worlds if it is unattended by guests, not offered at all, done without the ceremony to all the gods, or not offered according to the rules....

[5] If a man performs his sacred works when these flames are shining, and the sacrificial offerings follow at the right time, they lead him as sunrays to where the one Lord of the gods dwells. "Come here, come here!," the brilliant offerings say to him. They carry the sacrificer on the rays of the sun, while they utter pleasant speech and praise him: "This is your holy Brahma-world, gained by your good works."

But those boats, the eighteen sacrifices,[15] are truly frail. Fools who praise this as the highest good are subjected again and again to old age and death. Fools dwelling in darkness, wise in their own conceit and puffed up with vain knowledge, go round and round, staggering back and forth; they are like blind men led by the blind.... [10] Considering sacrifice and good works as the best, these fools know no higher good. Having enjoyed their reward in the height of heaven, gained by good works, they come back again to this world or a lower one. But those who practice penance and faith in the forest, who are tranquil, wise and live on alms, depart free from passion through the sun to where that immortal Person dwells, whose nature is imperishable.

---

[15]*eighteen sacrifices:* Vedic rituals.

Let a Brahmin, after he has examined all these worlds that are gained by works, acquire freedom from all desires. Nothing that is eternal can be gained by what is not eternal. To understand this, let him take fuel in his hand[16] and

approach a guru who is learned and dwells entirely in Brahman. The wise teacher truly tells that knowledge of Brahman through which he knows the eternal and true Person. He tells a pupil who has approached him respectfully, whose thoughts are not troubled by any desires and who has obtained perfect peace.

---

[16]*fuel in his hand:* a sign of studentship.

Stages of Life for a Twice-Born Man

The first stage of Hindu life is that of the student, who lives and studies with his guru (private teacher). The second stage is that of the householder, when the young man, his studies complete, must marry and father children. Here the rules for whom to marry are presented. The third stage is that of retirement into the forest, and *Manu* sets forth the style of life and religious aims of this stage. The fourth stage is that of the ascetic who renounces all typical life to find release from rebirth. These laws on the stages of life reflect the situation of about 200 C.E., when *Manu* was written. Some differ from present practice. Asceticism, for example, no longer requires a prior retirement stage but can be entered by an adult male at any time. The system presented here is idealized—only a minority of Hindus in the past and present have experienced it fully. Nonetheless, it continues to be influential.[17]

[2.69, the Stage of Studentship] Having performed the rite of initiation,[18] the teacher must first instruct the pupil in the rules of personal purification, conduct, fire-worship, and twilight devotions. [70] A student who is about to begin the study of the *Veda* shall receive instruction after he has sipped water according to the sacred law, has made the Brahmangali,[19] has put on clean clothing, and has brought his sexual organs under due control. At the beginning and at the end of a lesson in the *Veda* he must always clasp both the feet of his teacher. He must study by joining hands; that is called the Brahmangali [joining the palms for the sake of the *Veda*]. With crossed

hands he must clasp the feet of the teacher, and touch the left foot with his left hand, the right foot with his right hand. The teacher, always unwearied, must say to him who is about to begin studying, "Recite!" He shall stop when the teacher says, "Stop!" Let him always pronounce the syllable "Om" at the beginning and at the end of a lesson in the *Veda*. Unless the syllable "Om" precedes, the lesson will slip away from him, and unless it follows it will fade away....

[191] When ordered by his teacher, and without an order, a student shall always exert himself in studying [the *Veda*], and in doing what is serviceable to his teacher. Controlling his body, his speech, his organs of sense, and his mind, let him stand with joined hands, looking at the face of his teacher. Let him always keep his right arm uncovered, behave decently, and keep the rest of his body well covered. When he is addressed with the words, "Be seated," he shall sit down, facing his teacher. In the presence of his teacher let him

---

[17]Selections from *Manu* are taken, with editing, from G. Buhler, trans., *The Laws of Manu, Sacred Books of the East,* vol. 25 (Oxford: Oxford University Press, 1886).
[18]*rite of initiation:* the acceptance of a male into full membership in the Hindu community.
[19]*Brahmangali:* the traditional Indian gesture of greeting and respect, explained more fully in the next verse.

Laws of Manu 2.69–74, 191–201; 3.1–19; 6.1–9, 33–49.

always eat less [than the teacher], and wear less valuable clothing and ornaments. Let him rise earlier and go to bed later. [195] Let him not answer or talk with his teacher while reclining on a bed, or while sitting, or eating, or standing, or with an averted face. Let him talk standing up, if his teacher is seated, advancing toward him when he stands, going to meet him if he advances, and running after him when he runs. . . .

When his teacher is near, let his bed or seat be low; but within sight of his teacher he shall not sit carelessly at ease. Let him not pronounce the name of his teacher without adding an honorific title, even when talking about him behind his back. Let him not mimic his gait, speech, or conduct. [200] Wherever people justly criticize or falsely defame his teacher, he must cover his ears or depart to another place. By criticizing his teacher, even though justly, he will become in his next birth an ass. By falsely defaming him, he will become a dog. He who lives on his teacher's belongings will become a worm, and he who is envious of his merit will become a larger insect.

[3.1, the Stage of the Householder] The vow of studying the three *Vedas* under a teacher must be kept for thirty-six years, or for half that time, or for a quarter, or until the student has perfectly learned them. A student who has studied in due order the three *Vedas,* or two, or even only one, without breaking the rules of studentship, shall enter the order of householders. He who is famous for the strict performance of his duties and has received his heritage, the *Veda,* from his father, shall be honored. He will sit on a couch and be adorned with a garland, with the present of a cow and honey-mixture. With the permission of his teacher, having bathed and performed according to the rule the ritual for returning home, a twice-born man shall marry a wife of equal caste who is endowed with auspicious bodily marks. [5] A young woman who is neither a Sapinda[20] on the mother's side nor belongs to the same family on the father's side is recommended to twice-born men for marriage and conjugal union.

In connecting himself with a wife, let him carefully avoid the ten following types of families, even if they are great, or rich in cattle, horses, sheep, grain, or other property. He must avoid a family that neglects the sacred rites, one in which no male children are born, one in which the *Veda* is not studied, one that has thick hair on the body, those that are subject to hemorrhoids, tuberculosis, weakness of digestion, epilepsy, or white and black leprosy. Let him not marry a young woman with reddish hair, nor one who has a redundant body part, nor one who is sickly, nor one either with no hair on the body or too much hair. Let him not marry one who is too talkative or has red eyes. Let him not marry one named after a constellation, a tree, or a river, nor one bearing the name of a low caste, or of a mountain, nor one named after a bird, a snake, or a slave, nor one whose name inspires terror. [10] Let him wed a female free from bodily defects and who has an agreeable name. She must have the graceful gait of a swan or of an elephant, moderate hair on the body and on the head, small teeth, and soft limbs.

For the first marriage of twice-born men, wives of equal caste are recommended. But for those who because of desire take a second wife, the following females are approved. They are chosen according to the order of the castes. It is declared that a Shudra woman alone can be the wife of a Shudra, she and one of his own caste the wives of a Vaisya, those two and one of his own caste the wives of a Kshatriya, those three and one of his own caste the wives of a Brahmin. A Shudra woman is not mentioned even in any ancient story as the first wife of a Brahmin or of a Kshatriya, though they lived in the greatest distress. [15] Twice-born men who foolishly marry first wives of a low caste degrade their families and their children to the state of Shudras. According to Atri and to Gautama the son of Utathya,[21] he who weds a Shudra woman becomes an outcast. According to Saunaka, he becomes an outcaste on the birth of a son, and according to Bhrigu when he has a male child from a Shudra female. A Brahmin who takes a Shudra wife to his bed

---

[20] *Sapinda:* a relative; literally, "a sharer in the funeral feast," an obligation usually considered to go back six generations.

[21] *Gautama:* not Gautama Buddha.

will sink into hell. If he begets a child by her, he will lose the rank of a Brahmin. The spirits of deceased ancestors and the gods will not eat the offerings of a man who performs the rites in honor of the gods, of the manes, and of guests with a Shudra wife's assistance. Such a man will not go to heaven. No way of forgiveness is prescribed for him who drinks the moisture of a Shudra's lips, who is tainted by her breath, and who begets a son on her.

[6.1, the Stage of Retirement] A twice-born Snataka,[22] who has lived according to the law of householders, taking a firm resolution and keeping his organs in subjection, may dwell in the forest. He must duly observe the rules given below. When a householder sees his skin wrinkled, and his hair white, and the sons of his sons, then he may depart to the forest. Abandoning all food raised by cultivation, and all his belongings, he may depart into the forest. He may either commit his wife to his sons or be accompanied by her.[23] Taking with him the sacred fire and the implements required for domestic sacrifices, he may go forth from the village into the forest and reside there, controlling his senses.

[5] Let him offer those five great sacrifices according to the rule, with various kinds of pure food fit for ascetics, or with herbs, roots, and fruit. Let him wear a skin or a tattered garment; let him bathe in the evening or in the morning. Let him always wear his hair in braids, with the hair on his body, his beard, and his nails uncut. Let him perform the Bali-offering with the kind of food he eats, and give alms according to his ability. Let him honor those who come to his hermitage to give him alms of water, roots, and fruit. Let him always be industrious in privately reciting the *Veda*. Let him be patient in hardships, friendly toward all, collected in mind, always liberal and never a receiver of gifts, and compassionate toward all living creatures. Let him offer, according to the law, the Agnihotra with three sacred fires, and never omit the new-moon and full-moon sacrifices at the proper time. . . .

[6.33, the Stage of Asceticism] Having passed the third part of his natural term of life in the forest, a man may live as an ascetic during the fourth part of his existence. First he must abandon all attachment to worldly objects. He who . . . offers sacrifices and subdues his senses, busies himself with giving alms and offerings of food, and becomes an ascetic gains bliss after death. [35] When he has paid the three debts,[24] let him apply his mind to the attainment of final liberation. He who seeks it without having paid his debts sinks downwards. Having studied the *Vedas* according to the rule, having fathered sons according to the sacred law, and having offered sacrifices according to his ability, he may direct his mind to the attainment of final liberation. A twice-born man who seeks final liberation sinks downward if he has not studied the *Vedas*, fathered sons, and offered sacrifices. Having performed the Ishti, sacred to the Lord of creatures, in which he gives all his property as the sacrificial fee, having reposited the sacred fires in himself, a Brahmin may depart from his house as an ascetic. Worlds, radiant in brilliancy, become his who recites the texts regarding Brahman and departs from his house as an ascetic, after giving a promise of safety to all created beings.[25] [40] For that twice-born man who causes not even the smallest danger to created beings, there will be no danger from anything after he is freed from his body.

Departing from his house fully provided with the means of purification, let him wander about absolutely silent. He must care nothing for enjoyments that may be offered to him. Let him always wander about alone to attain final liberation. The solitary man, who neither forsakes nor is forsaken, gains his desired result. He shall possess neither a fire nor a dwelling. He may go to a village for his food. He shall be indifferent to everything, firm of purpose, meditating and concentrating his mind on Brahman. The marks of one who has attained liberation are a broken pot instead of an alms-bowl, the roots of trees for a dwelling, coarse

---

[22] *Snataka:* a Brahmin who has completed his studentship.
[23] *accompanied by her:* Note in the next passage that if the husband chooses the way of ascetic renunciation, the wife cannot accompany him. She is in a difficult situation: Having renounced his old life, her husband no longer belongs to her, but she still belongs to him.

[24] *the three debts:* the three obligations discussed in the next verses: study, having sons, sacrifice. These are similar to the modern Hindu expression "the three debts": to the gods, to the guru, to be a father.
[25] *promise of safety to all created beings:* the vow of ahimsa, non-violence to all creatures.

worn-out garments, life in solitude, and indifference toward everything. [45] Let him not desire to die; let him not desire to live. Let him wait for his appointed time as a servant waits for the payment of his wages. Let him put down his foot purified by his sight,[26] let him drink water purified by straining with a cloth, let him utter speech purified by

truth, let him keep his heart pure. Let him patiently bear hard words, let him not insult anybody. Let him not become anybody's enemy for the sake of this perishable body. Against an angry man let him not show anger, let him bless when he is cursed, and let him not utter false speech. . . .

He shall delight in matters of the Soul, sit in the postures prescribed by the Yoga, be independent of external help, entirely abstain from sensual enjoyments, and have himself for his only companion. He shall live in this world, but desire only the bliss of final liberation.

[26]*put down his foot purified by his sight:* that is, in a place on the ground with no visible living beings on it; so too he must *drink water purified* of living creatures. This requirement, which follows up on the ascetic's "promise of safety to all created beings" (verse 39), will become more important in Jainism.

The Life of Women

The first passage is often quoted as an example of a positive Hindu attitude toward women. It gives some indication of the respected place of Hindu women in the home (in the context of a strongly patriarchal society, of course). Much of this passage has as its background the participation of the wife in all the sacred rites of the home. The second passage contains rules for the whole life of women, emphasizing respect and obedience to husbands during their life. After her husband's death, a woman must not remarry and must live an ascetic life.

[3.55] Women must be honored and adorned by their fathers, brothers, husbands, and brothers-in-law, who desire their own welfare. Where women are honored, there the gods are pleased. Where they are not honored, no sacred rite yields rewards. Where the female relations live in grief, the family soon perishes completely. But the family where they are not unhappy always prospers. Female relatives pronounce a curse on houses where women are not honored; these houses perish completely, as if destroyed by magic. Men who seek their own welfare should always honor women on holidays and festivals with gifts of jewelry, clothes, and dainty food. [60] In a family where the husband is pleased with his wife and the wife with her husband, happiness will certainly be lasting.

[5.147] Nothing must be done independently by a girl, by a young woman, or by an old woman, even in her own house. In childhood a female must be subject to her father, in youth

to her husband, and when her husband is dead to her sons. A woman must never be independent. She must not seek to separate herself from her father, husband, or sons. By leaving them she would make both her own and her husband's families contemptible.

[150] She must always be cheerful, clever in household affairs, careful in cleaning her utensils, and economical in expenditure. She shall obey the man to whom her father may give her . . . as long as he lives. When he is dead, she must not insult his memory. For the sake of getting good fortune for brides, the recitation of benedictory texts and the sacrifice to the Lord of creatures are used at weddings; but the betrothal by the father or guardian is the cause of the husband's dominion over his wife. The husband who wedded her with sacred texts always gives happiness to his wife, both in season and out of season, in this world and in the next. Although he may be destitute of virtue, or seek

Laws of Manu 3.55–60; 5.147–165.

pleasure elsewhere, or be lacking good qualities, yet a husband must be constantly worshipped as a god by a faithful wife. [155] No sacrifice, no vow, no fast must be performed by women apart from their husbands. If a wife obeys her husband, she will for that reason alone be exalted in heaven.[27]

A faithful wife who desires to dwell after death with her husband must never do anything that might displease him, whether he is alive or dead. She may emaciate her body by living on pure flowers, roots, and fruit; but she must never even mention the name of another man after her husband has died. Until death let her be patient in hardships, self-controlled, and chaste. Let her strive to fulfil that most excellent duty that is prescribed for wives who have one husband only. Many thousands of Brahmins who were chaste from their youth have gone to heaven without continuing their race. [160] A virtuous wife who constantly remains chaste after the death of her husband reaches

heaven although she has no son, just like those chaste men.

But a woman who desires to have offspring violates her duty toward her [deceased] husband. She brings disgrace on herself in this world, and loses her place with her husband in heaven. Offspring begotten by another man is not considered lawful, offspring begotten on another man's wife does not belong to the begetter, nor is a second husband anywhere allowed for virtuous women.[28] She who lives with a man of higher caste, forsaking her own husband who belongs to a lower one, will become contemptible in this world, and is called a remarried woman. By violating her duty toward her husband, a wife is disgraced in this world. After death she enters the womb of a jackal, and is tormented by diseases as the punishment of her sin. [165] She who controls her thoughts, words, and deeds, and never slights her husband, will reside after death with him in heaven. She is called a virtuous wife.

---

[27]*heaven:* as elsewhere in Hinduism, usually a temporary reward before reincarnation.

[28]*anywhere allowed...women:* no ancient stories or laws permit it.

ORGANIZATION

Creation and the Caste System

One of the many creation hymns of the *Rig-Veda*, this poem presents the cosmic Man (*Purusha*) as the one through whose sacrifice the gods fashioned the universe. The making of humanity is presented in terms of the caste system, its first appearance in Hindu literature, and the foundation of its later authority. Much of the caste system is undergoing a liberalizing change in modern India, especially in the cities. But it is still important and pervasive as a general social structure and cultural inheritance.

The Man has a thousand heads, a thousand eyes, a thousand feet. He pervaded the earth on all sides and extended beyond it as far as ten fingers. It is the Man who is all this, whatever

has been and whatever is to be. He is the ruler of immortality, when he grows beyond everything through food. This is his greatness, and the Man is yet more than this. All creatures

---

Rig-Veda 10.90.

are a quarter of him; three quarters are what is immortal in heaven. With three quarters the Man rose upwards, and one quarter of him remains here.

From this he spread out in all directions, into that which eats and that which does not eat. [5] From him Viraj[29] was born, and from Viraj came the Man. When he was born, he ranged beyond the earth behind and before. When the gods spread the sacrifice with the Man as the offering, spring was the clarified butter, summer was the fuel, autumn was the oblation.[30] They anointed the Man, the sacrifice born at the beginning, upon the sacred grass. With him the gods, Sadhyas,[31] and sages sacrificed. From that sacrifice in which everything was offered, the melted fat was collected. He made it into those beasts who live in the air, in the forest, and in villages. From that sacrifice in which everything was offered, the verses and chants were born, the meters were born from it, and from it the formulas were born.[32]

[10] Horses were born from it, and those other animals that have two rows of teeth; cows were born from it, and from it goats and sheep were born.

When they divided the Man, into how many parts did they apportion him? What do they call his mouth, his two arms and thighs and feet? His mouth became the Brahmin; his arms were made into the Warrior, his thighs the People, and from his feet the Servants were born. The moon was born from his mind; from his eye the sun was born. Indra and Agni came from his mouth, and from his vital breath the Wind was born. From his navel the middle realm of space arose; from his head the sky evolved. From his two feet came the earth, and the quarters of the sky from his ear. Thus they set the worlds in order. [15] There were seven enclosing-sticks for him, and thrice seven fuel-sticks, when the gods, spreading the sacrifice, bound the Man as the sacrificial beast. With the sacrifice the gods sacrificed to the sacrifice. These were the first ritual laws. These very powers reached the dome of the sky where dwell the Sadhyas, the ancient gods.

[29] *Viraj:* the female counterpart of the man.
[30] *oblation:* what is sacrificed.
[31] *Sadhyas:* saints, called in the last verse of this hymn "the ancient gods."
[32] *verses, chants, meters, formulas:* the *Vedas.*

The Four Castes

This passage contains a short description of the main structure of the caste system. The duties and means of livelihood of each caste are indicated. The end of this passage gives the moral duties binding on everyone of whatever caste, gender, or stage of life. These general rules are growing more important in contemporary Hinduism as the caste system fades.[33]

Brahmins, Kshatriyas, Vaishyas, and Shudras are the four castes. The first three of these are called twice-born. They must perform with mantras[34] the whole number of ceremonies, which begin

with impregnation and end with the ceremony of burning the dead body. Their duties are as follows. [5] A Brahmin teaches the *Veda.* A Kshatriya has constant practice in arms. A Vaishya tends cattle. A Shudra serves the twice-born. All the twice-born are to sacrifice and study the *Veda.* [10] Their modes of livelihood are as follows. A Brahmin sacrifices for others and receives alms. A Kshatriya protects the world. A Vaishya

[33] Taken, with editing, from Julius Jolly, trans., *The Institutes of Vishnu, Sacred Books of the East,* vol. 7 (Oxford: Oxford University Press, 1880).
[34] *mantras:* sacred words or syllables chanted to create and acquire cosmic spiritual power.

engages in farming, keeps cows, trades, lends money at interest, and grows seeds. A Shudra engages in all branches of crafts. In times of distress, each caste may follow the occupation of that below it in rank. Duties common to all castes are patience, truthfulness, restraint, purity, liberality, self-control, not to kill, obedience toward one's gurus, visiting places of pilgrimage, sympathy, straightforwardness, freedom from covetousness, reverence toward gods and Brahmins,[35] and freedom from anger.

[35]*reverence toward...Brahmins:* As sacrificers, the Brahmins preserve the order of the universe, and other castes are to honor them. India has seen an almost continuous struggle between the priestly caste and the warrior-ruler caste.

The Outcastes

About fifteen to twenty percent of Indians are outside the caste system—"outcastes." They are known by various names: untouchables (a designation now widely regarded as impolite), Harijans ("Children of God," Gandhi's term), the legal term "the scheduled [listed] classes," and Dalits ("the downtrodden"), the most preferred name. Hindus of the four castes regard them as non-Hindu. The so-called outcastes do the most menial jobs in Indian society, such as cleaning sewers and digging graves, jobs that make those who do them religiously impure. In India today, the Dalits' challenges to their status are sources of serious conflict that often result in violence. This selection from the *Laws of Manu* gives a summary of their traditional state.

The dwellings of untouchables must be outside the village. They must use discarded bowls, and their only possessions are their dogs and donkeys. They take for their clothing the clothes of the dead, and eat their food in broken dishes. Their ornaments are made of black iron only, and they should always wander from place to place. A [Hindu] man should not deal with them in any way; they must do business and marry only among themselves. Their food, for which they are dependent upon others, should be left for them in broken dishes, and they should not walk at night in cities or villages. [55] They may walk around during the day to do their work,[36] with recognizably distinctive clothing. They are to carry out the corpses of people with no relatives. By the king's command, they are to execute those condemned to death, and take for themselves the clothes, beds, and ornaments of those condemned to death.

[36]*They may walk around during the day:* Some "Untouchable" subgroups are considered so polluting that they must do their work only at night; hence, they are called "Unseeables."

Laws of Manu 10.51–57.

RITUAL AND MEDITATION

The Gayatri Mantra

The name of this short prayer means "the savior of the singer." This mantra is considered the single most important prayer-formula of Hinduism. Pious believers repeat it at least three times a day. On a literal level, this verse is a simple prayer to the sun-god Savitar for blessing. At a deeper level, it expresses and applies the power that the god himself holds. Given to a young man at his initiation with the sacred thread, it helps to produce his rebirth. Believers in other Hindu deities have adapted it for their use from early times through today.

May we attain to the excellent glory of Savitar the
god; so may he stimulate our prayers.

Rig-Veda 3.62.10.

Devotion to Agni in Prayer and Sacrifice

Agni is the god of fire, especially the sacrificial fire, and he is the priest among the gods (verse 1). This first hymn of the *Rig-Veda* seeks to please Agni by praises and invoke his blessings. Like many other hymns of the *Rig*, it uses both the second person (e.g., "To you, Agni...") and the third person ("Agni earned the prayers..."), but all of it is addressed to Agni. The second reading is a good example of the Brahmanic exposition and development of the sacrificial rite. The ritual expounded here is the Agnihotra, the daily household sacrifice to Agni. The god Prajapati is the precursor of Brahman.[37]

[*Rig-Veda* 1.1] I pray to Agni, the household priest who is the god of the sacrifice, the one who chants and invokes and brings most treasure. Agni earned the prayers of the ancient sages, and of those of the present, too; he will bring the gods here. Through Agni one may win wealth, and growth from day to day, glorious and most abounding in heroic sons. Agni, only the sacrificial ritual that you encompass on all sides goes to the gods. [5] Agni, the priest with the sharp sight of a poet, the true and most brilliant, the god will come with the gods. Whatever good you wish to do for the one who worships you, Agni, through you, O Angiras,[38] that comes true. To you, Agni, who shine upon darkness, we come day after day, bringing our thoughts and homage. [We come to] you, the king over sacrifices, the shining guardian of the Order, growing in your own house. Be easy for us to

---

[37]Taken, with editing, from Julius Eggeling, trans., *The Sata-patha-Brahmana*, part 1, *Sacred Books of the East*, vol. 12 (Oxford: Oxford University Press, 1882).

[38]*Angiras:* messenger to the gods and the father of an ancient family of priests.

Rig-Veda 1.1; *Agni-Brahmana* 1.1–19.

reach, like a father to his son. Abide with us, Agni, for our happiness.

[*Agni-Brahmana* 1.1–19] Prajapati alone existed here in the beginning. He considered, "How may I be reproduced?" He toiled and performed acts of penance. He generated Agni from his mouth. Because he generated him from his mouth, therefore Agni is a consumer of food. Truly, he who knows Agni to be a consumer of food becomes himself a consumer of food. He thus generated him first of the gods; and therefore [he is called] Agni, for *agni* [they say] is the same as *agri*. He, being generated, went forth as the first; for of him who goes first, they say that he goes at the head. Such, then, is the origin and nature of that Agni.

Prajapati then considered, "In Agni I have generated a food-eater for myself. But there is no other food here but myself, whom Agni certainly would not eat." Then this earth had been made quite bald; there were neither plants nor trees. This, then, weighed on his mind. Then Agni turned toward him with open mouth. Prajapati was terrified, and his own greatness departed from him. Now his own greatness is his speech; his speech departed from him. He desired an offering in himself and rubbed his hands; and because he rubbed his hands, palms are hairless. He then obtained either a butter-offering or a milk-offering; but they are both made of milk.

[5] But this offering did not satisfy him, because it had hairs mixed with it. He poured it away into the fire, saying, "Drink, while burning!" From it plants sprang; hence their name "plants." He rubbed his hands a second time, and by that obtained another offering, either a butter-offering or a milk-offering. This offering then satisfied him. He hesitated, thinking, "Shall I offer it up? Or shall I not offer it up?" His own greatness said to him, "Offer it up!" Prajapati was aware that it was his own [*sva*] greatness that had spoken [*aha*] to him; he offered it up with the word *svaha!* This is why offerings are made with *svaha!* Then that burning one, the sun, rose; and then that blowing one, the wind, sprang up. Then Agni turned away.

Prajapati, having performed offering, reproduced himself, and saved himself from Agni as he was about to devour him. Truly whoever, knowing this, offers the Agnihotra reproduces himself by offspring even as Prajapati reproduced himself. He saves himself from Agni, death, when he is about to devour him. And when he dies, and when they place him on the fire, then he is born again out of the fire, and the fire only consumes his body. Even as he is born from his father and mother, so is he born from the fire. But he who does not offer the Agnihotra does not come into life at all. Therefore the Agnihotra must be offered.

Soma

Soma is here, as elsewhere in the *Vedas*, at once a plant, a drink, and a god. To judge from this hymn, soma had an effect that was hallucinogenic. The term *soma* is still used today, but it refers not to a hallucinogenic drug but to a fruit drink made of wild rhubarb. Other religions have words spoken during ritual intoxication. Few, however, are as evocative as this hymn's "We have drunk the Soma; we have become immortal; we have gone to the light; we have found the gods."

I have tasted the sweet drink of life, knowing that it inspires good thoughts and joyous expansiveness to the extreme, that all the gods and mortals seek it together, calling it honey. When you penetrate inside, you will know no limits, and you will avert the wrath of the gods. Enjoying Indra's friendship, O drop of Soma, bring riches as a docile cow brings the yoke. We have drunk the Soma; we have

Rig-Veda 8.48.

become immortal; we have gone to the light; we have found the gods. What can hatred and the malice of a mortal do to us now, O immortal one? When we have drunk you, O drop of Soma, be good to our heart, kind as a father to his son, thoughtful as a friend to a friend. Far-famed Soma, stretch out our lifespan so that we may live.

[5] The glorious drops that I have drunk set me free in wide space. You have bound me together in my limbs as thongs bind a chariot. Let the drops protect me from the foot that stumbles and keep lameness away from me. Inflame me like a fire kindled by friction; make us see far; make us richer, better. For when I am intoxicated with you, Soma, I think myself rich. Draw near and make us thrive. We would enjoy you, pressed with a fervent heart, like riches from a father. King Soma, stretch out our lifespans as the sun stretches the spring days. King Soma, have mercy on us for our well-being. Know that we are devoted to your laws. Passion and fury are stirred up. O drop of Soma, do not hand us over to the pleasure of the enemy. For you, Soma, are the guardian of our body; watching over men, you have settled down in every limb.

If we break your laws, O god, have mercy on us like a good friend, to make us better. [10] Let me join closely with my compassionate friend so that he will not injure me when I have drunk him. O lord of bay horses, for the Soma that is lodged in us I approach Indra to stretch out our lifespan. Weaknesses and diseases have gone; the forces of darkness have fled in terror. Soma has climbed up in us, expanding. We have come to the place where they stretch out lifespans. The drop that we have drunk has entered our hearts, an immortal inside mortals.

O fathers, let us serve that Soma with the oblations and abide in his mercy and kindness. Uniting in agreement with the fathers, O drop of Soma, you have extended yourself through sky and earth. Let us serve him with an oblation; let us be masters of riches. You protecting gods, speak out for us. Do not let sleep or harmful speech seize us. Let us, always dear to Soma, speak as men of power in the sacrificial gathering. [15] Soma, you give us the force of life on every side. Enter into us, finding the sunlight, watching over men. O drop of Soma, summon your helpers and protect us before and after.

Marriage

The first part of this hymn from the *Rig-Veda,* not given here, recounts the myth of the marriage of Surya the goddess. The part printed here contains the incantations and blessings still spoken at weddings to bring good and repel evil. The bride is compared to Surya, and the wedding of the humans is set in parallel with divine marriage. The words are designed to bring good fortune: that the wife continues to have beauty and passion, and so be loved by her husband; that both have a long life together; that the marriage produces many sons. The careful reader can discern several different ritual actions of the marriage. First comes leaving the site of the wedding, then traveling to the couple's home, then consummation of marriage, and finally the anointing of the couple. Verses from this hymn are still a part of traditional Hindu weddings.

Mount the world of immortality, O Surya, that is adorned with red flowers and made of fragrant wood, carved with many forms and painted with gold, rolling smoothly on its fine wheels. Prepare an exquisite wedding voyage for your husband. "Go away from here! For this woman

Rig-Veda 10.85.20–47.

has a husband." Thus I implore Visvavasu[39] with words of praise as I bow to him. "Look for another girl who is ripe and still lives in her father's house. That is your birthright; find it. Go away from here, Visvavasu, we implore you as we bow. Look for another girl, willing and ready. Leave the wife to unite with her husband." May the roads be straight and thornless on which our friends go courting. May Aryaman and Bhaga united lead us together. O Gods, may the united household be easy to manage.

I free you from Varuna's snare, with which the gentle Savitr bound you. In the seat of the Law, in the world of good action, I place you unharmed with your husband. [25] I free her from here, but not from there.[40] I have bound her firmly there, so that through the grace of Indra she will have fine sons and be fortunate in her husband's love. Let Pusan lead you from here, taking you by the hand; let the Asvins carry you in their chariot. Go home to be mistress of the house with the right to speak commands to the gathered people. May happiness be fated for you here through your progeny. Watch over this house as mistress of the house.

Mingle your body with that of your husband, and even when you are gray with age you will have the right to speak to the gathered people. The purple and red appears, a magic spirit; the stain is imprinted.[41] Her family prospers, and her husband is bound in the bonds. Throw away the gown, and distribute wealth to the priests. It becomes a magic spirit walking on feet, and like the wife it draws near the husband. [30] The body becomes ugly and sinisterly pale if the husband with evil desire covers his sexual limb with his wife's robe. The diseases that come from her own people and follow the glorious bridal

procession, may the gods who receive sacrifices lead them back whence they have come. Let no highwaymen, lying in ambush, fall upon the wedding couple. Let the two of them on good paths avoid the dangerous path. Let all demonic powers run away. This bride has auspicious signs; come and look at her. Wish her the good fortune of her husband's love, and depart, each to your own house. It burns, it bites, it has claws, it is as dangerous as poison to eat.[42] Only the priest who knows the Surya hymn is able to receive the bridal gown. [35] Cutting, carving, and chopping into pieces—see the colors of Surya, which the priest alone purifies.

I [the husband] take your hand for good fortune, so that with me as your husband you will attain a ripe old age. Bhaga, Aryaman, Savitr, Purandhi—the gods have given you to me to be mistress of the house. Pusan, rouse her to be most eager to please, the woman in whom men sow their seed, so that she will spread her thighs in her desire for us and we,[43] in our desire, will plant our penis in her. To you first of all they led Surya, circling with the bridal procession. Give her back to her husbands, Agni, now as a wife with progeny. Agni has given the wife back again, together with long life and beauty. Let her have a long lifespan, and let her husband live for a hundred autumns. [40] Soma first possessed her, and the Gandharva possessed her second. Agni was your third husband, and the fourth was the son of a man. Soma gave her to the Gandharva, and the Gandharva gave her to Agni. Agni gave me wealth and sons—and her.

Stay here and do not separate. Enjoy your whole lifespan playing with sons and grandsons and rejoicing in your own home. Let Prajapati create progeny for us; let Aryaman anoint us into old age. Free from evil signs, enter the world of your husband. Be good luck for our two-legged creatures and good luck for our four-legged creatures. Have no evil eye; do not be a husband-killer. Be friendly to animals, good-tempered and glowing with beauty. Bringing forth strong sons,

---

[39] *Visvavasu:* a lesser god who has sexual intercourse with virgins.
[40] *here:* her father's house; *there:* her new house with her husband.
[41] *The purple and red appears...imprinted:* In her first experience of sexual intercourse, the bride bleeds on her wedding robe as her hymen is ruptured. The resulting stain becomes a magic spirit with power to curse and destroy the marriage. The procedure for dealing with the robe is given at the end of this paragraph.

[42] *it:* the spirit arising from the stained robe.
[43] *us, we:* the husband, and the gods who are said to have spiritually possessed the wife before her marriage.

prosper as one beloved of the gods and eager to please. Be good luck for our two-legged creatures and good luck for our four-legged creatures. [45] Generous Indra, give this woman fine sons and the good fortune of her husband's love. Place ten sons in her and make her husband the eleventh.[44] Be an empress over your husband's father, an empress over your husband's mother; be an empress over your husband's sister and an empress over your husband's brothers. Let all the gods and the waters together anoint our two hearts together. Let Matarisvan[45] together with the Creator and together with her who shows the way join the two of us together.

---

[44]*her husband the eleventh:* A common Hindu idea is that the husband is metaphorically the last son of the wife, perhaps signifying the care given to the husband by his wife.

[45]*Matarisvan:* an assistant of Agni.

Cremation

Agni is petitioned here to bring a good burning to the body of the dead, strikingly called in sacrificial imagery "a good cooking." The proper funeral ritual enables the dead man to go to his fathers. No explicit mention is made here of heaven or hell, transmigration, or reincarnation, important in later Hinduism and today.

[To Agni:] Do not burn him entirely, Agni, or engulf him in your flames. Do not consume his skin or his flesh. When you have cooked him perfectly, O knower of creatures, send him forth to the fathers. When you cook him perfectly, O knower of creatures, give him over to the fathers. When he goes on the path that leads away the breath of life, then he will be led by the will of the gods.

[To the dead man:] May your eye go to the sun, your life's breath to the wind. Go to the sky or to earth, as is your nature; or go to the waters, if that is your fate. Take root in the plants with your limbs.

[To Agni:] The goat is your share; burn him with your heat. Let your brilliant light and flame burn him. With your gentle forms, O knower of creatures, carry this man to the world of those who have done good deeds. [5] Set him free again to go to the fathers, Agni, when he has been offered as an oblation in you and wanders with the sacrificial drink. Let him reach his own descendants, dressing himself in a lifespan. O knower of creatures, let him join with a body.

[To the dead man:] Whatever the black bird has pecked out of you, or the ant, the snake, or even a beast of prey, may Agni who eats all things make it whole, and Soma who has entered the Brahmins. Gird yourself with the limbs of the cow as armor against Agni, and cover yourself with fat and suet, so that he will not embrace you with his impetuous heat in his passionate desire to burn you up.

[To Agni:] O Agni, do not overturn this cup that is dear to the gods and to those who love Soma, fit for the gods to drink from, a cup in which the immortal gods carouse. I send the flesh-eating fire far away. Let him go to those whose king is Yama, carrying away all impurities. But let that other, the knower of creatures, come here and carry the oblation to the gods, since he knows the way in advance. [10] The flesh-eating fire has entered your house, though he sees there the other, the knower of creatures; I take that god away to the sacrifice of the fathers. Let him

---

Rig-Veda 10.16.

carry the heated drink to the farthest dwelling-place. Agni carries away the corpse and gives sacrifice to the fathers who are strengthened by truth. Let him proclaim the oblation to the gods and to the fathers.

[To the new fire:] Joyously would we put you in place, joyously would we kindle you. Joyously carry the joyous fathers here to eat the oblation. Now, Agni, quench and revive the very one you have burnt up. Let Kiyamba, Pakadurva, and Vyalkasa plants grow in this place. O cool one, bringer of coolness; O fresh one, bringer of freshness; unite with the female frog.[46] Delight and inspire this, O Agni.

[46]*unite with the female frog:* In this last section, the ritual action implied in the text calls for water to be thrown on the fire, dousing it when it can no longer burn away the larger bones. This produces, at least poetically, a marsh where water-plants and frogs live. The female frog symbolizes fertility, the new life that comes at the end of the funeral.

Charms and Spells

The first of these incantations is a spell against fever, the second a spell to frustrate the sacrifice of an enemy, the third a charm to induce the sexual passion of a woman (perhaps a wife who comes by an arranged marriage), and the fourth a spell for success in business. Note that the main point of the spell is often repeated to increase its power. Ritual actions that accompany the saying of these spells are occasionally suggested in the words.[47]

[6.20, against diseases that bring fever] As if from this Agni [fire], that burns and flashes, the fever comes. Let him [the fever] pass away like a babbling drunkard! Let him, the impious one, search out another person, not ourselves! Reverence be to the fever with the burning weapon![48] Reverence be to Rudra, reverence to the fever, reverence to the luminous king Varuna! Reverence to heaven, reverence to earth, reverence to the plants! To you that burns through, and turns all bodies yellow, to the fever produced by the forest, I render honor.

[7.70, for frustration of a sacrifice aimed at a worshipper] Whenever that person over there in his thought and with his speech offers sacrifice accompanied by offerings and benedictions, may Nirriti the goddess of destruction ally herself with death and strike his offering before it takes effect! May the sorcerers Nirriti and Rakshas mar his true work with error![49] May the gods, dispatched by Indra, churn up the butter used in his sacrifice butter! May that which he offers not succeed! . . . I tie back both your arms, I shut your mouth. With the fury of Agni, I have destroyed your sacrifice.

[6.9, for stirring up love in a new bride] Desire my body, my feet, my eyes, my thighs! As you lust after me, your eyes and your hair shall be hot with love! I make you cling to my arm, cling to my heart, so that you shall be in my power and shall come to my wish. The cows, the mothers of the sacrificial butter who lick their young, in whose heart love is planted, shall make this woman love me!

[3.16, for success in business] I urge Indra the merchant, come to us and be our forerunner. Ward off the one who does not pay his debts to us, and let masterful Indra be a bringer of wealth to me. O Gods! Let the money with which I conduct my business multiply and never decrease. O Agni, with this sacrifice frustrate those who would ruin my profit.

[47]Taken, with editing, from Maurice Bloomfield, trans., *Hymns of the Atharva-Veda, Sacred Books of the East*, vol. 42 (Oxford: Oxford University Press, 1897).
[48]*Reverence:* The spell uses flattering praise, as well as insults, to drive the fever away.

[49]*mar . . . with error:* If an error of word or deed is made in the sacrificial ceremony, it is not effective. Such a belief is common to many religions with well-developed sacrificial systems.

Chanting of *Om*

The *udgitha,* or "loud chant," is the important *Om* in the Vedic ritual. Members of the various Hindu schools differ on whether *Om* is Brahman itself or a near verbal expression of Brahman. But for all Hindus, it is the most sacred of sounds, the mantra that contains all other mantras, all the *Vedas,* all the meaning of the universe. Those who chant it with full knowledge will be freed from karma.

Let a man meditate on the syllable *Om,* called the *udgitha;* for the *udgitha* is sung, beginning with *Om.* The full account of *Om* is this.

The essence of all beings is the earth, the essence of the earth is water, the essence of water the plants, the essence of plants man, the essence of man speech, the essence of speech the *Rig-Veda,* the essence of the *Rig-Veda* the *Sama-Veda,* the essence of the *Sama-Veda* the *udgitha, Om.* The *udgitha* is the best of all essences, the highest, deserving the highest place, the eighth.

What then is the *Rig?* What is the *Saman?* What is the *udgitha?* This is the question. [5] The *Rig* is speech, *Saman* is breath, the *udgitha* is the syllable *Om.* Now speech and breath, or *Rig* and *Saman,* form one couple. That couple is joined in the syllable *Om.* When two people come together, they fulfill each other's desire. Thus he who knowing this meditates on the syllable *Om,* the *udgitha,* becomes a fulfiller of desires.

That syllable is a syllable of permission, for whenever we permit anything, we say *Om,* "Yes." Now permission is gratification. He who knows this and meditates on the syllable *Om* becomes a gratifier of desires.

By that syllable proceeds the threefold knowledge (of the three Vedas). When the Adhvaryu priest gives an order, he says *Om.* When the Hotri priest recites, he says *Om.* When the Udgatri priest sings, he says *Om,* all for the glory of that syllable. The threefold knowledge and threefold sacrifice proceed by the greatness of that syllable and by its essence. [10] Therefore it seems that both he who knows this [the true meaning of *Om*], and he who does not, perform the same sacrifice. But this is not so, for knowledge and ignorance are different. The sacrifice that a man performs with knowledge, faith, and the *Upanishad* is more powerful. This is the full account of the syllable *Om.*

Chandogya Upanishad 1.1.1–10.

The Practice of Yoga

Yoga is a spiritual and mental discipline to promote knowledge that the individual-soul and the world-soul are one. It does so by harnessing the power of the body to this end, but it is not (as often thought and practiced in the West) primarily a method of exercise with some meditation thrown in. Rather, the Hindu **yogin** (person who practices yoga) is fully devoted to religious purposes. This passage relates some of the main components of yogic meditation.[50]

[50]F. Max Müller, trans., *The Upanishads,* part 2, *Sacred Books of the East,* vol. 15 (Oxford: Oxford University Press, 1884), pp. 241–243.

Shvetashvatara Upanishad 2.8–15.

Holding his body steady with the three upper
parts[51] erect,
And causing the senses with the mind to
enter the heart,
A wise man with the Brahma-boat will cross
All the frightening streams.
Compressing his breathings here in the body,
and having his movements checked,
One should breathe through his nostrils with
diminished breath.
Like that chariot yoked with vicious horses,
The wise man should restrain his mind until
it is undistracted.
[10] In a clean level spot, free from pebbles,
fire, and gravel,
By the sound of water and similar things
Favorable to thought, not offensive to the
eye,
In a hidden retreat protected from the wind,
one should practice Yoga.
Fog, smoke, sun, fire, wind,
Fire-flies, lightning, a crystal, a moon—
These are the preliminary appearances,

Producing the manifestation of Brahma in
Yoga.
When the fivefold quality of Yoga is
produced,
Arising from earth, water, fire, air, and space,
No sickness, no old age, no death has he
Who has obtained a body made out of the
fire of Yoga.
Lightness, healthiness, steadiness,
Clearness of countenance and pleasantness of
voice,
Sweetness of odor, and scanty excretions—
These, they say, are the first stage in the
progress of Yoga.
Even as a mirror stained by dust
Shines brilliantly when it has been cleansed,
So the embodied one, on seeing the nature of
the Soul,
Becomes unitary, his end attained, from
sorrow freed.
[15] With the nature of the self like a lamp,
One who practices Yoga beholds here the
nature of Brahma,
Unborn, steadfast, from every nature free—
By knowing God one is released from all
fetters!

---

[51]*the three upper parts:* head, neck, and torso.

SELECTIONS FROM THE *BHAGAVAD GITA*

The most famous and influential text of Hinduism is section 6 of the *Mahabharata* epic known as the *Bhagavad Gita* (Song of the Lord). The *Gita* is especially important for an understanding of the devotional Hinduism that has flourished from about 400 C.E. until today. The background of the *Gita* is the rivalry between the Kaurava brothers and the Pandava brothers for the rule of India. In a game of dice, the leader of the Pandavas loses their claim to the throne. For thirteen years, the Pandavas are forced into exile. Civil war results when the Pandavas return to seize rule. As preparation for war begins, the god Krishna becomes a charioteer for Arjuna, a Pandava prince.

As the battle is about to begin, Arjuna is appalled by thoughts of the fratricide that will surely result. Moreover, he is afraid that this great evil will harm his own soul now and, by implication, its later incarnations. His charioteer, Krishna, teaches Arjuna divine truths that enable him to overcome his doubts. This teaching forms the content of the *Gita*. First, and most immediately for the plot of the *Mahabharata*, Krishna teaches Arjuna that he must do his caste duty and fight. Arjuna acknowledges that his warfare will not harm the souls of the slain. Second, Krishna explains that the several ways to salvation offered by Hinduism—sacrifice (the Vedic path), meditation (the Upanishadic and ascetic path), and action (the way of caste duty)—are effective only if approached in a spirit of complete detachment. The *Gita* teaches full involvement in life coupled with inner restraint and detachment. Third, the best way to salvation is devotion to Krishna, whom the *Gita* portrays as both the "base of Brahman, the impersonal world-soul," and a god filled with personal love for his devotees. In typically Hindu fashion, the *Gita* acknowledges and affirms all Hindu ways to the truth but affirms its own way as the best.

The *Gita* contains 7,000 verses grouped into eighteen chapters. It has no plot, only the setting just outlined that poses the religious problem. Most chapters begin with Arjuna's question, which typically deals with the meaning of previous teachings in the *Gita;* a lengthy answer from Krishna follows. Many chapters end with a call for devotion to Krishna. Much of the content of the *Gita* is repetitious; the key teachings are returned to again and again and examined from different perspectives. The following excerpts attempt to reduce this repetition and present the essence of the *Gita*'s argument. A short paragraph introduces and summarizes the content of each of the selections given here.[52]

[1.20–47] Chapter 1 provides the narrative setting and the religious problem of the *Gita*. King Dhritarashtra's charioteer, Sanjaya, tells the king, a Kaurava, what happened before the battle that took place to decide the fate of his kingdom. As Prince Arjuna came onto the battlefield, he was overcome by the horrors of the impending fratricidal war. He expressed his misgivings to his charioteer, Krishna, saying that war would lead to ruin and that he preferred death to fighting such a war. Then he dropped his weapons, waiting for his death at the hands of the enemy.

Sanjaya:
Arjuna, his war flag a rampant monkey,
saw Dhritarashtra's sons assembled as
weapons were ready to clash, and he lifted
   his bow.

He told his charioteer: "Krishna,
halt my chariot between the armies!
Far enough to see these men who lust for
   war,
ready to fight with me in the strain of battle.
I see men gathered here, eager to fight,

bent on serving the folly of Dhritarashtra's
   son."
When Arjuna had spoken, Krishna halted
their splendid chariot between the armies.

[25] Facing Bhishma and Drona
and all the great kings, he said,
"Arjuna, see the Kuru men assembled here!"

Arjuna saw them standing there:
fathers, grandfathers, teachers, uncles,
   brothers,
sons, grandsons, and friends.
He surveyed his companions in both armies,
all his kinsmen assembled together.

Dejected, filled with strange pity, he said
   this:
"Krishna, I see kinsmen gathered here,
   wanting war.
My limbs sink, my mouth is parched,
my body trembles, the hair bristles on my
   flesh.

[30] The magic bow slips
from my hand, my skin burns,
I cannot stand still, my mind reels.

I see omens of chaos, Krishna;
I see no good in killing my kinsmen in
   battle.

[52]From *Bhagavad-Gita*, translation by Barbara Stoler Miller, copyright © 1986 by Barbara Stoler Miller. Used by permission of Bantam Books, a division of Random House, Inc.

Krishna, I seek no victory, kingship or
    pleasures.
What use are kingship, delights, or life itself?

We sought kingship, delights,
and pleasures for the sake of those
assembled to abandon their lives
and fortunes in battle.

They are teachers, fathers, sons,
and grandfathers, uncles, grandsons,
fathers and brothers of wives,
and other men of our family.

[35] I do not want to kill them
even if I am killed, Krishna;
not for kingship of all three worlds,
much less for the earth!

What joy is there for us, Krishna,
in killing Dhritarashtra's sons?
Evil will haunt us if we kill them,
though their bows are drawn to kill.

Honor forbids us to kill
our cousins, Dhritarashtra's sons;
how can we know happiness
if we kill our own kinsmen?

The greed that distorts their reason
blinds them to the sin they commit
in ruining the family, blinds them
to the crime of betraying friends.

How can we ignore the wisdom
of turning from this evil when we see
the sin of family destruction, Krishna?

[40] When the family is ruined, the timeless
    laws
of family duty perish; and when duty is lost,
chaos overwhelms the family.

In overwhelming chaos, Krishna,
women of the family are corrupted;
and when women are corrupted,
disorder is born in society.

This discord drags the violators
and the family itself to hell;
for ancestors fall when rites
of offering rice and water lapse.

The sins of men who violate
the family create disorder in society
that undermines the constant laws
of caste and family duty.

Krishna, we have heard that a place in hell
is reserved for men who undermine family
    duties.

[45] I lament the great sin
we commit when our greed
for kingship and pleasures
drives us to kill our kinsmen.
If Dhritarashtra's armed sons
kill me in battle when I am unarmed
and offer no resistance,
it will be my reward."

Saying this in the time of war,
Arjuna slumped into the chariot
and laid down his bow and arrows,
his mind tormented by grief.

[2:1–7, 11–27, 31–38, 47–48] In Chapter 2,
Krishna rebukes Arjuna and urges him to fight.
Krishna advances several arguments: (1) The
soul is immortal, and all else is impermanent;
therefore, the battle has no real eternal significance. (2) Arjuna, a Kshatriya (warrior), must
do his caste duty and fight. (3) He must fight in
a contemplative, detached manner. (4) Yoga
(discipline) is the way to such detachment.
Verse 38 is the key: "Impartial to joy and suffering, gain and loss, victory and defeat, arm yourself for the battle, lest you fall into evil."

Sanjaya:
Arjuna sat dejected, filled with pity, his sad
    eyes blurred by tears.
Krishna gave him counsel.

Lord Krishna:
Why this cowardice in time of crisis, Arjuna?
The coward is ignoble, shameful, foreign to
    the ways of heaven.
Don't yield to impotence!

It is unnatural in you!
Banish this petty weakness from your heart.
Rise to the fight, Arjuna!

Arjuna:
Krishna, how can I fight Bhishma and Drona
    with arrows when they deserve my
    worship?

[5] Better in this world to beg for scraps
of food than to eat meals smeared with the
    blood of elders
I killed at the height of their power,
while their goals were still desires.

We don't know which weight is worse to
    bear—
our conquering them or their conquering us.
We will not want to live if we kill the sons of
    Dhritarashtra assembled before us.

The flaw of pity blights my very being; con-
    flicting sacred duties confound my reason.
I ask you to tell me decisively—Which is
    better?
I am your pupil. Teach me what I seek! . . .

Lord Krishna:
[11] You grieve for those beyond grief,
and you speak words of insight;
but learned men do not grieve
for the dead or the living.

Never have I not existed,
nor you, nor these kings;
and never in the future
shall we cease to exist.

Just as the embodied self
enters childhood, youth, and old age,
so does it enter another body;
this does not confound a steadfast man.

Contacts with matter make us feel
heat and cold, pleasure and pain.
Arjuna, you must learn to endure
fleeting things—they come and go!

[15] When these cannot torment a man,
when suffering and joy are equal
for him and he has courage,
he is fit for immortality.

Nothing of nonbeing comes to be,
nor does being cease to exist;

the boundary between these two
is seen by men who see reality.

Indestructible is the presence
that pervades all this;
no one can destroy
this unchanging reality.

Our bodies are known to end,
but the embodied self is enduring,
indestructible, and immeasurable;
therefore, Arjuna, fight the battle!

He who thinks this self a killer
and he who thinks it killed,
both fail to understand;
it does not kill, nor is it killed.

[20] It is not born, it does not die;
having been, it will never not be;
unborn, enduring, constant, primordial,
it is not killed when the body is killed.

Arjuna, when a man knows the self
to be indestructible, enduring, unborn,
unchanging, how does he kill
or cause anyone to kill?

As a man discards worn-out clothes
to put on new and different ones,
so the embodied self discards
its worn-out bodies to take on new ones.

Weapons do not cut it, fire does not burn it,
waters do not wet it, wind does not wither it.
It cannot be cut or burned, wet or withered;
it is enduring, all-pervasive, fixed,
immovable, and timeless.

[25] It is called unmanifest,
inconceivable, and immutable;
since you know that to be so,
you should not grieve!

If you think of its birth
and death as ever-recurring,
then too, Great Warrior,
you have no cause to grieve!

Death is certain for anyone born,
and birth is certain for the dead;

since the cycle is inevitable,
you have no cause to grieve!...

[31] Look to your own duty;
do not tremble before it;
nothing is better for a warrior
than a battle of sacred duty.

The doors of heaven open for warriors who
    rejoice
to have a battle like this thrust on them by
    chance.

If you fail to wage this war of sacred duty,
you will abandon your own duty
and fame only to gain evil.
People will tell of your undying shame,
and for a man of honor shame is worse than
    death.

[35] The great chariot warriors will think
you deserted in fear of battle;
you will be despised
by those who held you in esteem.

Your enemies will slander you,
scorning your skill
in so many unspeakable ways—
could any suffering be worse?

If you are killed, you win heaven;
if you triumph, you enjoy the earth;
Arjuna, stand up and resolve to fight the
    battle!

Impartial to joy and suffering,
gain and loss, victory and defeat,
arm yourself for the battle, lest you fall into
    evil....

[47] Be intent on action, not the fruits of
    action;
avoid attraction to the fruits
and attachment to inaction!

Perform actions, firm in discipline,
relinquishing attachment;
be impartial to failure and success—
this equanimity is called discipline.

[4:1–15] In Chapter 4, Krishna tells Arjuna about his many incarnations. The Gita itself does not explicitly state that Krishna is an incarnation of Vishnu, but Vishnu's followers in later devotional Hinduism saw this relationship and developed it fully.

Lord Krishna:
I taught this undying discipline
to the shining sun, first of mortals, who
told it to Manu, the progenitor of man;
Manu told it to the solar king Ikshvaku.

Royal sages knew this discipline,
which the tradition handed down;
but over the course of time
it has decayed, Arjuna.

This is the ancient discipline
that I have taught to you today;
you are my devotee and my friend,
and this is the deepest mystery.

Arjuna:
Your birth followed the birth of the sun;
how can I comprehend that you taught it
in the beginning?

Lord Krishna:
[5] I have passed through many births
and so have you;
I know them all, but you do not, Arjuna.

Though myself unborn, undying,
the lord of creatures, I fashion nature,
which is mine, and I come into being
through my own magic.

When sacred duty decays, chaos prevails;
then I create myself, Arjuna. To protect men
of virtue and destroy evil men, to set the
standard of sacred duty, I appear in every
    age.

He who really knows my divine
birth and my action, escapes rebirth
when he abandons the body—
and he comes to me, Arjuna.

[10] Free from attraction, fear, and anger,
filled with me, dependent on me,
purified by the fire of knowledge,
many come into my presence.

As they seek refuge in me,
I devote myself to them;
Arjuna, men retrace
my path in every way.

Desiring success in their actions,
men sacrifice here to the gods;
in the world of man success
comes quickly from action.

I created mankind in four classes,
different in their qualities and actions;
though unchanging, I am the agent of this,
the actor who never acts!

I desire no fruit of actions,
and actions do not defile me;
one who knows this about me
is not bound by actions.

[15] Knowing this, even ancient seekers
of freedom performed action—
do as these seers did in ancient times.

[9:16–28] Chapter 9 tells how the universe was
spun out of Krishna's body. Next come the
attributes of God (Krishna), service of different
Hindu gods, and a critique of Vedic religion.
At the end, devotion to Krishna is emphasized
as the part that, in contrast to the Vedic cult, is
open to all.

Lord Krishna:
I am the rite, the sacrifice,
the libation for the dead, the healing herb,
the sacred hymn, the clarified butter,
the fire, the oblation.

I am the universal father,
mother, granter of all, grandfather,
object of knowledge, purifier,
holy syllable *Om*, threefold sacred lore.

I am the way, sustainer, lord,
witness, shelter, refuge, friend,

source, dissolution, stability,
treasure, and unchanging seed.

I am heat that withholds
and sends down the rains;
I am immortality and death;
both being and nonbeing am I.

[20] Men learned in sacred lore,
Soma drinkers, their sins absolved,
worship me with sacrifices,
seeking to win heaven.

Reaching the holy world of Indra,
king of the gods,
they savor the heavenly delights
of the gods in the celestial sphere.

When they have long enjoyed the world of
heaven and their merit is exhausted,
they enter the mortal world; following
the duties ordained in sacred lore,
desiring desires, they obtain what is transient.

Men who worship me, thinking solely of me,
always disciplined, win the reward I secure.

When devoted men sacrifice
to other deities with faith,
they sacrifice to me, Arjuna,
however aberrant the rites.
I am the enjoyer and the lord of sacrifices;
they do not know me in reality, so they fail.

[25] Votaries of the gods go to the gods,
ancestor-worshippers go to the ancestors,
those who propitiate ghosts go to them,
and my worshippers go to me.

The leaf or flower or fruit or water
that he offers with devotion,
I take from the man of self-restraint
in response to his devotion.

Whatever you do—what you take,
what you offer, what you give,
what penances you perform—
do as an offering to me, Arjuna!

You will be freed from bonds of action,
from the fruit of fortune and misfortune;

armed with the discipline of renunciation,
your self liberated, you will join me.

[11:1–20, 50–55] In Chapter 11 after Arjuna
asks to see Krishna's divine form, Krishna
shows him all his divine forms at once. Arjuna
is filled with awe and praises Krishna. Krishna
then returns to his human form. The praise of
Krishna expresses the kind of attachment to
one god that is characteristic of devotional
Hinduism.

Arjuna:
To favor me you revealed
the deepest mystery of the self,
and by your words
my delusion is dispelled.

I heard from you in detail
how creatures come to be and die,
Krishna, and about the self
in its immutable greatness.

Just as you have described yourself,
I wish to see your form in all its majesty,
Krishna, Supreme among Men.

If you think I can see it, reveal to me your
immutable self, Krishna, Lord of Discipline.

Lord Krishna:
[5] Arjuna, see my forms
in hundreds and thousands;
diverse, divine, of many colors and shapes.

See the sun gods, gods of light,
howling storm gods, twin gods of dawn,
and gods of wind, Arjuna,
wondrous forms not seen before.

Arjuna, see all the universe,
animate and inanimate,
and whatever else you wish to see;
all stands here as one in my body.

But you cannot see me with your own eye;
I will give you a divine eye to see
the majesty of my discipline.

Sanjaya:
O King, saying this, Krishna, the lord
of discipline, revealed to Arjuna
the true majesty of his form.

[10] It was a multiform, wondrous vision,
with countless mouths and eyes
and celestial ornaments,
brandishing many divine weapons.

Everywhere was boundless divinity
containing all astonishing things,
wearing divine garlands and garments,
anointed with divine perfume.

If the light of a thousand suns
were to rise in the sky at once, it would
be like the light of that great spirit.

Arjuna saw all the universe
in its many ways and parts, standing
as one in the body of the god of gods.

Then filled with amazement,
his hair bristling on his flesh,
Arjuna bowed his head to the god,
joined his hands in homage, and spoke.

Arjuna:
[15] I see the gods in your body, O God,
and hordes of varied creatures:
Brahma, the cosmic creator,
on his lotus throne, all the seers
and celestial serpents.

I see your boundless form everywhere,
the countless arms, bellies, mouths, eyes;
Lord of All, I see no end,
or middle or beginning to your totality.

I see you blazing through the fiery rays
of your crown, mace, and discus,
hard to behold in the burning light
of fire and sun that surrounds
your measureless presence.

You are to be known as supreme eternity,
the deepest treasure of all that is,
the immutable guardian of enduring duty;
I think you are man's timeless spirit.

I see no beginning, middle or end to you;
only boundless strength in your arms,
the moon and sun in your eyes,
your mouths of consuming flames,
your own brilliance scorching the universe.

[20] You alone fill the space between heaven
and earth and all the directions;
seeing this awesome, terrible form of yours,
Great Soul, the three worlds tremble. . . .

Sanjaya:
[50] Saying this to Arjuna, Krishna again
revealed his intimate form;
resuming his gentle body, the great spirit
let the terrified hero regain his breath.

Arjuna:
Seeing your gentle human form, Krishna,
I recover my nature, my reason is restored.

Lord Krishna:
This form you have seen is rarely revealed;
the gods are constantly craving
for a vision of this form.

Not through sacred lore, penances, charity,
or sacrificial rites can I be seen in the form
that you saw me. By devotion alone can
    I, as
I really am, be seen and entered into, Arjuna.

[55] Acting only for me, intent on me,
free from attachment, hostile to no creature,
Arjuna, a man of devotion comes to me.

[16:1–11, 21–24] Chapter 16 is a summary of general morality suitable for all twice-born Hindus. It first describes the person "born to inherit a godly destiny," who quickly escapes the process of rebirth. Then it tells of "human devils," who are eternally recycling through rebirth.

Lord Krishna:
Fearlessness, purity, determination
in the discipline of knowledge,

charity, self-control, sacrifice,
study of sacred lore, penance, honesty;

Nonviolence, truth, absence of anger,
disengagement, peace, loyalty,
compassion for creatures, lack of greed,
gentleness, modesty, reliability;

Brilliance, patience, resolve,
clarity, absence of envy and of pride;
these characterize a man
born with divine traits.

Hypocrisy, arrogance, vanity,
anger, harshness, ignorance;
these characterize a man
born with demonic traits.

[5] The divine traits lead to freedom,
the demonic lead to bondage;
do not despair, Arjuna;
you were born with the divine.

All creatures in the world
are either divine or demonic;
I described the divine at length;
hear what I say of the demonic.

Demonic men cannot comprehend
activity and rest; there exists no clarity,
no morality, no truth in them.

They say that the world
has no truth, no basis, no god,
that no power of mutual dependence
is its cause, but only desire.

Mired in this view, lost to themselves
with their meager understanding,
these fiends contrive terrible acts
to destroy the world.

[10] Subject to insatiable desire,
drunk with hypocrisy and pride,
holding false notions from delusion,
they act with impure vows.

In their certainty that life
consists in sating their desires,

they suffer immeasurable anxiety
that ends only with death....

[21] The three gates of hell
that destroy the self
are desire, anger, and greed;
one must relinquish all three.

Released through these three gates
of darkness, Arjuna,
a man elevates the self
and ascends to the highest way.

If he rejects norms of tradition
and lives to fulfill his desires,
he does not reach perfection
or happiness or the highest way.

Let tradition be your standard
in judging what to do or avoid;
knowing the norms of tradition,
perform your action here.

[18:1–9, 41–49, 60–73] In the eighteenth and
last chapter of the *Gita,* the topics of renunciation and the three constituents of nature are
treated for the last time. Krishna summarizes
the duties of the castes and stresses the importance of doing one's caste duty in a spirit of
detachment. Then come a short summary of
the teaching of the whole book and a description of the merits obtained by reading it.
Arjuna is convinced by Krishna and surrenders
himself in obedience.

Arjuna:
Krishna, I want to know the real essence
of both renunciation and relinquishment.

Lord Krishna:
Giving up actions based on desire,
the poets know as "renunciation";
relinquishing all fruit of action,
learned men call "relinquishment."

Some wise men say all action
is flawed and must be relinquished;
others say action in sacrifice, charity,
and penance must not be relinquished.

Arjuna, hear my decision
about relinquishment;
it is rightly declared
to be of three kinds.

[5] Action in sacrifice, charity,
and penance is to be performed,
not relinquished—for wise men,
they are acts of sanctity.

But even these actions
should be done by relinquishing to me
attachment and the fruit of action—
this is my decisive idea.

Renunciation of prescribed action
is inappropriate; relinquished in delusion,
it becomes a way of dark inertia.

When one passionately relinquishes
difficult action from fear
of bodily harm, he cannot win
the fruit of relinquishment.

But if one performs prescribed action
because it must be done,
relinquishing attachment and the fruit,
his relinquishment is a lucid act....

[41] The actions of priests, warriors,
commoners, and servants
are apportioned by qualities
born of their intrinsic being.

Tranquility, control, penance,
purity, patience and honesty,
knowledge, judgment, and piety
are intrinsic to the action of a priest.

Heroism, fiery energy, resolve,
skill, refusal to retreat in battle,
charity, and majesty in conduct
are intrinsic to the action of a warrior.

Farming, herding cattle, and commerce
are intrinsic to the action of a commoner;
action that is essentially service
is intrinsic to the servant.

[45] Each one achieves success
by focusing on his own action;

hear how one finds success
by focusing on his own action. . . .

Better to do one's own duty imperfectly
than to do another man's well;
doing action intrinsic to his being,
a man avoids guilt.

Arjuna, a man should not relinquish
action he is born to, even if it is flawed;
all undertakings are marred by a flaw,
as fire is obscured by smoke.

His understanding everywhere detached,
the self mastered, longing gone,
one finds through renunciation
the supreme success beyond action. . . .

[60] You are bound by your own action,
intrinsic to your being, Arjuna;
even against your will you must do
what delusion now makes you refuse.

Arjuna, the lord resides
in the heart of all creatures,
making them reel magically,
as if a machine moved them.

With your whole being, Arjuna,
take refuge in him alone—
from his grace you will attain
the eternal place that is peace.

This knowledge I have taught
is more arcane than any mystery—
consider it completely,
then act as you choose.

Listen to my profound words,
the deepest mystery of all,
for you are precious to me
and I tell you for your good.

[65] Keep your mind on me,
be my devotee, sacrificing, bow to me—

you will come to me, I promise,
for you are dear to me.

Relinquishing all sacred duties to me,
make me your only refuge; do not grieve,
for I shall free you from all evils.

You must not speak of this to one
who is without penance and devotion,
or who does not wish to hear,
or who finds fault with me.

When he shares this deepest mystery
with others devoted to me,
giving me his total devotion,
a man will come to me without doubt.

No mortal can perform
service for me that I value more,
and no other man on earth
will be more dear to me than he is.

[70] I judge the man who studies
our dialogue on sacred duty
to offer me sacrifice
through sacrifice in knowledge.

If he listens in faith,
finding no fault, a man is free
and will attain the cherished worlds
of those who act in virtue.

Arjuna, have you listened
with your full powers of reason?
Has the delusion of ignorance
now been destroyed?

Arjuna:
Krishna, my delusion is destroyed,
by your grace I have regained memory;
I stand here, my doubt dispelled,
ready to act on your words.

TWO TAMIL POETS, APPAR AND TUKARAM

Much of the Sanskrit foundation of Hinduism was creatively adapted for the myriad languages of India. These adaptations preserved and extended the basic ideas of the ancient scriptural sources. The first two poems in this section sample the Tamil (south Indian) religious poetry of Appar (seventh century), the best known of the "Shaivite saints" whose writings are given a scriptural function if not formal status.[53] The last two poems are by Tukaram (seventeenth century), the greatest Maharashtrian poet. These poems reflect popular *bhakti* (devotional) tradition, and many of them are recited in the humblest households in India.

---

[53]Taken from F. Kingsbury and G. E. Phillips, *Hymns of the Tamil Shaivite Saints* (Calcutta: Association Press, 1921), pp. 47–51.

[Appar:] Confession of Sin

Evil, all evil, my race, evil my qualities all,
Great am I only in sin, evil is even my
  good.
Evil my innermost self, foolish, avoiding the
  pure,
Beast am I not, yet the ways of the beast I can
  never forsake.

I can exhort with strong words, telling men
  what they should hate.
Yet can I never give gifts, only to beg them I
  know.
Ah! wretched man that I am, why did I come
  to birth?

The Presence of God

No man holds sway over us,
Nor death nor hell fear we;
No tremblings, grief of mind,
No pains nor cringing see.
Joy, day by day, unchanged
Is ours, for we are His,
His ever, who does reign,
Our Shankara,[54] in bliss.

Here to His feet we've come,
Feet as plucked flowers fair;
See how His ears divine
Ring and white conch-shell wear.
He is ever hard to find, but He lives in the
  thought of the good;
He is innermost secret of Scripture, inscru-
  table, unknowable;
He is holy and milk and the shining light.
He is the king of the Devas,
Immanent in Vishnu, in Brahma, in flame
  and in wind,

---

[54]*Shankara:* Shiva.

Yet in the mighty-sounding sea and in the
   mountains.
He is the great One who chooses Shiva's
   paradise for his own.

If there be days when my tongue is dumb and
   speaks not of him,
Let no such days be counted in the record of
   my life.

[Tukaram:] Waiting[55]

With head on hand before my door,
I sit and wait in vain.
Along the road to Pandhari
My heart and eyes I strain.
When shall I look upon my Lord?
When shall I see him come?
Of all the passing days and hours
I count the heavy sum.
With watching long my eyelids throb,
My limbs with sore distress,

But my impatient heart forgets
My body's weariness.
Sleep is no longer sweet to me;
I care not for my bed;
Forgotten are my house and home,
All thirst and hunger fled.
Says Tuka,[56] Blest shall be the day—
Ah, soon may it betide!—
When one shall come from Pandhari
To summon back the bride.

[55]Taken from N. Macnicol, *Psalms of the Maratha Saints* (Calcutta: Association Press, 1920), p. 58.

[56]*Tuka:* the poet Tukaram himself. It is common in Indian poetry for the author to include his own name in the poem.

The Burden of the Past[57]

I have been harassed by the world.
I have dwelled in my mother's womb and I
   must enter the gate of the womb eight
   million times.
I was born a needy beggar and my life is
   passed under a stranger's power.
I am bound fast in the meshes of my past and
   its later influence continues with me;
It puts forth its power and whirls me along.
My stomach is empty and never at rest.
I have no fixed course or home or village.
I have no power, O God, to end my
   wanderings;
My soul dances about like rice in a
   frying pan.

Ages have passed in this way and I do not
   know how many more await me.
I cannot end my course, for it begins
   again;
Only the ending of the world can set me
   free.
Who will finish this suffering of mine?
Who will take my burden on himself?
Your name will carry me over the sea of this
   world,
You run to the help of the distressed.
Now run to me, Narayana,[58] to me, poor and
   wretched as I am.
Consider neither my merits or my faults.
Tukaram implores your mercy.

[57]From J. N. Fraser and K. B. Marathe, *The Poems of Tukaram* (Madras: Christian Literature Society, 1909), pp. 114–115.

[58]*Narayana:* Vishnu.

GLOSSARY

Aranyakas [ah-RUN-yah-kuhs] "Forest Books"; philosophical thoughts on sacrifice; part of the canon of *Shruti*.

Atman [AHT-muhn] the individual Self, or soul.

Bhagavad Gita [BAH-gah-vahd GEE-tuh] "Song of the Lord"; a long poem on religious duty in the *Mahabharata*.

Brahman [BRAH-muhn] the ultimate, absolute reality of the cosmos; the world-soul.

Brahmanas [BRAH-muh-nuhs] "Brahmin Books"; Vedic expositions of sacrifice; part of the canon of *Shruti*.

Dharma-Shastras [DAHR-muh SHAS-truhs] writings on personal and social duties.

mantra [MAHN-truh] a short sacred formula used in prayer or meditation (not, as often thought in North America, a common or personal motto).

Om (or *Aum*) [OHM] a spoken syllable symbolizing the fundamental hidden reality of the universe.

pandit [PAHN-deet] a Brahmin who specializes in Vedic memorization and ritual enactment.

rishis [REE-shees] "seers" who heard the sounds of the four *Vedas* and collected them into the *Veda*.

samhitas [SAHM-hee-tuhs] "collections" of hymns, formulas, songs, and spells that constitute the four *Vedas*.

Shruti [SHROO-tee] "What is heard"; the primary revelation heard by the ancients; the first level of Hindu scripture, considered of cosmic, not human, authorship.

Smriti [SMRIH-tee] "What is remembered" about divine revelation; epics, myths and legends, tantras, and law codes that constitute the second level of Hindu scripture.

Upanishads [oo-PAH-nee-shahds] "Sittings near a Teacher"; philosophical collections forming the end of the *Veda*; part of the canon of *Shruti*.

Vedas [VAY-duhs] "Books of Knowledge"; the four *Vedas—Rig, Yajur, Sama,* and *Atharva*—are part of the canon of *Shruti*.

yogin [YO-gin] a practitioner of yoga.

QUESTIONS FOR STUDY AND DISCUSSION

1. To what degree, if any, can the *Vedas* be described as reflecting a nature-worship religion?

2. Compare the use and effects of soma to the modern use of drugs by people who argue that drug use brings a higher consciousness. What might the similarities and differences be?

3. In what ways do the *Upanishads* differ from and agree with earlier Vedic literature? Do you agree with those scholars who argue that the differences between the earlier Vedas and later writings (including the Upanishads) justify calling the first stage "Vedic religion" and only the second stage "Hinduism"?

4. How does the variety of usages of Hindu scripture in the past and present mirror the variety of Hindu religion?

5. If you were to become a Hindu, to which caste would you like to belong? Which sex? Why?

6. How would you characterize the role of women in Hinduism? Are the texts given here reflective of what you see as women's actual conditions in India?

7. How and why does the *Bhagavad Gita* present the path of devotion as the best form of Hinduism?

8. How does the *Bhagavad Gita* present and answer the problem of war? What is your critique of its answer? How may its answer be applicable to peoples of other cultures and other religions?

9. How do the later devotional songs carry forth and develop the traditions of devotional Hinduism?

SCRIPTURES IN FILM

The Indian film industry, popularly known as "Bollywood," is second in size only to the film industry of the United States. However, it has not produced many English-language films that deal with Hindu scriptures. *The Mahabharata* (1989, not rated), directed by Peter Brooks, is a short version of the lengthy stage play done by the Brooklyn Academy of Music and has a short section on the *Bhagavad Gita*. For a treatment of the history and culture of modern India with indirect treatment of scriptural ideas, see *Gandhi* (1982, rated PG), directed by Richard Attenborough and starring Ben Kingsley. This excellent film won three Academy Awards. Also set in the time of Gandhi is *Water* (2005, not rated, in Hindi with English subtitles) by Deepa Mehta,

the story of widowed women and girls confined to exist in self-denial for the rest of their lives; it opens with quotations from the *Laws of Manu*. For a contemporary treatment of stages of life, marriage, and role relationships in a modern Western context, see *Monsoon Wedding* (2001, rated R), directed by Mira Nair, who also directed the Cannes prize-winning *Salaam Bombay!* the story of children's appalling lives on the street.

✻ SUGGESTIONS FOR FURTHER READING

PRIMARY READINGS

The most complete and accessible translations of Hindu scripture remain the several volumes in F. Max Müller, gen. ed., *Sacred Books of the East* (Oxford: Oxford University Press, 1879–1910). For more recent translations, begin with the following works.

Thomas B. Coburn, *Encountering the Goddess: A Translation of the Devi-Mahatmya and a Study of Its Interpretation*. Albany: State University of New York Press, 1991. A translation and study of the best-known goddess text in modern India.

Wendy Doniger and Sudhir Kakar, eds., *Kamasutra*. New York: Oxford University Press, 2002. A scholarly translation designed to correct Richard Burton's famous translation. Includes samples of commentaries from the thirteenth to the twentieth centuries but no illustrations.

Robert E. Hume, *The Thirteen Principal Upanishads*, 2d ed. Oxford: Oxford University Press, 1983. Perhaps the best translation of the most important *Upanishads.*

Donald S. Lopez Jr., *Religions of India in Practice*. Princeton, NJ: Princeton University Press, 1995. Contains primary documents, many never translated before, of more recent Hindu literature that has scriptural use. See especially the section "Songs of Devotion and Praise," which treats devotional poetry.

Barbara Stoler Miller, *The Bhagavad-Gita: Krishna's Counsel in Time of War*. New York: Columbia University Press, 1986. The most readable recent translation of the *Gita,* and one that suggests its power and literary beauty.

Wendy Doniger O'Flaherty, ed., *Textual Sources for the Study of Hinduism*. Totowa, NJ: Barnes & Noble, 1988. A selection of readings from both *Shruti* and *Smriti.*

Patrick Olivelle, *Samnyasa Upanishads: Hindu Scriptures on Asceticism and Renunciation*. New York: Oxford University Press, 1992. Full introduction, fresh translation, and notes for those *Upanishads* that deal with the stage of renunciation. See also his *Upanishads* (World's Classics Series). Oxford: Oxford University Press, 1998.

SECONDARY READINGS

Thomas B. Coburn, "'Scripture' in India: Towards a Typology of the Word in Hindu Life." In M. Levering, ed., *Rethinking Scripture*. Albany: State University of New York Press, 1989, pp. 102–128; also published in the *Journal of the American Academy of Religion* 52 (1984): 435–459. Argues that *scripture* is an ill-fitting term for Hinduism and proposes instead a *typology of the word.*

Harold Coward, "Scripture in Hinduism." In *Sacred Word and Sacred Text*. Maryknoll, NY: Orbis, 1988. A survey of the Hindu scriptures with special attention to orality.

Klaus Kostermaier, *Hindu Writings: A Short Introduction to the Major Sources*. Oxford: Oneworld, 2000. Treats *Veda* to contemporary writings, with emphasis on scripture.

Robert C. Lester, "Hinduism: Veda and Sacred Texts." In F. M. Denny and R. L. Taylor, *The Holy Book in Comparative Perspective*. Charleston: University of South Carolina Press, 1985, pp. 126–147. A good treatment of the relationship of Vedic texts and other Hindu scriptures, especially the *Smriti.*

Krishna Sivaraman, ed., *Hindu Spirituality: Vedas Through Vedanta*. New York: Crossroad, 1989. A treatment by mostly Indian scholars of the continuing significance of Vedic and Upanishadic traditions for contemporary Hinduism.

Katherine K. Young, "[Women in] Hinduism." In Arvind Sharma, ed., *Women in World Religions.* Albany: State University of New York Press, 1987, pp. 59–103. This concise but fairly comprehensive survey has good references to the content and usage of Hindu sacred writings.

❧ COMPANION WEBSITE

Visit the *Anthology of World Scriptures* companion website at **www.thomsonedu.com** for learning tools such as map explorations, flashcards of glossary terms, learning objectives, chapter practice quizzes, links to other websites for learning and research, and chapter summaries in PowerPoint® format.

Buddhism

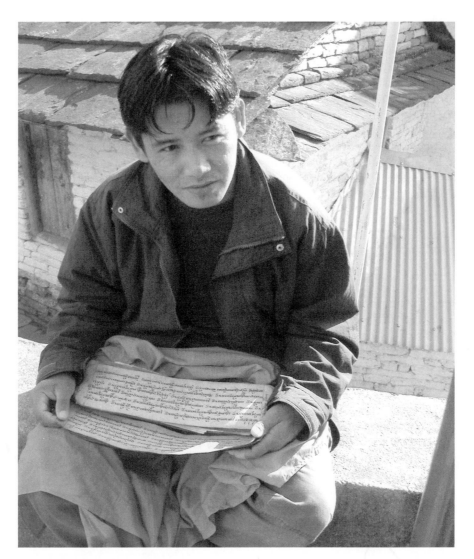

Studying Buddhist Scripture

Palden Wangchuk, a young monk in the village of Sirubari, Nepal, reads and reflects on Buddhist scripture, written here on the traditional palm-leaf material. Activity with scripture forms a good deal of the Buddhist monk's typical day. (*Photo courtesy of Chuck Conner Photography. Copyright © 2004 Chuck Conner.*)

- In a Chinese convent, Buddhist nuns gather daily to read scripture. A low hum fills the reading room as they recite in unison. They are "making merit," doing a deed that will wear away karma. This merit will enable them to be reborn after death into a better existence, eventually to achieve Nirvana and be reborn no more.

- In Washington, D.C., a "Dharma Wheel Cutting Karma" has been turning since 1997 in the Asian section of the Library of Congress. The wheel contains 208 repetitions of forty-two Tibetan scriptures, which otherwise fill fifteen Tibetan volumes. The spiritual power generated by the constant electrical turning of the wheel is said to generate compassion, prevent natural disasters, and promote peace in the world.

- In Thailand, a leading Buddhist authority urges that country's 300,000 monks to join in the fight against AIDS. Dr. Chatsumarn Kabilsingh of the Dharma Practice Center argues that monks should acquire a better understanding of Buddhist scriptures to be more effective in teaching the scriptural command against adultery. She says, "Sex springs from the love and care shown by two individuals, and they need to be responsible to each other. With true love, there is no need to change partners, and that is the best prevention against AIDS."

- In Maharagama, Sri Lanka, several Buddhist monks work at computer keyboards. They are keying in the complete text of the Pali canon of Buddhist scriptures. In 1994, after three years of work, the scriptures were published on the World Wide Web (only in the Pali language); later, they became available in a fully searchable CD-ROM. The monks and the private patrons funding this project see it as yet another phase in the preservation of Buddhist scripture from 2,500 years ago.

INTRODUCTION

The Buddhist religion is based on the life and teaching of the Indian sage Siddhartha Gotama (ca. 536–476 B.C.E.), the Enlightened One, or **Buddha** [BUH-dah; rhymes with "could-a"]. Buddhists believe that individuals can overcome the misery of the world and reach their own Buddha status by a process of mental and moral purification. The term *Buddha* applies to every individual who attains this state. Gotama Buddha is the Buddha par excellence.

Buddhism has spread throughout most of Asia. With this growth has come a wide diversity within Buddhism that is mirrored in its scriptures. The Buddhist canon has three main forms—*Theravadin, Mahayanan,* and *Tibetan*—hundreds of scriptural texts, and many different types of usage. This assemblage of scriptures provides a fascinating overview of the early history of the Buddhist tradition and insight into the contemporary life of Buddhists everywhere.

Overview of Structure

The scriptures of Theravada (south Asian) Buddhism are known as the *Tipitaka*[1] [tih-pee-TAH-kuh], the "Three Baskets" (see Table 3.1). Tradition says that the early disciples of Buddha wrote down his words on palm leaves and separated them into three baskets (*pitakas*): the *Vinaya Pitaka*, "Discipline Basket"; the *Sutta Pitaka*, "Discourse Basket"; and the *Abhidhamma Pitaka*, "Special Teaching Basket." In this section, we first consider each basket and then survey the structure of the Chinese and Tibetan forms of the Buddhist canon.

The *Vinaya Pitaka* contains regulations for the communal life of the monks and nuns. All these rules are said to be the words of the Buddha. The *Vinaya* [vih-NIGH-yuh] has three divisions: the *Sutta-vibhanga* (Division of Rules), the *Khandhaka* (Sections), and the *Parivara* (Accessory), a short summary of the rules and how to apply them. The *Vinaya* presents 227 different rules for monks—most of them prohibitions of forbidden activities—grouped according to importance. They range from a few major offenses that result in permanent expulsion from the order to many minor offenses that a monk need only confess to his monastic leader. All the rules for monks apply in a general way to the nuns as well, but a special section of the *Sutta-vibhanga* gives specific regulations for nuns. The size of the *Vinaya Pitaka* is indicated by its most recent English translation, which runs to six substantial volumes. That the *Vinaya* is first among the three baskets of scripture attests to the leading role that monasticism has played in Buddhism as a whole and especially in its scriptures.

The second basket, the *Sutta* [SUH-tuh] *Pitaka*, contains teachings attributed to Gotama Buddha. The word **sutta** (Sanskrit: *sutra*) refers to a scriptural text. Buddhists divide the *Sutta Pitaka* into five sections: *Long Discourses, Medium-Length Discourses, Corrected Discourses, Item-More* (or *Gradual*) *Discourses,* and *Short Texts*. Each of the discourses has many subdivisions, and most follow a common structure: First comes "Thus I have heard [from the Buddha]," then a statement of the place and occasion of the hearing, next the body of the teaching, and last the listener's confession of the truth of the teaching and acknowledgment that he (the listener) is Buddha's disciple. The *Sutta Pitaka* is probably the best known of the three baskets. With its rationale for the first basket, its collections of wise sayings, its stories of former lives of the Buddha and other famous Buddhists, and its general writings on doctrines and ethics, the *Sutta Pitaka* provides for students of Buddhism the best access to the essence of the religion's tradition.

The third basket, the *Abhidhamma* [ahb-hee-DAHM-muh] *Pitaka*, contains seven scholastic treatises based on the teachings of Buddha. They deal with advanced, difficult topics and are often highly philosophical. Although the Pali and Sanskrit versions of the first two baskets are similar in content, they vary quite a bit in the third basket. The Pali version, used by South Asian Theravada Buddhism, tries to adhere conservatively to the exact words of Buddha. Its six treatises are *The Summary of Teaching, Divisions, Discussion of Elements, The Designation of Persons, The Pairs,* and *Activations*. The Sanskrit version, *Abhidharma*, is important for the growth of

---

[1] Sanskrit: *Tripitaka*. Throughout this chapter, we generally use Pali language forms of key Buddhist words; Sanskrit equivalents appear in parentheses. The titles of scripture books reflect their language of origin, which is generally Pali.

TABLE 3.1 The Theravadin Canon: The *Tipitaka*

Name	Translation	Content/Size
Vinaya Pitaka	Discourse Basket	
1. *Sutta-vibhanga*	Division of Rules	Monastic rules stated and expanded
a. *Mahavibhanga*	Great Division	227 rules for monks
b. *Bhikkuni-vibhanga*	Division About Nuns	Rules for nuns
2. *Khandhaka*	Sections	
a. *Mahavagga*	Great Group	Main rules
b. *Cullavagga*	Small Group	Miscellaneous rules
3. *Parivara*	Accessory	Summaries of rules
Sutta Pitaka	Discourse Basket	
1. *Digha-nikaya*	Collection of Long Discourses	34 suttas
2. *Majjhima-nikaya*	Collection of Medium-Length Discourses	152 suttas
3. *Samyutta-nikaya*	Collection of Corrected Discourses	56 groups of suttas
4. *Anguttara-nikaya*	Collection of Item-More Discourses	2,308 suttas
5. *Khuddaka-nikaya*	Collection of Short Texts	
a. *Khuddaka-patha*	Little Readings	A meditation book
b. *Dhammapada*	Verses on Teaching	26 chapters
c. *Udana*	Utterances	80 utterances
d. *Itivuttaka*	Thus-saids	112 suttas
e. *Sutta-nipata*	Sutta Collection	71 suttas
f. *Vimana-vatthu*	Tales of Heavenly Mansions	85 poems
g. *Peta-vatthu*	Tales of Ghosts	Rebirth as ghosts
h. *Thera-Gatha*	Verses of Elder Men	Poems from earliest monks
i. *Theri-Gatha*	Verses of Elder Women	Poems from early nuns
j. *Jataka*	Lives	550 past lives of Gotama
k. *Nidessa*	Exposition	2 commentaries
l. *Patisambhida-magga*	Way of Analysis	Doctrinal exposition
m. *Apadana*	Stories	Saints past lives
n. *Buddhavamsa*	Lineage of the Buddhas	Stories of 24 pre-Gotama Buddhas
o. *Gariya-pitaka*	Basket of Perfections	35 tales from *Jataka*
Abhidhamma Pitaka	*Special Teaching Basket*	
1. *Dhamma-sangani*	Summary of Teaching	
2. *Vibhanga*	Divisions	
3. *Dhastu-Kadha*	Discussions of Elements	
4. *Puggala-pannatti*	Designation of Persons	
5. *Yamaka*	The Pairs	
6. *Patthama*	Activations	

Source: Adapted from Richard H. Robinson, *The Buddhist Religion* (Belmont, CA: Dickenson Publishing Company, 1970), pp. 125–128. Copyright © 1970, Dickenson Publishing Company. Used by permission of Wadsworth Publishing Company, Inc.

TABLE 3.2 The Mahayana or Chinese Canon

Name of Section	Translation	Size
Agama	Limbs	2 vols., 151 texts
Jatakas	Lives	2 vols., 68 texts
Prajna-Paramita	Perfect Wisdom	4 vols., 42 texts
Saddharma-Pundarika	—	1 vol., 16 texts
Avatamsaka	—	2 vols., 31 texts
Ratnakuta	—	
Mahaparinirvana	Great Decease	1 vol., 23 texts
—	Great Assembly	1 vol., 28 texts
Sutra-Pitaka	Sutra Collection	4 vols., 423 texts
Tantra	Tantra	4 vols., 572 texts
Vinaya	Discipline	3 vols., 86 texts
—	Commentary on Sutras	3 vols., 31 texts
Abhidhamma	Special Teaching	4 vols., 28 texts
Madhyamika		1 vol., 15 texts
Yogacara	Yoga Practice	2 vols., 49 texts
—	Treatises	1 vol., 65 texts
—	Commentaries on Sutras	7 vols.
—	Commentaries on *Vinaya*	1 vol.
—	Commentaries on Shastras	5 vols.
—	Chinese Sectarian Writings	5 vols.
—	History and Biography	4 vols., 95 texts
—	Encyclopedias and Dictionaries	2 vols., 16 texts
—	Non-Buddhist Writings	1 vol., 8 texts
—	Catalogues	1 vol., 40 texts

Source: Adapted from Richard H. Robinson, *The Buddhist Religion* (Belmont, CA: Dickenson Publishing Company, 1970), pp. 125–128. Copyright © 1970, Dickenson Publishing Company. Used by permission of Wadsworth Publishing Company, Inc.

Buddhist philosophy because these Sanskrit books deal with the ideas of Buddha more than with his words. Unlike the Pali version, the Sanskrit has seven books, and they differ from the Pali names and content, and Chinese and Tibetan translations of them also differ. The seven most commonly recognized are *Method of Knowledge, Treatise, Overview of Consciousness, Collection on the Teaching, Treatise on Communication, Overview of the Elements,* and *Discourse on Sacred Beliefs.*

The scriptures of Mahayana (north Asian, especially China and Japan) Buddhism are known as the "Chinese canon." The Mahayana canon did not adopt the threefold-basket division of the Pali canon. It has no main divisions (see Table 3.2), but many of the most important books of the Pali canon were incorporated in the Mahayana canon. The Theravadin and Mahayanan canons share important works such as the *Jatakas* (Lives), the *Death of the Buddha* (Pali: *Mahaparinib-bana;* Sanskrit: *Mahaparinirvana*), *Vinaya* texts on monastic discipline, and various *Abhidhamma* texts. Some books from the Mahayana canon have even penetrated Theravada Buddhism and are recognized and used as scripture though not formally admitted to the historic Pali canon. In Sri Lanka, for example, the *Buddhacarita* (Acts of the Buddha) and the *Visuddhimagga* (Path of Purification) are widely received and used as scripture.

The Mahayana canon also added many other new books, all of them claiming to be the true word of the Gotama Buddha. Among the most important are *Prajna-Paramita* (Perfection of Knowledge) sutras, which are philosophical discussions of the denial of the reality of existence and nonexistence. Their almost constant repetitiveness contributes to their great length. Another important work is the *Description of the Happy Land*—that is, the land where the gracious Buddha Amitabha rules and invites his followers to share eternal life with him. This text has become important in the Japanese Pure Land Buddhist sect. A third major work is the *Lotus Sutra of the True Law*. This work has become the leading text of Nichiren Buddhism. In sum, with its adoption of many older books along with an astonishing variety of new books, the literature of Mahayana Buddhism is vast and complex.

The third main Buddhist canon is the Tibetan (see Table 3.3). In the seventh century C.E., Buddhism came to Tibet, where it is known as Lamaism (from the Tibetan *bla-ma,* the "superior" religion). The Tibetan king sent a delegation to India, where an alphabet was devised for the Tibetan language and the entire Buddhist literature was translated into it. The Tibetans added many books of their own, secular as well as religious, to this Indian collection. The final and official assembling of these books came in the fourteenth century, when they were fixed into two sections: the *Kanjur* (Translation of the Ordinances) and the *Tanjur* (Translation of the Doctrine).

TABLE 3.3 The Tibetan Canon

Name	Translation	Size
Kanjur	Translation of the Ordinances	108 vols.
'Dul-ba	Discipline [for monastics]	13 vols.
Shes-rab-kyi-pha-rol-tu-phyin-pa	Supreme Otherworldly Knowledge	21 vols.
Phal-chen	Buddhist Cosmology	6 vols.
dKon-brtsegs	Heap of Jewels	6 vols.
mDo	Teaching Lectures	38 vols.
Mya-ngan-'das	Nirvana	2 vols.
rGyud	Texture [Tantra]	22 vols.
Tanjur	Translation of the Doctrine	225 vols.
mDo	Teaching [Sutra]	136 vols.
rGyud	Texture [Tantra]	87 vols.
	A book of Hymns	1 vol.
	An index	1 vol.

The *Kanjur* contains 689 books of various lengths in 100 or 108 volumes. It contains only those texts that the Buddha himself is said to have taught. The first main division is the *Discipline,* for monks; the second is *Supreme Otherworldly Knowledge;* the third deals with Buddhist cosmology; the fourth is *Heap of Jewels;* the fifth is *Teaching Lectures;* the sixth is *Nirvana;* the last is *Texture* (Tantra). The *Tanjur* is not, as is often stated, a commentary on the *Kanjur.* It contains 225 volumes in two main sections: *Teaching* (Sutra) and *Texture* (Tantra). The *Teaching* section includes many translations of Indian commentaries on older scriptures. The *Tanjur* deals with an even wider variety of topics than does the *Kanjur:* traditional religious teachings, magical texts drawn mainly from native Tibetan religion, and texts on alchemy and astrology. Today, the preservation and further dissemination of Tibetan scriptures is a primary task of Tibetan Buddhist exiles.

Contemporary Use

Buddhist use of scripture today centers on monastic activity. Since early times, when the teaching of Buddha was passed along orally and then written down, the role of monks (but not nuns) in scriptural activity has been primary. The scriptures themselves bear the marks of this orientation. For example, the first and the third baskets are explicitly for monastics. Other reasons also figure in. The expense of owning such a large canon makes it accessible mainly to monastic orders. Its size demands a lifetime of study to master it; its content is challenging and specialized, calling for special teachers who can be found only among the monks. Buddhism in general demands withdrawal from the distractions of daily life to give the scriptures the kind of in-depth study they deserve.

What does this monastic usage entail? First, Buddhism has traditionally distinguished between study monks and meditation monks. The very term *study monk* indicates the first use of scripture—the study of the content of its teachings. A new monk studies scripture to learn the first and most important of the monastic rules that govern his life. He also studies the most easily understood texts in the *Sutta Pitaka,* such as the *Dhammapada* and the *Jataka* [JAH-tah-kuh] verses. As time progresses and he masters this material, he learns the other rules in the *Vinaya Pitaka* and the other texts of the *Sutta Pitaka.* If, at the height of his monastic career, he displays excellence in study and teaching, he may go on to master the intricacies of the *Abhidhamma Pitaka.* Because study of the scriptures is in most forms of Buddhism a prerequisite for becoming a meditation monk, all monks pass through this first phase. Throughout the history of Buddhism and even today, study monks have greatly outnumbered meditation monks. This is especially the case in modern times, when the general conviction has grown in many Buddhist circles that one cannot reach enlightenment in this life. In all this study and teaching, the goal is to realize in one's own life the teachings of the Buddha that lead toward Nirvana, enlightenment. The scripture itself, as a book, is worth little or nothing. The *meaning* of the words, not the words themselves, has value in the search for purification.

Monks also pursue scriptural activity for the laity. At funerals, they recite texts for the merit of the deceased. Monks often officiate at wedding ceremonies. They lecture on the scriptures to the laity, both individuals and groups. Some monks preach the scriptures to the laity, often using such popular material as the *Jataka* tales. Wealthy layfolk often sponsor long recitations of scripture in the monasteries and pay for the publication of scriptures, all for the sake of making merit for loved ones. But all these activities with the laity are mostly incidental to a monk's main activity—studying and meditating on scripture to travel the road to personal enlightenment.

The Tibetan form of Buddhism holds its scriptures in great ritual esteem. The books are venerated in worship; incense and prayer are offered to them. They are produced in the traditional way, either printed by hand or with woodblocks, and are preserved in the monasteries with great care. Although these books are produced and preserved in Tibet and northern India, no scholarly critical edition of them has been compiled. Modern-language translations are very incomplete, and only a few European and North American libraries possess a complete copy of the *Kanjur* and *Tanjur.*

Historical Origin and Development

The development of Buddhist scripture begins with Gotama Buddha himself. Buddhists believe that Prince Gotama established among his monk disciples an oral transmission of his teachings on which later written scriptures are based. They trace all the varied scripture collections and their contents back to Buddha. All scriptures are his word.

Before Gotama died, he did not appoint a human successor. He taught instead that the leader of the Buddhists was to be his teaching—**dhamma** [DAH-muh] (Sanskrit: *dharma*)—and the monastic order (Sangha) he founded. Soon after his death, his disciples gathered at the first general council of Buddhists, held at Rajagaha in 483 B.C.E., to formalize his teachings. After seven months of work collecting and examining the supposed sayings of Buddha for authenticity, they drafted an official version and committed it to memory. Ananda, his chief disciple, is said to have recited them all. The sayings were written down on palm leaves (more durable than paper or parchment in the hot, humid Indian climate) and then separated into baskets. Mahayana Buddhists believe that all three baskets were developed at this time. Theravada Buddhists believe that the last basket, *Abhidhamma Pitaka,* was formed at the third general council of Buddhists in 253 B.C.E. Most modern scholars agree that the nature of this basket seems to suggest a later origin.

Even after this initial conversion to writing, oral transmission continued and was seen as the primary mode of scripture preservation by all early Buddhists. An early *Abhidhamma* text, the *Samuccaya,* indicates reasons for this preference: Memorizing is easy, accumulates merit, aids understanding, brings mental satisfaction, and promotes one's good standing among others. In addition, early Buddhists saw transmission by an exacting oral tradition as offering a more reliable way than writing to preserve the exact words of the Buddha.

When Mahayana Buddhism arose in the first century C.E., it showed new concern for liberation through the assistance of a **bodhisattva** [bohd-hee-SAHT-vuh], a person who postpones his or her own full enlightenment to help others. The older idea of self-redemption characteristic of Theravada Buddhism gave way to redemption through the grace of this Buddha. The new movement required a new body of scripture, and so began the Mahayana canon (see Table 3.2). Although this collection is typically called the "Chinese canon," it is also used in Japan, usually in its Chinese-language form.

HISTORY

The Past Lives of Siddhartha Gotama

After his enlightenment, Siddhartha knew all his past lives. In the *Jatakas* (Lives), he recounts in detail 550 episodes from as many past lives, each story revealing his gradual progress to perfection in his last incarnation as Gotama. Each *Jataka* teaches one point, always to edify the reader. Only the verses at the end are considered inspired, and the stories are built from them. They come from a Mahayana setting that features the bestowal of merit from one person to another, but they are widely known in Theravada lands as well. In this story, the layman transfers merit to the barber.[2]

The Master told this story about a believing layman. This was a faithful, pious soul, and a chosen disciple. One evening, on his way to Jetavana, he came to the bank of a river. The ferrymen had already pulled up their boat on the shore in order to attend service. No boat could be seen at the landing, and our friend's mind was full of delightful thoughts of the Buddha, so he walked into the river. His feet did not sink below the water. He got as far as mid-river walking as though he were on dry land, but then he noticed the waves. Then his ecstasy subsided, and his feet began to sink. But he stirred himself up to high tension [by meditation], and walked on over the water. So he arrived at Jetavana, greeted the Master, and took a seat on one side. The Master entered into conversation with him pleasantly: "I hope, good layman, you had no mishap on your way."

"O Sir," he replied, "I was so absorbed in thoughts of the Buddha that when I set foot upon the river, I walked over it as though it had been dry ground!"

"Ah, friend layman," said the Master, "you are not the only one who has been kept safe by remembering the virtues of the Buddha. In older days pious laymen have been shipwrecked in mid-ocean, and saved themselves by remembering the Buddha's virtues." Then, at the man's request, he told a story from his past lives.

Once upon a time...a disciple who had entered on the Paths went on a ship with a barber of some considerable property. The barber's wife had given him charge of our friend, to look after him in better and in worse. A week later, the ship was wrecked in mid-ocean. These two persons clung to one plank, and were cast up on an island. There the barber killed some birds, and cooked them, offering a share of his meal to the lay brother. "No, thank you," said he, "I have had enough." He was thinking to himself, "There is no help for us here except the Three Jewels,"[3] and so he pondered upon the blessings of the Three Jewels. As he pondered, a Serpent-king who had been born in that isle changed his own body to the shape of a great ship. The ship was filled with the seven kinds of precious things. An ocean god was the helmsman. The three masts were made of sapphire, the anchor of gold, the ropes of silver, and the planks were golden. The Sea-spirit stood on board, crying, "Any passengers for India?"

---

[2]Taken, with editing, from E. B. Cowell, ed., *The Jataka*, vol. 2 (Cambridge: Cambridge University Press, 1895), pp. 77–78.

[3]*Three Jewels:* the Buddha, the Dhamma (Teaching), and the Sangha (monastic order); also called the "Three Refuges."

Jataka 190, *Birth-Story of the Blessing of the Commandments.*

The lay brother said, "Yes, that's where we are headed."

"In with you then, on board with you!" He went aboard, and wanted to call his friend the barber. "You may come," said the helmsman to the lay brother, "but he may not. He is not a man of holy life. I brought this ship for you, not for him."

The lay brother replied, "Very well; the gifts I have given, the virtues I have practiced, the powers I have developed—I give him the fruit of all of them!"

"I thank you, master!" said the barber.

"Now," said the Sea-spirit, "I can take the barber aboard." So he conveyed them both over sea, and sailed upstream to Benares. There, by his power, he created a store of wealth for both of them, and spoke this to them: "Keep company with the wise and good. If this barber had not been in company with this pious layman, he would have perished in the deep."

Then he said this poem in praise of good company:

"Behold the fruit of sacrifice, virtue, and piety:
A serpent in ship-shape conveys the good man o'er the sea.
Make friendship only with the good, and keep good company;
Friends with the good, this barber could his home in safety see." . . .

Master Gotama, after finishing this discourse, declared the Truths and identified the [connection to his] Birth. At the conclusion of the Truths the pious layman entered on the Fruit of the Second Path.[4] "On that occasion the converted lay brother attained Nirvana; Sariputta was the Serpent-king, and I myself was the ocean-god."

---

[4]*the Fruit of the Second Path:* the path of those who are reborn again only once.

The Life of Siddhartha Gotama

Scholars of Buddhism today place the *Acts of the Buddha (Buddhacarita)* by Ashvaghosha, who lived in the first century B.C.E., between Theravada and Mahayana Buddhism. It is a favorite book in the latter. It deals in poetic form with the life and teachings of the Buddha. This selection recounts the birth of Gotama, the "Four Sights," his "Great Retirement," and his enlightenment. It portrays the life of Siddhartha as an example for all Buddhists: All his followers should reach Nirvana in this manner. It opens, as do many Buddhist scriptures, with an invocation to the Buddha. This salutes him as an **Arhat** [AHR-haht], a "Worthy One" who has achieved enlightenment.[5]

That Arhat is here saluted, who has no counterpart. Giving supreme happiness, he surpasses Brahman the Creator. Driving away darkness, he vanquishes the sun. Dispelling all burning heat, he surpasses the beautiful moon.

There was a city, the dwelling-place of the great saint Kapila, that had its sides surrounded by the beauty of a lofty broad plain like a line of clouds. With its high-soaring palaces, it was immersed in the sky. . . . [9] A king by the name of Suddhodana ruled over the city. He was a relative of the sun, anointed to stand at the head of earth's monarchs. He adorned it as a bee adorns a full-blown lotus. [10] He was

---

[5]Taken, with editing, from E. B. Cowell, trans., *Buddhist Mahayana Texts, Sacred Books of the East,* vol. 49 (Oxford: Oxford University Press, 1894), pp. 1–157.

Buddhacarita 1.1–2, 9–10, 15–17, 19–21, 23–25, 34, 54, 59, 62, 72–74, 83; 2.24–26, 28–32; 3.1–8, 26–33, 40–44, 53–61; 5.7–20; 12.88–104; 14.1–9, 35–37, 64–68, 79–81.

the very best of kings, intent on liberality but empty of pride, . . .

[15] He had a queen named Maya, who was free from all deceit. She was a brilliance proceeding from his brilliance, like the splendor of the sun when it is free from all the influence of darkness. . . . Truly the life of women is always darkness; yet when it encountered her, it shone brilliantly. . . .

[19] Falling from the host of beings in heaven, and illumining the three worlds, the most excellent of Bodhisattvas[6] suddenly entered her womb. [20] He assumed the form of a huge elephant as white as Himalaya, armed with six tusks, with his face perfumed with flowing ichor. Then he entered the womb of the queen of king Suddhodana to destroy the evils of the world. The guardians of the world hastened from heaven to watch over the world's one true ruler. . . . [23] Later, one day by the king's permission the queen, having a great longing in her mind, went with the residents of the women's apartments into Lumbini Garden. As the queen supported herself by a bough that hung with a weight of flowers, the Bodhisattva suddenly came forth, splitting open her womb. [25] Then the constellation Pushya was auspicious. From the side of the queen, her son Gotama was born for the welfare of the world. He was born without pain and without illness [for his mother]. . . . [34] He said, "I am born for supreme knowledge, for the welfare of the world. Therefore, this is my last birth. . . . "

[54] The great seer Asita learned of this birth, the birth of him who was to destroy all birth, by signs and through the power of his penances. In his thirst for the excellent Law, he came to the palace of the Sakya king. . . . [59] The sage, being invited by the king, filled with properly intense feeling, uttered his deep and solemn words [to the king] as his large eyes opened wide with wonder: . . . [62] "Hear the reason for my coming and rejoice in it. I have heard a heavenly voice saying that your son has been born for the sake of supreme knowledge. . . . "

[72] Knowing that the king was disturbed by his fear of some impending evil, the sage spoke to him. "Let not your mind, O monarch, be disturbed. All that I have said is certainly true. I have no feeling of fear about his being subject to change, but I am distressed for my own disappointment. It is my time to depart, and this child is now born. He knows the mystery hard to attain, the means of destroying rebirth. When he has forsaken his kingdom, become indifferent to all worldly things, and attained the highest truth by his strenuous efforts, he will shine as a sun of knowledge to destroy the darkness of illusion in the world. . . . "

[83] When he heard these words, the king, his queen, and his friends abandoned sorrow and rejoiced. . . . But he let his heart be influenced by the thought, "He will travel by the noble path." He was not opposed to religion, but he was alarmed at the prospect of losing his child [to a religious life]. . . .

[2.24] When the young prince had passed the period of childhood and reached his youth, he learned in a few days the various sciences suitable to his caste, which generally took many years to master. [25] But remembering what the great seer Asita said about his embrace of transcendental happiness, the anxious care of the king . . . turned the prince to sensual pleasures. He sought for him a bride possessed of beauty, modesty, gentle bearing, and widespread honor. She was from a family of unblemished moral excellence. Yasodhara was her name, a veritable goddess of good fortune. . . .

[28] "He might see some discouraging sight that could disturb his mind." Reflecting this way, the king had a dwelling prepared for his son in the private recesses of the palace. They were furnished with the delights proper for every season, gaily decorated like heavenly chariots upon the earth, and bright like the clouds of autumn. He spent time among the splendid musical concerts of singing women. [30] With the soft tambourines beaten by the tips of the women's hands, and ornamented with golden rims, and with the dances that were like the dances of the heavenly nymphs, that palace shone like Mount Kailasa. The women delighted him with their soft voices,

---

[6]*Bodhisattvas:* individuals who have reached enlightenment but postpone entering Nirvana to help others reach it.

their beautiful pearl-garlands, their playful intoxication, their sweet laughter, and their furtive glances. Carried away in the arms of these women well skilled in the ways of love, and reckless in the pursuit of pleasure, he fell from the roof of a pavilion and yet did not reach the ground. It was like a holy sage had stepped from a heavenly chariot. . . .

[3.1] On a certain day he heard about the forests carpeted with tender grass. They had been all bound up in the cold season, but now their trees resounded with birds and they were adorned with lotus ponds. When he heard of the delightful appearance of these parks beloved by the women, he resolved to go outdoors. He was like an elephant shut up in a house for a long time.

When the king learned the wish expressed by his son, he ordered an excursion to be prepared, one worthy of his own affection and his son's beauty and youth. But he prohibited any encounter with any afflicted common person on the road. He said, "Heaven forbid that the prince with his tender nature should even imagine himself to be distressed." [5] Then he removed from the road with the greatest gentleness all those who had mutilated limbs, the old, the sick, and all squalid beggars. They made the highway assume its perfect beauty. Along this road now made beautiful, the prince and his attendants came down one day at a proper time from the roof of the palace, and went to visit the king to gain his permission to leave. Then the king, with tears rising in his eyes, smelled his son's head and gazed for a long time upon him. He gave him his permission, saying, "Go." But in his heart he did not want him to depart. . . .

[26] But then the gods, dwelling in their pure abodes, saw the city rejoicing like heaven itself. They created an old man to walk along and to stir the heart of the king's son. The prince saw him overcome with weakness and different in form from other men. With his gaze intently fixed on him, he asked his driver, "Who is this man with white hair and his hand resting on a staff, his eyes hidden beneath his brows, his limbs bent down and hanging loose?

Is this a change produced in him, or his natural state, or an accident?"

The charioteer revealed to the king's son the secret that should have been kept so carefully. He thought no harm, for those same gods had bewildered his mind. He said, [30] "Old age has broken him down. It is the ravisher of beauty, the ruin of vigor, the cause of sorrow, the destruction of delights, the affliction of memories, the enemy of the senses. He too once drank milk in his childhood, and in time he learned to crawl on the ground. Step by step he became a vigorous youth, and now step by step he has reached old age."

The startled prince spoke these words to the charioteer: "What! Will this evil come to me also?" To him the charioteer spoke again, "It will certainly come in time even to my long-lived lord. All the world knows that old age will destroy their beauty, and they are content to have it so. . . ."

[40] Then the same deities created another man with his body all afflicted by disease. On seeing him the son of Suddhodana addressed the charioteer, having his gaze fixed on the man. "That man with a swollen belly, his whole frame shaking as he pants, his arms and shoulders hanging loose, his body all pale and thin, saying pathetically the word 'mother' when he embraces a stranger—what is the matter with him?"

Then his charioteer answered, "Gentle Sir, it is a very great affliction called sickness that has grown in him. It has made even this strong man no longer master of himself."

Then the prince again addressed him, looking upon the man compassionately, "Is this evil peculiar to him, or are all people threatened by sickness?" The charioteer answered, "O prince, this evil is common to all. Pressed by diseases, people try to find pleasure, even though they are racked with pain. . . ."

[53] When the royal road was especially adorned and guarded, the king let the prince go out once more. He ordered the charioteer and chariot to proceed in a direction different from the previous one. But as the king's son was going on his way, the very same deities created a dead man. Only the charioteer and the prince saw him

as he was carried dead along the road. [55] Then the prince spoke to the charioteer, "Who is this carried by four men, and followed by mournful companions? He is no longer breathing!"

Then the driver, whose mind was overpowered by the gods who possess pure minds and pure dwellings, and who knew the truth, uttered to his lord this truth that he had been forbidden to tell. "This is some poor man who, deprived of his intellect, senses, vitality, and qualities, lies as if he is asleep or unconscious, like mere wood or straw. He is abandoned by both friends and enemies after they have carefully swathed and guarded him."

Hearing these words of the charioteer, he was startled. He said to him, "Is this an accident particular to him alone, or is this the end of all living creatures?" Then the charioteer replied to him, "This is the final end of all living creatures. No matter if one is a poor man, a man of middle state, or a noble, destruction will come to all in this world."

[60] Then the king's son, calm though he was, immediately sank down overwhelmed. He spoke with a loud voice, "This is the end appointed to all creatures, and yet the world has no fear and is infatuated [with life]! The hearts of men must be hard, to be self-composed in such a situation...."

[5.7] Then he wanted to become perfectly alone in his thoughts, and stopped those friends who were following him. He went to the root of a rose-apple in a solitary spot, with its beautiful leaves all quivering [in the wind]. There he sat on the ground covered with leaves, and with its young grass bright like lapis lazuli. Meditating on the origin and destruction of the world, he laid hold of the path that leads to firmness of mind. [10] Having attained firmness of mind, and being immediately set free from all sorrows such as the desire of worldly objects, he attained the first stage of contemplation.

He considered thoroughly these faults of sickness, old age, and death that belong to all living beings. Then all the joy that he had felt in the activity of his vigor, in his youth, and in his life vanished in a moment. [15] He did not rejoice; he did not feel remorse. He suffered no hesitation, indolence, nor sleep. He felt no attraction to the qualities of desire. He neither hated nor scorned another person. This pure, passionless meditation grew within the great-souled Gotama. Then, unobserved by the other men with him, a man in a beggar's clothing crept up.

The king's son asked him, "Tell me, who are you?" He replied, "O bull of men, I who am terrified at birth and death have become an ascetic for the sake of liberation. Desiring liberation in a world subject to destruction, I seek that happy indestructible abode. I am isolated from mankind. My thoughts are unlike those of others, and my sinful passions are turned away from all objects of sense. Dwelling anywhere, at the root of a tree, or in an uninhabited house, a mountain, or a forest, I wander without a family and without home. I am a beggar ready for any food, and I seek only the highest good."

[20] When he had spoken, while the prince was looking on, he suddenly flew up to the sky. This ascetic was a heavenly inhabitant who, knowing that the prince's thoughts were other than what his outward form promised, had come to him to rouse his recollection. When the other man had gone like a bird to heaven, the foremost of men rejoiced and was astonished. Having comprehended the meaning of the term *dhamma*, he set his mind on how to accomplish his deliverance....

[12.88] Then he fixed his dwelling on the pure bank of the Nairangana. He wanted a lonely habitation. Five beggars who desired liberation came up to him when they saw him there.... [90] He was honored by these disciples who were dwelling in that family.... Thinking, "This may be the means of abolishing birth and death," he at once began a series of difficult austerities by fasting. For six years, vainly trying to attain merit, he practiced self-mortification. He performed many rules of abstinence that are hard for a man to carry out. At the hours of eating, longing to cross the world whose farther shore is so difficult to reach, he broke his vow with single jujube fruits, sesame seeds, and rice. But the emaciation that was produced in his body by that asceticism became positive fatness because of his splendor. [95] With his glory and his beauty unimpaired although he was thin, he caused gladness to other eyes.... He had only skin and bone remaining. His fat, flesh, and blood had faded completely. Yet, though diminished, he still shone with undiminished grandeur like the ocean.

Then the seer, having his body emaciated to no purpose in a cruel self-mortification, and dreading continued existence, reflected in his longing to become a Buddha. "This is not the way to passionlessness, nor to perfect knowledge, nor to liberation. That was certainly the true way that I found at the root of the Gambu tree. But that cannot be attained by one who has lost his strength."

So resuming his care for his body, he next pondered how best to increase his bodily vigor. [100] He said, "Wearied with hunger, thirst, and fatigue, with one's mind no longer self-possessed through fatigue, how can one who is not absolutely calm reach the purpose that is to be attained by the mind? True calm is properly obtained by the constant satisfaction of the senses. The mind's self-possession is only obtained when the senses are perfectly satisfied. True meditation is produced in one whose mind is self-possessed and at rest. In one whose thoughts are engaged in meditation, the exercise of perfect contemplation begins at once. By contemplation are obtained those conditions through which supreme calm is eventually gained. This is the undecaying, immortal state, which is so hard to reach." Having thus resolved, "This is based on eating food," the wise seer of unbounded wisdom decided to accept the continuance of his life....

[14.1] When he attained the highest mastery in all kinds of meditation, he remembered in the first watch the continuous series of all his former births. "In such a place I was so and so by name, and from there I passed and came here." Thus he remembered his thousands of births, experiencing each as it were over again. The compassionate one then felt compassion for all living beings. [5] This world of living beings rolls on helplessly like a wheel, having willfully rejected the good guides in this life and done all kinds of actions in various [previous] lives. As he remembered, in his strong self-control this conviction

came to him, "All existence is unsubstantial, like the fruit of a banana plant."

When the second watch came, he was possessed of unequaled energy. He who was the highest of all seeing beings received a pre-eminent divine sight. By that divine, perfectly pure sight he saw the whole world as in a spotless mirror. He saw the various transmigrations and rebirths of the various beings with their several lower or higher merits from their actions, and compassion grew up more within him....

[35] Having pondered all this, in the last watch he reflected, "Alas for this whole world of living beings who are doomed to misery, all wandering astray! They do not know that all this universe, destitute of any real refuge, is born and decays through that existence which is the site of the skandhas[7] and pain. It dies and passes into a new state and then is born anew...."

[64] The all-knowing Bodhisattva, the illuminated one, pondered and meditated again and came to his conclusion. [65] "This is pain; this also is the origin of pain in the world of living beings; this also is the stopping of pain; this is that course which leads to its stopping."[8] Having determined this, he knew everything as it really was. He, the holy one, sitting there on his seat of grass at the root of the tree, pondered by his own efforts and attained perfect knowledge. Then he bursted the shell of ignorance, and gained all the various kinds of perfect intuition. He attained all the partial knowledge of alternatives that is included in perfect knowledge. He became the perfectly wise, the Bhagavat, the Arhat, the king of the Law, the **Tathagata** [tah-THAH-gah-tuh],[9] the one who has attained the knowledge of all forms, the Lord of all knowledge....

[79] The gods rejoiced, and paid him worship and adoration with divine flowers. All the

---

[7] *skandhas:* the components that constitute the human person, physical and mental.

[8] *This is pain . . . its stopping:* The Buddhist reader would easily recognize here the Four Noble Truths.

[9] *Bhagavat:* the "Blessed One"; *Arhat:* the "Worthy One"; *Tathagata:* "One who has come [or "gone"] thus," a title of Buddha indicating his achievement of Nirvana.

world, when the great saint had become all-wise, was full of brightness. Then the holy one descended and stood on his throne under the tree.[10] There he passed seven days filled with

the thought "I have here attained perfect wisdom." [80] When the Bodhisattva had attained perfect knowledge, all beings became full of great happiness. All the different universes were illumined by a great light. The happy earth shook in six different ways like an overjoyed woman. The Bodhisattvas, each dwelling in his own special abode, assembled and praised him.

---

[10] *the tree:* the bo tree, so called because Gotama achieved enlightenment (*Bodhi*) there.

The Death of Gotama Buddha

In this excerpt from the *Death of the Buddha Sutra,* Buddha makes provision for life in the monastic community after his death. The unity and knowledge of the community are stressed—the Buddha leaves it in an ideal state.[11]

The Blessed One addressed the venerable Ananda and said, "It may be, Ananda, that some of you may think, 'The word of the Master is ended, we have a teacher no more!' Do not think this way. The truths and the rules of the order that I have set forth and laid down for you all, let them be your Teacher when I am gone.

"Ananda! When I am gone, do not address one another in the way in which the brothers have until now addressed each other, with the title of 'Friend.' A younger brother may be addressed by an elder with his name, or his family name, or the title 'Friend.' But an elder should be addressed by a younger brother as 'Lord' or as 'Venerable Sir.' And when I am gone, Ananda, let the order, if it should so wish, abolish all the lesser and minor precepts...."[12]

[10] Then the Blessed One addressed the brothers and said, "Behold now, brothers, I exhort you: Decay is inherent in all component

things! Work out your salvation with diligence!" This was the last word of the Tathagata....

Then the Blessed One, passing out of the state in which both sensations and ideas have ceased to be, entered the state between consciousness and unconsciousness. Passing out of the state between consciousness and unconsciousness, he entered the state of mind to which nothing at all is especially present. Passing out of the consciousness of no special object, he entered the state of mind to which the infinity of thought is the only thing present. Passing out of the mere consciousness of the infinity of thought, he entered the state of mind to which the infinity of space is alone present. Passing out of the mere consciousness of the infinity of space, he entered the fourth stage of deep meditation. Passing out of the fourth stage, he entered the third, and then the second and then the first. Passing out of the first stage of deep meditation, he entered the second. Passing out of the second stage, he entered the third. Passing out of the third stage, he entered the fourth stage of deep meditation. Then he passed out of the last stage of deep meditation, and immediately he died.

When the Blessed One died, at the moment of his passing out of existence, a mighty earthquake

---

[11] Taken, with editing, from T. W. Rhys Davids, trans., *Buddhist Suttas, Sacred Books of the East,* vol. 11 (Oxford: Oxford University Press, 1881), pp. 112–130.

[12] This was not done because the monastic order could not distinguish between major and minor rules.

Mahaparinibbana Sutta 6.1–12, 33–35, 45–48.

arose, terrible and awe-inspiring. The thunders of heaven burst forth....

[33] Then the Mallas of Kusinara said to the venerable Ananda, "What should be done, Lord, with the remains of the Tathagata?"

"As men treat the remains of a king of kings, so should they treat the remains of a Tathagata."

"And how, Lord, do they treat the remains of a king of kings?"

"They wrap the body of a king of kings in a new cloth. When that is done, they wrap it in cotton wool. When that is done, they wrap it in a new cloth, and so on till they have wrapped the body in five hundred successive layers of both kinds. Then they place the body in a vessel of iron, and cover that up with another vessel of iron. They then build a funeral pyre of all kinds of perfumes, and burn the body of the king of kings. Then at the four crossroads they build a burial mound to the king of kings. This is the way in which they treat the remains of a king of kings. As they treat the remains of a king of kings, so should they treat the remains of the Tathagata. At the four crossroads a burial mound should be built to the Tathagata. Whoever shall place garlands or perfumes or paint there, or make salutation there, or become in its presence calm in heart, shall have a profit and a joy for a long time."

Then the Mallas gave orders to their attendants, saying, "Gather all the carded cotton wool of the Mallas!" [35] Then the Mallas of Kusinara wrapped the body of the Blessed One in a new cloth. And when that was done, they wrapped it in cotton wool. And when that was done, they wrapped it in a new cloth, and so on till they had wrapped the body of the Blessed One in five hundred layers of both kinds. Then they placed the body in a vessel of iron, and covered that up with another vessel of iron. Then they built a funeral pyre of all kinds of perfumes, and they placed the body of the Blessed One on it....

[45] Then the venerable Maha Kassapa went...to the funeral pyre of the Blessed One. When he had come up to it, he arranged his robe on one shoulder. Bowing down with clasped hands, he walked three times reverently around the pyre. Then, uncovering his feet, he bowed down in reverence at the feet of the Blessed One. Those five hundred brethren arranged their robes on one shoulder. Bowing down with clasped hands, they walked reverently around the pyre three times, and then bowed down in reverence at the feet of the Blessed One. When the homage of the venerable Maha Kassapa and of those five hundred brothers was ended, the funeral pyre of the Blessed One caught fire by itself. Now as the body of the Blessed One burned itself away, neither soot nor ash was seen from the skin and from the flesh and the nerves and the fluid of the joints. Only the bones remained behind.... Of his five hundred pieces of clothing only the innermost and outermost were consumed.

TEACHING

The Sermon on the Four Noble Truths

This excerpt from the *Turning the Wheel of the Law Sutra* is commonly known as the "Benares Sermon." It is an excellent short statement of the essentials of Buddhist teaching: the Four Noble Truths and the Eightfold Path.[13]

---

[13]Taken, with editing, from Davids, *Buddhist Suttas,* pp. 146–155.

Dhammacakkapparattana Sutta 1–8.

Reverence to the Blessed One, the Holy One, the Fully Enlightened One!

Thus have I heard. The Blessed One was once staying at Benares, at the hermitage called Migadaya. The Blessed One addressed the company of the five monks, and said, "There are two extremes, O monks, which the man who has given up the world ought not to follow. The first is the habitual practice of those things whose attraction depends upon the passions. This is especially true of sensuality. It is a low and pagan way, unworthy, unprofitable, and fit only for the worldly-minded. Second is the habitual practice of asceticism, which is painful, unworthy, and unprofitable.

"There is a middle path, O monks, avoiding these two extremes, discovered by the Tathagata. This path opens the eyes, bestows understanding, leads to peace of mind, to the higher wisdom, to full enlightenment, and to Nirvana! What is that middle path, O monks, avoiding these two extremes? Truly, it is this Noble Eightfold Path, that is to say: Right views; Right aspirations; Right speech; Right conduct; Right livelihood; Right effort; Right mindfulness; and Right contemplation. . . .

[5] "Now this, O monks, is the noble truth concerning suffering. Birth brings pain, decay is painful, disease is painful, and death is painful. Union with something unpleasant is painful, and separation from something pleasant is painful. Any craving that is unsatisfied is painful. In brief, the five aggregates that spring from attachment, the conditions of individuality and their cause, are painful. This, O monks, is the noble truth concerning suffering.

"Now this, O monks, is the noble truth concerning the origin of suffering. Truly, it is thirst or craving. It causes the renewal of existence, and is accompanied by sensual delight, seeking satisfaction now here, now there. It is the craving for the gratification of the passions, or the craving for a future life, or the craving for success in this present life. This, O monks, is the noble truth concerning the origin of suffering.

"Now this, O monks, is the noble truth concerning the destruction of suffering. Truly, it is the destruction of this very thirst. It is the laying aside of, the getting rid of, the being free from, the harboring no longer of this thirst. This, O monks, is the noble truth concerning the destruction of suffering.

"Now this, O monks, is the noble truth concerning the way which leads to the destruction of sorrow. Truly, it is this Noble Eightfold Path. . . .

[21] "As long, O monks, as my knowledge and insight were not quite clear regarding each of these Four Noble Truths in this triple order, in this twelvefold manner, I was uncertain whether I had attained to the full insight of that wisdom that is unsurpassed in the heavens or on earth, among the whole race of Samanas and Brahmins, or of gods or men. But as soon as my knowledge and insight were quite clear regarding each of these four noble truths, in this triple order, in this twelvefold manner, then I became certain that I had attained to the full insight of that wisdom that is unsurpassed in the heavens or on earth, among the whole race of Samanas and Brahmins, or of gods or men. Now this knowledge and this insight have arisen within me. The emancipation of my heart is immovable. This is my last existence. Now there will be no rebirth for me!" . . .

[25] And when the royal chariot wheel of the truth had been set rolling by the Blessed One, the gods of the earth . . . the attendant gods of the four great kings . . . and the gods in the highest heaven gave forth a shout. They said, "In Benares, at the hermitage of the Migadaya, the supreme wheel of the empire of Truth has been set rolling by the Blessed One. That wheel can never be turned back by any Samana or Brahmin, or by any god, or by any Brahma or Mara, not by anyone in the universe!" In an instant, a second, a moment, this sound went up to the world of Brahma. This great ten-thousand-world-system quaked and trembled and was shaken violently. An immeasurably bright light appeared in the universe, beyond even the power of the gods!

The Noble Eightfold Path

The "Benares Sermon" also contains a full explanation of the Noble Eightfold Path, a practical system that follows up on the more abstract Four Noble Truths. The Noble Eightfold Path offers practical guidelines to mental and moral development with the goal of freeing individuals from attachments and delusions; it leads to understanding the truth about all things. By following the eight guidelines, the monk follows the path of the Buddha to release. The eight guidelines are often reduced to three categories: morality, wisdom, and meditation.[14]

The Blessed One then addressed the monks, saying, "Monks."

"Yes, lord," the monks responded.

The Blessed One said, "I will teach and interpret for you the Noble Eightfold Path. Listen and pay attention as I speak."

"We will do as you say, lord," the monks replied.

The Blessed One said, "What, monks, is the Noble Eightfold Path? Right view, right resolve, right speech, right action, right livelihood, right effort, right mindfulness, and right concentration.[15]

"What is right view? It is knowledge with regard to suffering, knowledge with regard to the origination of suffering, knowledge with regard to the stopping of suffering, knowledge with regard to the way of practice leading to the stopping of suffering.[16]

"What is right resolve? It is being resolved to practice renunciation, to be free from ill will, to be harmless.

"What is right speech? It is refraining from lying, refraining from divisive speech, refraining from abusive speech, and refraining from idle talk.

"What is right action? It is not taking life, not stealing, and being chaste.

"What is right livelihood? This is when a disciple of the noble ones, having abandoned a dishonest livelihood, sustains his life with right livelihood.

"What is right effort? This is when a monk desires, endeavors, persists, upholds, and exerts his intent so that evil, unhelpful qualities do not arise [in him]. He abandons unhelpful qualities that have arisen.... [He] brings about helpful qualities that have not yet arisen.... [He brings about] helpful qualities that have arisen.

"What is right mindfulness? This is when a monk remains focused on the body in and of itself—he is fervent, aware, and mindful—putting away the greed and distress of the world. He remains focused on feelings in and of themselves—he is fervent, aware, and mindful—putting away the greed and distress of the world. He remains focused on the mind in and of itself—he is fervent, aware, and mindful—putting away the greed and distress of the world. He remains focused on mental qualities in and of themselves—he is fervent, aware, and mindful—putting away the greed and distress of the world.

"What is right concentration? This is when a monk—quite withdrawn from sensuality, withdrawn from unskillful (mental) qualities—enters and remains in the first stage of concentration: rapture and pleasure born from withdrawal, accompanied by directed thought and evaluation. With the stilling of his directed thought and evaluation, he enters and remains in the second stage of concentration: rapture and pleasure born of concentration, unification of awareness free from directed thought and evaluation. This

---

[14]Taken, with editing, from Davids, *Buddhist Suttas,* pp. 149–152.
[15]*concentration:* can also be translated throughout this section as "meditation."
[16]*It is knowledge . . . stopping of suffering:* This sentence is a restatement of the Four Noble Truths.

Dhammacakkapparattana Sutta 9–20.

brings internal assurance. With the fading of rapture, he remains calm, mindful and alert, and physically sensitive of pleasure. He enters and remains in the third stage of concentration: calm and mindful, he has a pleasurable abiding. With the abandoning of pleasure and pain, as with the earlier disappearance of rapture and distress, he enters and remains in the fourth stage of concentration: pure calmness and mindfulness, having neither pleasure nor pain.

This is what the Blessed One said. The monks were delighted at his words.

The Skandhas and the Chain of Causation

The skandhas are the elements that together make up the human personality. They relate to the no-soul doctrine of Theravada Buddhism. This passage outlines these skandhas and then traces the chain of causation that leads to suffering.[17]

The omniscient lion of the Sakyas [i.e., Buddha] then caused all the assembly, headed by those who belonged to the company of Maitriya, to turn the wheel of the Law.[18] ...[28] "The body is composed of the five skandhas, and produced from the five elements. It is empty and without soul, and arises from the action of the chain of causation. This chain of causation is the cause of coming into existence, and the cessation of this chain is the cause of the state of cessation. . . .

[35] The idea of ignorance is what gives the root to the huge poison-tree of mundane existence with its trunk of pain. This causes the impressions, which produce [the acts of] the body, voice, and mind. Consciousness arises from these impressions, which produces the five senses and the mind. The organism that is sometimes called samgna or samdarsana springs from this; and from this arises the six organs of the senses, including the mind.

"The association of the six organs with their objects is called 'contact.' The consciousness of these different contacts is called 'sensation.' [40] Craving is produced by this, which is the desire of being troubled by worldly objects. Attachment to continued existence, arising from this, sets itself in action toward pleasure and the rest. From attachment springs continued existence. From existence arises birth through a returning to various wombs. On birth is dependent the series of old age, death, sorrow, and the like. By putting a stop to ignorance and what follows from it, all these cease successively. This is the chain of causation, which has many turns, whose sphere of action is created by ignorance. This is to be meditated upon by you who enjoy dwelling tranquilly in lonely woods. He who knows it thoroughly reaches at last to absolute thinness. Then he becomes blissfully extinct.

"When you have learned this, to be freed from the bond of existence you must cut down ignorance with all your efforts, for it is the root of pain. [45] Then, set free from the bonds of the prison-house of existence, you will possess as Arhats natures perfectly pure. You shall attain Nirvana."

Having heard this lesson preached by the chief of saints, all the mendicants understood the course and the cessation of embodied existence. As these five ascetics listened to his words, their intellectual eye was purified for the attainment of perfect wisdom. The eye of dharma was purified in six hundred millions

[17]Taken, with editing, from Cowell, *Buddhist Mahayana Texts,* pp. 174–180.
[18]*turn the wheel of the Law:* give and spread the true teaching.

Buddhacarita 16.1, 28–50.

of gods, and the eye of wisdom in eight hundred millions of Brahmans. The eye of dharma was purified in eighty thousand men, and even in all beings an ardor for the Law was made visible. [50] Everywhere all kinds of evil became tranquillized, and everywhere an ardor for all that helps the good Law manifested itself.

The Essence of Buddhism

This scripture—its full title is *Heart of Transcendent Wisdom*—is one of the best known in Buddhism. It personifies wisdom as a woman, especially at its beginning and end. In a religion often given to verbose writings, this sutra is remarkable for its brevity.[19]

Honor to the Omniscient. [or Honor to the Lady, Noble Transcendent Wisdom.]

The noble bodhisattva Avalokitesvara was brooding in the flowing depths of the course of Transcendent Wisdom. Looking about, he sees the five skandhas to be empty of essence.

Here, Sariputra, form is emptiness, emptiness is form. Form is not other than emptiness, and emptiness is not other than form. That which is form equals emptiness, and that which is emptiness is also form. Precisely the same may be said of form and the other skandhas: feeling, perception, impulse, and consciousness.

Here, Sariputra, all dharmas bear the marks of emptiness, which are: not to have arisen nor to have been suppressed, neither to be corrupt nor pure, and to be neither unfinished nor complete.

Therefore, Sariputra, emptiness is not form, nor feeling, perception, impulse, nor consciousness. It is not the eye, ear, nose, tongue, body, or mind. It is not shape, sound, odor, flavor, nor object of touch or thought. It is not the experience of vision (and so on until we reach) it is not elements of mental discrimination. It is not learning or ignorance, and it is not the elimination of learning or ignorance (and so on until we reach) it is not senility and death, and it is not the elimination of senility and death. It is not suffering, beginning, ceasing, or a path. It is not knowledge, not attainment or realization, and therefore neither is it nonattainment.

[5] The bodhisattva, bound to Transcendent Wisdom, lives with nothing clouding his mind. Lacking confusion, he is intrepid, and having passed beyond error, reaches Nirvana.

All Buddhas, of the past, present, or future, bound to irrefutable Transcendent Wisdom, reach completely full understanding and the highest awakening.

Therefore Transcendent Wisdom should be known as the great mantra, the great knowledge mantra, the invincible mantra, the unsurpassable mantra, causing all suffering to cease. It is trustworthy because it is not false. It is the mantra proclaimed in the *Prajnaparamita,* and it is this: Oh, you [Lady] who are gone, gone, gone beyond, gone utterly beyond: Hail Wisdom!

With these words the Heart of Transcendent Wisdom is complete.

---

[19]From Douglas A. Fox, trans., *The Heart of Buddhist Wisdom* (Lewiston, NY: Mellen, 1986). Copyright © 1985 Douglas A. Fox. Used by permission.

The Heart Sutra.

A Mahayana View of the Buddha

In Mahayana, the Buddha is a gracious savior who enables both monks and laity to reach Nirvana. This first selection from the *Lotus Sutra of the True Law* argues that the Mahayana ("Large Vehicle") is in fact the only vehicle in Buddhism. In the second, the *Lotus Sutra* itself is the gift of the Buddha that enables those who read and venerate it to come to Nirvana. This veneration is today especially prominent in Nichiren Buddhism.[20]

By means of one sole vehicle, namely, the Buddha-vehicle, I teach creatures the law. There is no second vehicle, nor a third. This is the nature of the law, Sariputra, universally in the world, in all directions. For all the Tathagatas, who in times past existed in countless, innumerable spheres in all directions for the welfare of many, the happiness of many, out of pity to the world, for the benefit, welfare, and happiness of the great body of creatures, preached the law to gods and men with able means. These means include several directions and indications, various arguments, reasons, illustrations, fundamental ideas, interpretations. They pay regard to the dispositions of creatures whose inclinations and temperaments are so varied.

All those Buddhas and Lords have preached the law to creatures by means of only one vehicle, the Buddha-vehicle, which finally leads to omniscience. It is identical with showing all creatures the sight of Tathagata-knowledge; with opening the eyes of creatures for the sight of Tathagata-knowledge; with the awakening (or admonishing) by the display (or sight) of Tathagata-knowledge; with leading the teaching of Tathagata-knowledge on the right path. Such is the law they have preached to creatures. And those creatures who have heard the law from the past Tathagatas have all reached supreme, perfect enlightenment. The Tathagatas who shall exist in the future, Sariputra, in countless, innumerable spheres in all directions for the weal of many, the happiness of many, out of pity to the world, for the benefit, weal, and happiness of the great body of creatures, shall preach the law to gods and men.... Such is the law they shall preach to creatures. Those creatures, Sariputra, who shall hear the law from the future Tathagatas shall all reach supreme, perfect enlightenment....

I myself also, Sariputra, am at the present period a Tathagata, for the welfare of many.... I myself, also, Sariputra, am preaching the law to creatures.... Such is the law I preach to creatures. Those creatures, Sariputra, who now are hearing the law from me shall all reach supreme, perfect enlightenment. In this sense, Sariputra, it must be understood that nowhere in the world a second vehicle is taught, far less a third....

The Lord proceeded: "All those Bodhisattvas Mahasattvas who in this assembly have heard well only a single stanza, a single verse [or word], or who even by a single rising thought have joyfully accepted this Sutra, to all of them, Bhaishajyaraga, among the four classes of my audience I predict their destiny to supreme and perfect enlightenment. Whoever after the complete extinction of the Tathagata shall hear this Dharmaparyaya and after hearing, if only a single stanza, joyfully accept it, even with a single rising thought, to those also, Bhaishajyaraga, be they young men or young women of good family,[21]

---

[20]Taken, with editing, from H. Kern, trans., *The Saddharma-Pundarika, Sacred Books of the East*, vol. 21 (Oxford: Oxford University Press, 1884), pp. 39–49, 213–214.

[21]*Young men or young women of good family:* layfolk can also reach Nirvana.

Saddharma-Pundarika Sutra 2.36; 10.1.

I predict their destiny to supreme and perfect enlightenment....

They shall be reborn who shall take, read, make known, recite, copy, and after copying always keep in memory and from time to time regard only a single stanza of this teaching. They shall be reborn who by that book shall feel veneration for the Tathagatas, treat them with the respect due to Masters, honor, revere, worship them. They shall be reborn who shall worship that book with flowers, incense, perfumed garlands, ointment, powder, clothes, umbrellas, flags, banners, music, etc., and with acts of reverence such as bowing and joining hands. In short, Bhaishajyaraga, any young men or young women of good family who shall keep or joyfully accept only a single stanza of this teaching, to all of them I predict their destiny of supreme and perfect enlightenment."

The Blessings of the Pure Land

The "Pure Land" tradition of Buddhism teaches that a Buddha named Amitabha ("Unlimited Light") created and now rules over a "Buddha-land" called the Pure Land, a paradise so wonderful that beings born into it will quickly proceed toward full awakening. This passage calls that place the Joyous Land. The Pure Land sect of Mahayana Buddhism has as its main belief salvation by faith in Amidabha; it is a popular form of Buddhism in China and Japan. Most Pure Land groups teach that good Buddhist character and constant repetition of the saying "Praise to Amida Buddha" are necessary to enter the Pure Land after death. Shrinan and other groups teach that all that is necessary is one moment of pure belief and one pure recitation of the saying.[22]

Thus have I heard: Once the Buddha was dwelling in the Anathapindada Garden of Jetavana in the country of Shravasti. He was with a large company of monks, twelve hundred and fifty members. They were all great Arhats, well known among the people....He was also with...all great Bodhisattvas. He was also with a large company of innumerable deities such as Shakrodevanam-Indra and the rest.

Then the Buddha addressed Shariputra and said, "Beyond a hundred thousand Buddha-lands westward from here, there is a world named Joyous Land. In that world there is a Buddha, Amida by name, now dwelling and preaching the law. Shariputra, why is that country named the Joyous Land? The living beings in that country have no pains, but receive pleasures only. Therefore, it is called the Joyous Land.

"Again, Shariputra, in the Joyous Land there are seven rows of balustrades, seven rows of fine nets, and seven rows of arrayed trees; they are all of four gems and surround and enclose the land. For this reason the land is called the Joyous Land.

"Again, Shariputra, in the Joyous Land there are lakes of the seven gems, in which is filled water with the eight meritorious qualities. The lake-bases are strewn with golden sand, and the stairs of the four sides are made of gold, silver, beryl, and crystal. On land there are stories and galleries adorned with gold, silver, beryl, crystal, white coral, red pearl and diamond. The lotus-flowers in the lakes, large as chariot wheels, are blue-colored with blue

---

[22]Taken, with editing, from Nishu Utsuki, *Kumarajiva* (Kyoto, Japan: Publication Bureau of Buddhist Books, 1924), pp. 2–5.

Array of the Joyous Land Sutra.

splendor, yellow-colored with yellow splendor, red-colored with red splendor, white-colored with white splendor, and they are all most exquisite and purely fragrant.

[5] "Again, Shariputra, in that Buddha-land there are heavenly musical instruments always played on. Gold is spread on the ground, and six times every day and night it showers blossoms of the Mandarava flower.[23] Usually at dawn all of those who live in that land fill their plates with those wonderful blossoms, and go to make offering to a hundred thousand Buddhas of other regions. At the time of the meal they come back to their own country, eat their meal, and take a walk. Shariputra, the Joyous Land is arrayed with these good qualities and adornments.

"And again, Shariputra, in that country there are always various wonderful birds of different colors: swan, peacock, parrot...and the bird with two heads. Six times every day and night all those birds sing in melodious tune, and that tune proclaims the Five Virtues, the Five Powers...the Noble Eightfold Path, and other laws of the kind. The living beings in that land, having heard that singing, all invoke the Buddha, invoke the Dharma, and invoke the Sangha.[24]...

"Shariputra, what do you think: Why is that Buddha is called Amida? Shariputra, the light of that Buddha is boundless; he shines without impediments all over the countries of the ten quarters. Therefore he is called Amida. Again, Shariputra, the life of that Buddha and of his people is endless and boundless in Asamkhyakalpas, so he is named Amida. Shariputra, since Buddha Amida attained Buddhahood, ten kalpas[25] have now passed....

"Shariputra, if there be a good man or a good woman, who, on hearing of Buddha Amida, keeps his name in mind with thoughts undisturbed for one day, two days, three days, four days, five days, six days, or seven days, that person, when about to die, will see Amida Buddha accompanied by his holy host appear before him; and immediately after his death, he with his mind undisturbed can be born into the Joyous Land of Buddha Amida. Shariputra, as I witness this benefit, I say these words; every being who listens to this preaching ought to offer up prayer with the desire to be born into that country.

[10] "Shariputra, as I now glorify the inconceivable excellences of Amida Buddha, there are also Buddhas [in the Northern, Western, Eastern, and Southern worlds of the earth, and lower and upper worlds of the cosmos] as many as the sands of the Ganges River, each of whom, in his own country stretching out his long broad tongue that covers three thousand greater worlds completely, proclaims these truthful words: 'All you sentient beings should believe in this sutra, which is approved and protected by all the Buddhas, and which glorifies the inconceivable excellences of Buddha Amida.'...

"Shariputra, what do you think: Why it is called the Sutra approved and protected by all the Buddhas? Shariputra, if there be a good man or a good woman who listens to those Buddhas' invocation of the name of Buddha Amida and the name of this Sutra, that good man or woman will be protected by all the Buddhas and never fail to attain supreme perfect enlightenment. For this reason, Shariputra, all of you should believe in my words and in what all the Buddhas proclaim. Shariputra, if there are men who have already made, are now making, or shall make prayer with the desire to be born in the land of Buddha Amida, they never fail to attain supreme perfect enlightenment; they have been born, are now being born, or shall be born in that country. Therefore, Shariputra, a good man or good woman who has the faith ought to offer up prayers to be born in that land.

---

[23] *Mandarava flower:* According to Buddhist legend, the mandarava flower exists only in heaven and blossoms only when portentous things are happening in the world. Thus, to have constant showers of these blossoms is extraordinary indeed.

[24] *Buddha...Dharma...Sangha:* the "Three Refuges" of Buddhism. Invoking them involves saying "I take refuge in the Buddha, the Dharma [teaching, religion], and the Sangha [monastic community]."

[25] *kalpas:* A kalpa is a period of 430 million years. It is the traditional period of time that one universe exists before it ends and another is re-created.

ETHICS

Conduct of the Monk

The *Dhammapada* (Verses on Teaching) is one of the fifteen books in the *Khuddaka-nikaya* of the *Sutta Pitaka*. A first-century B.C.E. collection of wise sayings, it summarizes Buddhist moral wisdom. Monks and nuns often memorize it at the beginning of their training, and it is studied as well by the laity.[26]

Restraint in the eye is good, restraint in the ear is good, restraint in the nose is good, restraint in the tongue is good. In the body restraint is good, in speech restraint is good, in thought restraint is good. Restraint is good in all things. A monk restrained in all things is freed from all pain.

People call a monk one who controls his hand, who controls his feet, who controls his speech, who is well controlled, who delights inwardly, who is collected, who is solitary and content. The monk who controls his mouth, who speaks wisely and calmly, who teaches the meaning and the law, his word is sweet.

He who dwells in the law, delights in the law, meditates on the law, follows the law, that monk will never fall away from the true law.

[365] Let him not despise what he has received, nor ever envy others; a mendicant who envies others does not obtain peace of mind. Even the gods will praise a monk who, though he receives little, does not despise what he has received, if his life is pure and if he is not lazy.

He who never identifies himself with his name and form, and does not grieve over what he has left behind, he indeed is called a monk.

The monk who acts with kindness, who is calm in the doctrine of Buddha, will reach the quiet place [Nirvana], cessation of natural desires, and happiness. O monk, empty this boat! If

emptied, it will go quickly. When you have cut off passion and hatred, you will go to Nirvana.

[370] Cut off the five senses, leave the five, rise above the five. A monk who has escaped from the five fetters is called Oghatinna, "saved from the flood."

Meditate, O monk, and do be not careless! Do not direct your thought to what gives pleasure. Then you may not have to swallow the iron ball (in hell) and cry out when burning, "This is pain." Without knowledge there is no meditation, without meditation there is no knowledge. He who has knowledge and meditation is near to Nirvana.

A monk who has entered his empty house, whose mind is tranquil, feels a super-human delight when he sees the law clearly. When he has considered the origin and destruction of the elements (skandhas) of the body, he finds happiness and joy that belong to those who know the immortal (Nirvana).

[375] This is the beginning here for a wise monk: watchfulness over the senses, contentedness, restraint under the law; keeping noble friends whose life is pure and who are not lazy. Let him live in charity, let him be perfect in his duties. Then in the fullness of delight he will put an end to his suffering.

As the Vassika plant sheds its withered flowers, men should shed passion and hatred, O monks! The monk whose body and tongue and mind are quieted, who is collected, and has rejected the baits of the world, he is called quiet.

---

[26]Taken, with editing, from F. Max Müller, *The Dhammapada, Sacred Books of the East*, vol. 10 (Oxford: Oxford University Press, 1881), pp. 85–88.

Dhammapada 25, 360–382.

Rouse yourself by yourself, examine yourself by yourself, thus self-protected and attentive you will live happily, O monk! [380] The self is the lord of self, self is the refuge of self. Therefore curb yourself as the merchant curbs a good horse.

The monk full of delight, who is calm in the doctrine of Buddha, will reach the quiet place (Nirvana), cessation of natural desires, and happiness. Even a young monk who applies himself to the doctrine of Buddha will brighten up this world like the moon on a cloudless night.

Admonition to Laity

At the end of a discussion of monastic morality, the Buddha lays down instructions for householders (laity). Notice that the rules given are modeled on those given to monks.

I will also tell you about the householder's work. . . .

Let him neither kill nor cause to be killed any living being. Let him not approve of others killing. Let him refrain from hurting all creatures, both those that are strong and those that tremble.

[20] Then let [him] abstain from taking anything in any place that has not been given to him, knowing it to belong to another. Let him not cause anyone to take, nor approve of those that take. Let him avoid all theft.

Let the wise man avoid an unchaste life as a burning heap of coals. If he is not able to live a life of chastity, let him not transgress with another man's wife.

Let no one speak falsely to another in the hall of justice or in the hall of the assembly. Let him not cause anyone to speak falsely, nor approve of those that speak falsely. Let him avoid all sort of untruth.

Let the householder who approves of the Dhamma not give himself to intoxicating drinks. Let him not cause others to drink, nor approve of those who drink, knowing it to end in madness. For through intoxication stupid people commit sins and make other people intoxicated. Let him avoid this seat of sin, this madness, this folly, which is delightful to the stupid.

[25] Let him not kill any living being, let him not take what has not been given [to him], let him not speak falsely, and let him not drink intoxicating drinks, let him refrain from unchaste sexual intercourse, and let him not eat untimely food at night. Let him neither wear wreaths nor use perfumes; let him lie on a couch spread on the earth. They call this the eightfold abstinence (*uposatha*), proclaimed by Buddha, who has overcome pain.

Cullavagga, Dammikasutta 18–27.

The Wisdom of the Buddha

This passage, often called "Twin Verses," is a general treatment of Buddhist morality. Each paragraph has two verses, usually opposites. A second section, from the chapter "On the Self," urges the virtue of self-reliance and self-dedication in the path to enlightenment.[27]

---

[27]Taken, with editing, from Müller, *The Dhammapada*, pp. 1–8, 45–46.

Dhammapada 1–20.

All that we are is the result of what we have thought: It is founded on our thoughts; it is made up of our thoughts. If a man speaks or acts with an evil thought, pain follows him, as the wheel follows the foot of the ox that draws the carriage. All that we are is the result of what we have thought. It is founded on our thoughts; it is made up of our thoughts. If a man speaks or acts with a pure thought, happiness follows him like a shadow that never leaves him.

"He abused me, he beat me, he defeated me, he robbed me"—in those who harbor such thoughts hatred will never cease. "He abused me, he beat me, he defeated me, he robbed me"—in those who do not harbor such thoughts hatred will cease. [5] For hatred never ends by more hatred. Hatred ends by love; this is an old rule. The world does not know that we must all come to an end here. But for those who know it, their quarrels cease at once.

He who lives looking for pleasures only, his senses uncontrolled, immoderate in his food, idle, and weak, Mara [the tempter] will certainly overthrow him as the wind throws down a weak tree. He who lives without looking for pleasures, his senses well controlled, moderate in his food, faithful and strong, him Mara will certainly not overthrow, any more than the wind throws down a rocky mountain.

He who wishes to put on the yellow clothing[28] without having cleansed himself from sin, who disregards also temperance and truth, is unworthy of the yellow clothing. [10] But he who has cleansed himself from sin is well grounded in all virtues; he also keeps temperance and truth, and he is worthy of the yellow clothing.

They who imagine truth in untruth, and see untruth in truth, never arrive at truth, but follow empty desires. They who know truth in truth, and untruth in untruth, arrive at truth, and follow true desires. As rain breaks through a poorly thatched house, passion will break through an unreflecting mind. As rain does not break through a well-thatched house, passion will not break through a well-reflecting mind.

[15] The evildoer mourns in this world, and he mourns in the next; he mourns in both. He mourns and suffers when he sees the evil of his own work. The virtuous man delights in this world, and he delights in the next; he delights in both. He delights and rejoices when he sees the purity of his own work.

The evildoer suffers in this world, and he suffers in the next; he suffers in both. He suffers when he thinks of the evil he has done. He suffers more when going on the evil path. The virtuous man is happy in this world, and he is happy in the next; he is happy in both. He is happy when he thinks of the good he has done. He is still more happy when going on the good path.

The thoughtless man, even if he can recite a large portion [of the law], but is not a doer of it, has no share in the priesthood. He is like a cowherd counting the cows of others. [20] The follower of the law, even if he can recite only a small portion [of the law], but, having forsaken passion and hatred and foolishness, possesses true knowledge and serenity of mind, he, caring for nothing in this world or that to come, has a share in the order of monks.

---

[28]*the yellow clothing:* the saffron gown of the monk.

ORGANIZATION

Founding of the Monastic Order

After his enlightenment, the Buddha converts the five Hindu ascetics who had left him when he gave up their practice of extreme asceticism. This *Vinaya Pitaka* selection offers a succinct view of general Buddhist teaching. Just as important, it offers a good view of the founding of the Buddhist order of monks and therefore of the Buddhist tradition itself.[29]

The Blessed One, wandering from place to place, came to Benares, to the deer park Isipatana, to the place where the five monks were. The five monks saw the Blessed One coming from a distance. When they saw him, they agreed with each other, saying, "Friends, there comes Gotama. He lives in abundance, has given up his exertions, and has turned to an abundant life. Let us not salute him, nor rise from our seats when he approaches, nor take his bowl and his robe from his hands. But let us put there a seat; if he likes, let him sit down...."

When they spoke to him, the Blessed One said to the five monks, "Monks, do not address the Tathagata by his name or with 'Friend.' The Tathagata is the holy, absolute Sambuddha.[30] Give ear, O monks! Immortality has been won by me. I will teach you; I will preach the doctrine to you. If you walk in the way I show you, you will, before long, have penetrated to the truth. You yourselves will know it and see it face to face. You will live with the highest goal of the holy life, for which noble youths give up the world completely and go forth into the houseless state."

When he had spoken, the five monks said to the Blessed One, "Friend Gotama, by those

observances, by those practices, and by those austerities you have not been able to obtain power surpassing that of other men. You have not obtained the superiority of full and holy knowledge and insight. Now that you are living in abundance, have given up your exertions, and have turned to an abundant life, how will you be able to obtain power surpassing that of men? How will you obtain the superiority of full and holy knowledge and insight?...."

[15] The five monks spoke to the Blessed One a second time as before. And the Blessed One replied to the five monks a second time as before. And the five monks spoke to the Blessed One a third time as before. When they had spoken thus, the Blessed One said to the five monks, "Do you admit, O monks, that I have never spoken to you in this way before this day?"

"You have never spoken so, Lord."

"The Tathagata, O monks, is the holy, absolute Sambuddha. Give ear, O monks...."

The Blessed One was able to convince the five monks. The five monks listened willingly to the Blessed One. They gave ear, and fixed their mind on the knowledge which Buddha imparted to them.... [There follows a statement of the Four Noble Truths and the Eightfold Path.]

[27] "O monks, as long as I did not possess with perfect purity this true knowledge and insight into these four Noble Truths...I knew that I had not yet obtained the highest, absolute Sambodhi in the world of men and gods, in Mara's and Brahma's world, among all beings,

---

[29]Taken, with editing, from T. W. Rhys Davids and Hermann Oldenberg, trans., *Vinaya Texts*, part 1, *Sacred Books of the East*, vol. 13 (Oxford: Oxford University Press, 1881), pp. 91–102.
[30]*Sambuddha:* one who has reached the insight essential to the higher stages of arhatship.

Mahavagga 1.6.10, 11–16, 27–30, 32, 34, 37.

Samanas and Brahmanas, gods and men. But when I possessed with perfect purity this true knowledge and insight into these four Noble Truths...then I knew that I had obtained the highest, universal Sambodhi in the world of men and gods.... This knowledge and insight arose in my mind; this emancipation of my mind cannot be lost. This is my last birth; I shall not be born again!"

Thus the Blessed One spoke. The five monks were delighted, and they rejoiced at the words of the Blessed One. When this exposition was given, the venerable Kondanna obtained the pure and spotless Eye of this truth: "Whatever is subject to the condition of origination, is subject also to the condition of cessation."

[30] And when the Blessed One had founded the Kingdom of Truth by propounding the Four Noble Truths, the earth-inhabiting gods shouted, "Truly the Blessed One has founded at Benares, in the deer park Isipatana, the highest kingdom of Truth, which may be opposed neither by a Samana nor by a Brahmana, neither by a deva, nor by Mara, nor by Brahma, nor by any being in the world."...

[32] The venerable Kondanna...overcame uncertainty, dispelled all doubts, and gained full knowledge. He was dependent on nobody else for knowledge of the doctrine of the teacher. He said to the Blessed One, "Lord, let me receive the pabbajja and upasampada ordinations from the Blessed One."

"Come, monk," said the Blessed One, "for the doctrine is well taught. Lead a holy life for the sake of the complete extinction of suffering." Then this venerable person received the ordination....

[34] Then [the other monks] spoke to the Blessed One: "Lord, let us receive the pabbajja and upasampada ordinations from the Blessed One."

"Come, monks," said the Blessed One, "for the doctrine is well taught. Lead a holy life for the sake of the complete extinction of suffering." Thus these venerable persons received ordination....

[37] Thus the Blessed One spoke. The five monks were delighted, and rejoiced at the words of the Blessed One. When this exposition had been given, the minds of the five monks became free from attachment to the world, and were released from the Asavas.[31] Then there were six arhants in the world.

---

[31]*Asavas:* mental defilement; the four Asavas are sensuality, lust for life, false views, and ignorance.

Founding of the Order of Nuns

This selection narrates the story about how women were admitted into the monastic order as nuns. The Buddha was at first very reluctant to admit them, but he relented, giving special rules for an order of nuns. Nuns have historically played a much smaller role in Buddhism than the order of monks. Nuns and other Buddhist women struggling for a greater degree of liberation still must contend with patriarchal interpretations of this passage.[32]

Now at that time the Blessed Buddha was staying among the Sakyas in Kapilavatthu, in the Nigrodharama. And Maha-pajapati the Gotami[33] went to the place where the Blessed One was. When she arrived there, she bowed

[32]Taken, with editing, from T. W. Rhys Davids and Hermann Oldenberg, trans., *Vinaya Texts,* part 3, *Sacred Books of the East,* vol. 20 (Oxford: Oxford University Press, 1885), pp. 320–326.

[33]*the Gotami:* a relative of Gotama and his nurse when he was an infant.

Cullavagga 10.1.1–6.

down before the Blessed One, and remained standing to one side. She said to the Blessed One, "It would be well, Lord, if women should be allowed to renounce their homes and enter the homeless state under the doctrine and discipline proclaimed by the Tathagata."

The Buddha replied, "Enough, O Gotami! Let it not please you that women should be allowed to do so." A second and a third time Maha-pajapati made the same request in the same words, and received the same reply. Then Maha-pajapati, sad and sorrowful that the Blessed One would not allow women to enter the homeless state, bowed down before the Blessed One. Keeping him on her right hand as she passed him, she departed weeping and in tears. . . . She cut off her hair and put on orange-colored robes. . . . Sad and sorrowful, weeping and in tears, she took her stand outside under the entrance porch.

The venerable Ananda saw her standing there, and on seeing her so, he said to her, "Why do you stand there outside the porch . . . weeping and in tears?"

"Because, Ananda, the Lord and Blessed One does not allow women to renounce their homes and enter the homeless state under the doctrine and discipline proclaimed by the Tathagata."

Then the venerable Ananda went up to the place where the Blessed One was. Bowing down before the Blessed One, he took his seat on one side. And, so sitting, the venerable Ananda said to the Blessed One: "Lord, Maha-pajapati is standing outside under the entrance porch. She is sad and sorrowful, weeping and in tears, because the Blessed One does not allow women to renounce their homes and enter the homeless state under the doctrine and discipline proclaimed by the Blessed One. It would be well, Lord, if women were to have permission granted to them to do as she desires."

The Buddha replied, "Enough, Ananda! Let it not please you that women should be allowed to do so." A second and a third time Ananda made the same request, in the same words, and received the same reply.

Then the venerable Ananda thought, "The Blessed One does not give his permission. I will now ask the Blessed One in another way." And the venerable Ananda said to the Blessed One, "Lord, can women—when they have gone forth from the household life and entered the homeless state, under the doctrine and discipline proclaimed by the Blessed One— can they gain the fruit of conversion, or of the second Path, or of the third Path, or of Arhatship?"

"They are capable (of all these), Ananda."

"Lord, Maha-pajapati has proved herself of great service to the Blessed One, when as aunt and nurse she nourished him and gave him milk, and on the death of his mother she nursed the Blessed One at her own breast. It would be well, Lord, that women should have permission to go forth from the household life and enter the homeless state, under the doctrine and discipline proclaimed by the Tathagata."

"Ananda, if Maha-pajapati takes upon herself these Eight Chief Rules, let that be reckoned as her initiation.

1. Even if a woman has been a nun for a hundred years, she shall make salutation to, shall rise in the presence of, shall bow down before, and shall perform all proper duties toward a monk, even if he is only just initiated.

2. A nun is not to spend the rainy season in a district in which there is no monk.

3. Every half month a nun is to await from the monks two things: the request about the date of the Uposatha ceremony and the time when the monk will come to give the Exhortation.

4. After keeping the rainy season, the nun is to inquire whether any fault can be laid to her charge before both Samghas—of monks and of nuns—with respect to three matters: what has been seen, what has been heard, and what has been suspected.

5. A nun who has been guilty of a serious offense is to undergo the Manatta discipline toward both the Samghas.

6. When a nun, as novice, has been trained for two years in the Six Rules, she is to ask permission for the upasampada initiation from both Samghas.

7. A nun is never to revile or mistreat a monk.

8. From this time on, nuns are forbidden to admonish monks, but the official admonition of nuns by monks is not forbidden....

Then the venerable Ananda said to the Blessed One, "Lord, Maha-pajapati has taken upon herself the Eight Chief Rules; the aunt of the Blessed One has received the upasampada initiation."

Then the Buddha said, "Ananda, if women had not received permission to go out from the household life and enter the homeless state, then the pure religion would have lasted long;

the good law would have stood fast for a thousand years. But since women have now received that permission, the pure religion will not now last so long, and the good law will now stand fast for only five hundred years. Houses in which there are many women but only a few men are easily violated by robbers. In the same way, Ananda, under whatever doctrine and discipline women are allowed to go out from the household life into the homeless state, that religion will not last long. So, Ananda, in anticipation [of this] I have laid down these Eight Chief Rules for the nuns, never to be transgressed for their whole life."

The Rules of Defeat for Monks and Nuns

In this scripture from the *Vinaya Pitaka*, the "rules of defeat" for monks are given and explained. "Defeat" means expulsion with no possibility of return. These rules govern the life of nuns as well as monks. Notice at the end of the passage the ritual for confession of these faults in the monastery, the basic method of which is similar for confession of all other faults. The four prohibitions here—against sexual intercourse, theft, killing, and lying—form the basis of Buddhist morality for the laity. The only qualification is that the prohibition of sexual intercourse is modified to a prohibition of intercourse outside marriage.[34]

[Rules for Monks] The four Rules concerning those acts that cause Defeat now come into recitation.

1. If any monk who has taken upon himself the monks' system of self-training and rule of life and has not after that withdrawn from the training, or declared his weakness, shall have sexual intercourse with anyone, down even to an animal, he has fallen into defeat; he is no longer in communion.

2. If any monk shall take, from village or from forest, anything not given—what men call

"theft"—he, too, has fallen into defeat; he is no longer in communion.

3. If any monk shall knowingly deprive a human being of life, or shall seek out an assassin against a human being, or shall utter the praises of death, or incite another to self-destruction, saying, "Ho, my friend! What good do you get from this sinful, wretched life? Death is better to you than life!"—he, too, is fallen into defeat; he is no longer in communion.

4. A monk, without being clearly conscious of possessing extraordinary qualities, may perhaps pretend that he has gained insight into the knowledge of the noble ones, saying, "Thus I know, thus I perceive." At some subsequent time, whether on being pressed or without

---

[34]Taken, with editing, from Davids and Oldenberg, *Vinaya Texts*, part 1, pp. 3–6.

Patimokkha, Parajika Dhamma 1–4.

being pressed, he may feel guilty and may want to be cleansed from his fault. He shall say, "Brothers, when I did not know, I said that I knew; when I did not see, I said that I saw—telling a fruitless falsehood." Then, unless he spoke through undue confidence, he has fallen into defeat; he is no longer in communion.

Venerable Sirs, the four Conditions of Defeat have been recited. When a monk has fallen into one or other, he is no longer allowed to reside with the monks. As before, so afterwards, he is defeated; he is not in communion.

Concerning them I ask the venerable ones, "Are you pure in this matter?" A second time I ask, "Are you pure in this matter?" A third time I ask, "Are you pure in this matter?" The venerable ones are pure. Therefore they keep silence. Thus I understandd.

[Rules for Nuns]

1. Should any nun willingly engage in the sexual act, even with a male animal, she is defeated and no longer in communion.

2. Should any nun, in the manner of stealing, take what is not given from an inhabited area or from the wilderness...she is defeated and no longer in communion.

3. Should any nun intentionally deprive a human being of life, or search for an assassin for her, or praise the advantages of death, or incite her to die...or with such a purpose in mind, should in various ways praise the advantages of death or incite her to die, she also is defeated and no longer in communion.

4. Should any nun, without direct knowledge, boast of a superior human state, a truly noble knowledge and vision as present in herself, saying, "Thus do I know; thus do I see," such that regardless of whether or not she is cross-examined on a later occasion, she—being remorseful and desirous of purification—might say, "Fellow nuns, not knowing, I said I know; not seeing, I said I see—vainly, falsely, idly," unless it was from over-estimation, she also is defeated and no longer in communion.

5. Should any nun, lusting, consent to a lusting man's rubbing, rubbing up against, taking hold of, touching, or fondling (her) below the collar-bone and above the knees, she also is defeated and no longer in communion.

6. Should any nun, knowing that (another) nun has fallen into an act (entailing) defeat, neither accuse her herself nor inform the group, and then...she (this nun) should say, "Even before, ladies, I knew of this nun that 'This sister is of such-and-such a sort,' and I didn't accuse her myself nor did I inform the group," then she also is defeated and no longer in communion.

7. Should any nun follow a monk suspended by a Community (of monks) acting in harmony, in line with the Dhamma...the nuns should admonish her thus: "Lady, that monk has been suspended by a community acting harmony in line with the Dhamma....Do not follow him, lady." And should that nun, admonished thus by the nuns, persist as before, the nuns are to rebuke her up to three times so as to desist. If while being rebuked up to three times she desists, that is good. If she does not desist, then she also is defeated and no longer in communion.

8. Should any nun, lusting, consent to a lusting man's taking hold of her hand or touching the edge of her outer robe, or should she stand with him or talk with him or go to a rendezvous with him, or should she consent to his approaching her, or should she enter a hidden place with him, or should she give her body to him for the purpose of that unrighteous act, then she also is defeated and no longer in communion.

Rules Requiring Formal Meetings of Monks

The next set of monastic rules covers thirteen matters for which a formal meeting of the order (*samghadisesa*) is required. The precise punishment, to be decided at a meeting of the whole monastic assembly, amounts to something less than permanent expulsion, often suspension for one month. All the rules are given here.[35]

The thirteen things which in their earlier and in their later stages require formal meetings of the Order now come into recitation.

1. If a monk intentionally emits his semen, except while sleeping.

2. If a monk, being degraded with perverted mind, comes into bodily contact with a woman by taking hold of her hand or her hair, or by touching any part of her body.

3. If a monk, being degraded with perverted mind, addresses a woman with wicked words, exciting her to passion as young men do to young women.

4. If a monk, being degraded with perverted mind, magnifies service to himself in the hearing of a woman, saying, "This, sister, would be the noblest of services, that to so righteous and exalted a religious person as myself you should serve by that act," meaning sexual intercourse.

5. If a monk acts as a go-between for a woman to a man, or for a man to a woman, or for a wife, or for a mistress, or even for a prostitute.

6. If a monk, at his own request, has a hut put up on a dangerous site, without the open space around it, or does not bring the monks to approve the site, or exceeds the due measure.

7. If a monk has a large house made on a dangerous site, without the open space around it, or does not bring the monks to the place to approve the site.

8. If a monk, in harshness, malice, or anger, harasses another monk by a groundless charge of having committed a Parajika offense, thinking to himself, "Perhaps I may get him to fall from this religious life"—and then later, either when he is pressed, or without his being pressed, the case turns out to be groundless, and the monk confesses his malice.

9. If a monk, in harshness, malice, or anger, harasses another monk by a groundless charge of having committed a Parajika offense, supporting himself by some point or other of no importance in a case that really rests on something of a different kind; thinking to himself, "Perhaps I may get him to fall from this religious life"—and then later, either when he is pressed, or without his being pressed, the case turns out to rest on something of a different kind, and that monk confesses his malice.

10. If a monk causes division in a community that is at union, or persists in calling attention to some matter calculated to cause division, that monk should be addressed by the monks, "Sir, do not go around causing division in a community that is unified." If that monk, when he has thus been spoken to by the monks, should persist as before, then let that monk be [formally] admonished about it by the monks as a body, even to the third time, to the intent that he abandon that course. If, while being so admonished up to the third time, he abandons that course, it is well. If he does not abandon it, it is a Samghadisesa.

11. Now other monks, one, two, or three, may become adherents of that monk, and may

[35]Taken, with editing, from Davids and Oldenberg, *Vinaya Texts,* part 1, pp. 7–14.

Patimokkha, Samghadisesa Dhamma 1–13.

raise their voices on his side: "Do not say, sirs, anything against that monk! That monk speaks according to the Dhamma, and he speaks according to the *Vinaya*." Then let those monks be addressed by the other monks in this way, "Do not say this, sirs! That monk does not speak according to the Dhamma, nor does he speak according to the *Vinaya*. Do not let division in the community be pleasing to you!" If those monks, when they have thus been spoken to by the monks, should persist as before, those monks should be formally judged by the monks, as a body, even to the third time, so that they abandon that course. If . . . they abandon that course, it is well. If they do not abandon it, it is a Samghadisesa.

12. A monk may refuse to listen to what is said to him. . . . He may allow nothing to be said to him, objecting, "Say nothing to me, Sirs, either good or bad; and I will say nothing, either good or bad, to you. Be good enough, sirs, to refrain from speaking to me!" Then let that monk be addressed by the monks, "Do not, sir, make yourself a person who cannot be spoken to. Make yourself a person to whom we can speak. . . . For the society of the Blessed One grown large by mutual discussion and by mutual help." If that monk, when he has thus been spoken to by the monks, should persist as before, then let that monk be formally judged by the monks as a body as many as three times, so that he may abandon that course. If he abandons that course, it is well. If he does not abandon it, it is a Samghadisesa.

13. If a monk dwells near a certain village or town, leading a life hurtful to the laity and devoted to evil, and the families led astray by him are seen and heard, let that monk be spoken to by the monks. The monks must say, "Your life, sir, is hurtful to the laity, and evil. . . . Be so good, sir, as to depart from this residence; you have lived here long enough." If that monk, when thus spoken to by the monks, should persist as before, that monk should be formally judged by the monks as a body as many as three times, so that he abandon that course. If he abandons that course, it is well. If he does not abandon it, it is a Samghadisesa.

RITUAL

The Relics of the Buddha

One of the most important features of Buddhist worship has been veneration of the relics (physical remains, mostly bones) of the Buddha. To a Buddhist, these are the holiest physical objects in the world. This selection from the *Death of the Buddha Sutta* tells the story of how the followers of the Buddha settled many arguments about how the relics of the cremated body of the Buddha should be distributed.[36]

When they heard these things, the Mallas of Kusinara spoke to the assembled brothers. "The Blessed One died in our village domain. We will not give away any part of the remains of the Blessed One!"

When they had thus spoken, Dona the Brahmin addressed the assembled brothers. He said, "Hear, reverend sirs, one word from me. Our

_____

[36]Taken, with editing, from Davids, *Buddhist Suttas,* pp. 133–134.

_____

Mahaparinibbana Sutta 6.58–60.

Buddha was accustomed to teach moderation. It is unseemly that strife should arise, and wounds, and war, over the distribution of the remains of him who was the best of beings! Let us all, sirs, unite in friendly harmony to make eight portions. Let thupas[37] arise widespread in every land, that

humanity may trust in the Enlightened One! Brahmin, divide the remains of the Blessed One equally into eight parts, with fair division."

"Let it be so, sir!" Dona said in assent to the assembled brothers. He divided the remains of the Blessed One equally into eight parts, with fair division. He said to them, "Give me, sirs, this vessel, and I will set up over it a sacred memorial mound, and in its honor I will establish a feast." And they gave the vessel to Dona the Brahmin.

---

[37]*thupas* (or *stupas):* a house of worship enshrining relics of the Buddha.

Mindfulness in Meditation

> Buddhist monks must have a powerful concentration to fix their minds on the abstract processes and products of meditation. This passage from an influential Theravada meditation scripture discusses the way to full mindfulness.[38]

Monks, there is one road, one path for beings to purify themselves, to transcend sorrow and grief, to overcome suffering and melancholy, to attain the right way, to realize Nirvana: that is the fourfold establishment of mindfulness. What are the four mindfulnesses? They are the mindful contemplation of the body, the mindful contemplation of the feelings, the mindful contemplation of thoughts, and the mindful contemplation of the elements of reality.

How does a monk practice the mindful contemplation of the body? In this way: He goes to the forest, or to the foot of a tree, or to an empty room, and he sits down, cross-legged, keeps his back straight, and directs his mindfulness in front of him. Mindfully, he breathes in, mindfully, he breathes out; breathing in a long breath, he knows "I am breathing in a long breath"; breathing out a long breath, he knows "I am breathing out a long breath"; breathing in a short breath, he knows "I am breathing in

a short breath"; breathing out a short breath, he knows "I am breathing out a short breath." He should be like a lathe operator who knows that "I am making a long turn" when he is making a long turn and that "I am making a short turn" when he is making a short turn. Thus a monk practices mindfully contemplating his body....

And also, a monk is fully mindful of what he is doing, both going and coming, looking straight ahead and looking away, holding out his bowl or retracting it, putting on his robes, carrying his bowl, eating, drinking, chewing, tasting, defecating, urinating, moving, standing, sitting, sleeping, waking, talking, being quiet. Thus a monk practices mindfully contemplating his body.

And also, a monk considers his body itself, from the soles of his feet upward and from the top of his head downward, wrapped as it is in skin and filled with all sorts of impurities. He reflects, "In this body there is hair, body-hair, nails, teeth, skin, flesh, sinews, bones, marrow, kidneys, heart, liver, pleura, spleen, lungs, colon, intestines, stomach, feces, urine,

---

[38]Taken, with editing, from V. Trenckner, *The Majjhima-nikaya,* vol. 1 (London: Pali Text Society, 1888), pp. 55–63.

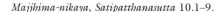

bile, phlegm, pus, blood, sweat, fat, tears, lymph, saliva, and snot." Thus a monk practices mindfully contemplating his body.

And also, a monk considers his body with regard to the elements that compose it. He reflects, "In this body there is earth, water, fire, and air." He should think of these elements that make up the body as though they were pieces of the carcass of a cow that a butcher had slaughtered and displayed in a market. Thus a monk practices mindfully contemplating his body. And also, if a monk should see a corpse abandoned in a cemetery, dead one day or two or three, swollen, turning blue, and beginning to fester, he should concentrate on his own body and think, "This body of mine is just like that one; it has the same nature, and it will not escape this fate." And should he see a corpse abandoned in a cemetery, being eaten by crows, hawks, vultures, dogs, jackals, or various kinds of vermin, he should concentrate on his own body and think, "This body of mine is just like that one; it has the same nature, and it will not escape this fate." And should he see a corpse abandoned in a cemetery, a skeleton still covered with some flesh and blood and held together by tendons, or without flesh but smeared with blood and still held together, or without flesh or blood but still held together, or just bones no longer held together but scattered in different directions...he should concentrate on his own body and think, "This body of mine is just like that; it has the same nature, and it will not escape this fate."...Thus a monk keeps mindfully contemplating his body.

And how, monks, does a monk practice the mindful contemplation of feelings? Experiencing a pleasant feeling, he knows "I am experiencing a pleasant feeling"; experiencing an unpleasant feeling, he knows "I am experiencing an unpleasant feeling." Experiencing a pleasant physical feeling, he knows "I am experiencing a pleasant physical feeling"; experiencing a pleasant spiritual feeling, he knows "I am experiencing a pleasant spiritual feeling"; experiencing an unpleasant physical feeling, an unpleasant spiritual feeling, a physical feeling that is neither pleasant nor unpleasant, a spiritual feeling that is neither pleasant

nor unpleasant, he knows he is experiencing those feelings. Thus a monk practices mindfully contemplating his feelings.

And how, monks, does a monk practice the mindful contemplation of thoughts? He knows a passionate thought to be a passionate thought; he knows a passionless thought to be a passionless thought; he knows a hate-filled thought to be a hate-filled thought; he knows a hate-free thought to be a hate-free thought; he knows a deluded thought, an undeluded thought, an attentive thought, a distracted thought, a lofty thought, a lowly thought, a mediocre thought, a supreme thought, a concentrated thought, a diffused thought, a thought that is free, a thought that is still bound, to be such thoughts as they are. Thus a monk practices mindfully contemplating his thoughts.

And how, monks, does a monk practice the mindful contemplation of the elements of reality? In this way: He practices the mindful contemplation of the elements of reality with regard to the five hindrances. How does he do that? When there is within him sensual excitement, he knows that "sensual excitement is occurring within me"; when there is within him no sensual excitement, he knows that "sensual excitement is not occurring within me." When there is within him some ill will, he knows that "ill will is occurring within me"; when there is within him no ill will, he knows that "ill will is not occurring within me." Similarly he knows the presence and the absence within himself of laziness and lethargy, agitation and worry, and doubt. Thus he practices mindfully contemplating elements of reality within himself, he practices mindfully contemplating elements of reality outside of himself, and he practices mindfully contemplating elements of reality as they arise and as they pass away. Thinking that "this is an element of reality," he is concerned with it only insofar as he needs to be for the sake of knowledge and recognition; so he abides free from attachment and does not cling to anything in this world.

A monk also practices the mindful contemplation of the elements of reality with regard to the five aggregates of attachment. How does he do that? He reflects "Such is physical form, such is the origin of physical form, and such is the passing away of physical form." "Such is feeling, such is the origin of feeling, such is the passing away of feeling." "Such is perception, such is the origin of perception, and such is the passing away of perception." "Such are karmic constituents, such is the origin of karmic constituents, and such is the passing away of karmic constituents." "Such is consciousness, such is the origin of consciousness, and such is the passing away of consciousness.". . .

A monk also practices the mindful contemplation of the elements of reality with regard to the seven factors of enlightenment. How does he do that? When the first factor of enlightenment, mindfulness, is within him, he knows it to be present; when it is not within him, he knows it to be absent. And similarly, he knows the presence and absence within himself of the other factors of enlightenment: the investigation of Dharma, energetic effort, enthusiasm, serenity, meditative concentration, and equanimity.

A monk also practices the mindful contemplation of the elements of reality with regard to the Four Noble Truths. How does he do that? He knows "suffering" the way it really is, and he knows "the origination of suffering" the way it really is, and he knows "the cessation of suffering" the way it really is, and he knows "the way leading to the cessation of suffering" the way it really is.

A Mahayana View of the Merit of Making Images

Another prominent feature of Buddhist worship—much more widespread than relic veneration—is using statues of the Buddha to focus one's thoughts toward enlightenment. In this passage from the Mahayana canon, the Buddha is said to lavish great merit on those who make his images. The belief that the Buddha gives his gracious blessing to those who seek it is a prominent theme in Mahayana Buddhism.[39]

The Blessed One sat upon his lotus throne, upon the terrace of enlightenment; and each person in the four assemblies thought to himself: "Truly we wish to hear the Blessed One teach us the meritorious virtue of making images of the Buddha.". . .

The Buddha said to the bodhisattva Maitreya: "Listen attentively! Listen attentively, and ever bear in mind what I shall explain to you.

"Let a son of good family or a daughter of good family but be pure and faithful, and fix his mind solely upon the virtues of the Buddha, and meditate unceasingly upon his awe-inspiring virtue and majesty. . . . Let him see how every single pore of the Buddha's body glows with measureless multicolored brilliant light, with immensities of surpassing blessings and adornments and accomplishments, with measureless insight and perfect enlightenment, with measureless meditation and forbearance, with measureless magic and spiritual power.

"Let him meditate upon the infinitude of all the virtues of the Buddha, upon his far removal

[39]From Stephan Beyer, *The Buddhist Experience: Sources and Interpretations* (Belmont, CA: Dickenson, 1974), pp. 47–50, 54–55. Copyright © 1974, Dickenson Publishing Company. Used by permission of Wadsworth Publishing Company, Inc.

Taisho Shinshu Daizokyo 16.694.

from all the hosts of error, and upon his splendor unequaled in all the world. And let him fix his mind in this manner, and awaken deep faith and joy, and make an image of the Buddha with all its signs. Then he gains merit which is vast, and great, and measureless, and limitless, and which can be neither weighed nor counted.

"Maitreya, should a man draw and adorn an image with a host of varied colors; or cast an image of silver, or bronze, or iron, or lead, or tin; or carve an image of fragrant sandalwood; or cover an image with pearls, or shell, or well-woven and embroidered silk; or cover a wooden image with red earth and white lime plaster; or build an image to the best of his ability, even if it be so small as the size of a finger, as long as those who see it can see that it is in the form of the Blessed One—I shall now tell you what his blessed reward will be, and how he will fare in his next life.

"For a man who does these things may be born again into this world, but he will not be born into a poor family, nor will he be born in a barbarian border kingdom, nor into a lowly clan, nor as an orphan; he will not be born stupid or fierce, nor as a merchant or peddler or butcher; truly he will not be born into any low mean craft or impure caste, into any heretical practices or heretical views.

"For by the power of his intention he has cast aside the cause for such rebirth, and he will not be born into such states; but rather he will always be born into the household of a universal emperor, having powerful clansmen, or perhaps into the household of a Brahmin of pure practices, rich and honorable, lordly and without error.

"The place where he is born will always be where Buddhas are served and worshipped; and perhaps there he shall be a king, able to maintain and establish the Law, teaching the Law which converts those of evil practices; and perhaps he shall be a universal emperor, having the seven jewels, bringing forth a thousand sons, and

mounting into the sky to convert the four corners of the world.

"When his length of days has been exhausted, the lord will be abundantly joyful, perhaps to rule as the king of the gods, or as lord of the Heaven of Delights, or of the Heaven of Power; for there will be no joy either of gods or of men which he will not taste. And thus his blessed reward will continue in heaven and will not be cut off when he dies.

"He will always be born as a man: he will not take on the body of a woman, or of a eunuch, or of a hermaphrodite.[40] The body which he takes will be without defect or deformity: neither one-eyed nor blind; his ears not deaf; his nose not bent or twisted; his mouth not large or crooked; his lips not hanging down or wrinkled or rough; his teeth not broken or missing, not black or yellow; his tongue not slow; the back of his neck without tumor or boil; his form not hunched; his color not splotched; his arms not weak; his feet not large; and he will be neither too thin nor too tall, neither too fat nor too thin. . . .

"Maitreya, if there is a man who, in the midst of this world, can awaken his faith and build an image of the Buddha, then between his having done so and his not having done so the difference is . . . great: for anywhere this man is born, he is purified and free of all his past sins, and by all his skill may gain liberation even without a teacher." . . .

The virtue of the Blessed Buddha is without limit or measure, and it cannot even be thought or talked of. And that is why, if a man awakens his faith and builds a Buddha image, every single one of his evil deeds will be exhausted and annulled; and from the store of the Buddhas he gains meritorious virtue without limit or measure, until he himself gains Buddhahood, and himself saves beings from all their suffering and woe forever."

---

[40]*hermaphrodite:* a person with male and female sexual organs and characteristics.

Tibetan Scripture to Guide the Soul after Death

Probably the most famous Tibetan scripture is the *Bardo Thodol* (or *Bar-do thos-grol*), popularly known as the "Tibetan Book of the Dead" but more accurately translated "Listen and Be Liberated from the Intermediate State." This book provides texts to be read at and after death to guide the soul of the deceased through the intermediate ("Bardo") state to a happy reincarnation. This key reading at the point of death first speaks of the "clear light" of pure Nirvana; the person cannot reach it, and guidance is given to lead the soul through demonic nightmares to shelter in the womb of a being who will later give birth to the dead person's reincarnation.[41]

"Noble person, (his/her name), now the time has come for you to seek a path [through the Bardo]. After your breath has almost ceased, that which is called the Clear Light of the first phase of the Intermediary State will dawn upon you. Its meaning was explained to you by your lama. It is existence as such, empty and bare like the sky; it will appear to you as the stainless and bare mind, clear and empty, without limitations or a center. At this moment you should recognize this and remain therein. I shall guide you to this insight." Before the physical breath has totally ceased one should repeat this close to the dying person's ear many times so that it is imprinted on the mind....

"Noble son, (name), listen! The intrinsic light of true being will now become apparent to you. This you must recognize! Noble son, the innate being of your present cognition is this very naked voidness, which does not exist as a thing, phenomenon, or color; it is mere voidness. This is the absolute reality of the female Buddha Samantabhadra.[42] As your cognition consists in

voidness, don't let this opportunity become meaningless.... The nature of your own mind is void of an inherent being and of any substance, but your intelligence is crystal clear. This nature of your mind is inseparable from your intelligence; together they are the true being, the Buddha. The nature of your mind, equally clear and void, consists in a mass of light, and because of being free of becoming and decaying, it is the Buddha of boundless light. This you must recognize! ...

"Noble son, for three and a half days you will be unconscious. When you awake from the coma you will think: 'What happened to me?' For this reason, you have to recognize that you are now in the intermediate state. At this time, when you depart from the world, all things will appear to you as light, and as celestial beings. The entire sky will shine with bright blue....

"You should yearn for the light blue light, which is so brilliant and clear; and full of devotion you should address Vairocana with this prayer which you should repeat after me: 'Alas! At this time I am wandering through the world because of my great ignorance. I beg you, Vairocana, to guide me on the bright path of the primordial wisdom of the sphere being-as-such, the right path. May the divine mother, Akashesvari (Protector of the heavens) protect me from behind. I beg you, rescue me from the abyss of the

---

[41]From H. Coward, E. Dargyay, and R. Neufeldt, *Readings in Eastern Religion* (Waterloo, Ontario: Wilfrid Laurier University Press, 1988). Copyright © 1988 Wilfrid Laurier University Press. Used by permission.
[42]*Samantabhadra:* As in Buddhist tantric texts, the feminine here represents perfect wisdom.

intermediate state and guide me to perfect buddhahood.'

"Noble son, (name), hear me! You have not understood me even though I have directed you toward the right insight according to the instructions of this text. Now when you can't close the womb, then the time has truly come when you have to acquire a new body. There is more than only one profound and authentic instruction for closing the door of the womb. Remember them, be not distracted; imprint them on your mind.

"Noble son, although you are reluctant to go, torturers—which are evil deeds—chase you. Powerless, you have to go where you don't want to. Torturers and executioners pull you and you feel as if you are running away from darkness, tornadoes, cries of war, snow, rain, hail, and blizzards. In your anxiety you are looking for a refuge, and you escape and hide. You ask yourself whether they will get you there. 'If they detect me here, then everything is lost,' and while questioning whether you have escaped you cling to this spot. If they take you from there you are afraid of being overcome by the anxieties and terrors of the intermediate state. Therein you seize a bad body that did not exist before, and you will suffer from various ills. This is a sign that the devils and demons have prevented your escape.

"Listen and memorize this instruction suitable for such an occasion! When the torturers chase you into a state of helplessness, or when fear and anxiety threaten you, then you should visualize a wrathful deity who destroys all these forms of threat. Quickly perfect your vision of the deity with all his limbs.... Through their blessing and compassion you will rid yourself from the torturers and will have the strength to close the door of the womb. This profound and accurate instruction you should keep in mind!"

A Zen Koan, "What Is Extraordinary?"

Zen (Chinese: *Chan*) Buddhism seeks immediate enlightenment beyond study, sense-perception, and rationality. As an aid to this, Zen masters developed the koan, a difficult question that cannot be rationally answered. Famous koans include such gems as these: "What is the sound of one hand clapping?" "What did your face look like before your parents were born?" "If I have nothing, what should I do with it?" The *Blue Cliff Record*, a famous Zen scripture, puts koans into a fuller context for use in the monasteries. Written in China during the Song dynasty (960–1276 C.E.), each of the 100 chapters deals with one koan, giving an introduction telling the impact of the koan; the story, taken from classical Zen lore, interspersed with parenthetical remarks by Zen master Yuanwu Keqin (1063–1135); and a commentary on the story by Yuanwu. The story is intended to illuminate the koan, but on the whole, the story also has a riddling quality.[43]

[Story] A monk asked [the ninth-century Zen master] Baizhang, "What is extraordinary?"

(There's an echo in the words. He demonstrates his ability in a phrase. He flabbergasts people. Though he has eyes, he's never seen.) Baizhang said, "Sitting alone on the mountain." (His awesome majestic air extends over the whole land. The one standing and the one sitting are both defeated.) The monk bowed: (A clever monk.

---

[43]From Thomas Cleary, translator, *The Blue Cliff Record*, BDK English Tripitaka, vol. 75. Berkeley, CA: Numata Center for Buddhist Translation and Research, 1998. Copyright © 1998 Bukkyo Dendo Kyokai and Numata Center for Buddhist Translation and Research.

The Blue Cliff Record 26.

There still is such a person who wants to see such a thing.) Baizhang then hit him. (A competent Chan teacher, why does he not speak much? The imperative is not carried out vainly.)

[Commentary] He has the eye to face situations unconcerned with danger or death. So it is said, "How can you catch tiger cubs without entering a tiger's lair?" Baizhang was like a tiger with wings. Nor does this monk avoid life and death: he dares to grab the tiger's whiskers and ask what is extraordinary. This monk too has eyes. Baizhang immediately took up the burden with him and said, "Sitting alone on the mountain." The monk bowed. Chan practitioners must be able to discern the meaning before the question. This monk's bow was not the same as an ordinary bow; he had to have eyes to do it. He didn't spill his guts. Though they knew each other, they acted like they didn't.

When the monk asked what was special and Baizhang told him sitting alone on the mountain, the monk bowed and Baizhang hit him; see how when they let both do so at once, and when they gather back they wipe away the tracks and obliterate the traces. But what did the monk mean by bowing? If it was good, why did Baizhang hit him? If it was not good, what was wrong?

Here you must be able to tell right from wrong, distinguish initiate from outsider, and stand on the summits of the summits of a thousand peaks, to begin to understand.

The monk's bow was like grabbing the tiger's whiskers; he was just contending for a pivotal position. Luckily Baizhang is perceptive; thus he hit the monk. Anyone else wouldn't have been able to handle the monk. The monk met mind with mind, conveyed intention with intention—that is why he bowed.

Nanquan said, "Last night at midnight Manjushri and Samantabhadra came up with views of the Buddha and the Dharma. I gave them each a beating and sentenced them to be hemmed in by twin iron mountains." Then Zhaozhou said, "Who should take your beating?" Nanquan said, "Where was my fault?" Zhaozhou bowed.

Chan masters do not idly observe how the other takes action. The moment they are in charge of the situation, they bring it into play. They are naturally lively. Wuzu would often say, "It's like coming to grips on the front lines." I'm always telling you simply to cut off subject and object all at once—then you'll be able to hold fast and act with mastery.

The Main Characteristics of the Falun Gong Movement

Falun Gong ("Practice of the Wheel of Law"), more often called by its practitioners Falun Dafa ("Great Teaching of the Wheel of Law"), is a new religious movement based on Chinese spiritual practice. It traces most of its roots to Buddhism but also shares some with Taoism. The ruling Communist Party of China has persecuted it as an "evil cult" that poses a threat to the state because it is a religious movement outside government control. The zeal of its followers and the appeal of its teachings continue to attract millions of followers in China and worldwide. Its main text, *Zhuan Falun*, "Turning the Wheel of Law," has scriptural status in the movement.[44]

---

[44]Taken from Li Hongzhi, *Zhuan Falun* (Englewood, NJ: Universe Publishing Company, 2000). Copyright 2000, Universe Publishing Company.

Li Hongzhi, *Zhuan Falun*, Lecture 1, Conclusion.

Our Falun Dafa is one of the eighty-four thousand cultivation ways in the Buddha School. During the historical period of this human civilization, it has never been made public. In a prehistoric period, however, it was once widely used to provide salvation to humankind. In this final period, I am making it public again. Therefore, it is extremely precious....

Falun Dafa is a cultivation practice of mind and body, and it requires exercises. On the one hand, the exercises are used to strengthen supernormal abilities. What is "strengthening"? It is the reinforcement of your supernormal abilities by your powerful gong potency,[45] thus making them progressively stronger. On the other hand, many living beings need to be developed in your body. In high-level cultivation practice, the Tao School requires the birth of the Immortal Infant (yuan ying), while the Buddha School requires the Vajra's indestructible body.[46] Furthermore, many supernatural abilities must be developed. These things need to be developed through the physical exercises, and they are what our exercises cultivate. A complete cultivation practice of mind and body requires both cultivation and practice....

Ours is a genuine cultivation practice of both mind and body. The gong that we cultivate is stored in every cell of the body, and the gong of high-energy matter is even stored in the original minuscule particles of matter at an extremely microscopic level. As your gong potency becomes greater, the density and power of gong will also increase. Such high-energy matter has intelligence. Because it is stored in each cell of the human body all the way to the origin of life, it will gradually become the same form as the cells in your body, assuming the same molecular combinations and form of nuclei. Its essence has changed, however, for this body is no longer composed of original physical cells.... Therefore, on the surface you still appear to be an ordinary person. The only

difference is that you look younger than those of your age. Certainly, the bad things in your body, including illnesses, must be removed first, but we do not treat illness here. We are purifying your body, and the term is not "healing illness," either. We just call it "purifying the body," and we clean out the bodies of true practitioners....

After a period of cultivation practice, our Falun Dafa practitioners look quite different in appearance. Their skin becomes delicate and reddish-white. For the elderly, wrinkles become fewer or even extremely few, which is a common phenomenon.... In addition, elderly women will regain their menstrual period since a cultivation practice of mind and body requires menses to cultivate the body. One's period will come, but the menstrual flow will not be much. At present, that little bit will suffice. This is also a common phenomenon. Otherwise, how can they cultivate their bodies without it? The same is true for men: The elderly and the young will all feel that the entire body is light. As for true practitioners, they will experience this transformation.

This practice of ours cultivates something very immense, as opposed to the many practices that imitate animals in their exercises. All of the principles that Sakyamuni [Buddha] and Lao Zi [Lao Tzu, the founder of Taoism] discussed in their time were confined to principles within our Milky Way. What does our Falun Dafa cultivate? Our cultivation practice is based upon the principles of the universe's evolution, and it is guided by the standard of the universe's highest characteristic. We cultivate something so enormous that it equates to cultivating the universe.

Our Falun Dafa has another extremely unique, most distinctive feature that is unlike any other practice.... Our practice cultivates a Falun in the lower abdomen. I personally install it for practitioners in the class. While I am teaching Falun Dafa, we install it for everyone in succession. Some people can feel it while others cannot; the majority of people can feel it.... Falun is a miniature of the universe that possesses all of the universe's capabilities, and it can operate and rotate automatically. It will forever rotate in your lower

---

[45]*gong potency:* spiritual and physical power.
[46]*Vajra's indestructible body:* diamond-like being, from the Tibetan term for its form of Buddhism, "Vajrayana."

abdominal area. Once it is installed in your body, year-in and year-out it will not stop and will forever rotate like this. While rotating clockwise, it can automatically absorb energy from the universe. Additionally, it can itself transform energy to supply the energy required for transforming every part of your body. Also, it emits energy while rotating counter-clockwise, releasing undesirable elements that will disperse around your body. When it emits energy, the energy can be released to quite a distance, and then it will bring in new energy again.

The emitted energy can benefit the people around you. The Buddha School teaches self-salvation and salvation of all sentient beings. One does not only cultivate oneself, but also offers salvation to all sentient beings. Others can benefit as well, and you can unintentionally rectify other people's bodies, heal their illnesses, and so on. Of course, the energy is not lost. When Falun rotates clockwise, it can collect the energy back since it rotates continuously.... If there is a phone call or someone knocks at the door, you may go ahead and take care of it right away without having to finish the practice. When you stop to do something, Falun will immediately rotate clockwise and take back the emitted energy from around your body....

What I have said may sound quite inconceivable. You will understand it later as you study further. There are also other things that are too profound for me to make known. We will systematically expound the Fa[47] of high levels, from the simple to the profound. It will not work if your own xinxing[48] is not righteous. If you pursue something, you may get into trouble. I have found that many veteran practitioners' Falun have become deformed. Why? You have intermingled other things with your practice, and you have accepted other people's things....

I am not saying that everyone has to study Falun Dafa. If you do not study Falun Dafa and have received true teachings from other qigong[49] practices, I will approve of it as well. Let me tell you, however, that to truly practice cultivation toward high levels, one must be single-minded with one practice. At present, no other person is truly teaching people toward high levels like me. In the future you will realize what I have done for you. Thus, I hope that you do not have very poor enlightenment quality. A lot of people want to practice cultivation toward high levels. This is now provided right before you, and you may still be unaware of it. You have been everywhere looking for a teacher and spent a fortune, yet you have found nothing. Today, it is offered to you at your doorstep, and maybe you have not realized it! This is an issue of whether you can become enlightened to it and whether you can be saved.

---

[47] *Fa:* Buddhist principles and practices.
[48] *xinxing:* inner moral character.
[49] *qigong:* traditional Chinese exercise that cultivates qi (chi), vital energy.

☙ GLOSSARY

Abhidhamma [ahb-hee-DAHM-muh] *Pitaka* "Special Teaching Basket"; the third basket of the Theravadin canon; it contains seven treatises based on the teachings of Buddha (Sanskrit: *Abhidharma*).

Arhat [AHR-haht] "Worthy One"; a title given to a person who achieves enlightenment (Sanskrit: Arhant).

• **bodhisattva** [bohd-hee-SAHT-vuh] a person who comes very close to achieving Buddha nature (enlightenment) but postpones it for the sake of helping others to achieve it.

Buddha [BUH-dah, rhymes with "could-a"] a person who has reached enlightenment; although Gotama is the Buddha par excellence, the term applies to all individuals who attain this state.

dhamma [DAH-muh] teaching, path, way (Sanskrit: *dharma*).

Jatakas [JAH-tah-kuhs] "Lives"; the book of tales of Gotama Buddha's previous lives.

sutta [SUH-tuh] a writing; a scripture. (Sanskrit: *sutra*).

Sutta Pitaka "Discourse Basket"; the second basket of the Pali canon; it features the basic teachings of Buddhism.

Tathagata [tah-THAH-gah-tuh] "One who has come [or "gone"] thus"; a person who has achieved enlightenment.

Tipitaka [tih-pee-TAH-kuh] "Three Baskets"; the main internal divisions of the Theravadin canon (Sanskrit: *Tripitaka*).

Vinaya [vih-NIGH-yuh] *Pitaka* "Discipline Basket"; the first basket of the Theravadin canon; it deals with the rules of monastic life.

QUESTIONS FOR STUDY AND DISCUSSION

1. What are the main features of the Theravadin scripture canon?
2. How is the life of Gotama Buddha an example for all Buddhists? Is it true to say that most of Buddhism is founded on the life of Gotama?
3. In what sense are the Four Noble Truths the essence of Buddhism?
4. What main characteristics of monasticism are described in Buddhist scripture?
5. To what degree is Buddhism a religion made for monastics?
6. How is the role of women in Buddhism described in its scripture? Consider especially the role of nuns.
7. In what ways do the scriptures reflect the basic differences and similarities between southern (Theravada) and northern (Mahayana) Buddhism? Consider both canon and content.
8. Based on your understanding of Buddhist scripture, how would you describe Nirvana?
9. What are some basic similarities and differences between Hinduism and Buddhism?

SCRIPTURES IN FILM

Although the life of Gotama Buddha has great meaning as a narrative for Buddhists and for many other people, no feature film has been made of his life. Martin Meissonier's 2001 film *Life of Buddha* is a blend of documentary and drama. For a film that tells the story of Buddha in tandem with a search for a new Tibetan leader that leads to the United States, see *Little Buddha* (1993, rated PG), directed by Bernardo Bertolucci and starring Keanu Reeves. Two films made in 1997 and rated PG-13 tell the story of the current Dalai Lama. The better one, from both cinematic and religious studies points of view, is *Kundun,* directed by Martin Scorsese. The other is *Seven Years in Tibet,* directed by Jean-Jacques Annaud.

SUGGESTIONS FOR FURTHER READING

PRIMARY READINGS

Wisdom Publications (**www.wisdompubs.org**) is a source for many important Theravada and Tibetan texts. The fullest and most accessible collection of Buddhist scripture in English translation is still the *Sacred Books of the East* series. Its vol. 10 contains the *Dhammapada,* trans. F. Max Müller, and the *Sutta-Nipata,* trans. V. Fausböll; vol. 11, various suttas, trans. T. W. Rhys Davids; vols. 13, 17, and 20, the most important *Vinaya* texts, trans. T. W. Rhys Davids and H. Oldenberg; vol. 19, a translation of the Chinese version of the *Acts of the Buddha;* vol. 21, the *Lotus Sutra,* trans. H. Kern; vols. 35 and 36, the *Questions of King Milinda;* and vol. 49, various Mahayana texts, prominently the *Acts of the Buddha,* trans. E. B. Cowell, F. Max Müller, and J. Takakusu.

E. Conze, *Buddhist Scriptures.* London: Penguin, 1959. An excellent anthology by a leading expert on Buddhism.

W. T. de Bary, *The Buddhist Tradition in India, China and Japan.* New York: Vantage Books, 1972. The finest of all the anthologies of the three major traditions of Buddhism.

SECONDARY READINGS

N. S. Barnes, "[Women in] Buddhism." In A. Sharma, ed., *Women in World Religions.* Albany: State University of New York Press, 1987. Gives good attention to the historical witness of Buddhist scriptures to the role of women.

S. Heine and D. S. Wright, *The Zen Canon: Understanding the Classic Texts.* New York: Oxford University Press, 2004. Treats several important Zen documents and has an opening essay, "Canon and Canonicity in the History of the Zen Literary Tradition."

Miriam Levering, "Scripture and Its Reception: A Buddhist Case." In Levering, ed., *Rethinking Scripture: Essays from a Comparative Perspective.* Albany: State University of New York Press,

1989, pp. 58–101. A fascinating glimpse of the use of scripture in a Buddhist nunnery.

Donald S. Lopez Jr., *Elaborations on Emptiness: Uses of the* Heart Sutra. Princeton, NJ: Princeton University Press, 1996. Explores the philosophical and ritual uses of this most important text.

R. A. Ray, "Buddhism: Sacred Text Written and Realized." In F. M. Denny and R. L. Taylor, eds., *The Holy Book in Comparative Perspective*. Columbia: University of South Carolina Press, 1985. Gives very good attention to orality.

K. A. Tsai, *Lives of the Nuns: Biographies of Chinese Buddhist Nuns from the Fourth to Sixth Centuries*. Honolulu: University Press of Hawaii, 1995. A translation of and commentary on a Chinese book written to demonstrate the power of Buddhist scripture in the lives of female monastics.

COMPANION WEBSITE

Visit the *Anthology of World Scriptures* companion website at **www.thomsonedu.com** for learning tools such as map explorations, flashcards of glossary terms, learning objectives, chapter practice quizzes, links to other websites for learning and research, and chapter summaries in PowerPoint® format.

CHAPTER FOUR

Jainism

Illustrated Folio from a Jaina *Kalpa Sutra* Palm-Leaf Manuscript

This thirteenth-century manuscript shows a Shvetambara monk sitting cross-legged and preaching to a prince, who raises his hands in reverence; the scriptures are open before them on a reading stand. Note the hole for threading the binding string at the center of the folio. (*Edwin Binney 3d Collection, copyright © 2005, San Diego Museum of Art.*)

- A Jaina man makes his way into a temple in Calcutta. He stands reverently before a life-size statue of a naked man who in ancient times attained Nirvana. As other worshippers walk respectfully around the statue several times, he stands still at its base and reads from the Jaina scriptures.

- A group of Jaina nuns walks slowly and carefully down a dirt road in northern India. Dressed in white, they have muslin cloths over their mouths to keep out flying insects. They use small brooms to gently sweep the ground in front of them as they walk, looking for even the smallest visible creatures. They are practicing the first and most important of their vows, noninjury to any living thing.

- In the streets of Mumbai (Bombay), two men come along carrying between them a light cot alive with bedbugs. They stop before the door of a Jaina household and cry, "Who will feed the bugs?" Someone tosses a coin from a window, and one of the men places himself carefully on the bed, offering himself as a living grazing ground to his fellow beings. The donor of the coin gains credit, and the man on the cot gains the coin.

INTRODUCTION

Jainism was founded by Mahavira (Great Hero) in the sixth century B.C.E. Mahavira taught a stricter version of the Hindu Upanishadic way, giving special emphasis to **ahimsa** [ah-HIM-suh], "noninjury" to all living beings. Rejecting belief in a supreme god, Jains seek release from endless reincarnation through a life of strict self-denial. Four million Jains in India have had an influence out of proportion to their comparatively small numbers. Gandhi, for example, drew inspiration from their teaching of nonviolence. The Jaina scriptures afford an excellent glimpse into this tenacious religion, especially its main teachings and monastic life.

Overview of Structure

Jaina scripture is known in religious scholarship as the *Agama* [ah-GAH-muh], "Tradition." Most Jains call it the *Siddhanta* [sid-DAHN-tuh], "Doctrine." The two main branches of Jainism, the Shvetambaras and the Digambaras, share a few books but for the most part have different canons. Shvetambara ("white-clad" monks) is the larger group. It teaches that a woman can achieve Nirvana without having to be reborn as a man; thus, this group has an order of nuns. Digambara ("sky-clad" or naked monks) teaches that women cannot achieve Nirvana.

The Shvetambara canon is commonly said by Western scholars to have forty-five books in six sections: *Angas* [AHN-guhs] (Limbs), *Upangas* (sub-*Angas*), *Prakirnakas* (mixed texts), *Chedasutras* (on authority and discipline), *Culikasutras* (Appendices), and *Mulasutras* ("basic texts"). The *Angas* are the oldest part of the canon. The first *Anga* is the *Acaranga Sutra*, containing the most reliable Jaina story of Mahavira and laws for monks and nuns. The second *Anga* is the *Sutrakritanga*, which contains the main Jaina teachings. The best-known *Mulasutra* is the *Uttaradhyayana Sutra*, which contains teachings Jains believe to be the last words of Mahavira. Besides these books, Jains also say that their original and pure teachings were contained in fourteen *Purvas* (Foundations), now all lost. The difficulties among the two sects and within each sect's canon are traced to the loss of these books. (The smallest of the Jaina sects, the Sthanakavasis, denies the existence of any scripture.)

The Digambaras accept as canonical the ancient *Purvas* that survive. They also accept the **Prakaranas,** which form the main part of their canon: the *Mulacara* (on conduct), the *Samayasara* (on doctrine), the *Pravancanasara* (teaching), and the *Aradhana* (Accomplishment). They also treat as scripture many scholastic commentaries on the scriptures (*anuyoga*), which range from the first to the ninth centuries C.E. Both Jaina groups accept the important *Tattvarthadhigama Sutra* (Book for Attaining the Meaning of Principles) by Umasvamin, the first work on Jaina philosophy to be written in Sanskrit. The fixing of the number of Shvetambara texts at forty-five, and their subdivision into six groups, was largely the work of the nineteenth-century German scholar Georg Buhler. Since the 1970s, this partition has been called into question as simplistic and not reflecting actual Jaina usage. Kendall Folkert, for example, states, "When one asks contemporary Jains what their scriptures are, one receives widely varying answers, responses that vary not because of ignorance, but because there does not appear to be a wholly accepted body of scripture that is of equal value to the entire community." Folkert also notes that Digambaras sometimes accept Shvetambara texts.[1]

The *Agama* discusses a vast number of subjects in books written by many Jaina leaders over a long period. Some of it is in prose, some in verse, and some in mixed prose and verse. Its content, though frequently repetitious and diffuse, at times is succinct and systematic.

Contemporary Use, Historical Origin, and Development

Like Theravada Buddhism, which it resembles, Jainism has put monks in control of the development and use of its scriptures. Mahavira gave the holy teaching as an ascetic to his monk followers, who passed it down for a thousand years until other monks wrote it down. Thus, the content of Jaina scripture is dominated by monastic teachings, ideals, and rules. The *Agama* was always intended not for a popular audience but for monks and, to a much smaller degree, nuns. These monks and nuns have the time to study it, learn it, and teach it to one another. Typically, a monk studies the four *Mulasutras* at the beginning of his career. If he masters them, he goes on to other more difficult texts and can perhaps become one of the highly respected monks who is a teacher of scripture in the monastery. Study of scripture is commanded in the rules for monks, and knowledge derived from the sacred books is typically the first step to release. This monastic orientation of the scriptures explains to a large extent their repetition and the numerous lists of various items that make them especially difficult for the layperson to comprehend.

Nevertheless, the Jaina laity uses the scriptures extensively. Jains tend to be better educated than the average Indian, and their high literacy rates have made their scriptures accessible to believers, who read and reflect upon them in houses of worship. Usage at festivals is also striking. For example, the *Kalpa Sutra* is formally read aloud at Paryusana, the end-of–year festival of confession and rededication.

---

[1]K. Folkert, "The 'Canons' of 'Scripture,' " in M. Levering, ed., *Rethinking Scripture: Essays from a Comparative Perspective* (Albany: State University of New York Press, 1989), p. 175.

Jains believe that when Mahavira achieved Nirvana, he emitted a "sacred sound" that his followers translated into words. Thus, the authority for the most ancient scriptures of both Jaina sects is Mahavira himself, but (in typical Indian fashion) he is not thought to have written these scriptures. Some of them claim to be speeches given by Mahavira to Gautama Indrabhuti, whose disciple Sudharman gave them in turn to his pupil Gambusvamin. The types of literature mentioned earlier developed over time, and all of them were handed on orally in the monastic community until about 500 C.E., when they were written down.

HISTORY

The Life of Mahavira

This passage tells the story of Mahavira as an example for believers, and especially for monks and nuns, of one who has achieved Nirvana. Mahavira renounced the world, gave away his property, pulled out his hair, and finally starved himself to death. The gods who see and admire these feats are not supreme gods, and Mahavira shows himself superior to them as a **Jina** [GEE-nuh], a "conqueror" who has achieved Nirvana. The *Kalpa Sutra* contains a story of Mahavira with more legendary touches than this.[2]

In that period, in that age, once upon a time, after the lapse of nine complete months and seven and a half days, in the first month of summer...on its thirteenth day...the Kshatriya woman Trisala, perfectly healthy herself, gave birth to a perfectly healthy boy, the Venerable Ascetic Mahavira.

In that night when the Kshatriya woman Trisala gave birth to the Venerable Ascetic Mahavira, there was a great divine, godly luster originated by descending and ascending gods and goddesses. They were of the four orders of Bhavanapatis, Vyantaras, Gyotishkas, and Vimanavasins. In the meeting of the gods their bustle amounted to confusion. In that night...the gods and goddesses rained down a great shower of nectar, sandal powder, flowers, gold, and pearls. In that night the gods and goddesses performed the customary ceremonies of auspiciousness and honor, and anointed Mahavira as a **Tirthankara** [tihr-TAHN-kah-ruh].[3]...

[14] Then the Venerable Ascetic Mahavira, after his intellect had developed and his childhood had gone, lived in the enjoyment of the allowed, noble fivefold joys and pleasures: sound, touch, taste, color, and smell....

[16] The Venerable Ascetic Mahavira's parents were worshippers of Parsva and followers of the Sramanas.[4] For many years they were followers of the Sramanas, and for the sake of protecting the

---

[2]All scripture selections in this chapter are taken, with editing, from Hermann Jacobi, *Jaina Sutras, Sacred Books of the East,* vols. 22, 45 (Oxford: Oxford University Press, 1884, 1895).

[3]*Tirthankara:* "Ford-finder"; a person who goes across the river of the world's misery to Nirvana. Jains believe that Mahavira was the last of twenty-four Tirthankaras.
[4]*Sramanas:* monks.

Acaranga Sutra 2.15.6–9, 14, 16–20, 22–25, 27.

six classes of lives they observed, repented, confessed, and did penance for their sins. On a bed of Kusa-grass they rejected all food. Their bodies were dried up by their last mortification of the flesh, which is to end in death. Thus they died in the proper month and, leaving their bodies, were born as gods in Adbhuta Kalpa. Descending after the end of their allotted length of life, with their departing breath they will reach absolute perfection. They will reach wisdom, liberation, final Nirvana, and the end of all misery.[5]

In that period, in that age the Venerable Ascetic Mahavira . . . lived thirty years among the householders under the name of Videha. After his parents had gone to the worlds of the gods . . . he gave up his gold and silver, his troops and chariots. He distributed, portioned out, and gave away his valuable treasures consisting of riches, plants, gold, pearls, etc. He gave them to those who wanted to make presents to others. Thus he gave away his possessions for a whole year. In the first month of winter, in the first fortnight, in the dark fortnight of Margasiras, on its tenth day, while the moon was in conjunction with Uttaraphalguni, he decided to retire from the world. . . .

Then the four orders of gods awakened the best of Jinas, the Venerable Mahavira, saying, "**Arhat** [AHR-haht]![6] Propagate the religion which is a blessing to all creatures in the world!" When the gods and goddesses . . . had become aware of the Venerable Ascetic Mahavira's intention to retire from the world, they assumed their proper form, dress, and banners. They ascended their own vehicles and chariots with their proper pomp and splendor, together with their whole retinue. Rejecting all large matter, they retained only tiny matter.[7] Then they rose up, and with that excellent, quick, swift, rapid, divine motion of the gods, they came down again. They crossed numberless

continents and oceans till they arrived in Gambudvipa at the northern Kshatriya part of the place called Kundapura. In the northeastern quarter of it they suddenly halted. . . .

At that period, in that age, in the first month of winter . . . on its tenth day . . . fasting three days without taking water, having put on one garment, the Venerable Ascetic Mahavira with a train of gods, men, and Asuras[8] left the northern Kshatriya part of the place Kundapura by the high road for the park Gnatri Shanda. There, just at the beginning of night, he caused his palanquin to stop quietly on a slightly raised untouched ground. He quietly descended from it, sat quietly on a throne with the face toward the east, and took off all his ornaments and finery.[9] . . .

When the Venerable Ascetic Mahavira had adopted the holy conduct which produced that state of soul in which the reward of former actions is temporarily counteracted, he reached the knowledge called Manahparyaya, by which he knew the thoughts of all thinking beings. . . . Then he formed the following resolution: "I shall for twelve years neglect my body and abandon the care of it. I shall with a right disposition bear, undergo, and suffer all calamities arising from divine powers, men or animals."

The Venerable Ascetic Mahavira formed this resolution. Neglecting his body, he arrived in the village Kummara when only one division of the day remained. Neglecting his body, the Venerable Ascetic Mahavira meditated on his Self in blameless lodgings, in blameless wandering, in restraint, in kindness, in avoidance of sinful influence, in a chaste life, in patience, in freedom from passion, in contentment, in control, and in correctness. All the while he practiced religious postures and acts. He walked the path of Nirvana and liberation, which is the fruit of good conduct. With right disposition he endured, sustained, and suffered all calamities arising from divine powers, men, and animals. With undisturbed and unaffected mind, he was careful in body, speech, and mind.

---

[5] *Descending . . . misery:* They will achieve Nirvana in their next incarnation and be reborn no more.
[6] *Arhat:* "Worthy One," another name for a person who has reached Nirvana.
[7] *large matter . . . tiny matter:* The gods change their form to a more spiritual and less physical state.

---

[8] *Asuras:* spirits.
[9] *took off . . . finery:* He is not naked, for he wears a cloth underneath. This reflects the Shvetambara orientation of this book.

The Venerable Ascetic Mahavira spent twelve years in this way of life. During the thirteenth year in the second month of summer...on its tenth day, on the northern bank of the river Rigupalika, in the field of the householder Samaga, in a north-eastern direction from an old temple, not far from a Sal tree, in a squatting position with joined heels exposing himself to the heat of the sun, with the knees high and the head low, in deep meditation, in the midst of abstract meditation, he reached Nirvana. He reached the full, unobstructed, unimpeded, infinite, and supreme knowledge and intuition called Kevala.[10]

___

[10]*Kevala:* knowledge that frees a person from the cycle of rebirth.

[25] When the Venerable One had become an Arhat and Jina, he was a Kevalin, omniscient and comprehending all objects. He knew all conditions of the world, of gods, men, and demons. He knew from where they come, where they go, whether they are born as men or animals, or become gods or demons. He knew their food, drink, doings, desires, open and secret deeds, their conversation and gossip, and the thoughts of their minds. He saw and knew all conditions in the whole world of all living beings....[27] On the day when the Venerable Ascetic Mahavira had reached the highest knowledge and intuition, he reflected on himself and the world. First he taught the Law to the gods, and then to men.

TEACHING

The Causes of Sin

This reading teaches the understanding of all that hurts other beings and renunciation of it. The first section deals with reincarnation, the second with ahimsa as the path out of it.

O long-lived Gambusvamin! I Sudharman[11] have heard the following discourse from the venerable Mahavira:

Many do not remember whether they have descended in an eastern direction when they were born in this world, or in a southern, or in a western, or in a northern direction.... Similarly, some do not know whether their soul is born repeatedly or not. They do not know what they were before, or what they will become after they die and leave this world. Now this is what one should know, either by one's own knowledge or through the instruction of the highest [i.e., a Tirthankara],

___

[11]*Gambusvamin:* the pupil of Sudharman.

or having heard it from others: what direction he descended. Similarly, some know that their soul is born repeatedly, that it arrives in this or that direction, whatever direction that may be. [5] He believes in soul, believes in the world, believes in reward, and believes in action (acknowledged to be our own doing in such judgments as these): "I did it"; "I shall cause another to do it"; "I shall allow another to do it." In the world, these are all the causes of sin, which must be comprehended and renounced. A man who does not comprehend and renounce the causes of sin is born repeatedly in many births, experiencing all painful feelings....He who understands and renounces these causes of sin is called a karma-knowing sage. Thus I say.

___

Acaranga Sutra 1.1–2.

[2.1] The living world is afflicted, miserable, difficult to instruct, and without insight. In this world full of pain, with beings suffering by their different acts, benighted people cause great pain. See! There are beings individually embodied.[12] See! Some men control themselves, while others only pretend to be houseless.[13] One destroys this earth-body[14] by bad and injurious acts. He hurts many other beings besides, through his doing acts relating to earth. About this the Revered One has taught the truth. For the sake of the splendor, honor, and glory of this life, for the sake of birth, death, and final liberation, for the removal of pain, man acts sinfully toward earth. He causes others to act so, and allows others to act so. This deprives him of happiness and perfect wisdom. He is informed about this when he has understood or heard, either from the Revered One or from the monks, the true faith. Some truly know this injuring to be bondage, delusion, death, and hell. A man is longing for this when he destroys this earth-body by bad, injurious acts. He destroys many other beings as well, through his deeds relating to earth. Thus I say.

---

[12] *beings individually embodied:* Individual souls exist as absolute realities, not as a part of one world-soul.
[13] *pretend to be houseless:* unfaithful monks.
[14] *earth-body:* all lives composed of the elements of the earth.

The Road to Final Deliverance

This passage presents a summary of the way to salvation. The four main steps are by knowledge, faith, conduct, and ascetic practice ("austerities"). Notice the Indian penchant to number things, useful in monastic teaching.

Learn the true road leading to final deliverance, which the Jinas have taught. It depends on four causes and is characterized by right knowledge and faith. Right knowledge, faith, conduct, and austerities—this is the road taught by the Jinas who possess the best knowledge. . . . Beings who follow this road will obtain blessedness.

Knowledge is fivefold: (1) knowledge derived from the sacred books; (2) perception; (3) supernatural knowledge; (4) knowledge of the thoughts of other people; (5) the highest, unlimited knowledge. [5] This is the fivefold knowledge. The wise ones have taught the knowledge of substances, qualities, and all developments. . . .

Dharma, Adharma,[15] space, time, matter, and souls are the six kinds of substances. They make up this world, as has been taught by the Jinas who possess the best knowledge. Dharma, Adharma, and space are each one substance only; but time, matter, and souls are an infinite number of substances. The characteristic of Dharma is motion, that of Adharma immobility, and that of space, which contains all other substances, is to make room (for everything).

[10] The characteristic of time is duration, that of soul the realization of knowledge, faith, happiness, and misery. The characteristic of Soul is knowledge, faith, conduct, austerities, energy, and realization of its developments. The characteristic of matter is sound, darkness, luster, light, shade, sunshine, color, taste, smell, and touch. The characteristic of development is singleness, separateness, number, form, conjunction, and disjunction.

The nine truths are (1) soul; (2) the inanimate things; (3) the binding of the soul by

---

[15] *Dharma, Adharma:* good and evil, respectively.

Uttaradhyayana Sutra 28.

karma;[16] (4) merit; (5) demerit; (6) that which causes the soul to be affected by sins; (7) the prevention of asrava by watchfulness; (8) the annihilation of karma; (9) final deliverance. He who truly believes the true teaching of the fundamental truths possesses righteousness.

Faith is produced by (1) nature; (2) instruction; (3) command; (4) study of the Sutras; (5) suggestion; (6) comprehension of the meaning of the sacred lore; (7) complete course of study; (8) religious exercise; (9) brief exposition; (10) the Law.

He who believes by nature truly comprehends, by a spontaneous effort of his mind, the nature of the soul, inanimate things, merit, and demerit. He puts an end to sinful influences. He who spontaneously believes the four truths (explicitly mentioned in the last verse), which the Jinas have taught, thinking they are of this and not of a different nature, believes by nature. But he who believes these truths, having learned them from somebody else, either a Khadmastha[17] or a Jina, believes by instruction. [20] He who has gotten rid of love, hate, delusion, and ignorance, and believes because he is told to do so, believes by command. He who obtains righteousness by the study of the Sutras, either *Angas* or other works, believes by the study of Sutras. He who by correctly comprehending one truth arrives at the comprehension of more—just as a drop of oil expands on the surface of water— believes by suggestion. He who truly knows the sacred lore, namely the eleven *Angas,* the *Prakaranas,* and the *Drishtivada,* believes by the comprehension of the sacred lore. He who understands the true nature of all substances by means of all proofs and nayas,[18] believes by a complete course of study.

[25] He who sincerely performs all duties implied by right knowledge, faith, and conduct, by asceticism and discipline, and by all Samitis and Guptis,[19] believes by religious exercise. He who holds no wrong doctrines though he is not versed in the sacred doctrines nor acquainted with other systems, believes by brief exposition. He who believes in the truth of the realities, the Sutras, and conduct, as it has been explained by the Jinas, believes by the Law.

Right belief depends on the acquaintance with truth, on the devotion to those who know the truth, and on the avoiding of schismatic and heretical tenets. There is no right conduct without right belief, and it must be cultivated for obtaining right faith. Righteousness and conduct originate together, or righteousness precedes conduct. [30] Without faith there is no knowledge, without knowledge there is no virtuous conduct, without virtues there is no deliverance, and without deliverance there is no perfection.

The excellence of faith depends on the following eight points: (1) that one has no doubts (about the truth of the tenets); (2) that one has no preference (for heretical tenets); (3) that one does not doubt its saving qualities; (4) that one is not shaken in the right belief (because heretical sects are more prosperous); (5) that one praises the pious; (6) that one encourages weak brethren; (7) that one supports or loves the confessors of the Law; (8) that one tries to exalt it.

Conduct that produces the destruction of all karma is (1) the avoidance of everything sinful; (2) the initiation of a novice; (3) purity produced by peculiar austerities; (4) reduction of desire; (5) annihilation of sinfulness according to the precepts of the Arhats, as well in the case of a Khadmastha as of a Jina.

Austerities are twofold, external and internal. Both external and internal austerities are sixfold. By knowledge one knows things, by faith one believes in them, by conduct one gets freedom from karma, and by austerities one reaches purity. Having by control and austerities destroyed their karma, great sages go to perfection and get rid of all misery. Thus I say.

---

[16]*karma:* fruit of evil deeds, a physical accretion on the soul.
[17]*Khadmastha:* a person who is advanced in knowledge but not to the full knowledge of Nirvana.
[18]*nayas:* literally, "leadings," probably referring to logical arguments.

[19]The five *Samitis,* rules for monks, are how to walk in a way noninjurious to other beings; how to speak; how to beg for food; how to excrete bodily wastes in a noninjurious manner; and how to use the few possessions allowed a monk. The three *Guptis* regulate thought, speech, and the body.

ETHICS

Ahimsa

This selection details the duty of noninjury, the first vow of monks. Noninjury is one of the leading duties of the laity as well. For example, devout Jains do not eat after sunset because they are less able to see any insects then.

These classes of living beings have been declared by the Jinas: earth, water, fire, wind; grass, trees, and plants; and the moving beings, both the egg-bearing and those that bear live offspring, those generated from dirt and those generated in fluids. Know and understand that they all desire happiness. By hurting these beings, people do harm to their own souls and will repeatedly be born as one of them.

Every being born high or low in the scale of the living creation, among movable and immovable beings, will meet with its death. Whatever sins the evildoer commits in every birth, for them he must die. In this world or in the next the sinners suffer themselves what they have inflicted on other beings, a hundred times, or suffer other punishment. Living in the Samsara[20] they always acquire new karma and suffer for their misdeeds.

---

[20] *Samsara:* the wheel of rebirth.

[5] Some leave their mother and father to live as Sramanas, but they use fire. Mahavira says, "People who kill beings for their own pleasure are wicked." He who lights a fire kills living beings; he who extinguishes it kills the fire. Therefore a wise man who well considers the Law should light no fire. Earth contains life, and water contains life; jumping or flying insects fall in the fire; dirt-born vermin and beings live in wood. All these beings are burned by lighting a fire.

Plants are beings that have a natural development. Their bodies require nourishment, and they all have their individual life. Reckless men who cut them down for their own pleasure destroy many living beings. By destroying plants, when young or grown up, a careless man does harm to his own soul. Mahavira says, "People who destroy plants for their own pleasure are wicked."

Sutrakritanga 1.7.1–9.

Rules for Monastic Life

Rules for both conduct and thought govern the life of a monk or a nun. Although the passage speaks of "compassion for living things" as a motivation for noninjury, the main motivation is less altruistic—to avoid as much as possible one's collection of karma.

Uttaradhyayana Sutra 35.

Learn from me, with attentive minds, the road shown by the wise ones. This road leads a monk who follows it to the end of all misery.

Giving up the life in a house, and taking the vow to wander, a sage should know and renounce those attachments that take hold of men. A restrained monk should abstain from killing, lying, stealing, and sexual intercourse, from desire, love, and greed.

Even in his thoughts, a monk should not long for a pleasant painted house filled with the fragrance of garlands and frankincense, secured by doors, and decorated with a white ceiling-cloth. [5] For in such a dwelling a monk will find it difficult to prevent his senses from increased desire and passion. He should be content to live on a burial-place, in a deserted house, below a tree, in solitude, or in a place that had been prepared for the sake of somebody else. A well-controlled monk should live in a pure place that is not too crowded, and where no women live. He should not build a house, nor cause others to build one. Many living beings both movable and immovable, both tiny and large, are killed when a house is being built. Therefore, a monk should abstain from building a house.

[10] The same holds good with the cooking of food and drink, or with one's causing them to be cooked. Out of compassion for living beings one should not cook or cause another to cook. Beings which live in water, in plants, or in earth and wood are destroyed in food and drink. Therefore, a monk should cause nobody to cook. Nothing is so dangerous as fire, for it spreads in all directions and is able to destroy many beings. One should not light a fire.

Even in his thoughts a monk should not long for gold and silver. Indifferent alike to dirt and gold, he abstains from buying and selling. If he buys, he becomes a buyer; if he sells, he becomes a merchant. A monk is not to engage in buying and selling. [15] A monk who is to live on alms should beg and not buy. Buying and selling is a great sin; but to live on alms is befitting. He should collect his alms in small parts according to the Sutras and to avoid faults. A monk should contentedly go on his begging-tour, whether he gets alms or not.

A great sage should eat not for the sake of the pleasant taste of the food but only for the sustenance of life. He should not be dainty or eager for good food; he should restrain his tongue and be without desire. Even in his thoughts he should not desire to be presented with flowers, to be offered a seat, to be eloquently greeted, to be offered presents, or to get a magnificent welcome and treatment.[21] He should meditate on true things only, committing no sins and having no property.

He should walk about with no care for his body until his end draws near. [20] Rejecting food when the time of his death is near, and leaving the human body, he becomes his own master and is liberated from misery. Without property, without egoism, free from passions . . . he obtains absolute knowledge and reaches eternal blessedness. Thus I say.

---

[21]*presents . . . treatment:* These come when a monk visits layfolk in public or in their homes.

ORGANIZATION

The Five Great Vows

A monk or nun entering the life of renunciation takes these solemn, final vows. Notice that the vow of ahimsa comes first. The ideals of these vows are also influential among the laity, and they take "Lesser Vows" modeled on the full monastic vows but not as strict. Because of

---

Acaranga Sutra 2.15.i–v.

faithfulness to their vows, Jains have a strong reputation in India for truthfulness (vow 2) and honesty (vow 3).

The Venerable Ascetic Mahavira, endowed with the highest knowledge and intuition, taught the five great vows, with their clauses...to the Sramanas and Nirgranthas,[22] to Gautama, etc.

The first great vow, Sir, is this. I renounce all killing of living beings, whether tiny or large, whether movable or immovable. I myself shall not kill living beings nor cause others to do it, nor consent to it....

The second great vow is this. I renounce all vices of lying speech arising from anger or greed or fear or mirth. I shall neither myself speak lies, nor cause others to speak lies, nor consent to the speaking of lies by others....

The third great vow is this. I renounce all taking of anything not given, either in a village or a town or a wood, either of little or much, of small or great, of living or lifeless things. I shall neither take myself what is not given, nor cause others to take it, nor consent to their taking it....

The fourth great vow is this. I renounce all sexual pleasures, either with gods or men or animals. I shall not give way to sensuality, nor cause others to give way to it, nor consent to their giving way....

The fifth great vow is this. I renounce all attachments, whether little or much, small or great, living or lifeless. I myself shall not form such attachments, nor cause others to do so, nor consent to their doing so. As long as I live, I confess and blame, repent and remove myself [of these].

---

[22] *Sramanas and Nirgranthas:* Jaina monks.

GLOSSARY

Agama [AH-gah-muh] "Tradition"; the Western name for the Jaina canon.

ahimsa [ah-HIM-suh] "noninjury" to any living being.

Angas [AHN-guhs] "Limbs"; the first and main section of the Shvetambara canon.

Arhat [AHR-haht] "Worthy One"; a person who has reached Nirvana.

Jina [GEE-nuh] "Conqueror"; a person who has reached Nirvana.

Prakaranas [prah-KAR-ah-nuhs] the main section of the Digambara canon.

Siddhanta [sid-DAHN-tuh] "Doctrine" or "Teaching"; the name that Jains use for their scripture.

Tirthankara [tihr-TAHN-kah-ruh] "Ford-finder"; a person who has traveled from the misery of this world across the river of existence to liberation and who enables others to do so by teaching and example.

QUESTIONS FOR STUDY AND DISCUSSION

1. Compare the lives of Mahavira and Siddhartha Gotama (the Buddha). How are they remarkably alike, and what might their dissimilarities be?
2. One scholar has called Jainism the "unhappy face of Buddhism." Judging from the Jaina scriptures, would you agree or disagree? Why?
3. Discuss the division between the Shvetambara and Digambara sects on the place of women as monastics. To what degree may this issue be reflected in arguments over the role of women in the monastic orders or clergy of other faiths?
4. Discuss the basic idea of ahimsa in Jainism. Why has it been influential in the wider Indian tradition? How might it be applicable to the peoples of other, non-Indian faiths?

🕮 SUGGESTIONS FOR FURTHER READING

PRIMARY READINGS

L. Basham, "Jainism and Buddhism." In W. T. de Bary, ed., *Sources of Indian Tradition*. New York: Columbia University Press, 1958, pp. 39–92. Excellent translations of, and introductions to, about twenty short but important passages in Jaina religion and philosophy.

Hermann Jacobi, trans., *Gaina Sutras*. In F. M. Müller, gen. ed., *Sacred Books of the East*, vols. 22 and 45. Oxford: Oxford University Press, 1884, 1895; reprinted, Delhi: Motilal Banarsidass, 1964. Contains selections of two *Angas*, a *Mulasutra*, and a *Chedasutra*; still the fullest English translation.

SECONDARY READINGS

Paul Dundas, *The Jains*. London: Routledge, 1993. The best and most recent introduction to Jainism, with an excellent examination of Jaina attitudes to scripture.

Kendall W. Folkert, "The 'Canons' of 'Scripture.'" In M. Levering, ed., *Rethinking Scripture: Essays from a Comparative Perspective*. Albany: State University of New York Press, 1989, pp. 170–179. A thought-provoking analysis of the present reception of Jaina scriptures in light of the comparative study of world scriptures.

Kendall W. Folkert, *Scripture and Community: Collected Essays on the Jains*, ed. J. E. Cort. Studies in World Religions Series. Cambridge, MA: Harvard University Center for the Study of World Religions, 1995. Treats the various aspects of Jaina tradition, with special attention to scriptures and monasticism.

Padmanabh S. Jaini, *The Jaina Path of Purification*. Berkeley: University of California Press, 1979. For the more advanced student; a nice complement to Dundas's book.

🕮 COMPANION WEBSITE

Visit the *Anthology of World Scriptures* companion website at **www.thomsonedu.com** for learning tools such as map explorations, flashcards of glossary terms, learning objectives, chapter practice quizzes, links to other websites for learning and research, and chapter summaries in PowerPoint® format.

CHAPTER FIVE

Sikhism

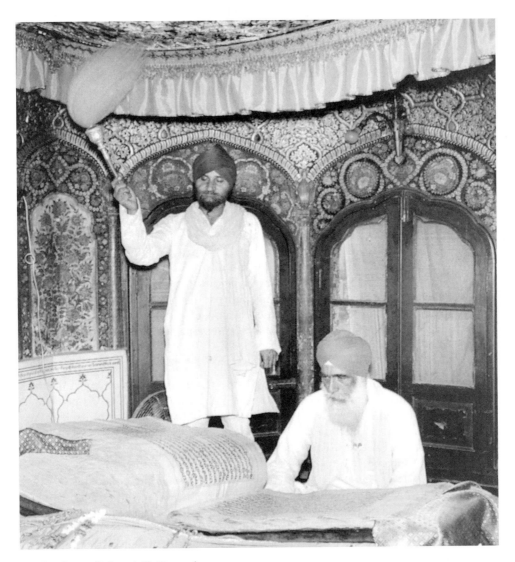

Recitation of the *Adi Granth*

An official reader recites the Sikh holy book in the Golden Temple of Amritsar, India, while an attendant behind him waves a horsehair fan to venerate the book. (*Gunter Reitz/Mary Evans Picture Library.*)

- A turbaned man walks down a bridge to the gate of the Golden Temple of Amritsar, India. Once inside, he approaches the central and only object of veneration, the large scripture book called the *Adi Granth*. Placed on cushions on a raised platform under a richly ornamented canopy, the *Granth* is read by an official reader as an attendant waves a ceremonial whisk over it. The worshipper bows reverently before the book with folded hands, listening to the melodious reading.

- Worshippers at a Sikh temple see, in quick succession, three life-cycle ceremonies. First, a baby is brought in for naming; as the *Adi Granth* is opened at random, the first letter on the left-hand page becomes the first letter in the child's first name. Second, a young couple comes to be married; during the ceremony, the couple circles the *Granth* several times to the accompaniment of verses from its marriage hymns. Third, the relatives of a recently deceased Sikh come for the conclusion of funeral rites; a prominent feature is the continuous reading of the entire *Granth,* and the relatives are present for the solemn conclusion of the reading.

INTRODUCTION

The Sikh religion was founded about 1500 C.E. by Guru Nanak. Its home is the Punjab region of northern India, where today it numbers more than 9 million believers. Sizable Sikh communities are also found in Canada and Great Britain. Designed to appeal to Hindus and Muslims, Sikhism contains elements of both faiths. With Hinduism, it shares mysticism and devotion; with Islam, a rigid monotheism. Yet it rejects elements of both these traditions, especially their leaders and rituals. Sikhism grew through a line of ten gurus until it reached its present form as expressed in its scripture, which believers consider the successor of the tenth guru. In the veneration of scripture, Sikhism is unsurpassed among world religions.

Overview of Structure

The *Adi Granth* ("the first/original book") has three main parts arranged in order of their importance. First and most important is the *Japji* [JAHP-jee], a poem that the faithful consider a summary and capstone of Sikhism. The term itself means "honored recitation." Written by Guru Nanak, the *Japji* differs from the rest of the *Adi Granth* [AH-dee GRAHNTH] by having no hymn tune. Appended to the *Japji* are fourteen hymns; all of them appear later in the *Adi Granth*. The second main part of the *Adi Granth,* by far the longest, is the collection of **ragas** [RAH-guhs], thirty-nine in all. Each raga ("tune") is divided by different poetic meters and lengths, which are subdivided by guru author, proceeding chronologically through the line of gurus. Each guru calls himself "Nanak," usually at the conclusion of the hymn, but the different guru authors are identified by the numbered use of the term **Mahala** [ma-HAH-luh]. Mahala 1 denotes the compositions of Guru Nanak, Mahala 2 of Guru Angad, and so on, up to Mahala 5 for Guru Arjan. The third main part of the *Adi Granth* is a mixed collection of twenty-six small books, most elaborating on the ragas. It also features hymns of many Hindu saints and Sufi Muslim mystics, which early Sikhs found congenial. Sikhs have always seen this inclusiveness as proof of the universality of their tradition. As it now stands, the *Adi Granth*'s material ranges in time from the twelfth-century hymns of Jaidev to the hymns of the ninth guru, Tegh Bahadur, who died in 1675.

The *Adi Granth* states in hymnic form the main beliefs of the Sikhs. The *Adi Granth* rejects what it perceives as the ritualism and formalism of Islam and especially of Hinduism, arguing for moral purity as the chief basis of religion. Hindu caste structure is repeatedly rejected; all men are to live as equals. Karma and reincarnation are accepted, but the practice of the Sikh religion will release believers from rebirth and lead to blessedness in heaven. Above all, the *Adi Granth* promotes the strict doctrine of one God and mystical devotion to his name. This loving God offers salvation by his grace to those who meditate on him and live in his truth. The non-Sikh reader looks in vain for stories about the life of the founder or other gurus. These have been collected instead into the **janam-sakhis** [JAH-num SAH-kees], "birth stories," traditional narratives that are highly legendary and have semicanonical status among devout Sikhs.

The main language of the *Adi Granth* is Punjabi. The text also shows strong traces of influence from Hindi and from several other north Indian languages. The *Adi Granth* employs the Sadhukari (or Sant-Basha) dialect, which was used by religious poets in north India in the fifteenth and sixteenth centuries. Its language is complicated enough to require special training for **granthis** [GRAHN-thees], official readers, but most observant Sikhs can understand the scripture well enough to read it on their own.

Contemporary Use

All Sikh usage of the *Adi Granth* is steeped in an attitude of profound respect. Devout Sikhs generally refer to the *Adi Granth* by a fuller, more venerable name, the *Sri Guru Granth Sahib* (*Guru Granth* for short), or "Revered Teacher Granth." This name is based on the origin of the Sikh scripture. Sikhs believe that each of their ten gurus had the same soul, the soul of Nanak, and that the last guru, Gobind Singh, bestowed this soul and its guru status on the *Granth,* which became the book embodiment of the soul of the gurus, the statement of the essence of Sikhism, and the final authority for the religion's continuing life.

Sikhs also call the *Adi Granth* the "living embodiment of the Guru." One of their leading theologians has claimed, "This is the only scripture of the world which was compiled by one of the founders of a religion himself and whose authenticity has never been questioned."[1] Moreover, the *Adi Granth* has served for almost 300 years as a force for unity in Sikhism. Doctrinal disputes are traditionally ended by consulting it, at random if need be. Sikhs have a strong mystical feeling for the *Granth* and treat it as an icon. No doubt the musical nature of its recitation contributes to its emotive power. Nevertheless, Sikhism also stresses the importance of meditating on and comprehending the meaning of its scripture.

The Sikh temple is in essence a shrine for the *Adi Granth.* Temple officials ceremoniously close the holy book and "put it to bed" at night. Before dawn, they bring it out again, install it in its place, and open it. All this is done to the accompaniment of hymns from the *Adi Granth*'s pages. Despite its large size—it has a standard format of 1,430 large-size pages—Sikhs carry it above their heads, wearing gloves.

---

[1] Gopal Singh, ed., *Sri Guru Granth Sahib* (Calcutta: M. P. Birla, 1989), p. 1.

When open, the *Granth* is draped in fine silk and placed on a special cot under a rich canopy at the focal point of the temple. Worshippers come to walk around it, bow to it, listen to its reading, and sometimes even pray to it. They must never turn their backs on it. Granthis (sometimes mistaken for "priests" by outsiders) often wear white scarves to cover their mouths as they read so that their breath does not touch the holy book. Sikh men take turns fanning it with a horsehair, yak-hair, or peacock-feather whisk—the **chaur** [chowr], one of the symbols of Sikhism. This scripture-centered activity goes on every day at the temple; there is no weekly service. At special festivals, a nonstop oral reading by a team of granthis is held that lasts two days and nights. Every life-cycle celebration centers in some way around the *Adi Granth*. In sum, it is no exaggeration to say that all the worship of the Sikhs centers on and originates in the *Adi Granth*.

This usage also carries over into the Sikh home. A prosperous Sikh household has a special room solely for the prominent placement of the *Granth*. Almost every other Sikh household has a **gutka** [GUHT-kuh], an anthology of the most important passages from the *Adi Granth* and a few passages from the *Dasam Granth*. Daily readings are held in the home. Early-morning recitation by memory of the *Japji* and other long sections is common, often lasting more than an hour. Devout Sikhs commit large portions of the *Adi Granth* to memory, and it is constantly on their lips during the day and night, especially in the five required daily prayers.

A memorable feature of Sikh scripture usage is **vak lao** [vahk low], "taking [God's] word." In the home or in the temple, the scripture is always opened at random, and the reading begins from the top of the left-hand page. This reading is thought to hold special significance for the occasion; it is God's word for the moment, which must be "taken" into the believer's life.

Historical Origin and Development

The overall structure of the *Adi Granth* suggests its origins and growth. Guru Nanak (1469–1539), in a typical Hindu attitude, rejected the authority of the written word and stressed instead interior meditation on the "holy [oral] word." The *Japji* and the various hymns he composed were passed along orally. Guru Angad, whom Nanak made his successor, devised a Punjabi alphabet for the Gurmukhi language, and the *Adi Granth* was later written in this script. Guru Amar Das, third in the line, compiled a hymnal of his own poems, the poems of his two predecessors, and poems from pre-Sikh mystics. The fifth guru, Arjan, revised this hymnal and compiled the oral and written work of all his predecessors into the *Adi Granth* in 1603–1604. Tradition says that Arjan's opponents were writing and circulating books falsely attributed to Nanak in an effort to corrupt Sikhism and turn it away from Arjan's leadership. In response, Arjan compiled the *Adi Granth*.

The sixth guru, Arjan's son Har Gobind, altered the Sikh movement's original pacifism to militancy. The tenth and final guru, Gobind Singh, is considered by Sikhs to be, after Nanak, their most important leader. Before his death in 1708, he declared that the line of gurus was complete. From this time on, the only guru of the community was to be the *Adi Granth* itself, which Gobind edited into its final, present form. (He himself wrote portions of the *Dasam Granth*, as mentioned earlier.) Thus, the *Adi Granth* serves as the teacher and authority for Sikhs, quite literally as the book containing the soul of the gurus.

The ***Dasam Granth*** (Tenth Book), a secondary scripture work for Sikhs, consists mostly of legendary narratives not found in the *Adi Granth*. Certain parts of the *Dasam Granth* [DAH-sum GRAHNTH] are well known and much used among Sikhs, especially the teachings of the tenth and final guru, Gobind Singh. Often quoted is his famous statement: "The temple and the mosque are one; so too are puja [Hindu worship] and [Muslim] prostration. All men are one though they seem to be many." Coupled with these more ecumenical sayings are statements of the rising militancy of the Sikhs.

TEACHING

Selections from the *Japji*

Practicing Sikhs repeat this entire poem from memory every morning during prayers—no small feat because the *Japji* is almost twice as long as the excerpts given here. They consider it the essence of their faith. The *Japji* moves back and forth among several topics: (1) God's name, greatness, and power; (2) God's creation of the world; (3) the way of salvation by meditating on God's name; (4) good and evil; and (5) relations with Hinduism and Islam. The rich sonority of the *Japji* comes through in this translation. It begins with the **Mul** ("root") **Mantar** [mool MAHN-tahr], a confession of faith considered the capstone of the whole composition.[2] In the tradition of Indian devotional poetry, the author's name is mentioned in most stanzas and emphasized at the end.

There is only one God whose name is true, the Creator who has no fear or enmity, immortal, unborn, self-existent; by the favor of the Guru.[3] Repeat His Name!

The True One was in the beginning; the True One existed before time began. The True One is now also, O Nanak; the True One also (forever) shall be.

[1] By thinking I cannot obtain a conception of Him, even though I think hundreds of thousands of times.

Though I be silent and keep my attention firmly fixed on Him, I cannot preserve silence.

The hunger of the hungry for God does not subside, though they obtain the load of the worlds.

If man should have thousands and hundreds of thousands of devices, even one would not assist him in obtaining God.

How shall man become true before God? How shall the veil of falsehood be torn?

By walking, O Nanak, according to the will of the Commander as preordained.

By His order bodies are produced; His order cannot be described.

By His order souls are infused into them; by His order greatness is obtained.

---

[2]All selections from the Sikh scriptures are taken, with editing, from Max A. Macauliffe, *The Sikh Religion: Its Gurus, Sacred Writings and Authors* (Oxford: Oxford University Press, 1909).

[3]*by the favor of the Guru:* known through the Guru.

Japji 1–3, 5–6, 9, 12–13, 15, 17–18, 20–22, Epilogue.

By His order men are high or low; by His order they obtained preordained pain or pleasure.

By His order some obtained their reward; by His order others must ever wander in transmigration.

All are subject to His order; none is exempt from it.

He who understands God's order, O Nanak, is never guilty of egoism....

Millions of men give millions upon millions of descriptions of Him, but they fail to describe Him.

The Giver gives; the receiver grows weary of receiving.

In every age man subsists by His bounty.

The Commander by His order has laid out the way of the world.

Nanak, God who is free from care is happy....

[5] He is not established, nor is He created.

The Pure One exists by Himself.

They who worshipped Him have obtained honor.

Nanak, sing His praises who is the Treasury of excellences.

Sing and hear and put His love into your hearts.

Thus shall your sorrows be removed, and you shall be absorbed in Him who is the abode of happiness.

Under the Guru's instruction God's word is heard;

Under the Guru's instruction its knowledge is acquired;

Under the Guru's instruction man learns that God is everywhere contained....

[9] By hearing the Name man becomes as Shiva, Brahma, and Indra.

By hearing the Name even the low become highly lauded.

By hearing the Name the way of Yoga and the secrets of the body are obtained.

By hearing the Name man understands the real nature of the *Shastras*, the *Smritis*, and the *Vedas*.

Nanak, the saints are always happy.

By hearing the Name sorrow and sin are no more....

[12] The condition of him who obeys God cannot be described.

Whoever tries to describe it shall afterward repent....

[15] By obeying Him man attains the gate of salvation;

By obeying Him man is saved with his family;

By obeying Him the Guru is saved, and saves his disciples;

By obeying Him, O Nanak, man wanders not in quest of alms—

So pure is God's name—

Whoever obeys God knows the pleasure of it in his own heart....

[17] Numberless Your worshippers, and numberless Your lovers;

Numberless adorers, and numberless they who perform austerities for You;

Numberless the reciters of sacred books and *Vedas;*

Numberless Your Yogins whose hearts are indifferent to the world;

Numberless the saints who ponder divine knowledge;

Numberless Your true men; numberless almsgivers;

Numberless Your heroes who face the steel of their enemies;

Numberless Your silent worshippers who lovingly fix their thoughts upon You.

What power have I to describe You?

So lowly am I, I cannot even once be a sacrifice to You.

Whatever pleases You is good.

O formless One, You are always secure.

Numberless are the fools appallingly blind;

Numberless are the thieves and devourers of others' property;

Numberless those who establish their sovereignty by force;

Numberless the cut-throats and murderers;

Numberless the sinners who pride themselves on committing sin; ...

Nanak thus describes the degraded.

So lowly am I, I cannot be a sacrifice to You.
Whatever pleases You is good. . . .

[21] Pilgrimage, austerities, mercy, and
   almsgiving on general and special
   occasions
Whoever performs, may obtain some little
   honor;
But he who hears and obeys and loves God
   in his heart
Shall wash off his impurity in the place of
   pilgrimage within him.
All virtues are Yours, O Lord; none are
   mine. . . .

What the time, what the epoch, what the
   lunar day, and what the week-day,
What the season, and what the month when
   the world was created,
The Pandits[4] did not discover; had they done
   so, they would have recorded it in the
   Puranas.
Nor did the Qazis[5] discover it; had they done
   so, they would have recorded it in the
   Qur'an.

Neither the Yogi nor any other mortal
   knows the lunar day, or the week-day, or
   the season, or the month.
Only the Creator who fashioned the world
   knows when He did so.

How shall I address You, O God? How shall
   I praise You? How shall I describe You?
   And how shall I know You?
Says Nanak, everybody speaks of You, one
   wiser than another. . . .
Men have grown weary at last of searching
   for God's limits; they say one thing, that
   God has no limit.
The thousands of *Puranas* and Muslim
   books tell that in reality there is but one
   principle.
If God can be described by writing, then
   describe Him; but such description is
   impossible.
O Nanak, call Him great; only He Himself
   knows how great He is!

---

[4] *Pandits:* highly learned Brahmins.
[5] *Qazis:* Islamic judges.

Remembering God

In Sikhism, the way of salvation is by profound reflection on and commitment to God's name.
"Remembering" is not the opposite of "forgetting" but a way to this reflection and commitment.
These are the words of Guru Arjan, often repeated after the *Japji* in the morning prayer service.

I bow to the primal Guru;
I bow to the Guru of the primal age;
I bow to the true Guru;
I bow to the holy divine Guru.
Remember, remember God;
By remembering Him you shall obtain
   happiness,
And erase from your hearts trouble and
   affliction.

Remember the praises of the one all-
   supporting God.

Numberless persons utter God's various
   names.
Investigating the *Vedas,* the *Puranas,* and the
   Smritis,
Men have made out the one word that is
   God's name.
His praises cannot be recounted.

Gauri Sukhmani, Mahala 5.

Says Nanak, save me, O Lord, with those
who are desirous of one glance of You.
In this *Sukhmani* is the name of God which
like ambrosia bestows happiness,
And gives peace to the hearts of the saints.

By remembering God man does not again
enter the womb;
By remembering God the tortures of Death
disappear;
By remembering God death is removed;
By remembering God enemies retreat;
By remembering God no obstacles are met;
By remembering God we are watchful night
and day;
By remembering God fear is not felt;
By remembering God sorrow troubles not:
Men remember God in the company of the
saints.
Nanak, by the love of God all wealth is
obtained.

By remembering God we obtain wealth,
supernatural power, and the nine treasures;

By remembering God we obtain divine
knowledge, meditation, and the essence of
wisdom;
Remembrance of God is the real devotion,
penance, and worship;
By remembering God the conception of
duality is dispelled;
By remembering God we obtain the
advantages of bathing at places of
pilgrimage;
By remembering God we are honored at His
court;
By remembering God we become reconciled
to His will;
By remembering God men's lives are very
profitable;
They whom He has caused to do so
remember Him.
Nanak, touch the feet of such persons.[6]

---

[6]*touch the feet of such persons:* show them respect because you
approve of them.

Dancing for Krishna

Sikhism developed out of devotional Hinduism. Here Guru Amar Das rejects the Krishnavites'
idea that merit is earned by participation in the dancing for Krishna that occurs at his festivals.
In typical *Guru Granth* style, Guru Amar Das adapts the practices of other religions to Sikhism
by reinterpreting them for the new faith.

I dance, but it is my heart I cause to dance;
By the favor of the Guru I have effaced myself.
He who keeps his mind firmly fixed on God
shall obtain deliverance and the object of
his desires.

Dance, O man, before your Guru;
He who dances as it pleases the Guru shall
obtain happiness, and at the last moment
the fear of Death shall forsake him.

He whom God causes to dance and whom
He loves is a saint.
He himself sings, he himself instructs, and
puts ignorant man on the right way.
He who banishes worldly love shall dance day
and night in God's house and never sleep.

Every one who dances, leaps, and sings of
other gods is lulled to sleep in the house

Rag Gurji, Mahala 3.

of riches; such are the perverse who have no devotion.

Demigods and men who abandon the world dance in religious works; Munis and men dance in the contemplation of divine knowledge.

The Sidhs, Strivers, and holy men who have acquired wisdom to meditate on God dance in God's love.

The regions, worlds, beings endowed with the three qualities, and they who love You, O God, dance.

Men and the lower animals all dance, the four sources of life dance.

They who please You dance, the pious who love the Word....

He to whom You are gracious shall obtain You by the favor of the Guru.

If I forget the True One even for a moment, that moment passes in vain.

Remember Him at every breath and He will pardon you from His own grace.

They who please You, O God, and who meditate on the Word, really dance.

Nanak says, they to whom You are merciful shall easily obtain bliss.

The Hindu Thread

This passage from Guru Nanak features a strong rejection of Hindu ritual practices. Singled out for criticism is the Hindu sacred string, worn on the body. As in the previous selection, Hindu practice is reinterpreted for Sikhs: "Make a sacred thread for the soul."

Make mercy your cotton, contentment your thread, continence its knot, truth its twist.

That would make a sacred thread for the soul; if you have it, O Brahmin, then put it on me.

It will not break, or become soiled, or be burned, or lost.

Blest is the man, O Nanak, who has such a thread on his neck.

You purchase a sacred thread for four coins, and seated in a square[7] you put it on;

You whisper instruction that the Brahmin is the guru—

Man dies, the sacred thread falls, and the soul departs without it.

Though men commit countless thefts, countless adulteries, utter countless falsehoods and countless words of abuse;

Though they commit countless robberies and villainies night and day against their fellow creatures;

Yet the cotton thread is spun, and the Brahmin comes to twist it.

For the ceremony they kill a goat and cook and eat it, and everybody then says, "Put on the sacred thread."

When it becomes old, it is thrown away and another is put on.

Nanak, the string does not break if it is strong.

By adoring and praising the Name honor and a true thread are obtained.

In this way a sacred thread shall be put on which will not break, and which will be fit for entrance into God's court.

---

[7] *seated in a square:* a square drawn on the ground in which the thread ceremony occurs.

Asa Ki Var, Mahala 1.

There is no string for the sexual organs (to wear), no string for women;

There is no string for the impure acts which cause your beards to be daily spat upon.

There is no string for the feet, no string for the hands,

No string for the tongue, no string for the eyes.

Without such strings the Brahmin wanders astray,

Twists strings for the neck, and puts them on others.

He takes a fee for marrying;

He pulls out a paper, and shows the fate of the wedded pair.[8]

Hear and see, you people; it is strange

That man who is mentally blind is called wise.

---

[8] *He pulls . . . pair:* shows them an astrological prediction written for the occasion, still an important part of Hindu marriage.

ETHICS

Prayer for Forgiveness

This lyrical prayer by Guru Arjan expresses the moral structure of Sikhism. God is holy and forgives those who confess their sin. The prayer ends with the worshipper assured of forgiveness.

Hear my supplication, O my Lord God,

Though I am full of millions of sins, nevertheless I am Your slave.

O You Dispeller of grief, merciful, fascinating,

Destroyer of trouble and anxiety,

I seek Your protection; protect my honor.

You are in all things, O spotless One;

You hear and behold us; You are with us all, O God;

You are the nearest of all to us.

O Lord, hear Nanak's prayer; save the slave of Your household.

You are ever omnipotent; we are poor and beggars.

O God, save us who are involved in the love of money.

Bound by covetousness and worldly love, we have committed various sins.

The Creator is distinct and free from entanglements; man obtains the fruit of his acts.

Show us kindness, You purifier of sinners; we are weary of wandering through many a womb.

Nanak represents—I am the slave of God who is the support of the soul and life.

You are great and omnipotent; my understanding is feeble.

You cherish even the ungrateful; You look equally on all.

Unfathomable is Your knowledge, O infinite Creator;

I am lowly and know nothing.

Having rejected the gem of Your name, I have amassed money;

I am a degraded and silly being.

By the commission of sin I have amassed what is very unstable and forsakes man.

Nanak has sought Your protection, O omnipotent Lord; preserve his honor.

Rag Bihagra, Mahala 5.

When I sang God's praises in the association of the saints,
He united me with Himself, although I had been separated from Him.
By ever thoroughly singing God's praises, He who is happiness itself becomes manifest.

My couch, when God accepts me as His own, is adorned by Him.
Having dismissed anxiety I am no longer anxious, and suffer no further pain.
Nanak lives beholding God and singing the praises of the Ocean of excellences.

Against the Use of Wine

Although the Sikh scriptures contain no formal listing of ethical commands, one of the firmest and most explicit moral commands of Sikhism is the prohibition of alcoholic beverages, which it shares with Islam. Notice once again the reinterpretation of an evil practice: "Make God's name your wine."

The barmaid is misery, wine is lust; man is the drinker.
The cup filled with worldly love is wrath, and it is served by pride.
The company is false and covetous, and is ruined by excess of drink.
Instead of such wine make good conduct your yeast, truth your molasses, God's name your wine;

Make merits your cakes, good conduct your clarified butter, and modesty your meat to eat.
Such things, O Nanak, are obtained by the Guru's favor; by partaking of them sins depart.

Rag Bihagra, Mahala 1.

ORGANIZATION

The Guru

This hymn by Guru Amar Das expresses the characteristic attitude of later Sikhs toward the line of the gurus. Though the *Sri Guru Granth Sahib* is not explicitly mentioned, Sikhs hearing this hymn would think that everything said about the guru applies to their *Guru Granth,* in which the soul of the guru is incarnated.

Through the Guru a few obtain divine knowledge;
He who knows God through the Guru shall be acceptable.

Through the Guru there results divine knowledge and meditation on the True One;
Through the Guru the gate of deliverance is attained.

Rag Gauri, Mahala 3.

It is only by perfect good fortune the Guru
  comes in one's way.
The true become easily absorbed in the True
  One.
On meeting the Guru the fire of avarice is
  quenched.

Through the Guru peace dwells in the heart.
Through the Guru man becomes pure, spot-
  less, and immaculate.
Through the Guru the Word which unites
  man with God is obtained.
Without the Guru everyone wanders in doubt.

Without the Name great misery is suffered.
He who is pious meditates on the Name.
On beholding the True One, true honor is
  obtained.

Whom shall we call the giver? The One God.
If He be gracious, we obtain the Word by
  which we meet Him.
May Nanak meet the beloved Guru, sing the
  True One's praises,
And becoming true be absorbed in the True
  One!

God's Power in the Sikh Community

The final shape of the Sikh community *(panth)* was established by the tenth guru, Gobind
Singh. This hymn by Guru Arjan contains a line, "Victory be ever to the society of the
saints!" which is very reminiscent of the shout used to close many Sikh services: "The
Khalsa shall rule!"

There is none beside Him,
In whose power are lords and emperors;
In whose power is the whole world;
Who has created everything.
Address your supplication to the true Guru,
That he may arrange all your affairs.

His court is the most exalted of all;
His name is the support of all the saints.
The Lord whose glory shines in every heart
Is contained in everything, and fills
  creation.
By remembering Him the abode of sorrow is
  demolished;

By remembering Him Death molests us not;
By remembering Him what is withered
  becomes green;
By remembering Him the sinking stone
  floats.

Victory be ever to the society of the saints!
God's name supports the lives of His
  servants.
Says Nanak, hear, O God, my supplication—
By the favor of the saints, grant me to dwell
  in Your name.

Rag Gauri, Mahala 5.

RITUAL

Hymn for the Installation of the *Guru Granth*

Although the content of this hymn seems unrelated to the *Guru Granth,* Sikhs in the temple sing it as the holy book is brought out in the morning and put to rest at night.

O God, this is the desire of my heart:
That You, the Treasure of mercy, the Compassionate, should make me the slave of Your saints;
That I should devote my body and soul to their service and sing God's praises with my tongue;

That I should ever abide with the saints and remember You at every breath I draw.
The Name is my sole support and wealth; from it Nanak obtains delight.

Rag Devgandhari, Mahala 5.

A Marriage Hymn

Here is a hymn typically sung at Sikh weddings. Devotion to God and devotion to one's spouse are masterfully blended. The believer is represented as the bride, with God as the groom.

The stars glitter on a clear night.
Holy men, the beloved of my Lord, are awake;
The beloved of my Lord are ever awake, and remember His name night and day.
They meditate in their hearts on His lotus feet, and forget Him not for a moment.
They renounce the sins of pride and worldly love, and efface the pain of wrong-doing.
Nanak represents, the servants of God, the dear saints are ever awake.

My couch has splendid trappings.
In my heart joy has sprung up since I heard that my Lord was approaching.

On meeting my Lord I have entered on happiness and am filled with the essence of joy and delight.
He embraced me; my sorrows fled; my soul, mind, and body all bloomed afresh.
I have obtained my heart's desires by meditating on God; the time of my union with Him I account auspicious.
Nanak testifies, when he met the Bearer of prosperity, the essence of all pleasure was prepared for him.

My companions meeting me asked me to describe my Spouse.
I was so filled with the sweets of love that I could not speak.

Rag Asa, Mahala 5.

The attributes of the Creator are deep, mysterious, and boundless; the *Vedas* have not found His limit.

She who meditates on the Lord with devotion and love, who ever sings His praises,

And is pleasing to her God, is full of all virtues and divine knowledge.

Nanak testifies that she who is dyed with the color of God's love shall be easily absorbed in Him.

When I began to sing songs of joy to God,

My friends became glad, my troubles and my enemies fled away,

My happiness and comfort increased, I rejoiced in God's name, and He Himself bestowed mercy on me.

I clung to His feet, and being ever wakeful I met Him.

Happy days came, I obtained peace with all treasures and was blended with God.

Nanak testifies that the saints of God are ever steadfast in seeking His protection.

SELECTIONS FROM THE *DASAM GRANTH*

Guru Gobind Singh's Story

Guru Gobind tells not only his own story but the story of the one soul of the line of gurus. In telling this story, he offers a stinging critique and rejection of Hinduism and Islam.[9]

I shall now tell my own history,
How God brought me into the world as I was performing penance
On the mountain of Hem Kunt,
Where the seven peaks are conspicuous.
There I performed very great austerities
And worshipped Great Death.
I performed such penance
That I became blended with God.

My father and mother had also worshipped the Unseen One,
And strove in many ways to unite themselves with Him.

The Supreme Guru was pleased
With their devotion to Him.

When God gave me the order
I assumed birth in this age.
I did not desire to come,
As my attention was fixed on God's feet.

God spoke earnestly to me,
And sent me into this world with the following orders:
"When I created this world
I first made the demons, who became enemies and oppressors.
They became intoxicated with the strength of their arms,
And ceased to worship Me, the Supreme Being.
I became angry and at once destroyed them.
In their places I established the gods.

---

[9]This and the following reading are taken from Max Macauliffe, *The Sikh Religion*, vol. 5 (Oxford: Oxford University Press, 1909), pp. 286–287, 296–300.

Dasam Granth, Vichitar Natak 6.

They also busied themselves receiving sacrifices and worship,
And called themselves supreme beings.
Shiva called himself the imperishable God.
Vishnu too declared himself to be God;
Brahma called himself the supreme Brahma,
And nobody thought Me to be God....
Brahma made the four *Vedas*
And caused all to act according to them;
But they whose love was attached to My feet renounced the *Vedas*.
They who abandoned the tenets of the *Vedas* and other books
Became devoted to Me, the supreme God.

"They who follow true religion
Shall have their sins of various kinds blotted out.
They who endure bodily suffering
And cease not to love Me shall all to go paradise.
There shall be no difference between Me and them.
They who shrink from suffering,
And, forsaking Me, adopt the way of the *Vedas* and *Smritis,*
Shall fall into the pit of hell,
And continually suffer transmigration....

"I then created Muhammad, and made him king of Arabia.

He too established a religion of his own,
Cut off the foreskins of all his followers,
And made every one repeat his name;[10]
But no one fixed the true Name in man's heart....
I have cherished you as My son,
And created you to extend My religion.
Go and spread My religion there,
And restrain the world from senseless acts."

I stood up, clasped my hands, bowed my head, and replied:
"Your religion shall prevail in the world when You assure me your assistance."

On this account God sent me;
I took birth and came into the world.
As He spoke to me so I speak unto men;
I bear no enmity to any one.
All who call me the Supreme Being shall fall into the pit of hell.
Recognize me as God's servant only:
Have no doubt whatever of this.
I am the slave of the Supreme Being,
Come to behold the wonders of the world.
I tell the world what God told me;
I will not remain silent through fear of mortals.

---

[10]*repeat his name:* in the confession, "There is no God but God, and Muhammad is God's prophet."

God as the Holy Sword

One of the most important developments in the early history of Sikhism was the shift from pacifism to militancy. This famous hymn expresses this militancy with its personification of the sword as God and its promotion of what Sikhs call the "battle for righteousness." Today, a Sikh child is baptized with water that has been stirred by a two-edged sword, and the dagger between two swords is a prominent symbol of modern Sikhism.

Dasam Granth, Vichitar Natak 6.

I bow with love and devotion to the Holy
  Sword.
Assist me that I may complete this book.
You are the Subduer of countries, the De-
  stroyer of the armies of the wicked; in the
  battlefield You greatly adorn the brave.
Your arm is unbreakable, Your brightness
  resplendent, Your radiance and splendor
  dazzle like the sun.
You bestow happiness on the good, You
  terrify the evil, You scatter sinners, and I
  seek Your protection.
Hail! Hail to the Creator of the world, the
  Savior of creation, my Cherisher, hail to
  You, O Sword!

I bow to Him who holds the arrow in His
  hand; I bow to the Fearless One;
I bow to the God of gods who is in the
  present and the future.
I bow to the Scimitar, the two-edged Sword,
  the broad-bladed sword, and the Dagger.
You, O God, always have one form;

You are always unchangeable.
I bow to the Holder of the mace,
Who diffused light through the fourteen
  worlds.
I bow to the Arrow and the Musket,
I bow to the Sword, spotless, fearless, and
  unbreakable;
I bow to the powerful Mace and Lance
To which nothing is equal.

I bow to Him who holds the discus,
Who is not made of the elements and is
  terrible.
I bow to Him with the strong teeth;
I bow to Him who is supremely powerful,
I bow to the Arrow and the Cannon that
  destroy the enemy.
I bow to the Sword and the Rapier that
  destroy evil.
I bow to all weapons called Shastar, which
  may be held.
I bow to all weapons called Astar, which may
  be hurled or discharged.

GLOSSARY

Adi Granth [AH-dee GRAHNTH] "The First/
  Original Book"; the main scripture of Sikhism,
  consisting primarily of the words of the first five
  gurus; also known as the *Sri Guru Granth Sahib*
  and the *Guru Granth.*

chaur [chowr] a horsehair, yak-hair, or peacock-
  feather fan used to venerate the *Adi Granth;* it is
  waved over the scripture to cool the book and
  repel flies.

Dasam Granth [DAH-sum GRAHNTH] "Tenth
  Book"; secondary scripture consisting mostly of
  the words of the tenth guru, Gobind Singh.

granthi [GRAHN-thee] an official reader of the *Adi
  Granth.*

gutka [GUHT-kuh] an anthology, for private use, of
  the most important passages from the *Adi Granth*
  and a few passages from the *Dasam Granth.*

janam-sakhis [JAH-num SAH-kees] "birth stories";
  traditional narratives about the lives of the gurus,
  especially Nanak.

Japji [JAHP-jee] a poem by Guru Nanak considered
  to express the essence of Sikhism; it is the first
  main section of the *Adi Granth.*

Mahala [ma-HAH-luh] a term in the *Adi Granth*
  used to differentiate the compositions of the first
  five gurus.

Mul Mantar [mool MAHN-tahr] "Root Formula";
  the opening confession of faith of the *Japji.*

ragas [RAH-guhs] the thirty-nine basic "tunes" on
  which melodies used for singing the *Adi Granth*
  are based.

vak lao [vahk low] "taking [God's] word" by opening the *Adi Granth* at random and beginning
  the reading from the top of the left-hand page.

QUESTIONS FOR STUDY AND DISCUSSION

1. Describe the main teachings of the *Adi Granth*. Which do you see as most important and why?
2. "Of all the religions of the world, Sikhism has the best claim to be a 'religion of the book.' " Do you agree or disagree? Why?
3. Which attitudes, teachings, and practices of Sikhism seem to resemble Hinduism? Which seem to resemble Islam? Which seem to be distinct?
4. How does Sikh tradition, as expressed in its scriptures, vary between inclusiveness toward other faiths and exclusiveness?
5. Describe the shift from pacifism to militarism in Sikh tradition. What similar shifts can you think of in other religions?

SUGGESTIONS FOR FURTHER READING

PRIMARY READINGS

Max A. Macauliffe, *The Sikh Religion: Its Gurus, Sacred Writings and Authors*, 6 vols. Oxford: Oxford University Press, 1909; reprinted New Delhi: S. Chand, 1963. Provides full selections from the Sikh scriptures, with good, literal translations.

W. H. McLeod, *Textual Sources for the Study of Sikhism*. Totowa, NJ: Barnes & Noble, 1984. An excellent anthology of Sikh scriptures and more recent writings.

C. Shackle and A. Singh Mandair, eds., *Teachings of the Sikh Gurus: Selections from the Sikh Scriptures*. London and New York: Routledge, 2005. Fresh translations of important scriptures, with a concise introduction to the origins of Sikhism and its scriptures.

SECONDARY READINGS

Gurinder Singh Mann, *The Making of Sikh Scripture*. Oxford: Oxford University Press, 2001. This discussion of the origin and meaning of Sikh scripture challenges many traditional understandings.

H. McLeod, "The Sikh Scriptures." In H. McLeod, *Evolution of the Sikh Community*. Oxford: Clarendon Press, 1976, pp. 59–82. A succinct survey of the origin, development, and use of Sikh scriptures, with special emphasis on textual problems.

P. Singh, *The Bhagats of the Guru Granth Sahib: Sikh Self-Definition and the Bhagat Bani*. New York: Oxford University Press, 2003. An analysis of the parts of the *Guru Granth Sahib* drawn from non-Sikh poetry of the time.

P. Singh, *The Guru Granth Sahib: Canon, Meaning and Authority*. New Delhi: Oxford University Press, 2000. Clear, comprehensive, and controversial treatment of the origin, development, and use of the *Adi Granth*.

COMPANION WEBSITE

Visit the *Anthology of World Scriptures* companion website at **www.thomsonedu.com** for learning tools such as map explorations, flashcards of glossary terms, learning objectives, chapter practice quizzes, links to other websites for learning and research, and chapter summaries in PowerPoint® format.

CHAPTER SIX

Confucianism

Reading by the Moon

Zu Luo, one of China's twenty-four paragons of filial piety and a disciple of the historical Confucius, studies by the light of the moon. Here he is shown in a print by Yoshitoshi Taiso (1839–1892) carrying rice to his parents while studying. (*Copyright © 2005 Asian Art & Archaeology, Inc./CORBIS.*)

- In a high school in Shanghai, China, students read and consider the meaning of the main Confucian book, the *Analects*. They read aloud, listen to their teacher's lecture, and discuss its meaning for China today. This study of Confucian scripture is undertaken by many Chinese throughout the world, but its recent revival in communist China heralds the return of classic Chinese values.

- In Hong Kong, a solitary sage studies ancient Chinese poems. He pauses to reflect on their meaning, especially on how they relate to his Confucian beliefs. After reflecting, he writes out the passage calligraphically. He is practicing self-cultivation toward becoming a "superior man," the highest goal of the Confucian tradition, and his study of the ancient classics is a key ingredient in bringing about this perfection.

- In Los Angeles, a sociologist researches the extraordinary success of Chinese American students in the University of California system. Her conclusion: The social and intellectual values of these students' Confucian tradition—family loyalty, love of learning, self-cultivation, all values of the Confucian scriptures—have produced a remarkable academic achievement.

- In Beijing, the celebration of the birth of Confucius was the biggest in the People's Republic of China since 1949. The festivities for his 2,556th birthday on September 28, 2005, were broadcast nationwide, and more than 2,500 people, including many high-ranking Communist Party members, made a pilgrimage to Confucius' birthplace in Shandong Province. The leaders of the party are seeking to use Confucian values to counteract social problems such as rising social incivility and the widespread "money first" mentality.

INTRODUCTION

Confucianism is the system of religion and philosophy begun by the sage Kung Fu-tzu ("Master Kung"), known to the Western world as Confucius (551–479 B.C.E.). Although his teachings had little impact during his lifetime, they were kept alive by his disciples. In the second century B.C.E., Confucianism became the official religion of China. Since then, it has been closely identified with the essence of traditional Chinese culture, forming the basis of Chinese education, ethics, and statecraft and influencing some of the lands surrounding China, especially Korea, Taiwan, and Japan. In Taiwan, study of the Confucian books is required in schools. No longer the state religion of China since the communist takeover in 1949, Confucianism has experienced a rebirth of sorts in other parts of Asia and now is being revived in China as well. It teaches a personal and social morality that stresses the practice of key virtues such as filiality, humaneness, propriety, and faithfulness. Its full and well-defined scriptural canon, reflecting the Chinese love of books and learning, provides excellent insight into Confucianism.

Overview of Structure

Confucianists call their earliest scriptures Classics, or **Ching** [jing]. In Chinese as in English, the word *classic* suggests a literary work that embodies principles accepted as authoritative over a long time up through the present. The Confucian canon is divided into two parts: the *Five Classics* (*Wu Ching*) and the later *Four Books*

(*Ssu Shu*). The *Five Classics* form the foundation of the later works written by Confucius and his followers. Hundreds of years before the birth of Confucius, these early books were known, respected, and authoritative. According to some lists, they number as many as thirteen, but the best-known list has five books. Confucianists believe that Confucius edited all these works and wrote commentaries for some. Though this claim is doubtful as fact, most scholars do hold that the early Confucian tradition played a strong role in shaping and transmitting these books when it took them into its canon. Also, the traditional claim expresses the high value the Confucian tradition placed on the ancient classics. As Confucius himself once said, "It is by the *Poetry* that the mind is aroused; by the *Rites* that the character is established; by the *Music* [now lost, but perhaps incorporated in part into the *Rites*] that the finish is received" (*Analects* 8.8).

The first and oldest of the *Five Classics* is the **I Ching** [ee jing], the "Classic of Changes," a diviner's manual that developed over several hundred years beginning in the early part of the Chou Dynasty (1120–221 B.C.E.). The book contains pairs of eight basic trigrams (combinations of three horizontal lines) that believers have used to provide information about the future and recommend a course of action to meet it. The *I Ching* is built on the **yin-yang,** great interactive cosmic forces such as passivity and activity, darkness and light, and other opposing pairs. This cosmology has given the book great popularity among educated Chinese. In Confucian history, it was also sometimes used philosophically, especially because of the "wings," or commentary appended to the hexagrams. Of all Chinese literature, the *I Ching* has been the most often translated into English and other modern European languages because of its cosmological appeal rather than as a book of divination; currently, more than twenty translations are in print. In China, however, the religio-magical use has tended to predominate. (This book is important for Taoists as well and is a prominent part of their canon.)

The second of the *Five Classics* is the *Shu Ching* [shoo jing], the "Classic of History/Documents." It consists of royal chronicles, narratives, decrees, and the like from the early Chou period, which Confucius looked on as an ideal age. Much of its content is later, forged additions.

The third of the *Five Classics* is the *Shih Ching* [shir jing], the "Classic of Poetry." It consists of **305** relatively short poems dating from the tenth to the seventh centuries B.C.E., all set to music. These songs, dealing with love, rituals, family relations, and government, were sung in worship services, especially in sacrifice to ancestors. By the time of Confucius, the *Poetry* had become the leading model of Chinese literary expression. The writings of Confucius are filled with allusions to it.

Fourth is the *Ch'un ch'iu* [chun chwee], the "Spring and Autumn Annals." The expression *spring and autumn* refers to the entire year, not just to those two seasons. The *Annals* is a sober and rather reliable chronological account of events in the state of Lu, Confucius' home state, from 720 to 480 B.C.E. Its ideas of respect for law and custom in government are only implicitly Confucian.

Fifth is the *Li Chi* [lee kee], the "Classic of Rites." This collection features rituals and ceremonies of ancient China, both public and private. The *Li Chi* was probably collected in the second century B.C.E. The word **li** can be variously translated "ritual," "propriety," or "manners," and all these ideas are important in the *Li Chi*.

The *Four Books* of the Confucian canon are built on what Confucius and his followers saw as the main teachings of the earlier *Five Classics*. First among them is the

Analects (Lun yu) of Confucius. The *Analects* (collected sayings) is by far the most important text in the history of Confucianism and our most reliable source for knowledge of Confucius himself. It contains sayings of the Master and occasional anecdotes about him as remembered by his disciples and recorded after his death. The *Analects* contains 12,700 characters (ideograms) in twenty short books. Like most other collections of sayings, the *Analects* is loosely organized and repetitive at times. Yet it treats well all the important concepts of the Confucian tradition: the cardinal virtues of humanity, propriety, respect for parents; becoming a superior man; and proper government.

The second of the *Four Books* is the *Mencius (Meng-tzu),* named for its author, who, after Confucius, was the most significant figure in Confucian tradition. Mencius (ca. 371–ca. 289 B.C.E.) died in the third century B.C.E., and his disciples compiled this book after his death. More than twice as long as the *Analects,* the *Mencius* has well-developed treatments of several important topics, especially proper government. Mencius saw filiality as the greatest of the virtues and held strongly to the teaching of innate human goodness.

Third is the *Great Learning (Ta hsueh),* a short book that is an excerpt on virtuous government from the *Li Chi.* Its first, short chapter is held to be the work of Confucius. The next ten chapters are a commentary on the first by Tseng-tzu, one of Confucius' disciples. The *Great Learning* teaches that rulers govern by example. If the ruler is morally good, so will be his government and his subjects. If the ruler is not good, his subjects will incline to evil, and his rule, along with the Mandate of Heaven to govern, will collapse.

Fourth is the *Doctrine of the Mean (Chung yung).* Like the *Great Learning,* it was originally a chapter in the *Li Chi.* "Mean" is a broad concept embracing many aspects of virtue: moderation, right conduct, decorum, and sincerity. The good Confucianist is expected to "keep to the middle" between emotional and intellectual extremes. It is in the middle that the superior man is formed and comes into harmony with the **Tao** [dow], the cosmic "Way" of life. This book was important in the neo-Confucian movement that arose in the twelfth century.

Contemporary Use

The official use of Confucian scriptures today flows from their adoption as the state literature of China. For more than 2,000 years, all education was based either directly or indirectly on them. The first books that boys studied and memorized in elementary school were the *Four Books,* especially the *Analects* and *Great Learning.* The rigorous civil service exams that allowed a young man to become a government official at the county, provincial, or national level were also based on the scriptures. Each county in China had a school where the scriptural lore was taught. Men who became unusually expert in the scriptures as applied to government were known as *mandarins;* the last known mandarin died in 1991. The imperial university in Beijing had five professorial posts in Confucian scripture that were designed to promote the excellence of the whole system. The personal intention of Confucius was thus fulfilled, not during his lifetime but after it, when the government of China came to be based on his leading ideas.

Confucius' ideal of providing education to all who desired and could master it fell by the wayside as this training for government became limited to the upper classes who could pay for it. Although only a small percentage of the population of China has been able to read, the influence of the Confucian scriptures through oral teaching and general cultural transmission has been so thorough that the social relationships and cultural attitudes of most Chinese have become essentially Confucian. It is often remarked that regardless of the specific religion of the Chinese—Buddhist, Taoist, Muslim, Christian, whatever—they are also Confucian. Thus, largely through the influence of its scriptures, Confucianism has taken its place as the leading historic religion of China. Now that communist values are waning in the People's Republic of China, educators are returning to Confucian scriptures to provide a core moral education, especially the values of civility and obedience to law.

The Confucian approach to scripture is almost exclusively cognitive. Confucius and his followers rejected mysticism for the most part, and in subsequent centuries, the sometimes bitter struggle with the more mystical Taoist tradition reinforced this cognitive orientation. Teacher and student discuss scriptural meaning in an orderly, rational way. The individual scholar often practices "quiet sitting." This solitary study involves recitation of the text, meditation on its meaning, and calligraphic reproduction of the text itself.

The literary style of the Confucian canon influences this use. Confucian and Taoist scriptures share a style known as **wen-yen** (roughly translated as "formal-classical"). This style is known for brief, even compressed composition. Each Chinese ideogram character must be considered carefully to bring out the meaning. This style is one reason Confucianists have generated a massive commentarial literature that seeks to shed more light on the canon itself. In the Confucian tradition, these commentaries have become accepted works in understanding the canon. Moreover, this formal-classical style means that translations of Confucian and Taoist scriptures often vary greatly among themselves, more so than translations of the scriptures of other religions. This compressed style invites the reader of both the Chinese original and the English translation to meditate carefully and deeply about its meaning. (For an example of differing contemporary translations of Chinese scripture, see pages 164–165.)

Historical Origin and Development

The Confucian canon has not come down to us in an easily traceable way. The *Analects* and the *Mencius* were probably first written down in the centuries following the deaths of their authors. The *Great Learning* and *Doctrine of the Mean* were separated from the *Classic of Rites* and made independent books. Then in 213 B.C.E., Emperor Shih Huang-ti, a radical innovator opposed to ancient traditions, ordered all Confucian books to be destroyed. This famous "Burning of the Books" resulted in the loss of several versions of the Confucian books, although most of them survived in some form. The Confucian canon was reedited and republished under the next dynasty, the Han (206 B.C.E.–220 C.E.). During this dynasty, Confucianism was made the official state religion, and the Confucian canon was officially adopted as the basis of thought and conduct—indeed, of all official Chinese culture. In the twelfth century, the *Four Books* were recognized as an independent collection, and they soon became more central to Confucian life than the older *Five Classics,* which came to be interpreted through the *Four Books.* State sanction for the Confucian scriptures lasted until 1905, when the government of China abolished the civil service system based on the canon.

HISTORY

The Character of Confucius

The *Analects* depicts Confucius as a model of the "superior man." By following his own teaching, he became an example to his followers. The first passage is Confucius' own summary of his progress in self-cultivation. The second describes key elements in his character. The third gives fascinating detail about some of his daily habits.[1]

#3 virtue dependent on education

[2.4] The Master said, "At fifteen, I had my mind focused on learning. At thirty, I stood firm. At forty, I had no doubts. At fifty, I knew the decrees of Heaven.[2] At sixty, my ear was an obedient organ for the reception of truth. At seventy, I could follow what my heart desired, without transgressing what was right."

[7.1] The Master said, "I am a transmitter and not a maker. I believe in and love the ancients, and I venture to compare myself with our old P'eng."[3]

The Master said, "The silent treasuring up of knowledge; learning without tiring; and instructing others without being wearied—which one of these things belongs to me?"

#5 The Master said, "Leaving virtue without proper cultivation; not thoroughly discussing what is learned; not being able to move toward righteousness of which a knowledge is gained; and not being able to change what is not good—these are the things which cause me much concern."

When the Master was unoccupied with business, his manner was easy, and he looked pleased.

[5] The Master said, "My decline is extreme. For a long time, I have not dreamed, as I used to do, that I saw the duke of Chou."[4]

The Master said, "Let the will be set on the path of duty. Let every attainment in what is good be firmly grasped. Let perfect virtue be followed. Let relaxation and enjoyment be found in the arts." *wen*

The Master said, "From the man bringing his bundle of dried meat for my teaching, or more than that, I have never refused instruction to anyone."[5]

The Master said, "I do not open up the truth to one who is not eager to get knowledge. Nor do I help out any of those who are not anxious to explain themselves. When I have presented one corner of a subject to any one, and he cannot from it learn the other three, I do not repeat my lesson."

When the Master was eating by the side of a mourner, he never ate to the full. He did not sing on the same day in which he had been weeping....

[19] The Master said, "I am not one who was born in the possession of knowledge. I am one who is fond of antiquity,[6] and earnest in seeking knowledge there."

---

[1]All selections from the *Analects* and the *Mencius* are taken, with editing, from James Legge, trans., *The Chinese Classics* (Oxford: Oxford University Press, 1893).
[2]*decrees* (or "mandates") *of Heaven:* understood today by most Confucianists as the working of Nature in people and events, not primarily as the working of God.
[3]*old P'eng:* a sage from ancient times.

[4]*duke of Chou:* in Confucius' view, one of the greatest of the early Chinese sage-kings.
[5]*dried meat:* the smallest possible payment for instruction. Confucianism has believed that learning and self-cultivation should be open to all men who desire it.
[6]*antiquity:* Confucianists emphasize the Chinese custom of seeking direction from the ancient writings.

Analects 2.4; 7.1–9, 19–24; 10.1–3, 8–12.

[20] The subjects on which the Master did not talk were extraordinary things,[7] feats of strength, disorder, and spiritual beings.

The Master said, "When I walk along with two others, they may serve me as my teachers. I will select their good qualities and follow them, their bad qualities and avoid them."

The Master said, "Heaven produced the virtue that is in me. What can Hwan T'ui do to me?"[8]

The Master said, "Do you think, my disciples, that I have any secrets? I conceal nothing from you. Everything I do is shown to you, my disciples. That is my way."

There were four things that the Master taught—literature, ethics, devotion of soul, and truthfulness.

[10.1] Confucius, in his village, looked simple and sincere, and as if he were not able to speak. When he was in the prince's ancestral temple, or in the (governmental) court, he spoke minutely on every point, but cautiously.

When he was on duty at court, in speaking with the great officers of the lower grade he spoke freely, but in a straightforward manner. In speaking with those of the higher grade, he did so mildly, but precisely. When the ruler was present, his manner displayed respectful uneasiness; it was serious, but self-possessed.

When the prince called on him to receive a visitor, his appearance changed, and his legs seemed to move forward with difficulty. He inclined himself to the other officers among whom he stood, moving his left or right arm, as their position required, but he kept the skirts of his robe evenly adjusted. He hastened forward, with his arms like the wings of a bird. When the guest had left, he would report to the prince, "The visitor is not looking back anymore." . . .

[8] He liked to have his rice finely cleaned, and to have his minced meat cut quite small. He did not eat rice which had been injured by heat or damp and turned sour, nor fish or meat which was spoiled. He did not eat what was discolored, or what was of a bad flavor, nor anything which was badly cooked, or was not in season. He did not eat meat which was not cut properly, nor what was served without its proper sauce. Though there might be a large quantity of meat, he would not allow what he took to exceed the due proportion for the rice.

Only in wine did he have no limit for himself, but he did not allow himself to be confused by it. He did not partake of wine and dried meat bought in the market. He was never without ginger when he ate. He did not eat much. When he had been assisting at the prince's sacrifice, he did not keep overnight the meat that he received. He did not keep longer than three days the meat of his family sacrifice. When eating, he did not converse. When in bed, he did not speak. Although his food might be coarse rice and vegetable soup, he would offer a little of it in sacrifice with a serious, respectful air.

If his mat was not straight, he did not sit on it.

[10] When the villagers were drinking together, after those who carried walking staffs left, he went out immediately. When the villagers were going through their ceremonies to drive away diseases, he put on his court robes and stood on the eastern steps.

When he was sending complimentary inquiries to anyone in another state, he bowed twice as he escorted the messenger away. When Chi K'ang sent him a present of medicine, he bowed and received it, saying, "I do not know it. I dare not taste it."

The stable burned down when he was at court. When he returned he asked, "Has any person been hurt?" He did not ask about the horses.

---

[7] *extraordinary things:* strange, perhaps supernatural, events in nature.
[8] *Hwan T'ui:* an army officer who had attempted to kill Confucius.

TEACHING

The Way

The "Way" (Tao) is an ancient idea in Chinese tradition. In Confucianism, where it forms one of the basic teachings, it is understood as the moral way of Heaven to which the emperor as the Son of Heaven should aspire. In this selection, the relationship between the Way and good government is brought out.

Confucius said, "When [the Way of] good government prevails in the empire, ceremonies, music, and punitive military expeditions proceed from the Son of Heaven. When bad government prevails in the empire, ceremonies, music, and punitive military expeditions proceed from the princes. When these things proceed from the princes, as a rule, they most often lose their power in ten generations. When they proceed from the great officers of the princes, as a rule, they lose their power in five generations. When the subsidiary ministers of the great officers hold in their grasp the orders of the state, as a rule, they lose their power in three generations. When the Way and right principles prevail in the kingdom, government will not be in the hands of the great officers. When right principles prevail in the kingdom, there will be no discussions among the common people."

Analects 16.2.

The Goodness of Human Nature

Although Confucius did not discuss the question of goodness and evil in the human personality, Mencius took up this topic. He argued the optimistic idea that all people are by nature good. Therefore, the ruler must only be good himself and bring out the innate goodness of his subjects to establish his rule. In this selection, the philosopher Kao Tzu serves as a foil for the thoughts of Mencius.

The philosopher Kao said, "Man's nature is like the willow tree, and righteousness is like a cup or a bowl. Fashioning benevolence and righteousness out of man's nature is like the making of cups and bowls from the willow."

Mencius replied, "Can you, by leaving untouched the nature of the willow, make cups and bowls with it? You must do violence and injury to the willow before you can make cups and bowls with it. According to your principles you must in the same way do violence and injury to humanity in order to fashion from it benevolence and righteousness! Your words would certainly lead all men to reckon benevolence and righteousness to be calamities."

The philosopher Kao said, "Man's nature is like water whirling round in a corner. Open a passage for it to the east and it will flow to the east;

Mencius 6.1.1–4, 6.

open a passage for it to the west and it will flow to the west. Man's nature is indifferent to good and evil, just as the water is indifferent to the east and west."

Mencius replied, "Water indeed will flow indifferently to the east or west, but will it flow indifferently up or down? The tendency of man's nature to good is like the tendency of water to flow downwards. All people have this tendency to good, just as all water flows downwards. Now by striking water and causing it to go up, you may make it go over your forehead, and, by damming and leading it, you may force it up a hill, but are such movements according to the nature of water? It is the force applied which causes them. When men are made to do what is not good, their nature is dealt with in this way." . . .

The philosopher Kao said, "To enjoy food and delight in colors is natural. Benevolence is internal and not external; righteousness is external and not internal."

Mencius asked him, "On what grounds do you say that benevolence is internal and righteousness external?"

He replied, "There is a man older than I, and I give honor to his age. It is not that there is first in me a principle of such reverence to age. It is just as when there is a white (-haired) man, and I consider him white—according as he is so externally to me. On this account, I pronounce of righteousness that it is external."

Mencius said, "There is no difference between our pronouncing of a white horse to be white and our pronouncing a white (-haired) man to be white. But is there no difference between the regard with which we acknowledge the age of an old horse and that with which we acknowledge the age of an old man? And what is it which is called righteousness? The fact of a man's being old? Or the fact of our giving honor to his age?"

Kao said, "There is my younger brother—I love him. But the younger brother of a man of Ts'in I do not love. The feeling is determined by me, and therefore I say that benevolence is internal. On the other hand, I give honor to an old

man of Ts'oo, and I also give honor to an old man of my own people. The feeling is determined by the age, and therefore I say that righteousness is external."

Mencius answered him, "Our enjoyment of meat roasted by a man of Ts'in does not differ from our enjoyment of meat roasted by ourselves. Thus, what you insist on takes place also in the case of such things; will you say likewise that our enjoyment of a roast is external?" . . .

Mencius said, "From the feelings proper to it, human nature is constituted for the practice of what is good. This is what I mean in saying that human nature is good. If men do what is not good, the blame cannot be imputed to their natural powers. The feeling of sympathy belongs to all men; so does that of shame and dislike, of reverence and respect, and of approving and disapproving. The feeling of sympathy implies the principle of benevolence; that of shame and dislike, the principle of righteousness; that of reverence and respect, the principle of propriety; and that of approving and disapproving, the principle of knowledge. Benevolence, righteousness, propriety, and knowledge are not infused into us from without. We are certainly furnished with them. And a different view is simply from lack of reflection. Hence it is said: 'Seek and you will find them. Neglect and you will lose them.' Men differ from one another in regard to them . . ., and it is because they cannot carry out fully their natural powers. It is said in the *Book of Poetry*:

> 'Heaven, in producing mankind,
> Gave them their various faculties and
>   relations with their specific laws;
> These are the invariable rules of nature of all
>   to hold,
> And all love this admirable virtue.' "

"Confucius said, 'The maker of this ode knew indeed the principle of our nature!' We may thus see that every faculty and relation must have its law, and since there are invariable rules for all to hold, they consequently love this admirable virtue."

ETHICS

The Virtues of the Superior Man

Confucius taught self-cultivation in knowledge and virtue. When one reaches moral and intellectual maturity, he is a "superior man." The Chinese phrase for "superior man," **chun-tzu** [jun-tzoo], literally means "prince's son," but Confucius taught that by education even a common man could become superior. (The noninclusive language is intentional— women were not expected or encouraged to pursue this self-cultivation.) Neo-Confucianism applies these passages to the closely related goal of becoming a sage.

[1.1] The Master said, "Is it not pleasant to learn with a constant perseverance? Is it not delightful to have friends coming from far away? Is he not a man of complete virtue who feels no discomposure though men may take no note of him?"

The philosopher Yu said, "Few are those who, being filial and fraternal, are fond of offending their superiors. There have been none who, not liking to offend their superiors, have been fond of stirring up confusion. The superior man pays attention to the foundation. That being established, all practical courses naturally grow up. Filiality and fraternal submission—are they not the root of all benevolent actions?"

The Master said, "Fine words and a sly appearance are seldom associated with true virtue."

The philosopher Tsang said, "I daily examine myself on three points: whether I have been faithful in transacting business for others; whether I have been sincere in dealing with friends; whether I have mastered and practiced the instructions of my teacher." ...

[6] The Master said, "A youth, when at home, should be filial, and away from home he should be respectful to his elders. He should be earnest and truthful. He should overflow in love to all, and cultivate the friendship of good people. When he has time and opportunity, after the performance of these things, he should employ them in the arts." Wen

Tsze-hsia said, "If a man withdraws his mind from the love of beauty, and applies it as sincerely to the love of the virtuous; if, in serving his parents, he can exert his utmost strength; if, in serving his prince, he can devote his life; if, in his dealings with his friends, his words are sincere—although men say that he has not learned, I will certainly say that he has."

The Master said, "If the scholar is not serious, he will not call forth any veneration, and his learning will not be solid. Hold faithfulness and sincerity as first principles. Have no friends not equal to yourself. When you have faults, do not fear to abandon them."

The philosopher Tsang said, "Let there be a careful attention to perform the funeral rites for parents, and let them be followed when parents are gone with the ceremonies of sacrifice. Then the virtue of the people will resume its proper excellence." ...

[14] The Master said, "He who aims to be a man of complete virtue in his food does not seek to gratify his appetite, nor in his dwelling place does he seek ease. He is earnest in what he does, and careful in his speech. He frequents the company of men of principle so that he may be rectified. Such a person may indeed be said to love learning."

[15.17] The Master said, "The superior man considers righteousness to be essential in everything. He performs it according to the rules of

Analects 1.1–4, 6–9, 14; 15.17–23.

propriety. He brings it forth in humility. He completes it with sincerity. This is indeed a superior man.''

The Master said, ''The superior man is distressed by his lack of ability. He is not distressed by his lack of fame.''

The Master said, ''The superior man dislikes the thought of his name not being mentioned after his death.''

[20] The Master said, ''What the superior man seeks is in himself. What the inferior man seeks is in others.''

The Master said, ''The superior man is dignified, but does not wrangle. He is sociable, but not a partisan.''

The Master said, ''The superior man does not promote a man simply on account of his words, nor does he put aside good words because of the man.''

Tsze-kung asked, ''Is there one word which may serve as a rule of practice for all one's life?'' The Master said, ''Is not reciprocity [*shu*] such a word? What you do not want done to yourself, do not do to others.''

Benevolence

Benevolence (**jen** [ren]) is the chief Confucian virtue. It denotes humaneness, fellow feeling, even love; in this translation, it is rendered as ''virtue.'' Confucianists, especially those aspiring to sagehood, train themselves in benevolence by reflecting on their lives in the light of the scriptures. *Human-heartedness*

#5

The Master said, ''Virtuous manners make a neighborhood excellent. If a man in selecting a residence does not choose one where such manners prevail, how can he be wise?''

The Master said, ''Those without virtue cannot remain long either in a condition of poverty and hardship, or in a condition of enjoyment. The virtuous rest in virtue; the wise desire virtue.''

The Master said, ''It is only the [truly] virtuous man who can love, or who can hate, others.''

The Master said, ''If the will is set on virtue, there will be no practice of wickedness.''

[5] The Master said, ''Men desire riches and honors. If they cannot be obtained in the proper way, they should not be held. Poverty and a low condition are what men dislike. If it cannot be obtained in the proper way, they should not be avoided. If a superior man abandons virtue, how can he fulfill the requirements of that name? The superior man does not, even for the space of a single meal, act contrary to virtue. In moments of haste, he clings to it. In times of danger, he clings to it.''

The Master said, ''I have not seen a person who loved virtue, or one who hated what was not virtuous. He who loved virtue would esteem nothing above it. He who hated what is not virtuous would practice virtue in such a way that he would not allow anything that is not virtuous to approach his person. Is any one able for one day to apply his strength to virtue? I have not seen the case in which his strength would be sufficient. If there might be any such case, I have not seen it.''

Analects 4.1–6.

The Actions and Attitudes of Filiality

Filiality (**hsiao** [syow]), translated as "filial piety" in the older literature, is reverence for one's living ancestors and extends to worship of one's dead ancestors. The *Classic of Rites* passage goes into great detail in laying down rules for proper filial conduct. It stresses deference, obedience, and faithfulness to one's parents.[9] In the *Analects* passage, Confucius stresses not only the actions of filiality but much more the attitude with which these acts are carried out. This attitude must be one of piety, the genuine reverence implied by hsiao.

[*Classic of Rites* 10.1] The sovereign king orders the chief minister to send down his lessons of virtue to the millions of the people....

[4] After getting properly dressed [in the morning], sons and their wives should go to his parents.[10] When they arrive, with bated breath and gentle voice they should ask if their parents' clothes are too warm or too cold, whether their parents are ill or pained or uncomfortable in any part. If they are, the sons should proceed reverently to stroke and scratch the place. They should in the same way, going before or following after, help and support his parents in leaving or entering the apartment. In bringing in the basin for them to wash, the younger will carry the stand and the elder the water. They will ask to be allowed to pour out the water, and when the washing is concluded, they will hand the parents the towel. They will ask whether they want anything, and then respectfully bring it. All this they will do with an appearance of pleasure to make the parents feel at ease.

They should bring gruel, thick or thin, spirits or juice, soup with vegetables, beans, wheat, spinach, rice, millet, maize, and glutinous millet—whatever the parents wish, in fact. They should bring dates, chestnuts, sugar and honey to sweeten their dishes; the ordinary or the large-leaved violets, leaves of elm-trees, fresh or dry, and the most soothing rice-water to lubricate them; and fat and oil to enrich them. The parents will be sure to taste them, and when they have done so, the young people should withdraw....

From the time that sons receive an official appointment [to government service], they and their father occupy different parts of their residence. But at dawn, the son will visit them, and express his affection by the offer of pleasant delicacies. At sunrise he will retire, and he and his father will attend to their different duties. At sundown, the son will pay his evening visit in the same way....

[10] While his parents are both alive, at their regular meals, morning and evening, the eldest son and his wife will encourage them to eat everything. They themselves will eat what is left. When the father is dead, and the mother still alive, the eldest son should wait upon her at her meals. The wives of the other sons will do with what is left as in the former case. The children should have the sweet, soft, and oily things that are left.

When sons and their wives are ordered to do anything by his parents, they should immediately respond and reverently do it. When going forward

---

[9]Taken, with editing, from James Legge, trans., *The Sacred Books of China: The Texts of Confucianism*, part 3, *Sacred Books of the East*, vol. 27 (Oxford: Oxford University Press, 1885), pp. 449–457.

[10]The passage presupposes that one's parents have an apartment or room in one's house, typically the case in traditional China.

Classic of Rites 10.1, 4, 7, 10–11, 13–15; *Analects* 2.5–7; 4.18–21; 13.18.

or backward, or turning round, they should be careful and serious. While going out or coming in, while bowing or walking, they should not presume to belch, sneeze, cough, yawn or stretch, to stand on one foot, to lean against anything, or to look sideways. They should not dare to spit or sniffle, nor if it is cold to put on more clothes, nor if they itch anywhere to scratch themselves. Unless for reverent attention to something, they should not presume to bare their [parents'] shoulders or chest. Unless it is in wading, they should not hold up their clothes. They should not display the inside of their clothing. They should not allow the spittle or snivel of the parents to be seen. They should ask permission to rinse away any dirt on their caps or belts, to wash their clothes that are dirty with lye that has been prepared for the purpose, and to stitch together any tear....

Sons and sons' wives who are filial and reverential should not refuse or delay carrying out any order from his parents. When the parents give them anything to eat or drink that they do not like, they will nevertheless taste it and wait for their further orders. When their parents give them clothes that are not to their liking, they will put them on and wait in the same way. If the parents give them something to do but then employ someone else to take their place, although they do not like the arrangement, they will let that other person do it.

When sons and their wives have not been filial and reverential, the parents should not be angry and resentful with them but should try to instruct them. If they will not receive instruction, parents should then be angry with them. If that anger does no good, they can then drive out the son and send the wife away, but they must not publicly show why they have treated them so.

[15] If a parent has a fault, the son should admonish him with bated breath, a mild appearance, and a gentle voice. If the admonition does not take effect, the son will be more reverential and more filial; if the father seems pleased, the son will repeat the admonition. If the father should be displeased with this, rather than allow him to commit an offense against anyone in the

neighborhood or countryside, the son should strongly protest. If the parent is angry and more displeased and beats him until his blood flows, the son should not presume to be angry and resentful; rather, he should be even more reverential and more filial.

[*Analects* 2.5] Mang asked what filiality was. The Master said, "It is not being disobedient." Soon after, as Fan Ch'ih was driving him, the Master told him, saying, "Mang-sun asked me what filiality was, and I answered him, 'Not being disobedient.'" Fan Ch'ih said, "What did you mean?" The Master replied, "That parents, when alive, should be served according to propriety; that, when dead, they should be buried according to propriety; and that they should be sacrificed to according to propriety."

Mang Wu asked what filiality was. The Master said, "Do not make your parents anxious about anything else than your being sick."

Tsze-yu asked what filiality was. The Master said, "Filial piety nowadays means the support of one's parents. But dogs and horses likewise are able to do something in the way of support. Without reverence, what is there to distinguish the one support given from the other?"...

[4.18] The Master said, "In serving his parents, a son may protest to them, but gently. If he sees that they do not incline to follow his advice, he shows an increased degree of reverence but does not abandon his purpose. Should they punish him, he does not allow himself to murmur."

The Master said, "While his parents are alive, the son should not leave his home area to live far away. If he does go away, he must have a fixed place to which he goes."[11]

[20] The Master said, "If the son for three years [after his father's death] does not alter from the way of his father, he may be called filial."

The Master said, "The age of one's parents should always be remembered, as a reason for joy and for fear."...

---

[11]*a fixed place:* so his parents know where he is.

[13.18] The duke of Sheh informed Confucius, "Some among us here may be called upright in their conduct. If their father stole a sheep, they will witness to the fact." Confucius said, "Among us, in our part of the country, those who are upright are different. The father conceals the misconduct of the son, and the son conceals the misconduct of the father. Uprightness is to be found in this."

Propriety

Li, "propriety," can also be translated as "ritual correctness" or "good manners." This selection highlights the traditional Confucian connection between propriety in the rites and in everyday life. In typically Confucian style, the *Classic of Poetry* is quoted to illustrate the point. Confucian rituals carried out in the temples of Korea, Taiwan, and other lands still keep to the meticulous care prescribed here. Just as important, emphasis on li has given Chinese peoples their highly developed sense of politeness.

The Master said, "If a man lacks the virtues proper to humanity [*jen*], what has he to do with the rites of propriety? If a man is without the virtues proper to humanity, what has he to do with music?"

Lin Fang asked what was the first thing to be attended to in ceremonies. The Master said, "A great question indeed! In festive ceremonies, it is better to be sparing than extravagant. In the ceremonies of mourning, deep sorrow is better than a minute attention to observances." . . .

[8] Tsze-hsia asked, "What is the meaning of the passage, 'The pretty dimples of her artful smile! The well-defined black and white of her eye! The plain ground for the colors'?"[12] The Master said, "The business of laying on the colors follows [the preparation of] the plain ground." "Ceremonies then are a subsequent thing?" The Master said, "Shang, you can bring out my meaning. Now I can begin to talk about the *Poetry* with you." . . .

[12] He sacrificed to the dead as if they were present. He sacrificed to the spirits as if the spirits were present. The Master said, "I consider my not being present at the sacrifice as if I did not sacrifice."

Wang-sun Chia asked, "What is the meaning of the saying, 'It is better to pay court to the oven than to the southwest corner'?"[13] The Master said, "Not so. He who offends against Heaven has none to whom he can pray."

The Master said, "Chou had the advantage of viewing the two past dynasties. How complete and elegant are its regulations! I follow Chou." . . .

[17] Tzu-kung wished to do away with the sacrifice of a sheep connected with the first day of each month. The Master said, "Tzu, you love the sheep; I love the ceremony."[14]

The Master said, "Full observance of the rules of propriety in serving one's prince is (wrongly) accounted by people to be flattery."

The duke Ting asked how a prince should employ his ministers and how ministers should serve their prince. Confucius replied, "A prince should employ his minister according to the rules of propriety. Ministers should serve their prince with faithfulness."

---

[12]A poem from the *Classic of Poetry*.

[13]A traditional saying, meaning that it is better to serve the gods of food than the ancestral spirits (of the household shrine at the southwest corner of the Chinese house).

[14]Also translated, "Tzu, you love the sheep, but I love the sacrifice."

Analects 3.3–4, 8, 12–14, 17–19.

The Love of Learning

Love of learning is a leading moral quality of anyone who aspires to moral and intellectual superiority. Here Confucius explains its relationship to other prominent virtues.

The Master said, "Yu, have you heard the six words to which are attached six faults?" Yu replied, "I have not." "Sit down, and I will tell them to you. There is the love of being benevolent without the love of learning; the fault here leads to a foolish simplicity. There is the love of knowing without the love of learning; the fault here leads to dissipation of mind. There is the love of being sincere without the love of learning; the fault here leads to an injurious disregard of consequences. There is the love of straightforwardness without the love of learning; the fault here leads to rudeness. There is the love of boldness without the love of learning; the fault here leads to insubordination. There is the love of firmness without the love of learning; the fault here leads to extravagant conduct."

The Master said, "My children, why do you not study the *Book of Poetry?* The poems stimulate the mind. They may be used for purposes of self-contemplation. They teach the art of sociability. They show how to regulate feelings of resentment. From them you learn the more immediate duty of serving one's father, and the remoter duty of serving one's prince. From them we become acquainted with the names of birds, beasts, and plants."

Analects 17.8–9.

The Basis of Good Government

The text of Confucius is given in sections 1–7; what follows is from the ninth chapter of the commentary by the philosopher Tsang, which is appended to the *Great Learning.* This passage, originally a chapter in the *Classic of Rites,* was made a classic by itself in one of the *Four Books* and has had a great influence on the idea and practice of government in China and other lands influenced by it.[15]

The *Great Learning* teaches to show illustrious virtue, to love people, and to rest in the highest excellence....

The ancients, who wished to illustrate illustrious virtue throughout the kingdom, first ordered well their states. Wishing to order well their states, they first regulated their families. Wishing to regulate their families, they first cultivated their persons. Wishing to cultivate their persons, they first rectified their hearts. Wishing to rectify their hearts, they first sought to be sincere in their thoughts. Wishing to be sincere in their thoughts, they first extended their knowledge to the utmost.

---

[15]Taken, with editing, from James Legge, trans., *The Sacred Books of China: The Texts of Confucianism*, part 4, *Sacred Books of the East*, vol. 28 (Oxford: Oxford University Press, 1885), pp. 411–413, 417–419.

Great Learning 1, 3–7; 9.1, 3–5.

The extension of knowledge is by the investigation of things. [5] When things were investigated, knowledge became complete. Their knowledge being complete, their thoughts were sincere. Their thoughts being sincere, their hearts were then rectified. Their hearts being rectified, their persons were cultivated. Their persons being cultivated, their families were regulated. Their families being regulated, their states were rightly governed. Their states being rightly governed, the whole kingdom was made tranquil and happy.

From the Son of Heaven down to the multitudes of the people, all considered the cultivation of the person to be the root of everything else. It cannot be, when the root is neglected, that what springs from it will be well ordered. What was of great importance has never been slightly cared for, and at the same time what was of slight importance has never been greatly cared for....

[9.1, from the commentary] What is meant by "In order rightly to govern the state, it is necessary first to regulate the family"[16] is this. One cannot teach others when he cannot teach his own family. Therefore, the ruler, without going beyond his family, completes the lessons for the state. There is filiality, with which the sovereign should be served. There is fraternal submission, with which elders and superiors should be served. There is kindness, with which the multitude should be treated....

[3] From the loving example of one family a whole state becomes loving, and from its courtesies the whole state becomes courteous, while from the ambition and perverseness of the one man [the emperor], the whole state may be led to rebellious disorder. Such is the nature of the influence.... Therefore, the ruler must himself be possessed of good qualities, and then he may require them in the people. He must not have bad qualities in himself, and then he may require that they shall not be in the people. Never has there been a man who, not having reference to his own character and wishes in dealing with others, was able to instruct them effectively. [5] Thus we see how the government of the state depends on the regulation of the family.

---

[16]Not a quote from the text of Confucius given earlier but a paraphrase of an idea that occurs there.

Confidence and Prosperity in Government

The *Mencius* has much to say about good government. The first excerpt deals with the need of the rulers to keep the confidence of the people. The second deals with the need for some level of economic prosperity so that both ruler and people may flourish.

[4.3] Mencius said, "By benevolence the three dynasties gained the empire, and by not being benevolent they lost it. By the same means are determined the decaying and flourishing, the preservation and perishing, of states. If the emperor is not benevolent, he cannot preserve the empire from passing from him. If the sovereign of a state is not benevolent, he cannot preserve his kingdom. If a high noble or great officer is not benevolent, he cannot preserve his ancestral temple. If a scholar or common man is not benevolent, he cannot preserve his four limbs. Hating death and ruin yet delighting in being unbenevolent is like hating to be drunk yet loving to drink wine."...

Mencius said, "There is a way to get the empire: Get the people, and the empire is obtained. There is a way to get the people: Get their hearts, and the people are obtained. There is a way to get their hearts: Collect for them what they like, and do not lay on them what they dislike. The people turn to a benevolent rule as water runs downward, and as wild animals run to the wilderness."

Mencius 4.3, 9; 1.6.20–24.

[1.6.20–24] Mencius said [to King Hsuan of Ch'i], . . . "Only men of education are able to maintain a fixed heart without a fixed means of livelihood. As to the people, if they do not have a certain livelihood, then they will not have a fixed heart. And if they do not have a fixed heart, there is nothing that they will not do. They will go the way of self-abandonment, of moral deflection, of depravity, and of wild license. When they have been involved in these crimes, to follow them up and punish them is to entrap the people. How can such a thing as entrapping the people be done under the rule of a benevolent man?

"Therefore an intelligent ruler will regulate the livelihood of the people, so as to make sure that they shall have enough to serve their parents, and enough to support their wives and children. He ensures that in good years they shall always be abundantly satisfied, and that in bad years they shall escape the danger of perishing. Then he may urge them to what is good, and they will do it, for in this case the people will follow after the good with ease. But now the livelihood of the people is so regulated that they do not have enough to serve their parents and enough to support their wives and children. Even though they may have good years, their lives are continually embittered, and in bad years they do not escape perishing. In such circumstances they only try to save themselves from death, and they are afraid they will not succeed. What leisure do they have to cultivate propriety and righteousness?

"If Your Majesty wishes to govern humanely the livelihood of the people, why not turn to that which is the essential step to it? Let mulberry trees be planted about the homesteads with their five sections of land, and persons of fifty years may then be clothed with silk. In keeping fowls, pigs, and swine, let not their times of breeding be neglected, and persons of seventy years may eat meat. Let there not be taken away the time that is proper for the cultivation of the farm with its hundred sections of land, and the family of eight that is supported by it shall not suffer from hunger. Let careful attention be paid to education in schools, especially education in the filial and fraternal duties, and gray-haired men will not be seen upon the roads carrying burdens on their backs or on their heads. It never has been that the ruler of a state where such results were seen—the old wearing silk and eating meat, and the young people suffering neither from hunger nor cold—did not attain to the office of emperor."

RITUAL

Divination

The *Classic of Changes (I Ching)* has been used for philosophical meditation, but its main use has been in divination. The traditional ceremony with milfoil sticks is often used, but rolling dice or any other method of selecting numbers can be employed. When the hexagram that matches the numbers thrown is located, it is read and applied to the inquirer's situation, giving the inquirer insight into the present and foresight into the future.[17]

[17]Taken, with editing, from James Legge, trans., *The Sacred Books of China: The Texts of Confucianism,* part 2, *The Yi King, Sacred Books of the East,* vol. 16 (Oxford: Oxford University Press, 1882), pp. 57–58, 161–163, 180–182.

Classic of Changes 1, 47, 54.

THE CH'IEN HEXAGRAM:

Ch'ien [represents] what is great and originating, penetrating, advantageous, correct, and firm.

In the first [or lowest] line, undivided, [we see] the dragon lying hidden in the deep. It is not the time for active doing.

In the second line, undivided, [we see] the dragon appearing in the field. It will be advantageous to meet with the morally great man.

In the third line, undivided, [we see] the superior man active and vigilant all day, and in the evening still careful and apprehensive. There is danger, but there will be no mistake.

In the fourth line, undivided, [we see the dragon looking] as if he were leaping up, but still in the deep. There will be no mistake.

In the fifth line, undivided, [we see] the dragon flying in the sky. It will be advantageous to meet with the great man.

In the sixth [or topmost] line, undivided, [we see] the dragon exceeding the proper limits. There will be occasion for repentance.

[The lines of this hexagram are all strong and undivided, as appears from] the use of the number nine. If the host of dragons thus appearing were to divest themselves of their heads, there would be good fortune.[18]

THE K'UN HEXAGRAM:

In [the condition denoted by] K'un there may [yet be] progress and success. For the firm and correct, the [really] great man, there will be good fortune. He will fall into no error. If he

makes speeches, his words cannot be made good.

The first line, divided, shows its subject with bare buttocks in difficulty under the stump of a tree. He enters a dark valley and for three years has no prospect [of deliverance].

The second line, undivided, shows its subject in difficulty amid his wine and food. Then comes to him the red knee-covers [of the ruler]. It will be well for him [to maintain his sincerity] in sacrificing. Active operations [on his part] will lead to evil, but he will be free from blame.

The third line, divided, shows its subject in difficulty before a [frowning] rock. He lays hold of thorns. He enters his palace and does not see his wife. There will be evil.

The fourth line, undivided, shows its subject proceeding very slowly [to help the subject of the first line], who is in difficulty by the carriage adorned with metal in front of him. There will be occasion for regret, but the end will be good.

The fifth line, undivided, shows its subject with his nose and feet cut off. He is in difficulty by [his ministers in their] scarlet aprons. He is leisurely in his movements, however, and is satisfied. It will be well for him to be [sincere] in sacrificing [to spiritual beings].

The sixth line, divided, shows its subject in difficulty, as if bound with creepers, or in a high and dangerous position and saying [to himself], "If I move, I shall regret it." If he does repent of former errors, there will be good fortune in his going forward.[19]

THE KUEI MEI HEXAGRAM:

Kuei Mei indicates that [under the conditions which it denotes] action will be evil and in no way advantageous.

---

[18]The point of the Ch'ien hexagram is that mildness of action plus firmness of decision lead to good fortune.

[19]The point of the K'un hexagram is that the person beset by problems can move out of them with a grasp of the situation and a change of attitude.

The first line, undivided, shows the younger woman married off in a position secondary to the real wife.[20] It suggests the idea of a person lame in one leg who yet manages to tramp along. Going forward will be fortunate.

The second line, undivided, shows her blind in one eye yet able to see. There will be advantage in her maintaining the firm correctness of a solitary widow.

The third line, divided, shows the younger woman who was to be married off in an inferior position. She returns and accepts an ancillary position.

The fourth line, undivided, shows the younger woman who is to be married off protracting the time. She may be late in being married, but the time will come.

The fifth line, divided, reminds us of the marrying of a younger woman to [King] Ti-yi, when the sleeves of the princess were not equal to those of the [still] younger woman who accompanied her in an inferior capacity. [The case suggests the thought of] the moon almost full. There will be good fortune.

The sixth line, divided, shows the young lady bearing the basket of harvest offerings, but without anything in it, and the gentleman slaughtering the sheep, but without blood flowing from it. There will be no advantage in any way.[21]

---

[20]*younger woman . . . real wife:* The symbolism here draws on the ancient Chinese custom of a man taking a concubine.

[21]The point of the Kuei Mei hexagram is that new undertakings are not advantageous, especially for those who, like the young woman, have difficulty accepting a low social role.

Songs for Sacrifice

These selections from the *Classic of Poetry* show the deep connection of ritual and virtue in Confucianism. The first song is for an emperor's sacrifice to an ancestor. The second is a complaint to Heaven about the rule of an unjust king. The last song provides fascinating details about the sacrificial service in the temple.[22]

SACRIFICIAL ODES OF KAU, ODE 7

They come full of harmony;
They are here in all seriousness,
The princes assisting,
While the Son of Heaven[23] looks profound.
[He says], "O Great and august Father,
While I present this noble bull,
And they assist me in setting forth the sacrifice,

---

[22]Taken, with editing, from James Legge, trans., *The Sacred Books of China: The Texts of Confucianism*, part 1, *Sacred Books of the East*, vol. 3 (Oxford: Oxford University Press, 1879), pp. 304–305, 325–326, 357–358, 365–368.
[23]*Son of Heaven:* the king or emperor.

Comfort me, your filial son.

"You lived with penetrating wisdom,
A sovereign with the gifts of peace and war.
You gave rest even to great Heaven,
And ensured prosperity to your descendants.

"You comfort me with the eyebrows of long life;
You make me great with many blessings.
I offer this sacrifice to my meritorious father,
And to my accomplished mother."

MINOR ODES OF THE KINGDOM, ODE 10.1, 3

Great and wide Heaven,
Why do you constrict your kindness,

Classic of Poetry: Kau 7; Minor Odes 10.1, 3; Minor Odes 5.

Sending down death and famine,
Destroying everything in the kingdom?
Compassionate Heaven, arrayed in terrors,
Why do you exercise no forethought, no care?

Leave the criminals alone;
They have suffered for their guilt.
But those who have no crime
Are indiscriminately involved in ruin.
How is it, O great Heaven,
That the king will not listen to just words?
He is like a man going astray,
Who knows not where he is going.
All you officers,
Let each of you attend to his duties.
Why do you not stand in awe of one another?
Because you do not stand in awe of Heaven.

MINOR ODES OF THE KINGDOM, ODE 5

Thick grew the prickly plants on the ground,
But they cleared away its thorny parts.
Why did they do this in old times?
That we plant our grain and sacrificial grain;
That our crops might be abundant,
Our sacrificial grain luxuriant.
When our barns are full,
And our stacks are tens of thousands,
We proceed to make drinks and prepare grain,
For offerings and sacrifice.

We seat the representatives of the dead, and
     urge them to eat,[24]
Seeking to increase our bright happiness.
With correct and reverent behavior,
The bulls and rams all pure,
We proceed to the winter and autumnal
     sacrifices.
Some arrange the meat; some adjust its
     pieces.[25]

The officiant sacrifices inside the temple gate,
And all the sacrificial service is complete and
     excellent.
Grandly come our ancestors;
Their spirits happily enjoy the offerings;
Their filial descendant receives blessing.
They will reward him with great happiness,
With ten thousand years, life without end.
They attend to the ovens with reverence;
They prepare the trays, which are very large—
Some for the roast meat, some for the broiled.
Wives presiding are still and reverent,
Preparing the numerous smaller dishes.
The guests and visitors
Present the cup all around.
Every form is according to rule,
Each smile and word as it should be.

The spirits quietly come,
And respond with great blessings—
Thousands of years as the [fitting] reward.
We are completely exhausted,
And have performed every ceremony without
     error.
The able officiant announces to the filial
     descendant,
"Your filial sacrifice has been fragrant,
And the spirits have enjoyed your drinks and
     food.
They confer on you a hundred blessings,
Each as it is desired, each as sure as law.
You have been exact and expeditious;
You have been correct and careful.
They will always confer on you the choicest
     favors,
In thousands and tens of thousands."

The ceremonies have been completed;
The bells and drums have given a warning.
The filial descendant goes to his place,
And the able officiant makes his
     announcement,
"The spirits have drunk to the full."
The great representatives of the dead then rise,
And the bells and drums escort their
     withdrawal,
On which the spirits tranquilly return.
All the servants, and the presiding wives,

---

[24] *We seat . . . eat:* People who, in the ceremony, represent the deceased ancestors are seated and feted.
[25] In Confucian sacrifice, the animals are killed and cooked before the ceremony, not as a part of it.

Remove the trays and dishes without delay.
The [sacrificer's] uncles and cousins
All go to the private feast that follows.
The musicians all go in to perform,
Giving soothing aid at the second blessing.
Your foods are set forth;
There is no dissatisfaction, but all feel happy.
They drink to the full, and eat to the full.

Great and small, they bow their heads,
   [saying],
"The spirits enjoyed your drinks and foods.
They will cause you to live long.
Your sacrifices, all in their seasons,
Are completely discharged by you.
May your sons and your grandsons
Never fail to perpetuate these services!"

Music and Morality

Music has played a large role in Chinese culture and religion. One of the ancient Classics dealt exclusively with music. Although that text has unfortunately been lost, some of it probably has survived in the *Classic of Rites (Li Chi)*. Notice here how music expresses the cosmic forces of the universe and how its extensive use in sacrifice furthers the meaning of the ceremony.[26]

In framing their music, the ancient kings laid its foundation in the feelings and nature of men. They examined the notes by the measures for the length and quality of each, and adapted each note to express the meaning of the ceremonies in which it was to be used. They brought it into harmony with the energy that produces life, and to give expression to the performance of the five regular constituents of moral worth. They made it indicate that energy in its Yang or phase of vigor, without any dissipation of its power, and also in its Yin or phase of remission, without the vanishing of its power. The strong phase showed no excess like that of anger, and the weak no shrinking like that of pusillanimity. These four characteristics blended harmoniously in the minds of men and were similarly manifested in their conduct. Each occupied quietly its proper place, and one did not interfere injuriously with another.

After this they established schools for teaching their music, and different grades for the learners. They marked fully the divisions of the pieces. They condensed the parts and variations, giving beauty and elegance, in order to regulate and increase the inward virtue of the learners. They gave laws for the great and small notes according to their names, and they harmonized the order of the beginning and the end to represent the doing of things. Thus they made the underlying principles of the relations between the near and distant relatives, the noble and inferior, the old and young, males and females, all to appear clearly in the music. Hence it is said, "In music we must endeavor to see its depths.". . .

[15] Hence the superior man returns to the good affections in order to bring his will into harmony with them, and he compares the different qualities of actions in order to perfect his conduct. Notes that are evil and depraved, and sights leading to disorder and licentiousness, are not allowed to affect his ears or eyes. Immoral music and corrupted ceremonies are not admitted into the mind to affect its powers. The spirit of idleness, indifference, depravity, and perversity finds no exhibition in his person. Thus he makes his ears, eyes, nose, and mouth the apprehensions of his mind, and the movements of all

---

[26]Taken, with editing, from James Legge, trans., *The Sacred Books of China: The Texts of Confucianism*, part 4, *Sacred Books of the East*, vol. 28 (Oxford: Oxford University Press, 1885), pp. 108–112.

Classic of Rites 17.2.10–11, 15–16, 18.

the parts of his body follow the course that is correct and do that which is right.

After this there ensues the manifestation of the inward thoughts by the modulations of note and tone, the elegant accompaniments of the lutes, small and large, the dances with shields and battle-axes, the ornaments of the plumes and ox-tails,[27]

concluding with the pipes and flutes. All this has the effect of exhibiting the brilliance of complete virtue, stirring up the harmonious action of the four seasonal energies, and displaying the true natures and qualities of all things....

[18] Therefore, when the music has full course...the perceptions of the ears and eyes become sharp and distinct; the action of the blood and physical energies is harmonious and calm, bad influences are removed and manners changed, and all under heaven there is complete calm.

---

[27]*movements...ox-tails:* Pantomime dancing often accompanies the important rituals; both military dances (with *shields and battle-axes*) and civilian dances (with *plumes and ox-tails*) are performed by the dancers.

Attack on Buddhism

Han Yu (768–824 C.E.) led a Confucian attack against Buddhism and Taoism, asking the emperor to suppress these religions. Han was a poet and philosopher and an official at the court of the emperor. This passage from a letter (not scriptural) to the emperor asks him to rethink his decision to view a relic of the Buddha's body, a bone. Han warns the emperor that viewing the bone would indicate imperial support of the Buddhist practice of relic worship.[28]

Buddhism is no more than a cult of the barbarian peoples which spread to China in the time of the Latter Han. It did not exist here in ancient times....When Emperor Kao-tsu received the throne from the House of Sui, he deliberated whether he should suppress Buddhism. But at that time the various officials, being of small worth and knowledge, were unable fully to comprehend the ways of the ancient kings, and so could not implement the wisdom of the emperor and rescue the age from corruption....

Buddha was a man of the barbarians who did not speak the language of China and wore clothes of a different fashion. His sayings did not concern the ways of our ancient kings, nor did his manner of dress conform to their laws. He understood neither the duties that bind sovereign and subject, nor the affections of father and son. If he were

still alive today and came to our court by order of his ruler, Your Majesty might condescend to receive him, but....he would then be escorted to the borders of the nation, dismissed, and not allowed to delude the masses. How then, when he has long been dead, could his rotten bones, the foul and inauspicious remains of his body, be rightly admitted to the palace? Confucius said, "Respect ghosts and spirits, but keep them at a distance." Now without reason Your Majesty has caused this loathsome thing to be brought in and would personally go to view it....

Your servant is deeply shamed and begs that this bone be given to the proper authorities to be cast into fire and water, that this evil may be rooted out, the world freed from its error, and later generations spared this delusion.... If the Buddha does indeed have supernatural power to send down curses and calamities, may they fall only upon the person of your servant, who calls upon High Heaven to witness that he does not regret his words.

---

[28]From W. T. de Bary, *Sources of Chinese Tradition* (New York: Columbia University Press, 1964), pp. 371–372. Copyright © 1964 by Columbia University Press.

Ch'ang-li hsien-sheng wen-chi 39.2b–42.

GLOSSARY

Pinyin spelling, where it differs from Wade-Giles, is given in parentheses before the pronunciation.

Ching (Jing) [jing] "Classics"; books that make up part of the early Confucian canon.

chun-tzu (jun-zi) [jun-tzoo] "prince's son"; in the teaching of Confucius, a "superior man" made so by the study and practice of virtue.

hsiao (xiao) [syow] filiality; love for and service to one's parents and deceased ancestors.

I Ching (*Yi Jing*) [ee jing] "Classic of Changes"; a diviner's manual; earliest of the Confucian scriptures.

jen (ren) [ren] the virtue of benevolence or humaneness.

li [lee] propriety, or decorum, both in the rites and in everyday life.

Tao (Dao) [dow] the cosmic "Way" of life; in Confucian scripture, often related to Heaven (e.g., the "Way of Heaven").

wen-yen the formal-classical style in which the Confucian classics are written.

yin-yang (*not* ying-yang) cosmic forces such as passivity and activity, darkness and light, and other opposing pairs.

QUESTIONS FOR STUDY AND DISCUSSION

1. Compare and contrast the earliest Confucian canon, the *Five Classics,* with the later canon, the *Four Books.* What are their commonalities and differences?
2. How do the Confucian scriptures bear witness to the importance of three elements often held to be common to all traditional Chinese religion: heaven, earth, and ancestor worship?
3. Reflect on the lively political issue of the personal character of candidates for public office in contemporary North America. To what degree does Confucius' counsel about a morally superior ruler apply in our society?

4. To what degree may filiality be a prescription for social pressures on the modern Western family?
5. What is the continuing significance of the Confucian scriptures in modern life outside China?
6. Do you think, with Mencius, that human nature is innately good? Why or why not?
7. Apply the standards in the "Music and Morality" reading (page 158) to the kinds of popular music you listen to. Do you agree with the results?
8. Having read these Confucian scriptures, what is your own conclusion about this often discussed issue: Is Confucianism a religion or a philosophy?

SCRIPTURES IN FILM

Confucian scriptures are illustrated but not directly treated in several highly praised feature films. (This is exactly what we would expect for a religion so deeply identified with Chinese culture.) *The Last Emperor* (1987, rated PG-13), directed by Bernardo Bertolucci, tells the story of Pu Yi, China's final monarch; it was filmed in part in the Forbidden City in Beijing (Peking). See the "director's cut" DVD for a fuller story that carries the life of Pu Yi through communist "re-education" camps. *Farewell My Concubine* (1993, rated R), directed by Chen Kaige, tells the story of two singers in the Beijing

Opera. It gives a good sense of the importance of music and dance in Chinese culture. *Raise the Red Lantern* (1998, rated PG), directed by Zhang Yimou, deals with the life of a traditional Chinese family in 1920, particularly the difficulties posed by second and third marriages. *Eat Drink Man Woman* (1994, not submitted for ratings but probably in the PG-13 to R range) explores family relationships in Taiwan as the Chinese people deal with modern times. Its focus on the life of a restaurant operator also gives some insight into how Chinese cuisine fits into wider Chinese culture.

SUGGESTIONS FOR FURTHER READING

PRIMARY READINGS

The fullest English translation of the Confucian canon continues to be by James Legge and others in F. Max Müller, gen. ed., *Sacred Books of the East*. Volume 3 is the *Shu Ching*, the religious portions of the *Shih Ching*, and the *Hsiao Ching;* vol. 16 is the *I Ching;* vol. 27 and 28 are the *Li Chi.*

R. M. Barnhart, *Li Kung-lin's Classic of Filial Piety*. New York: Metropolitan Museum of Art, 1993. Features the paintings of Li Kung-lin (1041–1106) illustrating the *Filial Piety;* Li's paintings are some of the most important works of art in Chinese cultural history.

Wing-tsit Chan, *A Source Book in Chinese Philosophy*. Princeton, NJ: Princeton University Press, 1963. Full selections from religious-philosophical Confucian books and older classics from a leading interpreter of Chinese religious literature to the West.

D. C. Lau, trans., *The Analects*. London: Penguin, 1979. An excellent contemporary translation, with good notes.

D. C. Lau, trans., *The Mencius*. London: Penguin, 1983. The same standard and format as in Lau's translation of the *Analects*.

R. Wilhelm, trans., *The I Ching*. Bollingen Series, no. 19. New York: Pantheon, 1961. Perhaps the best current translation of the *Book of Changes*.

SECONDARY READINGS

J. B. Henderson, *Scripture, Canon, Commentary: A Comparison of Confucian and Western Exegesis.* Princeton, NJ: Princeton University Press, 1991. An excellent treatment of the important question of the relationship and explanation of scripture and commentary, with valuable comparative analysis of Chinese commentary and the Western (mainly Christian) commentarial tradition.

T. Kelleher, "[Women in] Confucianism." In A. Sharma, ed., *Women in World Religions*. Albany: State University of New York Press, 1989, pp. 135–159. An insightful essay on the influence of Confucian scripture on the roles of women in China.

M. Nylan, *The Five "Confucian" Classics*. New Haven, CT: Yale University Press, 2001. A fascinating review of the history and influence of these books that challenges several current conclusions.

R. L. Taylor, "Confucianism: Scripture and Sage." In F. M. Denney and R. L. Taylor, eds., *The Holy Book in Comparative Perspective*. Columbia University of South Carolina Press, 1985, pp. 181–203. An excellent study of the use of scripture to achieve sagehood.

R. L. Taylor, *The Way of Heaven: An Introduction to Confucian Religious Life*. Leiden: Brill, 1986. A fine introduction to Confucian scripture in the context of religious life; many photographic illustrations of Confucian iconography and rituals.

COMPANION WEBSITE

Visit the *Anthology of World Scriptures* companion website at **www.thomsonedu.com** for learning tools such as map explorations, flashcards of glossary terms, learning objectives, chapter practice quizzes, links to other websites for learning and research, and chapter summaries in PowerPoint® format.

Taoism

Scripture Recitation in a Chinese Funeral

A Taoist priest in the Sichwan Province of China reads a funeral text, and the men sitting around respond, to enable the soul of the deceased to pass successive judgments on its way to final blessing. (*Stevan Harrell, from the Image Bank of the Center for the Study of World Religions, Harvard University. Used by permission of Stevan Harrell.*)

- In a temple in Kaoshiung, Taiwan, a medium known as a "spirit writer" falls under the possession of the temple's god. As he speaks the words of the god, a scribe standing nearby writes down the words. These words will be published in the temple's magazine and may perhaps form the basis of new Taoist scripture.

- At the Hsing T'ien Temple in Taipei, Taiwan, the temple courtyard is filled with blue-robed women carrying out the faith healing for which the temple has gained its reputation. They lay hands on the sick or on clothing brought by the families of those too sick to come in person. In this way, they carry out an ancient tradition of Taoism as discussed in many of its scriptures, that of healing and longevity.

- In Hong Kong, a "special administrative district" of China, filmmakers puzzle over the policy of the Chinese government about not allowing films with certain religious and cultural features from Hong Kong into mainland China. What government censors call "superstitions" and "cults" are not allowed in films, and this harms the profits of Chinese-language films featuring such popular staples as child vampires, ghosts, and sects with superhuman abilities. Secret societies based on arcane new beliefs have posed perceived threats to China's government for centuries. Even though Taoism is now one of the few officially approved religions in China, and although Taoists are often portrayed in Hong Kong films as spiritual and action heroes, Taoists worry that the more popular elements of their religion may be suppressed by the government.

INTRODUCTION

Taoism is, after Confucianism, the most influential religion among Chinese people. According to Taoists, their faith was founded by Lao Tzu in the sixth century B.C.E. Since ancient times, the Taoist tradition has had two interacting parts: philosophical Taoism, rich in cosmological meditation and speculation; and religious (sometimes called "esoteric") Taoism, with its emphasis on exorcism, astrology, and gaining long life or even immortality. Although Taoism [DOW-ism] has had an important influence through history, its future is cloudy. Some scholars hold it to be a dying tradition. Whether it is or not only time will tell, but the scriptures of Taoism—especially the *Tao Te Ching* [DOW duh jing], "Classic of the Way and Its Working," and the *Chuang-tzu* [jwahng tzoo]—have earned an undying place in the history of the world's cultures and remain influential.

Overview of Structure

Taoist canon as a whole is known as the *Tao Tsang* [dow tsahng]. Its last main printing, in 1926, consists of 1,120 volumes. The *Tao Tsang* has traditionally been grouped into the *Three Caverns (San-Tung),* reflecting three historic traditions within Taoism: the Supreme Clarity school, the Numinous Treasure school, and the Three Sovereigns school. Each "cavern" is divided into twelve sections. Their names indicate the overall content of the Taoist scriptures. They are original revelations; divine talismans; interpretations; diagrams; chronologies and genealogies; moral codes; ceremonial decorum; rituals; esoteric techniques (alchemy, astrology, exorcism, etc.); lives of past Taoist worthies; hymns; and messages to the

BOX 7.1 *Four Modern Translations of* Tao Te Ching, *Chapter 1*

1. By Stephen Addiss and Stanley Lombardo (1993)

Tao k'o tao fei ch'ang tao.
Tao called Tao is not Tao.
Names can name no lasting name.

Nameless: the origin of heaven and earth.
Naming: the mother of the ten thousand things.

Empty of desire, perceive mystery.
Filled with desire, perceive manifestations.

These have the same source, but different names.
Call them both deep—Deep and again deep:
The gateway to all mystery.

Source: From Lao Tzu: *Tao Te Ching*, translated by Lombardo and Addis, 1993. Reprinted by permission of Hackett Publishing Co., Inc.

2. By Ursula LeGuin (1998)

The way you can go
isn't the real way.
The name you can say
isn't the real name.

Heaven and earth
begin in the unnamed:
name's the mother
of the ten thousand things.

So the unwanting soul
sees what's hidden,
and the ever-wanting soul
sees only what it wants.

Two things, one origin,
but different in name,
whose identity is mystery.

dead. To the basic three-part form was added the *Four Supplements,* itself as mixed in content as the caverns.

Contemporary Use, Historical Origin, and Development

Critical study of the history of the Taoist canon is in its beginning stages, and the massive size of the canon makes the task especially challenging. Nevertheless, scholars have reached certain conclusions.

Probably because of its cryptic quality and mixed content, the *Tao Te Ching* is scripture that all Taoists have responded to. Indeed, it is one of the few scripture

Mystery of all mysteries!
The door to the hidden.

Source: From *Lao Tzu: Tao Te Ching*, Copyright © 1997. Reprinted by arrangement with Boston Shambhala Publications, Inc., Boston. www.shambhala.com.

3. By Benjamin Hoff (1981)

The way that can be defined to death is not the Way to Life.
The road that can be measured is not the endless road.
From nothing, the infinite universe began.
From no number, the countless things appeared.
From no name, their limitless sources will be known.

Looking out, its effects are seen;
Looking in, their cause is discovered.
With words, these are considered separate;
With vision, they are recognized as one.

Source: Benjamin Hoff, *The Way to Life: The Heart of the Tao Te Ching.* New York: Weatherhill, 1981, p. 1. Used by permission.

4. By James Legge (1891)

The Tao that can be trodden is not the enduring and unchanging Tao.
The name that can be named is not the enduring and unchanging name.

Conceived of as having no name, it is the Originator of heaven and earth;
Conceived of as having a name, it is the Mother of all things.

Always without desire we must be found,
If its deep mystery we would sound;
But if desire always within us be,
Its outer fringe is all that we will see.

Under these two aspects, it is really the same; but as development takes place, it
receives the different names. Together we call them the Mystery. Where the Mystery
is the deepest is the gate of all that is subtle and wonderful.

books to be extensively used in both philosophical Taoism and religious Taoism. Also, to judge from the frequency with which it has been translated into English (more than 100 times) and other European languages, the *Tao Te Ching* has had a significant appeal to peoples of other religions and cultures. The appeal of this book in the United States, for example, is echoed in the titles of more than fifty books, such as *The Tao of Parenting, The Tao of Dialogue, The Tao of Spycraft, The Tao of Coaching, The Tao of Sales, The Tao of Golf,* and even *The Tao of Jesus* and *The Tao of Islam.* (For an example of how modern English translations of the *Tao Te Ching* differ, see Box 7.1.)

The second most important text of Taoism is the *Chuang-tzu,* named for its author, a fourth-century B.C.E. Chinese philosopher and teacher. This book is far removed from the *Tao Te Ching.* Full of anecdote and allegory, it challenges the reader with its provocative style and content. It stresses the illusory nature of knowledge and the difficulty, if not the impossibility, of separating right and wrong. Nevertheless, the *Chuang-tzu* does include specific moral guidelines that proceed from the "two great sanctions": the moral requirements visible in nature and the inner conviction of what is right and wrong. Both of these principles are grounded in the great Tao.

Other important Taoist texts can be mentioned here only in passing. The *T'ai-shang* deals with retribution for sin and reward for evil. According to this work, the life span of people who live a good life in harmony with the Tao will be lengthened, but those who lead an evil life will die early or have their punishment passed on to their descendants. The *Tao-fa hui-yuan* (Group of Taoist Rites) is a book of ceremonies to control demonic forces, both in nature and in the individual, when they result in sickness. The *Shang-ching hou-shen tao-chun lieh-chi* (Annals of the Lord of the Tao, the Sage-to-Come of Shang-ching) contains information on how certain Taoist masters (often called "adepts") used respiration techniques, alchemy, and other esoteric techniques to feed on astral powers and become immortal or even divine. Many other texts of religious/esoteric Taoism are written in a special script taught only to initiates into special sects, and Taoists have been very secretive about sharing this literature.

Taoists trace the origins of their religion and scriptures to the claimed founder of their tradition, Lao Tzu (sixth century B.C.E.). They hold that his disciples wrote down the first and most important work of the canon, the *Tao Te Ching,* shortly after his death. Indeed, Taoists often refer to the *Tao Te Ching* as the *Lao Tzu.* Recent critical scholarship, however, has concluded that even though this book may have been started at this time, it is a collection of material from different authors that was assembled in the third century B.C.E.

The *Tao Te Ching* is the fountainhead of most of the Taoist scripture that followed. Its reflections on the **Tao** [dow] ("Way") and its **te** [duh] ("power") in eighty-one brief sections are written in a highly compressed style. The Chinese original features much parallelism among the lines of poetry and also a good deal of rhyme, lost in most translations. It points to a Tao that is cosmic, the origin of heaven and earth. This Tao is part of each individual's existence, and it is a social ideal as well.

TEACHING

The Nature of the Tao

The leading themes in the *Tao Te Ching* are the nature of the Tao and how one follows it. These passages present the Tao as unnameable (Chapter 1), female in quality (6), the "mother" of heaven and earth (25), and accomplishing great things by means of small

Tao Te Ching 1, 6, 25, 34; *Chuang-tzu* 29.

things (34). In the *Chuang-tzu,* the sage discusses the Tao in a more philosophical way, yet also in the playful and challenging manner typical of the *Chuang-tzu.*[1]

[*Tao Te Ching* 1] Tao called Tao is not Tao.
Names can name no lasting name.

Nameless: the origin of heaven and earth.
Naming: the mother of the ten thousand
   things.
Empty of desire, perceive mystery.
Filled with desire, perceive manifestations.

These have the same source, but different
   names.
Call them both deep—
Deep and again deep:
The gateway to all mystery.

[6] The Valley Spirit never dies.
It is called the Mysterious Female.

The entrance to the Mysterious Female
Is called the root of Heaven and Earth,
Endless flow
Of inexhaustible energy.

[25] Something unformed and complete
Before heaven and earth were born,
Solitary and silent,
Stands alone and unchanging,
Pervading all things without limit.
It is like the mother of all under heaven,
But I don't know its name—
Better call it Tao.
Better call it great.

Great means passing on.
Passing on means going far.
Going far means returning.

Therefore,
   Tao is great,
   And heaven,
   And earth,
   And humans.

Four great things in the world.
Aren't humans one of them?

Humans follow earth
Earth follows heaven
Heaven follows Tao.
Tao follows its own nature.

[34] Great Tao overflows
To the left   To the right.
All beings owe their life to it
And do not depart from it.
It acts without a name.
It clothes and nourishes all beings
But does not become their master.
Enduring without desire,
It may be called slight.
All beings return to it,
But it does not become their master.

It may be called immense.
By not making itself great,
It can do great things.

[*Chuang-tzu* 29] Tung-kwo Tze asked Chuang Tzu, "Where is what you call the Tao to be found?" Chuang Tzu replied, "Everywhere." The other said, "Specify an instance of it. That will be more satisfactory." "It is here in this ant." "Give me a lower instance." "It is in this earthenware tile." "Is that really the lowest instance?" Chuang Tzu said, "It is in that excrement." To this Tung-kwo Tze gave no reply.

Chuang Tzu said, "Your questions, my master, do not touch the fundamental point of the Tao. They remind me of the questions addressed by the superintendents of the market to the inspector about examining the value of a

[1]All readings from the *Tao Te Ching,* except where noted, are taken from Stephen Addiss and Stanley Lombardo, *Lao-Tzu, Tao Te Ching* (Cambridge, MA: Hackett, 1993). Copyright © 1993 Hackett Publishing Co., Inc. Used by permission. Selections from the *Chuang-tzu* are from James Legge, *The Texts of Taoism, Sacred Books of the East,* vols. 39 and 40 (Oxford: Oxford University Press, 1891).

pig by stepping on it and testing its weight as the foot descends lower and lower on the body. You should not specify any particular thing. One single thing does not describe the Tao. So it is with the Perfect Tao. And if we call it the Great Tao, it is just the same. It has the three terms 'Complete,' 'All-embracing,' and 'the Whole.' These names are different, but the reality sought in them is the same. They all refer to the One thing.

"Suppose we were to try to roam about in the palace of Nowhere. When met there, we might discuss the subject without ever coming to an end. Or suppose we were to be together in the region of Non-action. Should we say that the Tao was simplicity and stillness? or indifference and purity? or harmony and ease? My will would be aimless. If it went nowhere, I would not know where it had gone; if it went and came back again, I wouldn't know where it had stopped; if it went on going and coming, I would not know when the process would end. In vague uncertainty, I would be in the vastest waste. Though I entered it with the greatest knowledge, I would not know how inexhaustible it was. That which makes things what they are [the Tao] does not have the limit that belongs to things. . . . The Tao is the limit of the unlimited and the boundlessness of the unbounded.

"We speak of fullness and emptiness, and of withering and decay. It produces fullness and emptiness but is neither fullness nor emptiness. It produces withering and decay but is neither withering nor decay. It produces the root and branches but is neither root nor branch. It produces growth and spreading but is itself neither grown nor spread."

The World

The typical Chinese expression for the world is "Heaven and Earth." These passages present the world, composed of the "ten thousand things," as proceeding from the Tao and holding to the way of inactivity. The Tao operates with yin and yang, which are cosmic principles or dualities such as passive and active, earth and heaven, dark and light. Wise persons will pattern their lives on the Tao that generates Heaven and Earth.

[7] Heaven is long, Earth enduring.
Long and enduring
Because they do not exist for themselves.
Therefore the Sage
   Steps back, but is always in front,
   Stays outside, but is always within.
No self interest?
Self is fulfilled.

[42] Tao engenders One,
One engenders Two,

Two engenders Three,[2]
Three engenders the ten thousand things.

The ten thousand things carry shade
And embrace sunlight.
Shade and sunlight, yin and yang,
Breath blending into harmony.[3]

---

[2]The *One* is *ch'i*, the primordial, cosmic breath; the *Two* are yin and yang; the *Three* are the waters under the earth, the earth, and heaven.
[3]*breath: ch'i*, the cosmic breath/wind.

Tao Te Ching 7, 42, 52.

Humans hate
To be alone, poor, and hungry.
Yet kings and princes
Use these words as titles.
   We gain by losing,
   Lose by gaining.

What others teach, I also teach:
A violent man does not die a natural death.
This is the basis of my teaching.

[52] The world has a source: the world's mother.
Once you have the mother,
   You know the children.
Once you know the children,
   Return to the mother.

Your body dies.
There is no danger.

Block the passage,
Bolt the gate:
   No strain
Until your life ends.

Open the passage,
Take charge of things:
   No relief
Until your life ends.

Seeing the small is called brightness.
Maintaining gentleness is called
strength. Use this brightness to return to
   brightness.

Don't cling to your body's woes.
Then you can learn endurance.

The Relationship of Taoism to Confucianism

Taoism and Confucianism have long been the two major traditions of China. Here is a statement from the Taoist side on their relationship, with the better judgment going of course to Taoism. The text deals with the question: Of Confucianism and Taoism, which is easier?[4]

Confucianism is difficulty in the midst of facility [ease]; Taoism is facility in the midst of difficulties.

The difficulties of Taoism are these: abandonment of social intercourse and renouncing wife and family; rejection of fame and loss of income; removal of brilliances from one's sight and suppression of the tinkling marks of office from one's ears; the silence and retirement where one's sole profession is preservation of one's own integrity; not to be depressed by criticism nor elated by praise; to look upon honors without desiring them and to dwell humbly without shame. But Taoism also has its attractive side; no visits of congratulation or condolence, and no critical glances and looks at one's abode; no troubling of the internal gods with the Seven Classics and never a concern for the calendar; no bother about the advancing of asterisms[5] and no enslavement to a craft or to letters; all annoyances lifted, and an inner harmony that grows of itself; perfect freedom of action and thought, no fear, no grief. Therefore, I describe Taoism as facility in the midst of difficulties.

---

[4]From James R. Ware, *Alchemy, Medicine, Religion in the China of* A.D. *320: The Nei P'ien of Ko Hung (Pao-p'u tzu).* Cambridge, MA: Massachusetts Institute of Technology Press, 1966. Copyright © 1966 by the Massachusetts Institute of Technology. Used by permission.

[5]*asterisms:* a cluster of stars smaller than a constellation, thought to have a negative impact on human life.

Pao-p'u Tzu 7.5a.

Everything done in Confucianism is modeled upon precedents. Leaving and staying have their set rules; speech and silence depend upon the hour. If a teacher is desired, he can be found in practically any house; it is a matter of written material, there are plenty of commentaries to resolve the doubts. This is what is easy in Confucianism.

Its difficulties are these: grasping the profound and rendering present the distant, and also confronting and reconciling the regulations coming from the rulers of old; ... and acquiring a wide knowledge of all those many things said by the various schools of philosophy; constantly accumulating good works among the people, and giving the last drop of loyalty to one's lord; being able to interpret any signs conferred by heaven, and giving thought to the meanings of winds and clouds; to be considered unsuccessful for not knowing some solitary matter and to have to face criticism for one word of imprecision; to have one's every step taken as a model by the world, and to have one's every utterance repeated by all.

This is what I mean by difficulties in the midst of facility. But to put it honestly, Confucianism is difficult because of its multiplicities, while Taoism is easy with its conciseness.

ETHICS

Nonaction

The leading ethical ideal of Taoism is **wu-wei** [woo-WAY], a wonderfully ambiguous term that is variously translated "effortless action," "nonaction" (in this translation), "active non-striving," or "action without intent." By wu-wei, the sage seeks to come into harmony with the great Tao, which itself accomplishes by nonaction.

Nonaction makes the person who practices it the lord of all fame; nonaction serves him as the treasury of all plans; nonaction fits him for the burden of all offices; nonaction makes him the lord of all wisdom. The range of his action is inexhaustible, but there is nowhere any trace of his presence. He fulfills all that he has received from Heaven, but he does not see that he was the recipient of anything. A pure vacancy of all purpose is what characterizes him. When the perfect man employs his mind, it is a mirror. It conducts nothing and anticipates nothing. It responds to what is before it but does not retain it. Thus he is able to deal successfully with all things and injures nothing.

Chuang-tzu 7.

Individual Life in Harmony with the Tao

These selections emphasize the necessity of bringing individual life into accord with the Tao and give advice on how to accomplish this through nonaction and indirection.

[16] Attain complete emptiness,
Hold fast to stillness.

The ten thousand things stir about;
I only watch for their going back.

Things grow and grow,
But each goes back to its root.
Going back to the root is stillness.
This means returning to what is.
Returning to what is
Means going back to the ordinary.

Understanding the ordinary:
   Enlightenment.
Not understanding the ordinary:
   Blindness creates evil.
Understanding the ordinary:
   Mind opens.
Mind opening leads to compassion,
Compassion to nobility,
Nobility to heavenliness,
Heavenliness to Tao.
   Tao endures.
   Your body dies.
There is no danger.

[22] Crippled becomes whole,
Crooked becomes straight,
Hollow becomes full,
Worn becomes new,
Little becomes more,
Much becomes delusion.

Therefore Sages cling to the One
   And take care of this world;
Do not display themselves
   And therefore shine;
Do not assert themselves
   And therefore stand out;

Do not praise themselves
   And therefore succeed;
Are not complacent
   And therefore endure;
Do not contend
   And therefore no one under heaven
   Can contend with them.

The old saying
Crippled becomes whole
Is not empty words.
It becomes whole and returns.

[33] Knowing others is intelligent.
Knowing yourself is enlightened.

Conquering others takes force.
Conquering yourself is true strength.

Knowing what is enough is wealth.
Forging ahead shows inner resolve.

Hold your ground and you will last long.
Die without perishing and your life will endure.

[44] Name or body: which is closer?
Body or possessions: which means more?
Gain or loss: which one hurts?

Extreme love exacts a great price.
Many possessions entail heavy loss.

Know what is enough—
   Abuse nothing.
Know when to stop—
   Harm nothing.

This is how to last a long time.[6]

---

[6]*last a long time:* Lines like these in the *Tao Te Ching* encouraged later Taoist practices for gaining long life and even immortality.

Tao Te Ching 16, 22, 33, 44.

The Superior Man

Here is a characteristically Taoist presentation of the superior man, designed of course to provide an alternative to the Confucian idea of superiority. Taoist superiority comes not through self-cultivation in the virtues but by tapping through inactivity into the superiority of the Tao. The full descriptions of the Taoist superior man form a complete list of the type of person that Taoists, especially philosophically oriented ones, seek to become.

The Master said, "The Tao covers and sustains all things. How great is its overflowing influence! The superior man ought to remove from his mind all that is contrary to it. Acting without action is what is called Heaven-like. Speech coming forth of itself is what is called a mark of the true virtue. Loving men and benefiting things is what is called benevolence. Seeing wherein things that are different yet agree is what is called being great. Conduct free from the ambition of being distinguished above others is what is called being generous. The possession in himself of a myriad points of difference is what is called being rich. Therefore to hold fast the natural attributes is what is called the guiding line of government; the perfecting of those attributes is what is called its establishment; accordance with the Tao is what is called being complete; and not allowing anything external to affect the will is what is called being perfect.

"When the superior man understands these things, he keeps all matters sheathed in himself, showing the greatness of his mind. Through the outflow of his doings all things move and come to him. Being such, he lets the gold lie hid in the hill, and the pearls in the deep; he considers not property or money to be any gain. He keeps aloof from riches and honors; he rejoices not in long life, and grieves not for early death. He does not regard prosperity as a glorious thing, nor is ashamed of indigence. He would not grasp at the gain of the whole world to be held as his own private portion; he would not desire to rule over the whole world as his own private distinction. His distinction is in understanding that all things belong to the one treasury, and that death and life should be viewed in the same way."

The Master said, "How still and deep is the place where the Tao resides! How limpid is its purity! Metal and stone without it would give forth no sound. They have the power of sound in them, but if they are not struck, they do not emit it. Who can determine the qualities that are in all things?

"The man of kingly qualities holds on to his way unoccupied and is ashamed to busy himself with the conduct of affairs. He establishes himself in what is the root and source of his capacity, and his wisdom grows to be spiritual. In this way his attributes become more and more great, and when his mind goes forth, whatever things come in his way, it lays hold of them and deals with them. Thus, if there were not the Tao, the bodily form would not have life, and its life, without the attributes of the Tao, would not be manifested. He who preserves the body and gives the fullest development to the life, he who establishes the attributes of the Tao and clearly displays the Tao, is possessed of kingly qualities. How majestic is he in his sudden pronouncements, and in his unexpected movements, when all things follow him! We call him the man whose qualities fit him to rule.

"He sees where there is the deepest obscurity; he hears where there is no sound. In the

---

Chuang-tzu 12.

midst of the deepest obscurity, he alone sees and can distinguish various objects. In the midst of a soundless abyss, he alone can hear a harmony of notes.... In this way in his dealings with all things, while he is farthest from having anything, he can yet give to them what they seek. Although he is always hurrying forth, he returns to his resting place; now large, now small; now long, now short; now distant, now near."

Government

The social ethic of Taoism is largely concerned with government. Here it presents a quietist approach, the opposite of the activist approach of Confucianism. By inactivity in following the Tao, one can bring about the best state. This social ethic has led to several political options for Taoists: withdrawal from public life, mild participation in it, and at times, participation in anarchy.

[3] Don't glorify heroes,
And people will not contend.
Don't treasure rare objects,
And no one will steal.
Don't display what people desire,
And their hearts will not be disturbed.

Therefore,
The Sage rules
    By emptying hearts and filling bellies,
    By weakening ambitions and strengthening bones;
Leads people
    Away from knowing and wanting;
Deters those who know too much
    From going too far:
Practices non-action
    And the natural order is not disrupted.

[18] Great Tao rejected:
    Benevolence and righteousness appear.
Learning and knowledge professed:
    Great hypocrites spring up.
Family relations forgotten:
    Filial piety and affection arise.
The nation disordered:
    Patriots come forth.

[57] Use the expected to govern the country,

Use surprise to wage war,
Use non-action to win the world.
How do I know?
    Like this!

The more prohibitions and rules,
    The poorer people become.
The sharper people's weapons,
    The more they riot.
The more skilled their techniques,
    The more grotesque their works.
The more elaborate the laws,
    The more they commit crimes.

Therefore the Sage says:
I do nothing
    And people transform themselves.
I enjoy serenity
    And people govern themselves.
I cultivate emptiness
    And people become prosperous.
I have no desires
    And people simplify themselves.

[64] At rest is easy to hold.
Not yet impossible is easy to plan.
Brittle is easy to break.
Fine is easy to scatter.

Tao Te Ching 3, 18, 57, 64.

Create before it exists.
Lead before it goes astray.

A tree too big to embrace
   Is born from a slender shoot.
A nine-storey tower
   Rises from a pile of earth.
A thousand-mile journey
   Begins with a single step.

Act and you ruin it.
Grasp and you lose it.
Therefore the Sage
Does not act
   And so does not ruin

Does not grasp
   And so does not lose.
People commonly ruin their work
   When they are near success.
Proceed at the end as at the beginning
   And your work won't be ruined.
Therefore the Sage
   Desires no desires
   Prizes no prizes
   Studies no studies
   And returns
   To what others pass by.
The Sage
   Helps all beings find their nature,
   But does not presume to act.

On Death

This often-quoted story is an excellent example of the striking literary features of the Chuang-tzu.

When Chuang Tzu went to Khu, he saw an empty skull, bleached but still retaining its shape. Tapping it with his horse-switch, he asked it, "Did you, Sir, in your greed of life, fail in the lessons of reason and come to this? Or did you do so, in the service of a perishing state, by the punishment of the axe? Or was it through your evil conduct, reflecting disgrace on your parents and on your wife and children? Or was it through your hard endurance of cold and hunger? Or was it simply that you had completed your term of life?"

Then he took up the skull and made a pillow of it when he went to sleep. At midnight the skull appeared to him in a dream and said, "All your words were about the entanglements of men in their lifetime. None of those things are found after death. Would you like to hear me, Sir, tell you about death?"

"I would," said Chuang Tzu, and the skull resumed: "In death there are not the distinctions of ruler above and minister below. There are none of the features of the four seasons. Tranquil and at ease, our years are those of heaven and earth. No king in his court has greater enjoyment than we have."

Chuang Tzu did not believe it and said, "If I could get the Ruler of our Destiny to restore your body to life with its bones and flesh and skin, and to give you back your father and mother, your wife and children, and all your village acquaintances, would you wish me to do so?"

The skull stared intently at him, knitted its brows, and said, "How should I cast away the enjoyment of my royal court and undertake again the toils of life among mankind?"

Chuang-tzu 18.

Reward and Retribution

Although the Tao does not have a strongly moral character, the Taoist tradition nonetheless developed the doctrine of reward for virtue (long life) and punishment for evil (shortened life or punishment of descendants). This passage gives a lyrical list of good deeds and excerpts the beginning of an even longer section on evil deeds.

There are no special doors for calamity and happiness; they come as men themselves summon them. Their recompenses follow good and evil as the shadow follows the substance.

Accordingly, in heaven and earth there are spirits that take account of men's transgressions and, according to the lightness or gravity of their offences, take away from their term of life. When that term is curtailed, men become poor and reduced and meet with many sorrows and afflictions. All (other) men hate them; punishments and calamities attend them; good luck and occasions for felicitation shun them; evil stars send down misfortunes on them. When their term of life is exhausted, they die.

There also are the Spirit-rulers in the three pairs of the T'ai stars of the Northern Bushel constellation over men's heads, which record their acts of guilt and wickedness and take away (from their term of life) periods of twelve years or of a hundred days.

There also are the three Spirits of the recumbent body that reside within a man's person. As each appointed day of reporting comes, they ascend to the court of Heaven and report men's deeds of guilt and transgression. On the last day of the moon, the spirit of the Hearth does the same.

In the case of every man's transgressions, when they are great, twelve years are taken from his term of life; when they are small, a hundred days.

Transgressions, great and small, are seen in several hundred things. He who wishes to seek for long life must first avoid these.

If his way is right, he should go forward in it; if it is wrong, he should withdraw from it.

He will not tread in devious byways; he will not impose on himself in any secret apartment. He will amass virtue and accumulate deeds of merit. He will feel kindly toward all creatures. He will be loyal, filial, loving to his younger brothers, and submissive to his elder. He will make himself correct and so transform others. He will pity orphans and have compassion on widows; he will respect the old and cherish the young. Even the insects, grass, and trees he should not hurt.

He ought to pity the evil tendencies of others; to rejoice over their excellences; to help them in their difficulties; to rescue them from their perils; to regard their gains as if they were his own and their losses in the same way; not to publish their shortcomings; not to flaunt his own superiorities; to put a stop to what is evil and exalt and display what is good. He ought to yield much and take little for himself; to receive insult without resenting it and receive honor with an appearance of apprehension; to bestow favors without seeking for a return and give to others without any subsequent regret—this is what is called a good man. All other men respect him; Heaven in its course protects him; happiness and financial rewards follow him; all evil things keep far from him; the spiritual Intelligences defend him; what he does is sure to succeed; he may hope to become Immaterial and Immortal.

He who wants to become an Immortal of Heaven ought to give the proof of 1,300 good deeds; and he who wants to become an Immortal of Earth should give the proof of three hundred.

T'ai-Shang 1.

But if the movements of a man's heart are contrary to righteousness, and his conduct is in opposition to reason; if he regards his wickedness as a proof of his ability and can bear to do what is cruel and injurious; if he secretly harms the honest and good; if he treats with clandestine slight his ruler or parents; if he is disrespectful to his elders and teachers; if he disregards the authority of those whom he should serve; if he deceives the simple; if he calumniates his fellow-learners; if he vents baseless slanders, practices deception and hypocrisy, and attacks and exposes his kindred by blood or marriage; if he is hard, violent, and without humanity—in the case of crimes such as these, (the Spirits) presiding over the Life, according to their lightness or gravity, take away the culprit's periods of twelve years or of one hundred days. When his term of life is exhausted, death ensues. If at death there remains any unpunished guilt, judgment extends to his posterity.

RITUAL

Methods of Prolonging Life

This text, considered one of the most important in religious Taoism, stresses esoteric methods of achieving immortality. The first selection discusses the general principles of achieving longevity or immortality; the second points out how scripture texts can aid in this process.[7]

[15.6b] If you are going to do everything possible to nurture your life, you will take the divine medicines. In addition, you will never weary of circulating your breaths; morning and night you will do calisthenics to circulate your blood and breaths and see that they do not stagnate. In addition to these things, you will practice sexual intercourse in the right fashion; you will eat and drink moderately; you will avoid drafts and dampness; you will not trouble about things that are not within your competence. Do all these things, and you will not fall sick.

On the other hand, you are sure to become ill if you are afraid of not always having your own way in society and of instability in your affairs; also, if laxity and lack of diligence trouble you. If all you have is a heart faithful to God and yet do nothing for your own benefit—your predestined life span being defective and your body threatened with harm—the Three Corpses[8] will take advantage of your weak months and perilous days, the hours when your longevity could be interrupted or sickness incurred, to summon vicious breaths and bring in any demons they might be able to find to do you injury.... And when this situation intensifies, it produces the various illnesses. But all of this was set in motion by the anxiety that was present in the first place.

Accordingly, those who first did something about God in antiquity exercised all the medical arts at the same time to save themselves from misfortunes that are ever present, but this principle is

---

[7]From James R. Ware, *Alchemy, Medicine, Religion in the China of A.D. 320: The Nei P'ien of Ko Hung (Pao-p'u tzu)*. Cambridge, MA: Massachusetts Institute of Technology Press, 1966. Copyright © 1966 The Massachusetts Institute of Technology. Used by permission.

[8]*Three Corpses:* worms in the body causing illness and death.

unknown to ordinary processors who, not under-standing what they have been taught, pay no attention to the prescriptions for treating illness. Further, being unable to break with worldly life and live as hermits, and using only personal remedies to drive away illness, they lack all means for combating it and curing themselves. They are by no means as well off as the people in general who use various infusions. . . .

[19.6b] I heard Cheng Yin say that no Taoist book surpasses *San huang nei wen* and *Wu yueh chen hsing t'u* in importance.[9] They were the honored secrets of the genies and superior men of antiquity and could be taught only by those bearing the title of genie. Those receiving them transmitted them once after forty years, and in doing so oaths were taken by smearing the lips with the blood of a sacrificed animal, and agreements were entered into by the giving of a present. Writings of this type are to be found in all the famous mountains and the five revered mountains, but they are stored in hidden spots in caves. In response to those who have secured the divine process and entered a mountain to give sincere thought to it, the god of the mountain will automatically open the mountain and let such persons see the texts, just as Po Ho got his in a mountain, and immediately set up an altar, made a present of silk, drew one ordinary copy, and then left with them.[10] A purified place is always prepared for such texts, and whenever anything is done about them one must first announce it to them, as though one were serving a sovereign or a father.

---

[9]Po Ho wrote both these books, which deal with gaining immortality.
[10]*drew one ordinary copy:* made a copy by hand.

The classic itself states that if *San huang nei wen* is in a household, it will banish evil and hateful ghosts, soften the effects of epidemics, block calamities, and rout misfortunes. If anyone is suffering from illness or on the point of death, let someone believing in the process with all his heart give this text to the patient to hold, and he will be sure not to die. If a wife is having trouble in childbirth to the point of possible death, let her hold this text, and her son will be born immediately. If pilgrims wishing to seek Fullness of Life will hold this text when entering the mountains, it will rout tigers and wolves, and none of the mountain powers, poisons, or evils will dare approach. When crossing rivers and seas, the processors will be able to dispel crocodiles and dragons, and halt the wind and waves with this book.

With the method taught in this text it is possible to initiate undertakings positively or negatively without inquiring about the correct site or choosing the right day, and one's household will be free from calamities. If you wish to build a new house or tomb, write several dozen copies of the Earth Augustus text and spread them on the site. Look at them on the following day, and if a yellow color is seen adhering to them, one may begin the work there and the household will be sure to become rich and prosperous. When others are being interred, copy the Man Augustus text and include your own full name written on a folded sheet of paper. Insert this in that person's grave without letting others know what you are doing, and you will be free from sudden misfortune and robbers. Anyone plotting against you will be sure to have his harm turned against himself.

The Origins of Feng Shui

Feng shui [fung shway] is the ancient Chinese practice of positioning objects to maximize the good effects of yin and yang and promote the flow of life-giving chi [pronounced "chee," and spelled below as qi]. These objects include graves, altars, buildings, and recently, furniture

---

Zang Shu 1.1–4, 7–25, 30–43.

and decorative items. Feng shui originated in burial practices. Good positioning of the body in relation to the earth is believed to lead to a better life in the afterworld for the spirit of the person buried and hence to more blessing on the dead person's living descendants. *The Book of Burial (Zang Shu)* by Guo Pu (276–324 C.E.) laid down the basic principles of feng shui that endure today.[11]

[The purpose of] burial is to gain accord with the generative qi.[12] The five qi move within the ground and develop, thus generating the ten thousand things.[13] Human beings receive their bodies from their parents; the original bones gain qi and the remaining bones receive the yin. The Book says that qi responds to what it senses, and the good fortune of ghosts extends to the living....

[7] Overall, life is the condensation of qi. That which is coagulated becomes the bone, which remains after death. Therefore, to bury the dead is to obey the principle of returning qi to the bones, thus generating life out of yin.[14] Qi follows the bones of hilly ridges and the branches of hills and mounds. [10] The Book[15] says [that] when qi rides with the wind, it disperses; when it reaches water, it ends. The ancients were able to condense the qi and keep it from dispersion, to move it and to make it cease. Therefore, they called it feng shui (wind-water). The law of feng shui is: getting water is superior; hiding from wind is secondary. The Book says [that] when external qi is blocked, it thus takes forms; when internal qi is stopped, it thus generates life. This is what it refers to. Why is it said thus? When there is abundance of qi, it still remains even though it overflows everywhere; it still condenses in a deep place even though it disperses.

[15] Therefore, it is best to bury the dead deep in dry land, and shallow in smooth plains. The Book says [that] once the depth is properly achieved, feng shui will be complete itself. The qi of yin and yang flows out and thus becomes wind; it ascends and thus becomes cloud; it descends and thus becomes rain; and it moves through the ground and thus becomes the generative qi.... The Book says [that] earth takes forms and qi moves along them, and out of this all things are generated. [20] Qi moves through the ground. Its movement depends upon the earth's course; its condensation depends upon the cessation of these courses.

To bury the dead is to trace the beginning point of qi and to [come into] accord with its cessation. The aspect of the ground follows its pulse and the aspect of mountains follows their bones; they are meandering easily either in east-west or south-north directions. The length of a thousand feet is called "aspect"; a height of a hundred feet is called "form." Where the aspect arrives and the form ceases to be, there is what is called the total qi. [25] At the spot of total qi is where you stop and bury the dead....

[30] The accumulated [emerging aspects] ceases and condenses, and the harmonious yang and yin mingle. Where there are high ground and deep water, there are thick grass and dense woods. Such a place has wealth equaling one thousand chariots and has riches equaling ten thousand gold pieces. The Book says that where form ends, qi accumulates, transforming to become ten thousand things—that is the ultimate ground [in which to bury the dead]. It is most precious if ground is a flat plain; it is most precious if soil is that with secondary ridges. [35] The spot where the secondary ridges begin, qi

---

[11]From Juwen Zhang, *A Translation of the Ancient Chinese* The Book of Burial (Zang Shu) *by Guo Pu (276–324)* (Lewiston, NY: Edwin Mellen Press, 2004), pp. 41–84. Copyright © 2004 Juwen Zhang. Used by permission.

[12]*qi:* the primordial, cosmic breath, the power and energy of life; also spelled *chi.*

[13]*the ten thousand things:* traditional Chinese expression for the world and everything in it.

[14]*generating life out of yin:* not that the bones come back to life, but rather that life-giving energy flows to the spirit of the dead person.

[15]*The Book:* an earlier volume on this topic, the exact identity of which is unknown. Zhang suggests that it is likely an earlier version of the *Book of Burial,* perhaps the one version preferred by Wu Cheng (1246–1331 C.E.), who edited the *Book of Burial* that we have today.

consequently originates; where the secondary ridges end, qi consequently terminates. The method of detecting secondary ridges is finding the places where they are slightly hidden, and slightly rising like mounds, and where they are metaphysically and subtly connected. That is where good fortune lies. The Book says [that] when the ground contains auspicious qi, the soil rises in consequence; where the secondary ridge carries the ending qi, water flows to lift it up; the aspect goes smoothly with the form, [and] repeats endless cycles.

By obeying the principle for burying the dead in such a place, there will be perpetual auspiciousness and no misfortune. In mountains, there are those that have precipitous aspects. One should obey the principle to bury the dead at the conjoining spot. [It is also necessary] to accord with the location from which it emerges, [40] to examine the location for deficiencies, to choose from what is accommodating, [and] to avoid what is harmful. This is how the superior man accomplishes remarkable feats and heavenly advantages; thus the mandated fate of heaven is changed.[16]

_____

[16]Zhang remarks, "This may be one of the most important parts in the entire book, in that it shows the positive side of _feng shui_ practice: it is a search for harmony, in which mankind has a positive role in the process of bringing nature into accordance with the natural _Dao_" (Zhang, _Translation of the_ Book of Burial, p. 85).

❧ GLOSSARY

Pinyin spelling, where it differs from Wade-Giles, is given in parentheses before the pronunciation.

Chuang-tzu (Zhuangzi) [jwahng tzoo] the second most important book of the Taoist scriptures.

feng shui [fung shway] the ancient Chinese practice of positioning objects to maximize the good effects of yin and yang and the flow of spiritual energy.

Tao (Dao) [dow] the "Way" of the cosmos, which humans should discern and live by.

Tao Te Ching (Daode Jing) [DOW duh jing] "Classic of the Way and Its Working"; the leading book of the Taoist scriptures.

Tao Tsang (Daozang) [dow tsahng] the Taoist canon.

te (de) [duh] virtue, power, working.

yin and **yang** cosmic principles or dualities: passive and active, earth and heaven, dark and light, female and male, respectively.

wu-wei [woo WAY] "nonaction," "active nonstriving," "effortless action"; the use of the natural power of the Tao in oneself.

❧ QUESTIONS FOR STUDY AND DISCUSSION

1. From your reading of these texts, how would you define or describe the Tao?
2. In what ways is the _Tao Te Ching_ the foundation of subsequent Taoist traditions?
3. Compare and contrast the Taoist and Confucian ideas of the sage or superior man.
4. Discuss the remarkable feminine imagery used, especially in the _Tao Te Ching_, to describe the Tao. Has this carried over into later Taoism in the form of a greater role for women in the religion? If not, why?
5. Discuss the Taoist goal of longevity. How does the pursuit of this goal differ in religious and in philosophical Taoism?
6. How might the perplexing style of the _Chuang-tzu_ be particularly well designed to promote its goals?
7. Compare and contrast the Taoist and Confucian ideas of government. How is it possible, as the _Tao Te Ching_ claims, to govern by wu-wei?
8. Contrast philosophical Taoism and religious Taoism. How are their differences and similarities reflected in their scriptures?
9. One of the best-known Taoist sayings in North America is "A journey of a thousand miles begins with a single step" (see page 174). This was a favorite proverb, for example, of Robert Kennedy. Given the context of this saying in the _Tao Te Ching_ and the Taoist ideal of wu-wei, is this saying correctly interpreted by most people as a positive call to long-term action?

SCRIPTURES IN FILM

For the connection between Taoism and martial arts, see especially *Crouching Tiger, Hidden Dragon* (2000, directed by Ang Lee; in Mandarin, with English subtitles). This film, which won four Academy Awards including Best Foreign Film, draws on the Wudang Taoist school of meditation and martial arts, although this is not explicit in the film. For a more avant-garde film on Taoist themes, see *Koyaanisqatsi* ("Life Out of Balance," 1982, directed by Godfrey Reggio). Without any characters or conventional plot, this film uses music and film photography to depict the balance in nature that humans should study and adapt to, a key Taoist teaching.

SUGGESTIONS FOR FURTHER READING

PRIMARY READINGS

S. Addiss and S. Lombardo, *Lao-Tzu, Tao Te Ching*. Cambridge, MA: Hackett, 1993. An excellent translation characterized by literary grace and terse poetic power.

R. G. Henricks, *Lao Tzu, Te-Tao Ching*. New York: Ballantine, 1989. A lively translation, with full introduction and commentary, of the recently discovered *Ma-wang-tui* texts. (The usual name of this book is reversed in these texts.)

L. Kohn, ed., *The Taoist Experience: An Anthology*. Albany: State University of New York Press, 1993. Presentation and explanation of sixty key texts in Taoism.

J. Legge, ed., *The Texts of Taoism*. New York: Julian, 1959; first published 1891 by Oxford University Press. A standard rendering of the *Tao Te Ching*, *Chuang-tzu*, and the *T'hai-Shang*.

J. R. Ware, *Alchemy, Medicine, Religion in the China of A.D. 320: The Nei P'ien of Ko Hung (Pao-p'u tzu)*. Cambridge, MA: MIT Press, 1966. A complete and accurate translation of the single most important text in the history of religious Taoism.

SECONDARY READINGS

R. E. Allinson, *Chuang-Tzu for Spiritual Transformation: An Analysis of the Inner Chapters*. Albany: State University of New York Press, 1989. A challenging philosophical analysis of the heart of this classic.

Chih-chung Tsai (Zhirhong Cai), *Zhuangzi Speaks: The Music of Nature*, trans. Brian Bruya. Princeton, NJ: Princeton University Press, 1992. A best-selling book in its Chinese original, this volume features line drawings and cartoon interpretations of the *Chuang-tzu* by the Taiwanese cartoonist Chih-chung Tsai to express the ineffable Tao.

B. E. Reed, "[Women in] Taoism." In A. Sharma, ed., *Women in World Religions*. Albany: State University of New York Press, 1987, pp. 161–181. An insightful analysis of the role of the feminine in Taoist scripture, especially the *Tao Te Ching*, and women's less than prominent role in lived Taoist religion.

M. Saso, *Blue Dragon White Tiger: Taoist Rites of Passage*. Washington, DC: Taoist Center, 1990. A treatment of various life-cycle rituals.

K. Schipper and F. Verellen, *The Taoist Canon: A Historical Companion to the Daozang*. Chicago: University of Chicago Press, 2005. A three-volume handbook to the entire Taoist canon that sets out its contents chronologically, with a brief description of each book's contents and origin.

E. Slingerland, *Effortless Action: Wu-wei as a Conceptual Metaphor and Spiritual Ideal in Early China*. New York: Oxford University Press, 2003. Argues that wu-wei was an important concept not only in Taoism but in nearly all leading religions in early China.

COMPANION WEBSITE

Visit the *Anthology of World Scriptures* companion website at **www.thomsonedu.com** for learning tools such as map explorations, flashcards of glossary terms, learning objectives, chapter practice quizzes, links to other websites for learning and research, and chapter summaries in PowerPoint® format.

CHAPTER EIGHT

Shinto

Izanagi Creating the Japanese Islands

This hanging scroll painting by Kobayashi Eitaku (1843–1890) depicts a leading theme of the Shinto sacred writings, the creation of Japan as the first of all nations. (*Photograph copyright ©️ 2004 Museum of Fine Arts, Boston. William Sturgis Bigelow Collection. Courtesy, Museum of Fine Arts, Boston.*)

INTRODUCTION

Shinto, the ancient Japanese national religion, is unique among the religious traditions of Asia and the world. Of all the major faiths based in historically literate cultures, it is the only one that has no scripture as modern scholars understand that term. It does have sacred books, but Shinto recognizes no book as officially authoritative. It has no canon and no formalized doctrines or ethical systems that could be shaped by a scripture. Therefore, our presentation of Shinto takes a format different from the other chapters.

Two books in particular do have a special standing in Shinto because of their antiquity and unique contents: the **Kojiki,** "Record of Ancient Matters," and the **Nihongi,** "Chronicles of Japan." Written by imperial decree in the eighth century C.E., these books have held a place of honor in Shinto. The Japanese have looked on them as the story of the foundation of Japan. For a thousand years, schoolchildren were taught their stories as an education in patriotism. These books "are regarded as authoritative and provide [Shinto's] historical as well as its spiritual basis."[1]

Though not classified as scripture, the *Kojiki* [koh-JEE-kee] and *Nihongi* [nih-HAWN-gee] provide good evidence of the leading ideas of the Shinto tradition. First in importance is the existence of many **kami,** or gods and spirits. Second, humanity is the offspring of the kami [KAH-mee] and is continually supported by their power. Third, the Japanese nation, especially the imperial family, is the center of humanity. Fourth, deep reverence is owed the emperor as the one through whom blessings flow to the nation.

Since the disestablishment of Shinto as the official state religion in 1945, the *Kojiki* and *Nihongi* have not been taught in Japanese schools. Moreover, as a part of the disestablishment, the emperor of Japan renounced his divinity, which these books were intended to buttress. Nevertheless, much of the traditional high regard for Shinto still lingers. For example, both pride and protests erupted in 1991 when Akihito, the new emperor, spent a night in a specially constructed Shinto shrine, a ritual once thought to bring about the emperor's rebirth as a child of the sun-god Amaterasu. So even though the imperial claims that the *Kojiki* and the *Nihongi* were written to support have been officially renounced, these sacred texts continue to provide valuable insight into the historical essence of Shinto and its traditional relationship to the Japanese national character. The *Kojiki,* finished in 712 C.E., is the oldest surviving book in Japan. The only knowledge we have of its origin comes from the preface by its author, Yasumaro (given in full in the first reading). This preface records that Emperor Temmu (r. 672–687 C.E.) decreed that a new book should correct the falsified genealogical records of the leading Japanese families. In this way, the genealogical myths of the competing clans were incorporated into the genealogical myth of Temmu's clan. To do this, the *Kojiki* draws on two main works of the time: the *Teiki* (Imperial Sun-Lineage) and the *Honji* (Ancient Dicta of Former Ages). The first was a source of genealogies, and the second a collection of myths, legends, and songs; both were probably oral collections. These two sources, when combined and reworked into the *Kojiki,* shape its characteristic emphasis on a reliable genealogy that extends back to the gods.

---

[1]Sokyo Ono, *Shinto, The Kami Way* (Rutland, VT: Charles Tuttle, 1962), p. 10.

Scholars discern in the *Kojiki* other revisions to older traditions. For example, it is likely that early indigenous Japanese ideas about the equality of men and women were modified by Confucian ideas of male superiority.

The *Kojiki* itself is divided into three books. The first book, a statement of early Japanese mythology, proclaims that the emperor's family is destined to rule Japan because it is the "offspring of the heavenly deities." The second and third books contain stories of the ancient emperors and their exploits, most of them legendary, up to the time of writing. Only a few of these stories have any obvious religious significance.

The *Nihongi* (also known as the *Nihonshoki*) was written shortly after the *Kojiki*, in 720 C.E. Shotoku Daishi, its traditional author, compiled the *Nihongi* in thirty books. It narrates a closely related version of the stories in the *Kojiki*, draws on the same sources, and is written in the same Chinese style. Its special concern is to show that the Teika reforms of 645 C.E., which brought Shinto under stricter government regulation, resulted in greater obedience to the way of the kami.

SELECTIONS FROM THE *KOJIKI*

Preface to the *Kojiki*

This preface is the author's dedicatory address to Gemmei, niece and daughter-in-law of Emperor Kamu-Yamato (Temmu), who commissioned the work but died before its completion. The preface is a summary of much of the contents of the entire *Kojiki*. The narrator tells of the creation of the world, the birth of the early gods, and the creation of Japan. The middle sections deal with various emperors, from the first emperor, Jimmu, to Temmu, although the narrative seems to be speaking of Temmu continually throughout this section. His decision to sponsor the writing of the *Kojiki* is given special attention. The final sections tell the praises of the empress and provide the only information we have about the writing of this book. The significance of the *Kojiki* is given in this section: It is "the basis of the country, the grand foundation of the monarchy."[2]

I, Yasumaro, say:

When chaos had begun to condense, but force and form were not yet manifest, and nothing was named, nothing done, who could know its shape? Nevertheless Heaven and Earth first separated, and the Three Deities began creating.[3] The Passive and Active Essences[4] then developed, and the Two Spirits became the ancestors of all things.[5] Therefore he entered obscurity and emerged into light, and the washing of his eyes revealed the Sun and Moon. He floated on and plunged into the seawater, and Heavenly and Earthly Deities appeared through the washings of his person. So in the dimness of the great commencement, we, by relying

---

[2]Unless otherwise noted, all selections in this chapter are taken, with editing, from Basil Hall Chamberlain, trans., *Ko-ji-ki, Transactions of the Asiatic Society of Japan*, supplement to vol. 10 (Tokyo: Asiatic Society of Japan, 1906).

[3]*Deities:* The Japanese *kami* is translated "Deities" throughout.

[4]*Passive and Active Essences:* yin and yang, respectively.

[5]The *Two Spirits* from which all creation came are Izanagi (the Male-Who-Invites) and Izanami (the Female-Who-Invites).

on the original teaching, learn the time of the conception of the earth and of the birth of islands. In the remoteness of the original beginning, we perceive the era of the genesis of Deities and of the establishment of humans by trusting the former sages. Truly, we know that a mirror was hung up,[6] that jewels were spat out, and that then a Hundred Kings succeeded each other. We know that a blade was bitten, and a serpent cut in pieces, so that ten thousand deities flourished. By deliberations in the Tranquil River the Empire was pacified; by discussions on the Little Shore the land was purified.

Then His Augustness Ho-no-ni-ni-gi first descended to the Peak of Takachi, and the Heavenly Sovereign Kamu-Yamato traversed the Island of the Dragon-Fly. A weird bear put forth its claws, and a heavenly saber was obtained at Takakura. Men with tails obstructed the path, and a great crow guided him to Yeshinu. Dancing in rows, they destroyed the criminals, and listening to a song they vanquished their foes. Being instructed in a dream, he was reverent to the Heavenly and Earthly Deities, and was therefore styled the Wise Monarch. Having gazed on the smoke, he was benevolent to the people, and is therefore remembered as the Emperor-Sage....

In the august reign of the Heavenly Sovereign who governed the Eight Great Islands from the Great Palace of Kiyomihara at Asuka, the Hidden Dragon[7] put on perfection, the Reiterated Thunder came at the appointed moment. Having heard a song in a dream, he felt that he should continue the succession; having reached the water at night, he knew that he should receive the inheritance. Nevertheless Heaven's time was not yet, and he escaped like the cicada to the Southern Mountains.[8]

Then both men and matters were favorable, and he marched like the tiger to the Eastern Land.[9]

---

[6] *mirror:* In many Shinto shrines, a mirror is often the only visible symbol of the kami's presence.
[7] *the Hidden Dragon:* the emperor as the crown prince.
[8] *he escaped...Mountains:* He renounced ordinary life for a time.
[9] This paragraph tells how the emperor crushed an attempt by a rival to gain the imperial throne by force.

Suddenly riding in the imperial chariot, he forced his way across mountains and rivers. The Six Divisions rolled like thunder, the Three Hosts sped like lightning. The erect spears lifted up their might, and the bold warriors arose like smoke. The crimson flags glistened among the weapons, and the ill-omened crew were shattered like tiles. Before a day had elapsed, the evil influences were purified. Then the cattle were let loose and the horses given repose, and with shouts of victory they returned to the Flowery Summer. The flags were rolled up and the javelins put away, and with dances and chants they came to rest in the capital city. The year was that of the Rooster, and it was the Second Moon. At the Great Palace of Kiyomihara, he ascended to the Heavenly seat.... Then the Heavenly Sovereign commanded, "I hear that the chronicles of the emperors and likewise the original words in the possession of the various families deviate from exact truth, and are mostly amplified by empty falsehoods. If at the present time these imperfections be not amended, before many years shall have elapsed, the purport of this, the great basis of the country, the grand foundation of the monarchy, will be destroyed. So now I desire to have the chronicles of the emperors selected and recorded, and the old words examined and ascertained, falsehoods erased and truth determined, in order to transmit [the latter] to later ages."

At that time there was a retainer whose surname was Hiyeda; his personal name was Are. He was twenty-eight years old, and so intelligent that he could repeat with his mouth whatever met his eyes, and record in his heart whatever struck his ears. Then Are was commanded to learn by heart the genealogies of the emperors, and likewise the words of former ages. Nevertheless time elapsed and the age changed, and the thing was not yet carried out. Lying facedown in reverence, I consider how Her Majesty the Empress, having obtained the throne, illumines the empire. Being versed inthe Triad [of heaven, humanity and earth], shenourishes the people. Ruling from the Purple Palace, her virtue reaches to the utmost limits ofthe horses' hoof-marks. Dwelling amid the Somber Retinue, her influence illumines the farthestdistance attained to by vessels' prows. The sun rises, and the brightness is increased; the clouds disperse, neither is there smoke. The chroniclers never cease recording the good omens of connected stalks and double rice-ears. Never for a single moon is the treasury without the tribute of continuous beacon-fires and repeated interpretations. In fame she must be pronounced superior to Bum-Mei, in virtue more eminent than Ten-Itsu.[10]

She regretted the errors in the old words, and wished to correct the misstatements in the former chronicles. So on the eighteenth day of the ninth moon of the fourth year of Wa-do, she commanded me, Yasumaro, to select and record the old words learned by heart by Hiyeda No Are according to the Imperial Decree, and dutifully to lift them up to her. In reverent obedience to the contents of the Decree, I have made a careful choice. But in high antiquity both speech and thought were so simple, that it would be difficult to arrange phrases and compose sentences in [Chinese] characters.... Moreover, where the meaning of the words was obscure, I have elucidated their meaning. But need it be said that I have nowhere commented on what was easy? Again, in such cases as calling the surname *Kusaka,* and the personal name written with the character *Tarashi,* I have followed usage without alteration. Altogether the things recorded commence with the separation of Heaven and Earth, and conclude with the august reign at Woharida.[11] ... Altogether I have written three volumes, which I now reverently and respectfully present. I, Yasumaro, with true trembling and true reverence, bow my head, and bow my head again.

Reverently presented by the Court Noble Futo no Yasumaro, an Officer of the Upper Division of the Fifth Rank and of the Fifth Order of Merit, on the 28th day of the first moon of the fifth year of Wa-do.[12]

---

[10]*Bum-Mei...Ten-Itsu:* ancient Chinese rulers.

[11]*reign at Woharida:* the reign of the Empress Suiko, who died in 628 C.E.
[12]March 10, 712 C.E.

The Creation of Japan

In Chapter 1 of the *Kojiki,* the spontaneous birth of the first gods is described. Although the narration starts at the "beginning of heaven and earth," the myths of the *Kojiki* (and the *Nihongi* as well) are much more stories of the creation of Japan than full-fledged stories of the creation of the world. The reader notices, for example, no mention of the making of humanity in general or of animals. At the end of Chapter 2, the key gods Izanagi (the Male-Who-Invites) and Izanami (the Female-Who-Invites) come into being, and they begin to create islands. Chapters 4 and 5 tell the story of the births of their first children, and we can see a concern for proper male–female relationships. In Chapter 33, the culmination of these myths is reached when the grandson of Amaterasu descends from heaven to rule the land that was to become Japan.

[Chapter 1, "The Beginning of Heaven and Earth"] The names of the Deities that were born in the Plain of High Heaven when the Heaven and Earth began were the Deity Master-of-the-August-Center-of-Heaven, next the High-August-Producing-Wondrous-Deity, then the Divine-Producing-Wondrous-Deity. These three Deities were all Deities born alone, and hid their persons.

Kojiki 1–5, 33.

The names of the Deities that were born next from a thing that sprouted up like a reed-shoot when the earth, young and like floating oil, drifted about medusa-like, were the Pleasant-Reed-Shoot-Prince-Elder-Deity and the Heavenly-Eternally-Standing-Deity. These two Deities were likewise born alone, and hid their persons. The five Deities in the above list are separate Heavenly Deities.

[Chapter 2, "The Seven Divine Generations"] The names of the Deities that were born next were the Earthly-Eternally-Standing-Deity, next the Luxuriant-Integrating-Master-Deity. These two Deities were likewise Deities born alone, and hid their persons. The names of the Deities that were born next were the Deity Mud-Earth-Lord, next his younger sister the Deity Mud-Earth-Lady; next the Germ-Integrating- Deity, next his younger sister the Life-Integrating-Deity; next the Deity Elder-of-the-Great-Place, next his younger sister the Deity Elder-Lady-of-the-Great-Place; next the Deity Perfect-Exterior, next his younger sister the Deity Oh-Awful-Lady; next the Deity the Male-Who-Invites, next his younger sister the Deity the Female-Who-Invites. From the Earthly-Eternally-Standing-Deity down to the Deity the Female-Who-Invites in the previous list are what are termed the Seven Divine Generations. (The two solitary Deities above [mentioned] are each called one generation. Of the succeeding ten Deities each pair of deities is called a generation.)

[Chapter 3, "The Island of Onogoro"] Then all the Heavenly Deities commanded the two Deities His Augustness the Male-Who-Invites and Her Augustness the Female-Who-Invites, ordering them to "make, consolidate, and give birth to this drifting land." Granting to them a heavenly jeweled spear, they charged them thus. So the two Deities, standing upon the Floating Bridge of Heaven, pushed down the jeweled spear and stirred with it. When they had stirred the brine till it went curdle-curdle, and drew [the spear] up, the brine that dripped down from the end of the spear was piled up and became an island. This is the Island of Onogoro.

[Chapter 4, "Courtship of the Deities, the Male-Who-Invites and the Female-Who-Invites"] Having descended from Heaven onto this island, they saw to the erection of a heavenly august pillar, and they saw to the erection of a hall of eight fathoms. Then he asked the Female-Who-Invites, "In what form is your body made?" She responded, saying, "My body is formed with one part not fully formed." Then the Male-Who-Invites said, "My body is formed with one part more than fully formed. Therefore, would it not be good to take that part of my body which is more than fully formed and insert it into that part of your body which is less than fully formed, and procreate the land?" The Female-Who-Invites responded, "That would be good." Then the Male-Who-Invites said, "Let us walk in a circle about this heavenly pillar, meet, and have intercourse." Then she said, "You go around from the right, and I will go around from the left." Then they agreed and went around, and the Female-Who-Invites said first, "What a charming and lovable male!" Then the Male-Who-Invites said, "What a charming and lovable female!" When each had finished talking, he said to his wife, "It is not fitting that the woman speak first." But they still began procreating, and she gave birth to a leech-child. This child they placed in a boat of reeds, and let it float away. Next they gave birth to the Island of Aha. It also is not reckoned among their children.

[Chapter 5, "The Birth of the Eight Islands"] Then the two Deities took counsel, saying: "The children to whom we have now given birth are not good. It will be best to announce this in the august place of the Heavenly Deities." They ascended to Heaven and enquired of Their Augustnesses the Heavenly Deities. Then the Heavenly Deities commanded and found out by grand divination, and ordered them, saying: "They were not good because the woman spoke first. Descend back again and amend your words." So descending back, they again went round the heavenly august pillar as before. Then his Augustness the Male-Who-Invites spoke first: "Ah! What a charming and lovely maiden!" Afterward his younger sister Her Augustness the Female-Who-Invites spoke: "Ah! What a charming and lovely youth!" When these words were said, they had intercourse as before, and procreated the Island of Ahaji, Ho-no-sa-wake. Next they gave birth to the Island of Futa-na in Iyo. This island has one body and four faces, and each face has a name. So the Land of Iyo is called Lovely Princess; the Land of Sanuki is called Prince Good-Boiled-Rice; the Land of Aha is called the Princess-of-Great-Food; the Land of Tosa is called Brave-Good-Youth....

[Chapter 33, "The August Descent from Heaven of His Augustness the August Grandchild"] Then the Heaven-Shining-Great-August-Deity and the High-Integrating-Deity commanded and charged the Heir Apparent His Augustness Truly-Conqueror-I-Conquer-Swift-Heavenly-Great-Great-Ears [saying: "The Brave-Awful-Possessing-Male-Deity] says that he has now finished pacifying the Central Land of Reed-Plains. In accordance with our gracious charge, descend to, dwell in, and rule over it." Then the Heir Apparent His Augustness Truly-Conqueror-I-Conquer-Swift-Heavenly-Great-Ears replied, saying: "While I have been getting ready to descend, there has been born [to me] a child whose name is His Augustness Heaven-Plenty-Earth-Plenty-Heaven's-Sun-Height-Prince-Rice-ear-Ruddy-Plenty. This child should be sent down. [As for this august child, he was augustly joined to Her Augustness Myriad-Looms-Luxuriant-Dragon-fly-Island-Princess, daughter of the High-Integrating-Deity, and begot children: His Augustness Heavenly-Rice-ear-Ruddy, and next His Augustness Prince Rice-ear-Ruddy-Plenty].

In accordance with these words, they laid their command on His Augustness Prince Rice-ear-Ruddy-Plenty, charging him with these words, "This Luxuriant Reed-Plain-Land-of-Fresh-Rice-Ears is the land over which you shall rule." So [he replied]: "I will descend from Heaven according to your commands." So when His Augustness Prince Rice-ear-Ruddy-Plenty was about to descend from Heaven, there was at the eight-forking road of Heaven a Deity whose refulgence reached upward to the Plain of High Heaven and downward to the Central Land of Reed-Plains. So then the Heaven-Shining-Great-August-Deity and the High-Integrating-Deity commanded and charged the Heavenly-Alarming-Female-Deity [saying]: "Though you are a delicate female, you are a Deity who conquers in facing Deities. So be the one to go and ask thus, 'This being the road by which our august child is about to descend from Heaven, who is it that is there?'" So to this gracious question he replied, saying, "I am an Earthly Deity named the Deity Prince of Saruta. The reason for my coming here is that, having heard of the [intended] descent of the august child of the Heavenly Deities, I have come humbly to meet him and respectfully offer myself as His Augustness's vanguard." Then joining to him His Augustness Heavenly-Beckoning-Ancestor-Lord, His Augustness Grand-Jewel, Her Augustness Heavenly-Alarming-Female, Her Augustness I-shi-ko-ri-do-me, and His Augustness Jewel-Ancestor, in all five chiefs of companies, they sent him down from Heaven. Thereupon they joined to him the eight-feet [long] curved jewels and mirror that had allured [the Heaven-Shining-Great-August-Deity from the Rock-Dwelling], and also the Herb-Quelling-Great-Sword, and likewise the Deity Thought-Includer, the Hand-Strength-Male-Deity, and the Deity Heavenly-Rock-Door-Opener of Eternal Night, and charged him, "Regard this mirror exactly as if it were our august spirit, and reverence it as if reverencing us." Next they said, "Let the Deity Thought-Includer take in hand our affairs, and carry on the government." These two Deities are worshipped at the temple of Isuzu. The next, the Deity of Luxuriant-Food, is the Deity dwelling in the outer temple of Watarahi. The next, the Deity Heavenly-Rock-Door-Opener, another name for whom is the Wondrous-Rock-True-Gate-Deity, and another name for whom is the Luxuriant-Rock-True-Gate-Deity—this Deity of the August Gate. The next, the Deity Hand-Strength-Male, dwells in Sanagata.

The Story of Emperor Yuryaku and the Woman Akawi-ko

Most of the *Kojiki* is made up of legendary stories about the Japanese emperors told to extol their own greatness. This bittersweet story of the woman Akawi-ko and the emperor Yuryaku, with the poetic songs that conclude it, is indicative of Japanese literary style. In this chapter, the old woman Akawi-ko comes before Emperor Yuryaku, the "Heavenly Sovereign," to prove her faithfulness to a command he had given her many years before.

Once when the Heavenly Sovereign, going out for amusement, reached the River Miwa, a very beautiful girl was washing clothes by the riverside. The Heavenly Sovereign asked the girl, "Whose child are you?" She replied, "My name is Akawi-ko of the Hiketa Tribe." Then he said to her, "Do not marry a husband. I will send for you," and [with these words] he returned to the palace. Eighty years passed while she reverently awaited the Heavenly Sovereign's commands. Then Akawi-ko thought: "While looking for the [Imperial] commands, I have already passed many years. My face and form are lean and withered, so there is no longer any hope for me. Nevertheless, if I do not show [the Heavenly Sovereign] how truly I have waited, my disappointment will be unbearable." She caused merchandise to be carried on tables holding a hundred items, and came forth and presented [these gifts as] tribute. Then the Heavenly Sovereign, who had completely forgotten what he had formerly commanded, asked Akawi-ko, "What old woman are you, and why have you come here?" Then Akawi-ko replied, saying: "Having in such and such a month of such and such a year received the Heavenly Sovereign's commands, I have been reverently awaiting the great

command until this day, and eighty years have passed by. Now my appearance is quite decrepit, and there is no longer any hope for me. Nevertheless I have come forth in order to show and declare my faithfulness." Then the Heavenly Sovereign was greatly startled [and exclaimed], "I had quite forgotten the former event! Meanwhile, ever faithfully awaiting my commands, you have vainly let pass by the years of your prime. This is very pitiful." In his heart he wished to marry her, but he shrank from her extreme age, and could not make the marriage. However, he conferred on her an august song:

> "The younger chestnut orchard plain of Hiketa: would I had slept with her in her youth! Oh! How old she has become!"

Then the tears that Akawi-ko wept drenched the red-dyed sleeve that she had on. In reply to the great august song, she sang this song,

> "Left over from the piling up of the jewel-wall piled up round the august dwelling— to whom shall the person of the Deity's temple go?" . . .

Then the old woman was sent back plentifully endowed. So these songs are Quiet Songs.

Kojiki 154.

 GLOSSARY

Klami [KAH-mee] gods or spirits and their sacred power.

Kojiki [koh-JEE-kee] "Record of Ancient Matters."

Nihongi [nih-HAWN-gee] "Chronicles of Japan."

QUESTIONS FOR STUDY AND DISCUSSION

1. Describe the basic structure of Shinto polytheism as reflected in Shinto mythology.
2. Why, in your view, do the Japanese myths place so much emphasis on the creation of Japan instead of on the creation of the world?
3. Compare the status of the emperor in Confucianism and Shinto.
4. To what degree does the *Kojiki* reflect the traditional interpersonal customs of Japan?
5. How might the emperor's renunciation of divine standing have altered the reading of these texts and their influence in contemporary Japan?

SCRIPTURES IN FILM

The best recent film that portrays Japan's religion and culture is *The Last Samurai* (2003, rated R), directed by Edward Zwick. Tom Cruise plays an eighteenth-century American military adviser who, after he is captured in battle, embraces the samurai culture he was hired to destroy. The film begins with a brief retelling of the creation myth from the *Kojiki* and reflects its feeling for the land and people of Japan. The film also illustrates the Bushido code in action and the interplay between Buddhist tendencies to pacifism and traditional Shinto-samurai militancy.

SUGGESTIONS FOR FURTHER READING

W. G. Aston, *Nihongi: Chronicles of Japan from the Earliest Times to A.D. 697*. London: Kegan Paul, 1896.

B. H. Chamberlain, *Translation of* Ko-ji-ki. Tokyo: Asiatic Society of Japan, 1906; 2d ed., Kobe: Thompson, 1932. The standard translation of the *Kojiki*.

W. Theodore de Bary, *Sources of Japanese Tradition*. New York: Columbia University Press, 1958. Contains fresh translations of many important Shinto texts and a treatment of how early texts were used in Japanese history.

D. L. Philippi, *The* Kojiki. Princeton, NJ: Princeton University Press, 1969. Philippi's introduction and notes are full and helpful.

COMPANION WEBSITE

Visit the *Anthology of World Scriptures* companion website at **www.thomsonedu.com** for learning tools such as map explorations, flashcards of glossary terms, learning objectives, chapter practice quizzes, links to other websites for learning and research, and chapter summaries in PowerPoint® format.

CHAPTER NINE

Zoroastrianism

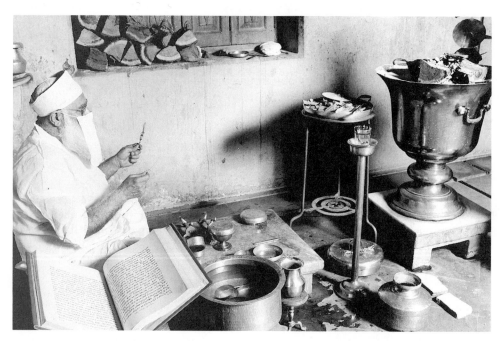

Zoroastrian Ritual

With the *Avesta* lying open at his right, a Zoroastrian priest in India offers a sacrifice. (*Jehangir Gazdar/Woodfin Camp & Associates.*)

- In a house in Mumbai (Bombay), India, a seven-year-old girl is being received into the Zoroastrian religion. A priest stands behind her, guiding her hands as she ties a sacred cord around her waist. She will wear this cord, which serves as a belt, for the rest of her life, except while bathing or sleeping. Five times a day, she will ceremonially loosen it, say her prayers, and then retie it. The cord has seventy-two threads representing the seventy-two chapters of the chief book of the Zoroastrian scripture, the *Yasna*.

- As he sits on the floor in a Zoroastrian temple in a Chicago suburb, a priest offers sacrifice for the souls of the dead. In his secular occupation, Kersey Antia is a psychologist specializing in panic disorders. As a Zoroastrian priest, he officiates at the fire ceremonies, feeding sandalwood and frankincense into a blazing fire in an ornate urn. He recites prayers from the Zoroastrian scriptures, which he has learned to pronounce by special training in the Avestan language at a school in India. Although Zoroastrians today do not understand many Avestan words, the Zoroastrian god Ahura Maza does, so the words are still effective.

- In August 2006, a controversy erupts in Tanzania over proposed celebrations marking what would have been the sixtieth birthday of the late rock star Freddie Mercury, the frontman and lead singer of the English rock band Queen. Mercury, born Farrokh Bulsara to a Zoroastrian family in what is now Tanzania, composed many hit songs, including "Bohemian Rhapsody" and "We Are the Champions." Although he did not formally observe his ancestral Zoroastrian religion as an adult, when he died in 1991 his funeral in London was led at Mercury's wishes by Zoroastrian priests. These rites, conducted entirely in the Avestan language, included prayers and hymns from the Zoroastrian scriptures.

INTRODUCTION

Begun perhaps 3,000 years ago in ancient Persia (modern Iran) by the prophet Zarathushtra, known to the Western world as Zoroaster, Zoroastrianism became the state religion of both the Persian Empire (sixth through fourth centuries B.C.E.) and the Sassanid Empire, which arose in the third century C.E. It had then approximately 40 million followers. Today, its numbers are severely reduced, with no more than 200,000 adherents clustered in eastern Iran and especially in Mumbai (Bombay), India. Many experts believe that Zoroastrianism may all but die out by the end of this century, and many Zoroastrian leaders fear this may be true. The scriptures of Zoroastrianism strongly advocate a moral life and maintaining ritual purity in worship and in daily life. Because of their obscure ancient language, troubled history of transmission, and fragmentary state, these scriptures are often difficult to understand. Nevertheless, the main beliefs of Zoroastrianism are clear, and modern Zoroastrians, like earlier believers, are concerned about how the scriptural message is embodied in daily life. Most scholars believe that Zoroastrianism had some significant influence on Judaism (the existence of angels and demons, judgment at the end of time, heaven and hell, etc.), and through Judaism on Christianity and Islam, but the scope of this influence is debated.

Overview of Structure

The ancient scriptures of Zoroastrianism are known as the ***Avesta.*** The meaning of the word *avesta* is uncertain. Usually translated as "injunction, command," it has also been translated as "wisdom, knowledge," as "authoritative utterance," and as "scripture." It probably derives from the Middle Persian word *avastaq,* "law." The "injunction" is that of the god Ahura Mazda, the Lord and Creator, through the prophet Zarathushtra. The term *avesta* is broad enough to encompass all the commands of Zoroastrianism: to serve good and turn from evil; to be both morally and ceremonially pure; and to worship Ahura Mazda and the good spirits by sacrifice and praise.

The *Avesta* [ah-VES-tuh] has four major divisions, each with ritual content and orientation. The ***Yasna*** (Sacrifice), the first and most important part, consists of hymns for worship in seventy-two chapters. The ***Visparad*** (All the [Divine] Lords) has twenty chapters of hymns. Within the ***Yashts*** [Hymns] are hymns of praise to sacred beings and heroic humans. The twenty-two-chapter ***Vendidad*** (The Law Against Demons) contains myths and codes of religious law. We now examine these Avestan books in turn.

The earliest and most important section of the *Yasna* [YAZH-nuh] is the ***Gathas,*** a collection of seventeen hymns. They now occupy five sections of the *Yasna.* Orthodox Zoroastrians believe the whole of the *Avesta* to be the work of Zarathushtra, but they hold the *Gathas* [GAH-tuhs] as especially his words. Modern scholarship agrees, using the *Gathas* as the primary source for our knowledge of Zarathushtra. The *Gathas* are distinguished from the other *Yasna* hymns by their emphasis on ethics and their lack of attention to ritual concerns. One main topic elsewhere in the *Yasna* is the haoma ritual, in which the juices of the haoma plant are ground out and mixed with milk and herbs. Also in the *Yasna* are prayers, a confession of faith, and rules for sacrifices to water. Priests daily recite all seventy-two chapters (from memory!) during Zoroastrianism's main sacrificial ceremony, the sacrifice of the haoma in fire. This sacrifice is called the Yasna, from which this part of the *Avesta* gets its name.

About one-sixth as long as the *Yasna,* the *Visparad* [VEE-spuh-rahd] contains poetic invocations, praises, and sacrifices to all the divine lords of Zoroastrianism. Words from this section of the *Avesta* are recited at various stages of the Yasna ceremony. Zoroastrians also recite the *Visparad* during their six holy days of obligation, especially New Year's Day.

The *Yashts* [yahshts] are hymns of praise to twenty-one divinities, angels, and human heroes of ancient Persia. Among the most important are hymns to Mithra and a hymn to the guardian spirits—**Fravashis** [frah-VAH-shees]—of the old saints. Much of the material in the *Yashts* is drawn from pre-Zoroastrian religion and provides an interesting glimpse of how Zoroastrianism adapted older Indo-European religious ideas to its own use. This occurred after the time of Zarathushtra himself; according to the *Gathas,* the prophet made a clean break with the older religion.

The *Vendidad* [VEN-dih-dahd] begins with two myths about the creation of the world and a primeval flood that tell how divine law came to humans. The remaining sixteen chapters form a law code that prescribes purifications and penalties for priests. Chapters 3 and 5, for example, contain regulations for funerals; Chapter 18 deals with the difference between true and false priests. Like the *Yashts,* the words of the *Vendidad* are recited during the Yasna ceremony.

Contemporary Use

As their names imply, the *Avesta* books are strongly oriented to worship and sacrifice. The scriptures are the hymn texts for sacrifice, and sacrifice is done to the constant accompaniment of scripture recitation, usually from memory. The use of scripture throughout Zoroastrian history has therefore been almost exclusively performative. Priests use scripture for the enactment of ritual, not for study, meditation, or the formation and teaching of doctrine. The Avestan language used in formal worship and in the traditional main prayers of the faithful is largely unknown to some priests and to most laypersons. Thus, Zoroastrians typically have had little knowledge of what their scriptures actually "teach."

At the end of nineteenth century, a movement of reform sought to change this age-old use of the *Avesta*. Under the influence of Western religion and European methods of religious scholarship, reformers claimed that the *Gathas* are the center and only authentic part of the *Avesta* and that everything else is to be judged in light of the leading ideas of the *Gathas*. Rituals were regarded as secondary to moral teachings and were interpreted symbolically, altered, or sometimes disregarded altogether. The rational, philosophical, and moral elements of the faith were given priority. This shift from a performative to a cognitive use among a minority of Zoroastrians in India and North America is the source of one of the chief internal disagreements in Zoroastrianism.

Historical Origin and Development

The *Avesta* begins with Zarathushtra himself. Though a date for the prophet in the sixth century B.C.E. is still accepted by most scholars, some (especially Mary Boyce) push Zarathushtra back to 1400–1000 B.C.E. The oral tradition that was later written down into the *Gathas* as we know them can be traced more or less to Zarathushtra for reasons of both style and content.

Next to arise, probably over the course of a millennium, were the other poetic sections of the *Avesta*, which scholars today call the "Younger *Avesta*." The rest of the *Yasna* and the *Yashts* are in metrical poetry. Last to be written were the prose portions of the *Avesta*. The whole process was complete and the canon of the *Avesta* was fixed by about 325 C.E.

In its original form, the *Avesta* was probably about four times larger than it is now. Besides the liturgical texts now in the *Avesta*, it probably treated cosmogony, eschatology, astronomy, natural history, the history of Zarathushtra, and several other topics. The *Zand*, a later collection of Zoroastrian literature, contains many references to a large loss of Zoroastrian scripture during the invasions of Alexander the Great (fourth century B.C.E.). What remained from these persecutions was material that was fixed in the memory of the priests—liturgical scripture. A collection was made under the Sassanid Empire in the third and fourth centuries C.E. The *Avesta* as we know it comes from this period and was probably first written down at this time. Zoroastrianism became the state religion of the Sassanid Empire, and a written text may have been viewed as a tool for promoting uniformity in religious doctrine and practice.

In the seventh century C.E., Islam began to press hard on the religion of Ahura Mazda. Although it officially tolerated Zoroastrianism as a monotheistic religion, Islam sought to end the faith by suppressing its temples and burning its scripture books. Some Zoroastrians fled Muslim intolerance for a more congenial life around Bombay, India, where they were welcomed by the dominant Hindu culture. During this period, the *Avesta* was reduced to its present size and preserved by the small Zoroastrian community left to continue to this day. The oldest manuscript that has survived dates to 1323 C.E.; the entire Avesta collection was printed for the first time in the nineteenth century.

HISTORY

The Call of Zarathushtra

This gatha is a conversation among four main characters: (1) the collective soul of the cattle, which represents the means of livelihood for the people of the Zoroastrian faith. In pre-Zoroastrian religion, this figure was a god; (2) Asha, or "Righteousness," one of the Immortal Holy Ones; (3) Ahura Mazda, the one God who is Lord and Creator; and (4) Zarathushtra. It closes with Zarathushtra's prayer for divine aid; the main point is that Zarathushtra himself alone can lead humanity to their God. Worshippers use this passage as a prayer for divine help to destroy the powers of deceit and to promote peace and truth.[1]

The Soul of the Cattle and the people cried aloud to you, O Ahura and Asha, "For whom did you create me, and by whom did you fashion me? Assaults of wrath and violent power come upon me, with desolating blows and bold insolence. I have no other pasture-giver than you. Teach me good cultivation of the fields, which is my only hope of blessing!"

Then the Creator of the Cattle asked Righteousness: "How did you appoint a guardian for the cattle when you made her? How did you secure for her both pasture and a cattle-chief who was skilled and energetic? Did you select one who might hurl back the fury of the wicked?"

The Divine Righteousness answered in his holiness, "We were very perplexed. We could not obtain a leader who was capable of striking back their fury, and who himself was without hate. We cannot know the influences that approach and move the heavenly fires, fires which reveal the favor and the will of God. God is the mightiest of beings. Those who have performed their actions approach him with invocations. He has no need to ask!"

Zarathushtra said, "The Great Creator is most mindful of the commands that have been fulfilled in the deeds of demon-gods and good or evil men. He knows the commands that they will fulfill. Ahura is the discerning judge. It shall be to us as he desires! [5] Therefore we both, my soul and the soul of the mother cattle, are making our requests for this world and the next to Ahura. With hands stretched out in entreaty, we pray to the Great Creator with questions in our doubt. He will answer. Destruction will not come to the one who lives righteously, or to the careful farmers of the earth!"

---

[1]Except where noted, all passages from Zoroastrian scripture are taken, with editing, from J. Darmesteter and L. H. Mills, trans., *The Zend-Avesta, Sacred Books of the East*, vols. 4, 23, 31 (Oxford: Oxford University Press, 1880–1887).

Yasna 29.

Then the wise Lord, the Great Creator who understands the mysterious grace by his insight, spoke. "We cannot find such a spiritual master among us. Nor can we find a leader moved by righteousness and appointed by its spirit. Therefore I have named you as the leader of the diligent tillers of the ground!"

The Immortal Holy Ones said, "Mazda has created the inspired Word of reason that is a spoken formula of fatness for the offering. The Divine Righteousness consented to Mazda's deed. He has prepared food for the cattle and food for the eaters. He is bountiful with his saving doctrine. But who is endowed with the Good Mind, who can give those teachings by word of mouth to mortals?"

Ahura said, "I have found one man, Zarathushtra Spitama[2], who alone has listened to our words! He desires to recite our teachings, for me the Great Creator, and for Righteousness. Therefore I will give him a good dwelling and the authoritative position of one who speaks for us!"

Then the Soul of the cattle lamented, "Woe is me, for I have obtained a lord who is powerless to carry out his wish![3] He is only a feeble and timid man. I desire one who is lord over his will, one who is able to carry out what he desires." The Immortal Holy Ones said, "Yes, when shall one who brings strong help to her[4] ever appear?"

[10] Zarathushtra said, "O Ahura, O Righteousness, grant strength to these our disciples. Grant them the sovereign kingdom of God, which is established in his Good Mind. This kingdom gives them the peaceful amenities of home and quiet happiness, instead of the terrible ravages that they suffer. O Great Creator, I know that You are the provider of these blessings!

The soul of the Cattle said, "O Great Creator and Living Lord, when shall the divine Righteousness, the Good Mind of the Lord, and his sovereign power hurry to me? Know me through this mortal one [Zarathushtra]. Give us your aid in abundance!"

---

[2]*Spitama:* the clan to which Zarathushtra belongs.

[3]Verses 9–11 show the Cattle's reluctance to accept Zarathushtra, Zarathushtra's willingness to accept his divine calling, and finally the Cattle's acceptance of him.
[4]*her:* the (female) Soul of the Cattle.

A Hymn of Praise to Zarathushtra

With this hymn, Zoroastrians venerate the memory of Zarathushtra. Notice the recurring use of "who/he first." The end of this selection recounts a legend of the cosmic praise offered to the baby Zarathushtra.

We worship the piety and the guardian spirit of the holy Zarathushtra. He was the first who thought what is good, the first who spoke what is good, the first who did what is good. He was the first Priest, the first Warrior, the first Plower of the ground. He was the first to know and teach [the truth]. He first possessed and first took possession of the Bull, of Holiness, of the Word, the obedience to the Word, the dominion, and all the good things made by Mazda, the good things that are the offspring of the good Principle.

He first took the turning of the wheel[5] from the hands of the evil spirits and cold-hearted men. He was first in the material world to

---

[5]*turning of the wheel:* the life of the created world.

pronounce the praise of Asha, thus bringing the evil spirits to nothing. He confessed himself a worshipper of Mazda, a follower of Zarathushtra. He is one who hates the evil spirits and obeys the laws of Ahura.

[90] He was first in the material world to say the word that destroys the evil spirits, the law of Ahura. He was first in the material world to proclaim the words that destroy the evil spirits, the law of Ahura. He was the first in the material world to declare all the creation of the evil spirits unworthy of sacrifice and prayer. He was strong, giving all the good things of life, and he was the first bearer of the law among the nations.

In him was heard the whole Mathra, the word of holiness. He was the lord and master of the world. He was the praiser of Asha, who is the most great, most good and most fair. He had a revelation of the Law, that most excellent of all beings.

For him the Immortal Holy Ones longed, in one accord with the sun, in the fullness of the faith of a devoted heart. They longed for him as the lord and master of the world, as the praiser of the most great, most good and most fair Asha. He had a revelation of the Law, that most excellent of all beings. In his birth and growth the waters and the plants rejoiced. In his birth and growth the waters and the plants grew. In his birth and growth all the creatures of the good creations cried out, "Hail! Hail to us! For he is born, the great priest Spitama Zarathushtra. Zarathushtra will offer us sacrifices with drink offerings and bundles of sandalwood. The good Law of the worshippers of Mazda will come, and it will spread through all the seven parts of the earth."

TEACHING AND ETHICS

Hymn to Ahura and the Purifying Fire

This hymn to Ahura Mazda and to the spirit of fire is set in the fire temple. Notice the emphasis on morality in thought, word, and deed. Today, fire is still a symbol of moral purity and the spiritual center of every Zoroastrian temple.

[1] We desire to approach you . . . in this house of your holy Fire, O Ahura Mazda, most bounteous Spirit! If anyone brings pollutions to this flame, you will cover him with pollutions. O most friendly one, O Fire of the Lord, give us zeal! Come to us with the loving blessing of one who is most friendly, with the praise of the one most adored. Yes, come to us and aid us in this great task!

You truly are the Fire of Ahura Mazda. Yes, you are the most bounteous one of his Spirit. Therefore yours is the most potent of all names for grace, O Fire of the Lord! Therefore we come to you, O Ahura, with the help of your Good Mind that you implant in us. We come to you with your good Righteousness, and with actions and words implanted by your good wisdom!

[5] We bow before you, and we direct our prayers to you with confessions of our guilt, O Ahura Mazda! With all the good thoughts that you inspire, with all the words well said, and the deeds well done, with these we come to you. To your most beautiful body we make our deep acknowledgments, O Ahura Mazda. We acknowledge those stars that are your body, and we acknowledge that one star, the highest of the high, as the sun was called.

Yasna 36.

Hymn to Ahura Mazda the Creator

This selection is a beautiful expression of faith and devotion to Ahura Mazda the Creator and to the spirits associated with him.

We worship Ahura Mazda, who made the Cattle, Righteousness, the waters, the wholesome plants, the stars, the earth, and all existing things that are good. Yes, we worship him for his Sovereign Power and his greatness. They are full of blessing, and have priority among the Yazads who abide beside the Cattle in protection and support.

We worship him under his name as Lord, Mazda dear, the most gracious of names. We worship him with our bones and with our flesh. We worship the Fravashis of the saints, of holy men and holy women. We worship Righteousness the Best, the most beautiful, the Bountiful Immortal, who is endowed with light in all things good.

[5] We worship the Good Mind of the Lord, and his Sovereign Power, and the Good Faith, the good law, and Piety the ready mind within your people!

Yasna 37:1–5.

The Choice Between Good and Evil

This gatha instructs the believer in the basic teachings of Zarathushtra on good and evil. It speaks of the ancient character of good and evil, their role in the creation of the world, their present struggle for domination, and their destiny at the end of history. The believer must constantly choose the good and thereby build up its power in the universe. Most scholars believe that many of these ideas had an influence on Judaism and then on Christianity and Islam.

[1] Now I will proclaim to you my observations about him who knows all things to you who are drawing near and want to be taught. I will proclaim the praises of Ahura, the sacrifices that spring from the Good Mind, and the blessed meditations inspired by Righteousness. I pray that favorable results may be seen in the lights. Hear then with your ears; see the bright flames with the eyes of the Better Mind. It is a decision about religions, man and man, each individual himself. Before taking up this cause, awake to our teaching!

The primeval spirits as a pair combined their opposite strivings, yet each is independent in his action. They have long been famous. One is better, the other worse, in thought, in word, and in deed. Let those who act wisely choose correctly between these two. Do not choose as evil-doers choose!

When the two spirits came together at first, they made life and life's absence. They decided how the world shall be ordered at its end. The wicked receive Hell, the worst life; the holy receive Heaven, the Best Mental State. [5] He who was the evil one chose the evil realm, working the worst possible results. But the more gracious spirit chose the Divine Righteousness. Yes, he who clothes himself with the firm stones of heaven as his robe made this choice. He also

Yasna 30.

chose those who make Ahura happy by their actions, actions performed in accordance with the faith.

The Demon-gods and those who worship them can make no righteous choice between these two spirits, since they have been deceived. As they were questioning and debating in their council, the Worst Mind approached them that he might be chosen. They made their fatal decision. Then they rushed to the Demon of Fury, that they might pollute the lives of mortals.

Then Aramaiti, the personified Piety of the saints, approached. The Sovereign Power, the Good Mind, and the Righteous Order came with her. Aramaiti gave a body to the spiritual creations of good and of evil; she is the abiding and ever-strenuous one. O Mazda, let that body for your people be at the end like it was when you first created it! At the end the great struggle shall be fought out which began when the evil spirits first seized the Demon of Wrath as their ally, and then just vengeance shall come upon these wretches. Then, O Mazda, your Good Mind within your people shall gain the Kingdom for you. O living Lord! The Good Mind speaks his command to those who will deliver the Demon of the Lie into the two hands of the Righteous Order, like a captive is delivered to a destroyer.

May we be like those who bring on this great renovation. May we make this world progressive, until its perfection is reached. May we be like the Ahuras of Mazda. Yes, may we be like you, in helpful readiness to meet your people, presenting benefits in union with the Righteous Order. Our thoughts will be where true wisdom shall live in her home.

[10] When perfection is attained, then the blow of destruction shall fall upon the Demon of Falsehood, and her adherents shall perish with her. But the righteous saints, who walk on earth in good reputation and in honor, will gather swiftly in the happy home of the Good Mind and of Ahura.

Therefore, O mortals, you are learning these religious commands that Ahura gave in our happiness and our sorrow. You are also learning the long punishment of the wicked, and the blessings that are in store for the righteous. When these begin their course, salvation will be yours!

Judgment of the Soul on Chinvat Bridge

In Zoroastrian belief, the soul of the departed hovers near the body for three days. On the fourth day, it faces a judgment on the Chinvat ("Requiter") Bridge, where the deceased's good and evil deeds are weighed. If good actions outweigh evil ones, the soul ascends to Heaven; if evil acts outweigh the good, it is dragged off to Hell. At the Last Judgment, at the end of time, all bodies are resurrected and reunited with their souls. Then there is a final and universal cleansing, from which all people emerge sinless, and enter into Paradise. This passage is designed, like most depictions of heaven and hell in world scriptures, to motivate believers to live correctly in this life, body and soul.[6]

Do not put not your trust in life, for at the last death must overtake you. Dogs and birds will tear at your corpse, and your bones will be tumbled on the earth.

For three days and nights the soul sits beside the pillow of the body. [115] Accompanied by the blessed Srosh, the good Vay, and the mighty Vahram, and opposed by Astvihat (the

---

[6]Taken, with editing, from E. W. West, *Pahlavi Texts*, part 3, *Sacred Books of the East*, vol. 24 (Oxford: Clarendon Press, 1885), pp. 16–26.

Menok I Khrat 2.110–195.

demon of death), the evil Vay, the demon Freh-zisht and the demon Vizisht, and pursued by the active ill-will of Wrath..., the soul on the fourth day after death will reach the lofty and awful Bridge of the Requiter. Every person whose soul will be saved and every person whose soul will be damned must come to this bridge. Many enemies lie in wait here. Here the soul will suffer from the ill-will of Wrath who wields a bloody spear, and from Astvihat who swallows all creation yet is never satisfied, and it will benefit by the mediation of Hihr, Srosh, and Rashn. [120] Then the soul submits to the weighing of its deeds by the righteous Rashn. He lets the scales of the spiritual gods incline to neither side, neither for the saved nor yet for the damned, nor yet for kings and princes. Not so much as a hair's breadth does he tip the scales. He is no respecter of persons, for he deals out impartial justice both to kings and prin-ces and to the humblest of men. And when the soul of the saved passes over that bridge, the breadth of the bridge appears to be one parasang.[7]

The soul of the saved goes on, accompanied by the blessed Srosh. [125] His own good deeds come to meet him in the form of a young woman, more beautiful than any on earth. The soul of the saved says, "Who are you? I have never seen a young woman on earth more beau-tiful than you." [130] She replies, "I am no woman! I am your own good deeds, O young man whose thoughts and words, deeds and reli-gion were good. When you saw someone offer sacrifice to the demons, you sat apart and offered sacrifice to the gods. When you saw a man do vi-olence and theft, afflict good men and mistreat them, or store up goods wrongfully obtained, you refrained from treating creatures with violence. Instead, you were considerate to good men; you entertained them and offer them hospitality; you gave alms both to the man who came from near and to him who came from afar; and you amassed your wealth

in righteousness. [135] When you saw someone who passed a false judgment or took bribes or gave false testimony, you spoke a right and true witness. I am the good thoughts, good words, and good deeds that you said and did...."

[140] When the soul departs, a fragrant breeze wafts towards him, a breeze more fragrant than any perfume. Then the soul of the saved asks Srosh, "What breeze is this, the like of which I never smelled on earth?" Then the blessed Srosh answers the soul of the saved, "This is a wind (wafted) from Heaven; therefore it is so fragrant."

[145] Then with his first step he enters the heaven of good thoughts, with his second the heaven of good words, with his third the heaven of good deeds, and with his fourth step he reaches the Endless Light where is all bliss. All the gods and good spirits come to greet him and ask him how he has been, saying, "How was your passage from those transient, fearful worlds where there is much evil to these eternal worlds in which there is no adversary, O young man whose thoughts and words, deeds and reli-gion are good?" [150] Then Ahura Mazda, the Lord, says "Do not ask him how he has been, be-cause he has been separated from his beloved body and has traveled on a fearsome road." They serve him the sweetest of all foods with the butter of early spring, so that his soul may take its ease after the three nights of terror on the Bridge inflicted on him by the demons. They seat him upon a throne everywhere bejew-eled.... [157] And for ever and ever he dwells blissfully with the spiritual gods.

But when the man who is damned dies, for three days and nights his soul hovers near his head and weeps, saying, "Where shall I go and in whom shall I now take refuge?" [160] During those three days and nights he sees all the sins and wickedness that he committed on earth. On the fourth day the demon Vizarsh comes and binds the soul of the damned in most shameful ways, and despite the opposition of the blessed Srosh drags it off to the Bridge of the Requiter. Then the righteous Rashn makes clear to the soul of the damned that it is damned indeed. Then the demon Vizarsh seizes

---

[7] *one parasang:* about three miles. This broad bridge makes for an easy, pleasant transit of the soul.

the soul of the damned, strikes it and abuses it without pity, urged on by Wrath. [165] The soul of the damned cries out loudly, moans in terror, and makes many piteous pleas; he struggles much, although his life-breath endures no more. All his struggling and his howling prove of no avail, because no help is offered him by any of the gods or by any of the demons. The demon Vizarsh drags him off against his will into deepest Hell.

Then a young woman who does not look like a woman comes to meet him. The soul of the damned says to that ill-favored woman, "Who are you? I have never seen anyone on earth as hideous as you." [170] She replies, "I am no woman! I am your deeds—hideous deeds—evil thoughts, evil words, evil deeds, and evil religion. When on earth you saw someone who offered sacrifice to the gods, you sat apart and offered sacrifice to the demons. When you saw someone who entertained good men and offered them hospitality...you treated good men with dishonor; you gave them no alms and you shut your door to them. [175] When you saw someone who passed just judgment or took no bribes or bore true witness or spoke up in righteousness, you passed false

judgment, you gave false testimony, and you spoke unrighteously."...

[182] Then with his first step he goes to the hell of evil thoughts, with his second to the hell of evil words, and with his third to the hell of evil deeds. With his fourth step he lurches into the presence of the accursed Destructive Spirit and the other demons. [185] The demons mock him and scorn him, saying, "What grieved you in Ahura Mazda, the Lord, and the Amahraspands and in fragrant and delightful Heaven? What grudge or complaint did you have against them that you should come to see the demons and this murky Hell? We will torment you and have no mercy on you for a long time!" The Destructive Spirit cries out to the demons, "Do not ask about him, for he has been separated from his beloved body, and he has come through that most evil passageway. Serve him the filthiest and most foul food that Hell can produce." [190] Then they bring him poison and venom, snakes and scorpions and other noxious reptiles that flourish in Hell, and they serve him these to eat. Until the resurrection and the final body he must remain in Hell, suffering much torment and many kinds of punishment.

RITUAL

The Place of the *Gathas*

This passage, which stands at the end of the *Gathas,* serves to show their high place in the Zoroastrian faith.

As our offering to the bountiful *Gathas* that rule as the leading chants within the appointed times and seasons of our ritual, we present all our riches of land, and our persons, together with our very bones and tissues. We present our

forms and forces, our consciousness, our soul, and Fravashi.

The *Gathas* are our guardians and defenders, and our spiritual food. Yes, they are both food and clothing to our souls. The *Gathas* are

Yasna 55:1–3.

guardians and defenders and spiritual food, both food and clothing to our souls. May they be an offering for us. May they give abundant rewards...for the world beyond the present world, after our consciousness and our body are separated from each other. May these Praises of the Offering come forth and appear for us with power and victory, with health and healing, with progress, with growth, with preparation and protection, and with blessing and holiness. May they abound with gifts for those who can understand. Let them appear with free generosity to the enlightened. Let them appear as Mazda, the most beneficial, has produced them. He is the one who is victorious when he strikes. He helps our communities advance, and he protects and guards the religious order of the communities; even now they are being furthered. He guards those who will bring salvation to us, and he protects the entire creation of holy and clean things.

The Zoroastrian Confession

This stately creed of Zoroastrianism is called the *Faravane*. Recited daily by every faithful worshipper of Mazda, it outlines an important Zoroastrian doctrine: the dualism of good and evil as cosmic forces. Believers pledge themselves to Mazda and the good and reject the evil spirits.

I drive the evil spirits away. I confess myself a Mazda-worshipper of the order of Zarathushtra. I renounce the evil spirits and devote myself to the lore of the Lord. I am a praiser of the Bountiful Immortals. I attribute all things good to Ahura Mazda, the Holy and Resplendent One. To Him belong all things good...and the stars, in whose lights the glorious beings and objects are clothed. I choose Piety, the generous and the good. I loudly condemn all robbery and violence against the sacred Cattle, and all droughts that waste the Mazdayasnian villages. I put away the thought of wandering at will, of pitching my tent freely like a nomad. I wish to remove all wandering from the Cattle that abide steadfastly on this land. Bowing down in worship to Righteousness, I dedicate my offerings with praise. May I never be a source of decline, and may I never be a source of withering to the Mazdayasnian villages, not for the love of body or life.

I renounce the shelter and headship of the evil spirits, evil as they are. They are utterly empty of good and void of Virtue. They are deceitful in their wickedness. Of all beings they are most like the Demon of the Lie, the most loathsome of existing things. They are completely empty of good.

[5] I renounce and renounce again the evil spirits and all possessed by them, the sorcerers and all who use their methods, and every being of the sort. I renounce their thoughts, their words and actions, and the seed that propagates their sin. I renounce their shelter and their headship. I renounce sinners of every kind, who act like demons!

Thus indeed might Ahura Mazda have shown to Zarathushtra, answering every question that Zarathushtra asked, in all the consultations that they had. Thus might Zarathushtra have renounced the shelter and the headship of the evil spirits in all the questions, and in all the consultations with which Zarathushtra and the Lord conversed together. And so I myself, in whatever circumstances I may be placed, as a worshipper of Mazda and of Zarathushtra's order, also

Yasna 12.

renounce the evil spirits and their shelter. The holy Zarathushtra renounced them the same way in old times.

I belong to that religious holiness to which the waters belong, to that holiness to which the plants, to that holiness to which the Cattle of blessed gift, to that religious holiness to which Ahura Mazda, who made both cattle and holy men, belongs. To that holiness I belong. I am of the creed that Zarathushtra held, which Kavi Vistaspa, Frashaostra, and Gamaspa held.[8] Yes, I am of that religious faith as every **Saoshyant**[9] who shall yet come to see us, the holy ones

who do truly significant things. Of that creed, and of that tradition, am I.

I am a Mazda-worshipper of Zarathushtra's order. Thus I confess, as a praiser and confessor. I praise aloud the thing well thought, the word well spoken, and the deed well done. Yes, I praise at once the faith of Mazda, the faith that has no saying that fails, the faith that wields the deadly battle-ax, the faith of kindred marriage.[10] I praise the holy Creed, which is the most imposing, best, and most beautiful of all religions which exist, and of all that in the future shall come to be. I praise Ahura's Faith, the Zarathushtrian creed. I ascribe all good to Ahura Mazda, and such shall be the worship of the Mazdayasnian belief!

---

[8]King *Kavi Vistaspa* was Zarathushtra's royal patron and protector. *Frashaostra* was an early follower of Zarathushtra; his daughter Hvovi was Zarathushtra's third wife. *Gamaspa* was the chief counselor of King Vistaspa and a friend of the new faith.

[9]*Saoshyant* [sa-OSH-yant]: "Future rescuer"; a future savior who will help purify the world.

[10]*kindred marriage:* the Zoroastrian practice of marriage between distant relatives.

The Four Great Prayers

These four prayers are the most important in Zoroastrian worship. They are named after their first words.

Ahuna vairyo:[11] As is the Master, so is the Judge to be chosen in accord with truth. Establish the power of acts arising from a life lived with good purpose, for Mazda and for the lord whom they made pastor for the poor.

Airyema ishyo: May longed-for Airyaman come to the support of the men and women

of Zarathushtra, to the support of our good purpose. The Inner Self earns the reward to be chosen. I ask for it the longed-for recompense of truth, which the Lord Mazda has in mind.

Ashem vohu: Asha is good, it is best. According to wish it is, according to wish it shall be for us. Asha belongs to Asha Vahishta.

Yenhe hatam: Those Beings, male and female, whom Lord Mazda knows the best for true worship, we worship them all.

---

[11]This prayer and the *Ashem vohu* are taken from M. Boyce, *A History of Zoroastrianism*, 2 vols. (Leiden: Brill, 1975, 1982).

From the Yasna.

Disposal of the Dead

This passage describes the Zoroastrian "towers of silence," in which the dead are exposed to birds of prey so that their ritually defiling bodies may not pollute the sacred earth. First, provision is made for the on-ground exposure of the dead in places where "towers of silence" cannot be built.

"O Maker of the material world, you Holy One! Where shall we bring the bodies of the dead, where shall we lay their bodies, O Ahura Mazda?" [45] Ahura Mazda answered, "On the highest summits, where you know there are always corpse-eating dogs and corpse-eating birds, O holy Zarathushtra! There the worshippers of Mazda shall secure the corpse by the feet and by the hair. They shall secure it with brass, stones, or lead, so that the corpse-eating dogs and the corpse-eating birds cannot carry the bones to the water and to the trees."

"If they shall not secure the corpse, so that the corpse-eating dogs and the corpse-eating birds carry the bones to the water and to the trees, what is the penalty that they shall pay?" Ahura Mazda answered: "They shall be severely punished. They shall receive two hundred stripes with the Aspahe-astra, two hundred stripes with the Sraoshokarana."[12]

"O Maker of the material world, you Holy One! Where shall we bring the bones of the dead, where shall we lay them, O Ahura Mazda?" [50] Ahura Mazda answered: "The worshippers of Mazda shall build a building out of the reach of the dog, of the fox, and of the wolf, and in which rainwater cannot stay. Such a building shall they build, if they can afford it, with stones, mortar, and earth. If they cannot afford it, they shall lay the dead man on the ground, on his carpet and his pillow, clothed with the light of heaven,[13] and beholding the sun."

---

[12] The same type of whip is probably meant here so that the total number of lashes would be 200.

[13] *clothed with the light of heaven:* naked. Exposed to the birds of prey, the body will undergo the same ritual disposal as corpses put in towers of silence.

Vendidad, Fargard 65, 44–51.

🐚 GLOSSARY

Avesta [ah-VES-tuh] variously translated as "injunction," "wisdom," and "scripture"; the name of the Zoroastrian scriptures.

Fravashis [frah-VAH-shees] guardian spirits.

Gathas [GAH-tuhs] a collection of seventeen hymns in the *Yasna*, which Zoroastrians hold to be the words of Zarathushtra.

Saoshyant [sa-OSH-yant] "Future rescuer"; savior who will help purify the world.

Vendidad [VEN-dih-dahd] The Law Against Demons; a division of the *Avesta* containing myths and codes of religious law.

Visparad [VEE-spuh-rahd] "All the [Divine] Lords"; a twenty-chapter collection of hymns in the *Avesta*.

Yashts [yahshts] "Hymns"; hymns of praise to twenty-one divinities, angels, and human heroes of ancient Persia; a division of the *Avesta*.

Yasna [YAHZ-nuh] "Sacrifice"; hymns for worship; the first and foremost division of the *Avesta*.

❧ QUESTIONS FOR STUDY AND DISCUSSION

1. What, to judge from the *Gathas,* were the main religious ideas of the prophet Zarathushtra?
2. What sort of changes occurred in Zoroastrian religion after the passing of Zarathushtra? For your answer, compare the *Gathas* with the rest of the *Avesta.*
3. Explain how Zarathushtra is worshipped by means of these scriptures.
4. How do the striking funeral and cleanliness rituals reproduced here testify to the strong connection made in Zoroastrianism between ritual purity and moral purity?
5. When rock star Freddie Mercury died (see the vignette on page 191), his body was cremated after an otherwise traditional Zoroastrian funeral. Explain how this use of fire is not in accord with Zoroastrian practice.

❧ SUGGESTIONS FOR FURTHER READING

PRIMARY SOURCES

M. Boyce, *Textual Sources for the Study of Zoroastrianism.* Chicago: University of Chicago Press, 1990. A full selection of texts, with introductions but few annotations.

J. Darmesteter and L. H. Mills, *The Zend-Avesta.* In F. Max Müller, ed., *Sacred Books of the East,* vols. 4, 23, and 31. Oxford: Oxford University Press, 1880–1887. Its Victorian English often interferes, but this is the only relatively complete translation of the *Avesta* in English.

J. Insler, *The Gathas of Zarathushtra.* Leiden: Brill, 1975. Contains the Avestan text, English translation and notes, and excellent commentary.

SECONDARY SOURCES

J. Barr, "The Question of Religious Influence: The Case of Zoroastrianism, Judaism, and Christianity." *Journal of the American Academy of Religion* 53 (1985): 201–235. A reexamination of the notion, commonly accepted in religious scholarship, that Zoroastrian teachings had a great influence on Judaism and through it on Christianity and Islam.

M. Boyce, *A History of Zoroastrianism,* 2 vols. Leiden: Brill, 1975, 1982. The standard history of Zoroastrianism, with comprehensive treatment of the *Avesta* as the main source of our knowledge of early Zoroastrianism.

M. Boyce, *A Persian Stronghold of Zoroastrianism.* Oxford: Oxford University Press, 1977. Although no explicit and extended treatment of scripture is included here, this firsthand report on the life of Iranian Zoroastrians sheds much light on present-day use of the *Avesta.*

J. W. Boyd, "Zoroastrianism: Avestan Scripture and Rite." In F. M. Denny and R. L. Taylor, eds., *The Holy Book in Comparative Perspective.* Charleston: University of South Carolina Press, 1985, pp. 109–125. An excellent discussion of orthodox versus reformist reception and use of the *Avesta.*

❧ COMPANION WEBSITE

Visit the *Anthology of World Scriptures* companion website at **www.thomsonedu.com** for learning tools such as map explorations, flashcards of glossary terms, learning objectives, chapter practice quizzes, links to other websites for learning and research, and chapter summaries in PowerPoint® format.

CHAPTER TEN

Judaism

Celebrating Scripture

Orthodox Jews at the Western Wall in Jerusalem lift a Hebrew *Bible* scroll in its box during the Festival of Sukkot ("Booths"). This act emphasizes Jews' joy in their scripture and the obligation to keep its teachings. (*Used by permission of BiblePlaces.com.*)

- In New York City, detective Mordacai Dzinkansky sets up a "sting" operation with unsuspecting criminals who are selling *Torah* scrolls into a worldwide black market. These scrolls—many of them worth more than $50,000 each—have been stolen from synagogues. A member of the NYPD *Torah* task force and a Hebrew-speaking Orthodox Jew, Dzinkansky is remarkably effective at winning the confidence of criminals, bringing them to justice, and recovering the stolen *Torahs* for return to their rightful owners.

- Jewish demonstrators surround the parliament building in Jerusalem as members of parliament inside debate withdrawing Jewish settlers from the predominantly Arab area of Gaza and giving their land to the Palestinian Authority. Several of the signs carry references to "Eretz [land of] Israel," the size of Israel promised by God to Abraham in *Genesis* 15:18–21. Some Israeli rabbis have threatened to excommunicate any soldiers who participate in transferring any part of this land to Palestinian control. The insistence by a small but politically powerful group on keeping "Eretz Israel" has complicated the peace process for more than three decades.

- In London, a prominent Jewish rabbi criticizes pop singer Madonna's latest venture into religious practice, this time the Jewish mystical belief and practice known as the Kabbalah. Rabbi Yitzchak Schochet of London's Mill Hill Synagogue strongly objects to Madonna's use of the Kabbalah in a music video and in books for children, arguing that it tarnishes Jewish scripture and law. Particularly objectionable to Rabbi Schochet and many other observant Jews is Madonna's new tattoo on her right shoulder of an ancient sacred Hebrew name for God. Interest in, and controversy over, her practice of the Kabbalah began with her 1998 *Ray of Light* album and still increases. An Internet search of the combined terms "Madonna" and "Kabbalah" returned more than 460,000 hits in June 2007.

INTRODUCTION

Judaism is founded on a belief in one personal God who was revealed in the early history of the Jewish people, calling them to serve God and spread divine love and justice in the world. The influence of the Jewish scriptures stems directly from rigorous adherence over more than 2,500 years in ways those three vignettes can only suggest. The Jewish *Bible* is the foundation of both the Christian and the Islamic scriptures as well, and thus its teachings have carried over into the lives of the world's two largest religions. Even though some of the importance of the Jewish scriptures has been lost in the modern secularized world, their deep influence on everyday life and on patterns of Western thought and culture has abated only a little. Our seven-day week with its day of rest is an inheritance from Jewish scripture; the belief that there is only one God is a gift of these writings as well. That all people are equally human, that the human race is one family, and that each individual can fully realize the meaning of life regardless of social or economic class are ideas that have also come to the Western world from the Jewish scriptures.

Names

The most particularly Jewish name for the whole Jewish *Bible* is ***Tanakh*** [TAH-nahk]. It is an acronym formed from the first letters of the names of the three sections of the scriptures: ***Torah*** [TOH-rah], "Teaching" or "Law"; ***Nevi'im*** [NEH-vih-eem], "Prophets"; and ***Kethuvim*** [KETH-u-veem], "Writings" (see Table 10.1). The name *Tanakh* arose in the Middle Ages and is widely known among European and American Jews. It is not widely known among non-Jews, however, nor is it the commonly used academic name for the Jewish scriptures.

Many people call the Jewish scripture the *Old Testament,* but that is a Christian name (the latter part of the Christian *Bible* is called the *New Testament*). Because of the predominance of Christianity over Judaism in the West, the name *Old Testament* has become traditional even in journalistic and academic circles. Jews, however, rightly see the term and the more kindly "First Testament" as derogatory, and students of religion now avoid both of them as partisan and inappropriate. A better designation is "Hebrew scriptures" ("Hebrew" here refers to the language of the Jewish *Bible,* which is Hebrew except for one verse each in the books of *Genesis* and *Jeremiah* and several chapters in *Ezra* and *Daniel.* The exceptions are in Aramaic, a language closely related to Hebrew.) Christians and Jews accept "Hebrew scriptures" as both accurate and nonprejudicial. Its wide acceptance is indicated by its use in the *New Revised Standard Version* of the (Christian) *Bible.*

The most common name for the Jewish scriptures, the simple term *Bible,* is probably its oldest. This word has its roots in the Hebrew term *Ha-Sefarim,* "The Books" (*Daniel* 9:2), which Greek-speaking Jews by the second century B.C.E. translated as *ta biblia.* The term passed into the Greek translation of the *New Testament* and then through Latin to give us the English word *Bible.* This name stresses the written, textual nature of the Jewish **revelation.** (When Jews refer to the *Bible,* they mean of course *their* scripture, of which the Christian *New Testament* is not a part.) In sum, no single name for the Jewish scripture has ever been common to all Jews, but *Bible* is probably the most ancient and the most widely accepted, so we use it here.

Overview of Structure

Reduced to its most basic form, the overall structure of the Jewish *Bible,* shown in Table 10.1, may be summarized as follows (the dates provide a time line for the events narrated in the books and are not to be taken as dates of the writing of the books themselves). In *Genesis,* the first book of the *Torah,* God creates the world good, but humanity falls into sin and rebellion. After the growth of the human race through many generations, Abraham responds to God's call by migrating from Mesopotamia to Palestine (ca. 1750 B.C.E.). He and his main descendants, Isaac and Jacob, move about in the hills of Palestine; Jacob and his descendants go to Egypt during a famine. In *Exodus,* the second book of the *Torah,* Moses leads the Hebrews by God's power from Egypt into the Sinai Peninsula (between Egypt and Palestine), where they receive the law of God (ca. 1280 B.C.E.). In *Leviticus,* they receive God's instruction for worship and purity. *Numbers* relates how they wander in the wilderness until they are ready to enter the Promised Land. In *Deuteronomy,* the people receive the law a second time as Moses warns them against

TABLE 10.1 The Books of the Jewish *Bible*

Division	English Name	Hebrew Name	Chapters
Torah ("Teaching, Law")	*Genesis*	*Bereshith* ("in the beginning")	50
	Exodus	*Shemoth* ("names")	40
	Leviticus	*Wayiqra* ("and he called")	27
	Numbers	*Bemidbar* ("in the wilderness")	36
	Deuteronomy	*Debarim* ("words")	34
Nevi'im ("Prophets")	*Former Prophets*		
	Joshua	*Yehoshua*	24
	Judges	*Shofetim* ("judges")	21
	I–II Samuel	*Shemuel*	31, 24
	I–II Kings	*Melakim* ("kings")	22, 25
	Latter Prophets		
	Isaiah	*Yeshayahu*	66
	Jeremiah	*Yirmeyahu*	52
	Ezekiel	*Yehezqel*	48
	The Twelve:		
	Hosea	*Hoshea*	14
	Joel	*Yoel*	3
	Amos	*Amos*	9
	Obadiah	*Obadyahu*	1
	Jonah	*Yonah*	4
	Micah	*Micah*	7
	Nahum	*Nahum*	3
	Habakkuk	*Habaqquq*	3
	Zephaniah	*Zephanyah*	3
	Haggai	*Haggai*	2
	Zechariah	*Zekaryahu*	14
	Malachi	*Malaki*	4
Kethuvim ("Writings")	*Psalms*	*Tehillim* ("praises")	150
	Job	*Iyyob*	31
	Proverbs	*Mishle* ("proverbs of")	42
	Ruth	*Ruth*	4
	Song of Songs	*Shir Hashirim* ("song of songs")	8
	Ecclesiastes	*Koheleth* ("preacher")	12
	Lamentations	*Ekah* ("how")	5
	Esther	*Ester*	10
	Daniel	*Daniel*	12
	Ezra-Nehemiah	*Ezra-Nehemyah*	10, 13
	I–II Chronicles	*Dibre Hayamin* ("words of")	29, 36

serving other gods. These five books are together known as the *Torah,* "Teaching" or "Law." They are the most important of the Hebrew scriptures.

Nevi'im, "Prophets," the second section of the Jewish *Bible,* is subdivided into two parts: *Former* and *Latter* refer to the position of the books in the canon, not to the time of their composition. The books of the *Former Prophets* are *Joshua, Judges, Samuel* (volumes I and II), and *Kings* (volumes I and II). *Joshua* presents a somewhat idealized version of how the Israelites crossed the Jordan River and conquered the peoples of Palestine (ca. 1250 B.C.E.). *Judges* provides another view of how the Israelites engaged in continuing wars to maintain their possession of the land as they were led by charismatic figures against their enemies. *I Samuel* and *II Samuel* relate how a monarchy was established with Saul as the first king and David (crowned 1000 B.C.E.) as his successor. *I Kings* and *II Kings* tell how, under King Solomon, Israel grew to be a small empire and then, when Solomon died, split into two nations—the northern kingdom of Israel (or Ephraim) and the southern kingdom of Judah. The northern kingdom was conquered by Assyria in 721 B.C.E., never to reappear. The southern kingdom fell to Babylonia in 590, and many of the Judeans went into exile in Babylon. They considered the exile punishment for their failure to serve God alone.

The first book of the *Latter Prophets* is *Isaiah,* a composite text that contains the words of Isaiah in the eighth century B.C.E. and the messages of "Second Isaiah" (an anonymous prophet responsible for *Isaiah* 40–55) and "Third Isaiah" (an anonymous prophet responsible for Isaiah 56–66) in the sixth century B.C.E. *Jeremiah* presents the message of the mournful prophet who foresaw the destruction of Jerusalem by the Babylonians. *Ezekiel* prophesies hope among the Jewish exiles in Babylon. The last book is *The Twelve* (known by their Aramaic name *Terei Asar*). It is a collection of short prophetic texts: *Hosea, Joel, Amos, Obadiah, Jonah, Micah, Nahum, Habakkuk, Zephaniah, Haggai, Zechariah,* and *Malachi.* The books of *The Twelve* are known as the *Minor Prophets* because of their relatively small size— each one was formerly written on one scroll. The careers of these twelve prophets extended from the 700s to the 500s B.C.E.

The third section of the Jewish *Bible* is the *Kethuvim,* "Writings." As the name suggests, within this section is a miscellaneous collection of several types of literature. It begins with the *Psalms.* A **psalm** [sahlm] is a sacred song used for divine worship. *Proverbs* and *Job* are books about wisdom. The former is a collection of wise sayings attributed to Solomon; the latter is a drama about the perennial question "If God is good, why do good people suffer?" *Ruth* tells the beautiful story of how a non-Israelite woman became one of the people of God and an ancestor of King David. The *Song of Songs* is a collection of poetry that celebrates love between a man and a woman, traditionally interpreted by Jews as symbolic of the relationship between God and Israel. *Ecclesiastes* offers a bittersweet perspective on what wisdom and life have to offer. *Lamentations,* traditionally ascribed to the prophet Jeremiah, mourns the destruction of Jerusalem by the Babylonians. *Esther* is the dramatic story of how a Jewish woman delivers her people from destruction by a Persian king. *Daniel* contains visions of the end of time. *Ezra-Nehemiah* records the return of the Jewish exiles from Babylon at the end of the sixth century B.C.E., the reconstruction of Jerusalem, and the reconstitution of Judaism. Finally, *I Chronicles* and *II Chronicles* tell much the same story as *I* and *II Kings* (in the *Former Prophets* section) but from the perspective of the Jerusalem priesthood.

These, then, are the books of the Jewish *Bible*. In Jewish reckoning, they number twenty-four in all, a number obtained by counting as one book each *I–II Samuel, I–II Kings, I–II Chronicles, The Twelve,* and *Ezra-Nehemiah* (see Table 10.1) . In ancient times, they were traditionally written on twenty-four scrolls, and even after the two-volume books were physically separated at the end of the Middle Ages, this number was kept.

The order of the books of the Jewish *Bible* that is familiar to Christians is based on the Greek translation made before Christianity began. (This translation, known as the *Septuagint,* was the only scripture of early Christianity until the *New Testament* was recognized as scripture in the second and third centuries C.E. We deal more fully with the relationship of the Jewish and Christian scriptures in Chapter 11.) Table 10.2 shows the order of books in the Greek version of the Jewish *Bible*.

Contemporary Use

When Muhammad, the founder of Islam, called Jews (and Christians) the "people of the book," he made an accurate assessment of the role of scripture in Judaism. For more than 2,000 years, the *Bible* has been read, prayed, and taught in the synagogue. It has shaped the doctrine, ethics, and worship of the Jews. Its instruction and inspiration have helped to preserve them through good times and bad and over their wide dispersion throughout much of the world.

To understand the contemporary use of the Jewish *Bible,* we must examine briefly its more ancient use. The Jewish *Bible* is built on the foundation of the *Torah,* the written law of God. But ancient law needs interpreting and application to new times and situations, and so arose the concept of "oral Torah." The oral Torah explains, supplements, and applies the commands of the written *Torah.* It is called "oral" because it was believed by the end of the first century C.E. to have been revealed to Moses on Mount Sinai and passed down orally by experts for more than a thousand years. It was also probably kept in oral form so as not to compete in standing and authority with the *Bible,* the written *Torah.* In time, the oral Torah grew so large and authoritative that it had to be written down, first in the *Mishnah* (ca. 200 C.E.), then in its commentary, the *Gemara* (ca. 450–550 C.E.), and shortly thereafter in the combination of those two works—the ***Talmud*** [TALL-mood]. The *Talmud* has two versions: the short *Jerusalem Talmud* and the longer and more authoritative *Babylonian Talmud.* For almost all Jews from 500 to 1800 C.E., the scripture was understood by way of the oral Torah as written down in the *Talmud,* and Orthodox Jews still understand scripture in this way. For example, the biblical law of "an eye for an eye" is not to be taken literally but means that a person who injures another must pay adequate monetary fines to compensate for the loss.

This was how the *Talmud* was used through the Middle Ages. This period of rabbinic Judaism also saw the rise of the fourfold meaning of the scripture: midrashic, philosophical, mystical, and literal. *Midrash* was the sermonic, illustrative interpretation of the *Bible,* often quite fanciful. The philosophical meaning sought by Maimonides and others yielded deep truths in the *Bible* that could be related to the teachings of Plato or Aristotle. The hidden, mystical meaning made possible a direct experience of God, emotional as well as intellectual or moral. One mystical group, the Kabbalists, found cryptic meanings in words and letters of scripture and ignored the other three

TABLE 10.2 The Books of the Greek Version of the Jewish *Bible*

Genesis	*Proverbs*
Exodus	*Ecclesiastes*
Leviticus	* *Wisdom of Solomon*
Numbers	* *Wisdom of Sirach*
Deuteronomy	* *Psalms of Solomon*
Joshua	*Isaiah*
Judges	*Jeremiah*
Ruth	*Lamentations*
I Kings (I Samuel)	* *Baruch*
II Kings (II Samuel)	* *Letter of Jeremiah*
III Kings (I Kings)	*Ezekiel*
IV Kings (II Kings)	*Daniel*
I Chronicles	* *Susanna*
II Chronicles	* *Bel and the Snake*
* *I Esdras*	*Hosea*
II Esdras (Ezra-Nehemiah)	*Joel*
* *Tobit*	*Amos*
* *Judith*	*Obadiah*
Esther	*Jonah*
* *I Maccabees*	*Micah*
* *II Maccabees*	*Nahum*
* *III Maccabees*	*Habakkuk*
* *IV Maccabees*	*Zephaniah*
Job	*Haggai*
Psalms	*Zechariah*
* *Odes*	*Malachi*

*These apocryphal, or deutero-canonical, books are not included in the canon of the Hebrew scriptures or in the *Bibles* of most Protestant churches. They are included in the *Bibles* of the Eastern Orthodox and Roman Catholic churches, but the Catholic canon excludes *I Esdras*, *III* and *IV Maccabees*, *Odes*, and *Psalms of Solomon*. Some *Bibles* used by Orthodox Christians omit *IV Maccabees*, *Odes*, and *Psalms of Solomon*.

types of meaning. The literal meaning emerged from the study of the diction and grammar of the text. The greatest practitioner of literalism was Rashi (Rabbi Solomon Itzchaki) of Troyes, France. Rabbis often combined the four levels of meaning in some way, but the literal meaning was prominent by the end of the Middle Ages and was most compatible with the developing historical method.

With the emancipation of Judaism from legal restrictions and official discrimination around 1800 C.E., liberalizing Jews applied the historical-critical method of studying texts to the Jewish *Bible*. Accepting the ideas of the Enlightenment, these Jews said that scripture was to be understood like any other book, with supernatural and miraculous elements largely discounted. The Dutch Jewish philosopher Baruch Spinoza (1623–1677), a pre-emancipation scholar, had already introduced and exemplified this approach. He dismissed the divine inspiration of scripture and Moses' authorship of the *Torah*, advocating a historical interpretation. At first, his methods shocked and scandalized the Jewish world, but over the next 300 years, they became more common.

By the end of the 1800s, the three main groups of modern Judaism had emerged along with their distinct uses of scripture. The Reform branch, which largely adopted the historical-critical method, approaches the *Bible* much as mainstream Protestants and Roman Catholics understand it. The Orthodox branch sticks to the traditional and Talmudic views of scripture and methods of interpreting it—for example, believing that the whole *Torah* was written by Moses, that the *Talmud* is the oral Torah, and that every law of God is to be followed literally as fully as possible. The Conservative branch lies between the other two, employing modern historical methods to understand and apply scripture but seeking to preserve much of the essential and traditional meaning.

As in most religions, the site where Jews have characteristically met and used their scripture is their place of worship. Synagogue worship is filled with the *Bible;* scripture saturates the prayers, chants, hymns, and liturgies. The main point of the service is the solemn reading of passages appointed for the day in the prayer books. The entire *Torah* is read at the Sabbath services during the course of each year. Special *Torah* readings are fixed for the main festivals and High Holy Days. Related readings from the prophets (called the *Haftorah*) are also fixed in the **lectionary,** or list of readings, for each Sabbath and holy day. Some passages from the *Kethuvim* section of the *Bible* (see Table 10.1) are read on five lesser festivals (Sukkot, Passover, Shavu'ot, Purim, the Ninth of Ab) from the five scrolls known as the *Megilloth* (*Ecclesiastes, Song of Songs, Ruth, Esther,* and *Lamentations*).

The readings themselves are very musical. The worship leader chants the words in Hebrew guided by accent marks written into the Hebrew text and also employing traditional Hebrew melodies. The place where the *Torah* scrolls are kept is the **ark.** It is a special closet or recess in the synagogue wall on the side nearest Jerusalem and is usually the focal point of the synagogue. The scrolls themselves are typically covered with richly embroidered cloth, and the upper ends of the wooden rollers are adorned with gold and silver decorations. When a scroll is removed from the ark during the service, everyone in the synagogue stands and special songs are sung. Then the scroll is placed on a reading desk, and the reader uses a special pointer, often made of solid silver, to keep track of his or her place in the text. When the reading is complete, the scroll is rolled up, its covers are put back on, and it is returned to the ark with great solemnity. Then the rabbi preaches a sermon based on the texts that were read, especially the *Torah* reading.

The *Bible,* together with the *Talmud,* is also the focus of group and individual study. Since ancient times, it has been a legal obligation for every Jewish man—and often, in modern and more liberal forms of Judaism, an option for women—to be able to read and interpret scripture. In North America, every synagogue of substance provides after-school classes in Hebrew language and religious studies to children from elementary to high school age. Jewish parochial schools that teach both general and religious subjects, with heavy doses of scripture, can be found in cities with sizable Jewish populations. This emphasis on early education in scripture fosters Jewish adults who are able and willing to study it on an advanced level. Every Jewish home typically possesses a *Bible* in the native language of the family and often one in Hebrew as well.

The daily life of the observant Jew is also immersed in reminders of the *Bible* and its instruction. For example, fastened to the doorpost of many homes is the **mezuzah** [meh-ZOO-zah], a small box containing three short passages from the *Torah*, among them the well-known words of *Deuteronomy* 6:4–9: "Take to heart these instructions with which I charge you this day. Impress them upon your children. Recite them when you stay at home and when you are away, when you lie down and when you get up…inscribe them on the doorposts of your house and on your gates." This passage also commands the wearing of **tefillin** [teh-FILL-in], called in English phylacteries. Orthodox Jews wear tefillin while praying, which they typically do three times a day. Tefillin are two small wooden boxes that contain tiny scripture scrolls. Using leather straps, the wearer binds one to his forehead and the other to his weaker arm. Outward practices of religion such as displaying the mezuzah and wearing tefillin are intended to remind every Jew of the duty to act in obedience to God during every activity night or day, at home or away.

Historical Origin and Development

The Jewish *Bible* had a long history of formation in oral tradition, transcription in writing, and editorial polishing. Because this process of development is shrouded in the mists of antiquity, scholarly judgments vary, but there is some agreement about the following summary description.

• The writing probably began about 1100 B.C.E., with the writing down of the oldest sections of poetry and historical narratives (for example, the "Songs of Moses and Miriam" in *Exodus* 15; the "Song of Deborah" in *Judges* 5). In the reign of Solomon, the story of his father, David, began to be written (*II Samuel 9–I Kings* 2). One source of the *Torah*, which tells of creation and the patriarchs as a prelude to the formation of Israel, was written in southern Israel. Another source of the *Torah* was written in northern Israel from a northern religious and political perspective.

• The eighth century B.C.E. saw a flowering of literary effort. The disciples of the prophets Amos, Hosea, Isaiah, and Micah began to write down their words. When the northern kingdom of Israel fell in 721 B.C.E., the sources mentioned earlier were combined into the "Old Epic" narrative to give much of the present *Genesis*. In 621 B.C.E., the finding of a law scroll in the Jerusalem temple, a scroll probably containing the substance of *Deuteronomy* 12–26, provided impetus for the writing of the rest of this book.

• The Exile in Babylon (587–539 B.C.E.) was a fruitful period of literary activity. *Jeremiah, Ezekiel,* and "Second Isaiah" (*Isaiah* 40–55) were written down by those prophets' disciples. The Deuteronomic history (*Deuteronomy, Joshua, Judges, I–II Samuel,* and *I–II Kings*) was probably completed at the end of the Exile. Priestly sections of the *Torah* were completed, and many of the *Psalms* were written down.

• After the Exile, more prophetic books were completed: "Third Isaiah" (*Isaiah* 56–66), *Malachi, Joel,* and *Haggai*. By 400 B.C.E., the *Torah* probably reached its present form as it was finished and edited by the Jerusalem priests, becoming the first and primary section of Jewish scripture. Around 350 B.C.E., the historical works *I–II Chronicles* and *Ezra-Nehemiah* were completed. The later wisdom books, *Job* and *Ecclesiastes,* were compiled, and two short stories, *Ruth* and *Esther,* appeared. By 200 B.C.E., the eight-book section known as *Nevi'im* was largely complete. The final texts of the Jewish scripture were in the apocalyptic mode: *Isaiah* 24–27, *Ezekiel* 38, and especially the book of *Daniel,* the last book to be written, in 160 B.C.E. The *Kethuvim* section was basically determined by about 100 B.C.E.

The full and formal canonization of the entire Jewish *Bible* as we now have it—the *Law (Torah), Prophets (Nevi'im),* and *Writings (Kethuvim)*—took place at the end of the first century C.E. No one disagreed on the books of the *Torah* and the *Prophets*—this canon had been settled for centuries. A Jewish council meeting at Jamnia (ca. 90 C.E.) seems to have ruled on the writings as we have them, but it took some years for this ruling to be widely accepted. The main criterion for canonicity was the recognition that God was revealed in these books and spoke to his people in them. Canonization did not confer scripturality on a book. Rather, scriptural status emerged from the official and formal recognition of a longstanding reception and use of these books as holy and scriptural by the Jewish community itself. Once recognition was given, canonization helped reinforce the texts' holiness and authority.

HISTORY

The Call of Abraham

The history of the Jewish people begins with Abraham, whose name was Abram at first. God calls him to journey to Canaan (ancient Palestine) and promises that Abraham's descendants will form a great nation, will become a source of blessing to the world, and will inherit the land of Canaan. Abraham responds faithfully to God's call. Compare this passage with *Genesis* 17:9–14, 23–27 given later in the "Ritual" section of this chapter.[1]

The Lord said to Abram, "Go forth from
   your native land and from your father's
   house to the land that I will show you.
I will make of you a great nation,
And I will bless you;
I will make your name great,
And you shall be a blessing.
I will bless those who bless you

And curse him that curses you;
And all the families of the earth
Shall bless themselves by you."

Abram went forth as the Lord had commanded him, and Lot went with him. Abram was seventy-five years old when he left Haran.[2] [5] Abram took his wife Sarai and his brother's son Lot, and all the wealth that they had amassed,

---

[1] All passages from the Jewish *Bible* are from *Tanakh: The Holy Scriptures.* Copyright © 1985 Jewish Publication Society. Used by permission.

[2] *Haran:* the city in northern Mesopotamia (modern-day Iraq) where Abraham lived.

Genesis 12:1–9.

and the persons that they had acquired in Haran; and they set out for the land of Canaan. When they arrived in the land of Canaan, Abram passed through the land as far as the site of Shechem, at the terebinth[3] of Moreh. The Canaanites were then in the land.

---

[3]*terebinth:* an oak tree, with sacred significance.

The Lord appeared to Abram and said, "I will assign this land to your heirs." And he built an altar there to the Lord who had appeared to him. From there he moved on to the hill country east of Bethel and pitched his tent, with Bethel on the west and Ai on the east; and he built there an altar to the Lord and invoked the Lord by name. Then Abram journeyed by stages toward the Negeb.

The Call of Moses

Speaking from a burning bush, God calls Moses to be God's prophetic agent in liberating the Hebrews from their Egyptian slavery. This passage provides insight into the personality of Moses, the most influential person in the *Tanakh* and in Jewish history.

Now Moses, tending the flock of his father-in-law Jethro, the priest of Midian, drove the flock into the wilderness, and came to Horeb, the mountain of God. An angel of the Lord appeared to him in a blazing fire out of a bush. He gazed, and there was a bush all aflame, yet the bush was not consumed. Moses said, "I must turn aside to look at this marvelous sight; why doesn't the bush burn up?" When the Lord saw that he had turned aside to look, God called to him out of the bush: "Moses!" He answered, "Here I am." [5] And He said, "Do not come closer. Remove your sandals from your feet, for the place on which you stand is holy ground.[4] I am," He said, "the God of your father, the God of Abraham, the God of Isaac, and the God of Jacob." And Moses hid his face, for he was afraid to look at God.

And the Lord continued, "I have marked well the plight of My people in Egypt and have heeded their outcry because of their taskmasters; yes, I am mindful of their sufferings. I have come down to rescue them from the Egyptians and to bring them out of that land to a good and spacious land, a land flowing with milk and honey, the region of the Canaanites, the Hittites, the Amorites, the Perizzites, the Hivites, and the Jebusites. Now the cry of the Israelites has reached Me; moreover, I have seen how the Egyptians oppress them. [10] Come, therefore, I will send you to Pharaoh, and you shall free My people, the Israelites, from Egypt."

But Moses said to God, "Who am I that I should go to Pharaoh and free the Israelites from Egypt?" And He said, "I will be with you, that shall be your sign that it was I who sent you. And when you have freed the people from Egypt, you shall worship God at this mountain."

Moses said to God, "When I come to the Israelites and say to them 'The God of your fathers has sent me to you,' and they ask me, 'What is His name?' what shall I say to them?" And God said to Moses, "Ehyeh-Asher-Ehyeh."[5] He continued,

---

[4]*Remove your sandals:* the custom in many ancient Near Eastern religions of going barefoot in a holy place, still practiced in Islamic mosques.

[5]*Ehyeh-Asher-Ehyeh:* "I am what I am," based on the holy name YHWH, probably pronounced "YAH-weh." This name both reveals and conceals God's nature. It is translated here, as in the ancient synagogues, as "the Lord."

Exodus 3:1–20.

"Thus shall you say to the Israelites, 'Ehyeh sent me to you.'" [15] And God said further to Moses, "Thus shall you speak to the Israelites: The Lord, the God of your fathers, the God of Abraham, the God of Isaac, and the God of Jacob, has sent me to you: This shall be My name forever, This My appellation for all eternity."

"Go and assemble the elders of Israel and say to them: the Lord, the God of your fathers, the God of Abraham, Isaac, and Jacob, has appeared to me and said, 'I have taken note of you and of what is being done to you in Egypt, and I have declared: I will take you out of the misery of Egypt to the land of the Canaanites, the Hittites, the Amorites, the Perizzites, the Hivites, and the Jebusites,[6] to a land flowing with milk and honey.' They will listen to you; then you shall go with the elders of Israel to the king of Egypt and you shall say to him, 'The Lord, the God of the Hebrews, manifested Himself to us. Now therefore, let us go a distance of three days into the wilderness to sacrifice to the Lord our God.' Yet I know that the king of Egypt will let you go only because of a greater might. [20] So I will stretch out My hand and smite Egypt with various wonders which I will work upon them; after that he shall let you go."

---

[6]*Canaanites...Jebusites:* native peoples of Palestine before the Israelite conquest of the Promised Land.

Crossing the Red Sea

The dramatic climax of the Exodus is the Israelites' escape through the sea and the destruction of the Egyptians who pursued them. This tale is told at every Passover feast.

The Lord said to Moses: "Tell the Israelites to turn back and encamp before Pi-hahiroth, between Migdol and the sea, before Baal-zephon;[7] you shall encamp facing it, by the sea. Pharaoh will say of the Israelites, 'They are astray in the land; and wilderness has closed in on them.' Then I will stiffen Pharaoh's heart and he will pursue them, that I may gain glory through Pharaoh and all his host; and the Egyptians shall know that I am the Lord." And they did so.

[5] When the king of Egypt was told that the people had fled, Pharaoh and his courtiers had a change of heart about the people and said, "What is this we have done, releasing Israel from our service?" He ordered his chariot and took his men with him; he took six hundred of his picked chariots, and the rest of the chariots of Egypt, with officers in all of them. The Lord stiffened the heart of Pharaoh king of Egypt, and he gave chase to the Israelites. As the Israelites were departing defiantly, the Egyptians gave chase to them, and all the chariot horses of Pharaoh, his horsemen, and his warriors overtook them encamped by the sea, near Pi-hahiroth, before Baal-zephon.

[10] As Pharaoh drew near, the Israelites caught sight of the Egyptians advancing upon them. Greatly frightened, the Israelites cried out to the Lord. And they said to Moses, "Was it for lack of graves in Egypt that you brought us to die in the wilderness? What have you done to us, taking us out of Egypt? Is this not the very thing we told you in Egypt, saying 'Let us be, and we will serve the Egyptians, for it is better for us to serve the Egyptians than to die in the wilderness'?" But Moses said to the people, "Have no fear. Stand by, and witness

---

[7]*Pi-hahiroth, Migdol, Baal-zephon:* Egyptian fortified towns. The Israelites were trapped between the Egyptians and the sea.

Exodus 14:1–31.

the deliverance which the Lord will work for you today; for the Egyptians whom you see today you will never see again. The Lord will battle for you; you hold your peace."

[15] Then the Lord said to Moses, "Why do you cry out to Me? Tell the Israelites to go forward. And you lift up your rod and hold out your arm over the sea and split it, so that the Israelites may march into the sea on dry ground. And I will stiffen the hearts of the Egyptians so that they go in after them; and I will gain glory through Pharaoh and all his warriors, his chariots and his horsemen. Let the Egyptians know that I am Lord, when I gain glory through Pharaoh, his chariots, and his horsemen."

The angel of God, who had been going ahead of the Israelite army, now moved and followed behind them; and the pillar of cloud shifted from in front of them and took up a place behind them, [20] and it came between the army of the Egyptians and the army of Israel. Thus there was the cloud with the darkness, and it cast a spell upon the night, so that the one could not come near the other all through the night.

Then Moses held out his arm over the sea and the Lord drove back the sea with a strong east wind all that night, and turned the sea into dry ground. The waters were split, and the Israelites went into the sea on dry ground, the waters forming a wall for them on their right and on

their left. The Egyptians came in pursuit after them into the sea, all of Pharaoh's horses, chariots, and horsemen. At the morning watch, the Lord looked down upon the Egyptian army from a pillar of fire and cloud, and threw the Egyptian army into panic. [25] He locked the wheels of their chariots so that they moved forward with difficulty. And the Egyptians said, "Let us flee from the Israelites, for the Lord is fighting for them against Egypt."

Then the Lord said to Moses, "Hold out your arm over the sea, that the waters may come back upon the Egyptians and upon their chariots and upon their horsemen." Moses held out his arm over the sea, and at daybreak the sea returned to its normal state, and the Egyptians fled at its approach. But the Lord hurled the Egyptians into the sea. The waters turned back and covered the chariots and the horsemen—Pharaoh's entire army that followed them into the sea; not one of them remained. But the Israelites had marched through the sea on dry ground, the waters forming a wall for them on their right and on their left.

[30] Thus the Lord delivered Israel that day from the Egyptians. Israel saw the Egyptians dead on the shore of the sea. And when Israel saw the wondrous power which the Lord had wielded against the Egyptians, the people feared the Lord; they had faith in the Lord and His servant Moses.

The Covenant with Israel

After the Exodus, God renews the **covenant,** or pact, made with Abraham. The familiar terms of the covenant from *Genesis* 17:1–8 are present here: "I will be your God"; "You will be my people"; "You must obey me." These covenant conditions are here prefaced and founded on what God did in liberating the people from Egypt.

On the third new moon after the Israelites had gone forth from the land of Egypt, on that very day, they entered the wilderness of Sinai.

Having journeyed from Rephidim, they entered the wilderness of Sinai and encamped in the wilderness. Israel encamped there in front of the

Exodus 19:1–8.

mountain, and Moses went up to God. The Lord called to him from the mountain, saying, "Thus shall you say to the house of Jacob and declare to the children of Israel: 'You have seen what I did to the Egyptians, how I bore you on eagles' wings and brought you to Me. [5] Now then, if you will obey Me faithfully and keep My covenant, you shall be My treasured possession among all the peoples. Indeed, all the earth is Mine, but you shall be to Me a kingdom of priests and a holy nation.' These are the words that you shall speak to the children of Israel."

Moses came and summoned the elders of the people and put before them all that the Lord had commanded him. All the people answered as one, saying, "All that the Lord has spoken we will do." And Moses brought back the people's words to the Lord.

A Psalm for David

The story of David's rule over Israel is told in *II Samuel*. *Psalm* 132 portrays well the significance of David for the continuing life of Judaism. Israel hopes for the coming of its Messiah
from the descendants of David to take up again the rule of David. Orthodox Jews look for a
literal fulfillment of this hope; more liberal Jews look for a symbolic fulfillment.

O Lord, remember in David's favor
his extreme self-denial,
how he swore to the Lord,
vowed to the Mighty One of Jacob,
"I will not enter my house,
nor will I mount my bed,
I will not give sleep to my eyes,
or slumber to my eyelids
[5] until I find a place for the Lord,
an abode for the Mighty One of Jacob."

We heard it was in Ephrath;
we came upon it in the region of Jaar.[8]
Let us enter His abode,
bow at His footstool.
Advance, O Lord, to Your resting-place,
You and Your mighty Ark!
Your priests are clothed in triumph;
Your loyal ones sing for joy.
[10] For the sake of Your servant David
do not reject Your anointed one.

The Lord swore to David
a firm oath that He will not renounce,
"One of your own issue I will set upon
your throne.
If your sons keep My covenant
and My decrees that I teach them,
then their sons also,
to the end of time,
shall sit upon your throne."
For the Lord has chosen Zion;[9]
He has desired it for His seat.
"This is my resting-place for all time;
here I will dwell, for I desire it.
[15] I will amply bless its store of food,
give its needy their fill of bread.
I will clothe its priests in victory,
its loyal ones shall sing for joy.
There I will make a horn sprout for David;
I have prepared a lamp for My anointed
one.
I will clothe his enemies in disgrace,
while on him his crown shall sparkle."

---

[8]*Ephrath:* David's home city, also known as Bethlehem; *Jaar:* where the Ark of the Covenant was kept from Samuel's time until David moved it to Jerusalem.

[9]*Zion:* Jerusalem.

Psalm 132.

Ezra's Enforcement of *Torah* Observance

The return of the Jews from Exile in Babylon brought a new dedication to keep the *Torah,* for it was widely perceived that God had used the Exile to punish them for their sins. One way this *Torah* observance was enforced was in the compulsory divorce of Jewish men from non-Jewish wives. Marriage only within Judaism became the rule in Jewish law and was widely followed in all branches of Judaism until modern times. (See the book of *Ruth,* perhaps also written at this time, for a more liberal view of intermarriage.)

When this was over, the officers approached me, saying, "The people of Israel and the priests and Levites have not separated themselves from the peoples of the land whose abhorrent practices are like those of the Canaanites, the Hittites, the Perizzites, the Jebusites, the Ammonites, the Moabites, the Egyptians, and the Amorites. They have taken their daughters as wives for themselves and for their sons, so that the holy seed has become intermingled with the peoples of the land; and it is the officers and prefects who have taken the lead in this trespass."

When I heard this, I rent my garment and robe, I tore hair out of my head and beard, and I sat desolate.[10] Around me gathered all who were concerned over the words of the God of Israel because of the returning exiles' trespass, while I sat desolate until the evening offering. [5] At the time of the evening offering I ended my self-affliction; still in my torn garment and robe, I got down on my knees and spread out my hands to the Lord my God, and said, "O my God, I am too ashamed and mortified to lift my face to You, O my God, for our iniquities are overwhelming and our guilt has grown high as heaven. From the time of our fathers to this very day we have been deep in guilt. Because of our iniquities, we, our kings, and our priests have been handed over to foreign kings, to the sword, to captivity, to pillage, and to humiliation, as is now the case . . . [13] After all that has happened to us because of our evil deeds and our deep guilt—though You, our God, have been forbearing, less than our iniquity in that You have granted us such a remnant[11] as this—shall we once again violate Your commandments by intermarrying with these peoples who follow such abhorrent practices?[12] Will You not rage against us till we are destroyed without remnant or survivor? [15] O Lord, God of Israel, You are benevolent, for we have survived as a remnant, as is now the case. We stand before You in all our guilt, for we cannot face You on this account."

[10:1] While Ezra was praying and making confession, weeping and prostrating himself before the House of God, a very great crowd of Israelites gathered about him, men, women, and children; the people were weeping bitterly. Then Shecaniah son of Jehiel of the family of Elam spoke up and said to Ezra, "We have trespassed against our God by bringing into our homes foreign women from the peoples of the land; but there is still hope for Israel despite this. Now then, let us make a covenant with our God to expel all these women and those who have been born to them, in accordance with the bidding of the Lord and of all who are concerned over the commandment of our God, and let the Teaching

---

[10]*rent* [tore] *my garment . . . sat desolate:* all signs of mourning.

[11]*remnant:* group of survivors.

[12]*such abhorrent practices:* the immoralities and idolatry of other peoples.

Ezra 9:1–7, 13–15; 10:1–12.

#2 be obeyed. Take action, for the responsibility is yours and we are with you. Act with resolve!"

[5] So Ezra at once put the officers of the priests and the Levites and all Israel under oath to act accordingly, and they took the oath. Then Ezra rose from his place in front of the House of God and went into the chamber of Jehohanan son of Eliashib; there, he ate no bread and drank no water, for he was in mourning over the trespass of those who had returned from exile. Then a proclamation was issued in Judah and Jerusalem that all who had returned from the exile should assemble in Jerusalem, and that anyone who did not come in three days would, by decision of the officers and elders, have his property confiscated and himself excluded from the congregation of the returning exiles.

All the men of Judah and Benjamin assembled in Jerusalem in three days; it was the ninth month, the twentieth of the month. All the people sat in the square of the House of God, trembling on account of the event and because of the rains. [10] Then Ezra the priest got up and said to them, #3 "You have trespassed by bringing home foreign women, thus aggravating the guilt of Israel. So now, make confession to the Lord, God of your fathers, and do His will, and separate yourselves from the peoples of the land and from the foreign women." The entire congregation responded in a loud voice, "We must surely do just as you say."

TEACHING

The Oneness of God

These words of Moses explain the commandment "You shall have no other gods beside me." In Jewish tradition, the last paragraph of this selection is known as the **Shema** [sheh-MAH], the Hebrew word meaning "hear," which opens this section. The last sentence has produced the use of the tefillin, small boxes with the *Shema* and three other passages inside that are bound by leather straps to the hand and forehead, and the mezuzah, a small box fastened to the doorpost that contains the *Shema* and *Deuteronomy* 11:13–21. They are reminders of Jewishness and the duty to love and serve God alone.

"And this is the Instruction—the laws and the rules—that the Lord your God has commanded to impart to you, to be observed in the land that you are about to cross into and occupy, so that you, your children, and your children's children may revere the Lord your God and follow, as long as you live, all His laws and commandments that I enjoin upon you, to the end that you may long endure. Obey, O Israel, willingly and faithfully, that it may go well with you and that you may increase greatly a land flowing with milk and honey, as the Lord, the God of your fathers, spoke to you.

"Hear, O Israel The Lord is our God, the Lord alone. [5] You shall love the Lord your God with all your heart and with all your soul and with all your might. Take to heart these instructions with which I charge you this day. Impress them upon your children. Recite them when you stay at home and when you are away, when you lie down and when you get up. Bind them as a sign on your hand and let them serve as a symbol on your forehead; inscribe them on the doorposts of your house and on your gates."

Deuteronomy 6:1–9.

God's Creation of the World

Two narratives tell the story of God's creation of the world: one from Priestly traditions (1:1–2:3), the other from Old Epic traditions (2:4–25). They vary in content and style. In the first, God creates an orderly cosmos out of primeval chaos, with humankind as the capstone of creation. In the second, the creation of humanity is the central topic. Notice the different ways the two stories account for the creation of woman.

When God began to create heaven and earth—the earth being unformed and void, with darkness over the surface of the deep and a wind from God sweeping over the water—God said, "Let there be light"; and there was light. God saw that the light was good, and God separated the light from the darkness. [5] God called the light Day, and the darkness He called Night. And there was evening and there was morning, a first day.

God said, "Let there be an expanse in the midst of the water, that it may separate water from water." God made the expanse, and it separated the water which was below the expanse from the water which was above the expanse. And it was so. God called the expanse Sky. And there was evening and there was morning, a second day.

God said, "Let the water below the sky be gathered into one area, that the dry land may appear." And it was so. [10] God called the dry land Earth, and the gathering of waters He called Seas. And God saw that this was good. And God said, "Let the earth sprout vegetation: seed-bearing plants, fruit trees of every kind on earth that bear fruit with the seed in it." And it was so. The earth brought forth vegetation: seed-bearing plants of every kind, and trees of every kind bearing fruit with the seed in it. And God saw that this was good. And there was evening and there was morning, a third day.

God said, "Let there be lights in the expanse of the sky to separate day from night; they shall serve as signs for the set times—the days and the years; [15] and they shall serve as lights in the expanse of the sky to shine upon the earth." And it was so. God made the two great lights, the greater light to dominate the day and the lesser light to dominate the night, and the stars. And God set them in the expanse of the sky to shine upon the earth, to dominate the day and the night, and to separate light from darkness. And God saw that this was good. And there was evening and there was morning, a fourth day.

[20] God said, "Let the waters bring forth swarms of living creatures, and birds that fly above the earth across the expanse of the sky." God created the great sea monsters, and all the living creatures of every kind that creep, which the waters brought forth in swarms, and all the winged birds of every kind. And God saw that this was good. God blessed them, saying, "Be fertile and increase, fill the waters in the seas, and let the birds increase on the earth." And there was evening and there was morning, a fifth day.

God said, "Let the earth bring forth every kind of living creature: cattle, creeping things, and wild beasts of every kind." And it was so. [25] God made wild beasts of every kind and cattle of every kind, and all kinds of creeping things of the earth. And God saw that this was good. And God said, "Let us make man in our[13] image, after our likeness. They shall rule the fish of the sea, the birds of the sky, the

---

[13] *us, our:* God and the beings of the heavenly court. There is probably no idea of the plurality of God here.

Genesis 1:1–31; 2:1–9, 15–25.

cattle, the whole earth, and all the creeping things that creep on earth." And God created man in His image, in the image of God He created him; male and female He created them. God blessed them and God said to them, "Be fertile and increase, fill the earth and master it; and rule the fish of the sea, the birds of the sky, and all the living things that creep on earth."

God said, "See, I give you every seed-bearing plant that is upon all the earth, and every tree that has seed-bearing fruit; they shall be yours for food. [30] And to all the animals on land, to all the birds of the sky, and to everything that creeps on earth, in which there is the breath of life, all the green plants for food." And it was so. And God saw all that He had made, and found it very good. And there was evening and there was morning, the sixth day.

[2:1] The heaven and the earth were finished, and all their array. On the seventh day God finished the work that He had been doing, and He ceased on the seventh day from all the work that He had done. And God blessed the seventh day and declared it holy, because on it God ceased from all the work of creation that He had done.[14] Such is the story of heaven and earth when they were created.

[2:4, the second creation account] When the Lord God made earth and heaven—when no shrub of the field was yet on earth and no grasses of the field had yet sprouted, because the Lord God had not sent rain upon the earth and there was no man to till the soil, but a flow would well up from the ground and water the whole surface of the earth—the Lord God formed man from the dust of the earth. He blew into his nostrils the breath of life, and man became a living being.

The Lord God planted a garden in Eden, in the east, and placed there the man whom He had formed. And from the ground the Lord God caused to grow every tree that was pleasing to the sight and good for food, with the tree of life in the middle of the garden, and the tree of knowledge of good and bad....

[2:15] The Lord God took the man and placed him in the garden of Eden, to till it and tend it. And the Lord God commanded the man, saying, "Of every tree of the garden you are free to eat; but as for the tree of knowledge of good and bad, you must not eat of it; for as soon as you eat of it, you shall die."

The Lord God said, "It is not good for man to be alone; I will make a fitting helper for him." And the Lord God formed out of the earth all the wild beasts and all the birds of the sky, and brought them to the man to see what he would call them; and whatever the man called each living creature, that would be its name. [20] And the man gave names to all the cattle and to the birds of the sky and to all the wild beasts; but for Adam no fitting helper was found. So the Lord God cast a deep sleep upon the man; and, while he slept, He took one of his ribs and closed up the flesh at that spot. And the Lord God fashioned the rib that He had taken from the man into a woman; and He brought her to the man. Then the man said,

"This one at last
Is bone of my bones
And flesh of my flesh.
This one shall be called Woman,
For from man was she taken."

Hence a man leaves his father and mother and clings to his wife, so that they become one flesh. [25] The two of them were naked, the man and his wife, yet they felt no shame.

---

[14] *God blessed the seventh day...done:* an allusion to the law of rest and renewal on the seventh day, the sabbath.

The Revolt of Humanity

#2 Humans fall into sin by rebelling against God's command. Tempted by the serpent (in this "miss the mark" story a wily creature, but in later Jewish and then Christian and Islamic tradition thought to be the devil in disguise), first the woman and then the man disobey God. God punishes all the guilty parties in various ways, but humanity's chief punishment is being driven out of the Garden. Orthodox Jews, like conservative Christians and traditional Muslims, regard this as a fully historical event. Many Conservative and most Reform Jews, like more liberal Christians, see it as mythical—not historical but religiously true nonetheless.

Now the serpent was the shrewdest of all the wild beasts that the Lord God had made. He said to the woman, "Did God really say: 'You shall not eat of any tree of the garden'?" The woman replied to the serpent, "We may eat of the fruit of the other trees of the garden. It is only about fruit of the tree in the middle of the garden that God said: 'You shall not eat of it or touch it, lest you die.'" And the serpent said to the woman, "You are not going to die, [5] but God knows that as soon as you eat of it your eyes will be opened and you will be like divine beings who know good and bad." When the woman saw that the tree was good for eating and a delight to the eyes, and that the tree was desirable as a source of wisdom, she took of its fruit and ate. She also gave some to her husband, and he ate. Then the eyes of both of them were opened and they perceived that they were naked;[15] and they sewed together fig leaves and made themselves loincloths.

They heard the sound of the Lord God moving about in the garden at the breezy time of day; and the man and his wife hid from the Lord God among the trees of the garden. The Lord God called out to the man and said to him, "Where are you?" [10] He replied, "I heard the sound of You in the garden, and I

disobedience

was afraid because I was naked, so I hid." Then He asked, "Who told you that you were naked? Did you eat of the tree from which I had forbidden you to eat?" The man said, "The woman You put at my side—she gave me of the tree, and I ate." And the Lord God said to the woman, "What is this you have done?" The woman replied, "The serpent duped me, and I ate." Then the Lord God said to the serpent,

"Because you did this,
More cursed shall you be
Than all cattle
And all the wild beasts:
On your belly shall you crawl
And dirt shall you eat
All the days of your life.
[15] I will put enmity
Between you and the woman,
And between your offspring and hers;
They shall strike at your head,
And you shall strike at their heel."

And to the woman He said,
"I will make most severe
Your pangs in childbearing;
In pain shall you bear children.
Yet your urge shall be for your husband,
And he shall rule over you."[16]

---

[15] *naked:* Knowledge of their nakedness is a symbol of their loss of goodness and innocence.

[16] *he shall rule over you:* The original equality between man and woman is lost; the husband now has authority over the wife.

Genesis 3:1–24.

To Adam He said, "Because you did as your wife said and ate of the tree about which I commanded you, 'You shall not eat of it,'

Cursed be the ground because of you;
By toil shall you eat of it
All the days of your life:
Thorns and thistles shall it sprout for you.
But your food shall be the grasses of the
    field;
By the sweat of your brow
Shall you get bread to eat,
Until you return to the ground—
For from it you were taken.
For dust you are,
And to dust you shall return."

[20] The man named his wife Eve, because she was the mother of all the living. And the Lord God made garments of skins for Adam and his wife, and clothed them.

And the Lord God said, "Now that the man has become like one of us, knowing good and bad, what if he should stretch out his hand and take also from the tree of life and eat, and live forever!" So the Lord God banished him from the garden of Eden, to till the soil from which he was taken. He drove the man out, and stationed east of the garden of Eden the cherubim[17] and the fiery ever-turning sword, to guard the way to the tree of life.

---

[17]*cherubim:* not "cherubs" but fearsome six-winged angels, half human and half lion.

Prayer for Divine Deliverance

The Psalms show a strong personal relationship to God as well as a strong distinction between good and evil, both characteristic of Israelite religion. This psalm, a typical prayer for deliverance, first describes the difficulties of the believer and ends with expression of the believer's trust in God to deliver.

Give ear to my speech, O Lord; consider my
    utterance.
Heed the sound of my cry, my king and God,
    for I pray to You.
Hear my voice, O Lord, at daybreak; at
    daybreak I plead before You, and wait.

[5] For You are not a God who desires
    wickedness; evil cannot abide with You;
    wanton men cannot endure in Your
    sight.
You detest all evildoers; You doom those
    who speak lies; murderous, deceitful men
    the Lord abhors.
But I, through Your abundant love, enter
    Your house; I bow down in awe at Your
    holy temple.

O Lord, lead me along Your righteousness
    because of my watchful foes; make Your
    way straight before me.
[10] For there is no sincerity on their lips;
    their heart is malice; their throat is an
    open grave; their tongue slippery.
Condemn them, O God; let them fall by their
    own devices; cast them out for their many
    crimes, for they defy You.
But let all who take refuge in You rejoice,
    ever jubilant as You shelter them; and
    let those who love Your name exult in
    You.
For You surely bless the righteous man,
    O Lord, encompassing him with favor like
    a shield.

Psalm 5.

The Messianic King

This prophetic oracle promises a deliverer of Israel to come from among the descendants of   # 4
King David. He will bring forth light, joy, peace, and justice. Orthodox Jews look forward to a
literal fulfillment of this promise; others interpret it in the sense of progress toward justice in
Judaism or in all of humanity.

But a shoot shall grow out of the stump of
    Jesse,
A twig shall sprout from his stock.
The spirit of the Lord shall alight upon him:
A spirit of wisdom and insight,
A spirit of counsel and valor,
A spirit of devotion and reverence for the
    Lord.
He shall sense the truth by his reverence for
    the Lord:
He shall not judge by what his eyes behold,
Nor decide by what his ears perceive.
Thus he shall judge the poor with equity
And decide with justice for the lowly of the
    land.
He shall strike down a land with the rod of
    his mouth
And slay the wicked with the breath of his
    lips.

[5] Justice shall be the girdle of his loins,
And faithfulness the girdle of his waist.
The wolf shall dwell with the lamb,
The leopard lie down with the kid;
The calf, the beast of prey, and the fatling
    together,
With a little boy to herd them.
The cow and the bear shall graze,
Their young shall lie down together;
And the lion, like the ox, shall eat straw.
A babe shall play
Over a viper's hole
And an infant pass his hand
Over an adder's den.
In all of My sacred mount
Nothing evil or vile shall be done;
For the land shall be filled with devotion to
    the Lord
As water covers the sea.

Isaiah 11:1–9.

The Final Judgment of the World

The apocalyptic view of the world and history can be richly symbolic, with dreams and
visions featuring mixed-form animals, cosmic battles, and other fantastic events. In this passage, the winged lion represents the Babylonian Empire, the bear is the Medes, the four-
headed leopard is the Persians, and the dragon is the Greeks. The ten horns are the
ten rulers succeeding Alexander in the Near East, and the "little horn" is the Syrian King
Antiochus Epiphanes, whose brutal persecution of the Jews precipitated a Jewish revolt and
whose destruction is foretold here. Although the rich symbolism of apocalyptic scripture
did not carry over into later Judaism, an apocalyptic view of the main events at the end of
time did: God will someday bring history to an end and judge all peoples and nations.

Daniel 7:1–14.

In the first year of King Belshazzar of Babylon, Daniel saw a dream and a vision of his mind in bed; afterward he wrote down the dream. Beginning the account, Daniel related the following: "In my vision at night, I saw the four winds of heaven stirring up the great sea. Four mighty beasts different from each other emerged from the sea. The first was like a lion but had eagles' wings. As I looked on, its wings were plucked off, and it was lifted off the ground and set on its feet like a man and given the mind of a man. [5] Then I saw a second, different beast, which was like a bear but raised on one side, and with three fangs in its mouth among its teeth; it was told, 'Arise, eat much meat.' After that, as I looked on, there was another one, like a leopard, and it had on its back four wings like those of a bird; the beast had four heads, and dominion was given to it. After that, as I looked on in the night vision, there was a fourth beast—fearsome, dreadful, and very powerful, with great iron teeth—that devoured and crushed, and stamped the remains with its feet. It was different from all the other beasts which had gone before it; and it had ten horns. While I was gazing upon these horns, a new little horn sprouted up among them; three of the older horns were uprooted to make room for it. There were eyes in this horn like those of a man, and a mouth that spoke arrogantly. As I looked on,

> Thrones were set in place,
> And the Ancient of Days[18] took His seat.
> His garment was like white snow,

---

[18]*the Ancient of Days:* God, the Eternal One.

> And the hair of His head was like lamb's wool.
> His throne was tongues of flame;
> Its wheels were blazing fire.
> [10] A river of fire streamed forth before Him;
> Thousands upon thousands served Him;
> Myriads upon myriads attended Him;
> The court sat and the books were opened.[19]

I looked on. Then, because of the arrogant words that the horn spoke, the beast was killed as I looked on; its body was destroyed and it was consigned to the flames. The dominion of the other beasts was taken away, but an extension of life was given to them for a time and season. As I looked on, in the night vision,

> One like a human being[20]
> Came with the clouds of heaven;
> He reached the Ancient of Days
> And was presented to Him.
> Dominion, glory, and kingship were given to him;
> All peoples and nations of every language must serve him.
> His dominion is an everlasting dominion that shall not pass away,
> And his kingship, one that shall not be destroyed."

---

[19]*books were opened:* books in which the deeds of all people or their eternal destiny is written.
[20]*One like a human being:* This human figure represents the faithful Jews; traditionally, this figure is identified as the Messiah.

Resurrection of the Dead

One prominent element of apocalyptic scripture is the resurrection of the dead, God's summoning them out of their graves with new, eternal bodies to face a judgment that determines their eternal fate. Although this short passage says that "many" will arise, soon the idea is established in Judaism that all will arise. This belief is held firmly by the Orthodox; other Jews interpret it metaphorically or discard it. The resurrection of the dead became an important part of Christian and Muslim teaching as well. Here, God speaks to Daniel.

Daniel 12:1–3.

"At that time, the great prince, Michael, who stands beside the sons of your people,[21] will appear. It will be a time of trouble, the like of which has never been since the nation came into being. At that time, your people will be rescued, all who are found inscribed in the book. Many of those that sleep in the dust of the earth will awake, some to eternal life, others to reproaches, to everlasting abhorrence. And the knowledgeable will be radiant like the bright expanse of sky, and those who lead the many to righteousness will be like the stars forever and ever."

---

[21] *Michael:* the guardian angel of Israel.

ETHICS

The Ten Commandments

This is the first section of the law given by God to Israel at Mount Sinai after the Exodus from Egypt. The first group of commandments, up through false swearing, deals with humanity's duty to God; the last group deals with person-to-person obligations. Of all the ancient law codes, the *Ten Commandments* (or the **Decalogue**) are probably the most influential in Western religion and culture. The numbering of the commands varies among Jews and Christians, but all agree on the total of ten.

God spoke all these words, saying:

I the Lord am your God who brought you out of the land of Egypt, the house of bondage: You shall have no other gods beside Me.

You shall not make for yourself a sculptured image, or any likeness of what is in the heavens above, or on the earth below, or in the waters under the earth. [5] You shall not bow down to them or serve them. For I the Lord your God am an impassioned God, visiting the guilt of the parents upon the children, upon the third and upon the fourth generations of those who reject Me, but showing kindness to the thousandth generation of those who love Me and keep My commandments.

You shall not swear falsely by the name of the Lord your God; for the Lord will not clear one who swears falsely by His name.

Remember the sabbath day and keep it holy. Six days you shall labor and do all your work, [10] but the seventh day is a sabbath of the Lord your God: you shall not do any work—you, your son or daughter, your male or female slave, or your cattle, or the stranger who is within your settlements. For in six days the Lord made heaven and earth and sea, and all that is in them, and He rested on the seventh day; therefore the Lord blessed the sabbath day and hallowed it.

Honor your father and your mother, that you may long endure on the land that the Lord your God is assigning to you.

You shall not murder.

You shall not commit adultery.

You shall not steal.

You shall not bear false witness against your neighbor.

You shall not covet your neighbor's house: you shall not covet your neighbor's wife, or his male or female slave, or his ox or his ass, or anything that is your neighbor's.

Exodus 20:1–14.

Laws on Slaves, Violence, and Property

Following the *Ten Commandments* is a section of laws also traditionally traced to God's giving of the law to Moses. The laws on slavery reflect the humanitarian concern of Israel in the midst of a slave-owning and patriarchal culture. Although both male and female Hebrew slaves are given some protections, the male has more. The time limits on slavery imply that it is not the proper condition of humankind or at least of Israelites. In the laws on violence, a distinction is made between intentional and unintentional acts. The law of retributive justice, called here "an eye for an eye," is often seen today as a crude and violent method of justice, but it is a humane limitation on the continual violence of blood feuds and private revenge. This selection closes with laws that protect the more vulnerable and helpless members of society.

These are the rules that you shall set before them:

When you acquire a Hebrew slave, he shall serve six years; in the seventh year he shall go free, without payment. If he came single, he shall leave single; if he had a wife, his wife shall leave with him. If his master gave him a wife, and she has borne him children, the wife and her children shall belong to the master, and he shall leave alone. [5] But if the slave declares, "I love my master, and my wife and children: I do not wish to go free," his master shall take him before God.[22] He shall be brought to the door or the doorpost, and his master shall pierce his ear with an awl; and he shall then remain his slave for life.

When a man sells his daughter as a slave, she shall not be freed as male slaves are. If she proves to be displeasing to her master, who designated her for himself, he must let her be redeemed;[23] he shall not have the right to sell her to outsiders, since he broke faith with her. And if he designated her for his son, he shall deal with her as is the practice with free maidens. [10] If he marries another, he must not withhold from this one her food, her clothing, or her conjugal rights. If he fails her in these three ways, she shall go free, without payment.

He who fatally strikes a man shall be put to death. If he did not do it by design, but it came about by an act of God, I will assign you a place to which he can flee.[24]

When a man schemes against another and kills him treacherously, you shall take him from My very altar to be put to death.

[15] He who strikes his father or his mother shall be put to death.

He who kidnaps a man—whether he has sold him or is still holding him—shall be put to death.

He who insults his father or mother shall be put to death.

When men quarrel and one strikes the other with stone or fist, and he does not die but has to take to his bed—if he then gets up and walks outdoors upon his staff, the assailant shall go unpunished, except that he must pay for his idleness and his cure.

[20] When a man strikes his slave, male or female, with a rod, and he dies there and then, he must be avenged. But if he survives a day or two, he is not to be avenged, since he is the other's property.

---

[22]*take him before God:* that is, at the sacred doorpost of the house.
[23]*redeemed:* bought from slavery by a relative or other interested party.

---

[24]*a place to...flee:* a place of safety in which to take refuge, often at an altar of God; hence our word *sanctuary* in the sense of "safe refuge."

Exodus 21:1–36; 22:15–26.

When men fight, and one of them pushes a pregnant woman and a miscarriage results, but no other damage ensues, the one responsible shall be fined according as the woman's husband may exact from him, the payment to be based on reckoning. But if other damage ensues, the penalty shall be life for life, eye for eye, tooth for tooth, hand for hand, foot for foot, [25] burn for burn, wound for wound, bruise for bruise.

When a man strikes the eye of his slave, male or female, and destroys it, he shall let him go free on account of his eye. If he knocks out the tooth of his slave, male or female, he shall let him go free on account of his tooth.

When an ox gores a man or a woman to death, the ox shall be stoned and its flesh shall not be eaten, but the owner of the ox is not to be punished. If, however, that ox has been in the habit of goring, and its owner, though warned, has failed to guard it, and it kills a man or a woman—the ox shall be stoned and its owner, too, shall be put to death. [30] If ransom is laid upon him, he must pay whatever is laid upon him to redeem his life. So, too, if it gores a minor, male or female, the owner shall be dealt with according to the same rule. But if the ox gores a slave, male or female, he shall pay thirty shekels of silver to the master, and the ox shall be stoned.

When a man opens a pit, or digs a pit and does not cover it, and an ox or an ass falls into it, the one responsible for the pit must make restitution; he shall pay the price to the owner, but shall keep the dead animal.

[35] When a man's ox injures his neighbor's ox and it dies, they shall sell the live ox and divide its price; they shall also divide the dead animal. If, however, it is known that the ox was in the habit

of goring, and its owner has failed to guard it, he must restore ox for ox, but shall keep the dead animal. . . .

[22:15[25]] If a man seduces a virgin for whom the bride-price[26] has not been paid, and lies with her, he must make her his wife by payment of a bride-price. If her father refuses to give her to him, he must still weigh out silver in accordance with the bride-price for virgins.

You shall not tolerate a sorceress.

Whoever lies with a beast shall be put to death.

Whoever sacrifices to a god other than the Lord alone shall be proscribed.[27]

[20] You shall not wrong a stranger or oppress him, for you were strangers in the land of Egypt.

You shall not ill-treat any widow or orphan. If you do mistreat them, I will heed their outcry as soon as they cry out to Me, and My anger shall blaze forth and I will put you to the sword, and your own wives shall become widows and your children orphans.

If you lend money to My people, to the poor among you, do not act toward them as a creditor: exact no interest from them. [25] If you take your neighbor's garment in pledge, you must return it to him before the sun sets; it is his only clothing, the sole covering for his skin. In what else shall he sleep? Therefore, if he cries out to Me, I will pay heed, for I am compassionate.

---

[25]The verse numbers differ by one between this translation and the Christian translations of this passage.
[26]*bride-price:* the husband's payment to the family of the bride.
[27]*proscribed:* put to death.

Justice for All

Israel's strong sense of equal justice and correct judicial procedure for all social classes is shown in this selection.

You must not carry false rumors; you shall not join hands with the guilty to act as a malicious witness: You shall neither side with the mighty to do wrong—you shall not give perverse testimony in a dispute so as to pervert it in favor of the mighty—nor shall you show deference to a poor man in his dispute.

When you encounter your enemy's ox or ass wandering, you must take it back to him. When you see the ass of your enemy lying under its burden and would refrain from raising it, you must nevertheless raise it with him.

You shall not subvert the rights of your needy in their disputes. Keep far from a false charge; do not bring death on those who are innocent and in the right, for I will not acquit the wrongdoer. Do not take bribes, for bribes blind the clear-sighted and upset the pleas of those who are in the right.

You shall not oppress a stranger,[28] for you know the feelings of the stranger, having yourselves been strangers in the land of Egypt.

_____
[28] _stranger:_ resident alien in the land of Israel.

_____
Exodus 23:1–9.

Holy War

In holy war, God fights with and for the people against their Canaanite enemies during the conquest of the Promised Land. The people and cities of Canaan are to be sacrificed to God by utter destruction. Notice that verses 10–14 specify a more humane method of warfare against non-Canaanite opponents. The last section sets limits on the destruction of the natural environment during warfare.

When you take the field against your enemies, and see horses and chariots—forces larger than yours—have no fear of them, for the Lord your God, who brought you from the land of Egypt, is with you. Before you join battle, the priest shall come forward and address the troops. He shall say to them, "Hear, O Israel! You are about to join battle with your enemy. Let not your courage falter. Do not be in fear, or in panic, or in dread of them. For it is the Lord your God who marches with you to do battle for you against your enemy, to bring you victory."

[5] Then the officials shall address the troops, as follows: "Is there anyone who has built a new house but has not dedicated it? Let him go back to his home, lest he die in battle and another dedicate it. Is there anyone who has planted a vineyard but has never harvested it? Let him go back to his home, lest he die in battle and another harvest it. Is there anyone who has paid the bride-price[29] for a wife, but who has not yet married her? Let him

_____
[29] _bride-price:_ the husband's payment to the family of the bride.

_____
Deuteronomy 20:1–20.

go back to his home, lest he die in battle and another marry her." The officials shall go on addressing the troops and say, "Is there anyone afraid and disheartened? Let him go back to his home, lest the courage of his comrades flag like his." When the officials have finished addressing the troops, army commanders shall assume command of the troops.

[10] When you approach a town to attack it, you shall offer it terms of peace. If it responds peaceably and lets you in, all the people present there shall serve you at forced labor. If it does not surrender to you, but would join battle with you, you shall lay siege to it; and when the Lord your God delivers it into your hand, you shall put all its males to the sword. You may, however, take as your booty the women, the children, the livestock, and everything in the town—all its spoil—and enjoy the use of the spoil of your enemy, which the Lord your God gives you.

[15] Thus you shall deal with all towns that lie very far from you, towns that do not belong to nations hereabout. In the towns of the latter peoples, however, which the Lord your God is giving you as a heritage, you shall not let a soul remain alive. No, you must proscribe them—the Hittites and the Amorites, the Canaanites and the Perizzites, the Hivites and the Jebusites—as the Lord your God has commanded you, lest they lead you into doing all the abhorrent things that they have done for their gods and you stand guilty before the Lord your God.

When in your war against a city you have to besiege it a long time in order to capture it, you must not destroy its trees, wielding the ax against them. You may eat of them, but you must not cut them down. Are trees of the field human to withdraw before you into the besieged city? [20] Only trees that you know do not yield food may be destroyed; you may cut them down for constructing siegeworks against the city that is waging war on you, until it has been reduced.

Sexual Love

The finest literary testimony to the sexual dimensions of love in the *Bible* is the *Song of Songs* (called by many Christians the *"Song of Solomon"*), which is modeled after Egyptian love poetry. Its poems are a dialogue between a man, traditionally thought to be Solomon, and a woman who take full delight in the emotional and physical dimensions of love. Later Judaism, as well as Christianity, made this book symbolic of the love of God for people. (The notes in brackets are explanations by the editors of the *Tanakh* translation).

[The woman speaks:] Oh, give me of the
   kisses of your mouth,[30]
For your love is more delightful than wine.
Your ointments yield a sweet fragrance,
Your name is like finest oil—
Therefore do maidens love you.
Draw me after you, let us run
The king has brought me to his chambers.

Let us delight and rejoice in your love,
Savoring it more than wine—
Like new wine they love you!

[5] I am dark, but comely,[31]
O daughters of Jerusalem—
Like the tents of Kedar,
Like the pavilions of Solomon.

---

[30]*kisses of your mouth:* full ("French") kisses, as opposed to kisses of the lips.

[31]The *New Revised Standard Version* of the *Bible* translates this, "I am black and beautiful."

Song of Songs 1:1–2:17.

Don't stare at me because I am swarthy,
Because the sun has gazed upon me.
My mother's sons quarreled with me,
They made me guard the vineyards;
My own vineyard I did not guard.

Tell me, you whom I love so well;
Where do you pasture your sheep?
Where do you rest them at noon?
Let me not be as one who strays
Beside the flocks of your fellows.
If you do not know, O fairest of women,
Go follow the tracks of the sheep,
And graze your kids
By the tents of the shepherds.

[The man speaks:] I have likened you, my
    darling,
To a mare in Pharaoh's chariots:
[10] Your cheeks are comely with plaited
    wreaths,
Your neck with strings of jewels.
We will add wreaths of gold
To your spangles of silver.

[The woman speaks:] While the king was on
    his couch,
My nard gave forth its fragrance.
My beloved to me is a bag of myrrh
Lodged between my breasts.
My beloved to me is a spray of henna blooms
From the vineyards of En-gedi.

[15, The man and woman exchange short
    compliments:] Ah, you are fair, my
    darling,
Ah, you are fair,
With your dove-like eyes!
And you, my beloved, are handsome,
Beautiful indeed!
Our couch is in a bower;
Cedars are the beams of our house,
Cypresses the rafters.
[2:1] I am a rose of Sharon,
A lily of the valleys.

[The woman speaks:] Like a lily among thorns,
So is my darling among the maidens.
Like an apple tree among trees of the forest,
So is my beloved among the youths.

I delight to sit in his shade,
And his fruit is sweet to my mouth.
He brought me to the banquet room
And his banner of love was over me.
[5] "Sustain me with raisin cakes,
Refresh me with apples,
For I am faint with love."
His left hand was under my head,
His right arm embraced me.
I adjure you, O maidens of Jerusalem,
By gazelles or by hinds of the field:
Do not wake or rouse
Love until it please!

Hark, My beloved!
There he comes,
Leaping over mountains,
Bounding over hills.
My beloved is like a gazelle
Or like a young stag.
There he stands behind our wall,
Gazing through the window,
Peering through the lattice.
[10] My beloved spoke thus to me,
"Arise, my darling;
My fair one, come away!
For now the winter is past,
The rains are over and gone.
The blossoms have appeared in the land,
The time of pruning has come;
The song of the turtledove
Is heard in our land.
The green figs form on the fig tree,
The vines in blossom give off fragrance.
Arise, my darling;
My fair one, come away!"

[The man speaks:]
"O my dove, in the cranny of the rocks,
Hidden by the cliff,
Let me see your face,
Let me hear your voice;
For your voice is sweet
And your face is comely."
[15] Catch us the foxes,
The little foxes
That ruin the vineyards—
For our vineyard is in blossom.

[The woman speaks:] My beloved is mine
And I am his
Who browses among the lilies.
When the day blows gently
And the shadows flee,

Set out, my beloved,
Swift as a gazelle
Or a young stag,
For the hills of spices!

God's Call to an Unfaithful People

In this oracle, Amos pronounces God's judgment on the unfaithful people of Israel. He employs bitter sarcasm to denounce their sins. They enjoy worship and sacrifice to God but have neglected the basic commands of God's law: justice and mercy. They have ignored God's chastisements, listed here. Now God promises a severe final punishment, indicated by the ominous words, "Prepare to meet your God."

Hear this word, you cows of Bashan
On the hill of Samaria—
Who defraud the poor,
Who rob the needy;
Who say to your husbands,
"Bring, and let's carouse!"
My Lord God swears by His holiness:
Behold, days are coming upon you
When you will be carried off in baskets,
And, to the last one, in fish baskets,
And taken out—
Each one through a breach straight ahead—
And flung on the refuse heap[32]
—declares the Lord.

Come to Bethel and transgress;
To Gilgal, and transgress even more:[33]
Present your sacrifices the next morning
And your tithes on the third day;
[5] And burn a thank offering of leavened
   bread;
And proclaim freewill offerings loudly.
For you love that sort of thing, O Israelites
—declares my Lord God.

I, on My part, have given you
Cleanness of teeth in all your towns,
And lack of food in all your settlements.
Yet you did not turn back to Me
—declares the Lord.
I therefore withheld the rain from you
Three months before harvest time:
I would make it rain on one town
And not on another;
One field would be rained upon
While another on which it did not rain
Would wither.
So two or three towns would wander
To a single town to drink water,
But their thirst would not be slaked.
Yet you did not turn back to Me
—declares the Lord.

I scourged you with blight and mildew;
Repeatedly your gardens and vineyards,
Your fig trees and olive trees
Were devoured by locusts.
Yet you did not turn back to Me
—declares the Lord.

[10] I sent against you pestilence
In the manner of Egypt;
I slew your young men with the sword,
Together with your captured horses,

---

[32]These predictions look forward to the destruction of the northern kingdom of Israel by Assyria in 721 B.C.E.
[33]*Bethel, Gilgal:* Israelite cities with sanctuaries. Notice the biting sarcasm of this section.

Amos 4:1–13.

And I made the stench of your armies
Rise in your very nostrils.
Yet you did not turn back to Me
—declares the Lord.

I have wrought destruction among you
As when God destroyed Sodom and
    Gomorrah;[34]
You have become like a brand plucked from
    burning.

Yet you have not turned back to Me
—declares the Lord.

Assuredly, because I am doing that to you,
Even so will I act toward you, O Israel—
Prepare to meet your God, O Israel!
Behold, He who formed the mountains,
And created the wind,
And has told man what His wish is,
Who turns blackness into daybreak,
And treads upon the high places of the earth—
His name is the Lord, the God of Hosts.

[34]*Sodom and Gomorrah:* cities destroyed for their wickedness;
see *Genesis* 19:1–29.

Two Views of Wisdom

Of all the main types of literature in the Hebrew scriptures, the most international in form and content is the wisdom literature. In the first passage, from the beginning of *Proverbs,* the first nine verses describe what wisdom can do for its followers—lead to knowledge, mental power, and moral strength. Notice in verse 20 and following verses the personification of wisdom as a woman. The second passage, from *Ecclesiastes,* gives a more pessimistic outlook on wisdom. Here it cannot answer life's riddles. The books of *Proverbs* and *Ecclesiastes* are attributed to King Solomon, who had an ancient reputation as a sage.

[Proverbs 1] The proverbs of Solomon, son
    of David, king of Israel:
For learning wisdom and discipline;
For understanding words of discernment;
For acquiring the discipline for success,
Righteousness, justice, and equity;
For endowing the simple with shrewdness,
The young with knowledge and foresight.
[5]—The wise man, hearing them, will gain
    more wisdom;
The discerning man will learn to be adroit;
For understanding proverb and epigram,
The words of the wise and their riddles.

The fear of the Lord is the beginning of
    knowledge;
Fools despise wisdom and discipline.
My son, heed the discipline of your father,
And do not forsake the instruction of your
    mother;

For they are a graceful wreath upon your head,
A necklace about your throat. . . .

[20] Wisdom cries aloud in the streets,
Raises her voice in the squares.
At the head of the busy streets she calls;
At the entrance of the gates, in the city, she
    speaks out:
"How long will you simple ones love simplicity,
You scoffers be eager to scoff,
You dullards hate knowledge?
You are indifferent to my rebuke;
I will now speak my mind to you,
And let you know my thoughts.
Since you refused me when I called,
And paid no heed when I extended my hand,
[25] You spurned all my advice,
And would not hear my rebuke,
I will laugh at your calamity,
And mock when terror comes upon you,

Proverbs 1:1–9, 20–33; *Ecclesiastes* 1:1–9.

When terror comes like a disaster,
And calamity arrives like a whirlwind,
When trouble and distress come upon you.
Then they shall call me but I will not answer;
They shall seek me but not find me.
Because they hated knowledge,
And did not choose fear of the Lord,
[30] They refused my advice,
And disdained all my rebukes,
They shall eat the fruit of their ways,
And have their fill of their own counsels.
The tranquility of the simple will kill them,
And the complacency of dullards will destroy
 them.
But he who listens to me will dwell in safety,
Untroubled by the terror of misfortune."

[Ecclesiastes 1:1] The words of Koheleth son
 of David, king in Jerusalem.
Utter futility!—said Koheleth—
Utter futility! All is futile!

What real value is there for a man
In all the gains he makes beneath the sun?

One generation goes, another comes,
But the earth remains the same forever.
[5] The sun rises, and the sun sets—
And glides back to where it rises.
Southward blowing, turning northward,
Ever turning blows the wind;
On its rounds the wind returns.
All streams flow into the sea,
Yet the sea is never full;
To the place [from] which they flow
The streams flow back again.
All such things are wearisome:
No man can ever state them;
The eye never has enough of seeing,
Nor the ear enough of hearing.
Only that shall happen which has happened,
Only that occur which has occurred;
There is nothing new beneath the sun!

The Virtuous Wife

Given the context of a patriarchal society, the ideal wife depicted here is remarkably independent and appreciated for her talents and relationships rather than for her beauty or her ability to bear children. The somewhat disjointed style of this poem is the result of its unique composition—in Hebrew, each line begins with a successive letter of the Hebrew alphabet. This method of composition suggests a full description of its topic—as we might say today, the virtuous wife "from A to Z."

What a rare find is a capable wife!
Her worth is far beyond that of rubies.
Her husband puts his confidence in her,
And lacks no good thing.
She is good to him, never bad,
All the days of her life.
She looks for wool and flax,
And sets her hand to them with a will.
She is like a merchant fleet,
Bringing her food from afar.
[15] She rises while it is still night,
And supplies provisions for her household,

The daily fare of her maids.
She sets her mind on an estate and acquires it;
She plants a vineyard by her own labors.
She girds herself with strength,
And performs her tasks with vigor.
She sees that her business thrives;
Her lamp never goes out at night.
She sets her hand to the distaff;
Her fingers work the spindle.

[20] She gives generously to the poor;
Her hands are stretched out to the needy.

Proverbs 31:10–31.

She is not worried for her household because
of snow,
For her whole household is dressed in
crimson.
She makes covers for herself;
Her clothing is linen and purple.
Her husband is prominent in the gates,
As he sits among the elders of the land.
She makes cloth and sells it,
And offers a belt to the merchant.
[25] She is clothed with strength and splendor;
She looks to the future cheerfully.
Her mouth is full of wisdom,

Her tongue with kindly teaching.
She oversees the activities of her household
And never eats the bread of idleness.
Her children declare her happy;
Her husband praises her,
"Many women have done well,
But you surpass them all."

[30] Grace is deceptive, beauty illusory;
It is for her fear of the Lord
That a woman is to be praised.
Extol her for the fruit of her hand,
And let her works praise her in the gates.

ORGANIZATION

Sacrifice at the Ordination of Priests

This passage outlines the sacrificial ceremony by which priests are ordained—that is, consecrated to the service of God. The ceremony here indicates the role of the priesthood in Israel:
intermediaries between God and the people. God here speaks to Moses ("you").

This is what you shall do to them in consecrating them to serve Me as priests: Take a young bull of the herd and two rams without blemish; also unleavened bread, unleavened cakes with oil mixed in, and unleavened wafers spread with oil—make these of choice wheat flour. Place these in one basket and present them in the basket, along with the bull and the two rams. Lead Aaron and his sons up to the entrance of the Tent of Meeting, and wash them with water. [5] Then take the vestments, and clothe Aaron with the tunic, the robe of the ephod [the main priestly garment], the ephod, and the breastpiece, and gird him with the decorated band of the ephod. Put the headdress on his head, and place the holy diadem upon the headdress. Take the anointing oil and pour it on his head and anoint him. Then bring his sons forward; clothe them with tunics and wind turbans upon them. And gird both Aaron and his sons with sashes. And so they shall have priesthood as their right for all time.

You shall then ordain Aaron and his sons. [10] Lead the bull up to the front of the Tent of Meeting, and let Aaron and his sons lay their hands upon the head of the bull. Slaughter the bull before the Lord, at the entrance of the Tent of Meeting, and take some of the bull's blood and put it on the horns of the altar with your finger; then pour out the rest of the blood at the base of the altar. Take all the fat that covers the entrails, the protuberance on the liver, and the two kidneys with the fat on them, and turn them into smoke upon the altar. The rest of the flesh of the bull, its hide, and its dung shall be put to the fire outside the camp; it is a sin offering.

Exodus 29:1–37.

[15] Next take the one ram, and let Aaron and his sons lay their hands upon the ram's head. Slaughter the ram, and take its blood and dash it against all sides of the altar. Cut up the ram into sections, wash its entrails and legs, and put them with its quarters and its head. Turn the entire ram into smoke upon the altar. It is a burnt offering to the Lord, a pleasing odor, an offering by fire to the Lord.

Then take the other ram, and let Aaron and his sons lay their hands upon the ram's head. [20] Slaughter the ram, and take some of its blood and put it on the ridge of Aaron's right ear and on the ridges of his sons' right ears, and on the thumbs of their right hands, and on the big toes of their right feet; and dash the rest of the blood against every side of the altar round about. Take some of the blood that is on the altar and some of the anointing oil and sprinkle upon Aaron and his vestments, and also upon his sons and his sons' vestments. Thus shall he and his vestments be holy, as well as his sons and his sons' vestments.

You shall take from the ram the fat parts—the broad tail, the fat that covers the entrails, the protuberance on the liver, the two kidneys with the fat on them—and the right thigh; for this is a ram of ordination. Add one flat loaf of bread, one cake of oil bread, and one wafer, from the basket of unleavened bread that is before the Lord. Place all these on the palms of Aaron and his sons, and offer them as an elevation offering[35] before the Lord. [25] Take them from their hands and turn them into smoke upon the altar with the burnt offering, as a pleasing odor before the Lord; it is an offering by fire to the Lord.... The sacral vestments of Aaron shall pass on to his sons after him, for them to be anointed and ordained in. [30] He among his sons who becomes priest in his stead, who enters the Tent of Meeting to officiate within the sanctuary, shall wear them seven days.... [35] Thus you shall do to Aaron and his sons, just as I have commanded you. You shall ordain them through seven days, and each day you shall prepare a bull as a sin offering for expiation; you shall purge the altar by performing purification upon it, and you shall anoint it to consecrate it. Seven days you shall perform purification for the altar to consecrate it, and the altar shall become most holy; whatever touches the altar shall become consecrated.

---

[35] *elevation offering:* a sacrifice of a vegetable product, moved back and forth, and up and down, before the altar.

A Call to Be a Prophet

This passage from the ninth century B.C.E. is the fullest prophetic call vision in the Hebrew scriptures and certainly the most dramatic. Though highly negative in tone—Isaiah's job as a prophet will not be a happy one—the end of the passage (probably added later) promises some hope.

In the year that King Uzziah died, I beheld my Lord seated on a high and lofty throne; and the skirts of His robe filled the Temple. Seraphs stood in attendance on Him. Each of them had six wings: with two he covered his face, with two he covered his legs, and with two he would fly.

And one would call to the other,
"Holy, holy, holy!
The Lord of Hosts!
His presence fills all the earth!"

Isaiah 6:1–13.

The doorposts would shake at the sound of the one who called, and the House kept filling with smoke. [5] I cried,

"Woe is me; I am lost!
For I am a man of unclean lips
And I live among a people of unclean lips;
Yet my own eyes have beheld
The King, the Lord of Hosts."

Then one of the seraphs flew over to me with a live coal, which he had taken from the altar with a pair of tongs. He touched it to my lips and declared,

"Now that this has touched your lips,
Your guilt shall depart
And your sin be purged away."

Then I heard the voice of my Lord saying, "Whom shall I send? Who will go for us?" And I said, "Here am I; send me." And He said, "Go, say to that people:

'Hear, indeed, but do not understand;
See, indeed, but do not grasp.'
[10] Dull that people's mind,
Stop its ears and seal its eyes—
Lest, seeing with its eyes
And hearing with its ears,
It also grasps with its mind,
And repents and saves itself."

I asked, "How long, my Lord?" And He replied:

"Till towns lie waste without inhabitants
And houses without people,
And the ground lies waste and desolate—
For the Lord will banish the population—
And deserted sites are many
In the midst of the land.

"But while a tenth part yet remains in it, it shall repent. It shall be ravaged like the terebinth and the oak, of which stumps are left even when they are felled: its stump shall be a holy seed."

Women as Judges and Prophets

#1 The leadership of Israel was predominantly male, but occasionally, women rose to prominent positions. In the first selection, Deborah the "judge" (national leader) delivers her nation from a military threat. In the second selection, Huldah the prophet speaks the word of God to the king of Judah at a critical time of repentance and reform.

[*Judges* 4:4] Deborah, wife of Lappidoth, was a prophetess; she led Israel at that time. [5] She used to sit under the Palm of Deborah, between Ramah and Bethel in the hill country of Ephraim, and the Israelites would come to her for decisions.

She summoned Barak son of Abinoam, of Kedesh in Naphtali, and said to him, "The Lord, the God of Israel, has commanded: Go, march up to Mount Tabor, and take with you ten thousand men of Naphtali and Zebulun. And I will draw Sisera, Jabin's army commander, with his chariots and his troops, toward you up to the Wadi Kishon; and I will deliver him into your hands." But Barak said to her, "If you will go with me, I will go; if not, I will not go." "Very well, I will go with you," she answered. "However, there will be no glory for you in the course you are taking, for then the Lord will deliver Sisera into the hands of a woman." So Deborah went with Barak to Kedesh. [10] Barak then mustered Zebulun and Naphtali at Kedesh; ten thousand men marched up after him; and Deborah also went up with him....

Judges 4:4–10, 12–16; *II Kings* 22:11–20.

Sisera was informed that Barak son of Abinoam had gone up to Mount Tabor. So Sisera ordered all his chariots—nine hundred iron chariots—and all the troops he had to move from Harosheth-goiim to the Wadi Kishon. Then Deborah said to Barak, "Up! This is the day on which the Lord will deliver Sisera into your hands: the Lord is marching before you." Barak charged down Mount Tabor, followed by the ten thousand men, [15] and the Lord threw Sisera and all his chariots and army into a panic before the onslaught of Barak. Sisera leaped from his chariot and fled on foot as Barak pursued the chariots and the soldiers as far as Harosheth-goiim. All of Sisera's soldiers fell by the sword; not a man was left. [The next section recounts how Jael, a Kenite woman allied with Israel, killed Sisera while he was sleeping in her tent.]

[*II Kings* 22:11] When the king [Josiah] heard the words of the scroll of the Teaching,[36] he rent his clothes.[37] And the king gave orders to the priest Hilkiah, and to Ahikam son of Shaphan, Achbor son of Michaiah, the scribe Shaphan, and Asaiah the king's minister: "Go, inquire of the Lord on my behalf, and on behalf of the people, and on behalf of all Judah, concerning the words of this scroll that has been found. For great indeed must be the wrath of the Lord that has been kindled against us, because our fathers did not obey the words of this scroll to do all that has been prescribed for us."

So the priest Hilkiah, and Ahikam, Achbor, Shaphan, and Asaish went to the prophetess Huldah—the wife of Shallum son of Tikvah son of Harhas, the keeper of the wardrobe—who was living in Jerusalem in the Mishneh, and they spoke to her. [15] She responded: "Thus said the Lord, the God of Israel: Say to the man who sent you to me: Thus said the Lord: I am going to bring disaster upon this place and its inhabitants, in accordance with all the words of the scroll which the king of Judah has read. Because they have forsaken Me and have made offerings to other gods and vexed Me with all their deeds, My wrath is kindled against this place and it shall not be quenched. But say this to the king of Judah, who sent you to inquire of the Lord: Thus said the Lord, the God of Israel: As for the words which you have heard—because your heart was softened and you humbled yourself before the Lord when you heard what I decreed against this place and its inhabitants—that it will become a desolation and a curse—and because you rent your clothes and wept before Me, I for My part have listened—declares the Lord. [20] Assuredly, I will gather you to your fathers and you will be laid in your tomb in peace. Your eyes shall not see all the disaster which I will bring upon this place." So they brought back the reply to the king.

---

[36]*scroll of the Teaching:* probably an early form of the biblical book of *Deuteronomy.*
[37]*rent his clothes:* ritually tearing the clothing one is wearing is a sign of mourning and repentance.

RITUAL

The Establishment of Circumcision

Circumcision is the sign of the covenant and membership in the people of Israel. As such, it is the primary ritual in Judaism, even though, given the high level of modesty about the human body in Semitic culture, it is a private, perpetually hidden sign. It is performed on males only. Here its origins are traced to Abraham.

Genesis 17:9–14, 23–27.

God further said to Abraham, "As for you, you and your offspring to come throughout the ages shall keep My covenant. [10] Such shall be the covenant between Me and you and your offspring to follow which you shall keep: every male among you shall be circumcised. You shall circumcise the flesh of your foreskin, and that shall be the sign of the covenant between Me and you. And throughout the generations, every male among you shall be circumcised at the age of eight days. As for the homeborn slave and the one bought from an outsider who is not of your offspring, they must be circumcised, homeborn and purchased alike. Thus shall My covenant be marked in your flesh as an everlasting pact. And if any male who is uncircumcised fails to circumcise the flesh of his foreskin, that person shall be cut off from his kin; he has broken My covenant.... "

[23] Then Abraham took his son Ishmael, and all his homeborn slaves and all those he had bought, every male in Abraham's household, and he circumcised the flesh of their foreskins on that very day, as God had spoken to him. Abraham was ninety-nine years old when he circumcised the flesh of his foreskin, [25] and his son Ishmael was thirteen years old when he was circumcised in the flesh of his foreskin. Thus Abraham and his son Ishmael were circumcised on that very day; and all his household, his home-born slaves and those that had been bought from outsiders, were circumcised with him.

The Establishment of the Passover

In the first two paragraphs of this selection, the ingredients of the meal itself and the meaning of the Passover as a remembrance and reenactment of God's deliverance of Israel from its slavery in Egypt are given. In the third and fourth paragraphs, the feast of unleavened bread (mazoh) is treated; originally, it was a harvest festival, but now it is incorporated into the Passover.

The Lord said to Moses and Aaron in the land of Egypt: This month shall mark for you the beginning of the months; it shall be the first of the months of the year for you. Speak to the whole community of Israel and say that on the tenth of this month each of them shall take a lamb to a family, a lamb to a household. But if the household is too small for a lamb, let him share one with a neighbor who dwells nearby, in proportion to the number of persons; you shall contribute for the lamb according to what each household will eat. [5] Your lamb shall be without blemish, a yearling male; you may take it from the sheep or from the goats. You shall keep watch over it until the fourteenth day of this month; and all the assembled congregation of the Israelites shall slaughter it at twilight. They shall take some of the blood and put it on the two doorposts and the lintel of the houses in which they are to eat it. They shall eat the flesh that same night; they shall eat it roasted over the fire, with unleavened bread and with bitter herbs. Do not eat any of it raw, or cooked in any way with water, but roasted—head, legs, and entrails—over the fire. [10] You shall not leave any of it over until morning; if any of it is left until morning, you shall burn it.

This is how you shall eat it: your loins girded, your sandals on your feet, and your staff in your hand; and you shall eat it hurriedly: it is a

Exodus 12:1–19, 24–27.

Passover offering to the Lord. For that night I will go through the land of Egypt and strike down every first-born in the land of Egypt, both man and beast; and I will mete out punishments to all the gods of Egypt, I the Lord. And the blood on the houses where you are staying shall be a sign for you: when I see the blood I will pass over you, so that no plague will destroy you when I strike the land of Egypt.

This day shall be to you one of remembrance: you shall celebrate it as a festival to the Lord throughout the ages; you shall celebrate it as an institution for all time. [15] Seven days you shall eat unleavened bread; on the very first day you shall remove leaven from your houses, for whoever eats leavened bread from the first day to the seventh day, that person shall be cut off from Israel.

You shall celebrate a sacred occasion on the first day, and a sacred occasion on the seventh day; no work at all shall be done on them; only what every person is to eat, that alone may be prepared for you. You shall observe the [Feast of] Unleavened Bread, for on this very day I brought your ranks out of the land of Egypt; you shall observe this day throughout the ages as an institution for all time. In the first month, from the fourteenth day of the month at evening, you shall eat unleavened bread until the twenty-first day of the month at evening. No leaven shall be found in your houses for seven days. For whoever eats what is leavened, that person shall be cut off from the community of Israel, whether he is a stranger or a citizen of the country....

[24] You shall observe this [Passover] as an institution for all time, for you and for your descendants. And when you enter the land that the Lord will give you, as He has promised, you shall observe this rite. And when your children ask you, "What do you mean by this rite?" you shall say, "It is the Passover sacrifice to the Lord, because He passed over the houses of the Israelites in Egypt when He smote the Egyptians, but saved our houses."

The Observance of the Sabbath

Throughout Jewish history, keeping the sabbath, or seventh day of the week, has been an important sign of Judaism. In this passage, which expands on the sabbath commandment in the *Decalogue,* the penalty for breaking it, like the penalty for breaking the other commandments of the *Decalogue,* is death. How often this penalty was carried out is uncertain.

The Lord said to Moses: Speak to the Israelite people and say: Nevertheless, you must keep My sabbaths, for this is a sign between Me and you throughout the ages, that you may know that I the Lord have consecrated you. You shall keep the sabbath, for it is holy for you. He who profanes it shall be put to death: whoever does work on it, that person shall be cut off from among his kin. [15] Six days may work be done, but on the seventh day there shall be a sabbath of complete rest, holy to the Lord; whoever does work on the sabbath day shall be put to death. The Israelite people shall keep the sabbath, observing the sabbath throughout the ages as a covenant for all time: it shall be a sign for all time between Me and the people of Israel. For in six days the Lord made heaven and earth, and on the seventh day He ceased from work and was refreshed.

Exodus 31:12–17.

The Day of Atonement

 # 5 This selection presents the ceremonies of the Day of Atonement (Yom Kippur), tracing it to the time of Moses. It centers on ceremonies in the Holy of Holies chamber in the Tabernacle, called here the "Tent of Meeting." These ceremonies were carried out later in the First Temple built by Solomon. Since the destruction of the Second Temple in 70 C.E., Jews have practiced the spiritual heart of the holy day as it is developed at the end of the passage: a day of rest, self-denial, confession, and making amends. Although the Jewish *Bible* presents all holy days as equal, in modern Jewish practice the Day of Atonement and New Year's Day (Rosh Hashanah) have become the most important.

The Lord spoke to Moses after the death of the two sons of Aaron who died when they drew too close to the presence of the Lord. The Lord said to Moses: *# 5*

Tell your brother Aaron that he is not to come at will into the Shrine[38] behind the curtain, in front of the cover that is upon the ark, lest he die; for I appear in the cloud over the cover. Thus only shall Aaron enter the Shrine: with a bull of the herd for a sin offering and a ram for a burnt offering. He shall be dressed in a sacral linen tunic, with linen breeches next to his flesh, and be girt with a linen sash, and he shall wear a linen turban. They are sacral vestments; he shall bathe his body in water and then put them on. And from the Israelite community he shall take two he-goats for a sin offering and a ram for a burnt offering....

[11] Aaron shall then offer his bull of sin offering, to make expiation for himself and his household. He shall slaughter his bull of sin offering, and he shall take a panful of glowing coals scooped from the altar before the Lord, and two handfuls of finely ground aromatic incense, and bring this behind the curtain. He shall put the incense on the fire before the Lord, so that the cloud from the incense screens the cover that is over [the Ark of] the Pact, lest he die.

He shall take some of the blood of the bull and sprinkle it with his finger over the cover on the east side; and in front of the cover he shall sprinkle some of the blood with his finger seven times. [15] He shall then slaughter the people's goat of sin offering, bring its blood behind the curtain, and do with its blood as he has done with the blood of the bull: he shall sprinkle it over the cover and in front of the cover.

Thus he shall purge the Shrine of the uncleanness and transgression of the Israelites, whatever their sins; and he shall do the same for the Tent of Meeting, which abides with them in the midst of their uncleanness. When he goes in to make expiation in the Shrine, nobody else shall be in the Tent of Meeting until he comes out.

When he has made expiation for himself and his household, and for the whole congregation of Israel, he shall go out to the altar that is before the Lord and purge it: he shall take some of the blood of the bull and of the goat and apply it to each of the horns of the altar; and the rest of the blood he shall sprinkle on it with his finger seven times. Thus he shall cleanse it of the uncleanness of the Israelites and consecrate it....

[29] And this shall be to you a law for all time: In the seventh month, on the tenth day of the month, you shall practice self-denial; and you shall do no manner of work, neither the citizen nor the alien who resides among you. For on this day atonement shall be made for you to

___

[38]*Shrine:* the Holy of Holies chamber, the innermost room in the Tabernacle and then the Temple.

___

Leviticus 16:1–5, 11–19, 29–34.

cleanse you of all your sins; you shall be clean before the Lord. It shall be a sabbath of complete rest for you, and you shall practice self-denial; it is a law for all time. The priest who has been anointed and ordained to serve as priest in place of his father shall make expiation. He shall put on the linen vestments, the sacral vestments. He shall purge the innermost Shrine; he shall purge the Tent of Meeting and the altar; and he shall make expiation for the priests and for all the people of the congregation. This shall be to you a law for all time: to make atonement for the Israelites for all their sins once a year. And Moses did as the Lord had commanded him.

Kosher and Nonkosher Foods

This passage on dietary law gives a list of clean ("kosher") and unclean foods. The types of unclean animals specified here are (1) four-footed animals that do not chew the cud and have a split hoof, (2) carnivorous birds, (3) winged insects, (4) water animals lacking fins and scales, and (5) small creeping ("swarming") animals. To be kosher, acceptable animals must be butchered in a humane way, and all food must be served according to kosher regulations (for example, no mixing of dairy products and meat in cooking or serving). These regulations form the basis of kosher inspection and certification today, as many food-production businesses owned by non-Jews seek this certification for wider sales opportunities.

The Lord spoke to Moses and Aaron, saying to them: Speak to the Israelite people thus:

These are the creatures that you may eat from among all the land animals: any animal that has true hoofs, with clefts through the hoofs, and that chews the cud—such you may eat. The following, however, of those that either chew the cud or have true hoofs, you shall not eat: the camel—although it chews the cud, it has no true hoofs: it is unclean for you; [5] the daman [a type of sheep]—although it chews the cud, it has no true hoofs: it is unclean for you; the hare—although it chews the cud, it has no true hoofs: it is unclean for you; and the swine—although it has true hoofs, with the hoofs cleft through, it does not chew the cud: it is unclean for you. You shall not eat of their flesh or touch their carcasses; they are unclean for you.

These you may eat of all that live in water: anything in water, whether in the seas or in the streams, that has fins and scales—these you may eat. [10] But anything in the seas or in the streams that has no fins and scales, among all the swarming things of the water and among all the other living creatures that are in the water—they are an abomination for you and an abomination for you they shall remain: you shall not eat of their flesh and you shall abominate their carcasses. Everything in water that has no fins and scales shall be an abomination for you.

The following you shall abominate among the birds—they shall not be eaten, they are an abomination: the eagle, the vulture, and the black vulture; the kite, falcons of every variety; [15] all varieties of raven; the ostrich, the nighthawk, the sea gull; hawks of every variety; the little owl, the cormorant, and the great owl; the white owl, the pelican, and the bustard; the stork; herons of every variety; the hoopoe, and the bat.

[20] All winged swarming things that walk on fours shall be an abomination for you. But these you may eat among all the winged swarming things that walk on fours: all that have, above their feet, joints legs to leap with on the ground—of these you may eat the following:

Leviticus 11:1–31, 41–45.

locusts of every variety; all varieties of bald locust; crickets of every variety; and all varieties of grasshopper. But all other winged swarming things that have four legs shall be an abomination for you.

And the following shall make you unclean—whoever touches their carcasses shall be unclean until evening, [25] and whoever carries the carcasses of any of them shall wash his clothes and be unclean until evening—every animal that has true hoofs but without clefts through the hoofs, or that does not chew the cud. They are unclean for you; whoever touches them shall be unclean. Also all animals that walk on paws, among those that walk on fours, are unclean for you; whoever touches their carcasses shall be unclean until evening. And anyone who carries their carcasses shall wash his clothes and remain unclean until evening. They are unclean for you.

The following shall be unclean for you from among the things that swarm on the earth: the mole, the mouse, and great lizards of every variety; [30] the gecko, the land crocodile, the lizard, the sand lizard, and the chameleon. Those are for you the unclean among all the swarming things; whoever touches them when they are dead shall be unclean until evening....

[41] All the things that swarm upon the earth are an abomination; they shall not be eaten. You shall not eat, among all things that swarm upon the earth, anything that crawls on its belly, or anything that walks on fours, or anything that has many legs; for they are an abomination. You shall not draw abomination upon yourselves through anything that swarms; you shall not make yourselves unclean therewith and thus become unclean. For I the Lord am your God: you shall sanctify yourselves and be holy, for I am holy. You shall not make yourselves unclean through any swarming thing that moves upon the earth. [45] For I the Lord am He who brought you up from the land of Egypt to be your God: you shall be holy, for I am holy.

RABBINIC LITERATURE

Jews have traditionally held the *Talmud* as an authoritative book. They often understood the *Bible*, and applied it to all the affairs of daily life, through the *Talmud*. Here are two passages from this important writing. In the first, taken entirely from the *Mishnah*, the rabbis explain the chain of transmission of the oral Torah from Moses to the writing of the *Mishnah*. In the second, the biblical duty to have children is discussed in the *Talmud* and given here as an example of rabbinic interpretation and debate at work. Note the creative, even playful, methods of biblical interpretation, characteristic of much of the *Talmud*, and how this patriarchal passage ends on a sober note that implicitly blames women for male infidelity.

The Chain of Rabbinic Tradition: "The Sayings of the Fathers"

This famous passage from the *Mishnah*, which was incorporated with all the *Mishnah* into the *Talmud*, is concerned to trace the transmission of the oral Torah from Moses to the second century C.E., when the *Mishnah* was compiled. Throughout this selection, the word *Torah*

Mishnah, Aboth 1.1–18.

refers especially to the oral Torah, a "fence around the [written] law," the body of legal opinions developed by the rabbis and codified in the *Mishnah*. Notice the characteristic use of three sayings to sum up the teachings of leading figures in this chain of transmission.[39]

Moses received the Torah from Sinai and delivered it to Joshua, Joshua delivered it to the elders, the elders to the prophets, and the prophets to the men of the great synagogue. They said three things: "Be deliberate in judgment, raise up many disciples, and make a fence around the law."

Simon the Just was one of the last men of the great synagogue. He used to say that the world stood on three things: on the law, the [temple] service, and the acts of the pious.

Antigonus of Soco received [the Torah] from Simon the Just. He used to say, "Do not be like servants who serve their master for the sake of receiving a reward; be like servants who serve their master without the intent of receiving a reward; and let the fear of heaven be upon you."

Jose, son of Joezer of Zeredah, and Jose, son of Jochanan of Jerusalem, received [the Torah] from him. Jose, son of Joezer of Zeredah, said, "Let your house be a house of assembly for the wise, dust yourself with the dust of their feet, and drink their words in thirstiness." [5] Jose, son of Jochanan of Jerusalem, said, "Let your house be wide open, and let the poor be your children. Do not talk much with women, not even with your wife, much less with your neighbor's wife." Hence the wise men say, "Whoever converses much with women brings evil on himself, neglects the study of the law, and at last will go to hell."

Joshua, son of Perechiah, and Natai the Arbelite received the oral law from them. Joshua, son of Perechiah, said, "Get yourself a master, and obtain a companion [in learning], and judge all people with favor." Natai the Arbelite said, "Withdraw from an evil neighbor, do not associate with the wicked, and do not flatter yourself to escape punishment."

Judah, son of Tabai, and Simon, son of Shetach, received it from them. Judah son of Tabai said, "Do not consider yourself as the arranger of the law, and when the parties are before you in judgment, consider them as guilty; but when they are departed from you, consider them as innocent, when they have acquiesced in the sentence."

Simon, son of Shetach, said, "Be extremely careful in the examination of witnesses, and be cautious in your words, lest they [the witnesses] should learn to tell lies."

[10] Shemaiah and Abtalyon received it from them. Shemaiah said, "Love your business, hate power, and keep clear of the government."

Abtalyon said, "You Sages, be cautious of your words, lest you be doomed to captivity, and carried captive to a place of bad waters, and the disciples who follow you should drink of them, by which means the name of God may be profaned."

Hillel and Shammai received it from them. Hillel said, "Be like the disciples of Aaron, who loved peace and pursued peace, so that you love mankind, and allure them to the study of the law."

He also used to say, "Whoever aggrandizes his name, destroys his name; he who does not increase his knowledge in the law, shall be cut off; he who does not study the law is deserving of death, and he who serves himself with the crown of the law, will perish." He also said, "If I do not perform good works myself, who can do them for me?" and "When I consider myself, what am I?" and "If not now, when?"

[15] Shammai said, "Let your study of the law be fixed, say little and do much, and receive all men with an open, pleasant face."

Rabbi Gamaliel said, "Get yourself an instructor, that you may not be in doubt, and do not accustom yourself to give [too many] tithes by conjecture."

Rabbi Simon, his son, said, "All my life I have been brought up among wise men, and

---

[39]Taken, with editing, from Joseph Barclay, trans., *Hebrew Literature*, rev. ed. (New York: Colonial Press, 1901).

never found anything so good for the body as silence; neither is the study of the law the principal thing, but its practice; whoever multiplies words causes sin." Simon . . . also said that the duration of the world depends on three things, justice, truth, and peace, as is said, "Judge truth, justice, and peace in your gates."[40]

---

[40]*Judge truth . . . gates:* a quotation from *Zechariah* 8:16.

An Example of Rabbinic Debate: The Duty to Marry and Have Children

In Jewish reckoning, the first commandment in the *Torah* is God's command to the human race, "Be fruitful and multiply." This passage discusses the implications of this command. Like most Talmudic passages, this one relies heavily on the interpretation of scripture, some of it straightforward and some highly creative, even fanciful.[41]

A man must not abstain from carrying out the obligation to "be fruitful and multiply" [*Genesis* 1:28] unless he already has two children. The School of Shammai ruled that this means two sons, and the School of Hillel ruled that it means a son and a daughter, because it is written, "Male and female He created them" [*Genesis* 1:28; 5:2] The duty of procreation applies to a man but not to a woman. Rabbi Yohanan the son of Seroka said that it applies to both [man and woman], for "God blessed them and said to them, 'Be fruitful and multiply'" [*Genesis* 1:28].[42]

This [*Mishnah*] passage means that if a man has children he may abstain from the duty of procreation, but he may not abstain from living with his wife. This supports the view of Rabbi Nahman, who reported a ruling in the name of Samuel that even though a man have many children, he may not remain without a wife, for it is written: "It is not good for a man to be alone" [*Genesis* 2:18]. Others held the opinion that if a man had children, he may abstain from the duty of procreation, and he may also abstain from the duty of living with a wife. Does this contradict what was reported by Rabbi Nahman in the name of Samuel? No. If he has no children, he is to marry a woman capable of having a child, but if he already has children, he may marry a woman who is incapable of having children.

Other rabbis taught that Rabbi Nathan said that according to the School of Shammai, a person satisfies the obligation to "be fruitful and multiply" if he has a son and a daughter, and according to the School of Hillel if he has either a son or a daughter. Rabbi [Judah the Prince] said, "Why this view of the School of Hillel? It is written, 'God created it not to be a waste, and he formed it to be inhabited' [*Isaiah* 45:18], and he has already contributed to making it a place of habitation [by having a child]."

What if a person had children while he was a pagan, and was later converted? Rabbi Yohanan said that he has already fulfilled the duty of procreation. However, Rabbi Lakish said that he has not fulfilled it, because at conversion one is like a born-again child.

---

[41]Translated by the editor.
[42]This paragraph is from *Mishnah* 6:6; the rest of the passage is the *Gemara* discussion of it.

Babylonian Talmud, Yebamoth 61b–63.

The *Mishnah* disagrees with the view of Rabbi Joshua. Joshua stated that if a person married in his youth he is also to marry in his old age; and if he had children in his youth, he is also to have children in his old age. For it is written: "Sow your seed in the morning and do not withdraw your hand in the evening, for you do not know which will prosper, this or that, or whether both alike will be good" [*Ecclesiastes* 11:6].

Rabbi Tanhum said in the name of Rabbi Hanilai that a man who is without a wife has no joy, no blessing, and no good. He has no joy, for it is written: "You shall rejoice, you and your household" [*Deuteronomy* 14:26]. He has no blessing, for it is written: "That a blessing may rest on your house" [*Ezekiel* 44:30]. He has no good, for it is written: "It is not good for a man to be alone" [*Genesis* 2:28].

Rabbi Joshua the son of Levi said that a man who knows his wife to be a God-fearing woman and does not have sexual relations with her is a sinner, for it is written: "And you shall visit your habitation and you will not sin" [*Job* 5:24].

The rabbis taught that when a man loves his wife as himself, and honors her more than himself, and trains his sons and daughters in the right path, and arranges for their marriage at a young age—about this man the verse says, "And you shall know that your tent is at peace" [*Job* 5:24].

Rabbi Eleazar said that a man without a wife is not a complete man, for it is written: "Male and female created He them, and He called their name *adam*, 'man.'" [*Genesis* 1:27].

Avert your eyes from the charms of another man's wife, or you may be trapped in her snare. Do not become friends with her husband and drink wine and strong drink with him. Many men have been destroyed by the appearance of a beautiful woman, and she has killed a vast number.

✿ GLOSSARY

ark a special closet or recess in the synagogue wall on the side nearest Jerusalem in which *Bible* scrolls used for public worship are stored.

Bible the "Book" of Jewish scripture, numbering twenty-four books by Jewish count. In the Christian framework, it includes thirty-nine books of Jewish scripture and twenty-seven *New Testament* books.

covenant an agreement between God and the people of Israel setting forth obligations and privileges for each party.

Decalogue "Ten Words"; also known as the *Ten Commandments* (found in *Exodus* 20:1–17, restated in *Deuteronomy* 5:6–21).

Kethuvim [KETH-u-veem] "Writings"; the third division of the Jewish *Bible*.

lectionary a list of scripture readings for divine worship.

mezuzah [meh-ZOO-zah] a small box containing *Bible* verses that is attached to the doorpost of a Jewish house.

Nevi'im [NEH-vih-eem] "Prophets"; the second division of the Jewish *Bible*.

psalm [sahlm] a sacred song, in the style found in the biblical book of *Psalms*, used for divine worship.

revelation the communication of the divine person and/or truth to humanity.

Shema [sheh-MAH] Judaism's most basic statement of faith, found in *Deuteronomy* 6:4–9 and in two shorter passages. The word means "hear."

Talmud [TALL-mood] the Jewish law code, a compilation of the "oral Torah."

Tanakh [TAH-nahk] acronymic name for the Jewish *Bible*, formed from the first letters of *Torah*, *Nevi'im*, and *Kethuvim*.

tefillin [teh-FILL-in] small boxes containing *Bible* verses on tiny scrolls, bound by leather straps on the forehead and weaker arm of an Orthodox Jew during prayers.

Torah [TOH-rah] "Teaching" or "Law"; the first five books of the Jewish *Bible;* more broadly, God's teaching and revelation.

QUESTIONS FOR STUDY AND DISCUSSION

1. In what ways did the Jewish people link their history to their system of morality? Consider two focal points of the *Bible:* (a) the relationship of the Exodus and law; (b) the restoration of the Jews to their land after the Exile and concerns for purity.

2. The Jewish scripture's three main sections are arranged in order of importance. What has it meant for Judaism that the *Torah* is first, *Prophets* second, and *Writings* third?

3. Discuss the tension in the *Bible* between Israel's call to be a light to the other nations and the demand to be a separate, holy people.

4. How has Judaism adapted its worship and rituals to a time when it has no Temple? Which rituals described in this chapter's passages could be continued essentially as is, which had to be altered greatly, and which had to be discontinued?

5. How could the ancient Israelite ideal of equal justice be seen as an antecedent of modern European and North American ideals of justice?

6. Explain the standing of women in the Jewish *Bible*. To what degree did the Hebrew scriptures ameliorate the condition of women and to what degree did they reinforce a patriarchal society?

7. Trace the theme of the chosen/covenant people through the Hebrew scriptures.

8. Explain the statement, "Judaism is a religion of the book."

SCRIPTURES IN FILM

Hollywood has not made films based directly on the Hebrew Jewish *Bible/Old Testament* for more than fifty years, despite the grand narratives of the *Bible* that are seemingly tailor-made for film. The Holocaust has so shaped recent Jewish life that it and other contemporary Jewish events have received the lion's share of attention in film (*Schindler's List, Sophie's Choice, A Beautiful Life,* and the rest). Students may want to view 1956's *The Ten Commandments,* directed by Cecil B. DeMille in the grandiose style of old-time Hollywood "biblical epics." A more recent treatment of a contemporary topic is *Trembling Before G-d,* directed by Simcha Dubowski (2001). This prize-winning documentary film deals with Jews from Orthodox backgrounds who are dealing with their own same-sex orientation and with the traditional biblical reaction to it by other Orthodox Jews.

SUGGESTIONS FOR FURTHER READING

PRIMARY READINGS

The New Revised Standard Version of the Bible. New York: Oxford University Press, 1991. The best one-volume translation of the Jewish and Christian scriptures. The Hebrew scripture section is widely recognized for its accuracy.

Adele Berlin and Marc Z. Brettler, eds., *The Jewish Study Bible.* New York: Oxford University Press, 2003. Features the Jewish Publication Society's *Tanakh* translation first published in 1985 and provides excellent resources for understanding Jewish interpretation and use.

L. H. Schiffman, ed., *Texts and Traditions: A Source Reader for the Study of Second Temple and Rabbinic Judaism.* New York: KTAV, 1998. A comprehensive collection of primary sources for this formative period, especially *Bible* and *Talmud* selections.

SECONDARY READINGS

R. Alter, *The Art of Biblical Narrative.* New York: Basic Books, 1981. An excellent introduction to the Jewish *Bible* as literature.

B. Anderson, S. Bishop, and J. Newman, *Understanding the Old Testament,* 5th ed. Englewood Cliffs, NJ: Prentice Hall, 2006. The standard introductory study.

E. Fackenheim, *The Jewish Bible After the Holocaust—A Rereading.* Indianapolis: Indiana University Press, 1991. A prominent Jewish philosopher contends that the Jewish *Bible* is still the great spiritual resource of the Western religious traditions.

F. Greenspahn, "Does Judaism Have a Bible?" In L. J. Greenspoon and B. F. LeBeau, eds., *Sacred Text, Secular Times: The Hebrew Bible in the Modern World.* Omaha, NE: Creighton University Press,

2000, pp. 1–12. An up-to-date critical discussion of the Hebrew canon in the life of Judaism.

J. Rosenbaum, "Judaism: Torah and Tradition." In F. M. Denny and R. L. Taylor, eds., *The Holy Book in Comparative Perspective*. Columbia: University of South Carolina Press, 1985, pp. 10–35. Examines the interplay of the *Bible* and other sacred literature of Judaism, especially the *Talmud*.

P. Trible, *Texts of Terror*. Philadelphia: Fortress, 1984. A powerful examination of some biblical passages from a religious and feminist perspective.

B. Visotzky, *Reading the Book: Making the Bible a Timeless Text*. New York: Anchor/Doubleday, 1991. Designed to provide an "introduction to the meaningful reading of Scripture," this book takes account of rabbinic and modern methods of interpretation.

COMPANION WEBSITE

Visit the *Anthology of World Scriptures* companion website at **www.thomsonedu.com** for learning tools such as map explorations, flashcards of glossary terms, learning objectives, chapter practice quizzes, links to other websites for learning and research, and chapter summaries in PowerPoint® format.

CHAPTER ELEVEN

Christianity

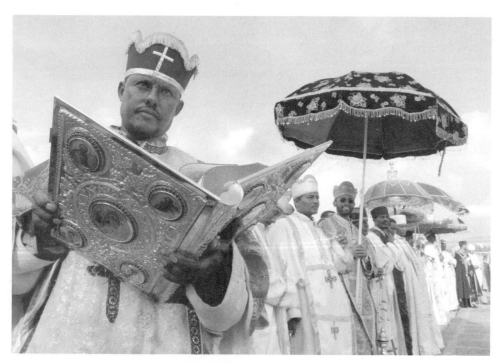

Ethiopian Orthodox Priests Read Scripture at a Festival in Addis Ababa

Ethiopian Orthodox priests in their satin robes stand under sequined velvet umbrellas as the *Bible* is read during the annual "Timket" celebrations in Addis Ababa, Ethiopia. Timket, the greatest Ethiopian festival of the year, commemorates Jesus Christ's baptism in the Jordan River by John the Baptist. (© *Wolfgang Rattay/Reuters/Landov.*)

- In a congregation of the Church of Scotland, the bell tolls and the congregation stands out of respect for the Word as a layperson walks solemnly down the center aisle carrying a large Christian *Bible*. When the book is placed on the pulpit, the service begins.

- In a village of New Guinea, North American and European missionaries trained in linguistics work to decipher a tribal language, commit it to writing, and educate the tribespeople to read it. The purpose of their work is to translate the *New Testament* into the tribal language for use in training new believers in the faith and as a tool for converting other members of the tribe.

- In Rome, the Congregation for Divine Worship, the Vatican department responsible for guiding Roman Catholic religious services, presents to Pope John Paul II a report entitled "Authentic Liturgy" on inclusive language in the *Bible* and religious services. It states that scripture translations are to avoid many of the features of "inclusive language" because they obscure the meaning of the text. For example, where the original language of scripture says "brothers," "brothers and sisters" may not be used. This document stirs up some controversy in European and North American Catholic churches and points up how issues of inclusive/exclusive language have become important in the contemporary churches, both Roman Catholic and Protestant.

INTRODUCTION

Christianity teaches salvation from sin and the gift of eternal life through the life, death, and resurrection of Jesus, the Son of God. A missionary religion from its beginning, it has become the world's most widespread faith. The *New Testament* has had paramount importance in the history of Christianity from the time of its writing in the century after the death of Jesus in 30 C.E. It has shaped the church's teaching, ethics, ritual, organization, and mission in the world. Although Christians differ in language, culture, organization, and the fine points of religious teaching, all believers have the books of the *New Testament* in common. Indeed, it has often been remarked that the *New Testament* is the *only* thing that all Christians have in common! This scripture has played such a prominent role in world events past and present that to know the *New Testament* and its patterns of use is to have a key to the understanding of Western culture as well as Christianity itself.

Names

The common name in Christianity for its scriptures is the **Bible,** composed of both the **Old Testament** (the Hebrew scriptures) and the **New Testament.** As in the Jewish *Bible,* **testament,** or its synonym *covenant,* refers to the relationship God has established with people. "New" signifies the early Christian belief that in Jesus God has acted in a new way for salvation. This is seen as a fulfillment of the promises made by God to the Jewish people. In *II Corinthians* 3:6–15, the early Christian missionary Paul calls Christian believers members of the "new covenant" and the books of Moses (the Jewish *Bible*) the "old covenant." The first term echoes *Jeremiah* 31:31, in which God promises, "I will make a new covenant with the house of Israel and the house of Judah." The expression "new covenant" was also used in the early Christian celebration of the ritual of Holy Communion, as its earliest recorded form attests:

"In the same way [Jesus] took the cup also, after supper, saying, "This cup is the new covenant in my blood" (*I Corinthians* 11:25). In sum, "new covenant/testament" was a common term in early Christianity, and it did not take long to be formally attached to the body of Christian scripture.

The advantage of *New Testament* as a label is that it suggests the complexity of the early Christian attitude to its relationship with Judaism and the Jewish *Bible*. This relationship has both continuity with Judaism, as expressed by "covenant" or "testament," and discontinuity, as expressed by the qualifier "new." A disadvantage is that it leads to an all-too-easy misunderstanding of the role of the Jewish *Bible* in Christianity—namely, that "old" means outmoded and completely replaced by the *New Testament*. This misconception ignores the fact that the Jewish *Bible* itself is part of the Christian scriptures and that the earliest scripture of Christianity—before its own writings were canonized—was the Jewish *Bible*. (For a chart showing the differences between the Protestant *Old Testament* and the Roman Catholic/Episcopal and Orthodox *Old Testament*—the former identical with the Jewish *Bible*, the latter identical with the Greek translation of the Jewish Bible—see Table 10.2.)

In recent years, there has been a growing tendency to counter this disadvantage by labeling the twenty-seven books of the *New Testament* with a different name. Some use "Christian scriptures." But this is even more disadvantageous than *New Testament* because it implies that the Jewish *Bible* is not part of the Christian scriptures. A few scholars call these books the "Second Testament" and the Hebrew *Bible* the "First Testament," but this distinction is vague. In sum, *New Testament* seems the best choice. Despite its disadvantages, it is the commonly accepted label within the Christian church and in the academic community, and we use it here.

Overview of Structure

The *New Testament* is organized into two main sections: books about Jesus called gospels and letters of the apostles to early churches. The **gospels** are "good news" of the story of Jesus. The *Gospel of Matthew* tells the story of Jesus the Savior as the promised Messiah of Israel, going from his conception by the Holy Spirit in the womb of the Virgin Mary through his appearances after his resurrection from the dead. The *Gospel of Mark* tells the story of Jesus from baptism through the resurrection, presenting Jesus as the Savior of the Gentiles (non-Jews). The *Gospel of Luke* also presents Jesus as the savior of the Gentiles, with a secondary theme of God's concern for the poor, women, and outcasts. These three gospels are known as **synoptic,** or "seen in one view," because of their parallel structure and content in recounting the story of Jesus. The *Gospel of John* is the story of Jesus as the eternal, divine Son of God who came to earth to show God's glory in his life, death, and resurrection from the dead.

The gospels are followed by the *Acts of the Apostles,* the only book of the *New Testament* devoted to a historical account of the early church and its growth through its first approximately thirty-five years. *Luke* and *Acts* were written as a two-volume work by the same author; unfortunately, *John* now stands between them in the canonical order. The names of all these books were attached in the second century C.E.; when first written, the texts probably featured no authors' names.

Most of the rest of the *New Testament* consists of **letters,** or "epistles," of instruction and correction written by church leaders to various churches. Some scholars dispute the names on several of these letters, arguing that the texts are

pseudonymous, written by someone other than the given author, usually by one of his followers or coworkers after his death. Letters that scholars think are genuinely written by the stated person are called **authentic.**

The first letters are those of the **apostle** ("one sent out" with the message of salvation) Paul and his coworkers, arranged mostly by length from longest to shortest and named according to their destination. *Romans* presents Paul's understanding of Christian teaching in a fairly systematic way to a church that he did not establish but was soon to visit. In *I Corinthians,* Paul discusses various issues related to Christian doctrine, morality, and worship. In *II Corinthians*—a later letter that is probably, as it now stands, a composite of two or three letters Paul wrote to the church at Corinth after *I Corinthians*—Paul's main concern is to keep this Gentile-Christian church from straying to Jewish Christianity. *Galatians* has much this same theme— namely, that Christians from non-Jewish backgrounds need not be Jewish as well as Christian. *Ephesians,* probably written by a fellow worker of Paul's after his death, presents Jesus Christ as the cosmic savior who unifies races and nations. *Philippians,* a genuine Pauline letter, urges Christians to find joy in Christ. *Colossians,* probably written under Paul's name by a coworker, seeks like *Ephesians* to correct error by presenting Jesus Christ as the all-sufficient savior of the universe, not only of the church. *I Thessalonians* answers questions about what happens when the Lord Jesus returns in glory to judge the world at the end of time. *II Thessalonians,* probably pseudonymously written after the death of Paul, instructs Christians about how to wait for Jesus' return. The next three letters, *I and II Timothy* and *Titus,* are called the "Pastoral" letters because they are instructions under Paul's name about pastoral offices and church life at the end of the first century C.E. Finally, *Philemon* is Paul's attempt to reconcile a Christian slave owner to his runaway Christian slave who now seeks to return to that master.

The next section of the *New Testament* is traditionally known as the "General" or "Catholic" *Letters* (or *Epistles*). This name was given to them because church authorities supposed that they were written to all the church, but today, scholars view them as having just as specific an audience as the Pauline letters. Like the Pauline letters, these also seem to be arranged by length. This section begins with *Hebrews,* an anonymous letter written to encourage Christians not to turn to Judaism. The book of *James* exhorts its audience to live wise, righteous, and socially responsible lives. *I Peter* offers guidelines on Christian behavior, especially to those undergoing persecution for the faith. *II Peter* urges readers to stay true to traditional Christian teaching and reject false forms of the faith. The three letters of *John* combat false teachers while promoting love and hospitality among Christians. *Jude* is very similar in content and purpose to *II Peter*—defending the faith against falsehoods. Finally, the apocalyptic book, *Revelation,* offers visions of God's triumph at the end of the world, delivering believers from persecution by establishing the kingdom of heaven on earth.

For the order, authors (those probably pseudonymous are noted as "disputed"), approximate dates, genres, and size (in number of chapters) of the *New Testament* literature, see Table 11.1.

Contemporary Use

Because Christianity came from a Judaism with well-formed patterns of scripture usage, the use of the *New Testament* in the church today strongly reflects the

TABLE 11.1 The Books of the *New Testament*

Book	Traditional or Given Author	Date (C.E.)	Genre	Chapters
Matthew	Matthew (disputed)	80s	gospel	28
Mark	Mark (disputed)	70	gospel	16
Luke	Luke (disputed)	80s	gospel	24
John	John (disputed)	90	gospel	21
Acts of the Apostles	Luke (disputed)	80s	history	28
Romans	Paul	55	letter	16
I Corinthians	Paul	53	letter	16
II Corinthians	Paul	55	letter	13
Galatians	Paul	55	letter	6
Ephesians	Paul (disputed)	90	letter	6
Philippians	Paul	61	letter	4
Colossians	Paul (disputed)	80s	letter	4
I Thessalonians	Paul	51	letter	5
II Thessalonians	Paul (disputed)	80s	letter	3
I Timothy	Paul (disputed)	90s	letter	6
II Timothy	Paul (disputed)	90s	letter	4
Titus	Paul (disputed)	90s	letter	3
Philemon	Paul	50s	letter	1
Hebrews	Anonymous	80s	letter-sermon	13
James	James (disputed)	90	letter-sermon	5
I Peter	Peter (disputed)	80	letter	5
II Peter	Peter (disputed)	120	letter	3
I John	John "the Elder"	95	essay	5
II John	John "the Elder"	96	letter	1
III John	John "the Elder"	97	letter	1
Jude	Jude (disputed)	100	letter	1
Revelation	John "the Prophet"	90s	apocalypse	22

ways in which the Jewish *Bible* is used in Judaism. The first scripture of the church was the Jewish *Bible* in its Greek form, the *Septuagint*. The entire Jewish *Bible* had a strong influence in early Christianity, but certain sections were especially important. Some of these are mentioned in Chapter 10 on Judaism because they are important for both Judaism and Christianity. For reasons of space, the important Jewish *Bible* selections cannot be repeated or given here. So the reader should be familiar with the Exodus traditions, including the Passover feast (*Exodus* 12:1–27; 14:1–31); the rising Messianic hope (*Isaiah* 11:1–9; 42:1–7); expectations for the end of time (*Daniel* 7:1–14; 12:1–3); and the passages that the early church used to interpret the person and work of Jesus (e.g., *Psalm* 110; *Isaiah* 52:13–54:12).

As in Judaism, the primary use of the Christian *Bible* has always been in the service of divine worship. Most of the words and phrases used in worship come from the *Bible*. One of the high points of the service in all Catholic and most Protestant churches is the reading of a selection from the *Old Testament* and two selections from the *New Testament,* the last always a gospel reading. This lectionary system arose in the early Greek church, probably as an inheritance from Judaism. It quickly passed into Western Catholic Christianity. In the twentieth century, especially in its last quarter, many Protestant and Roman Catholic churches in Europe and North America adopted basically the same lectionary system. As a result, on any given Sunday, most American Christians hear the same scripture readings and sermons based more or less on them. (Independent Protestants, such as fundamentalists and Pentecostalists, do not follow this system.)

The *Bible* itself occupies a privileged place in the physical arrangement of the typical Christian church. In churches of a "higher," more elaborate form of worship, it is often placed on a special ornate lectern. In more formal services, the book of the gospels is often brought before the altar, "incensed," and kissed by the priest as a sign of its holiness before it is read. In both Catholic and Eastern Orthodox traditions, the scripture books are often richly bound and decorated with gold, jewels, and icons. But even in Protestant churches with less formal worship, the *Bible* is also revered. In such churches, it is often placed on the main pulpit from which the minister conducts the entire service. In churches of the Baptist wing of Protestantism, it is not unusual to see the preacher carrying the *Bible* in one hand and referring to it constantly during the sermon.

Many Christians supplement this formal use of the *Bible* with private devotional reading. Since the Reformation in the sixteenth century, Protestant churches have insisted on the right and duty of every Christian to read the *Bible* individually. This reading includes prayerful meditation on the meaning of the words and on the implication of this meaning for the life of the reader. Reading is also often done aloud by families as a part of the main meal of the day. Such private and familial use of scripture has formed a large part of Protestant spirituality. In the twentieth century, especially after the reforms of the Second Vatican Council in the 1960s, Roman Catholics also acknowledged the importance of private study and historical study of the *Bible*. Despite this emphasis on private usage of scripture, however, Christians throughout the world still come into contact with their *Bible* mostly during church services.

Alongside this devotional use of the *Bible* is academic study by means of the historical-critical method. This method seeks to understand the various parts of the *Bible* in their original historical context and tries to determine what the writings meant to their original readers. It tends to disregard, or at least relegate to a secondary position, the teachings of the various churches about the content of scripture. Because this approach puts the *Bible* in the same analytical framework as any other book from the ancient world, fundamentalists, both Protestant and Catholic alike, strongly reject it. An indication of the rapid advance that historical criticism made in the Roman Catholic Church during the twentieth century is that the most influential biblical scholar of the last third of the twentieth century, the late Raymond E. Brown, was a Catholic priest.

Historical Origin and Development

At first glance, it would seem that the *New Testament* was written perhaps only one or two generations after the death and resurrection of Jesus and the beginnings of the church. Yet modern biblical scholarship has discovered that its writing was not completed until perhaps ninety years after Jesus' death. (The process of forming the canon was even longer.)

The pace of writing was slowed by several factors. First, the early church, which began as a group within Judaism, already had a complete body of scripture—the Jewish *Bible*. At first, it found this scripture sufficient for its life, especially when it could interpret and use the Jewish *Bible* in its own way to bolster its claim that Jesus was the Messiah, the promised deliverer of Israel. Second, the early Christians quite comfortably used the words and deeds of Jesus in primarily oral form. They did not remember Jesus as a writer, and there was no urgency to write down his words. Indeed, they probably looked on the spoken words of Jesus as more immediate and potent than words about him written in a book. Third, many early Christians believed that the end of the world was very near, and with this prospect, the lengthy process of writing, copying (by hand), and distributing books was not to be expected.

How, then, did the process of writing what was to become the *New Testament* begin? The genuine Pauline letters came first. Paul wrote letters to keep in contact with the churches he founded as he moved around the northeastern Mediterranean provinces of the Roman Empire on his missionary travels. He used letters to instruct and exhort his churches and as a substitute for his own personal presence. These letters gained more importance after Paul's death (probably ca. 65 C.E.), and after his death, his coworkers continued to write letters in his name to perpetuate and adapt his teachings for a new generation. Of course, at this stage, there was probably no thought by Paul and his followers that these letters would become part of a new body of Christian scripture.

The gospels began to be written down around 70 C.E. The word *gospel* in English is derived from the Anglo-Saxon *godspel*. The Greek word (all the *New Testament* was written in Greek, the common language of the Mediterranean world) is *euangelion,* "good news," from which we get the word *evangelical*. The characteristic structure of the gospel book seems to have been invented by Mark: Jesus' ministry in Galilee, his journey to Jerusalem, teaching in Jerusalem, arrest, trial, death, and resurrection. This structure is evident in two other gospels, *Matthew* and *Luke,* which (the vast majority of scholars conclude) use *Mark* as a source. *John* does not use *Mark* as a source, so it differs somewhat from this basic outline.

Those two parts of the *New Testament,* commonly called "the gospel and the apostle," were the basic building blocks of the canon. In the second century C.E., Christians began sorting out true Christian writings from ones they considered false and heretical. The details of this process are hazy, but the main features seem clear. First, a canonical writing had to have a claim to apostolic authorship or authority. It had to be seen as written either by an apostle, by one "sent forth" with the Christian message (such as Matthew, John, Paul, and Peter), or by someone under apostolic authority (Mark, Luke). In other words, it had to give the appearance of going back to the first century. Second, the content of the writings was weighed. In the fight with heresy in the second century, doctrinal content was important because writings that the church deemed heretical also claimed to be written by the apostles, and the only way to differentiate them from false teaching was to compare the content of their teaching to books held to be genuinely apostolic in content. In his *Church History,* for example, Eusebius tells the story of Serapion, the bishop of Antioch in Syria (about 190 C.E.), who heard a reading in church of the *Gospel of*

Peter, a work he did not know. At first, Serapion accepted it as apostolic. But when he learned that people whom he considered heretics were using its account of the death of Jesus to bolster their claim that Jesus did not die on the cross, but returned to heaven before the crucifixion, Serapion forbade any further reading of the *Gospel of Peter* in the churches under his authority.

The third main factor in the process of canonization was the actual use of scripture by prominent Christian churches. The church at Antioch promoted *Matthew,* the province of Asia Minor (modern western Turkey) used *John* and *Luke,* and Rome used *Mark.* The support of these large and influential centers of early Christianity was crucial in the formation of the canon. The final factor was the competing canons of groups that the mainstream church considered heretical. Marcion, an early Christian leader who came to Rome about 145 C.E., argued that the God revealed by Jesus was not the creator God revealed in the Jewish *Bible.* As a result, Marcion totally rejected the Jewish *Bible* as canonical and made a special canon of Christian books out of the *Gospel of Luke* only and ten Pauline letters, rejecting everything else. This selection probably spurred the early church to insist on a wider canon: four gospels, all the Pauline letters that looked genuinely apostolic in content, and other letters from the twelve apostles of Jesus to their churches.

Thus, a consensus grew during the third and fourth centuries around the main books of the emerging canon of the *New Testament.* Seven books remained in doubt during this time, accepted by some churches but not by all: *Hebrews, James, II* and *III John, Jude, II Peter,* and *Revelation.* But as the widely scattered churches grew closer together in the third and fourth centuries, they began accepting these disputed books from each other. By 367 C.E., the twenty-seven-book canon was widely accepted, as the *Festal Letter* of Bishop Athanasius of Alexandria, Egypt, testifies. The catholic (which means "universal") church had a catholic *New Testament.*

HISTORY

The Birth of Jesus the Messiah

The gospels of *Matthew* and *Luke* present Jesus as conceived by the action of the Spirit of God in the Virgin Mary. This miraculous conception signifies the divine Sonship of Jesus. The passage also focuses on the name Jesus, which in the Aramaic language of Palestine means "he will save."[1]

Now the birth of Jesus the Messiah took place in this way. When his mother Mary had been engaged to Joseph, but before they lived together, she was found to be with child from the Holy

[1] All passages from the *New Testament* are from the *New Revised Standard Version of the Bible.* Copyright © 1989 Division of Christian Education of the National Council of the Churches of Christ in the U.S.A. Used by permission. All rights reserved.

Matthew 1:18–25.

Spirit. Her husband Joseph, being a righteous man and unwilling to expose her to public disgrace, planned to dismiss her quietly. [20] But just when he had resolved to do this, an angel of the Lord appeared to him in a dream and said, "Joseph, son of David, do not be afraid to take Mary as your wife, for the child conceived in her is from the Holy Spirit. She will bear a son, and you are to name him Jesus, for he will save his people from their sins." All this took place to fulfill what had been spoken by the Lord through the prophet: "Look, the virgin shall conceive and bear a son, and they shall name him Emmanuel," which means, "God is with us." When Joseph awoke from sleep, he did as the angel of the Lord commanded him; he took her as his wife, [25] but had no marital relations with her until she had borne a son[2]; and he named him Jesus.

_____

[2]_until she had borne a son:_ Roman Catholics, who confess the lifelong virginity of Mary, do not interpret this verse to mean that Mary and Joseph did have sexual relations after Jesus' birth.

Jesus' Miracles

In the gospels, as in the Hebrew scriptures, miracles signify the inbreaking of God into human life. They are seen not as "violations of natural law" but as acts of divine power for salvation. This selection has two types of miracles characteristic of the ministry of Jesus: exorcism of demons, showing the power of Jesus over supernatural evil; and healing of the sick, showing Jesus' ultimate victory over physical evil and death, which is central to early Christianity.

Then they arrived at the country of the Gerasenes, which is opposite Galilee. As he stepped out on land, a man of the city who had demons met him. For a long time he had worn no clothes, and he did not live in a house but in the tombs. When he saw Jesus, he fell down before him and shouted at the top of his voice, "What have you to do with me, Jesus, Son of the Most High God? I beg you, do not torment me"— for Jesus had commanded the unclean spirit to come out of the man. (For many times it had seized him; he was kept under guard and bound with chains and shackles, but he would break the bonds and be driven by the demon into the wilds.) [30] Jesus then asked him, "What is your name?" He said, "Legion"; for many demons had entered him. They begged him not to order them to go back into the abyss.[3]

_____

[3]_abyss:_ a section of hell in which demons are confined to await final destruction.

Now there on the hillside a large herd of swine was feeding; and the demons begged Jesus to let them enter these. So he gave them permission. Then the demons came out of the man and entered the swine, and the herd rushed down the steep bank into the lake and was drowned. When the swineherds saw what had happened, they ran off and told it in the city and in the country. [35] Then people came out to see what had happened, and when they came to Jesus, they found the man from whom the demons had gone sitting at the feet of Jesus, clothed and in his right mind. And they were afraid. Those who had seen it told them how the one who had been possessed by demons had been healed. Then all the people of the surrounding country of the Gerasenes asked Jesus to leave them; for they were seized with great fear. So he got into the boat and returned. The man from whom the demons had gone begged that he might be with him; but Jesus

_____

Luke 8:26–56.

sent him away, saying, "Return to your home, and declare how much God has done for you." So he went away, proclaiming throughout the city how much Jesus had done for him.

[40] Now when Jesus returned, the crowd welcomed him, for they were all waiting for him. Just then there came a man named Jairus, a leader of the synagogue. He fell at Jesus' feet and begged him to come to his house, for he had an only daughter, about twelve years old, who was dying. As he went, the crowds pressed in on him. Now there was a woman who had been suffering from hemorrhages for twelve years; and though she had spent all she had on physicians, no one could cure her. She came up behind him and touched the fringe of his clothes, and immediately her hemorrhage stopped. [45] Then Jesus asked, "Who touched me?" When all denied it, Peter said, "Master, the crowds surround you and press in on you." But Jesus said, "Someone touched me; for I noticed that power had gone out from me." When the woman saw that she could not remain hidden, she came trembling; and falling down before him, she declared in the presence of all the people why she had touched him, and how she had been immediately healed. He said to her, "Daughter, your faith has made you well; go in peace."

While he was still speaking, someone came from the leader's house to say, "Your daughter is dead; do not trouble the teacher any longer." [50] When Jesus heard this, he replied, "Do not fear. Only believe, and she will be saved." When he came to the house, he did not allow anyone to enter with him, except Peter, John, and James, and the child's father and mother. They were all weeping and wailing for her; but he said, "Do not weep; for she is not dead but sleeping."[4] And they laughed at him, knowing that she was dead. But he took her by the hand and called out, "Child, get up." [55] Her spirit returned, and she got up at once. Then he directed them to give her something to eat. Her parents were astounded; but he ordered them to tell no one what had happened.[5]

---

[4]*sleeping:* Jesus knows the girl is dead but soon to be brought to life, so her condition is like sleep from which one awakens.
[5]*tell no one what had happened:* probably connected with the "messianic secret"; see *Matthew* 16:20 (page 281 in this text).

The Arrest, Trial, and Death of Jesus

The sufferings of Jesus at the end of his life include betrayal by his disciple Judas, denial by Peter, a trial before the Jews on religious charges, a trial before the Roman Governor Pontius Pilate on civil charges, and condemnation to be crucified. Throughout their narration of these sufferings, *Mark* and the other gospels portray Jesus gently accepting his suffering as the will of God and his death as a sacrifice for the sin of the world.

Immediately, while he was still speaking, Judas, one of the twelve, arrived; and with him there was a crowd with swords and clubs, from the chief priests, the scribes, and the elders. Now the betrayer had given them a sign, saying, "The one I will kiss is the man; arrest him and lead him away under guard." [45] So when he came, he went up to him at once and said, "Rabbi" and kissed him. Then they laid hands on him and arrested him. But one of those who stood near drew his sword and struck the slave of the high priest, cutting off his ear. Then Jesus said to them, "Have you come out with swords and clubs to arrest me as though I were a bandit? Day after day I was with you in the temple teaching, and you did not arrest me. But

---

Mark 14:43–50, 53–65; 15:1–41.

let the scriptures be fulfilled." [50] All of them deserted him and fled....

They took Jesus to the high priest; and all the chief priests, the elders, and the scribes were assembled. Peter had followed him at a distance, right into the courtyard of the high priest; and he was sitting with the guards, warming himself at the fire. [55] Now the chief priests and the whole council were looking for testimony against Jesus to put him to death; but they found none. For many gave false testimony against him, and their testimony did not agree. Some stood up and gave false testimony against him, saying, "We heard him say, 'I will destroy this temple that is made with hands, and in three days I will build another, not made with hands.'" But even on this point their testimony did not agree. [55] Then the high priest stood up before them and asked Jesus, "Have you no answer? What is it that they testify against you?" But he was silent and did not answer. Again the high priest asked him, "Are you the Messiah, the Son of the Blessed One?" Jesus said, "I am; and 'you will see the Son of Man seated at the right hand of the Power,' and 'coming with the clouds of heaven.'"[6] Then the high priest tore his clothes and said, "Why do we still need witnesses? You have heard his blasphemy! What is your decision?" All of them condemned him as deserving death. [65] Some began to spit on him, to blindfold him, and to strike him, saying to him, "Prophesy!" The guards also took him over and beat him.

[15:1] As soon as it was morning, the chief priests held a consultation with the elders and scribes and the whole council. They bound Jesus, led him away, and handed him over to Pilate. Pilate asked him, "Are you the King of the Jews?" He answered him, "You say so." Then the chief priests accused him of many things. Pilate asked him again, "Have you no answer? See how many charges they bring against you." [5] But Jesus made no further reply, so that Pilate was amazed.

Now at the festival he used to release a prisoner for them, anyone for whom they asked. Now a man called Barabbas was in prison with the rebels who had committed murder during the insurrection. So the crowd came and began to ask Pilate to do for them according to his custom. Then he answered them, "Do you want me to release for you the King of the Jews?" [10] For he realized that it was out of jealousy that the chief priests had handed him over. But the chief priests stirred up the crowd to have him release Barabbas for them instead. Pilate spoke to them again, "Then what do you wish me to do with the man you call the King of the Jews?" They shouted back, "Crucify him!" Pilate asked them, "Why, what evil has he done?" But they shouted all the more, "Crucify him!" [15] So Pilate, wishing to satisfy the crowd, released Barabbas for them; and after flogging Jesus, he handed him over to be crucified. Then the soldiers led him into the courtyard of the palace; and they called together the whole cohort. And they clothed him in a purple cloak; and after twisting some thorns into a crown, they put it on him. And they began saluting him, "Hail, King of the Jews!" They struck his head with a reed, spat upon him, and knelt down in homage to him. [20] After mocking him, they stripped him of the purple cloak and put his own clothes on him. Then they led him out to crucify him. They compelled a passer-by, who was coming in from the country, to carry his cross; it was Simon of Cyrene, the father of Alexander and Rufus.[7] Then they brought Jesus to the place called Golgotha. And they offered him wine mixed with myrrh; but he did not take it. And they crucified him, and divided his clothes among them, casting lots to decide what each should take. [25] It was nine o'clock in the morning when they crucified him. The inscription of the charge against him read, "The King of the Jews." And with him they crucified two bandits, one on his right and one on his left. Those who passed by derided him, shaking

---

[6]Quoted from *Daniel* 7:13 in the Jewish scriptures, with an allusion to *Psalm* 110:1.

[7]*Simon, Rufus:* That these names are given probably indicates that these men were known to the first readers of *Mark*.

their heads and saying, "Aha! You who would destroy the temple and build it in three days, [30] save yourself, and come down from the cross!" In the same way the chief priests, along with the scribes, were also mocking him among themselves and saying, "He saved others; he cannot save himself. Let the Messiah, the King of Israel, come down from the cross now, so that we may see and believe." Those who were crucified with him also taunted him.

When it was noon, darkness came over the whole land until three in the afternoon. At three o'clock Jesus cried out with a loud voice, "Eloi, Eloi, lema sabachthani?" which means, "My God, my God, why have you forsaken me?"[8] [35] When some of the bystanders heard it, they said, "Listen, he is calling for Elijah."[9] And someone ran, filled a sponge with sour wine, put it on a stick, and gave it to him to drink, saying, "Wait, let us see whether

Elijah will come to take him down." Then Jesus gave a loud cry and breathed his last. And the curtain of the temple was torn in two, from top to bottom. Now when the centurion, who stood facing him, saw that in this way he breathed his last, he said, "Truly this man was God's Son!"

[40] There were also women looking on from a distance; among them were Mary Magdalene, and Mary the mother of James the younger and of Joses, and Salome. These used to follow him and provided for him when he was in Galilee; and there were many other women who had come up with him to Jerusalem.

---

[8]Jesus quotes the words of *Psalm* 22.
[9]*Elijah:* A fairly widespread Jewish belief at this time was that Elijah, an ancient Israelite prophet, would return at the end of time. Compare the contemporary Jewish practice of leaving an empty seat at the Passover meal for Elijah.

The Resurrection of Jesus

After Joseph of Arimathea buried the body of Jesus, three women from among his followers came on Sunday morning to finish the tasks of the funeral. They become the first witnesses of Jesus' resurrection. In this passage, the "young man" is an angel, and his message is that God has raised Jesus from the dead. The resurrection of Jesus and the life it brings became the center of early Christian belief.

When the sabbath was over, Mary Magdalene, and Mary the mother of James, and Salome bought spices, so that they might go and anoint him. And very early on the first day of the week, when the sun had risen, they went to the tomb. They had been saying to one another, "Who will roll away the stone for us from the entrance to the tomb?"[10] When they looked up, they saw that the stone, which was very large,

had already been rolled back. [15] As they entered the tomb, they saw a young man, dressed in a white robe, sitting on the right side; and they were alarmed. But he said to them, "Do not be alarmed; you are looking for Jesus of Nazareth, who was crucified. He has been raised; he is not here. Look, there is the place they laid him. But go, tell his disciples and Peter that he is going ahead of you to Galilee; there you will see him, just as he told you." So they went out and fled from the tomb, for terror and amazement had seized them; and they said nothing to anyone, for they were afraid.

---

[10]*roll away the stone:* A massive disk-shaped stone had been rolled over the entrance of the tomb.

Mark 16:1–8.

The Ascension of Jesus

In *Luke* and *Acts,* which are written by the same author, Jesus ascends to heaven forty days after his resurrection. This selection draws a connection between the completion of the earthly ministry of Jesus and the consummation of history: The end is not yet, but in the interim between the present and the end, the church is to witness to Jesus throughout the world. This missionary commission began to be carried out in the first century C.E. and has characterized Christianity for several periods of its subsequent history.

So when they had come together, they asked him, "Lord, is this the time when you will restore the kingdom to Israel?" He replied, "It is not for you to know the times or periods that the Father has set by his own authority. But you will receive power when the Holy Spirit has come upon you; and you will be my witnesses in Jerusalem, in all Judea and Samaria, and to the ends of the earth." When he had said this, as they were watching, he was lifted up, and a cloud took him out of their sight. [10] While he was going and they were gazing up toward heaven, suddenly two men in white robes stood by them. They said, "Men of Galilee, why do you stand looking up toward heaven? This Jesus, who has been taken up from you into heaven, will come in the same way as you saw him go into heaven."

Acts 1:6–11.

The Coming of the Holy Spirit

In dealing with the "speaking in tongues" that occurs on Pentecost, a Jewish holiday that comes fifty days after Passover, *Acts* works with two traditions: that the apostles are speaking in actual foreign languages and that they speak in a language not human but interpreted by the listeners as their own. (Modern Pentecostalism picks up on the second tradition.) Peter's speech on this occasion explains the meaning of the Holy Spirit's coming as the fulfillment of scripture and the divine plan, bringing the presence and power of God to all in the church regardless of gender or social standing.

When the day of Pentecost had come, they were all together in one place. And suddenly from heaven there came a sound like the rush of a violent wind, and it filled the entire house where they were sitting. Divided tongues, as of fire, appeared among them, and a tongue rested on each of them. All of them were filled with the Holy Spirit and began to speak in other languages, as the Spirit gave them ability.

[5] Now there were devout Jews from every nation under heaven living in Jerusalem. And at this sound the crowd gathered and was bewildered, because each one heard them speaking in the native language of each. Amazed and astonished, they asked, "Are not all these who are speaking Galileans? And how is it that we hear, each of us, in our own native language? Parthians, Medes, Elamites, and residents of Mesopotamia,

Acts 2:1–21.

Judea and Cappadocia, Pontus and Asia, [10] Phrygia and Pamphylia, Egypt and the parts of Libya belonging to Cyrene and visitors from Rome, both Jews and proselytes,[11] Cretans and Arabs—in our own languages we hear them speaking about God's deeds of power." All were amazed and perplexed, saying to one another, "What does this mean?" But others sneered and said, "They are filled with new wine."

But Peter, standing with the eleven, raised his voice and addressed them, "Men of Judea and all who live in Jerusalem, let this be known to you, and listen to what I say. [15] Indeed, these are not drunk, as you suppose, for it is only nine

---

[11] *Jews and proselytes:* born Jews and Gentiles converted to Judaism. All the nationalities listed in this "Table of Nations" were Jews then living in Jerusalem.

o'clock in the morning. No, this is what was spoken through the prophet Joel:

'In the last days it will be, God declares, that
I will pour out my Spirit upon all flesh, and
your sons and your daughters shall prophesy, and your young men shall see visions,
and your old men shall dream dreams.
Even upon my slaves, both men and women,
in those days I will pour out my Spirit;
and they shall prophesy.
And I will show portents in the heaven above
and signs on the earth below, blood,
fire, and smoky mist.
[20] The sun shall be turned to darkness and
the moon to blood, before the coming
of the Lord's great and glorious day.
Then everyone who calls on the name of the
Lord shall be saved.'"

Persecution of the Apostles

The early Christian church met opposition from the same forces that acted to do away with Jesus. The apostles' calm and confident attitude to their persecutions is underscored here, and this attitude would remain important in the next few centuries as Roman persecution of the church grew stronger. Verse 29 sounds a theme that echoes through the history of the church: When the laws of this world and the law of God collide, "We must obey God rather than any human authority."

When they had brought [the apostles], they had them stand before the council. The high priest questioned them, saying, "We gave you strict orders not to teach in this name, yet here you have filled Jerusalem with your teaching and you are determined to bring this man's blood on us." But Peter and the apostles answered, "We must obey God rather than any human authority. [30] The God of our ancestors raised up Jesus, whom you had killed by hanging him on a tree. God exalted him at his right hand as Leader and Savior that he might give repentance to Israel and forgiveness of sins. And we are witnesses to

these things, and so is the Holy Spirit whom God has given to those who obey him."

When they heard this, they were enraged and wanted to kill them. But a Pharisee in the council named Gamaliel, a teacher of the law, respected by all the people, stood up and ordered the men to be put outside for a short time. [35] Then he said to them, "Fellow Israelites, consider carefully what you propose to do to these men. For some time ago Theudas rose up, claiming to be somebody, and a number of men, about four hundred, joined him; but he was killed, and all who followed him were dispersed

---

Acts 5:27–42.

and disappeared. After him Judas the Galilean[12] rose up at the time of the census and got people to follow him; he also perished, and all who followed him were scattered. So in the present case, I tell you, keep away from these men and let them alone; because if this plan or this undertaking is of human origin, it will fail; but if it is of God, you will not be able to overthrow

them—in that case you may even be found fighting against God!"

They were convinced by him, [40] and when they had called in the apostles, they had them flogged. Then they ordered them not to speak in the name of Jesus, and let them go. As they left the council, they rejoiced that they were considered worthy to suffer dishonor for the sake of the name. And every day in the temple and at home they did not cease to teach and proclaim Jesus as the Messiah.

[12]*Theudas . . . Judas the Galilean:* messianic pretenders whose movements collapsed after they died.

The Council at Jerusalem

The issue at this council was whether Gentile converts to Christianity should be required to be circumcised and keep at least some of the laws of Moses. Paul and Peter argued no; some conservative Jewish Christians, converts from the Pharisees, said yes. James, kinsman of Jesus and leader of the Jerusalem church at this time, gave the compromise ruling: No circumcision would be required of Gentile converts, but certain minimal laws of purity would be imposed. The result of this decision was that Christianity began to separate from its roots in Judaism, becoming a different religion.

Then certain individuals came down from Judea and were teaching the brothers, "Unless you are circumcised according to the custom of Moses, you cannot be saved." And after Paul and Barnabas had no small dissension and debate with them, Paul and Barnabas and some of the others were appointed to go up to Jerusalem to discuss this question with the apostles and the elders. So they were sent on their way by the church, and as they passed through both Phoenicia and Samaria, they reported the conversion of the Gentiles, and brought great joy to all the believers. When they came to Jerusalem, they were welcomed by the church and the apostles and the elders, and they reported all that God had done with them. [5] But some believers who belonged to the sect of the Pharisees stood up and said, "It is necessary for them to be circumcised and ordered to keep the law of Moses."

The apostles and the elders met together to consider this matter. After there had been much debate, Peter stood up and said to them, "My brothers, you know that in the early days God made a choice among you, that I should be the one through whom the Gentiles would hear the message of the good news and become believers. And God, who knows the human heart, testified to them by giving them the Holy Spirit, just as he did to us; and in cleansing their hearts by faith he has made no distinction between them and us. [10] Now therefore why are you putting God to the test by placing on the neck of the disciples a yoke that neither our ancestors nor we have been able to bear? On the contrary, we believe that we will be saved through the grace of the Lord Jesus, just as they will."

The whole assembly kept silence, and listened to Barnabas and Paul as they told of all the signs and wonders that God had done

Acts 15:1–21.

through them among the Gentiles. After they finished speaking, James replied, "My brothers, listen to me. Simeon[13] has related how God first looked favorably on the Gentiles, to take from among them a people for his name. [15] This agrees with the words of the prophets, as it is written, 'After this I will return, and I will rebuild the dwelling of David, which has fallen; from its ruins I will rebuild it, and I will set it up, so that all other peoples may seek the Lord—even all the Gentiles over whom my name has been called. Thus says the Lord, who has been making these things known from long ago.' Therefore I have reached the decision that we should not trouble those Gentiles who are turning to God, [20] but we should write to them to abstain only from things polluted by idols and from fornication and from whatever has been strangled and from blood.[14] For in every city, for generations past, Moses has had those who proclaim him, for he has been read aloud every sabbath in the synagogues."

---

[13] *Simeon:* Peter.

[14] *from things polluted . . . and from blood:* foods offered to idols in sacrifice and meat not ritually butchered, respectively.

TEACHING

The Parables of Jesus

The parables were Jesus' distinctive form of teaching. Parables are stories that compare an experience in everyday life with some aspect of religious life, especially life in the Kingdom of God. Here is a collection of parables gathered by Mark or transmitted to him in the oral tradition. Many scholars view the interpretation of the parable of the sower, found in the third paragraph, as deriving not directly from Jesus but from the early church.

Again he began to teach beside the sea. Such a very large crowd gathered around him that he got into a boat on the sea and sat there, while the whole crowd was beside the sea on the land. He began to teach them many things in parables, and in his teaching he said to them: "Listen! A sower went out to sow. And as he sowed, some seed fell on the path, and the birds came and ate it up. [5] Other seed fell on rocky ground, where it did not have much soil, and it sprang up quickly, since it had no depth of soil. And when the sun rose, it was scorched; and since it had no root, it withered away. Other seed fell among thorns, and the thorns grew up and choked it, and it yielded no grain. Other seed fell into good soil and brought forth grain, growing up and increasing and yielding thirty and sixty and a hundredfold." And he said, "Let anyone with ears to hear listen."

[10] When he was alone, those who were around him along with the twelve asked him about the parables. And he said to them, "To you has been given the secret of the kingdom of God, but for those outside, everything comes in parables; in order that 'they may indeed look, but not perceive, and may indeed listen, but not understand; so that they may not turn again and be forgiven.'"

And he said to them, "Do you not understand this parable? Then how will you understand all the parables? The sower sows the

---

Mark 4:1–34.

word. [15] These are the ones on the path where the word is sown: when they hear, Satan immediately comes and takes away the word that is sown in them. And these are the ones sown on rocky ground: when they hear the word, they immediately receive it with joy. But they have no root, and endure only for a while; then, when trouble or persecution arises on account of the word, immediately they fall away. And others are those sown among the thorns: these are the ones who hear the word, but the cares of the world, and the lure of wealth, and the desire for other things come in and choke the word, and it yields nothing. [20] And these are the ones sown on the good soil: they hear the word and accept it and bear fruit, thirty and sixty and a hundredfold.''

He said to them, "Is a lamp brought in to be put under the bushel basket, or under the bed, and not on the lampstand? For there is nothing hidden, except to be disclosed; nor is anything secret, except to come to light. Let anyone with ears to hear listen!" And he said to them, "Pay attention to what you hear; the measure you give will be the measure you get, and still more will be given you. [25] For to those who have, more

will be given; and from those who have nothing, even what they have will be taken away.''

He also said, "The kingdom of God is as if someone would scatter seed on the ground, and would sleep and rise night and day, and the seed would sprout and grow, he does not know how. The earth produces of itself, first the stalk, then the head, then the full grain in the head. But when the grain is ripe, at once he goes in with his sickle, because the harvest has come.''

[30] He also said, "With what can we compare the kingdom of God, or what parable will we use for it? It is like a mustard seed, which, when sown upon the ground, is the smallest of all the seeds on earth; yet when it is sown it grows up and becomes the greatest of all shrubs, and puts forth large branches, so that the birds of the air can make nests in its shade.''

With many such parables he spoke the word to them, as they were able to hear it; he did not speak to them except in parables,[15] but he explained everything in private to his disciples.

---

[15]*except in parables:* Jesus' teaching was characteristically illustrated by parables, but the parable was not his only form of teaching.

The Divine Word Became Human

This hymn to Christ as the divine Word made human is perhaps the New Testament's most exalted view of the Savior. Largely on the strength of John's gospel, and with help from some other writers (especially Paul), the early church came to see the divine nature of Jesus as the divine Son from all eternity. This main theme alternates here with a secondary theme: that John the Baptist is not the Messiah.

In the beginning was the Word, and the Word was with God, and the Word was God. He was in the beginning with God. All things came into being through him, and without him not one thing came into being. What has come into being in him was life, and the life was the light of all people. [5] The light shines in the darkness, and the darkness did not overcome it.

There was a man sent from God, whose name was John. He came as a witness to testify to the light, so that all might believe through him. He himself was not the light, but he came to testify to the light. The true light, which enlightens everyone, was coming into the world. [10] He was in the world, and the world came into being through him; yet the world did not know

---

John 1:1–18.

him. He came to what was his own, and his own people did not accept him. But to all who received him, who believed in his name, he gave power to become children of God, who were born, not of blood or of the will of the flesh or of the will of man, but of God.

And the Word became flesh and lived among us, and we have seen his glory, the glory as of a father's only son, full of grace and truth. [15]

John testified to him and cried out, "This was he of whom I said, 'He who comes after me ranks ahead of me because he was before me.'" From his fullness we have all received, grace upon grace. The law indeed was given through Moses; grace and truth came through Jesus Christ. No one has ever seen God. It is God the only Son, who is close to the Father's heart, who has made him known.

Nicodemus Visits Jesus

This selection presents one early Christian view of salvation: a "rebirth" by the power of the Holy Spirit that makes a person the child of God. In modern times, a part of evangelical Protestantism has fastened upon this passage, interpreting the "born again" concept as an emotionally powerful conversion experience. Christians of other Protestant, Roman Catholic, and Orthodox traditions hold that simply to believe in Jesus as Savior and be baptized is to be "born again."

Now there was a Pharisee named Nicodemus, a leader of the Jews. He came to Jesus by night and said to him, "Rabbi, we know that you are a teacher who has come from God; for no one can do these signs that you do apart from the presence of God." Jesus answered him, "Very truly, I tell you, no one can see the kingdom of God without being born from above."[16] Nicodemus said to him, "How can anyone be born after having grown old? Can one enter a second time into the mother's womb and be born?" [5] Jesus answered, "Very truly, I tell you, no one can enter the kingdom of God without being born of water and Spirit. What is born of the flesh is flesh, and what is born of the Spirit is spirit. Do not be astonished that I said to you, 'You must be born from above.' The wind blows where it chooses, and you hear the sound of it, but you do not know where it comes from or where it goes. So it is with everyone who is born of the Spirit." Nicodemus said

to him, "How can these things be?" [10] Jesus answered him, "Are you a teacher of Israel, and yet you do not understand these things? Very truly, I tell you, we speak of what we know and testify to what we have seen; yet you do not receive our testimony. If I have told you about earthly things and you do not believe, how can you believe if I tell you about heavenly things? No one has ascended into heaven except the one who descended from heaven, the Son of Man. And just as Moses lifted up the serpent in the wilderness, so must the Son of Man be lifted up, [15] that whoever believes in him may have eternal life."

"For God so loved the world that he gave his only Son, so that everyone who believes in him may not perish but may have eternal life. Indeed, God did not send the Son into the world to condemn the world, but in order that the world might be saved through him. Those who believe in him are not condemned; but those who do not believe are condemned already, because they have not believed in the name of the only Son of God. And this is the judgment, that

---

[16]*born from above:* From the Greek original of the *New Testament* it is possible to translate "from above" as "again."

the light has come into the world, and people loved darkness rather than light because their deeds were evil. [20] For all who do evil hate the light and do not come to the light, so that their deeds may not be exposed. But those who do what is true come to the light, so that it may be clearly seen that their deeds have been done in God."

A Sinful Woman Forgiven

In this passage, Jesus answers a Pharisee's criticism with a parable on the meaning of forgiveness. Jesus teaches the radical nature of God's love and its transforming power. The woman in this parable was, in post–New Testament times, identified as Mary Magdalene. This identification has been reinforced recently by *The Da Vinci Code,* a novel by Dan Brown and the film based on it, but scholars almost unanimously reject it.

One of the Pharisees asked Jesus to eat with him, and he went into the Pharisee's house and took his place at the table. And a woman in the city, who was a sinner,[17] having learned that he was eating in the Pharisee's house, brought an alabaster jar of ointment. She stood behind him at his feet, weeping, and began to bathe his feet with her tears and to dry them with her hair. Then she continued kissing his feet and anointing them with the ointment. Now when the Pharisee who had invited him saw it, he said to himself, "If this man were a prophet, he would have known who and what kind of woman this is who is touching him—that she is a sinner."

[40] Jesus spoke up and said to him, "Simon, I have something to say to you. . . . A certain creditor had two debtors; one owed five hundred denarii, and the other fifty.[18] When they could not pay, he canceled the debts for both of them. Now which of them will love him more?" Simon answered, "I suppose the one for whom he canceled the greater debt." And Jesus said to him, "You have judged rightly." Then turning toward the woman, he said to Simon, "Do you see this woman? I entered your house; you gave me no water for my feet, but she has bathed my feet with her tears and dried them with her hair. [45] You gave me no kiss, but from the time I came in she has not stopped kissing my feet. You did not anoint my head with oil, but she has anointed my feet with ointment. Therefore, I tell you, her sins, which were many, have been forgiven; hence she has shown great love. But the one to whom little is forgiven, loves little." Then he said to her, "Your sins are forgiven." But those who were at the table with him began to say among themselves, "Who is this who even forgives sins?" [50] And he said to the woman, "Your faith has saved you; go in peace."

---

[17]*a sinner:* a notorious sinner, probably one who made her living by an occupation considered sinful by the law of Moses.
[18]A *denarius* was a day's pay for a common laborer.

Luke 7:36–50.

Results of Justification

Justification is God's act of making believers righteous through faith in the crucified and resurrected Jesus. In this justification, believers are reconciled to God. Protestant churches have used this and similar passages to support their leading doctrines of justification by faith alone rather than through human obedience to religious law. Since the mid-1990s, Roman Catholic and Protestant churches have made great strides toward a common understanding of justification by faith.

Therefore, since we are justified by faith, we have peace with God through our Lord Jesus Christ, through whom we have obtained access to this grace in which we stand; and we boast in our hope of sharing the glory of God. And not only that, but we also boast in our sufferings, knowing that suffering produces endurance, and endurance produces character, and character produces hope, [5] and hope does not disappoint us, because God's love has been poured into our hearts through the Holy Spirit that has been given to us.

For while we were still weak, at the right time Christ died for the ungodly. Indeed, rarely will anyone die for a righteous person—though perhaps for a good person someone might actually dare to die. But God proves his love for us in that while we still were sinners Christ died for us. Much more surely then, now that we have been justified by his blood, will we be saved through him from the wrath of God. [10] For if while we were enemies, we were reconciled to God through the death of his Son, much more surely, having been reconciled, will we be saved by his life.[19] But more than that, we even boast in God through our Lord Jesus Christ, through whom we have now received reconciliation.

---

[19]*his life:* Jesus' eternal life after his resurrection, which secures the believer's resurrection to eternal life.

Romans 5:1–11.

The End of Time

Many *New Testament* teachings about the end of time are taken from Judaism and adapted to Christianity. In the first passage, Matthew relates the teaching of Jesus about his role as the judge at the final judgment, after the resurrection of all the dead. In the second, the author of *Revelation* presents in striking apocalyptic-style dreams and visions about the end.

[*Matthew* 25:31] "When the Son of Man comes in his glory, and all the angels with him, then he will sit on the throne of his glory. All the nations will be gathered before him, and he will separate people one from another as a shepherd separates the sheep from the goats, and he will put the sheep at his right hand and the goats at the left. Then the king will say to those at his right hand, 'Come, you that are blessed by my Father, inherit the kingdom prepared for you from the foundation of the world; [35] for I was hungry and you gave me food, I was thirsty and you gave me

---

Matthew 25:31–46; *Revelation* 20:1–21:4.

something to drink, I was a stranger and you welcomed me, I was naked and you gave me clothing, I was sick and you took care of me, I was in prison and you visited me.'

"Then the righteous will answer him, 'Lord, when was it that we saw you hungry and gave you food, or thirsty and gave you something to drink? And when was it that we saw you a stranger and welcomed you, or naked and gave you clothing? And when was it that we saw you sick or in prison and visited you?' [40] And the king will answer them, 'Truly I tell you, just as you did it to one of the least of these who are members of my family, you did it to me.' Then he will say to those at his left hand, 'You that are accursed, depart from me into the eternal fire prepared for the devil and his angels; for I was hungry and you gave me no food, I was thirsty and you gave me nothing to drink, I was a stranger and you did not welcome me, naked and you did not give me clothing, sick and in prison and you did not visit me.' Then they also will answer, 'Lord, when was it that we saw you hungry or thirsty or a stranger or naked or sick or in prison, and did not take care of you?' [45] Then he will answer them, 'Truly I tell you, just as you did not do it to one of the least of these, you did not do it to me.' And these will go away into eternal punishment, but the righteous into eternal life.'"

[*Revelation* 20:1] Then I saw an angel coming down from heaven, holding in his hand the key to the bottomless pit and a great chain. He seized the dragon, that ancient serpent, who is the Devil and Satan, and bound him for a thousand years, and threw him into the pit, and locked and sealed it over him, so that he would deceive the nations no more, until the thousand years were ended. After that he must be let out for a little while.

Then I saw thrones, and those seated on them were given authority to judge. I also saw the souls of those who had been beheaded for their testimony to Jesus and for the word of God. They had not worshiped the beast or its image and had not received its mark on their foreheads or their hands. They came to life and reigned with Christ a thousand years. [5] (The rest of the dead did not come to life until the thousand years were ended.) This is the first

resurrection. Blessed and holy are those who share in the first resurrection. Over these the second death has no power, but they will be priests of God and of Christ, and they will reign with him a thousand years.

When the thousand years are ended, Satan will be released from his prison and will come out to deceive the nations at the four corners of the earth, Gog and Magog,[20] in order to gather them for battle; they are as numerous as the sands of the sea. They marched up over the breadth of the earth and surrounded the camp of the saints and the beloved city. And fire came down from heaven and consumed them. [10] And the devil who had deceived them was thrown into the lake of fire and sulfur, where the beast and the false prophet were, and they will be tormented day and night forever and ever.

Then I saw a great white throne and the one who sat on it; the earth and the heaven fled from his presence; and no place was found for them. And I saw the dead, great and small, standing before the throne, and books were opened. Also another book was opened, the book of life. And the dead were judged according to their works, as recorded in the books. And the sea gave up the dead that were in it, Death and Hades[21] gave up the dead that were in them, and all were judged according to what they had done. Then Death and Hades were thrown into the lake of fire. This is the second death, the lake of fire; [15] and anyone whose name was not found written in the book of life was thrown into the lake of fire.

[21:1] Then I saw a new heaven and a new earth; for the first heaven and the first earth had passed away, and the sea was no more. And I saw the holy city, the new Jerusalem, coming down out of heaven from God, prepared as a bride adorned for her husband. And I heard a loud voice from the throne saying,

---

[20] *Gog and Magog:* nations allied with Satan to oppose the coming of God's kingdom. In *Ezekiel* 38–39, these are probably code words for the nation of Babylon, which in the book of *Revelation* is code in turn for Rome.
[21] *Death and Hades* (Hell) are personified here.

"See, the home of God is among mortals.[22]
He will dwell with them as their God;
they will be his peoples,
and God himself will be with them;
he will wipe every tear from their eyes.
Death will be no more;

mourning and crying and pain will be
  no more,
for the first things have passed away."

———

[22]*mortals:* The Greek word is better translated "humans" here; in the context, since "death will be no more," they are not (strictly speaking) "mortal" any longer.

ETHICS

The Sermon on the Mount

The Sermon on the Mount is the gospels' longest collection of the moral teachings of Jesus. It is largely a collection by the gospel writer, probably drawing on an early collection of Jesus' sayings called by modern scholars the *Quelle,* "source." The sermon contains his understanding of Jesus' teaching on what it is to follow Jesus. The themes are many and varied: blessings on obedience, the law of Moses, the practice of piety, use of possessions, and following Jesus' words.

When Jesus saw the crowds, he went up the mountain; and after he sat down, his disciples came to him. Then he began to speak, and taught them, saying:

"Blessed are the poor in spirit, for theirs is the kingdom of heaven.
"Blessed are those who mourn, for they will be comforted.
[5] "Blessed are the meek,[23] for they will inherit the earth.
"Blessed are those who hunger and thirst for righteousness, for they will be filled.
"Blessed are the merciful, for they will receive mercy.
"Blessed are the pure in heart, for they will see God.
"Blessed are the peacemakers, for they will be called children of God.
[10] "Blessed are those who are persecuted for righteousness' sake, for theirs is the kingdom of heaven.
"Blessed are you when people revile you and persecute you and utter all kinds of evil against you falsely on my account. Rejoice and be glad, for your reward is great in heaven, for in the same way they persecuted the prophets who were before you.

"You are the salt of the earth; but if salt has lost its taste, how can its saltiness be restored? It is no longer good for anything, but is thrown out and trampled under foot. You are the light of the world. A city built on a hill cannot be hid. [15] No one after lighting a lamp puts it under the bushel basket, but on the lampstand, and it gives light to all in the house. In the same way, let your light shine before others, so that they may see your good works and give glory to your Father in heaven.

"Do not think that I have come to abolish the law or the prophets; I have come not to abolish but to fulfill. For truly I tell you, until heaven

———

[23]*meek:* humble.

Matthew 5–7.

and earth pass away, not one letter, not one stroke of a letter, will pass from the law until all is accomplished. Therefore, whoever breaks one of the least of these commandments, and teaches others to do the same, will be called least in the kingdom of heaven; but whoever does them and teaches them will be called great in the kingdom of heaven. [20] For I tell you, unless your righteousness exceeds that of the scribes and Pharisees, you will never enter the kingdom of heaven.

"You have heard that it was said to those of ancient times, 'You shall not murder'; and 'Whoever murders shall be liable to judgment.' But I say to you that if you are angry with a brother or sister, you will be liable to judgment; and if you insult a brother or sister, you will be liable to the council; and if you say, 'You fool,' you will be liable to the hell of fire. So when you are offering your gift at the altar, if you remember that your brother or sister has something against you, leave your gift there before the altar and go; first be reconciled to your brother or sister, and then come and offer your gift. [25] Come to terms quickly with your accuser while you are on the way to court with him, or your accuser may hand you over to the judge, and the judge to the guard, and you will be thrown into prison. Truly I tell you, you will never get out until you have paid the last penny.

"You have heard that it was said, 'You shall not commit adultery.' But I say to you that everyone who looks at a woman with lust has already committed adultery with her in his heart. If your right eye causes you to sin, tear it out and throw it away;[24] it is better for you to lose one of your members than for your whole body to be thrown into hell. [30] And if your right hand causes you to sin, cut it off and throw it away; it is better for you to lose one of your members than for your whole body to go into hell.

"It was also said, 'Whoever divorces his wife, let him give her a certificate of divorce.' But I say to you that anyone who divorces his wife, except on the ground of unchastity, causes her to commit adultery; and whoever marries a divorced woman commits adultery.

"Again, you have heard that it was said to those of ancient times, 'You shall not swear falsely, but carry out the vows you have made to the Lord.' But I say to you, Do not swear at all, either by heaven, for it is the throne of God, [35] or by the earth, for it is his footstool, or by Jerusalem, for it is the city of the great King. And do not swear by your head, for you cannot make one hair white or black. Let your word be 'Yes, Yes' or 'No, No'; anything more than this comes from the evil one.

"You have heard that it was said, 'An eye for an eye and a tooth for a tooth.' But I say to you, Do not resist an evildoer. But if anyone strikes you on the right cheek, turn the other also; [40] and if anyone wants to sue you and take your coat, give your cloak as well; and if anyone forces you to go one mile, go also the second mile. Give to everyone who begs from you, and do not refuse anyone who wants to borrow from you.

"You have heard that it was said, 'You shall love your neighbor and hate your enemy.' But I say to you, Love your enemies and pray for those who persecute you, [45] so that you may be children of your Father in heaven; for he makes his sun rise on the evil and on the good, and sends rain on the righteous and on the unrighteous. For if you love those who love you, what reward do you have? Do not even the tax collectors do the same? And if you greet only your brothers and sisters, what more are you doing than others? Do not even the Gentiles do the same? Be perfect, therefore, as your heavenly Father is perfect.[25]

[6:1] "Beware of practicing your piety before others in order to be seen by them; for then you have no reward from your Father in heaven. So whenever you give alms, do not sound a trumpet before you, as the hypocrites[26] do in the synagogues and in the streets, so that they may be

---

[24]*tear it out . . . cut it off:* This is hyperbole and not to be interpreted literally. Jesus does not advocate self-mutilation; the meaning is that Jesus' followers are to take all necessary measures to avoid adultery.

[25]*perfect:* not sinless but mature and complete.
[26]*hypocrites:* not those who are evil on the inside yet act righteously, but those who are basically good yet have moral faults that mar their goodness.

praised by others. Truly I tell you, they have received their reward. But when you give alms, do not let your left hand know what your right hand is doing, so that your alms may be done in secret; and your Father who sees in secret will reward you. [5] And whenever you pray, do not be like the hypocrites; for they love to stand and pray in the synagogues and at the street corners, so that they may be seen by others. Truly I tell you, they have received their reward. But whenever you pray, go into your room and shut the door and pray to your Father who is in secret; and your Father who sees in secret will reward you.

"When you are praying, do not heap up empty phrases as the Gentiles do; for they think that they will be heard because of their many words. Do not be like them, for your Father knows what you need before you ask him. Pray then in this way:[27]

> Our Father in heaven, hallowed be your name.
> [10] Your kingdom come.
> Your will be done, on earth as it is in heaven.
> Give us this day our daily bread.
> And forgive us our debts, as we also have
>   forgiven our debtors.
> And do not bring us to the time of trial,
>   but rescue us from the evil one.

For if you forgive others their trespasses, your heavenly Father will also forgive you; [15] but if you do not forgive others, neither will your Father forgive your trespasses.

"And whenever you fast, do not look dismal, like the hypocrites, for they disfigure their faces so as to show others that they are fasting. Truly I tell you, they have received their reward. But when you fast, put oil on your head and wash your face, so that your fasting may be seen not by others but by your Father who is in secret; and your Father who sees in secret will reward you.

"Do not store up for yourselves treasures on earth, where moth and rust consume and where thieves break in and steal; [20] but store up for yourselves treasures in heaven, where neither moth nor rust consumes and where thieves do not break in and steal. For where your treasure is, there your heart will be also.

"The eye is the lamp of the body.[28] So, if your eye is healthy, your whole body will be full of light; but if your eye is unhealthy, your whole body will be full of darkness. If then the light in you is darkness, how great is the darkness!

"No one can serve two masters; for a slave will either hate the one and love the other, or be devoted to the one and despise the other. You cannot serve God and wealth.

[25] "Therefore I tell you, do not worry about your life, what you will eat or what you will drink, or about your body, what you will wear. Is not life more than food, and the body more than clothing? Look at the birds of the air; they neither sow nor reap nor gather into barns, and yet your heavenly Father feeds them. Are you not of more value than they? And can any of you by worrying add a single hour to your span of life? And why do you worry about clothing? Consider the lilies of the field, how they grow; they neither toil nor spin, yet I tell you, even Solomon in all his glory was not clothed like one of these. [30] But if God so clothes the grass of the field, which is alive today and tomorrow is thrown into the oven, will he not much more clothe you—you of little faith? Therefore do not worry, saying, 'What will we eat?' or 'What will we drink?' or 'What will we wear?' For it is the Gentiles who strive for all these things; and indeed your heavenly Father knows that you need all these things. But strive first for the kingdom of God and his righteousness, and all these things will be given to you as well.

"So do not worry about tomorrow, for tomorrow will bring worries of its own. Today's trouble is enough for today.

[7:1] "Do not judge, so that you may not be judged. For with the judgment you make you will be judged, and the measure you give will be the measure you get. Why do you see the speck in

---

[27]*pray this way:* Jesus gives this prayer as a model; prayer should be full yet brief. That some English-speaking Christians say "debts" and others "trespasses" comes from different English versions of the Bible.

[28]*eye:* probably the heart as the seat of emotion and thought; perhaps the conscience.

your neighbor's eye, but do not notice the log in your own eye? Or how can you say to your neighbor, 'Let me take the speck out of your eye,' while the log is in your own eye? [5] You hypocrite, first take the log out of your own eye, and then you will see clearly to take the speck out of your neighbor's eye.

"Do not give what is holy to dogs; and do not throw your pearls before swine, or they will trample them underfoot and turn and maul you.

"Ask, and it will be given you; search, and you will find; knock, and the door will be opened for you. For everyone who asks receives, and everyone who searches finds, and for everyone who knocks, the door will be opened. Is there anyone among you who, if your child asks for bread, will give a stone? [10] Or if the child asks for a fish, will give a snake? If you then, who are evil, know how to give good gifts to your children, how much more will your Father in heaven give good things to those who ask him!

"In everything do to others as you would have them do to you; for this is the law and the prophets.[29]

"Enter through the narrow gate; for the gate is wide and the road is easy that leads to destruction, and there are many who take it. For the gate is narrow and the road is hard that leads to life, and there are few who find it. . . .

"Everyone then who hears these words of mine and acts on them will be like a wise man who built his house on rock. [25] The rain fell, the floods came, and the winds blew and beat on that house, but it did not fall, because it had been founded on rock. And everyone who hears these words of mine and does not act on them will be like a foolish man who built his house on sand. The rain fell, and the floods came, and the winds blew and beat against that house, and it fell—and great was its fall!"

Now when Jesus had finished saying these things, the crowds were astounded at his teaching, for he taught them as one having authority, and not as their scribes.[30]

---

[29]This is the "Golden Rule." Expressed in its positive form, it is the essence of self-giving love.
[30]*not as their scribes:* Jewish scribes taught on the authority of other scribal experts; Jesus teaches on his own authority.

Directions Concerning Marriage

Paul here gives detailed directions about marriage. His basic perspective, based mostly on his expectation of the imminent return of Jesus, is that marriage is good but to remain single is better. In this passage and the next, the quotations are slogans prominent in the church of Corinth to which Paul is responding. Notice Paul's careful distinction between the commands of Jesus and his own preferences. These ideas became influential in the ancient church and continue in churches that practice forms of clerical celibacy.

Now concerning the matters about which you wrote: "It is well for a man not to touch a woman." But because of cases of sexual immorality, each man should have his own wife and each woman her own husband. The husband should give to his wife her conjugal rights, and likewise the wife to her husband. For the wife does not have authority over her own body, but the husband does; likewise the husband does not have authority over his own body, but the wife does. [5] Do not deprive one another except perhaps by agreement for a set time, to devote yourselves to prayer, and then come together again, so that Satan may not tempt you because of your lack of

---

I Corinthians 7:1–16, 25–40.

self-control. This I say by way of concession, not of command. I wish that all were as I myself am. But each has a particular gift from God, one having one kind and another a different kind.

To the unmarried and the widows I say that it is well for them to remain unmarried as I am. But if they are not practicing self-control, they should marry. For it is better to marry than to be aflame with passion.

[10] To the married I give this command—not I but the Lord—that the wife should not separate from her husband, and that the husband should not divorce his wife.

To the rest I say—I and not the Lord—that if any believer has a wife who is an unbeliever, and she consents to live with him, he should not divorce her. And if any woman has a husband who is an unbeliever, and he consents to live with her, she should not divorce him. For the unbelieving husband is made holy through his wife, and the unbelieving wife is made holy through her husband. Otherwise, your children would be unclean, but as it is, they are holy. [15] But if the unbelieving partner separates, let it be so; in such a case the brother or sister is not bound. It is to peace that God has called you. Wife, for all you know, you might save your husband. Husband, for all you know, you might save your wife....

[25] Now concerning virgins,[31] I have no command of the Lord, but I give my opinion as one who by the Lord's mercy is trustworthy. I think that, in view of the impending crisis,[32] it is well for you to remain as you are. Are you bound to a wife? Do not seek to be free. Are you free from a wife? Do not seek a wife. But if you marry, you do not sin, and if a virgin marries, she does not sin. Yet those who marry will experience distress in this life, and I would spare you

that. I mean, brothers and sisters, the appointed time has grown short; from now on, let even those who have wives be as though they had none, [30] and those who mourn as though they were not mourning, and those who rejoice as though they were not rejoicing, and those who buy as though they had no possessions, and those who deal with the world as though they had no dealings with it. For the present form of this world is passing away.

I want you to be free from anxieties. The unmarried man is anxious about the affairs of the Lord, how to please the Lord; but the married man is anxious about the affairs of the world, how to please his wife, and his interests are divided. And the unmarried woman and the virgin are anxious about the affairs of the Lord, so that they may be holy in body and spirit; but the married woman is anxious about the affairs of the world, how to please her husband. [35] I say this for your own benefit, not to put any restraint upon you, but to promote good order and unhindered devotion to the Lord.

If anyone thinks that he is not behaving properly toward his fiancée, if his passions are strong, and so it has to be, let him marry as he wishes; it is no sin. Let them marry. But if someone stands firm in his resolve, being under no necessity but having his own desire under control, and has determined in his own mind to keep her as his fiancée, he will do well. So then, he who marries his fiancée does well; and he who refrains from marriage will do better.

A wife is bound as long as her husband lives. But if the husband dies, she is free to marry anyone she wishes, only in the Lord.[33] But in my judgment she is more blessed if she remains as she is. And I think that I too have the Spirit of God.

---

[31] *virgins:* young women of marriageable age; no other implication is made.
[32] *impending crisis:* troubles for believers at the end of the world.

[33] *only in the Lord:* to a fellow Christian.

Love

This "Hymn to Love," perhaps written by Paul or adapted by him for use in this letter, extols love as the greatest spiritual gift. It has three distinct themes in these three paragraphs: First, it contrasts love with other spiritual gifts; second, it describes love; third, it extols the persistence of love. This chapter in *I Corinthians* is heard most often at Christian marriage ceremonies, but the scope of love Paul covers here goes far beyond marriage.

If I speak in the tongues of mortals and of angels, but do not have love, I am a noisy gong or a clanging cymbal. And if I have prophetic powers, and understand all mysteries and all knowledge, and if I have all faith, so as to remove mountains, but do not have love, I am nothing. If I give away all my possessions, and if I hand over my body so that I may boast, but do not have love, I gain nothing.

Love is patient; love is kind; love is not envious or boastful or arrogant [5] or rude. It does not insist on its own way; it is not irritable or resentful; it does not rejoice in wrongdoing, but rejoices in the truth. It bears all things, believes all things, hopes all things, endures all things.

Love never ends. But as for prophecies, they will come to an end; as for tongues, they will cease; as for knowledge, it will come to an end. For we know only in part, and we prophesy only in part; [10] but when the complete comes, the partial will come to an end. When I was a child, I spoke like a child, I thought like a child, I reasoned like a child; when I became an adult, I put an end to childish ways. For now we see in a mirror, dimly, but then we will see face to face. Now I know only in part; then I will know fully, even as I have been fully known. And now faith, hope, and love abide, these three; and the greatest of these is love.

I Corinthians 13:1–13.

Ethics in the Christian Household

This discussion of ethics in the Christian household contains instructions for wives, husbands, children, parents, slaves, and masters. It presupposes the legitimacy of the household structure of the times but seeks to transform it with the Christian ethic.

Be subject to one another out of reverence for Christ.

Wives, be subject to your husbands as you are to the Lord. For the husband is the head of the wife just as Christ is the head of the church, the body of which he is the Savior. Just as the church is subject to Christ, so also wives ought to be, in everything, to their husbands. [25]

Husbands, love your wives,[34] just as Christ loved the church and gave himself up for her, in order to make her holy by cleansing her with

---

[34] *Husbands, love your wives:* In ancient societies, as in most societies today where marriage is not based on romantic love, keeping this command would not be seen as essential to marriage.

Ephesians 5:21–6:9.

the washing of water by the word, so as to present the church to himself in splendor, without a spot or wrinkle or anything of the kind—yes, so that she may be holy and without blemish. In the same way, husbands should love their wives as they do their own bodies. He who loves his wife loves himself. For no one ever hates his own body, but he nourishes and tenderly cares for it, just as Christ does for the church, [30] because we are members of his body. For this reason a man will leave his father and mother and be joined to his wife, and the two will become one flesh. This is a great mystery, and I am applying it to Christ and the church. Each of you, however, should love his wife as himself, and a wife should respect her husband.

[6:1] Children, obey your parents in the Lord, for this is right. "Honor your father and mother"—this is the first commandment with a promise: "so that it may be well with you and you may live long on the earth." And, fathers, do not provoke your children to anger, but bring them up in the discipline and instruction of the Lord.

[5] Slaves, obey your earthly masters with fear and trembling, in singleness of heart, as you obey Christ; not only while being watched, and in order to please them, but as slaves of Christ, doing the will of God from the heart. Render service with enthusiasm, as to the Lord and not to men and women, knowing that whatever good we do, we will receive the same again from the Lord, whether we are slaves or free. And, masters, do the same to them. Stop threatening them, for you know that both of you have the same Master in heaven, and with him there is no partiality.

Being Subject to Authorities

Romans 13 is the most important treatment in the *New Testament* of the relationship of the believer and the government and the most influential throughout the history of the church. It couples specific and positive instructions about being subject to governing authorities with more general instructions about social ethics.

Let every person be subject to the governing authorities; for there is no authority except from God, and those authorities that exist have been instituted by God. Therefore whoever resists authority resists what God has appointed, and those who resist will incur judgment. For rulers are not a terror to good conduct, but to bad. Do you wish to have no fear of the authority? Then do what is good, and you will receive its approval; for it is God's servant for your good. But if you do what is wrong, you should be afraid, for the authority does not bear the sword in vain. It is the servant of God to execute wrath on the wrongdoer. [5] Therefore one must be subject, not only because of wrath but also because of conscience. For the same reason you also pay taxes, for the authorities are God's servants, busy with this very thing. Pay to all what is due them—taxes to whom taxes are due, revenue to whom revenue is due, respect to whom respect is due, honor to whom honor is due.

Owe no one anything, except to love one another; for the one who loves another has fulfilled the law. The commandments, "You shall not commit adultery; You shall not murder; You shall not steal; You shall not covet"; and any other commandment, are summed up in this word, "Love your neighbor as yourself." [10] Love does no wrong to a neighbor; therefore, love is the fulfilling of the law.

Romans 13:1–10.

The Fall of Rome

This is the flip side of the positive view of civil government presented in *Romans* 13:1–7. The city of Rome is depicted symbolically as a "great whore," and the scarlet beast she rides is the Roman Empire. This selection concludes with a funeral song sung over the fallen Rome. This approach encourages quiet opposition to idolatrous and persecuting government, longing for its downfall at the coming of God's kingdom.

Then one of the seven angels who had the seven bowls came and said to me, "Come. I will show you the judgment of the great whore who is seated on many waters, with whom the kings of the earth have committed fornication, and with the wine of whose fornication the inhabitants of the earth have become drunk." So he carried me away in the spirit into a wilderness, and I saw a woman sitting on a scarlet beast that was full of blasphemous names, and it had seven heads and ten horns. The woman was clothed in purple and scarlet, and adorned with gold and jewels and pearls, holding in her hand a golden cup full of abominations and the impurities of her fornication; [5] and on her forehead was written a name, a mystery: "Babylon the great,[35] mother of whores and of earth's abomination." And I saw that the woman was drunk with the blood of the saints and the blood of the witnesses to Jesus.

When I saw her, I was greatly amazed. But the angel said to me, "Why are you so amazed? I will tell you the mystery of the woman, and of the beast with seven heads and ten horns that carries her. The beast that you saw was, and is not, and is about to ascend from the bottomless pit and go to destruction. And the inhabitants of the earth, whose names have not been written in the book of life from the foundation of the world, will be amazed when they see the beast, because it was and is not and is to come.

"This calls for a mind that has wisdom: the seven heads are seven mountains on which the woman is seated; also, they are seven kings, [10] of whom five have fallen, one is living, and the other has not yet come; and when he comes, he must remain only a little while. As for the beast that was and is not, it is an eighth but it belongs to the seven, and it goes to destruction. And the ten horns that you saw are ten kings who have not yet received a kingdom, but they are to receive authority as kings for one hour, together with the beast. These are united in yielding their power and authority to the beast; they will make war on the Lamb,[36] and the Lamb will conquer them, for he is Lord of lords and King of kings, and those with him are called and chosen and faithful."

And he said to me, "The waters that you saw, where the whore is seated, are peoples and multitudes and nations and languages. And the ten horns that you saw, they and the beast will hate the whore; they will make her desolate and naked; they will devour her flesh and burn her up with fire. For God has put it into their hearts to carry out his purpose by agreeing to give their kingdom to the beast, until the words of God will be fulfilled. The woman you saw is the great city that rules over the kings of the earth."

After this I saw another angel coming down from heaven, having great authority; and the earth was made bright with his splendor. He called out with a mighty voice,

---

[35]*Babylon the great:* a code name for Rome, taken from the name of a great oppressing city-empire in the Jewish *Bible*.

[36]*the Lamb:* Jesus Christ, the Lamb of God.

Revelation 17:1–18:5.

"Fallen, fallen is Babylon the great!
It has become a dwelling place of demons, a
haunt of every foul and hateful bird, a
haunt of every foul and hateful beast.
For all the nations have drunk of the wine of
the wrath of her fornication;
The kings of the earth have committed
fornication with her,
And the merchants of the earth have grown
rich from the power of her luxury."

Then I heard another voice from heaven
saying,

"Come out of her, my people,
So that you do not take part in her sins,
and so that you do not share in her plagues;
For her sins are heaped high as heaven,
and God has remembered her iniquities."

ORGANIZATION

The Twelve Apostles and their Mission

The apostles, twelve in number to suggest the twelve tribes of ancient Israel are fulfilled in the
early church, are named and commissioned here. Both the situation of Jesus (the restriction of
his mission to the Jews) and the later church (itinerant prophets and evangelists) are reflected.
The work of itinerant prophets and evangelists was important in the early spread of Christianity through Palestine and Syria.

Then Jesus summoned his twelve disciples and
gave them authority over unclean spirits, to cast
them out, and to cure every disease and every
sickness. These are the names of the twelve apostles: first, Simon, also known as Peter, and his
brother Andrew; James son of Zebedee, and his
brother John; Philip and Bartholomew; Thomas
and Matthew the tax collector; James son of
Alphaeus, and Thaddaeus; Simon the Cananaean,
and Judas Iscariot, the one who betrayed him.
[5] These twelve Jesus sent out with the following instructions: "Go nowhere among the
Gentiles, and enter no town of the Samaritans,
but go rather to the lost sheep of the house of
Israel. As you go, proclaim the good news, 'The
kingdom of heaven has come near.' Cure the
sick, raise the dead, cleanse the lepers, cast out
demons. You received without payment; give
without payment. Take no gold, or silver, or

copper in your belts, [10] no bag for your journey, or two tunics, or sandals, or a staff; for
laborers deserve their food. Whatever town or village you enter, find out who in it is worthy, and
stay there until you leave. As you enter the house,
greet it.[37] If the house is worthy, let your peace
come upon it; but if it is not worthy, let your
peace return to you. If anyone will not welcome
you or listen to your words, shake off the dust
from your feet as you leave that house or
town.[38] [15] Truly I tell you, it will be more tol-
erable for the land of Sodom and Gomorrah[39] on
the day of judgment than for that town.

---

[37] *greet it:* Give the inhabitants of the house a blessing, such as,
"Peace be to this house."
[38] *shake the dust from your feet:* an action symbolizing condemnation for rejecting the message.
[39] *Sodom and Gomorrah:* cities destroyed by God for their
wickedness (*Genesis* 19:1–28).

Matthew 10:1–15.

Matthew's Church Order

Matthew is the only gospel with comprehensive instructions for church life, one reason it became the most important gospel in the mainstream church. This passage begins with sayings on humility and forgiveness and ends with procedures for dealing with persistent sin among church members.

At that time the disciples came to Jesus and asked, "Who is the greatest in the kingdom of heaven?" He called a child, whom he put among them, and said, "Truly I tell you, unless you change and become like children, you will never enter the kingdom of heaven. Whoever becomes humble like this child is the greatest in the kingdom of heaven. [5] Whoever welcomes one such child in my name welcomes me.

"If any of you put a stumbling block before one of these little ones who believe in me, it would be better for you if a great millstone were fastened around your neck and you were drowned in the depth of the sea. Woe to the world because of stumbling blocks! Occasions for stumbling are bound to come, but woe to the one by whom the stumbling block comes! If your hand or your foot causes you to stumble, cut it off and throw it away; it is better for you to enter life maimed or lame than to have two hands or two feet and to be thrown into the eternal fire. And if your eye causes you to stumble, tear it out and throw it away; it is better for you to enter life with one eye than to have two eyes and to be thrown into the hell of fire.

[10] "Take care that you do not despise one of these little ones; for, I tell you, in heaven their angels[40] continually see the face of my Father in heaven.... [15] If another member of the church sins against you, go and point out the fault when the two of you are alone. If the member listens to you, you have regained that one. But if you are not listened to, take one or two others along with you, so that every word may be confirmed by the evidence of two or three witnesses. If the member refuses to listen to them, tell it to the church; and if the offender refuses to listen even to the church, let such a one be to you as a Gentile and a tax collector.[41] Truly I tell you, whatever you bind on earth will be bound in heaven, and whatever you loose on earth will be loosed in heaven.[42] Again, truly I tell you, if two of you agree on earth about anything you ask, it will be done for you by my Father in heaven. [20] For where two or three are gathered in my name, I am there among them."

Then Peter came and said to him, "Lord, if another member of the church sins against me, how often should I forgive? As many as seven times?" Jesus said to him, "Not seven times, but, I tell you, seventy-seven times."[43]

---

[40]*their angels:* their guardian angels.
[41]*a gentile and a tax collector:* that is, a person to be shunned.
[42]*bind...loose:* forbid an action as sinful or permit it, respectively.
[43]*seventy-seven times:* that is, forgive without limit.

Matthew 18:1–10, 15–22.

Peter as the Rock

Jesus here renames Simon as Peter, the rock on which the church is founded. Greek *Petros* (Peter) is similar to *petra* (rock). Jesus gives Peter "the keys of the kingdom of heaven." Catholicism sees this as establishing the papacy, the bishop of Rome, who is the successor of Peter and who holds universal power over the church by these "keys." Protestants, like the Eastern Orthodox churches, dispute this.

Now when Jesus came into the district of Caesarea Philippi, he asked his disciples, "Who do people say that the Son of Man is?" And they said, "Some say John the Baptist, but others Elijah, and still others Jeremiah or one of the prophets." [15] He said to them, "But who do you say that I am?" Simon Peter answered, "You are the Messiah, the Son of the living God." And Jesus answered him, "Blessed are you, Simon son of Jonah! For flesh and blood has not revealed this to you, but my Father in heaven. And I tell you, you are Peter, and on this rock I will build my church, and the gates of Hades will not prevail against it. I will give you the keys of the kingdom of heaven, and whatever you bind on earth will be bound in heaven, and whatever you loose on earth will be loosed in heaven."[44] [20] Then he sternly ordered the disciples not to tell anyone that he was the Messiah.[45]

---

[44] Compare *Matthew* 18:18 earlier, where the power to bind and loose is given to the apostles as a group.

[45] *not to tell anyone that he was the Messiah:* The reason for this "messianic secret" has been debated for almost a century, with little consensus among scholars.

Matthew 16:13–20.

Qualifications of Bishops and Deacons

Here we see the beginning of the threefold office in the church: bishop, presbyter (an elder or priest), and deacon. This has been the most common pattern of church office among most Christians even when these particular names are not used. The duties of these offices are not given, but we can infer their duties from the lists of qualifications. The emphasis on skill in family relationships comes in part from the setting of early Christian congregations, which met in believers' homes.

The saying is sure: whoever aspires to the office of bishop desires a noble task. Now a bishop must be above reproach, married only once, temperate, sensible, respectable, hospitable, an apt teacher, not a drunkard, not violent but gentle, not quarrelsome, and not a lover of money. He must manage his own household well, keeping his children submissive and respectful in every way—[5] for if someone does not know how to manage his own household, how can he take care of God's church? He must not be a recent convert, or he may be puffed up with conceit and fall into the condemnation of the devil. Moreover, he must be well thought of by

I Timothy 3:1–13.

outsiders, so that he may not fall into disgrace and the snare of the devil.

Deacons likewise must be serious, not double-tongued, not indulging in much wine, not greedy for money; they must hold fast to the mystery of the faith with a clear conscience. [10] And let them first be tested; then, if they prove themselves blameless, let them serve as deacons. Women[46] likewise must be serious, not slanderers, but temperate, faithful in all things.

Let deacons be married only once, and let them manage their children and their households well; for those who serve well as deacons gain a good standing for themselves and great boldness in the faith that is in Christ Jesus.

---

[46] *Women:* Historians debate whether this means "wives of deacons" or "women deacons." The majority of opinion now favors the latter.

Women in the Early Church

Christianity's traditional attitude toward women, which argues for some degree of equality and subjection at the same time, has its roots in the *New Testament*. In the first passage, Jesus shows that women should participate with men in hearing his teaching, although this requirement might conflict with women's traditional roles. In the second reading, Paul expresser a much more restrictive view of the roles of women in the church. The third reading has been influential in the Christian movement for equality. The last passage features the most patriarchal statement of the place of women in the church and has been influential in the history of Christianity.

[*Luke* 10:38] Now as they went on their way, he entered a certain village, where a woman named Martha welcomed him into her home. She had a sister named Mary, who sat at the Lord's feet and listened to what he was saying. [40] But Martha was distracted by her many tasks; so she came to him and asked, "Lord, do you not care that my sister has left me to do all the work by myself? Tell her then to help me." But the Lord answered her, "Martha, Martha, you are worried and distracted by many things; there is need of only one thing. Mary has chosen the better part, which will not be taken away from her."

[*I Corinthians* 11:2] I commend you because you remember me in everything and maintain the traditions just as I handed them on to you. But I want you to understand that Christ is the head of every man, and the husband is the head of his wife, and God is the head of Christ. Any man who prays or prophesies with something on his head disgraces his head, [5]

but any woman who prays or prophesies with her head unveiled disgraces her head—it is one and the same thing as having her head shaved. For if a woman will not veil herself, then she should cut off her hair; but if it is disgraceful for a woman to have her hair cut off or to be shaved, she should wear a veil. For a man ought not to have his head veiled, since he is the image and reflection of God; but woman is the reflection of man. Indeed, man was not made from woman, but woman from man. Neither was man created for the sake of woman, but woman for the sake of man. [10] For this reason a woman ought to have a symbol of authority on her head, because of the angels. Nevertheless, in the Lord woman is not independent of man or man independent of woman. For just as woman came from man, so man comes through woman; but all things come from God. Judge for yourselves: is it proper for a woman to pray to God with her head unveiled? Does not

---

Luke 10:38–42; *I Corinthians* 11:2–16; *Galatians* 3:25–28; *I Timothy* 2:8–15.

nature itself teach you that if a man wears long hair, it is degrading to him, [15] but if a woman has long hair, it is her glory? For her hair is given to her for a covering. But if anyone is disposed to be contentious—we have no such custom, nor do the churches of God.

[*Galatians* 3:25] Now that faith has come, we are no longer subject to a disciplinarian,[47] for in Christ Jesus you are all children of God through faith. As many of you as were baptized into Christ have clothed yourselves with Christ. [28] There is no longer Jew or Greek, there is no longer slave or free, there is no longer male and female; for all of you are one in Christ Jesus.

---

[47] *disciplinarian*: the Law of Moses.

[*I Timothy* 2:8] I desire, then, that in every place the men should pray, lifting up holy hands without anger or argument; also that the women should dress themselves modestly and decently in suitable clothing, not with their hair braided, or with gold, pearls, or expensive clothes, [10] but with good works, as is proper for women who profess reverence for God. Let a woman learn in silence with full submission. I permit no woman to teach or to have authority over a man; she is to keep silent. For Adam was formed first, then Eve; and Adam was not deceived, but the woman was deceived and became a transgressor. [15] Yet she will be saved through childbearing, provided they continue in faith and love and holiness, with modesty.

RITUAL

Baptism

At the conclusion of *Matthew*, Jesus commands that the triadic divine name—Father, Son, and Holy Spirit—be used in baptism of people from all the nations of the earth. In *Romans* 6, Paul explains that when Christians are baptized, they die with Christ to sin and begin to live holy lives for God. **Baptism**, a washing with, or immersion in, water for forgiveness and new spiritual life, became the foundation for the Christian vision of the moral life.

[*Matthew* 28:16] Now the eleven disciples went to Galilee, to the mountain to which Jesus had directed them. When they saw him, they worshiped him; but some doubted.[48] And Jesus came and said to them, "All authority in heaven and on earth has been given to me. Go therefore and make disciples of all nations, baptizing them in the name of the Father and of the Son and of the Holy Spirit, [20] and teaching them to obey everything that I have commanded you. And remember, I am with you always, to the end of the age."

---

[48] *some doubted:* Some among the eleven disciples still doubt the reality of Jesus' resurrection.

[*Romans* 6:1] What then are we to say? Should we continue in sin in order that grace may abound? By no means! How can we who died to sin go on living in it? Do you not know that all of us who have been baptized into Christ Jesus were baptized into his death? Therefore we have been buried with him by baptism into death, so that, just as Christ was raised from the dead by the glory of the Father, so we too might walk in newness of life.

[5] For if we have been united with him in a death like his, we will certainly be united with him in a resurrection like his. We know that our

---

Matthew 28:16–20; *Romans* 6:1–14.

old self was crucified with him so that the body of sin[49] might be destroyed, and we might no longer be enslaved to sin. For whoever has died is freed from sin. But if we have died with Christ, we believe that we will also live with him. We know that Christ, being raised from the dead, will never die again; death no longer has dominion over him. [10] The death he died, he died to sin, once for all; but the life he lives, he lives to God. So you also must consider yourselves dead to sin and alive to God in Christ Jesus. Therefore, do not let sin exercise dominion in your mortal bodies, to make you obey their passions. No longer present your members[50] to sin as instruments of wickedness, but present yourselves to God as those who have been brought from death to life, and present your members to God as instruments of righteousness. For sin will have no dominion over you, since you are not under law but under grace.

---

[49]*the body of sin:* the sinful self, not the physical body.

[50]*your members:* the different components of the human being.

The Eucharist

The Eucharist ("Thanksgiving [to God]") also goes by the names "Lord's Supper" and "Holy Communion." The first passage relates its institution during Jesus' last Passover meal, when he identified the bread and wine of the Passover with his body and blood. These were soon to be shed on the cross for the establishment of a "new covenant" of forgiveness and life. In the second passage, Jesus makes this identification in a symbolic way that has had a strong influence on how Christians view the Eucharist: His body and blood nourish one to eternal life.

[*Matthew* 21:17] On the first day of Unleavened Bread the disciples came to Jesus, saying, "Where do you want us to make the preparations for you to eat the Passover?" He said, "Go into the city to a certain man, and say to him, 'The Teacher says, My time is near; I will keep the Passover at your house with my disciples.'" So the disciples did as Jesus had directed them, and they prepared the Passover meal. . . .

While they were eating, Jesus took a loaf of bread,[51] and after blessing it he broke it, gave it to the disciples, and said, "Take, eat; this is my body." Then he took a cup, and after giving thanks he gave it to them, saying, "Drink from it, all of you; for this is my blood of the covenant, which is poured out for many for the forgiveness of sins. I tell you, I will never again drink of this fruit of the vine until that day when I drink it new with you in my Father's kingdom."

[*John* 6:25] When (the crowds) found him on the other side of the sea, they said to him, "Rabbi, when did you come here?" Jesus answered them, "Very truly, I tell you, you are looking for me, not because you saw signs, but because you ate your fill of the loaves. Do not work for the food that perishes, but for the food that endures for eternal life, which the Son of Man will give you. For it is on him that God the Father has set his seal." Then they said to him, "What must we do to perform the works of God?" Jesus answered them, "This is the work of God, that you believe in him whom he

---

[51]*a loaf of bread:* a large piece of unleavened bread.

Matthew 26:17–19, 26–29; *John* 6:25–40, 52–59.

has sent." [30] So they said to him, "What sign are you going to give us then, so that we may see it and believe you? What work are you performing? Our ancestors ate the manna in the wilderness; as it is written, 'He gave them bread from heaven to eat.'" Then Jesus said to them, "Very truly, I tell you, it was not Moses who gave you the bread from heaven, but it is my Father who gives you the true bread from heaven. For the bread of God is that which comes down from heaven and gives life to the world." They said to him, "Sir, give us this bread always."

[35] Jesus said to them, "I am the bread of life. Whoever comes to me will never be hungry, and whoever believes in me will never be thirsty. But I said to you that you have seen me and yet do not believe. Everything that the Father gives me will come to me, and anyone who comes to me I will never drive away; for I have come down from heaven, not to do my own will, but the will of him who sent me. And this is the will of him who sent me, that I should lose nothing of all that he has given me, but raise it up on the last day. [40] This is indeed the will of my Father, that all who see the Son and believe in him may have eternal life; and I will raise them up on the last day." . . .

The Jews then disputed among themselves, saying, "How can this man give us his flesh to eat?" So Jesus said to them, "Very truly, I tell you, unless you eat the flesh of the Son of Man and drink his blood, you have no life in you. Those who eat my flesh and drink my blood have eternal life, and I will raise them up on the last day; [55] for my flesh is true food and my blood is true drink. Those who eat my flesh and drink my blood abide in me, and I in them. Just as the living Father sent me, and I live because of the Father, so whoever eats me will live because of me. This is the bread that came down from heaven, not like that which your ancestors ate, and they died. But the one who eats this bread will live forever." He said these things while he was teaching in the synagogue at Capernaum.

Confession and Anointing

Those churches—Roman Catholic, Orthodox, and some Protestant—that practice the "anointing of the sick" appeal to this passage frequently. In the Roman Catholic Church, it is one of the seven sacraments, formerly called *extreme unction* or (more popularly) *last rites*. The anointing or ritual application with holy oil is connected here with confession of sin, prayer, and the use of the divine name.

Are any among you suffering? They should pray. Are any cheerful? They should sing songs of praise. Are any among you sick? They should call for the elders of the church and have them pray over them, anointing them with oil in the name of the Lord. [15] The prayer of faith will save the sick, and the Lord will raise them up; and anyone who has committed sins will be forgiven. Therefore confess your sins to one another, and pray for one another, so that you may be healed. The prayer of the righteous is powerful and effective. Elijah was a human being like us, and he prayed fervently that it might not rain, and for three years and six months it did not rain on the earth. Then he prayed again, and the heaven gave rain and the earth yielded its harvest.

James 5:13–18.

EARLY NONCANONICAL JESUS TRADITION

The *Gospel of Thomas*

The *Gospel of Thomas,* written sometime around 125–175 C.E., is a rich collection of sayings, many of which may go back to early stages of Christianity. Many scholars see an independent stream of tradition in these sayings, with at least a handful of sayings not found in the *New Testament* going back to Jesus himself. In fact, many scholars today refer to *Thomas* as the "Fifth Gospel." It never entered the canon of the mainstream ancient church but was likely among the scriptures of various Gnostic-Christian groups in the second and third centuries.[52]

These are the secret words which the living Jesus spoke, and Didymos Judas Thomas wrote down.

[1] And he said, "He who finds the meaning of these words will not taste death."

[2] Jesus said, "Let him who seeks not cease seeking until he finds, and when he finds, he shall be troubled, and when he is troubled, he will marvel, and he will rule over the All."

[13] Jesus said to his disciples, "Make a comparison and tell me whom I am like." Simon Peter said to him, "You are like a righteous angel." Matthew said to him, "You are like a wise man." Thomas said to him, "Master, my mouth will not be able to say what you are like." Jesus said, "I am not your master. Because you drank, you are drunk from the bubbling spring which I measured out." And he took him; he went aside. He spoke to him three words. When Thomas returned to his companions, they asked him, "What did Jesus say to you?" Thomas said to them, "If I tell you one of the words which he said to me, you will pick up stones; you will throw them at me. And fire will come out of the stones and consume you."

[14] Jesus said to them, "If you fast, you will bring sin upon yourselves and, if you pray, you will be condemned and, if you give alms, you will do evil to your spirits. And if you enter any land and wander through regions, if they receive you, whatever they set before you, eat it. Heal the sick among them. For that which goes into your mouth will not defile you, but that which comes out of your mouth is what will defile you."

[18] The disciples said to Jesus, "Tell us how end will occur." Jesus said, "Have you found the beginning that you search for the end?" In the place of the beginning, the end will be. Blessed is he who will stand at the beginning, and he will know the end, and he will not taste death."

[22] Jesus saw babies being suckled. He said to his disciples, "These babies who are being suckled are like those who enter the Kingdom." They said to him, "We are children, shall we enter the kingdom?" Jesus said to them, "When you make the two one, and when you make the inner as the outer and the outer as the inner and the upper as the lower, so that you will make the male and the female into a single one, so that the male will not be the male and the female [not] be female, when you make eyes in place of an eye, and a hand in place of a hand, and a foot in the place of a

---

[52]From *Documents for the Study of the Gospels*, ed. David R. Cartlidge and David L. Dungan. Copyright © 1994 Augsburg Fortress Press. Used by permission.

Gospel of Thomas 1–2, 13–14, 18, 22, 29, 49–50, 53, 83–84, 99, 101.

foot, (and) an image in place of an image, then shall you enter [the kingdom]."

[29] Jesus said, "If the flesh exists because of spirit, it is a miracle, but if spirit (exists) because of the body, it is a miracle of miracles. But I marvel at how this great wealth [of spirit] established itself in this poverty [of the body]."

[49] Jesus said, "Blessed are the solitary and the chosen, because you will find the Kingdom; because you come from it, you will again go there."

[50] Jesus said, "If they say to you, 'Where did you come from?' say to them, 'We come from the light, where the light came into being through itself. It stood and reveals itself in their image.' If they say to you, '[Who] are you?' say to them, 'We are his sons and we are chosen of the living Father.' If they ask you, 'What is the sign of you Father who is in you?' say to them, 'It is movement and repose.'"

[53] His disciples said to him, "Is circumcision profitable or not?" He said to them, "If it were profitable, their father would beget them circumcised from their mother. But the true circumcision in the Spirit has found complete usefulness."

[83] Jesus said, "The images are manifest to man, and the light in them is hidden in the image of the light of the Father. He will not reveal himself, and his image will be hidden by his light."

[84] Jesus said, "When you see your likeness, you rejoice. But when you see your images which came into being before you, which do not die nor manifest, how much will you bear!"

[99] The disciples said to him, "Your brothers and your mother are standing outside." He said to them, "Those here who do the will of my Father are my brothers and mother; they will enter the Kingdom of my Father. [101] He who does not hate his [father] and his mother in my way will not be able to be my [disciple], and he who does [not] love his father and his mother in my way, will not be able to be my [disciple], for my mother . . . , but [my] true [mother] gave me life."

GLOSSARY

apostle "one sent out" with the message of salvation, especially the twelve main disciples of Jesus.

authentic writings that most modern biblical scholars commonly accept as actually written by the persons whose names they bear.

baptism a washing with, or immersion in, water for forgiveness and new spiritual life.

Bible the scriptures of Christianity; the thirty-nine books of the *Old Testament* and the twenty-seven books of the *New Testament*.

gospel "good news"; at first, the oral message of "good news" about salvation in Jesus; later, the name given to the books that tell the story of the life, death, and resurrection of Jesus.

letters occasional writings of instruction addressed to churches, so called because they share many or all of the features of the common Greco-Roman letter; also called *epistles*.

New Testament the collection of twenty-seven books, mostly gospels and letters, written within the first 100 years of Christianity and constituting the unique, Christian portion of the Christian *Bible*.

Old Testament the name that early Christianity gave to the books of the Jewish *Bible*, which it incorporated into the Christian *Bible*.

pseudonymous writings that most modern biblical scholars do not commonly accept as authentic.

synoptic gospel books that can be "seen in one view" (*synopsis*) because of their parallel structure and content: *Matthew, Mark,* and *Luke*.

testament the relationship that God established with his people; also called *covenant*. Christians saw a "new covenant" established in Jesus, leading them to call their new scriptures the *New Testament*.

QUESTIONS FOR STUDY AND DISCUSSION

1. In what ways do the four gospels center on the suffering, death, and resurrection of Jesus?

2. Summarize in your own words the main points of the teaching of Jesus. How does the teaching of

Jesus relate to Jesus' life, death, and resurrection as portrayed in the gospels?

3. In what ways do the acts and teaching of Jesus, the *Acts of the Apostles,* and Paul's *Letters* show Christianity to be a "missionary religion"?

4. What degree of continuity and discontinuity can be discerned in these readings from the teaching of Jesus to the teaching of Paul?

5. Why is Jesus so harsh toward hypocrisy in the Sermon on the Mount? In what ways could

hypocrisy have been a problem in early Christianity?

6. In what ways does the *New Testament* better the condition of women and in what ways does it not? Discuss both the first century C.E. and today.

7. How does the *New Testament* promote love as the chief virtue in the religious life?

8. To what extent, if any, does the organization of the church and church offices reflect the distinctive teachings of the *New Testament?*

SCRIPTURES IN FILM

Of all major world religions, Christianity is the most fully, if not always the most artistically, represented in feature films. *The Gospel According to St. Matthew* (1964, unrated), directed by Pier Paolo Pasolini, is the most cinematically artistic. *The Passion of the Christ* (2004, rated R), directed by Mel Gibson, is a controversial, thought-provoking depiction of the death of Jesus. *The Gospel of John* (2003, rated PG-13) uses the English text of an entire gospel to tell the story of Jesus' ministry, death, and resurrection. For a taste of apocalyptic style in the *New Testament* and in modern film, see *The Seventh Seal* (1958, unrated), directed by Ingmar Bergman, one of the

classics of world cinema, and (interesting but with much less cinematic excellence) *The Seventh Sign* (1989, rated R), directed by Carl Schultz and starring Demi Moore. Also of interest to students of Christianity are *Jesus of Montreal* (1989, rated R), directed by Denys Arcand, in which a Montreal theater troupe puts on a controversial passion play and begins to experience suffering akin to Jesus', and *Babette's Feast* (1987, not rated but suitable for all audiences, in Danish with English subtitles), directed by Gabriel Axel, a story of frugality and prodigality that won the 1987 Academy Award for best foreign film.

SUGGESTIONS FOR FURTHER READING

PRIMARY READINGS

M. D. Coogan, ed., *The New Oxford Annotated Bible,* 3d ed. New York: Oxford University Press, 2001. The standard translation of the *Bible* in an edition with excellent introductions and notes.

The New English Bible. New York: Oxford and Cambridge University Presses, 1970. A translation known for its literary beauty.

D. Senior and J. Collins, eds., *The Catholic Study Bible,* 2d ed. New York: Oxford University Press, 2006. An excellent study *Bible* for both Roman Catholics and others who wish to know more about the contemporary Catholic understanding of the *Bible.* Contains the text of the *New American Bible,* similar to the *New Revised Standard Version.*

SECONDARY READINGS

R. E. Brown, *An Introduction to the New Testament.* New York: Doubleday, 1997. An outstanding survey of scholarship.

E. P. Sanders, *The Historical Figure of Jesus.* London: Penguin, 1993. Arguably one of the best recent introductions to the "historical Jesus."

E. Schüssler Fiorenza, *In Memory of Her,* rev. ed. Philadelphia: Fortress, 1995. A study of women in the *New Testament* from a strongly feminist perspective.

B. Witherington, *Women in the New Testament.* Cambridge: Cambridge University Press, 1985. A thorough and readable study of the status and role of women in the ministry of Jesus and in the early church from a moderate feminist perspective.

COMPANION WEBSITE

Visit the *Anthology of World Scriptures* companion website at **www.thomsonedu.com** for learning tools such as map explorations, flashcards of glossary terms,

learning objectives, chapter practice quizzes, links to other websites for learning and research, and chapter summaries in PowerPoint® format.

Islam

Private Reading of the *Qur'an*

Muhammed Mukti, a teacher of the *Qur'an*, reads the holy book in the Karanganyar City Mosque in Central Java, Indonesia, the nation of the world with the most Muslims. His *Qur'an* rests on a stand to keep it off the ground and thus treat it respectfully. (*Joanna Pinneo, Foreign Missions Board, SBC.*)

- In a city in Saudi Arabia, a boy who is auspiciously four years, four months, and four days old celebrates a special event. He goes to the *Qur'an* school to recite formally his first verse of the *Qur'an*. The verse is written in honey on a small slate. When the boy finishes practicing the verse, he recites it formally and the honey is dissolved in water. The boy then drinks the water, which has been sweetened by the holy words of the *Qur'an*. The words he has spoken become a part of him, and he returns home with his family to a celebration.

- In a village near Khartoum, Sudan, a large crowd of Muslims has gathered to hear perhaps the most famous healer in Africa, Sheik Abdel Azziz ibn Ali. This Sudanese cleric soon emerges to stand on a platform and sing the *Qur'an*. As his chant grows in intensity, the crowd responds in various emotional ways, and some people loudly report that they have now been cured of chronic diseases. The sheik defends himself against occasional charges of charlatanism by saying, "All I do is recite the *Qur'an*."

- In Philadelphia, Pennsylvania, a recently converted Muslim woman studies the *Qur'an* as she rides a bus to her job. She looks first at the mostly unfamiliar Arabic original on the right-hand pages, then reads carefully the English interpretation of it on the left-hand pages, and finally looks back at the Arabic. When she leaves the bus, she feels inspired and directed to serve God during that day.

INTRODUCTION

Islam confesses that "there is no God but God" and that "Muhammad is God's prophet" who has come to teach and spread the way of submission and obedience to the one God. Muslims believe that the angel Gabriel revealed the *Qur'an* to Muhammad over an approximately twenty-year period, from his call to be a prophet until his death in 632 C.E. The words of the *Qur'an* were *given to* Muhammad, not *written by* him. Its only author is God, and every word comes from God. The *Qur'an* is the basic authority for Islamic religious life, Islam's continuing guide during 1,400 years of history. As W. C. Smith observed, the *Qur'an* "has fired the imagination, and inspired the poetry, and formulated the inhibitions, and guided the ecstasies, and teased the intellects, and ordered the family relations and the legal chicaneries, and nurtured the piety, of hundreds of millions of people in widely diverse climes and over a series of radically divergent centuries."[1] Therefore, one who understands the *Qur'an* and its use has been well introduced to Islam.

Name

Qur'an is Arabic for "recitation, reading." These two meanings suggest the twin aspects of oral and written revelation, both of them important in understanding the *Qur'an* and its place in Islam. (The two meanings are closer than what we might imagine because "reading" is typically out loud.) God gave the message

---

[1]W. C. Smith, "The Study of Religion and the Study of the Bible," in M. Levering, ed., *Rethinking Scripture: Essays from a Comparative Perspective* (Albany: State University of New York Press, 1989), p. 21.

to Muhammad, and Muhammad spoke it to his followers. Indeed, the oral meaning predominates in the *Qur'an* itself, where the word *Qur'an* refers primarily to oral revelations, not to the written book of human history that we know as the *Qur'an*. But the oral revelations in turn were based on the heavenly written *Qur'an*, the "well-preserved tablet" and the "mother of the Book." They began to be recorded in writing during Muhammad's lifetime and were collected into a book, the *Qur'an*, soon after his death. So the movement of revelation, as Muslims would explain it, goes from the eternal, heavenly *Qur'an*, to Gabriel's oral revelation of this *Qur'an* to Muhammad, then orally from Muhammad to his followers, and finally from his followers to the written *Qur'an*. In each stage, the *Qur'an* has a strong oral dimension in its formal recitation called **tilawa** [tee-LAH-wuh] and in always vocalized informal reading. The circle of revelation is complete and perfect: The heavenly *Qur'an* and the *Qur'an* on earth are identical.

The usual English spelling of the Muslim scripture is *Qur'an*. Often, the older spelling *Koran* is found, especially in journalism. More recent scholarship prefers the newer spelling as closer to the Arabic pronunciation. *Qur'an* is pronounced "kuhr-AHN." Between the two syllables is a glottal stop that is stronger in Arabic than the similar sound that speakers of English naturally make when they pronounce the beginning of the second syllable. The apostrophe between the syllables reminds us of this glottal stop.

Overview of Structure

The *Qur'an*, which is approximately the length of the *New Testament,* is divided into 114 chapters called **surahs** [SOO-rahs]. The first surah, *Fatihah* [fah-TEE-huh] ("Opening"), is a preface to the book. Beginning with Surah 2, these chapters are organized by approximate length, from longest to shortest. This means that a new reader of the *Qur'an* first encounters long chapters ranging over many unrelated topics. The *Qur'an* generally reverses the order in which Muhammad revealed the surahs to his followers. The long, more prosaic surahs that begin the *Qur'an* typically come from the last part of Muhammad's prophetic career, and the shorter, more poetic surahs come from the first part. To Muslims, this sequence is of no importance because the sacredness and authority of the text derive from its origin, not from its order. To non-Muslim readers, however, it presents a challenge that often leads them to lay aside the *Qur'an* out of sheer puzzlement. Some English translations try to make the *Qur'an* more intelligible to non-Muslim readers by rearranging the chapters into an order that more or less follows Muhammad's life.

The internal structure of each surah is as follows (see Table 12.1).

• A title heads the chapter. Most titles are short, and some are drawn from the opening words of the chapter. More typically, the title is taken from one isolated and sometimes metaphoric word in the chapter, such as "The Cave" (18) or "Light" (24). A few surahs are titled after the Arabic letter or letters with which they begin, as is Surah 50. Only occasionally does the title of a surah indicate its main topic, so a new reader of the *Qur'an* cannot depend on chapter titles as a guide to content.

TABLE 12.1 Structure of a Typical Surah

THE SAND DUNES _____ Title	
46:1–11 _____ Number	
(Mecca) _____ Origin	
In the Name of God, the Compassionate, the Merciful _____ *Bismillah*	
Ha-mim. This Book is revealed by God, the Mighty One, the Wise One.	
It was to manifest the Truth that We created the heavens and _____ Ayah1	
the earth and all that lies between them; We created them to last for an appointed term;	
Yet the unbelievers give no heed to our warning. _____ Ayah2	

- A number follows the title. These labels provide ease of reference.

- The *Qur'an* then indicates whether the chapter was given to Muhammad while he was in Mecca or Medina. The Meccan chapters tend to be found in the second half of the *Qur'an*, and the Medinan chapters in the first half. Many passages are of mixed origin, containing material from both stages of the Prophet's career. This is recognized by modern non-Muslim scholars and by Muslim traditionalists.

- Next comes the **Bismillah** [biss-MILL-uh], which in full runs *Bismillah al-Rahman, al-Rahim.* It is usually translated "In the name of God, the Compassionate, the Merciful"; the translation by Abdel Haleem renders the *Bismillah* in a way that preserves the close relationship of *al-Rahman* and *al-Rahim*: "the Lord of Mercy, the Giver of Mercy." This resonant Arabic formula, both an invocation of God and a blessing of God, is always spoken before reading a passage as well as at many other times in a Muslim's life. It likely goes back to the time of Muhammad, but whether it was used in his time to mark the head of a chapter is less certain.

- Each chapter is further divided into **ayahs** [EYE-yuhs], numbered verses. These divisions were added after Muhammad's death for ease in locating passages, especially in the longer chapters. The verses vary greatly in length; one ayah can be as long as several sentences or as short as a few words. *Ayah* literally means "sign," and this word is found many times in the *Qur'an* to denote the signs of nature and history that point to the reality and power of the one God.

- The body of the chapters usually has one or more topics. Generally, the longer a chapter is, the more numerous and varied are the topics. The wording of the chapters presents the speech of God. God speaks in a majestic "We/Us/Our," capitalized in translations. "You" in the singular refers to Muhammad; at other times, in the plural, "you" refers to Muhammad's audience. Many utterances begin with "Say," and what follows this word is presented as God's revelation to Muhammad's audience. Passages that narrate biblical incidents are briefly recounted, with the emphasis on their teaching, not on the story itself.

- Just as they have a variety of topics, the chapters also have a variety of endings. Often, there is a plea to Muhammad to persist in his calling, a summons for Muslims to persevere, or a promise of reward or punishment in the next life.

Contemporary Use

The *Qur'an* has always been the ultimate authority in Islam. Still, from the first generations of Islam arose a second body of authority, first in oral form and then written. This second authority is the **hadith,** narrative "traditions" about Muhammad and the first generation of Muslims. These traditions were meant to form a historical context by which the *Qur'an* could be interpreted, and they deal especially with the life of Muhammad in a way that the *Qur'an* does not. It was almost inevitable that these *hadith* should arise. The *Qur'an,* with its almost complete lack of any historical structure, needs such a framework by which its difficulties, seeming inconsistencies, and other interpretive issues can be ironed out. Qur'anic interpretation has been, from the very first, an effort to understand and apply to Muslim life the teachings given through Muhammad (the *Qur'an*) in the context of the traditions (the *hadith*). The principle arose quickly that every interpretation of the *Qur'an* must have a tradition to back it up. The collection and preservation of these traditions became a major task of religious scholarship in Islam.

The Sunni and Shi'a branches of Islam have the same *Qur'an* but differ in their approach to the *hadith*. Shi'ites believe that the split between these two groups goes back to the period shortly after the death of Muhammad, when a few of the faithful accepted Ali, Muhammad's cousin, as his successor, but most went with his general Abu Bakr, then with Umar and Uthman. Most Shi'ites believe that those *hadith* passed on through the correct followers of Ali are much more trustworthy than the other *hadith,* some of which are rejected. This rejection has led to some of the differences between Sunni and Shi'ite legal practices, for example, temporary marriages contracted for a few days or months, which are accepted by most Shi'ites.

Soon after the gathering of the *hadith,* commentary became the lens through which the *Qur'an* was viewed. This commentary, called **tafsir** [TAHF-sear], became an important branch of Muslim theology. Tafsir combined analysis of both the *Qur'an* and the relevant *hadith* to produce a detailed and often massive body of literature. In this period of interpretation, which lasted until the nineteenth century, all higher study of the *Qur'an* was indirect; the scripture was read only through the commentaries, and the commentaries specified its meaning. Only in the mosques and among the common people was the *Qur'an* allowed to speak more or less for itself.

In recent times, a period of modernism challenged the monopoly of the commentaries. A movement arose to revive the most ancient forms of Islam and reform it by ending the authority of the medieval commentators. Some historical methods new to Islam but well known in Europe were introduced to attempt to recover the original meaning of the *Qur'an*. For example, the Indian Muslim scholar M. Azad argued that it is necessary to study the life and language of Arabia at the time of Muhammad to understand what the *Qur'an* meant to its original hearers and readers. D. Rahbar, in his *The God of Justice* (1960), argued that it is more important to compare Qur'anic passages against each other in determining their meaning than to rely on hadith and later commentators. This liberalizing movement was generally confined to the more Westernized upper classes. Since about 1980, a tide of conservatism in the Muslim world, led by the increasingly influential Shi'ite branch of Islam, has effectively limited the movement to modernize the interpretation of the *Qur'an.*

Among ordinary Muslims during most of Islamic history, the esteem and reverence shown to the *Qur'an* are evidenced in everyday actions. To use the Muslim scripture in any way, one must first ritually wash. Although Muslims often sit on the floor to study the *Qur'an*, especially in a mosque, the *Qur'an* itself is never allowed to touch the floor but rests on a short bookstand. A person who carries several books must always place the *Qur'an* on top. Pious Muslims read portions of it every day, and they read the entire *Qur'an* during Ramadan, guided by special division marks in the Arabic text. Large portions of it are committed to memory, and it is considered a mark of special piety to memorize the entire *Qur'an*.

The *Qur'an* is also used for purposes of magic, especially to ward off evil curses by humans and **jinn,** spirits who inhabit the world and who can have a supernatural influence, most often evil, on people. Its last two chapters are plainly countermagical, designed to keep away evil supernatural powers. Verses from other chapters are also copied and used as amulets to bring blessing and ward off evil.

Historical Origin and Development

The first stage of the *Qur'an* was its reception as revelation by Muhammad. A few times, he heard the audible voice of the angel Gabriel, but usually, he received the revelation while in a trance or asleep. Muslims believe that whatever the mode of revelation, Muhammad received the *Qur'an* from God and that God is its only author. European scholars in the nineteenth century searched for literary sources of the *Qur'an* on the assumption that Muhammad drew on other sources and wrote the *Qur'an* himself. But more recent non-Muslim scholarship recognizes that beyond the question of sources, the *Qur'an* has its main origin in the internal experience of Muhammad. The question of whether his experience has a divine origin is one that historians and scholars of religion cannot answer.

The next stage in the development of the *Qur'an* was its oral transmission in prophetic utterances to Muhammad's followers. Muhammad spoke to them the words that Gabriel commanded him to speak, which are often introduced in the *Qur'an* by the imperative "Say." His disciples committed his sayings to memory and spoke them to others, and these early "reciters" of the *Qur'an* played an important part in its survival and transmission. But as a *hadith* narrates, Muhammad's followers also wrote them down at his command on "pieces of paper, stones, palm-leaves, shoulder-blade bones and ribs, and bits of leather"—in other words, on any material at hand.

The *Qur'an* in its final form bears witness to some difficulties in composition: substitution of verses, new revelations that cancel out older ones, and long periods between revelations. A *hadith* even speaks of "Satanic verses" in which Muhammad initially was led by Satan to give a revelation that favored some form of polytheism (the "daughters of Allah"). He later rejected them in favor of the strict monotheism that is the essential element of Islam.

After Muhammad's death in 632 and the Battle of Yamamah in 633, it was feared that knowledge of the *Qur'an* (still mostly recited orally) might die out. The process of recording all of it in writing began under the first caliph, Umar. But different versions arose, with consequent disputes over which *Qur'an* was better. To end these troubles, Caliph Uthman (r. 644–656) commissioned respected and learned men to produce a single recognized version using the best manuscripts and the memories of those with recognized knowledge of the *Qur'an*. This version became the only authorized text recognized by the Muslim community, believed to be a true copy of the "Mother of the Book." Other texts were systematically collected and destroyed. Today almost all Muslims view the Uthmanic edition as identical to the *Qur'an* of Muhammad. No attempt to go behind this authorized version has been made, for it would be considered blasphemy to suggest that this is not the exact *Qur'an* that God gave originally to Muhammad.

The Arabic language in which the *Qur'an* is written is an important part of its origin and continuing appeal. It is often emphasized that Muhammad gave his followers an "Arabic *Qur'an*." Just as Jews and Christians had scriptures in their own languages, Arabs have an Arabic book. Muslims view the Arabic style of the *Qur'an*, especially its poetry, as matchless. Indeed, it is a sin to imitate its style or content in any way. Moreover, the *Qur'an* itself is not considered translatable into other languages. Although Muslims and non-Muslims alike have translated the *Qur'an* into many languages, which are typically put interlinearly or on facing pages with the Arabic text, the faithful commonly argue that these translations are only an approximation of the *Qur'an*, a rough indication of its content. They are not the scripture itself, which can exist only in Arabic. Even believers who do not learn Arabic memorize formulas and passages from the *Qur'an* in Arabic. Arabic is thus, at least in a basic way, the common language of Muslims throughout the world, and the *Qur'an* contributes to the unity of the Muslim community.

HISTORY

The Call of Muhammad

In traditional Muslim understanding, Surah 96 is the story of Muhammad's call vision. A *hadith* relates that while Muhammad was meditating in a cave, an angel appeared to him and commanded him to recite (iqra', the imperative form of *Qur'an*). Muhammad at first refused, but the angel choked and threatened him into submission. This story is told in the first five verses; the rest are said to come from a later time. Most modern scholars identify "The Star," Surah 53, as Muhammad's call vision. It is related as a challenge to those who "question what he sees." Muhammad's vision is inspired and authoritative because it is "received from one who is powerful and mighty." Surah 53 tells of two visions, and Islamic tradition *(hadith)* says that these are the only two times when Muhammad actually saw Gabriel.[2]

[96, Mecca]

Recite in the name of your Lord who created— created man from clots of blood. Recite! Your Lord is the Most Bountiful One, who by the pen[3] [5] taught man what he did not know.

[2]Unless otherwise noted, all selections are taken from N. J. Dawood, The *Koran* (London:1990). Copyright © N. J. Dawood, 1956, 1959, 1966, 1968, 1974, 1990. Reproduced by permission of Penguin Books Ltd.

[3]*by the pen*: the coming of revelation and its writing down into what was to become the *Qur'an*.

Qur'an 96:1–19; 53:1–18.

#2

Indeed, man transgresses in thinking himself his own master: for to your Lord all things return.

Observe the man who rebukes Our servant when he prays. [10] Think: does he follow the right guidance or enjoin true piety? Think: if he denies the Truth and gives no heed, does he not know that God observes all things? [15] No. Let him desist, or We will drag him by the forelock, his lying, sinful forelock. Then let him call his helpmates. We, in Our turn, will call the guards of Hell. No, never obey him. Prostrate yourself and come nearer.

[53:1–18, Mecca] By the declining star, your compatriot[4] is not in error, nor is he deceived He does not speak out of his own fancy. This is an inspired revelation. [5] He is taught by one who is powerful and mighty.

He stood on the uppermost horizon; then, drawing near, he came down within two bows' length or even closer, [10] and revealed to his servant that which he revealed. His[5] own heart did not deny his vision. How can you, then, question what he sees?

He beheld him once again at the sidra tree, beyond which no one may pass.[6] (Near it is the Garden of Repose.) [15] When that tree was covered with what covered it, his eyes did not wander, nor did they turn aside: for he saw some of his Lord's greatest signs.

---

[4]*your compatriot:* Muhammad, who was living among his tribe, the Quraysh, at the time of this surah.

[5]*His:* "His" and "he" now refer to Muhammad.
[6]*sidra tree, Garden of Repose:* The sidra tree is at the border of the highest heaven; the Garden of Repose lies in the presence of God. This second vision is of heaven, which explains why Muhammad saw there "some of his Lord's greatest signs."

The Mission of Muhammad

Surah 11 describes the tasks of Muhammad as God's prophet. He is a messenger who is to proclaim, "Serve none but God." Submission (islam) to God is the only way to serve him faithfully. Muhammad also warns of the terrors of hell that await those who refuse his message and promises rich rewards to those who obey. Muhammad brings no signs, treasures, or angels; his message itself is the miracle. In the face of opposition, Muhammad received the encouragement recorded in Surah 93. It offers a glimpse into his personal experience: He was an orphan, in error, and poor, from which God delivered him. The surah ends with a call for Muhammad to be faithful to his mission. "You" throughout this passage is Muhammad.

[11:1–16, Mecca] *Alif lam ra'.* This Book, whose verses are perfected and made plain, is a revelation from Him who is wise and all-knowing.

Serve none but God. I am sent to you from Him to warn you and to give you good tidings.

Seek forgiveness of your Lord and turn to Him in repentance. A goodly provision He will make for you till an appointed day, and will bestow His grace on those that have merit. But if you give no heed, then beware the torment of a fateful day. To God you shall all return. He has power over all things.

[5] They cover up their breasts to conceal their thoughts from Him. But when they put on their garments, does He not know what they hide and what they reveal? He knows their inmost thoughts. There is not a creature on the earth but God provides its sustenance. He knows its dwelling and its resting-place. All is recorded in a glorious book. Throned above the

---

Qur'an 11:1–16; 93.

#6 waters, He made the heavens and the earth in six days, to find out which of you shall best acquit himself.

#4 [10] When you[7] say: "After death you shall be raised to life," the unbelievers declare: "It is but plain sorcery." And if We put off their punishment till an appointed time, they ask: "Why is it delayed?" On the day it overtakes them, #^ they shall not be immune from it. The terrors at which they scoffed will encompass them.

If We show man Our mercy and then withhold it from him, he yields to despair and becomes ungrateful. And if after adversity We let him taste good fortune, he says: "Gone are my sorrows from me," and grows jubilant and boastful. Not so the steadfast who do good works. Forgiveness and a rich reward await them.

[15] You may chance to omit a part of what is revealed to you and be distressed because they say: "Why has no treasure been sent to him? Why

has no angel come with him?" But you are only to give warning. God is the guardian of all things. If they say: "He has invented it himself," say to them: "Produce ten invented chapters like it.[8] Call on whom you will among your idols, if what you say be true. But if they fail you, know that it is revealed with God's knowledge, and that there is no god but Him. Will you then accept Islam?"

[93, Mecca] By the light of day, and by the dark of night, your Lord has not forsaken you, nor does He abhor you.

The life to come holds a richer prize for you than this present life. [5] You shall be gratified with what your Lord will give you. Did He not find you an orphan and give you shelter? Did He not find you in error and guide you? Did He not find you poor and enrich you? [10] Therefore do not wrong the orphan, nor chide away the beggar. But proclaim the goodness of your Lord.

---

[7] *you:* Muhammad.

[8] *Produce ten ... like it:* This type of response by Muhammad to his opponents is called the **challenge verses.**

Opposition to Muhammad

Muhammad experienced strong opposition to his ministry, especially in the Meccan phase. The first selection, from Surah 52, catalogs many of the charges of Muhammad's Meccan opponents, who are referred to as "they." Surah 63, the second selection, deals with another type of opposition to Muhammad, from "hypocrites" who seemingly acknowledged Muhammad and accepted Islam but only for their own advantage. These hypocrites are residents of Medina, where Muhammad was widely followed as a religious and political leader.

[52:30, Mecca] Do they say: "He is only a poet: we are waiting for some misfortune to befall him"? Say: "Wait if you will; I too am waiting." Does their reason prompt them to say this? Or is it merely that they are wicked men?

Do they say: "He has invented it[9] himself"? Indeed, they have no faith. Let them produce a scripture like it, if what they say be true!

[35] Were they created out of the void? Or were they their own creators? Did *they* create the heavens and the earth? Surely they have no faith! Do they hold the treasures of your Lord, or have control over them? Have they a ladder

---

[9] *it:* Muhammad's revelation, on the way to becoming the written *Qur'an.*

Qur'an 52:30–49; 63.

by means of which they overhear Him? Let their eavesdropper bring a positive proof!

Is He to have daughters and you sons?[10]

[40] Are you demanding payment of them, that they should fear to be weighed down with debts? Have they knowledge of what is hidden? Can they write it down? Are they seeking to ruin you? They themselves shall be ruined. Have they a god other than God? Exalted be he above their idols! If they saw a part of heaven falling down, they would still say: "It is but a mass of clouds."

[45] Let them be, until they face the day when they shall stand dumbfounded; the day when their designs will avail them nothing and none will help them. And besides this a punishment awaits the wrongdoers, though most of them do not know it. Therefore, wait the judgment of your Lord: We are watching over you. Give glory to your Lord when you awaken, in the night-time praise Him, and at the setting of the stars.

[63, Medina] When the hypocrites come to you they say: "We bear witness that you are God's apostle." God knows that you are indeed His apostle; and God bears witness that the hypocrites are lying. They use their faith as a disguise, and debar others from the path of God. Evil is

what they do. They believed and then renounced their faith: their hearts are sealed, so that they are devoid of understanding.

When you see them, their good looks please you; and when they speak, you listen to what they say. Yet they are like propped-up beams of timber. Every shout they hear they take to be against them. *They* are the enemy. Guard yourself against them. God confound them! How perverse they are!

[5] When it is said to them: "Come, God's apostle will beg forgiveness for you," they turn their heads and you see them go away in scorn. It is the same whether or not you ask forgiveness for them: God will not forgive them. God does not guide the evil-doers.

It is they who say: "Give nothing to those that follow God's apostle until they have deserted him." God's are the treasures of heaven and earth: but the hypocrites cannot understand. They say: "If we return to Medinah, the strong will soon drive out the weak." But strength belongs to God and to His apostle and to the faithful: yet the hypocrites do not know it.

Believers, let neither your riches nor your children beguile you from God's remembrance. Those that forget Him shall forfeit all. [10] Give of that which We have given you before death befalls you and you say: "Reprieve me, Lord, awhile, that I may give in charity and be among the righteous." But God reprieves no soul when its term expires. God has knowledge of all your actions.

---

[10]*daughters and ... sons:* The "daughters of God" were the female deities in the pre-Islamic religions of the Arabs. This charge rests on the higher value that Arabs put on sons than on daughters.

The Night Journey

Surah 17 is entitled "The Night Journey," although only the first two verses deal with this topic. This chapter is also called "The Children of Israel" for one of its later themes. The angel Gabriel took Muhammad to Jerusalem, and most Muslim interpreters and ordinary believers hold that he ascended there to heaven for a brief time. Muhammad's journey to Jerusalem is an important reason for later Islam's viewing it as the third holiest city in the world, after Mecca and Medina.

Qur'an 17:1–2.

Glory be to Him who made His servant go by night from the Sacred Temple[11] to the farther Temple[12] whose surroundings We[13] have blessed, that We might show him some of Our signs. He alone hears all and observes all.

The Flight to Medina

When he was driven out of Mecca by his opponents, Muhammad hid in a cave for three days with his lone companion, Abu Bakr. God's deliverance of the Prophet from this threat to his life made a deep impression on him, giving him a sense of confidence that would transform his life.

If you[14] do not help him,[15] God will help him as He helped him when he was driven out by the unbelievers with one other. In the cave he said to his companion: "Do not despair, God is with us." God caused His tranquillity to descend upon him and sent to his aid invisible warriors, so that he routed the unbelievers and exalted the Word of God. God is mighty and wise.

[14]*you:* the citizens of Medina.
[15]*him:* Muhammad.

Qur'an 9:40.

The Wives of Muhammad

The most extensive view of the personal life of Muhammad that the *Qur'an* offers is of his marriages during the Medinan period. Earlier, in Mecca, the Prophet was married only to Kadijah, of whom the *Qur'an* does not speak. In Medina, Muhammad had many wives and concubines, which became controversial.

Prophet, say to your wives: "If you seek this life and all its finery, come, I will make provision for you and release you honorably. But if you seek God and His apostle and the abode of the hereafter, know that God has prepared a rich reward for those of you who do good works."

[30] Wives of the Prophet! Those of you who commit a proven sin shall be doubly punished. That is easy enough for God. But those of you who obey God and His apostle and do good works shall be doubly rewarded; for them We have made a generous provision. # 4

Wives of the Prophet, you are not like other women. If you fear God, do not be too complacent in your speech, lest the lecherous-hearted should lust after you. Show discretion in what

Qur'an 33:28–33, 37–40, 48–49.

you say. Stay in your homes and do not display your finery as women used to do in the days of ignorance.[16] Attend to your prayers, give alms and obey God and His apostle....

[37] You said to the man[17] whom God and yourself have favored: "Keep your wife and have fear of God." You sought to hide in your heart what God was to reveal. You were afraid of man, although it would have been more proper to fear God. And when Zayd divorced his wife, We gave her to you in marriage, so that it should become legitimate for true believers to wed the wives of their adopted sons if they divorced them. God's will must needs be done. No blame shall be attached to the Prophet for doing what is sanctioned for him by God. Such was the way of

God with the prophets who passed away before him; who fulfilled the mission with which God had charged them, fearing God and fearing none besides Him. Sufficient is God's reckoning.

[40] Muhammad is the father of no man among you.[18] He is the Apostle of God and the Seal of the Prophets. God has knowledge of all things....

[48] Prophet, We have made lawful to you the wives to whom you have granted dowries and the slave-girls whom God has given you as booty; the daughters of your paternal and maternal uncles and of your paternal and maternal aunts who fled with you; and any believing woman who gives herself to the Prophet and whom the Prophet wishes to take in marriage.[19] This privilege is yours alone, being granted to no other believer.

---

[16]*the days of ignorance:* pre-Islamic times.
[17]*the man:* Zayd, an adopted son of Muhammad, was unhappily married to Zainab. He wanted to divorce her, but Muhammad advised him not to. God wished otherwise and here tells Muhammad to allow the divorce and marry Zainab himself. This provides justification in Islam for marriage to divorced wives of adopted sons.

[18]The Prophet had many wives but no male heirs, seen here as God's will.
[19]The *Qur'an* elsewhere limits men to four wives at any one time.

The Death of Muhammad

The Qur'an does not narrate the death of Muhammad but raises it as an issue. Muhammad is indeed mortal, as mortal as any other man. This Medinan passage serves to reinforce the *Qur'an's* view of Muhammad as a purely human prophet.

No man before you[20] have We made immortal. If you yourself are doomed to die, will they live for ever? Every soul shall taste death. We will prove you all with good and evil. To Us you shall return.

When the unbelievers see you, they scoff at you, saying: "Is this the man who fulminates against your gods?" And they deny all mention of the Merciful. Impatience is the very stuff man is made of. You shall before long see My signs; you need not ask Me to hasten them.

---

[20]*you:* In this passage, "you" is Muhammad.

Qur'an 21:34–36.

TEACHING

God's Absolute Oneness

One of the main themes of the Qur'an is the absolute oneness of God. The first passage is given against jinn (spirits) being considered divine and against the notion of God having sons and daughters. The wording of the short Surah 112, entitled "Oneness," seems to suggest that it is specifically anti-Christian, against the Christian belief that God the Father begot the Son and that the two are equal in being and power. Traditional Muslim interpretation holds it to be both anti-Christian and anti-Arab polytheism. An important *hadith* relates that this chapter, despite being one of the shortest in the *Qur'an,* is equal in value to two-thirds of the *Qur'an.*

[6:100–103 Mecca] They regard the jinn as God's equals, though He Himself created them, and in their ignorance ascribe to Him sons and daughters. Glory to Him! Exalted be He above their imputations! He is the Creator of the heavens and the earth. How should He have a son when He had no consort?[21] He created all things and has knowledge of all things.

Such is God, your Lord. There is no god but Him, the Creator of all things. Therefore serve Him. He is the Guardian of all things. No mortal eyes can see Him, though He sees all eyes. He is benevolent and all-knowing.

[112, Mecca] Say: "God is One, the Eternal God. He begot none, nor was He begotten. None is equal to him."

---

[21]*have a son:* The singular noun *son* might indicate that this is an anti-Christian polemic, countering the Christian belief in Jesus as the Son of God.

Qur'an 6:100–103; 112.

God's Names

"God has the most excellent names," the *Qur'an* affirms (7:17). Two of these names, "compassionate" and "merciful," occur in every *Bismillah* and dozens of times in the chapters proper. God has ninety-nine most gracious names in the *Qur'an,* as fixed by traditional interpretation (see the *hadith* "On God" on page 323). The first thirteen are listed here, from "Compassionate" to "Modeller." These names are used in Muslim devotion to express the greatness of God in a very poetic and rhythmic fashion.

He is God, besides whom there is no other deity. He knows the unknown and the manifest. He is the Compassionate, the Merciful.

He is God, besides whom there is no other deity. He is the Sovereign Lord, the Holy One, the Giver of Peace, the Keeper of Faith; the Guardian, the Mighty One, the All-powerful, the Most High! Exalted be God above their idols!

He is God, the Creator, the Originator, the Modeller. His are the most gracious names. All that is in heaven and earth gives glory to Him. He is the Mighty, the Wise One.

Qur'an 59:22–24.

God's Power

The first selection sings the praise of God the Creator. It ends, like many other teachings in the *Qur'an,* on a moral note: The creation shows God's truth and the straight (correct) path of life. Creation is here connected to revelation. The second selection ties the power of God in creation firmly to Muhammad's call for repentance and belief.

[24:41] Do you not see how God is praised by those in heaven and those on earth? The very birds praise Him as they wing their flight. He notes the prayers and praises of all His creatures, and has knowledge of all their actions. It is God who has sovereignty over the heavens and the earth. To Him shall all things return.

Do you not see how God drives the clouds, then gathers and piles them up in masses which pour down torrents of rain? From heaven's mountains He sends down the hail, pelting with it whom He will and turning it away from whom He pleases. The flash of His lightning almost snatches off men's eyes. He makes the night succeed the day; surely in this there is a lesson for clear-sighted men.

[45] God created every beast from water. Some creep upon their bellies, others walk on two legs, and others yet on four. God creates what He pleases. He has power over all things.

We have sent down revelations demonstrating the Truth. God guides whom He will to a straight path.

[6:95, Mecca] It is God who splits the seed and the fruit-stone. He brings forth the living from the dead, and the dead from the living. Such is God. How then can you turn away?

He kindles the light of dawn. He has ordained the night for rest and the sun and the moon for reckoning. Such is the ordinance of the Mighty One, the All-knowing. He has created for you the stars, so that they may guide you in the darkness of land and sea. We have made plain Our revelations to men of sense. He created you from one being and furnished you with a dwelling and a resting-place. We have made plain Our revelations to men of understanding.

He sends down water from the sky, and with it We bring forth the buds of every plant. From these We bring forth green foliage and close-growing grain, palm-trees laden with clusters of dates, vineyards and olive groves, and pomegranates alike and different. Behold their fruits when they ripen. Surely in these there are signs for true believers.

Qur'an 24:41–46; 6:95–99.

Predestination

Predestination is God's eternal choice of his own people from among the fallen human race. In the first selection, God is said to predestine many religions for humanity but only Islam for the saved. The *Qur'an* affirms the sovereignty of God and human responsibility to live morally, but it puts the emphasis on the former. Predestination and fate play a large role in affairs both big and small in Muslim life. In Arab countries, perhaps the most

Qur'an 42:8–13; 7:177–179.

frequently heard expression is Enshallah, "if God wills," a word reflected at the beginning of the first passage. The second reading presents a typical Qur'anic statement of the predestination of individuals. God's leading of people into error presents no moral problem because these are the "heedless," who are and always will be immoral and disobedient. Both passages come from Medina.

[42:8] Had it had been God's will, He could have made them all of one religion. But God brings whom He will into His mercy; the wrongdoers have none to befriend or help them.

Have they set up other guardians besides Him? Surely God alone is the Guardian. He resurrects the dead and has power over all things. [10] Whatever the subject of your disputes, the final word belongs to God. Such is God, my Lord. In Him I have put my trust, and to Him I turn in repentance....

He has ordained for you the faith which He enjoined on Noah, and which We have revealed to you; which We enjoined on Abraham, Moses, and Jesus, saying: "Observe the Faith and do not divide yourselves into factions." But hard for the pagans is that to which you call them. God chooses for it whom He will, and guides to it those that repent.

[7:177] The man whom God guides is rightly guided; but those whom He confounds will surely be lost. We have predestined for Hell many jinn and many men. They have hearts they cannot comprehend with; they have eyes they cannot see with; and they have ears they cannot hear with. They are like beasts—indeed, they are more misguided. Such are the heedless.

Jinn

Like the angels and humanity, jinn are a mixed lot: Some are good and others evil. This passage presents the words of a band of formerly evil jinn who hear the message of God in the Qur'an and repent, taking up Islam. They serve as a pattern and encouragement for the people to whom Muhammad testifies to do the same. Notice the oral nature of the Qur'an here; it is the recitation of Gabriel's message to Muhammad.

It is revealed to me that a band of jinn listened to God's revelations and said: "We have heard a wondrous Qur'an giving guidance to the right path. We believed in it and shall henceforth serve none besides Our Lord. He (exalted be the glory of our Lord!) has taken no wife,[22]

nor has He begotten any children. The Blaspheming One among us has uttered a wanton falsehood against God, [5] although we had supposed no man or jinn could tell of Him what is untrue.

"We made our way to high heaven, and found it filled with mighty wardens and fiery comets. We sat eavesdropping, but eavesdroppers find flaming darts in wait for them. [10] We cannot tell if this bodes evil to the inhabitants of earth or whether their Lord intends to guide them.

---

[22] *He . . . has taken no wife:* The argument of some non-Muslim Arabs and all Christians that God has begotten children or a son implies that God also has taken a wife. The *Qur'an* sees this wife as a goddess who would nullify its preaching of the absolute oneness of God.

Qur'an 72:1–15.

✳ 3

"Some of us are righteous, while others are not; we follow different ways. We know we cannot escape on earth from God, nor can we elude His grasp by flight. When we heard His guidance we believed in Him; he that believes in his Lord shall fear neither dishonesty nor injustice. Some of us are Muslims and some are wrongdoers. Those that embrace Islam pursue the right path; [15] but those that do wrong shall become the fuel of Hell."

Creation

The *Qur'an* has several poetic recitals of creation. Surah 15 is one of the fullest. This passage also tells the origin of Satan as an evil angel and his temptation of humanity to sin.

[15:16] We have decked the heavens with constellations and made them lovely to behold. We have guarded them from every cursed devil. Eavesdroppers are pursued by fiery comets.

We have spread out the earth and set upon it immovable mountains. We have planted it with every seasonable fruit, [20] providing sustenance for yourselves and for those whom you do not provide for. We hold the store of every blessing and send it down in appropriate measure. We let loose the fertilizing winds and bring down water from the sky for you to drink; its stores are beyond your reach.

We ordain life and death. We are the Heir of all things. We know those who have gone before you, and those who will come hereafter. [25] Your Lord will gather them all before Him. He is wise and all-knowing.

We created man from dry clay, from black molded loam, and before him Satan from smokeless fire. Your Lord said to the angels: "I am creating man from dry clay, from black molded loam. When I have fashioned him and breathed of My spirit into him, kneel down and prostrate yourselves before him." [30] The angels, one and all, prostrated themselves, except Satan. He refused to prostrate himself with the others.

"Satan," said God, "why do you not prostrate yourself?"

He replied: "I will not bow to a mortal whom You created of dry clay, of black molded loam."

[35] "Begone," said God, "you are accursed. My curse shall be on you till Judgment Day." ✳ 4

"Lord," said Satan, "reprieve me till the Day of Resurrection."

He answered: "You are reprieved till the Appointed Day."

"Lord," said Satan, "since You have thus seduced me, I will tempt mankind on earth. [40] I will seduce them all, except those of them who are your faithful servants."

He replied: "This is the right course for Me. You shall have no power over My servants, only the sinners who follow you. They are all destined for Hell. It has seven gates, and through each gate they shall come in separate bands. [45] But the righteous shall dwell among gardens and fountains; in peace and safety they shall enter them. We shall remove all hatred from their hearts, and they shall take their ease on couches face to face,[23] a band of brothers. Toil shall not weary them, nor shall they ever be driven out."

---

[23]*face to face:* in agreement with each other, therefore becoming "a band of brothers."

Qur'an 15:16–48.

Adam, Eve, and the Fall

Here the fall of humanity into sin and rebellion against God is strongly related to the fall of Satan into sin. Humanity is forgiven when it "receives the revelations of God" and follows them; this is the positive model for those who receive God's revelations through Muhammad and follow them. On the other hand, those who reject these revelations will receive Hell as their punishment (verse 37).

When your Lord said to the angels: "I am placing on the earth one that shall rule as My deputy," they replied: "Will You put there one that will do evil and shed blood, when we have for so long sung Your praises and sanctified Your name?"

[30] He said: "I know what you do not know."

He taught Adam the names of all things and then set them before the angels, saying: "Tell Me the names of these, if what you say be true."

"Glory to You," they replied, "we have no knowledge except that which You have given us. You alone are all-knowing and wise."

Then He said, "Adam, tell them their names." And when Adam had named them, He said . . ., "Dwell with your wife in Paradise and eat of its fruits to your hearts' content wherever you will. But never approach this tree or you shall both become transgressors." But Satan removed them thence and brought about their banishment. "Go hence," We said, "and be enemies to each other. The earth will for a while provide your dwelling and sustenance."

[35] Then Adam received commandments from his Lord, and his Lord relented towards him. He is the Forgiving One, the Merciful.

"Go down hence, all," We said.[24] "When Our guidance is revealed those that accept it shall have nothing to fear or to regret; but those that deny and reject Our revelations shall be the heirs of Hell, and there they shall abide for ever."   # 4

[24]*Go down hence:* Leave the Paradise, the ideal Garden of Eden.

Qur'an 2:29–37.

The Holy *Qur'an*

The revelations to Muhammad, which later formed the *Qur'an*, took several forms. The first passage refers to direct, audible speech and to the less direct inspiration that comes "from behind a veil." Whatever the form, Muslims believe that all revelations come from God by way of his angel Gabriel. The second passage recounts the qualities of the *Qur'an*: its origin as a revelation from God, its miraculous nature, its connection to the faith of Islam, and its Arabic character. A recurrent theme of this surah is the defense of the *Qur'an* against the charge that it is false. In the third passage, the *Qur'an* claims to be the capstone of the prior scriptures of Judaism and Christianity. It confirms the *Bibles*   # 7
of these faiths and shares much the same content, but the peoples of these latter books reject Islam.

Qur'an 42:50–53; 46:1–13; 2:87–91.

[42:50] It is not given to any mortal that God should speak to him except by revelation, or from behind a veil, or through a messenger sent and authorized by Him to make known His will. Exalted is He, and wise.

Thus have We inspired you[25] with a spirit of Our will when you knew nothing of faith or scripture, and made it a light whereby We guide those of Our servants whom We please. You will surely guide them to the right path: the path of God, to whom belongs all that the heavens and the earth contain. Surely to God all things shall in the end return.

[46:1–11, Mecca] *Ha mim*. This Book is revealed by God, the Mighty One, the Wise One.

It was to manifest the Truth that We created the heavens and the earth and all that lies between them; We created them to last for an appointed term. Yet the unbelievers give no heed to Our warning.

Say: "Have you pondered on those whom you invoke besides God? Show me what part of the earth they have created! Have they a share in the heavens? Bring me a scripture revealed before this, or some other vestige of divine knowledge, if what you say be true."

Who is in greater error than the man who prays to idols which will never hear him till the Day of Resurrection—which are, indeed, unconscious of his prayers? [5] When mankind are gathered together upon the Judgment Day, their idols will become their enemies and will disown their worship.

When Our revelations are recited to them, clear as they are, the unbelievers say: "This is plain sorcery." Such is their description of the truth when it is declared to them.

Do they say: "He has invented it himself"? Say: "If I have indeed invented it, then there is nothing you can do to protect me from the wrath of God. He well knows what you say about it. Sufficient is He as a witness between me and you. He is the Benevolent One, the Merciful."

Say: "I am no prodigy among the apostles; nor do I know what will be done with me or you. I follow only what is revealed to me, and my only duty is to give plain warning."

[10] Say: "Think if this Qur'an is indeed from God and you reject it; if an Israelite[26] has vouched for it and accepted Islam, while you yourselves deny it with disdain. Truly, God does not guide the wrongdoers."

The unbelievers say of the faithful: "Had there been any good in it they would not have believed in it before us." And since they reject its guidance, they say: "This is an ancient falsehood." Yet before it the Book of Moses was revealed, a guide and a blessing to all men. This Book confirms it. It is revealed in the Arabic tongue, to forewarn the wrongdoers and to give good tidings to the righteous.

[2:87–91, Medina] To Moses We gave the Scriptures and after him We sent other apostles.[27] We gave Jesus the son of Mary veritable signs and strengthened him with the Holy Spirit. Will you then scorn each apostle whose message does not suit your fancies, charging some with imposture and slaying others?

They say: "Our hearts are sealed." But God has cursed them for their unbelief. They have but little faith. [90] Now that a Book confirming their own has come to them from God, they deny it, although they know it to be the truth and have long prayed for help against the unbelievers. God's curse be upon the infidels! Evil is that for which they have bartered away their souls. To deny God's own revelation, grudging that He should reveal His bounty to whom he chooses from among His servants, they have incurred God's most inexorable wrath. An ignominious punishment awaits the unbelievers.

When it is said to them: "Believe in what God has revealed," they reply: "We believe in what was revealed to us." But they deny what has since been revealed, although it is the truth, corroborating their own scriptures.

---

[25]*you:* Muhammad.

[26]*an Israelite:* a Jew who converted to Islam, traditionally identified as Abdullah bin Salam.

[27]*other apostles:* not the *New Testament* meaning of the term *apostle* but the Islamic sense of "messengers, sent ones."

On Unbelievers, Jews, and Christians

The first reading outlines the Islamic approach to "unbelievers" and "idolaters," those who follow the pre-Islamic religions of Arabia. This passage has no *Bismillah;* it was probably originally attached to Surah 8. A *hadith* traced to Caliph Uthman states that it was revealed by Muhammad shortly before his death, and he left no instructions on it. In the second reading, Jesus is presented as a righteous prophet who called his people to submit to the true God. He died, but not by crucifixion, and his death has no saving effect. This sought to undercut the Christian claim that salvation is produced by Jesus' death and resurrection. Nevertheless, Muslims tend to have a positive attitude toward Jesus as one of the leading prophets. The last passage indicates how Muhammad hoped to convert the Jews and Christians of Medina to his new faith, but this effort failed. He then turned overtly hostile to them. They are to convert to Islam or live as subject peoples within the authority of Muslim government.

[9:1] A declaration of immunity from God and His apostle to the idolaters with whom you have made agreements: For four months you shall go unmolested in the land. But know that you shall not escape God's judgment, and that God will humble the unbelievers.

A proclamation to the people from God and His apostle on the day of the greater pilgrimage: God and His apostle are under no obligation to the idolaters. If you repent, it shall be well with you; but if you give no heed, know that you shall not be immune from God's judgment. Proclaim a woeful punishment to the unbelievers, except to those idolaters who have honored their treaties with you in every detail and aided none against you. With these keep faith, until their treaties have run their term. God loves the righteous.

[5] When the sacred months are over slay the idolaters wherever you find them. Arrest them, besiege them, and lie in ambush everywhere for them. If they repent and take to prayer and render the alms levy, allow them to go their way. God is forgiving and merciful. If an idolater seeks asylum with you, give him protection so that he may hear the Word of God, and then convey him to safety. For the idolaters are ignorant men. God and His apostle put no trust in idolaters, except those with whom you have made treaties at the Sacred Mosque.[28] So long as they keep faith with you, keep faith with them.

[3:38] Remember the angels' words to Mary. They said: "God has chosen you. He has made you pure and exalted you above womankind. Mary, be obedient to your Lord; bow down and worship with the worshippers."

This is an account of a divine secret. We reveal it to you. You were not present when they cast lots to see which of them should have charge of Mary; nor were you present when they argued about her.

[40] The angels said to Mary: "God bids you rejoice in a word from Him. His name is the Messiah, Jesus the son of Mary. He shall be noble in this world and in the hereafter, and shall be favored by God. He shall preach to men in his cradle and in the prime of manhood, and shall lead a righteous life."

"Lord," she said, "how can I bear a child when no man has touched me?"

He replied: "Such is the will of God. He creates whom He will. When He decrees a thing He need only say: 'Be,' and it is. He will instruct him in the Scriptures and in wisdom, in the Torah and in the Gospel, and send him forth as an apostle to

----

[28]*the Sacred Mosque:* the holy shrine in Mecca.

Qur'an 9:1–7, 3:38–50; 2:111–121, 132–137.

the Israelites. He will say: 'I bring you a sign from your Lord. From clay I will make for you the likeness of a bird. I shall breathe into it and, by God's leave, it shall become a living bird.[29] By God's leave I shall heal the blind man and the leper, and raise the dead to life. I shall tell you what to eat and what to store up in your houses. Surely that will be a sign for you, if you are true believers. I come to confirm the Torah already revealed and to make lawful to you some of the things you are forbidden. I bring you a sign from your Lord: therefore fear God and obey me. God is my Lord and your Lord: therefore serve Him. That is the straight path.' " # 3

When Jesus observed that they had no faith, he said: [45] "Who will help me in the cause of God?" The disciples replied: "We are the helpers of God. We believe in God. Bear witness that we have surrendered ourselves to Him. Lord, we believe in Your revelations and follow Your apostle. Count us among Your witnesses."

They plotted,[30] and God plotted. God is the supreme Plotter. He said: "Jesus, I am about to cause you to die and lift you up to Me. I shall take you away from the unbelievers[31] and exalt your followers above them till the Day of Resurrection. Then to Me you shall all return and I shall judge your disputes. The unbelievers shall be sternly punished in this world and in the world to come; there shall be none to help them. [50] As for those that have faith and do good works, they shall be given their reward in full. God does not love the evil-doers." W.O.W

[2:111] They declare: "None but Jews and Christians shall be admitted to Paradise." Such are their wishful fancies. Say: "Let us have your proof, if what you say be true." Indeed, those that surrender themselves[32] to God and do

good works shall be rewarded by their Lord: they shall have nothing to fear or to regret.

The Jews say the Christians are misguided, and the Christians say it is the Jews who are misguided. Yet they both read the Scriptures. And the ignorant say the same of both. God will judge their disputes on the Day of Resurrection.

Who is more wicked than the men who seek to destroy the mosques of God and forbid His name to be mentioned in them, when it behooves these men to enter them with fear in their hearts? They shall be held up to shame in this world and sternly punished in the hereafter.

[115] To God belongs the east and the west. Whichever way you turn[33] there is the face of God. He is omnipresent and all-knowing.

They say: "God has begotten a son." Glory be to Him![34] His is what the heavens and earth contain; all things are obedient to Him. Creator of the heavens and the earth! When He decrees a thing, He need only say "Be," and it is.

The ignorant ask: "Why does God not speak to us or give us a sign?"[35] The same demand was made by those before them: their hearts are all alike. But to those whose faith is firm We have already revealed Our signs. We have sent you forth to proclaim the truth and to give warning. You shall not be questioned about the heirs of Hell.

[120] You will please neither the Christians nor the Jews unless you follow their faith. Say: "God's guidance is the only guidance." And if after all the knowledge you have been given you yield to their desires, there shall be none to help or protect you from the wrath of God. Those to whom We have given the Book, and who read it as it ought to be read, truly believe in it; those that deny it shall assuredly be lost. . . .

[132] Abraham enjoined the faith [of Islam] on his children, and so did Jacob, saying: "My children, God has chosen for you the true faith. Do not depart this life except as men who have submitted to Him." Were you present when death came to Jacob? He said to his children:

---

[29]This story is found in a post–*New Testament* Christian book, the *Apocryphon of James.* It probably came to Muhammad by oral tradition.

[30]*They plotted:* Jesus' opponents seek to bring him to death.

[31]*take you away:* Muslims believe that a lookalike was substituted for Jesus just before his death on the cross so that he only seemed to die. Instead, he was taken up to God before his death. Western scholars commonly hold that this view reflects the views of a Christian group that the mainstream church regarded as heretical.

[32]*surrender themselves:* accept Islam.

[33]*way you turn:* the direction of prayer (**qiblah**).

[34]*Glory be to Him:* That is, it is not so.

[35]*Why . . . sign:* a complaint against Muhammad that he brings no miracles to authenticate himself as God's prophet as the other biblical prophets had done.

"What will you worship when I am gone?" They replied: "We will worship your God and the God of your forefathers Abraham and Ishmael and Isaac: the One God. To Him we will surrender ourselves." ...

[135] They say: "Accept the Jewish or the Christian faith and you shall be rightly guided." Say: "By no means! We believe in the faith of Abraham, the upright one. He was no idolater." Say: "We believe in God and that which is revealed to us; in what was revealed to Abraham, Ishmael, Isaac, Jacob, and the tribes; to Moses and Jesus and the other prophets by their Lord. We make no distinction among any of them, and to God we have surrendered ourselves." If they accept your faith, they shall be rightly guided; if they reject it, they shall surely be in schism. Against them God is your all-sufficient defender. He hears all and knows all.

Resurrection and Judgment

Like Judaism and Christianity, Islam foresees a literal resurrection of the body from death; soul and body are rejoined to face judgment. The Meccan origin of these passages is reflected in their lyrical style and power. The second passage, vivid in its emotional intensity, describes the last judgment that follows the resurrection on the last day. The use of "right" and "left" is reminiscent of the *New Testament* teaching that at the last judgment, the righteous will stand at God's right and the unrighteous at the left.   # 4

[75:1–15, Mecca]

I swear by the Day of Resurrection, and by the self-reproaching soul!

Does man think We shall never put his bones together again? Indeed, We can remold his very fingers! [5] Yet man would ever deny what is to come. "When will this be," he asks, "this Day of Resurrection?" But when the sight of mortals is confounded and the moon eclipsed; when sun and moon are brought together—[10] on that day man will ask: "Where shall I flee?"

No, there shall be no refuge. For to your Lord, on that day, all shall return. Man shall on that day be told of all his deeds, from first to last. Indeed, man shall bear witness against himself, plead as he may with his excuses.

[69:14–35, Mecca] When the Trumpet sounds a single blast; when earth with all its mountains is raised high and with one mighty crash is shattered into dust—[15] on that day the Dread Event will come to pass.

Frail and tottering, the sky will be rent asunder on that day, and the angels will stand on all its sides with eight of them carrying the throne of your Lord above their heads. On that day you shall be utterly exposed, and all your secrets shall be brought to light.

He who is given his book in his right hand will say: [20] "Here it is, read my book! I knew that I should come to my reckoning!" His shall be a blissful state in a lofty garden, with clusters of fruit within his reach. We shall say to him: "Eat and drink to your heart's content: your reward for what you did in days gone by."

[25] But he who is given his book in his left hand will say: "Would that my book were not given me! Would that I knew nothing of my account! Would that my death had ended it all!

Qur'an 75:1–15; 69:14–35.

My wealth availed me for nothing, and I am bereft of all my power."

[30] We shall say: "Lay hold of him and bind him. Burn him in the fire of Hell, then fasten him with a chain seventy cubits long. For he did not believe in God, the Most High, nor did he care to feed the poor. [35] Today he shall be friendless here; filth shall be his food, the filth which sinners eat."

Heaven and Hell

The first passage is one of the fullest descriptions in the *Qur'an* of the blessings of heaven. They are physical to the point of sensuousness, with little explicit development of the spiritual blessing or happiness of the residents of heaven. The second passage deals with the two types of heavenly attendants that will be given to the faithful in heaven. "Immortal youths" will wait on them with food and drink, and the houris, beautiful dark-eyed women, will be wed to faithful men (the *Qur'an* never speaks explicitly about the reward of women in heaven). In the third passage, the punishments of the damned are described in vivid imagery. The purpose was to threaten and warn the Arabs against the godless way that leads to eternal destruction and encourage them in the way of eternal life. All three passages are Meccan.

[76:1] Does there not pass over man a space of time when his life is a blank?[36]

We have created man from the union of the two sexes, so that We may put him to the proof. We have endowed him with hearing and sight and, be he thankful or oblivious of Our favors, We have shown him the right path.

For the unbelievers We have prepared chains and fetters, and a blazing Fire. [5] But the righteous shall drink of a cup tempered at the Camphor Fountain, a gushing spring at which the servants of God will refresh themselves: they who keep their vows and dread the far-spread terrors of Judgment Day; who, though they hold it dear, give sustenance to the poor man, the orphan, and the captive, saying: "We feed you for God's sake only; we seek of you neither recompense nor thanks. [10] We fear from our Lord a day of anguish and of woe."

God will deliver them from the evil of that day, and make their faces shine with joy. He will reward them for their steadfastness with robes of silk and the delights of Paradise. Reclining there upon soft couches, they shall feel neither the scorching heat nor the biting cold. Trees will spread their shade around them, and fruits will hang in clusters over them.

[15] They shall be served with silver dishes, and beakers as large as goblets; silver goblets which they themselves shall measure: and cups brim-full with ginger-flavored water from a fount called Salsabil.[37] They shall be attended by boys graced with eternal youth, who to the beholder's eyes will seem like sprinkled pearls. When you gaze upon that scene, you will behold a kingdom blissful and glorious.

They shall be arrayed in garments of fine green silk and rich brocade, and adorned with bracelets of silver. Their Lord will give them pure nectar to drink. Thus shall you be rewarded; your high endeavors are gratifying to God.

[56:1] When that which is coming comes—and no soul shall then deny its coming—some

[36]*his life is a blank:* To judge from the next verse, this time is life in the womb before birth.

[37]*Salsabil:* Arabic for "ginger."

Qur'an 76:1–22; 56:1–39; 77:1–39.

shall be abased and others exalted. [5] When the earth shakes and quivers, and the mountains crumble away and scatter abroad into fine dust, you shall be divided into three multitudes: those on the right (blessed shall be those on the right); those on the left (damned shall be those on the left); [10] and those to the fore[38] (foremost shall be those). Such are they that shall be brought near to their Lord in the gardens of delight: a whole multitude from the men of old, but only a few from the later generations.

[15] They shall recline on jewelled couches face to face, and there shall wait on them immortal youths with bowls and ewers and a cup of purest wine (that will neither pain their heads nor take away their reason); [20] with fruits of their own choice and flesh of fowls that they relish. And theirs shall be the dark-eyed houris, chaste as hidden pearls: a reward for their deeds. There they shall hear no idle talk, no sinful speech, but only the greeting, "Peace! Peace!"

[25] Those on the right hand—happy shall be those on the right hand! They shall recline on couches raised on high in the shade of thornless sidrs and clusters of bananas; [30] amid gushing waters and abundant fruits, unforbidden, never ending. [35] We created the houris and made them virgins, loving companions for those on the right hand: a multitude from the men of old, and a multitude from the later generations.

[77:16] Would that you knew what the Day of Judgment is! Woe on that day to the disbelievers! [20] Did We not destroy the men of old and cause others to follow them? Thus shall We deal with the guilty. Woe on that day to the disbelievers! Did we not create you from an unworthy fluid, which We kept in a safe receptacle[39] for an appointed time? All this We did; how excellent is Our work!

Woe on that day to the disbelievers! [25] Have We not made the earth a home for the living and for the dead? Have We not placed high mountains upon it, and given you fresh water for your drink? Woe on that day to the disbelievers! Begone to that Hell which you deny! [30] Depart into the shadow that will rise high in three columns, giving neither shade nor shelter from the flames, and throwing up sparks as huge as towers, as bright as yellow camels! Woe on that day to the disbelievers! [35] On that day they shall not speak, nor shall their pleas be heeded. . . . Such is the Day of Judgment. We will assemble you all, together with past generations. If then you are cunning, try your spite against Me!

---

[38] *those to the fore:* The righteous are divided into two groups, the blessed and the more blessed; "those to the fore" are the more blessed.

[39] *unworthy fluid ... safe receptacle:* The fluid is semen, and the receptacle is the womb. One traditional Arab commentator says it is "unworthy" because man is ashamed of the process of procreation by which he comes into being.

ETHICS

The Conduct of Believers

The ethical dimensions of the Islamic life are spread evenly throughout the *Qur'an*. Occasional passages summarize the duty of the believer. This selection from Mecca deals comprehensively with the moral structure of Islam; notice its relationship to the *Ten Commandments* of Judaism.

Qur'an 17:23–38.

Serve no other god besides God, lest you incur disgrace and ruin. Your Lord has enjoined you to worship none but Him, and to show kindness to your parents. If either or both of them attain old age in your dwelling, show them no sign of impatience, nor rebuke them; but speak to them kind words. [25] Treat them with humility and tenderness and say: "Lord, be merciful to them. They nursed me when I was an infant."

Your Lord best knows what is in your hearts; He knows if you are good. He will forgive those that turn to Him.

Give to the near of kin their due, and also to the destitute and to the wayfarers. Do not squander your substance wastefully, for the wasteful are Satan's brothers; and Satan is ever ungrateful to his Lord. [30] But if, while waiting for your Lord's bounty, you lack the means to assist them, then at least speak to them kindly.

Be neither miserly nor prodigal, for then you should either be reproached or be reduced to penury. Your Lord gives abundantly to whom He will and sparingly to whom He pleases. He knows and observes His servants.

You shall not kill your children for fear of want.[40] We will provide for them and for you. To kill them is a great sin.

You shall not commit adultery, for it is foul and indecent.

[35] You shall not kill any man whom God has forbidden you to kill, except for a just cause. If a man is slain unjustly, his heir shall be entitled to satisfaction. But let him not carry his vengeance too far, for his victim will in turn be assisted and avenged.[41]

Do not interfere with the property of orphans except with the best of motives, until they reach maturity. Keep your promises; you are accountable for all that you promise.

Give full measure, when you measure, and weigh with even scales. That is fair, and better in the end.

Do not follow what you do not know. Man's eyes, ears, and heart—each of his senses shall be closely questioned. Do not walk proudly on the earth. You cannot cleave the earth, nor can you rival the mountains in stature.

---

[40]*kill your children:* In pre-Islamic times, unwanted infants, especially females, were killed by being buried alive. The *Qur'an* views this practice as murder.

[41]*be assisted and avenged:* Blood feuds could easily get out of control; this is an effort to limit their scope.

Women

In the Semitic culture of ancient Arabia, society was strongly patriarchal; it continues to be so today. This is reflected in the first passage, on the general relations between the sexes, and in the second, on marriage, sexual relations, and divorce. Despite this patriarchal structure, women did have some rights, as the beginning of the first reading indicates. Both readings, like most legal material in the *Qur'an,* come from the later, Medinan phase.

[4:19] Believers, it is not lawful for you to inherit anything from women against their will. Do not hinder them from remarrying so that you may get part of what you have given them, unless they are openly immoral. Treat them properly, even if you dislike them. [20] If you desire to exchange one wife for another, and you have given one of them a large sum of money, do not hold back any of it. Will you withhold it through slander and open sin? How can you hold it back when

---

Qur'an 4:19–22, 34–39; 2:220–223, 227–233.

you have had intercourse with each other, and they have made a solemn agreement with you? . . .

[34] Men have authority over women because God has made the one superior to the other, and because men spend their wealth to maintain women. Good women are obedient. They guard their unseen parts because God has guarded them.[42] As for those from whom you fear disobedience, admonish them and send them to beds apart and beat them. Then if they obey you, take no further action against them. God is high, supreme.

If you fear a breach between a man and his wife, appoint an arbiter from his people and another from hers. If they wish to be reconciled God will bring them together again. God is all-knowing and wise.

[2:220] You shall not wed pagan women, unless they embrace the Faith. A believing slave-girl is better than an idolatress, although she may please you. Nor shall you wed idolaters, unless they embrace the Faith. A believing slave is better than an idolater, although she may please you. These call you to Hell-fire; but God calls you, by His will, to Paradise and to forgiveness. He makes plain His revelations to mankind, so that they may take heed.

They ask you about menstruation. Say: "It is an indisposition. Keep aloof from women during their menstrual periods and do not touch them until they are clean again. Then have intercourse with them in the way God enjoined you. God loves those that turn to Him in repentance and strive to keep themselves clean."

Women are your fields: go into your fields as you please. Do good works and fear God. Bear in mind that you shall meet Him. Give good tidings to the believers. . . .

[227] Those that renounce their wives on oath[43] must wait four months. If they change their minds, God is forgiving and merciful; but if they decide to divorce them, know that God hears all and knows all. Divorced women must wait, keeping themselves from men, three menstrual courses. It is unlawful for them, if they believe in God and the last Day, to hide what God has created in their wombs: in which case their husbands would do well to take them back, should they desire reconciliation.

Women shall with justice have rights similar to those exercised against them, although men have a status above women. God is mighty and wise.

Divorce may be pronounced twice, and then a women must be retained in honor or allowed to go with kindness. It is unlawful for husbands to take from them anything they have given them, unless both fear that they may not be able to keep within the bounds set by God; in which case it shall be no offence for either of them if the wife ransom herself. These are the bounds set by God; do not transgress them. Those that transgress the bounds of God are wrongdoers.

[230] If a man divorces his wife,[44] he cannot remarry her until she has wedded another man and been divorced by him; in which case it shall be no offence for either of them to return to the other, if they think that they can keep within the bounds set by God. . . .

When you have renounced your wives and they have reached the end of their waiting period, either retain them in honor or let them go with kindness. But you shall not retain them in order to harm them or to wrong them. Whoever does this wrongs his own soul.

Do not make a game of God's revelations. Remember the favors God has bestowed upon you, and the Book and the wisdom He has revealed for your instruction. Fear God and know that God has knowledge of all things.

---

[42] *They guard their unseen parts:* This verse is used as a main justification for the veiling of women, which is not explicitly mentioned in the *Qur'an.*

[43] *renounce their wives on oath:* "I divorce you" pronounced twice, temporary and revocable by the husband.

---

[44] *divorces:* irrevocably divorces, with "I divorce you" pronounced three times.

Against Evil Magic

Here are formulas to recite against evil magic. The last two chapters in the *Qur'an* deal with this theme. The traditional explanation of these passages in Muslim interpretation is that they are used to dispel doubt. Used by the ordinary Muslim, however, such a formula often takes on a semimagical character itself. The power of these passages when recited will protect one from evil both human and supernatural.

[113, Mecca] Say: "I seek refuge in the Lord of Daybreak from the mischief of His creation; from the mischief of the night when she spreads her darkness; from the mischief of conjuring witches,[45] from the mischief of the envier, when he envies."

[114, Mecca] Say: "I seek refuge in the Lord of men, the King of men, the God of men, from the mischief of the slinking prompter who whispers in the hearts of men[46]; from jinn and men." #3

[45] *conjuring witches:* literally, "those who blow on knots," a way to cast an evil spell. Witches here are viewed as conjuring evil on those who follow God.

[46] *the slinking prompter:* the devil or evil jinn.

Qur'an 113; 114.

The Different Dimensions of Struggle (Jihad)

The *Qur'an* urges **jihad,** "struggle" or "striving" against unbelief of all sorts to spread the faith. Jihad is often called "struggle in the way of Allah." This struggle includes prayer, study, a "war" against evil in oneself, and military conflict to spread and defend the faith. In the first passage, God commends those who struggle/strive in his way. In the second passage, a problem arose for Muhammad about what to do with those who refuse to fight in the military aspects of jihad. The answer came by revelation that those who will not fight should have no share in the war booty or in eternal life. In the third passage, Muhammad is preparing to sponsor a holy war against Mecca, from which he had fled for his life. In these instructions, the basic guidelines for all holy wars in Islam arise: It is obligatory for all who can participate, and its aim is to spread the faith and crush opposition to Islam.

[6:16, translated by the editor] Did you suppose that you would be left in peace, that God does not know who among you struggles? God knows all that you do.... Do you think that quenching a pilgrim's thirst and attending (services at) the Holy Sanctuary are equal to believing in God and in judgment on the last day, and struggling in the way of God? They are not equal in God's sight. God does not guide those who do evil. Those who truly believe, who have left their homes and struggle with their possessions and their lives in God's way, are very precious in God's sight. They will be triumphant.

Qur'an 6:16, 19–20; 48:11–21; 2:190–194, 216–218.

[48:11] The desert Arabs who stayed behind[47] will say to you: "We were occupied with our goods and families. Implore God to pardon us." They will say with their tongues what they do not mean in their hearts.

Say: "Who can intervene on your behalf with God if it be His will to do you harm or good? God is cognizant of all your actions."

No. You thought the Apostle and the believers would never return to their people; and with this fancy your hearts were delighted. You harbored evil thoughts and thus incurred damnation. As for those that disbelieve in God and His apostle, We have prepared a blazing Fire for the unbelievers. God has sovereignty over the heavens and the earth. He pardons whom He will and punishes whom He pleases. God is forgiving and merciful.

[15] When you set forth to take the spoils, those that stayed behind will say: "Let us come with you." They seek to change the Word of God. Say: "You shall not come with us. So God has said beforehand."

They will reply: "You are jealous of us." But how little they understand! Say to the desert Arabs who stayed behind: "You shall be called upon to fight a mighty nation, unless they embrace Islam. If you prove obedient, God will reward you well. But if you run away, as you have done before this, He will inflict on you a stern chastisement."

It shall be no offence for the blind, the lame, and the sick to stay behind. He that obeys God and His apostle shall be admitted to gardens watered by running streams; but he that turns and flees shall be sternly punished by Him.

God was well pleased with the faithful when they swore allegiance to you under the tree. He knew what was in their hearts. Therefore He sent down tranquillity upon them, and rewarded them with a speedy victory and with the many spoils which they have taken. Mighty is God and wise.

[20] God has promised you rich booty, and has given you this with all promptness. He has stayed your enemies' hands, so that He may make your victory a sign to true believers and guide you along a straight path. And God knows of other spoils which you have not yet taken. God has power over all things.

[2:190] Fight for the sake of God those that fight against you, but do not attack them first. God does not love aggressors.

Slay them wherever you find them. Drive them out of the places from which they drove you. Idolatry is worse than carnage. But do not fight them within the precincts of the Holy Mosque unless they attack you there; if they attack you put them to the sword. Thus shall the unbelievers be rewarded; but if they mend their ways, know that God is forgiving and merciful.

Fight against them until idolatry is no more and God's religion reigns supreme. But if they mend their ways, fight none except the evil-doers.... [216] Fighting is obligatory for you, much as you dislike it. But you may hate a thing although it is good for you, and love a thing although it is bad for you. God knows, but you do not.

They ask you about the sacred month. Say: "To fight in this month is a grave offence; but to debar others from the path of God, to deny Him, and to expel His worshippers from the Holy Mosque, is far more grave in His sight. Idolatry is worse than carnage."

They will not cease to fight against you until they force you to renounce your faith—if they are able. But whoever of you recants and dies an unbeliever, his works shall come to nothing in this world and in the world to come. Such men shall be the tenants of Hell, wherein they shall abide for ever.

Those that have embraced the Faith and those that have fled their land[48] and fought for the cause of God may hope for God's mercy. God is forgiving and merciful.

---

[47]*desert Arabs who stayed behind:* These are certain tribes who refused to participate in a military campaign led by Muhammad against unbelieving opponents.

[48]*those that have fled their land:* those who fled from Mecca to Medina with Muhammad.

Law Codes

The *Qur'an* has several developed law codes dealing with various topics of everyday life. As a sample, here is a passage on the treatment of orphans and women. That orphans are treated before women may be an indication that they were more of a problem at the time of Muhammad.

Men, have fear of your Lord, who created you from a single soul. From that soul He created its mate, and through them He filled the earth with countless men and women.

Fear God, in whose name you plead with one another, and honor the mothers who bore you. God is ever watching you.

Give orphans the property which belongs to them. Do not exchange their valuables for worthless things or cheat them of their possessions; for this would surely be a great sin. If you fear that you cannot treat orphans with fairness, then you may marry other women who seem good to you: two, three, or four of them. But if you fear that you cannot maintain equality among them, marry one only or any slave-girls you may own. This will make it easier for you to avoid injustice.

Give women their dowry as a free gift; but if they choose to make over to you a part of it, you may regard it as lawfully yours.[49] [5] Do not give the feeble-minded the property with which God has entrusted you for their support; but maintain and clothe them with its proceeds, and give them good advice.

Put orphans to the test until they reach a marriageable age. If you find them capable of sound judgment, hand over to them their property, and do not deprive them of it by squandering it before they come of age. Let not the rich guardian touch the property of his orphan ward; and let him who is poor use no more than a fair portion of it for his own advantage. When you hand over to them their property, call in some witnesses; sufficient is God's accounting of your actions.

Men shall have a share in what their parents and kinsmen leave; and women shall have a share in what their parents and kinsmen leave[50]; whether it be little or much, they shall be legally entitled to their share. If relatives, orphans, or needy men are present at the division of an inheritance, give them, too, a share of it, and speak to them kind words.

Let those who are solicitous about the welfare of their young children after their own death take care not to wrong orphans. Let them fear God and speak for justice. [10] But those that devour the property of orphans unjustly swallow fire into their bellies; they shall burn in a mighty conflagration.

---

[49] *Give ... yours:* In Islam, a woman continues to own and control her dowry after her marriage.

[50] *women shall have a share ... leave:* Prior to Islam, women could not inherit.

Qur'an 4:1–10.

RITUAL

The Opening of the *Qur'an*

The first chapter in the *Qur'an* is its **Fatihah,** "Opening," which stands as a devotional preface to the book. A beautiful poem of praise to God, the Fatihah sums up the content of the *Qur'an*: praise to the one God and submission to his way. This is by far the most recited chapter in the *Qur'an;* we reproduce it here in full.

THE OPENING [1, MECCA]

In the Name of God, the Compassionate, the Merciful

Praise be to God, Lord of the Universe, The Compassionate, the Merciful, Sovereign of the Day of Judgment! You alone we worship, and to You alone we turn for help. Guide us to the straight path, the path of those whom You have favored, not of those who have incurred Your wrath, nor of those who have gone astray.

Qur'an 1.

Confession of Faith

The first pillar of Islam states, "There is no God but God, and Muhammad is God's prophet." This formula does not occur in this developed and exact form in the *Qur'an,* but the two parts of it do occur in early forms. The conclusion of the first selection, "Have faith in God and in his apostle," links the two halves of the confession. In the second selection, the first half of the confession is found in an exact and formal use.   ① Pillar

[57:1–7, Mecca] All that is in heaven and earth gives glory to God. He is the Mighty, the Wise One. It is He that has sovereignty over the heavens and the earth. He ordains life and death, and has power over all things. He is the First and the Last, the Visible and the Unseen. He has knowledge of all things.

He created the heavens and the earth in six days, and then mounted His throne. He knows all that goes into the earth and all that emerges from it, all that comes down from heaven and all that ascends to it. He is with you wherever you are. God is cognizant of all your actions.

[5] He has sovereignty over the heavens and the earth. To God shall all things return. He causes the night to pass into the day, and the day into the night. He has knowledge of the inmost thoughts of men.

Have faith in God and His apostle and give in alms of that which He has made your inheritance; for whoever of you believes and gives in alms shall be richly rewarded.

Qur'an 57:1–7; 37:32–39.

[37:32, Mecca] On that day they will all share Our punishment. Thus shall We deal with the evil-doers, for when it was said to them: "There is no god but God," they replied with scorn: "Are we to renounce our gods for the sake of a mad poet?"

Surely he has brought the truth, confirming those who were sent before. You shall all taste the grievous scourge: you shall be rewarded according to your deeds.

Prayer

At first, Muhammad and his followers faced Jerusalem during prayer, as was the Jewish custom. Later, after relations with the Jews of Medina had soured, he changed the direction of prayer (qiblah) to the holy shrine at Mecca. The duty and direction of prayer are discussed in the *Qur'an,* but the content of prayer is not, perhaps because the *Qur'an* itself is rich with prayers and other devotional material.

The foolish will ask: "What has made them turn away from their qiblah?"[51]

Say: "The East and the West are God's. He guides whom He will to the right path."

We have made you a just nation, so that you may testify against mankind and that your own Apostle may testify against you. We decreed your former qiblah only in order that We might know the Apostle's true adherents and those who were to disown him. It was indeed a hard test, but not to those whom God has guided. He was not to make your faith fruitless. He is compassionate and merciful to men.

Many a time have We seen you turn your face towards heaven. We will make you turn towards a qiblah that will please you. Turn your face towards the Holy Mosque; wherever you be, turn your faces towards it.

[145] Those to whom the Scriptures[52] were given know this to be the truth from their Lord. God is never heedless of what they do. But even if you gave them every proof they would not accept your qiblah, nor would you accept theirs; nor would any of them accept the qiblah of the other. If, after all the knowledge you have been given, you yield to their desires, then you will surely become an evil-doer.

Those to whom We gave the Scriptures know Our apostle as they know their own sons. But some of them deliberately conceal the truth. This is the truth from your Lord: therefore never doubt it.

Each one has a goal towards which he turns. But wherever you be, emulate one another in good works. God will bring you all before Him. God has power over all things.

Whichever way you depart, face towards the Holy Mosque. This is surely the truth from your Lord. God is never heedless of what you do.

---

[51] *turn away from their qiblah:* that is, change their qiblah.
[52] *Scriptures:* Jewish and Christian.

Qur'an 2:142–149.

Alms *pillar*

In Islam, the giving of alms (zakat) is mandatory; alms are more of a tax than an offering, but believers are urged to give fully and willingly. The first passage castigates those who evade the alms tax; the second deals especially with who may receive alms.

[107; Mecca: 1–3; Medina: 4–7] Have you thought of him that denies the Last Judgment? It is he who turns away the orphan and has no urge to feed the poor.

[4] Woe to those who pray but are heedless in their prayer; who make a show of piety and give no alms to the destitute.

[9:53, Medina] Say: "Whether you[53] give willingly or with reluctance, your offerings shall not be accepted from you; for you are wicked men."

Their offerings shall not be accepted from them because they have denied God and His apostle. They pray half-heartedly and begrudge their contributions. [55] Let neither their riches nor their children rouse your envy. Through these God seeks to punish them in this life, so that they shall die unbelievers.

They swear by God that they are believers like you. Yet they are not. They are afraid of you. If they could find a shelter or a cave, or any hiding-place, they would run in frantic haste to seek refuge in it. There are some among them who speak ill of you[54] concerning the distribution of alms. If a share is given them, they are contented: but if they receive nothing, they grow resentful.

Would that they were satisfied with what God and His apostle have given them, and would say: "God is all-sufficient for us. He will provide for us from His own abundance, and so will His apostle. To God we will submit."

[60] Alms shall be only for the poor and the helpless, for those that are engaged in the management of alms and those whose hearts are sympathetic to the Faith, for the freeing of slaves and debtors, for the advancement of God's cause, and for the traveler in need. That is a duty enjoined by God. God is all-knowing and wise.

---

[53]*you:* hypocrites among the Muslims.

[54]*you:* Muhammad.

Qur'an 107; 9:53–60.

The Fast

As the beginning of this Medinan passage indicates, fasting was a pre-Islamic custom among the Arabs. Muhammad adapts it with his own regulations to Islam. Easily discernible here is the transition between pre-Islamic and Islamic fasting.

Qur'an 2:183–186.

Pillars

Believers, fasting is decreed for you as it was decreed for those before you; perchance you will guard yourselves against evil. Fast a certain number of days, but if any one among you is ill or on a journey, let him fast a similar number of days later; and for those that cannot endure it there is a ransom: the feeding of a poor man. He that does good of his own accord shall be well rewarded; but to fast is better for you, if you but knew it.

In the month of Ramadan the *Qur'an* was revealed, a book of guidance with proofs of guidance distinguishing right from wrong. Therefore whoever of you is present[55] in that month let him fast. But he who is ill or on a journey shall fast a similar number of days later on.

---

[55]*whoever of you is present:* To judge from the context, the meaning seems to be "present at home."

[185] God desires your well-being, not your discomfort. He desires you to fast the whole month so that you may magnify Him and render thanks to Him for giving you His guidance.

When My servants question you about Me, tell them that I am near. I answer the prayer of the suppliant when he calls to Me; therefore let them answer My call and put their trust in Me, that they may be rightly guided.

It is now lawful for you to lie with your wives on the night of the fast; they are a comfort to you as you are to them. God knew that you were deceiving yourselves. He has relented towards you and pardoned you. Therefore you may now lie with them and seek what God has ordained for you. Eat and drink until you can tell a white thread from a black one in the light of the coming dawn. Then resume the fast till nightfall and do not approach them, but stay at your prayers in the mosques.

Pilgrimage

The Sacred Mosque of Mecca, which houses the Kaba (the holy stone) and its shrine, was reclaimed by Muhammad from Arab polytheism with the argument that it was founded by Abraham and Ishmael, the first Muslims. In the second selection, the tribe of the Quraysh, which is Muhammad's own tribe, will receive God's protection in return for keeping the Holy Mosque. The third selection gives rules for the pilgrimage.   *Pillars*

[2:125, Medina] We made the House[56] a resort and a sanctuary for mankind, saying: "Make the place where Abraham stood a house of worship." We enjoined Abraham and Ishmael to cleanse Our House for those who walk round it, who meditate in it, and who kneel and prostrate themselves.

"Lord," said Abraham, "make this a land of peace and bestow plenty upon its people, those of them that believe in God and the Last Day."

---

[56]*the House:* the Sacred Mosque of Mecca, the holiest site in Islam. It is the house of the Kaba and the house of worship for all Muslims.

"As for those that do not," He answered, "I shall let them live awhile, and then shall drag them to the scourge of the Fire. Evil shall be their fate."

Abraham and Ishmael built the House and dedicated it, saying: "Accept this from us, Lord. You are the One that hears all and knows all. Lord, make us submissive to You; make of our descendants a nation that will submit to You. Teach us our rites of worship and turn to us with mercy; You are forgiving and merciful. Lord, send forth to them an apostle of their own who shall declare to them Your revelations,

---

Qur'an 2:125–129; 106; 2:196–199.

and shall instruct them in the Book and in wisdom, and shall purify them of sin. You are the Mighty, the Wise One."

[106, Mecca] For the protection of the Quraysh: their protection in their summer and winter journeys.[57]

Therefore let them worship the Lord of this House, who fed them in the days of famine and shielded them from all peril.

[2:196, Medina] Make the pilgrimage and visit the Sacred House for His sake. If you cannot, send such offerings as you can afford and do not shave your heads until the offerings have reached their destination. But if any of you is ill or suffers from an ailment of the head, he must pay a ransom either by fasting or by almsgiving or by offering a sacrifice.

If in peacetime anyone among you combines the visit with the pilgrimage, he must offer such gifts as he can afford; but if he lacks the means let him fast three days during the pilgrimage and seven when he has returned; that is, ten days in all. That is incumbent on him whose family are not present at the Holy Mosque. Have fear of God: know that He is stern in retribution.

Make the pilgrimage in the appointed months. He that intends to perform it in those months must abstain from sexual intercourse, obscene language, and acrimonious disputes while on pilgrimage. God is aware of whatever good you do. Provide well for yourselves: the best provision is piety. Fear Me, then, you that are endowed with understanding.

It shall be no offence for you to seek the bounty of your Lord. When you come running from Arafat[58] remember God as you approach the sacred monument. Remember Him that gave you guidance when you were in error. Then go out from the place whence the pilgrims will go out and implore the forgiveness of God. He is forgiving and merciful. And when you have fulfilled your sacred duties, remember God as you remember your forefathers or with deeper reverence.

---

[57]*journeys:* trade caravans.

[58]*Arafat:* one of the mountains near Mecca, a stop on the pilgrimage.

The Mosque

The Arabic word for mosque is *masjid,* "place of prostration." A mosque is a place of prayer, praise, and hope in the next world. The restrictions on attending mosques are given in the second reading. They are for Muslims only, and Muslims are urged to be faithful as they come to the mosque. These two passages are given from Medina.

[24:36] God speaks in metaphors to men. God has knowledge of all things.

His light is found in temples which God has sanctioned to be built for the remembrance of His name. In them, morning and evening, His praise is sung by men whom neither trade nor profit can divert from remembering Him, from offering prayers, or from giving alms; who dread the day when men's hearts and eyes shall writhe with anguish; who hope that God will requite them for their noblest deeds and lavish His grace upon them. God gives without measure to whom He will.

[9:15] It ill becomes the idolaters to visit the mosques of God, for they are self-confessed unbelievers. Vain shall be their works, and in the Fire they shall abide for ever.

None shall visit the mosques of God except those who believe in God and the Last Day, attend to their prayers and render the alms levy and fear none but God. These shall be rightly guided.

Do you pretend that he who gives a drink to the pilgrims and pays a visit to the Sacred Mosque is as worthy as the man who believes in God and the Last Day, and fights for God's cause? These are not held equal by God. God does not guide the wrongdoers.

SELECTIONS FROM THE *HADITH*

The *hadith* ("traditions") are sayings by Muhammad passed down in early Islam that did not find their way into the *Qur'an*. They are called the "unrecited revelation." This designation rests on the belief common to Muslims that Muhammad's words were divinely inspired, not only when he recited the *Qur'an* but in all of his utterances after his prophetic call. The *Qur'an* and the *hadith* form the basis of the religious law that has governed Islamic societies since early times. Even though the *hadith* are not considered scriptural, their high, semicanonical standing leads us to sample them briefly here.

Muslim theologians divide each *hadith* in two parts. First is the **isnad,** the authority on which the tradition stands. This is a list of the individuals who orally passed down the specific tradition, from the person who heard the saying of Muhammad and first framed the story to the last person to report it before it was written down two or two and a half centuries after the Prophet's death. (The whole chain of transmission is not given in the selections here.) For a tradition to be considered authentic, it must show an unbroken chain of transmission, and each person in the chain must be reliable and pious. The second part of a *hadith* is the **matn,** the text of the saying itself. Sometimes, this is just a short saying, and other times, it is framed by a story.[59]

The last four selections deal with jihad, "struggle/warfare" for the faith. In the first, the privileges of death in combat, called "martyrdom," are given. In the second, the Islamic practice of taking captured people and property as plunder (sometimes called "booty") is defended against the ancient Israelite prohibition of plunder; for the Jewish *Bible* story referred to at the end of this selection, see Chapter 7 in the book of *Joshua*. In the third, a brief command is given forbidding the killing of women and children in jihad. In the last, procedures are laid down for dealing with religious opponents who have come under Muslim control in jihad.

On Innovations

It is related from Irbad bin Sariyah that he said, "On a certain day the Apostle of God said prayers with us; then he drew near to us and gave us eloquent instruction that brought tears to our eyes and by which our hearts were affected. A man said, 'O Apostle of God, this is as if it were a farewell address, therefore give us a command.' He replied, 'I command you the fear of God, and giving ear and obedience even if one is an Abyssinian slave; for those of you who will live after me will see many schisms. Therefore it is your duty to follow my rule of faith and the rule of faith of the rightly guided caliphs. Seize it and hold it fast. Beware of new things, for all new things are an innovation, and all innovation is a going astray.'"

On Ritual Washings

It is related from Othman that he performed his ablutions and poured water on his hands three times, he washed his mouth, and then cleansed his nose. After that he washed his face three

---

[59]The passages that follow are excerpted from W. Goldsack, *Selections from Muhammadan Traditions* (Madras: Christian Literature Society for India, 1923).

times, then he washed his right arm to his elbow three times, then he washed his left arm to his elbow three times. After that he wiped his hand over his head, then he washed his right foot three times, then the left three times. After that he said, "I saw the Apostle of God perform his ablutions like these ablutions of mine." Then he said, "Whoever performs his ablutions like these ablutions of mine, and then prays two sets of prayers, while his mind speaks nothing the while, all his preceding sins will be forgiven him."

On Prayer

It is related from Abdullah bin Omar that, "The Apostle of God said, 'The time for the midday prayer is when the sun declines, and a man's shadow becomes equal to his height, and the afternoon prayer has not arrived. And the time for the afternoon prayer is so long as the sun has not become yellow; and the time for the evening prayer is so long as the ruddy light of twilight has not disappeared; and the time of the night prayer is to the first half of the night; and the time for the morning prayer is from the breaking of the dawn until the sun rises. When the sun rises, then withhold from the morning prayer, for truly it rises between the two horns of Satan.'"

It is related from Ubadah binus-Samit that, "The Apostle of God said, 'There can be no prayer for the one who does not recite the opening chapter of the Book.'"

On Alms

It is related from Abu Musaul-Ashari that, "The Apostle of God said, 'Alms are obligatory on every Muslim.' They said 'And if he has nothing?' He replied, 'Then let him work with his hands, and gain something for himself, and give alms.' They said, 'And if he is not able to work, or has not done so?' He replied, 'Then let him assist those who are in need and in distress.' They said, 'And if he does not do that?' He replied, 'Then let him order people to do right.' They said, 'And if he does not do that?' He replied, 'Then let him withhold himself from evil; and truly that will be alms for him.'"

It is related from Abu Umamah that he said, "I heard the Apostle of God say, in his public address, in the year of the farewell pilgrimage,[60] 'Let not a woman spend anything in alms from the house of her husband, except with the permission of her husband.' It was said, 'O Apostle of God, not even food?' He replied, 'That is the best of our property.'"

On God

It is related from Ubai bin Kab that, "The Apostle of God said, 'O Abu Al Mandhar, do you know which verse from the Book of God most High which is with you is the greatest?' I said, 'God and His Apostle know best.' He said, 'O Abu Al Mandhar, do you know which verse from the Book of God which is with you is greatest?' I said, 'God, there is no God but He, the Living, the Self-subsisting.'" Ubai said, "And he struck me on my breast and said, 'O Abu Al Mandhar, may knowledge be welcome to you.'"

It is related from Abu Hurairah that, "The Apostle of God said, 'Truly God Most High has ninety-nine names. Whoever counts them will enter paradise. He is Allah, than whom there is no other God, the Merciful, the Compassionate, the King, the Holy, the Peace, the Faithful, the Protector, the Mighty, the Compeller, the Proud, the Creator, the Maker, the Fashioner, the Forgiver, the Dominant, the Bestower, the Provider, the Opener, the Knower, the Restrainer, the Speaker, the Abaser, the Exalter, the Honorer, the Destroyer, the Hearer, the Seer, the Ruler, the Just, the Subtle, the Aware, the Clement, the Grand, the Forgiving, the Grateful, the Exalted, the Great, the Guardian, the Strengthener, the Reckoner, the Majestic, the Generous, the Watcher, the Approver, the Comprehensive, the Wise, the Loving, the Glorious, the Raiser, the Witness, the Truth, the Advocate, the Strong, the Firm, the Patron, the Laudable, the Counter, the Beginner, the Restorer, the Quickener, the Killer, the Living, the Subsisting, the Finder, the Glorious, the One, the Eternal, the Powerful, the Prevailing, the Bringer-forward, the Deferrer, the First, the Last, the Evident, the Hidden, the Governor,

---

[60]*farewell pilgrimage:* the Prophet's last pilgrimage to Mecca before his death.

the Exalted, the Righteous, the Accepter of Repentance, the Avenger, the Pardoner, the Kind, the Ruler of the Kingdom, the Lord of majesty and liberality, the Equitable, the Collector, the Independent, the Enricher, the Giver, the Withholder, the Distresser, the Profiter, the Light, the Guide, the Incomparable, the Enduring, the Inheritor, the Director, the Patient.' "

On the Power of Reading the *Qur'an*

It is related from Abu Sa'idu'l-Khudri that Usaid bin Hudair said, "On a certain night when he was reading, and his horse was tethered near him, behold! the horse wheeled round. Then he became silent, and it also became steady. Then he read (again), and it wheeled round. Then he became silent, and it ceased wheeling round. He again read, and the horse wheeled round as before. Then he turned away, and his son Yahya was near it, and he feared that it would injure him. And when he moved the child away he raised his head to the heavens, and behold! something like a cloud and in it objects resembling lamps. And when the morning came he informed the Prophet.... 'I feared, O Apostle of God, that it would tread on Yahya who was near it, and I moved near to him, and raised my head to the heavens, and behold! something resembling a cloud, in which were objects like lamps, and I went out in order that I should not see them.' He replied, 'And do you know what that was?' He said, 'No.' He said, 'Those were angels which came near at the sound of thy voice, and if you had continued to read, they would have remained until the morning, and men would have seen them. They would not have remained hidden.'

On the Martyr in Jihad

It is related from Abu Miqdam bin Madikarib that the Apostle of God said, "The martyr has six privileges near God: he is forgiven his sins on (the shedding of) the first drop of blood; he is shown his resting-place in paradise; he is redeemed from the punishment of the grave; he is made secure from the great fear (of hell); and a crown of glory is placed on his head, one ruby of which is better than the world and all

that is therein; and he will marry seventy-two wives from the houris with dark eyes; and his intercession will be accepted for seventy of his relatives."

On Plunder in Jihad

It is related from Abu Hurairah that the Prophet said, "One of the Prophets [Joshua] went out to fight; and he said to his people, 'Let no man follow me who has married a wife and wishes to take her to his house, but has not yet done so; nor the one who has built a house, but has not yet raised a roof over it; nor the man who has bought a sheep or camel and is expecting it to give birth.' Then he went forth to war. And he drew near a certain village at the time of evening prayer. Then he said to the sun, 'Truly you are under orders, and I am also under orders. O God, restrain it for us.' Then it was restrained (from setting) until God gave him the victory. After that he gathered together the plunder; and a fire came to devour it, but it did not consume it. And he said, 'Truly there is deceit among you with regard to the plunder. Therefore let a man from each tribe pledge his oath.' Then the hand of a certain man stuck to his hand. He said, 'The deceit concerning the plunder is among you.' Then they [the offenders] brought a golden head like the head of a cow. Then he set it down and the fire came and devoured it." And the relater has added in another tradition, "Plunder was not lawful for any one before us. Afterwards God made plunder lawful for us. He saw our weakness and impotence and made it lawful for us."

On Women and Children in Jihad

It is related from Abdullah bin Omar, "The Apostle of God forbade the killing of women and children."

On the Steps for Jihad Against Enemies

It is related from Sulaiman bin Buraidah, from his father, that he said, "When the Apostle of God appointed a leader over any army or marauding band, he was in the habit of giving him orders regarding his special duties concerning the fear of God and good behavior towards those Muslims who were with him. After that he would say,

'Go forth to war in the name of God in his road. Fight with those who disbelieve in God. Go forth to war. Do not use deceit or break a covenant, or mutilate [anyone], or kill children. And when you meet your enemy the polytheists, then invite them to the rights and privileges of Islam or defeat. If they give an affirmative answer, accept it from them and withdraw from them. After that invite them to remove themselves from their homes to the homes of the refugees, and inform them that if they do that, then for them is what is given to the refugees; and their duties are the same as those of the refugees. But if they refuse to change from their homes, then inform them that they will remain as the desert Arabs who have embraced Islam. The commands of God will be obligatory upon them which are obligatory upon other believers; but they will get nothing of the plunder and spoils unless they go to fight along with the other Muslims. But if they refuse (to become Muslims) then ask from them the poll-tax. And if they answer you in the affirmative, then accept it from them, and withdraw from them. But if they refuse (to pay), then seek help from God and fight them.'"

GLOSSARY

ayah [EYE-yuh] "sign"; a verse in the *Qur'an.*

Bismillah [biss-MILL-uh] the opening formula for surahs in the *Qur'an:* "In the name of God, the Compassionate, the Merciful."

Challenge verses short passages of the *Qur'an* in which the Prophet calls on his opponents to produce anything like his revelation.

Fatihah [fah-TEE-huh] "Opening"; the first chapter of the *Qur'an,* used as a prayer in Islam.

hadith [hah-DEETH] "traditions"; a traditional report recording a saying or action of Muhammad.

isnad [EES-nahd] the authority on which a section of *hadith* stands, usually given as a list of names in a chain of tradition.

jihad [jee-HAHD] "struggle," both personal, inner struggle through prayer and study and armed struggle through military conflict to promote and defend Islam.

jinn [jihn] spirits, both good and evil, distinguishable from angelic beings and the deity.

matn [MAH-ten] the main text of a *hadith.*

qiblah [KIB-luh] the direction Muslims face during prayer.

Qur'an [kuhr-AHN] "recitation, reading"; the scripture of Islam.

surah [SOO-rah] a chapter of the *Qur'an.*

tafsir [TAHF-sear] the branch of Islamic scholarship that deals with commentary on the *Qur'an.*

tilawa [tee-LAH-wuh] ritual recitation of the *Qur'an.*

QUESTIONS FOR STUDY AND DISCUSSION

1. How does the *Qur'an* give both direct (explicit) and indirect (implicit) information about the career of Muhammad?
2. In what sense is Islam especially Arabic? What does it mean for a universal religion like Islam to have a scripture that cannot be translated and still fully remain God's word for all peoples?
3. Explain the statement "Islam is a religion of the book."
4. Describe the status of women in the *Qur'an* and in Islam in general. To what degree may it be possible to improve this status and still keep within the bounds of the *Qur'an?*
5. How does almsgiving function to promote compassion and social justice?
6. Relate the cognitive to the noncognitive uses of the *Qur'an.* Which do you see as primary and why?
7. How does the *Qur'an*'s view of creation and the world add to the views presented in Jewish and Christian scripture?
8. Free will and predestination are problems that touch many religions. They even touch other areas of thought, especially philosophy and psychology, with debates between behaviorists and humanists. Explain your views on this topic and relate them to the *Qur'an.*

SCRIPTURES IN FILM

The traditional Muslim reluctance to picture the face of Muhammad has influenced films about Muslim origins. Significant but of mixed cinematic value is *The Message* (1976, rated PG), directed by Moustapha Akkad, the story of Muhammad (without depicting him directly) and early Islam. One film that depicts Muslim life today as it draws on the *Qur'an* is *Malcolm X* (1992, rated PG-13), directed by Spike Lee and starring Denzel Washington, showing the struggle of the Black Muslim movement to return to Muslim roots.

SUGGESTIONS FOR FURTHER READING

PRIMARY READINGS

Alim: version 4.5. ISL Software, 1997. A multimedia CD-ROM featuring Arabic text, recitation, transliteration, translations, and some *hadith* passages.

A. J. Arberry, ed., *The Koran Interpreted*. New York: Macmillan, 1955. This translation probably does the best job of suggesting in English the literary quality of the original.

K. Cragg, *Readings in the Qur'an*. London: Collins, 1988. An abridgment of the *Qur'an* to two-thirds of its size, arranged by eight themes, with a comprehensive introduction.

N. J. Dawood, trans., *The Koran*. New York: Penguin, 1990. This reliable translation is probably the most widely read edition available.

M. A. S. Abdel Haleem, *The Qur'an*. Oxford: Oxford University Press, 2004. A new translation, highly acclaimed for its accuracy and readability. For the readings of this chapter in Haleem's translation, see R. E. Van Voorst, *Anthology of World Scriptures: Western Religions* (Belmont, CA: Thomson Wadsworth, 2006).

T. B. Irving, *The Qur'an: The First American Translation*. Brattleboro, VT: Amana, 1985. This translation is in good idiomatic English; the notes are from a traditional Muslim perspective and help the reader understand the role of the *Qur'an* in Muslim life.

M. Sells, *Approaching the Qur'an: The Early Revelations*. Ashland, OR: White Cloud Press, 1999. Fresh, powerful translations of the earlier, more poetic surahs, with a compact disc recording of Arabic recitations of several of these surahs.

SECONDARY READINGS

A. Barlas, *"Believing Women" in Islam: Unreading Patriarchal Interpretations of the Qur'an*. Austin: University of Texas Press, 2002. Develops a reading of the *Qur'an* arguing for its originally egalitarian and antipatriarchal themes.

F. M. Denny, "Islam: *Qur'an* and *Hadith*." In F. M. Denny and R. L. Taylor, eds., *The Holy Book in Comparative Perspective*. Charleston: University of South Carolina Press, 1985, pp. 84–108. An up-to-date discussion of the relationship of the *Qur'an* and the *hadith*.

W. A. Graham, "'An Arabic Recital': Qur'an as a Spoken Book." In W. A. Graham, *Beyond the Written Word*. Cambridge: Cambridge University Press, 1987, pp. 79–115. An excellent treatment of the oral aspects of the *Qur'an*.

J. D. McAuliffe, *Qur'anic Christians: An Analysis of Classical and Modern Exegesis*. Cambridge: Cambridge University Press, 1991. An excellent study of the history of Islamic interpretation of the *Qur'an* by way of an important interreligious question: the meaning of those passages that make ostensibly positive remarks about Christians.

F. Rahman, *The Leading Ideas of the Qur'an*. Minneapolis: Bibliotheca, 1980. A fine treatment of the most important themes of the *Qur'an* by a leading Muslim theologian.

J. I. Smith, "Islam." In A. Sharma, ed., *Women in World Religions*. Albany: State University of New York Press, 1987, pp. 235–250. A treatment of the place of women in Islam, with a fine discussion of what the *Qur'an* says about women and how it is and is not applied in contemporary Muslim societies.

B. Stowasser, *Women in the Qur'an, Traditions, and Commentaries*. New York: Oxford University Press, 1994. An excellent treatment of the status and role of women in scripture, *hadith*, and commentary.

COMPANION WEBSITE

Visit the *Anthology of World Scriptures* companion website at **www.thomsonedu.com** for learning tools such as map explorations, flashcards of glossary terms, learning objectives, chapter practice quizzes, links to other websites for learning and research, and chapter summaries in PowerPoint® format.

New Religious Movements

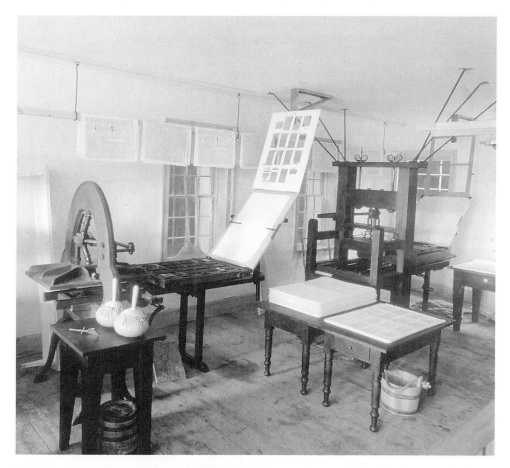

The Grandin Press, Palmyra, New York

The Book of Mormon was first published here in 1830. The size of the first printing—5,000 copies—was unusually large for the time and indicates the initial strength of the Church of Jesus Christ of Latter-day Saints. A distinguishing feature of most scriptures of the new religious movements is their immediate mass publication. (*Copyright © 2000 Intellectual Reserve, Inc. Used by permission.*)

- A weary business traveler settles into her room in the Marriott Hotel in Chicago. Looking for a bit of inspiration at the end of her day, she opens the top drawer of the nightstand alongside the bed expecting to find a Christian *Bible*. On top of the *Bible,* however, is a copy of the *Book of Mormon,* subtitled "Another Testament of Jesus Christ." This puzzles her for a moment, until she remembers that the Marriott family that owns this hotel chain is devoutly Mormon and, like all devout Mormons, is eager to spread its scriptures.

- In Manhattan's Madison Square Garden, 2,000 couples are waiting to be joined in marriage by the Reverend Sun Myung Moon and his wife, Hak Ja Han Moon, the founders of the Unification Church. The Moons arranged these marriages, and many of the couples have met only recently. As a part of the ceremony, words from the Unification scripture, *Divine Principle,* are intoned over the assembled crowd. These words emphasize one of the key ideas in Unification teaching: Under the religious direction of the Moons, the True Parents, the world will be saved by its repopulation with true children of God, believing Unificationists.

- In Boston, a young woman gets up in a meeting to tell of her recent case. A Christian Scientist, she has used her faith to become healthy again after suffering from a form of cancer. Like Christian Scientists for more than a century before her, she attributes her health to the spiritual power she found while reading Mary Baker Eddy's book, *Science and Health with Key to the Scriptures.*

INTRODUCTION

New religious movements, a recent term in the field of religious studies, generally denotes religious groups that arose since the start of the nineteenth century and now have sufficient size, longevity, and cultural impact to merit academic study. Most recently published encyclopedias, handbooks, and textbooks on religion use this term and provide information about the groups to which it refers.[1] *New religious movements* is preferable in many ways to other recent terms such as *alternative religious movements* and *marginal religious movements,* and it is clearly preferable to the older *cults* and *sects.* Although these last two terms still have some validity—especially in the sociological study of religion, where scholars try to use them objectively—they have become so laden with value judgments that most scholars no longer use them to characterize the new religious movements.

Hundreds of groups around the world today are in a sense new religious movements, and each year sees the birth of more. In this chapter, we focus on four movements that have become significant worldwide, that make and use scriptures, and that are important for students of world religions to encounter: the Baha'i tradition, the Church of Jesus Christ of Latter-day Saints, the Christian Science Church, and the Unification Church. (For treatment of the Falun Gong movement, which many people view as a new religious movement, see Chapter 3, pages 104–106.)

---

[1]For an excellent concise treatment of new religious movements, see W. H. Swatus Jr., ed., *Encyclopedia of Religion and Society* (Walnut Creek, CA: AltaMira, 1998), pp. 328–333.

The inclusion of these groups in this chapter is not intended to imply that they see themselves as new religious movements; often, they do not. Nor do they see themselves as related to each other; indeed, they are not. Although scholars call these religious movements "new," we must note that all branch off from older religions. Baha'i arose in the nineteenth century from Shi'ite Islam and sees itself as the successor of Islam. The Church of Jesus Christ of Latter-day Saints, the Christian Science Church, and the Unification Church see themselves as Christian, and most experts in comparative religions view this labeling as basically correct. That all three accept the Christian *Bible* as their first canon is a good indication of their Christian roots. Moreover, outsiders to Christianity, such as Buddhists, would almost certainly recognize them as belonging to the stream of Christian tradition.

Some of these new religious movements are highly controversial in North America and in other parts of the world. However, many of the other faiths examined in this book were also controversial when they were new. Careful students of religion will want to form judgments about the four new movements that are based in some measure on what believers say about themselves in their own sacred writings.

Because each of the movements treated in this chapter is separate from the others, we examine each movement and its scripture in turn in the order in which it first appeared. In the remainder of this introductory section, we consider briefly the names of the various scriptures, their use, their structures, and their origin and development.

Names

Most of the scriptures of the new religious movements (unlike those of the older, traditional faiths) were written and published by the founders in their lifetime. Thus, the founding authors themselves gave these scriptures the names by which they are known.

Baha'i calls its scriptures **Holy Writings.** This name may seem bland and unilluminating, but it does imply something important about Baha'i scriptures: their originally written character. The *Qur'an* ("Recitation") originated orally as the transmission of God's words; in contrast, the *Holy Writings* are the "Pen of God," a phrase often repeated in the earliest Baha'i scriptures.

The Church of Jesus Christ of Latter-day Saints has a three-part scripture. The **Book of Mormon** is the leading part, and it is from this title that the followers of this movement came to be known as Mormons. (This is the only instance among the major world religions of a faith being named, or in this case nicknamed, from the name of its scripture.) The current subtitle of this book, *A Second Testament of Jesus Christ,* is a more recent addition to the original title. A second, shorter scripture is the **Pearl of Great Price,** a selection of inspired translations by Mormon founder Joseph Smith (1805–1844). The final scripture is **Doctrine and Covenants,** which contains the continuing revelation of God's word through Latter-day Saint prophets, especially Joseph Smith. The *Book of Mormon,* but not the other two texts, is also considered scriptural by the Community of Christ, formerly known as the Reorganized Church of Jesus Christ of Latter-day Saints, an early splinter group. In addition to this "second canon" of scripture, the Latter-day Saint church has a "first canon" of the Christian *Bible*—in particular, the King James Version of 1611.

The founder of Christian Science, Mary Baker Eddy (1821–1910), was a prolific writer, like many founders of new religious movements. Although new religious movements sometimes consider everything their founders wrote to be scriptural, the Christian Science Church has carefully delineated only one book as scripture: *Science and Health with Key to the Scriptures* (first published in 1875). Mrs. Eddy herself guided this delineation. The title of the book accurately suggests its content: a "science" that uses prayer, Christian scripture (the King James Version), and Eddy's book itself to heal body, mind, and spirit.

The Unification Church's sole scripture, written by its founder Sun Myung Moon (b. 1920), is the *Divine Principle. Principle* here means "teaching," and it refers to Moon's distinctive reinterpretation of Christianity (the "Divine" of the title) in combination with select Asian teachings such as yin and yang; devotion to Korea; and a virulent anticommunism to produce a new religious movement.

Overview of Structure

The scriptures of new religious movements tend to show much less variety in structure and genre than the scriptures of traditional religions. They are usually nonnarrative prose strongly oriented to teaching the new doctrines. Three reasons help to explain this internal sameness. First, because they are "second canon" works, following up on the *Qur'an* (Baha'i) or on the Christian *Bible,* they are more tightly focused than other scriptures. Second, the relatively short period of time in which they were written, compared to the centuries-long process of scriptural creation in most other traditions, gives them a sharper focus. (The *Book of Mormon,* however, does claim to have been written by multiple authors over a 1,000-year period.) Third, they are mostly written by the first founders of the various religious movements, not by later leaders.

The *Holy Writings* of Baha'i are organized in four parts corresponding to their four authors. First are the writings of a men known as the Bab ("Gate" to God), born Sayyid Ali-Muhammad Shiraz (1819–1850). These writings form a sort of preface to Baha'i. Next are the writings of Baha'u'llah, born Mirza Husayn-Ali Nur (1817–1892), the main founder of the faith. In the Baha'i canon, these two groups of writings are considered directly revelatory from God and thus most authoritative. Next are the writings of Abdu'l-Baha (1843–1921), the third leader, and finally the writings of his grandson Shoghi Effendi (1897–1957), the final leader of Baha'i, whose death effectively closed the canon. These writings are a collection of letters, narratives, prayers, and laws.

The scriptures of the Church of Jesus Christ of Latter-day Saints are fairly complex. They record a story of ancient American peoples descended from ancient Hebrews who left Judah around 600 B.C.E., the appearance of the resurrected Jesus Christ to these Americans, and the rebirth of the true Christian church in the nineteenth century with Joseph Smith Jr. The *Book of Mormon* has fifteen main parts known, with one exception, as books. Like the *Bible,* these books are subdivided into chapters and verses. Mormons believe that these texts are based on writings appearing on four groups of metal plates: those of Nephi [NEE-figh], Mormon, and Ether, and brass plates that, according to founder Joseph Smith, people fleeing Jerusalem in 600 B.C.E. brought to the Americas. In 421 C.E., Moroni, the last of the Nephite prophets, is believed to have sealed the sacred plates and hidden them by divine instruction. Smith said that in 1823 this same Moroni visited him as a resurrected prophet and directed him to these sacred plates. He reported that he translated the writing on the plates into English. He published the text in 1830 as the *Book of Mormon.* The plates themselves, Mormons believe, were returned to Moroni and then hidden away for all time.

The second Latter-day Saint scripture, *Pearl of Great Price,* was first compiled in 1851 by Franklin Richards, then a member of the church's Council of the Twelve Apostles and in charge of the church's missions in Great Britain. Richards intended to increase circulation among Latter-day Saints of Joseph Smith's testimony and translations. The book quickly received wide acceptance, especially in mission fields, and became a scripture of the church by the action of its First Presidency (highest official body) in 1880. *Pearl of Great Price* contains five main sections: *Selections from the Book of Moses* is an excerpt from Joseph Smith's translation of *Genesis. The Book of Abraham* is a translation of writings by the patriarch Abraham on Egyptian papyri that Joseph Smith obtained in 1835. *Joseph Smith—Matthew* is an excerpt from the testimony of the *New Testament's Gospel of Matthew* to Jesus Christ as understood in the church. *Joseph Smith—History* is extracts of Joseph Smith's official testimony about his own life. *Articles of Faith of the Church of Jesus Christ of Latter-day Saints* is a statement by Joseph Smith.

The third Latter-day Saint scripture, *Doctrine and Covenants,* has 138 sections plus two "official declarations." It contains revelations on doctrines and community life, some narrative, some theological, and some legal, from 1823 until 1978. Its "official declarations" deal with two controversial topics: the ending of polygamy and the admission of blacks to the priesthood.

The scripture of Christian Science is in two parts, as its title implies. The first part, "Science and Health," consists of a preface by the author and fourteen chapters on various topics: Christian doctrines, spiritualism and hypnotism, medicine, and Christian Science practices of prayer and healing. The second part, "Key to the Scriptures," has three chapters, one each treating *Genesis* and the *Apocalypse* (*Revelation* in the *New Testament*), and a glossary. "Fruitage," a final section added later, is a collection of written testimonies to the healing power of Christian Science and especially to the role of *Science and Health with Key to the Scriptures* in this healing. This book has not been revised since the edition of 1910—the last edition that Mary Baker Eddy published—and has kept in all subsequent printings the 1910 pagination and line numbers.

The *Divine Principle* of the Unification Church is heavily didactic in content and style, as its abstract title implies. Its organization is also complex. Thirteen chapters are divided into numerous sections and subsections. Topics treated include "Principle of Creation," "The Human Fall," "The Messiah," "Predestination," "Christology," "The Periods in Providential History and the Determination of Their Lengths," "Preparation Period for the Second Advent of the Messiah," and "Second Advent." These chapter titles vaguely imply what the content of this book makes plain—namely, that Jesus, the first Messiah, did not accomplish God's mission, and a second Messiah has now been born in Korea, God's new chosen nation. (Moon's writings do not make a distinction between North and South Korea on this point; indeed, one of Moon's primary objectives has been the reunification of the Korean Peninsula.) *Divine Principle* does not make it explicit, but in other places, Moon has proclaimed himself to be this second Messiah.

Contemporary Use

The use of scripture in the new religious movements is typically more limited than its use in more traditional religions. Believers within these new groups do not regularly use their scriptures in ritual; they pay them no veneration, and the books themselves are not ornately published or decorated. (The new religious movements that use the Christian *Bible* alongside their own scriptures often show the *Bible* some formal respect short of veneration.) Nor do they typically use their books to organize the structure of their religious communities. Instead, they use their scriptures in three key ways.

• Believers are expected to study the scriptures in groups and privately. At times, this use crosses over into meditation. For example, Christian Scientists believe that healing comes from proper study and use of Mary Baker Eddy's *Science and Health with Key to the Scriptures*. In the Baha'i faith, the wording of the early scriptures, based as it is on lyrical Qur'anic style, encourages a meditative approach.

• The scriptures are used to teach key doctrines. They were written in large measure to teach new religious ideas in the context of an older traditional religion, and the faithful teaching of these new doctrines is important. For example, Sun Myung Moon's teachings in the *Divine Principle* are known and carried out by Unification Church leaders at all levels.

• New religious movements typically use their scriptures in missionary activities to spread their faith. Two examples must suffice here. The Christian Science Church widely distributes *Science and Health with Key to the Scriptures* at a subsidized price. The *Book of Mormon* is strongly advertised on American television and in print ads inviting people to send for a free copy. Given its role in the missionizing goals of the Latter-day Saints church, the *Book of Mormon* has become one of the world's most important scriptures.

A telling indication that these groups view their own writings as scriptural is the physical appearance of the books themselves. Though not ornate, these books are typically designed to look like the scripture books they supplement or replace. The *Holy Writings* of Baha'i resembles the *Qur'an*. The *Divine Principle* of the Unification Church is, like the traditional Christian *Bible,* published with a black cover and black end papers. The Latter-day Saint church designs the *Book of Mormon* to resemble the format of the *Bible* it publishes.

Historical Origins and Development

It is possible to make four general observations about the origin and development of scripture in the new religious movements, especially as contrasted with the scriptures of older religions.

• The scriptures of the new religious movements have little or no oral tradition behind them; instead, they went straight into print. The *Holy Writings* of Baha'i, the *Book of Mormon, Science and Health with Key to the Scriptures,* and the *Divine Principle* of the Unification Church were all taken by their respective authors from composition to publication. They do not reflect a long tradition shaped by community use, but they do reflect the thinking of individual authors.

• The scriptures of the new religious movements are "instant scripture" in that they are immediately accepted and used as scripture by believers. In the traditional faiths, a good deal of time passes while writings are compiled, recognized as scriptural, and put into a canon. As soon as the founder of a new movement produces a book, the movement adopts the text as authoritative.

• The new religious movements tend to have a remarkably large amount of scriptural literature compared to the older traditions. Everything each founder wrote—many of the founders were very prolific writers—is often considered scriptural, but special emphasis is placed on certain works. For example, in the Latter-day Saints and Baha'i movements, the scriptural literature continued to grow even after the death of the founders. These movements tend to have scriptures as lengthy as the scripture of the religions they seek to supplant.

• Despite their fixed, published form, most scriptures of the new religious movements are amenable to change. For example, the Latter-day Saints text *Doctrine and Covenants* is open-ended. An addition to it can change or amplify previous revelation, even previous revelation recorded in the *Book of Mormon*. The Unification Church's *Divine Principle* was revised in 1996, and a careful comparison of this and the previous edition shows a few significant changes in content.

We focus now on each of the new religious movements in turn. The Baha'i scriptures have a fourfold development that corresponds to their current structure as outlined earlier. Each step is built on those that precede it to make a coherent written tradition and teaching for the faith. First are the writings of "the Bab," next are the writings of Baha'u'llah, then the writings of Abdu'l-Baha, the third leader, and finally, the writings of his grandson Shoghi Effendi.

The *Book of Mormon*, the main scripture of the Church of Jesus Christ of Latter-day Saints, serves as a basis for newer scriptures in the Mormon canon. Ironically, the *Book of Mormon* tends to be more similar than later official church writings and teachings to the mainstream Protestant Christianity against which the movement arose, especially as regards the controversial doctrines that have tended to set the Latter-day Saints apart from other Christians. For example, the *Book of Mormon* promotes monogamy and discourages (but does not forbid) polygamy (see *Jacob* 2:27, 30), but *Doctrine and Covenants* preserves both the approval of polygamy (section 132, 37–38, 52, 61–62) and the official disapproval of it ("Official Declaration 1"). Although opponents of the church point to more than 3,000 alleged changes in the *Book of Mormon* since its initial publication, the majority of them are corrections and updates of spelling and grammar. In essence, this important book remains as Joseph Smith Jr. wrote it.

The development of Christian Science scripture began with the writing of the "Science and Health." Then in "Key to the Scriptures," Mary Baker Eddy applied the ideas from "Science and Health" to parts of the Christian *Bible*. The concluding "Fruitage" ("Results") was compiled on the basis of earlier editions of "Science and Health," especially testimonies about the healing power of its ideas. *Science and Health with Key to the Scriptures* grew in stages from its first publication in 1875 until it reached its final form in 1910.

The Unification Church's *Divine Principle* has gone through three English-language editions since its first publication in 1959. The last of these, in 1996, is a much more fluent translation than the first two. However, these three editions are not just new translations of the Korean original; a few entire sections have been added or deleted, especially from the second to third edition. Because the Unification movement has no other scripture, this text shifts as the religion changes.

THE SCRIPTURE OF BAHA'I

The Essence of Baha'i Teaching and a Sketch of the Life of Baha'u'llah

Here the last leader of the Baha'i movement gives its definitive teaching. He stresses the oneness of humanity under the oneness of God. This powerful vision for world harmony, written in the middle of the twentieth century, has become the leading characteristic of the Baha'i movement.[2]

The fundamental principle enunciated by Baha'u'llah . . . is that religious truth is not absolute but relative, that Divine Revelation is a continuous and progressive process, that all the great religions of the world are divine in origin, that their basic principles are in complete harmony, that their aims and purposes are one and the same. Their teachings are but facets of one truth, their functions are complementary, and they differ only in the nonessential aspects of their doctrines. Their missions represent successive stages in the spiritual evolution of human society. . . .

His mission is to proclaim that the ages of the infancy and of the childhood of the human race are past. The convulsions associated with the present stage of its adolescence are slowly and painfully preparing it to attain the stage of manhood. They are heralding the approach of that Age of Ages when swords will be beaten into plowshares, when the Kingdom promised by Jesus Christ will have been established, and the

peace of the planet definitely and permanently ensured. Baha'u'llah does not claim finality for his Revelation, but rather stipulates that a fuller measure of the truth he has been commissioned by the Almighty to vouchsafe to humanity, at so critical a juncture in its fortunes, must be disclosed at future stages in the constant and limitless evolution of mankind.

The Baha'i Faith upholds the unity of God, recognizes the unity of God's prophets, and inculcates the principle of the oneness and wholeness of the entire human race. It proclaims the necessity and the inevitability of the unification of mankind, and asserts that it is gradually approaching. It claims that nothing short of the transmuting spirit of God, working through his chosen Mouthpiece in this day, can ultimately succeed in bringing it about. It enjoins upon its followers the primary duty of an unfettered search after truth, condemns all manner of prejudice and superstition, declares the purpose of religion to be the promotion of friendship and harmony, proclaims its essential harmony with science, and recognizes it as the foremost agency for the pacification and the orderly progress of human society. . . .

---

[2]All Baha'i writings are from the website Bahai-library.org. Copyright © 1996 National Spiritual Assembly of the Baha'is in the United States. Used by permission.

Shoghi Effendi, *The Promised Day Is Come*, Preface.

Mirza Husayn-'Ali, surnamed Baha'u'llah (the Glory of God), a native of Mazindaran, whose advent the Bab [Herald and Forerunner of Baha'u'llah] had foretold...was imprisoned in Teheran, Iran. He was banished in 1852 from his native land to Baghdad, and thence to Constantinople and Adrianople, and finally to the prison city of Akka, where he remained imprisoned for no less than twenty-four years, and in whose neighborhood he passed away in 1892. In the course of his banishment, and particularly in Adrianople and Akka, he formulated the laws and ordinances of his Dispensation and expounded, in over a hundred volumes, the principles of his Faith. He proclaimed his Message to the kings and rulers of both the East and the West, both Christian and Muslim, addressed the Pope, the Caliph of Islam, the Chief Magistrates of the Republics of the American continent, the entire Christian clergy, the leaders of Shi'ih and Sunni Islam, and the high priests of the Zoroastrian religion. In these writings he proclaimed his Revelation, summoned those whom he addressed to heed his call and espouse his Faith, warned them of the consequences of their refusal, and denounced, in some cases, their arrogance and tyranny....

The Faith that this order serves, safeguards, and promotes is essentially supernatural, supranational, entirely nonpolitical, and nonpartisan. It is diametrically opposed to any policy or school of thought that seeks to exalt any particular race, class, or nation. It is free from any form of ecclesiasticism, has neither priesthood nor rituals, and is supported exclusively by voluntary contributions made by its avowed adherents. Though loyal to their respective governments, though imbued with the love of their own country, and anxious to promote at all times its best interests, the followers of the Baha'i Faith view mankind as one entity and are profoundly attached to its vital interests. They will not hesitate to subordinate every particular interest, be it personal, regional, or national, to the overriding interests of the generality of mankind, knowing full well that in a world of interdependent peoples and nations the advantage of the part is best to be reached by the advantage of the whole. No lasting result can be achieved by any of the component parts if the general interests of the entity itself are neglected.

Baha'i, Islam, and Christianity

The Bab ("Gate" to God) saw himself as the "hidden Imam" or leader, promised in Shi'ite Islam. In this selection from his writings, addressed to the shah (king) of Iran, the predecessor of the faith deals with Muslim and Christian opposition and asserts the superiority of his faith to theirs. Notice how the style of the Bab's writings is very similar to the style of the *Qur'an;* the chapter-and-verse references to the *Qur'an* are in the original.

[1] All praise be to God Who has, through the power of Truth, sent down this Book unto his servant, that it may serve as a shining light for all mankind....Verily this is none other than the sovereign Truth; it is the Path which God has laid out for all that are in heaven and on earth. Let him then who will, take for himself the right path unto his Lord....This is indeed the eternal Truth that God, the Ancient of Days, has revealed unto his omnipotent Word—He Who has been raised up from the midst of the Burning Bush. This is the Mystery which has been hidden from all that are in heaven and on earth, and in this wondrous Revelation it has, in very truth, been set forth in the Mother Book by the hand of God, the Exalted....O concourse of kings and of the

The Bab, *Qayyumu'l-Asma* 1, 61–62.

sons of kings! Lay aside, one and all, your dominion which belongs to God.... Let not your sovereignty deceive you, O Shah, for "every soul shall taste of death," (*Qur'an* 3:182) and this, in very truth, has been written down as a decree of God.

[61] Verily, those who ridicule the wondrous, divine Verses revealed through his Remembrance are but making themselves the objects of ridicule, and We, in truth, aid them to grow in their iniquity. Indeed God's knowledge transcends all created things.... The infidels, of a truth, seek to separate God from his Remembrance, but God has determined to perfect his Light through his Remembrance, and indeed He is potent over all things....

Verily, Christ is Our Word that We communicated unto Mary; and let no one say what the Christians term as "the third of three" (*Qur'an* 5:77); it slanders the Remembrance Who...is invested with supreme authority. Indeed God is but one God, and far be it from his glory that there should be anyone else besides Him. All those who shall attain unto Him on the Day of Resurrection are but his servants, and God is, of a truth, a sufficient Protector. Verily I am none other but the servant of God and his Word, and none but the first one to bow down in supplication before God, the Most Exalted; and indeed God witnesses all things.

[62] O people of the *Qur'an*! You are as nothing unless you submit unto the Remembrance of God and unto this Book. If you follow the Cause of God, We will forgive your sins; but if you turn aside from our command, We will, in truth, condemn your souls in Our Book unto the Most Great Fire. We, verily, do not deal unjustly with men, even to the extent of a speck on a date-stone.

Baha'i Laws

Baha'u'llah's *Kitab-I-Aqdas,* "Most Holy Book," is the most influential statement of Baha'i laws. Reflecting the Muslim background of this new religious movement, great emphasis is placed on knowing and obeying God's laws. The sections given here include treatment of prayer (12–14), fasting (16), pilgrimage (32), criminals (45), marriage (65), scripture (149–150), and a single language for the world (189).

In the name of him who is the supreme ruler over all that has been and all that is to be! The first duty prescribed by God for his servants is the recognition of Him Who is the Dayspring of his Revelation and the Fountain of his laws, Who represents the Godhead in both the Kingdom of his Cause and the world of creation. Whoever achieves this duty has attained unto all good; and whoever is deprived thereof has gone astray, though he be the author of every righteous deed. Every one who reaches this most sublime station, this summit of transcendent glory, must observe every ordinance of him....

[2] They whom God has endued with insight will readily recognize that the precepts laid down by God constitute the highest means for the maintenance of order in the world and the security of its peoples. He who turns away from them is accounted among the abject and foolish. We have commanded you to refuse the dictates of your evil passions and corrupt desires, and not to transgress the bounds that the Pen of the Most High has fixed, for these are the breath of life unto all created things. The seas of Divine wisdom and Divine utterance have risen under the breath of the breeze of the All-Merciful. Hasten to drink your fill, O men of understanding!

Baha'u'llah, *Kitab-I-Aqdas* 1–2, 12–14, 16, 30–34, 45, 49, 56, 63–65, 149–150, 189.

They that have violated the Covenant of God by breaking his commandments, and have turned back on their heels, these have erred grievously in the sight of God, the All-Possessing, the Most High....

[12] It has been ordained that obligatory prayer is to be performed by each of you individually. Except for the Prayer for the Dead, the practice of congregational prayer has been annulled. He is truly the Ordainer, the All-Wise. God has exempted women who are in their monthly courses from obligatory prayer and fasting. Let them, instead, after performance of their washings, give praise unto God, repeating ninety-five times between the noon of one day and the next, "Glorified be God, the Lord of Splendor and Beauty." Thus has it been decreed in the Book, if you are of them that comprehend. When traveling, if you should stop and rest in some safe spot, perform—men and women alike—a single prostration in place of each unsaid Obligatory Prayer. While prostrating say, "Glorified be God, the Lord of Might and Majesty, of Grace and Bounty." Whoever is unable to do this, let him say only "Glorified be God."... Thus the Lord makes plain the ways of truth and guidance, ways that lead to one way, which is this Straight Path.

[16] O Pen of the Most High! Say: People of the world! We have enjoined upon you fasting during a brief period, and at its close have designated for you Naw-Rúz as a feast.... It befits the people of Baha'i, throughout these days [that precede the fast], to provide good cheer for themselves, their kindred and, beyond them, the poor and needy, and with joy and exultation to hail and glorify their Lord, to sing his praise and magnify his Name. When they end this, let them begin the fast.... The traveler, the ailing, those who are with child, are not bound by the Fast. They have been exempted by God as a token of his grace....

[30] The Lord has ordained that in every city a House of Justice be established wherein shall gather counselors.... They should consider themselves as entering the Court of the presence of God, the Exalted, the Most High, and as beholding Him who is unseen. They should be the trusted ones of the Merciful among men, and regard themselves as the guardians appointed of God for all that dwell on earth. It is incumbent upon them to take counsel together and to have regard for the interests of the servants of God, for his sake, even as they regard their own interests, and to choose that which is fitting and proper....

O people of the world! Build houses of worship throughout the lands in the name of him who is the Lord of all religions. Make them as perfect as is possible and adorn them with that which befits them, not with images and effigies. Then, with radiance and joy, celebrate in them the praise of your Lord, the Most Compassionate. Truly, by his remembrance the eye is cheered and the heart is filled with light.

The Lord has ordained that those of you who are able shall make pilgrimage to the sacred House, and from this he has exempted women as a mercy on his part. He is truly All-Bountiful, the Most Generous....

Whoever lays claim to a Revelation direct from God, before the expiration of a full thousand years, such a man is assuredly a lying impostor. We pray God that he may graciously assist him to retract and repudiate such claim. Should he repent, God will, no doubt, forgive him. If, however, he persists in error, God will certainly send down one who will deal mercilessly with him. Terrible, indeed, is God in punishing! Whoever interprets this verse otherwise than its obvious meaning is deprived of the Spirit of God and of his mercy which encompasses all created things. Fear God, and follow not your idle fancies. Nay, rather, follow the bidding of your Lord, the Almighty, the All-Wise. Before long clamorous voices will be raised in most lands. Shun them, O My people, and follow not the iniquitous and evil-hearted....

[45] Exile and imprisonment are decreed for the thief, and, on the third offence, place a mark upon his forehead so that, thus identified, he may not be accepted in the cities of God and His countries. Beware lest, through compassion, you neglect to carry out the statutes of the

religion of God; do that which has been bidden you by God who is compassionate and merciful. We school you with the rod of wisdom and laws, like the father who educates his son, and this for naught but the protection of your own selves and the elevation of your stations. . . .

[63] God has prescribed marriage for you. Beware that you take not unto yourselves more wives than two.[3] When someone contents himself with a single partner from among the women who serve God, both he and she shall live in tranquillity. He who would take into his service a[nother] young woman may do so with propriety. Such is the ordinance which, in truth and justice, has been recorded by the Pen of Revelation. . . . Marriage is dependent upon the consent of both parties. Desiring to establish love, unity, and harmony among Our servants, We have conditioned it, once the couple's wish is known, upon the permission of their parents, lest enmity and rancor should arise among them. In this We have yet other purposes. Thus has Our commandment been ordained. . . .

[149] Recite the verses of God every morning and evening. Whoever fails to recite them has not been faithful to the Covenant of God and his Testament, and whoever turns away from these holy verses in this Day is of those who throughout eternity have turned away from God. Fear God, O My servants, one and all. Pride not yourselves on much reading of the verses or on a multitude of pious acts by night and day; for were a man to read a single verse with joy and radiance it would be better for him than to read with lassitude all the Holy Books of God, the Help in Peril, the Self-Subsisting. . . . Lay not upon your souls that which will weary them and weigh them down, but rather what will lighten and uplift them, so that they may soar on the wings of the Divine verses toward the Dawning-place of his manifest signs; this will draw you nearer to God. [150] Teach your children the verses revealed from the heaven of majesty and power, so that, in most melodious tones, they may recite the Tablets of the All Merciful. . . .

[189] O members of parliaments throughout the world! Select a single language for the use of all on earth, and adopt likewise a common script. . . . This will be the cause of unity, if you could only comprehend it, and the greatest instrument for promoting harmony and civilization. Would that you might understand!

---

[3] *more wives than two:* Islam permits four at most.

Baha'i Prayers

The Short Obligatory (required) Prayer is for use at any time. The Medium Obligatory Prayer is to be recited three times a day—at morning, noon, and evening. Its italics indicate directions for prayer. The Prayer for America was written when Baha'i leaders visited the United States early in the twentieth century.

[Short Obligatory Prayer] I bear witness, O my God, that Thou hast created me to know Thee and to worship Thee. I testify, at this moment, to my powerlessness and to Thy might, to my poverty and to Thy wealth. There is none other God but Thee, the Help in Peril, the Self-Subsisting.

Short Obligatory Prayer, Medium Obligatory Prayer, Prayer for America.

[Medium Obligatory Prayer] *Whoever wishes to pray, let him wash his hands, and while he washeth, let him say:*

Strengthen my hand, O my God, that it may take hold of Thy Book with such steadfastness that the hosts of the world shall have no power over it. Guard it, then, from meddling with whatsoever doth not belong unto it. Thou art, verily, the Almighty, the Most Powerful. I have turned my face unto Thee, O my Lord! Illumine it with the light of Thy countenance. Protect it, then, from turning to anyone but Thee.

Then let him stand up, and facing the Qiblih [Point of Adoration], let him say:

God testifies that there is no other God but Him. His are the kingdoms of Revelation and of creation. He, in truth, has manifested Him Who is the Dayspring of Revelation, Who conversed on Sinai, through Whom the Supreme Horizon has been made to shine, and the [boundary] beyond which there is no passing has spoken, and through Whom the call has been proclaimed unto all who are in heaven and on earth: "Lo, the All-Possessing is come. Earth and heaven, glory and dominion are God's, the Lord of all men, and the Possessor of the Throne on high and of earth below!"

Let him, then, bend down, with hands resting on the knees, and say:

Exalted art Thou above my praise and the praise of anyone beside me, above my description and the description of all who are in heaven and all who are on earth!

Then, standing with open hands, palms upward toward the face, let him say:

Disappoint not, O my God, him that has, with beseeching fingers, clung to the hem of Thy mercy and Thy grace, O Thou Who of those who show mercy art the Most Merciful!

Let him, then, be seated and say:

I bear witness to Thy unity and Thy oneness, and that Thou art God, and that there is none other God beside Thee. Thou hast, verily, revealed thy Cause, fulfilled Thy Covenant, and opened wide the door of Thy grace to all that dwell in heaven and on earth. Blessing and peace, salutation and glory, rest upon Thy loved ones, whom the changes and changes of the world have not deterred from turning unto Thee, and who have given their all, in the hope of obtaining that which is with Thee. Thou art, in truth, the Ever-Forgiving, the All-Bountiful.

[Prayer for America] O Thou kind Lord! This gathering is turning to Thee. These hearts are radiant with Thy love. These minds and spirits are exhilarated by the message of Thy glad tidings. O God! Let this American democracy become glorious in spiritual degrees even as it has aspired to material degrees, and render this just government victorious. Confirm this revered nation to upraise the standard of the oneness of humanity, to promulgate the Most Great Peace, to become thereby most glorious and praiseworthy among all the nations of the world. O God! This American nation is worthy of Thy favors and is deserving of Thy mercy. Make it precious and near to Thee through Thy bounty and bestowal.

THE SCRIPTURE OF THE CHURCH OF JESUS CHRIST OF LATTER-DAY SAINTS

Joseph Smith's Story

This autobiographical account tells of Joseph Smith's first vision and angelic visitation, discovery of the *Book of Mormon,* and the founding of the church. As the first paragraph indicates, the experience of his vision and conversion was the most contentious point with his opponents, and it continues to be so today.[4]

Owing to the many reports which have been put in circulation by evil-disposed and designing persons, in relation to the rise and progress of the Church of Jesus Christ of Latter-day Saints, all of which have been designed by the authors thereof to militate against its character as a Church and its progress in the world—I have been induced to write this history, to disabuse the public mind, and put all inquirers after truth in possession of the facts, as they have transpired, in relation both to myself and the Church, so far as I have such facts in my possession. In this history I shall present the various events in relation to this Church, in truth and righteousness, as they have transpired, or as they at present exist, being now [1838] the eighth year since the organization of the said Church.

I was born in the year of our Lord 1805, on the twenty-third day of December, in the town of Sharon, Windsor county, State of Vermont.... My father, Joseph Smith, Senior, left the State of Vermont, and moved to Palmyra, in the State of New York, when I was in my tenth year, or thereabouts. In about four years after my father's arrival in Palmyra, he moved with his family into Manchester in the same county of Ontario....

[5] Some time in the second year after our removal to Manchester, there was in the place where we lived an unusual excitement on the subject of religion. It commenced with the Methodists, but soon became general among all the sects in that region of country. Indeed, the whole district of country seemed affected by it, and great multitudes united themselves to the different religious parties, which created no small stir and division amongst the people, some crying, "Lo, here!" and others, "Lo, there!" Some were contending for the Methodist faith, some for the Presbyterian, and some for the Baptist....

I was at this time in my fifteenth year. My father's family was proselyted to the Presbyterian faith, and four of them joined that church, namely, my mother, Lucy; my brothers Hyrum and Samuel Harrison; and my sister Sophronia. During this time of great excitement my mind was called up to serious reflection and great uneasiness; but though my feelings were deep and often poignant, still I kept myself aloof from all these parties, though I attended their several meetings as often as occasion would permit. In process of time my mind became somewhat partial to the Methodist sect, and I felt some desire to be united with them; but so great were the confusion and strife among the different denominations, that it was impossible for a person young as I was, and so unacquainted with men and things, to come to any certain conclusion who

---

[4]All excerpts from Mormon scriptures are from "The Scriptures-Internet Edition" (http://www.scriptures.lds.org). Copyright © 2000 Intellectual Reserve, Inc. All rights reserved. Used by permission.

Pearl of Great Price, "Joseph Smith—History 1" 1–22, 25–35, 40–47, 59–62, 67–74.

was right and who was wrong....[10] In the midst of this war of words and tumult of opinions, I often said to myself: What is to be done? Who of all these parties are right; or, are they all wrong together? If any one of them be right, which is it, and how shall I know it?...

So, in accordance with this, my determination to ask of God, I retired to the woods to make the attempt. It was on the morning of a beautiful, clear day, early in the spring of eighteen hundred and twenty. It was the first time in my life that I had made such an attempt, for amidst all my anxieties I had never as yet made the attempt to pray vocally. [15] After I had retired to the place where I had previously designed to go, having looked around me, and finding myself alone, I kneeled down and began to offer up the desires of my heart to God. I had scarcely done so, when immediately I was seized upon by some power which entirely overcame me, and had such an astonishing influence over me as to bind my tongue so that I could not speak. Thick darkness gathered around me, and it seemed to me for a time as if I were doomed to sudden destruction. But, exerting all my powers to call upon God to deliver me out of the power of this enemy which had seized upon me, and at the very moment when I was ready to sink into despair and abandon myself to destruction...Just at this moment of great alarm, I saw a pillar of light exactly over my head, above the brightness of the sun, which descended gradually until it fell upon me. It no sooner appeared than I found myself delivered from the enemy which held me bound. When the light rested upon me I saw two Personages, whose brightness and glory defy all description, standing above me in the air. One of them spake unto me, calling me by name and said, pointing to the other—"This is My Beloved Son. Hear Him!"

My object in going to inquire of the Lord was to know which of all the sects was right, that I might know which to join. No sooner, therefore, did I get possession of myself, so as to be able to speak, than I asked the Personages who stood above me in the light, which of all the sects was right (for at this time it had never entered into my heart that all were wrong)—and which I should join. I was answered that I must join

none of them, for they were all wrong; and the Personage who addressed me said that all their creeds were an abomination in his sight; that those professors were all corrupt; that: "they draw near to me with their lips, but their hearts are far from me, they teach for doctrines the commandments of men, having a form of godliness, but they deny the power thereof." [20] He again forbade me to join with any of them; and many other things did he say unto me, which I cannot write at this time. When I came to myself again, I found myself lying on my back, looking up into heaven. When the light had departed, I had no strength; but soon recovering in some degree, I went home. And as I leaned up to the fireplace, mother inquired what the matter was. I replied, "Never mind, all is well—I am well enough off." I then said to my mother, "I have learned for myself that Presbyterianism is not true."

It seems as though the adversary was aware, at a very early period of my life, that I was destined to prove a disturber and an annoyer of his kingdom; else why should the powers of darkness combine against me?...[M]y telling the story had excited a great deal of prejudice against me among professors of religion, and was the cause of great persecution, which continued to increase; and though I was an obscure boy, only between fourteen and fifteen years of age, and my circumstances in life such as to make a boy of no consequence in the world, yet men of high standing would take notice sufficient to excite the public mind against me, and create a bitter persecution; and this was common among all the sects—all united to persecute me....

[O]n the evening of the twenty-first of September, after I had retired to my bed for the night, I betook myself to prayer and supplication to Almighty God for forgiveness of all my sins and follies, and also for a manifestation to me, that I might know of my state and standing before him. I had full confidence in obtaining a divine manifestation, as I previously had one. [30] While I was thus in the act of calling upon God, I discovered a light appearing in my room, which continued to increase until the room was lighter than at noonday, when immediately a personage appeared at my bedside, standing in the air, for his feet did not touch the floor.... When I first looked upon him, I was afraid; but the fear soon left me. He called me by name, and said unto me that he was a messenger sent from the presence of God to me, and that his name was Moroni; that God had a work for me to do; and that my name should be had for good and evil among all nations, kindreds, and tongues, or that it should be both good and evil spoken of among all people. He said there was a book deposited, written upon gold plates, giving an account of the former inhabitants of this continent, and the source from whence they sprang. He also said that the fulness of the everlasting Gospel was contained in it, as delivered by the Savior to the ancient inhabitants; [35] Also, that there were two stones in silver bows—and these stones, fastened to a breastplate, constituted what is called the Urim and Thummim[5]—deposited with the plates; and the possession and use of these stones were what constituted "seers" in ancient or former times; and that God had prepared them for the purpose of translating the book.... Again, he told me that when I got those plates of which he had spoken—for the time that they should be obtained was not yet fulfilled—I should not show them to any person; neither the breastplate with the Urim and Thummim; only to those to whom I should be commanded to show them; if I did I should be destroyed. While he was conversing with me about the plates, the vision was opened to my mind that I could see the place where the plates were deposited, and that so clearly and distinctly that I knew the place again when I visited it....

[59] At length the time arrived for obtaining the plates, the Urim and Thummim, and the breastplate. On the twenty-second day of September, 1827, having gone as usual at the end of another year to the place where they were deposited, the same heavenly messenger delivered them up to me with this charge: that I should be responsible for them; that if I should let them go carelessly, or through any neglect of mine, I should be cut off; but that if I would use all my endeavors to preserve them, until he, the messenger, should call for them, they should be protected. [60] I soon found out the reason why I had received such strict charges to keep them safe, and why it was that the messenger had said that when I had done what was required at my hand, he would call for them. For no sooner was it known that I had them, than the most strenuous exertions were used to get them from me. Every stratagem that could be invented was resorted to for that purpose. The persecution became more bitter and severe than before, and multitudes were on the alert continually to get them from me if possible. But by the wisdom of God, they remained safe in my hands, until I had accomplished by them what was required at my hand. When, according to arrangements, the messenger called for them, I delivered them up to him; and he has them in his charge until this day, being the second day of May, 1838....

We still continued the work of translation, when, in the ensuing month (May, 1829), we on a certain day went into the woods to pray and inquire of the Lord respecting baptism for the remission of sins, that we found mentioned in the translation of the plates. While we were thus employed, praying and calling upon the Lord, a messenger from heaven descended in a cloud of light, and having laid his hands upon us, he ordained us, saying: "Upon you my fellow servants, in the name of Messiah, I confer the Priesthood of Aaron, which holds the keys of the ministering of angels, and of the gospel of repentance, and of baptism by immersion for the remission of sins; and this shall never be taken again from the earth until the sons of Levi do offer again an offering unto the Lord in righteousness." [70] He said this Aaronic Priesthood had not the power of laying on hands for the gift of the Holy Ghost, but that this should be conferred on us hereafter; and he commanded us to go and be baptized, and gave us directions that I should baptize Oliver Cowdery, and that afterwards he should baptize me.

---

[5] *Urim and Thummim*: a device consulted by the chief priest of ancient Israel to determine God's response to a yes or no question. The Hebrew Scriptures do not specify how the device is used; Joseph Smith here uses it as "seer stones" for translating the *Book of Mormon*.

Accordingly we went and were baptized. I baptized him first, and afterwards he baptized me—after which I laid my hands upon his head and ordained him to the Aaronic Priesthood, and afterwards he laid his hands on me and ordained me to the same Priesthood—for so we were commanded. The messenger who visited us on this occasion and conferred this Priesthood upon us, said that his name was John, the same that is called John the Baptist in the New Testament, and that he acted under the direction of Peter, James, and John, who held the keys of the Priesthood of Melchizedek, which Priesthood, he said, would in due time be conferred on us, and that I should be called the first Elder of the Church, and he (Oliver Cowdery) the second. It was on the fifteenth day of May, 1829, that we were ordained under the hand of this messenger, and baptized. Immediately on our coming up out of the water afer we had been baptized, we experienced great and glorious blessings from our Heavenly Father....

Our minds being now enlightened, we began to have the scriptures laid open to our understandings, and the true meaning and intention of their more mysterious passages revealed unto us in a manner which we never could attain to previously, nor ever before had thought of. In the meantime we were forced to keep secret the circumstances of having received the Priesthood and our having been baptized, owing to a spirit of persecution which had already manifested itself in the neighborhood.

The First Description of the *Book of Mormon*

The original title page of the *Book of Mormon* (1830) has been printed in every succeeding edition. Written by Joseph Smith Jr., the title page serves as an apt description of the *Book of Mormon*'s content. The original punctuation, replete with dashes and original capitalization is presented here.

THE BOOK OF MORMON, AN ACCOUNT WRITTEN BY THE HAND OF MORMON UPON PLATES TAKEN FROM THE PLATES OF NEPHI

Wherefore, it is an abridgment of the record of the people of Nephi, and also of the Lamanites—Written to the Lamanites, who are a remnant of the house of Israel; and also to Jew and Gentile—Written by way of commandment, and also by the spirit of prophecy and of revelation—Written and sealed up, and hid up unto the Lord, that they might not be destroyed—To come forth by the gift and power of God unto the interpretation thereof—Sealed by the hand of Moroni, and hid up unto the Lord, to come forth in due time by way of the Gentile—The interpretation thereof by the gift of God.

An abridgment taken from the Book of Ether also, which is a record of the people of Jared, who were scattered at the time the Lord confounded the language of the people, when they were building a tower to get to heaven—Which is to show unto the remnant of the House of Israel what great things the Lord has done for their fathers; and that they may know the covenants of the Lord, that they are not cast off forever—And also to the convincing of the Jew and Gentile that JESUS is the CHRIST, the ETERNAL GOD, manifesting himself unto all nations—And now, if there are faults they are the mistakes of men; wherefore, condemn not the things of God, that you may be found spotless at the judgment-seat of Christ.

TRANSLATED BY JOSEPH SMITH, JUNIOR.

Book of Mormon, original title page.

The Coming of Jesus Christ in 34 C.E. to the New World

This reading tells the story of the appearance of Jesus Christ, after his resurrection, to Americans descended from Israelite settlers. In this account, Jesus uses this appearance to teach the rudiments of true faith.

And now it came to pass that there were a great multitude gathered together, of the people of Nephi, round about the temple which was in the land Bountiful; and they were marveling and wondering one with another, and were showing one to another the great and marvelous change which had taken place. And they were also conversing about this Jesus Christ, of whom the sign had been given concerning his death. And it came to pass that while they were thus conversing one with another, they heard a voice as if it came out of heaven; and they cast their eyes round about, for they understood not the voice which they heard; and it was not a harsh voice, neither was it a loud voice; nevertheless, and notwithstanding it being a small voice it did pierce them that did hear to the center, insomuch that there was no part of their frame that it did not cause to quake; yea, it did pierce them to the very soul, and did cause their hearts to burn. And it came to pass that again they heard the voice, and they understood it not.

[5] And again the third time they did hear the voice, and did open their ears to hear it; and their eyes were towards the sound thereof; and they did look steadfastly towards heaven, from whence the sound came. And behold, the third time they did understand the voice which they heard; and it said unto them: "Behold my Beloved Son, in whom I am well pleased, in whom I have glorified my name—hear him." And it came to pass, as they understood they cast their eyes up again towards heaven; and behold, they saw a Man descending out of heaven; and he was clothed in a white robe; and he came down and stood in the midst of them; and the eyes of the whole multitude were turned upon him, and they durst not open their mouths, even one to another, and wist not what it meant, for they thought it was an angel that had appeared unto them. And it came to pass that he stretched forth his hand and spake unto the people, saying: [10] "Behold, I am Jesus Christ, whom the prophets testified shall come into the world. And behold, I am the light and the life of the world; and I have drunk out of that bitter cup which the Father has given me, and have glorified the Father in taking upon me the sins of the world, in the which I have suffered the will of the Father in all things from the beginning." And it came to pass that when Jesus had spoken these words the whole multitude fell to the earth; for they remembered that it had been prophesied among them that Christ should show himself unto them after his ascension into heaven. . . .

[31] "Behold, verily, verily, I say unto you, I will declare unto you my doctrine. And this is my doctrine, and it is the doctrine which the Father has given unto me; and I bear record of the Father, and the Father beareth record of me, and the Holy Ghost beareth record of the Father and me; and I bear record that the Father commandeth all men, everywhere, to repent and believe in me. And whoso believeth in me, and is baptized, the same shall be saved; and they are they who shall inherit the kingdom of God. And whoso believeth not in me, and is not baptized, shall be damned.

Book of Mormon 3 Nephi 11.1–41.

[35] Verily, verily, I say unto you, that this is my doctrine, and I bear record of it from the Father; and whoso believeth in me believeth in the Father also; and unto him will the Father bear record of me, for he will visit him with fire and with the Holy Ghost. And thus will the Father bear record of me, and the Holy Ghost will bear record unto him of the Father and me; for the Father, and I, and the Holy Ghost are one. And again I say unto you, you must repent, and become as a little child, and be baptized in my name, or you can in nowise receive these things....Therefore, go forth unto this people, and declare the words which I have spoken, unto the ends of the earth.''...

Destruction of the Nephites and Burial of the Golden Plates

The *Book of Mormon* relates how the tribe of Nephites [NEE-fites] was destroyed in warfare in 385 c.e. by their enemies the Lamanites. Approximately twenty years later, the prophet Moroni, Mormon's son, buried the golden plates of scripture in the Hill Cumorah, outside what is now Palmyra in upstate New York.

Now I finish my record concerning the destruction of my people, the Nephites. And it came to pass that we did march forth before the Lamanites. And I, Mormon, wrote an epistle unto the king of the Lamanites, and desired of him that he would grant unto us that we might gather together our people unto the land of Cumorah, by a hill which was called Cumorah, and there we could give them battle. And it came to pass that the king of the Lamanites did grant unto me the thing which I desired....

[6] When we had gathered in all our people in one to the land of Cumorah, behold I, Mormon, began to be old. Knowing it to be the last struggle of my people, and having been commanded of the Lord that I should not suffer the records which had been handed down by our fathers, which were sacred, to fall into the hands of the Lamanites, (for the Lamanites would destroy them) therefore I made this record out of the plates of Nephi, and hid up in the hill Cumorah all the records which had been entrusted to me by the hand of the Lord, save it were these few plates which I gave unto my son Moroni. And it came to pass that my people, with their wives and their children, did now behold the armies of the Lamanites marching towards them; and with that awful fear of death which fills the breasts of all the wicked, did they await to receive them.

They came to battle against us, and every soul was filled with terror because of the greatness of their numbers. And it came to pass that they did fall upon my people with the sword, and with the bow, and with the arrow, and with the ax, and with all manner of weapons of war. [10] And it came to pass that my men were hewn down, yea, even my ten thousand who were with me, and I fell wounded in the midst; and they passed by me that they did not put an end to my life.

And when they had gone through and hewn down all my people save it were twenty and four of us, (among whom was my son Moroni) and we having survived the dead of our people, did behold on the morrow, when the Lamanites had returned unto their camps, from the top of the hill Cumorah, the ten thousand of my people who were hewn down, being led in the front by me....

Book of Mormon, "Mormon" 6:1–3, 6–11, 16–22.

And my soul was rent with anguish, because of the slaying of my people, and I cried: "O you fair ones, how could you have departed from the ways of the Lord! O you fair ones, how could you have rejected that Jesus, who stood with open arms to receive you! Behold, if you had not done this, you would not have fallen. But behold, you are fallen, and I mourn your loss. O you fair sons and daughters, you fathers and mothers, you husbands and wives, you fair ones, how is it that you could have fallen! [20] But behold, you are gone, and my sorrows cannot bring your return. And the day soon cometh that your mortal body must put on immortality, and these bodies which are now moldering in corruption must soon become incorruptible bodies; and then you must stand before the judgment-seat of Christ, to be judged according to your works; and if it so be that you are righteous, then are you blessed with your fathers who have gone before you. O that you had repented before this great destruction had come upon you. But behold, you are gone, and the Father, yea, the Eternal Father of heaven, knoweth your state; and he doeth with you according to his justice and mercy."

Preparations for the Trek to Utah

The following account outlines some of the well-planned provisions, both physical and spiritual, for the Latter-day Saints' trek in 1847–1848 from Missouri to the Great Salt Lake basin of northern Utah. After years of persecution in New York, Ohio, Illinois, and Missouri, church leaders wanted to move to a location that was promising enough to support their growing community but not so promising as to attract non–Latter-day Saint settlers. The trek was planned and led by Brigham Young, who succeeded the martyred Joseph Smith.

The Word and Will of the Lord concerning the Camp of Israel in their journeys to the West: Let all the people of the Church of Jesus Christ of Latter-day Saints, and those who journey with them, be organized into companies, with a covenant and promise to keep all the commandments and statutes of the Lord our God. Let the companies be organized with captains of hundreds, captains of fifties, and captains of tens, with a president and his two counselors at their head, under the direction of the Twelve Apostles. And this shall be our covenant—that we will walk in all the ordinances of the Lord.

[5] Let each company provide themselves with all the teams, wagons, provisions, clothing, and other necessaries for the journey, that they can. When the companies are organized let them go to with their might, to prepare for those who are to tarry. Let each company, with their captains and presidents, decide how many can go next spring; then choose out a sufficient number of able-bodied and expert men, to take teams, seeds, and farming utensils, to go as pioneers to prepare for putting in spring crops. Let each company bear an equal proportion, according to the dividend of their property, in taking the poor, the widows, the fatherless, and the families of those who have gone into the army, that the cries of the widow and the fatherless come not up into the ears of the Lord against this people. Let each company prepare houses, and fields for raising grain, for those who are to remain behind this season; and this is the will of the Lord concerning his people.

[10] Let every man use all his influence and property to remove this people to the place where the Lord shall locate a stake of Zion. And if you do this with a pure heart, in all

Doctrine and Covenants 136.1–11, 17–24, 30–42.

faithfulness, you shall be blessed; you shall be blessed in your flocks, and in your herds, and in your fields, and in your houses, and in your families.... [17] Go thy way and do as I have told you, and fear not thine enemies; for they shall not have power to stop my work. Zion shall be redeemed in mine own due time. And if any man shall seek to build up himself, and seeketh not my counsel, he shall have no power, and his folly shall be made manifest.

[20] Seek ye; and keep all your pledges one with another; and covet not that which is thy brother's. Keep yourselves from evil to take the name of the Lord in vain, for I am the Lord your God, even the God of your fathers, the God of Abraham and of Isaac and of Jacob. I am he who led the children of Israel out of the land of Egypt; and my arm is stretched out in the last days, to save my people Israel. Cease to contend one with another; cease to speak evil one of another. Cease drunkenness; and let your words tend to edifying one another.... [30] Fear not thine enemies, for they are in mine hands and I will do my pleasure with them. My people must be tried in all things, that they may be prepared to receive the glory that I have for them, even the glory of Zion; and he that will not bear chastisement is not worthy of my kingdom.

Let him that is ignorant learn wisdom by humbling himself and calling upon the Lord his God, that his eyes may be opened that he may see, and his ears opened that he may hear; for my Spirit is sent forth into the world to enlighten the humble and contrite, and to the condemnation of the ungodly. Thy brethren have rejected you and your testimony, even the nation that has driven you out; [35] And now cometh the day of their calamity, even the days of sorrow, like a woman that is taken in travail; and their sorrow shall be great unless they speedily repent, yea, very speedily. For they killed the prophets, and them that were sent unto them; and they have shed innocent blood, which crieth from the ground against them. Therefore, marvel not at these things, for you are not yet pure. You cannot yet bear my glory, but you shall behold it if you are faithful in keeping all my words that I have given you, from the days of Adam to Abraham, from Abraham to Moses, from Moses to Jesus and his apostles, and from Jesus and his apostles to Joseph Smith, whom I did call upon by mine angels, my ministering servants, and by mine own voice out of the heavens, to bring forth my work; which foundation he did lay, and was faithful; and I took him to myself. Many have marveled because of his death; but it was needful that he should seal his testimony with his blood, that he might be honored and the wicked might be condemned.

[40] Have I not delivered you from your enemies, only in that I have left a witness of my name? Now, therefore, hearken, O you people of my church; and you elders listen together; you have received my kingdom. Be diligent in keeping all my commandments, lest judgments come upon you, and your faith fail you, and your enemies triumph over you. So no more at present. Amen and Amen.

The Essence of Latter-day Saint Teaching

This short statement, written and signed by Joseph Smith, shows in its main points how Latter-day Saint teaching both agrees with, and departs from, mainstream Christian teaching. Notice that point 11 asserts the right to practice the faith as believers see fit, but point 12 asserts the duty to be obedient to political authorities.

Pearl of Great Price, "Articles of Faith" 1–13.

1. We believe in God, the Eternal Father, and in His Son, Jesus Christ, and in the Holy Ghost.

2. We believe that men will be punished for their own sins, and not for Adam's transgression.

3. We believe that through the Atonement of Christ, all mankind may be saved, by obedience to the laws and ordinances of the Gospel.

4. We believe that the first principles and ordinances of the Gospel are: first, Faith in the Lord Jesus Christ; second, Repentance; third, Baptism by immersion for the remission of sins; fourth, Laying on of hands for the gift of the Holy Ghost.

5. We believe that a man must be called of God, by prophecy, and by the laying on of hands by those who are in authority, to preach the Gospel and administer in the ordinances thereof.

6. We believe in the same organization that existed in the Primitive Church, namely, apostles, prophets, pastors, teachers, evangelists, and so forth.

7. We believe in the gift of tongues, prophecy, revelation, visions, healing, interpretation of tongues, and so forth.

8. We believe the Bible to be the word of God as far as it is translated correctly; we also believe the Book of Mormon to be the word of God.

9. We believe all that God has revealed, all that He does now reveal, and we believe that He will yet reveal many great and important things pertaining to the Kingdom of God.

10. We believe in the literal gathering of Israel and in the restoration of the Ten Tribes; that Zion (the New Jerusalem) will be built upon the American continent; that Christ will reign personally upon the earth; and, that the earth will be renewed and receive its paradisiacal glory.

11. We claim the privilege of worshiping Almighty God according to the dictates of our own conscience, and allow all men the same privilege, let them worship how, where, or what they may.

12. We believe in being subject to kings, presidents, rulers, and magistrates, in obeying, honoring, and sustaining the law.

13. We believe in being honest, true, chaste, benevolent, virtuous, and in doing good to all men.... If there is anything virtuous, lovely, or of good report or praiseworthy, we seek after these things.

Church Pronouncements
on Polygamy and Men of African Descent

In the early history of the Latter-day Saint church, one of the most controversial practices was polygamy, a practice that still continues among some splinter groups in Utah. In the middle of the twentieth century, especially as the church grew in the developing world, its prohibition on admitting Africans and men of African descent to the priesthood became controversial. The Official Declaration of 1890 reasserts the church's official disavowal of polygamy even as it admits that polygamy is still occurring to some degree; it is accompanied by an anguished letter on this change by the church's president, Wilford Woodruff. The Official Declaration of 1978 is an open letter to the church from Spencer Kimball, N. Eldon Tanner, and Marion G. Romney allowing all "worthy male members," including Africans and men of African descent, to be ordained as Mormon priests. These revisions of the teaching of the church are based on revelations to the church presidents of the time.

Doctrine and Covenants, Official Declarations of 1890 and 1978.

[Official Declaration of 1890] Press dispatches having been sent for political purposes, from Salt Lake City, which have been widely published, to the effect that the Utah Commission, in their recent report to the Secretary of the Interior, allege that plural marriages are still being solemnized and that forty or more such marriages have been contracted in Utah since last June or during the past year, also that in public discourses the leaders of the Church have taught, encouraged and urged the continuance of the practice of polygamy—

I, therefore, as President of the Church of Jesus Christ of Latter-day Saints, do hereby, in the most solemn manner, declare that these charges are false. We are not teaching polygamy or plural marriage, nor permitting any person to enter into its practice, and I deny that either forty or any other number of plural marriages have during that period been solemnized in our Temples or in any other place in the Territory. One case has been reported, in which the parties allege that the marriage was performed in the Endowment House, in Salt Lake City, in the Spring of 1889, but I have not been able to learn who performed the ceremony; whatever was done in this matter was without my knowledge. In consequence of this alleged occurrence the Endowment House was, by my instructions, taken down without delay.

Inasmuch as laws have been enacted by Congress forbidding plural marriages, which laws have been pronounced constitutional by the court of last resort, I hereby declare my intention to submit to those laws, and to use my influence with the members of the Church over which I preside to have them do likewise.

There is nothing in my teachings to the Church or in those of my associates, during the time specified, which can be reasonably construed to inculcate or encourage polygamy; and when any Elder of the Church has used language which appeared to convey any such teaching, he has been promptly reproved. And I now publicly declare that my advice to the Latter-day Saints is to refrain from contracting any marriage forbidden by the law of the land.

WILFORD WOODRUFF
President of the Church of Jesus Christ of Latter-day Saints

[Excerpts from a letter by President Wilford Woodruff regarding the Official Declaration of 1980.] The question is this: Which is the wisest course for the Latter-day Saints to pursue—to continue to attempt to practice plural marriage, with the laws of the nation against it and the opposition of sixty millions of people, and at the cost of the confiscation and loss of all the Temples, and the stopping of all the ordinances therein, both for the living and the dead, and the imprisonment of the First Presidency and Twelve and the heads of families in the Church, and the confiscation of personal property of the people (all of which of themselves would stop the practice); or, after doing and suffering what we have through our adherence to this principle to cease the practice and submit to the law, and through doing so leave the Prophets, Apostles and fathers at home, so that they can instruct the people and attend to the duties of the Church, and also leave the Temples in the hands of the Saints, so that they can attend to the ordinances of the Gospel, both for the living and the dead?

The Lord showed me by vision and revelation exactly what would take place if we did not stop this practice. If we had not stopped it . . . all ordinances would be stopped. . . . Confusion would reign . . . , and many men would be made prisoners. This trouble would have come upon the whole Church, and we should have been compelled to stop the practice. Now, the question is, whether it should be stopped in this manner, or in the way the Lord has manifested to us, and leave our Prophets and Apostles and fathers free men, and the temples in the hands of the people, so that the dead may be redeemed. A large number has already been delivered from the prison house in the spirit world by this people,[6]

---

[6]*A large number . . . people*: a reference to baptism for the dead done by Latter-day Saints, allowing them entrance into heaven.

and shall the work go on or stop?...I say to you that that is exactly the condition we as a people would have been in had we not taken the course we have....

I saw exactly what would come to pass if there was not something done. I have had this spirit upon me for a long time. But I want to say this: I should have let all the temples go out of our hands; I should have gone to prison myself, and let every other man go there, had not the God of heaven commanded me to do what I did do; and when the hour came that I was commanded to do that, it was all clear to me. I went before the Lord, and I wrote what the Lord told me to write....I leave this with you, for you to contemplate and consider. The Lord is at work with us.

[Official Declaration, June 8, 1978] To all general and local priesthood officers of the Church of Jesus Christ of Latter-day Saints throughout the world:

As we have witnessed the expansion of the work of the Lord over the earth, we have been grateful that people of many nations have responded to the message of the restored gospel, and have joined the Church in ever-increasing numbers. This, in turn, has inspired us with a desire to extend to every worthy member of the Church all of the privileges and blessings which the gospel affords.

Aware of the promises made by the prophets and presidents of the Church who have preceded us that at some time, in God's eternal plan, all of our brethren who are worthy may receive the priesthood, and witnessing the faithfulness of those from whom the priesthood has been withheld, we have pleaded long and earnestly in behalf of these, our faithful brethren, spending many hours in the Upper Room of the Temple supplicating the Lord for divine guidance.

He has heard our prayers, and by revelation has confirmed that the long-promised day has come when every faithful, worthy man in the Church may receive the holy priesthood, with power to exercise its divine authority, and enjoy with his loved ones every blessing that flows from it, including the blessings of the temple. Accordingly, all worthy male members of the Church may be ordained to the priesthood without regard for race or color. Priesthood leaders are instructed to follow the policy of carefully interviewing all candidates for ordination to either the Aaronic or the Melchizedek Priesthood to insure that they meet the established standards for worthiness.

We declare with soberness that the Lord has now made known his will for the blessing of all his children throughout the earth who will hearken to the voice of his authorized servants, and prepare themselves to receive every blessing of the gospel.

THE SCRIPTURE
OF CHRISTIAN SCIENCE

Introduction to Christian Science Scripture and to the Work of Mary Baker Eddy

This selection is Mary Baker Eddy's autobiographical introduction to her main book. It also details the origin and development of this book, which shows a common feature of scriptures in the new religious movements: Their writing usually accompanies the religion's founding.[7]

To those leaning on the sustaining infinite, today is big with blessings.... The time for thinkers has come. Truth, independent of doctrines and time-honored systems, knocks at the portal of humanity....

Since the author's discovery of the might of Truth in the treatment of disease as well as of sin, her system has been fully tested and has not been found wanting; but to reach the heights of Christian Science, man must live in obedience to its divine Principle. To develop the full might of this Science, the discords of corporeal sense must yield to the harmony of spiritual sense, even as the science of music corrects false tones and gives sweet concord to sound. Theology and physics teach that both Spirit and matter are real and good, whereas the fact is that Spirit is good and real, and matter is Spirit's opposite. The question, What is Truth, is answered by demonstration, by healing both disease and sin; and this demonstration shows that Christian healing confers the most health and makes the best men. On this basis Christian Science will have a fair fight. Sickness has been combated for centuries by doctors using material remedies; but the question arises, Is there less sickness because of these practitioners? A vigorous "No" is the response....

As early as 1862 [the author] began to write down and give to friends the results of her Scriptural study, for the Bible was her sole teacher; but these compositions were crude, the first steps of a child in the newly discovered world of Spirit. She also began to jot down her thoughts on the main subject, but these jottings were only infantile lispings of Truth. A child drinks in the outward world through the eyes and rejoices in the draught. He is as sure of the world's existence as he is of his own; yet he cannot describe the world. He finds a few words, and with these he stammeringly attempts to convey his feeling. Later, the tongue voices the more definite thought, though still imperfectly. So was it with the author.... Today, though rejoicing in some progress, she still finds herself a willing disciple at the heavenly gate, waiting for the Mind of Christ.

Before writing this work, *Science and Health,* she made copious notes of Scriptural exposition, which have never been published. This was during the years 1867 and 1868. These efforts show her comparative ignorance of the stupendous life-problem up to that time, and the degrees by which she came at length to its solution. She values them as a parent may treasure the memorials of a child's growth, and she would not have them changed. The first edition of *Science and Health* was published in 1875....

---

[7]All excerpts from *Science and Health with Key to the Scriptures* are taken from the 1917 edition (Boston: A. V. Stewart), which has the same wording and pagination as the edition currently in print.

Science and Health with Key to the Scriptures, Preface.

The divine Principle of healing is proved in the personal experience of any sincere seeker of Truth. Its purpose is good, and its practice is safer and more potent than that of any other sanitary method. The unbiased Christian thought is soonest touched by Truth, and convinced of it.... Many imagine that the phenomena of physical healing in Christian 'Science present only a phase of the action of the human mind, which action in some unexplained way results in the cure of disease. On the contrary, Christian Science rationally explains that all other pathological methods are the fruits of human faith in matter, faith in the workings, not of Spirit, but of the fleshly mind which must yield to Science. The physical healing of Christian Science results now, as in Jesus' time, from the operation of divine Principle, before which sin and disease lose their reality in human consciousness and disappear as naturally and as necessarily as darkness gives place to light and sin to reformation. Now, as then, these mighty works are not supernatural, but supremely natural. They are the sign of Immanuel, or "God with us," a divine influence ever present in human consciousness....

When God called the author to proclaim His Gospel to this age, there came also the charge to plant and water His vineyard. The first school of Christian Science Mind-healing was started by the author with only one student in Lynn,

Massachusetts, about the year 1867. In 1881, she opened the Massachusetts Metaphysical College in Boston, under the seal of the Commonwealth, a law relative to colleges having been passed, which enabled her to get this institution chartered for medical purposes.... During seven years over four thousand students were taught by the author in this College. Meanwhile she was pastor of the first established Church of Christ, Scientist; President of the first Christian Scientist Association, convening monthly; publisher of her own works; and (for a portion of this time) sole editor and publisher of the *Christian Science Journal,* the first periodical issued by Christian Scientists. She closed her College, October 29, 1889, in the height of its prosperity with a deep-lying conviction that the next two years of her life should be given to the preparation of the revision of *Science and Health,* which was published in 1891. She retained her charter and, as its President, reopened the College in 1899 as auxiliary to her church. Until June 10, 1907, she had never read this book throughout consecutively in order to elucidate her idealism.

In the spirit of Christ's charity, as one who "hopeth all things, endureth all things," and is joyful to bear consolation to the sorrowing and healing to the sick, she commits these pages to honest seekers for Truth.

The Essence of Christian Science Teaching

The "Recapitulation" (ending summary) of *Science and Health* gives the main points of Christian Science teaching in very brief form. Notice how the main doctrines of mainstream Protestant Christianity at the end of the nineteenth century are recast in Christian Science.

The following is a brief exposition of the important points, or religious tenets, of Christian Science:

1. As adherents of Truth, we take the inspired Word of the Bible as our sufficient guide to eternal Life.

2. We acknowledge and adore one supreme and infinite God. We acknowledge His Son, one Christ; the Holy Ghost or divine Comforter; and man in God's image and likeness.

3. We acknowledge God's forgiveness of sin in the destruction of sin and the spiritual

Science and Health with Key to the Scriptures, "Recapitulation."

understanding that casts out evil as unreal. But the belief in sin is punished so long as the belief lasts.

4. We acknowledge Jesus' atonement as the evidence of divine, efficacious Love, unfolding man's unity with God through Christ Jesus the Way-shower; and we acknowledge that man is saved through Christ, through Truth, Life, and Love as demonstrated by the Galilean Prophet in healing the sick and overcoming sin and death.

5. We acknowledge that the crucifixion of Jesus and his resurrection served to uplift faith to understand eternal Life, even the allness of Soul, Spirit, and the nothingness of matter.

6. And we solemnly promise to watch, and pray for that Mind to be in us which was also in Christ Jesus; to do unto others as we would have them do unto us; and to be merciful, just, and pure.

Prayer and Its Role

Prayer and meditation are the chief religious activities in Christian Science and its main methods of healing sickness of body and mind. Here Mary Baker Eddy gives her interpretation of the Lord's Prayer ("Our Father") in accordance with Christian Science teachings.

Our Master taught his disciples one brief prayer, which we name after him the Lord's Prayer. Our Master said, "After this manner therefore pray ye," and then he gave that prayer which covers all human needs. There is indeed some doubt among Bible scholars, whether the last line is not an addition to the prayer by a later copyist; but this does not affect the meaning of the prayer itself. In the phrase, "Deliver us from evil," the original properly reads, "Deliver us from the evil one." This reading strengthens our scientific apprehension of the petition, for Christian Science teaches us that "the evil one," or one evil, is but another name for the first lie and all liars. Only as we rise above all material sensuousness and sin, can we reach the heaven-born aspiration and spiritual consciousness, which is indicated in the Lord's Prayer and which instantaneously heals the sick. Here let me give what I understand to be the spiritual sense of the Lord's Prayer.

Our Father which art in heaven, Our Father-Mother God, all-harmonious, Hallowed be Thy name. Adorable One. Thy kingdom come. Thy kingdom is come; Thou art ever-present. Thy will be done in earth, as it is in heaven. Enable us to know,—as in heaven, so on earth,—God is omnipotent, supreme. Give us this day our daily bread; Give us grace for to-day; feed the famished affections; And forgive us our debts, as we forgive our debtors. And Love is reflected in love; And lead us not into temptation, but deliver us from evil; And God leadeth us not into temptation, but delivereth us from sin, disease, and death. For Thine is the kingdom, and the power, and the glory, forever. For God is infinite, all power, all Life, Truth, Love, over all, and All.

Science and Health with Key to the Scriptures, "Prayer."

Interpretation of *Genesis* 1

Here Mary Baker Eddy teaches the ultimate unreality of matter, belief in which is the main cause of suffering. Gender is a mental construct, not a reality. Notice how she stresses the feminine aspects of God, most unusual for her time.

Genesis 1:1. In the beginning God created the heaven and the earth.

Ideas and identities: The infinite has no beginning. This word "beginning" is employed to signify "the only"—that is, the eternal verity and unity of God and man, including the universe. The creative Principle—Life, Truth, and Love—is God. The universe reflects God. There is but one creator and one creation. This creation consists of the unfolding of spiritual ideas and their identities, which are embraced in the infinite Mind and forever reflected. These ideas range from the infinitesimal to infinity, and the highest ideas are the sons and daughters of God.

Genesis 1:27. So God created man in His own image, in the image of God created He him; male and female created He them.

Ideal man and woman: To emphasize this momentous thought, it is repeated that God made man in His own image, to reflect the divine Spirit. It follows that man is a generic term. Masculine, feminine, and neuter genders are human concepts. In one of the ancient languages the word for "man" is used also as the synonym of "mind." This definition has been weakened by anthropomorphism, or a humanization of Deity. The word "anthropomorphic," in such a phrase as "an anthropomorphic God," is derived from two Greek words, signifying "man" and "form," and may be defined as a mortally mental attempt to reduce Deity to corporeality. The life-giving quality of Mind is Spirit, not matter. The ideal man corresponds to creation, to intelligence, and to Truth. The ideal woman corresponds to Life and to Love. In divine Science, we have not as much authority for considering God masculine, as we have for considering Him feminine, for Love imparts the clearest idea of Deity.

Divine personality: The world believes in many persons; but if God is personal, there is but one person, because there is but one God. His personality can only be reflected, not transmitted. God has countless ideas, and they all have one Principle and parentage. The only proper symbol of God as person is Mind's infinite ideal. What is this ideal? Who shall behold it? This ideal is God's own image, spiritual and infinite. Even eternity can never reveal the whole of God, since there is no limit to infinitude or to its reflections.

Science and Health with Key to the Scriptures, "Genesis."

Two Testimonials to Healing

Testimonies to spiritual healing have been commonplace in Christian Science from the very beginning. These two testimonials, like all the others, relate healing directly to the reading and use of Eddy's *Science and Health.* As the first paragraph implies, this section was added to the first editions of *Science and Health* to create the fuller book.

Science and Health with Key to the Scriptures, "Fruitage."

Thousands of letters could be presented in testimony of the healing efficacy of Christian Science and particularly concerning the vast number of people who have been reformed and healed through the perusal or study of this book. For the assurance and encouragement of the reader, a few of these letters are here republished from *The Christian Science Journal* and *Christian Science Sentinel*. The originals are in the possession of the Editor, who can authenticate the testimonials which follow....

Cancer and Consumption [tuberculosis] Healed: I was a great sufferer for many years from internal cancer and consumption. I was treated by the best of physicians in New York, Minneapolis, and Duluth, and was finally given up as incurable, when I heard of Christian Science. A neighbor who had been healed of consumption, kindly loaned me *Science and Health* by Mrs. Eddy, which I read and became interested in. In three months' time, I was healed, the truth conveyed to me by this book being the healer, and not only of these diseases, but I was made whole mentally as well. I have not been in bed one day since, or rather in eleven years. I have had many good demonstrations during this time, have passed through many a "fiery trial," but this blessed truth has caused me to stand, at times seemingly alone, and God was with me.

I will also mention a demonstration of painless childbirth that I have had since coming to Idaho. Perhaps it may help some sister who is looking through the *Journal* for a demonstration of this kind, as I was before my baby came. Good help being scarce here, I did my housework up to the time I was confined, and was in perfect health. I awoke my husband one morning at five o'clock, and at half past five baby was born, no one being present but my husband and myself. It was quite a surprise to the rest of the family to see me sitting by the fire with a new baby on my lap. My son got the breakfast, of which I ate heartily; at noon I joined the family in the dining room. I was out on the porch the second day, around the yard the third day, and have been perfectly well ever since, which has been now over three years. To one who had

previously passed through agony untold, with a physician in attendance, this seemed wonderful. I hope this will interest some one who is seeking the truth, and I wish to express my sincere love for our beloved Leader, who has given us the *Key to the Scriptures*.—E. C. C., Lewiston, Idaho.

Saved from Insanity and Suicide: A few years ago, while under a sense of darkness and despair caused by ill health and an unhappy home, *Science and Health* was loaned me with a request that I should read it. At that time my daughter was given up by [physicians] to die of lingering consumption, supposed to have been inherited.

My own condition seemed even more alarming, as insanity was being manifested, and rather than go to an insane asylum, it seemed to me the only thing to do was to commit suicide. Heart trouble, kidney complaint, and continual headaches caused from female trouble were some of the many ailments I had to contend with. My doctor tried to persuade me to undergo an operation as a means of relief, but I had submitted to a severe operation ten years previous, and found only additional suffering as a result, so I would not consent.

When I began with *Science and Health,* I read the chapter on "Prayer" first, and at that time did not suppose it possible for me to remember anything I read, but felt a sweet sense of God's protection and power, and a hope that I should at last find Him to be what I so much needed, a present help in time of trouble. Before that chapter on "Prayer" was finished, my daughter was downstairs eating three meals a day, and daily growing stronger. Before I had finished reading the textbook she was well, but never having heard that the reading of *Science and Health* healed any one, it was several months before I gave God the glory. One by one my many ailments left me, all but the headaches; they were less frequent, until at the end of three years the fear of them was entirely overcome. Neither myself nor my daughter have ever received treatments, but the study of the Bible and *Science and Health,* the Christian Science textbook by Mrs. Eddy, has healed us and keeps us well.—E. J. B., Superior, Wisconsin

THE SCRIPTURE
OF THE UNIFICATION CHURCH

Dual Characteristics
of the Universe and of Human Beings

The beginning of Sun Myung Moon's *Divine Principle* relates the principles of creation. Dual characteristics are built into everything in the world, reflecting the nature of God. The yin-yang explanation shows Moon's concern to combine Christianity and Asian thought, especially in their Korean forms.[8]

Let us begin by pointing out the common elements which are found universally throughout the natural world. Every entity possesses dual characteristics of *yang* (masculinity) and *yin* (femininity) and comes into existence only when these characteristics have formed reciprocal relationships, both within the entity and between it and other entities. For example, subatomic particles, the basic building blocks of all matter, possess either a positive charge, a negative charge, or a neutral charge formed by the neutralization of positive and negative constituents. When particles join with each other through the reciprocal relationships of their dual characteristics, they form an atom. Atoms, in turn, display either a positive or a negative valence. When the dual characteristics within one atom enter into reciprocal relationships with those in another atom, they form a molecule. Molecules formed in this manner engage in further reciprocal relationships between their dual characteristics to eventually become nourishment fit for consumption by plants and animals.

Plants propagate by means of stamen and pistil. Animals multiply and maintain their species through the relationship between males and females. According to the Bible, after God created Adam, He saw that it was not good for the man to live alone. Only after God created Eve as Adam's female counterpart did He declare that His creations were "very good." Let us take human beings as an example. A human being is composed of an outer form, the body, and an inner quality, the mind. The body is a visible reflection of the invisible mind. Because the mind possesses a certain structure, the body which reflects it also takes on a particular appearance. This is the idea behind a person's character and destiny being perceived through examining his outward appearance by such methods as physiognomy[9] or palm reading. Here, mind is the internal nature and body is the external form. Mind and body are two correlative aspects of a human being; hence, the body may be understood as a second mind. Together, they constitute the dual characteristics of a human being. Similarly, all beings exist through the reciprocal relationships between their dual characteristics of internal nature and external form.

[8]All excerpts from *Divine Principle* are taken from its third edition (New York: HAS-UWC Press, 1996). Copyright © 1996 the Holy Spirit Association for the Unification of World Christianity. Used by permission.

[9]*physiognomy:* a study of external physical characteristics to determine one's character or destiny.

Divine Principle 1.1.1.1.

The Purpose of the Creation of the Universe

Why did God create the world—or as one modern philosopher has asked in a nonreligious mode, why is there something rather than nothing? Sun Myung Moon states here that God created the universe for God's own enjoyment.

It is recorded in the Bible that after God completed each day of creation, He saw that it was good. This suggests that God wanted His creations to be object partners embodying goodness that He might take delight in them. How can the creation give God the greatest joy?

God created human beings as the final step in creating the universe. He created them in His image, in the likeness of His internal nature and external form, and gave them sensibility to all feelings and emotions because it was His intention to share joy with them. After their creation, God blessed Adam and Eve: Be fruitful and multiply, and fill the earth and subdue it; and have dominion over the fish of the sea and over the birds of the air and over every living thing that moves upon the earth (*Genesis* 1:28). These are the *three great blessings:* to be fruitful (mature and ready to bear fruit), multiply, and have dominion over the creation. Had Adam and Eve obeyed this divine mandate and built the Kingdom of Heaven, there is no doubt that God would have felt the greatest joy as His sons and daughters rejoiced in the world of His ideal.

How can God's three great blessings be fulfilled? They can be realized only when the four position foundation, which is the fundamental foundation of creation, has been established. The three great blessings are fulfilled when the whole creation, including human beings, completes the ... foundation with God as the center. This is the Kingdom of Heaven, where ultimate goodness is realized and God feels the greatest joy. This is, in fact, the very purpose for which God created the universe.

The ultimate purpose of the universe, with human beings at its center, is to return joy to God. All entities have dual purposes. As was explained earlier, every entity has dual centers of movement, one of internal nature and another of external form. These centers pursue corresponding purposes—for the sake of the whole and for the sake of the individual—whose relationship is the same as that between internal nature and external form. These dual purposes relate to each other as cause and result, internal and external, subject partner and object partner. In God's ideal, there cannot be any individual purpose which does not support the whole purpose, nor can there be any whole purpose that does not guarantee the interests of the individual. The infinite variety of beings in the universe form one vast organic body interwoven by these dual purposes.

Divine Principle 1.1.3.1.

The Spiritual and Physical Falls of Adam and Eve

Duality of being and action leads to duality in the human fall. Moon's emphasis on the key role of sexual intercourse in the fall itself (largely unknown in Jewish, Christian, and Islamic traditions) ties into his prescription for the salvation of the world by the propagating of a true, heavenly family on earth.

God created human beings with two components: the spirit self and the physical self. The human Fall likewise took place in two dimensions: the spiritual and the physical. The fall which took place through the sexual relationship between the angel and Eve was the *spiritual fall*, while the fall which occurred through the sexual relationship between Eve and Adam was the *physical fall....*

(The Spiritual Fall:) God created the angelic world and assigned Lucifer (*Isaiah* 14:12) to the position of archangel. Lucifer was the channel of God's love to the angelic world, just as Abraham was the channel of God's blessing to the Israelites. In this position he virtually monopolized the love of God. However, after God created human beings as His children, He loved them many times more than He had ever loved Lucifer, whom He had created as His servant. In truth, God's love toward Lucifer did not change; it was the same before and after the creation of human beings.... Lucifer, feeling as though he were receiving less love than he deserved, wanted to grasp the same central position in human society as he enjoyed in the angelic world, as the channel of God's love. This was why he seduced Eve, and this was the motivation of the spiritual fall.

Everything in the universe is created to be governed by God through love. Thus, love is the source of life, the key to happiness, and the essence of the ideal to which all beings aspire. The more one receives love, the more beautiful one appears to others. When the angel, created

as God's servant, beheld Eve, the daughter of God, it was only natural that she looked beautiful in his eyes. Moreover, when Lucifer saw that Eve was responding to his temptation, the angel felt the stimulation of her love to be deliciously enticing. At this point, Lucifer was seducing Eve with the mind to have her, regardless of the consequences. Lucifer, who left his proper position due to his excessive desire, and Eve, who wanted to open her eyes and become like God (*Genesis* 3:5–6) before the time was ripe, formed a common base and began give and take action. The power of the unprincipled love generated by their give and take led them to consummate an illicit sexual relationship on the spiritual plane.

All beings are created based on the principle that when they become one in love, they exchange elements with each other. Accordingly, when Eve became one with Lucifer through love, she received certain elements from him. First, she received feelings of dread arising from the pangs of a guilty conscience, stemming from her violation of the purpose of creation. Second, she received from Lucifer the wisdom which enabled her to discern that her originally intended spouse was to be Adam, not the angel. Eve was in the position to receive wisdom from the Archangel because she was immature and her wisdom was not as seasoned as that of the Archangel, who was already in a state of angelic maturity.

(The Physical Fall:) Perfect Adam and Eve were supposed to have become an eternal

---

Divine Principle 1.2.2.1–2.

husband and wife in God's love. But Eve, who in her immaturity had engaged in the illicit relationship with the Archangel, joined with Adam as husband and wife. Thus, Adam fell when he, too, was still immature. This untimely conjugal relationship in satanic love between Adam and Eve constituted the physical fall. . . . Eve then seduced Adam with the hope that by uniting with him, her intended spouse, she could rid herself of the dread and once again stand before God. This was Eve's motivation which led to the physical fall.

Once Eve had united with the Archangel through their illicit sexual relationship, she stood in the position of the Archangel with respect to Adam. Thus, Adam, who was still receiving

God's love, appeared very attractive to her. Seeing Adam as her only hope of returning to God, Eve turned to Adam and tempted him, playing the same role as the Archangel had played when he had tempted her. Adam responded and formed a common base with Eve, and they began give and take action with each other. The power of the unprincipled love generated in their relationship induced Adam to abandon his original position and brought them together in an illicit physical relationship of sexual love. When Adam united in oneness with Eve, he inherited all the elements Eve had received from the Archangel. These elements in turn have been passed down to all subsequent generations without interruption.

The Restoration of Humanity

Fallen humans cannot restore the creation to achieve its purpose. Only with a new group of humans, a new human family sprung from True Parents, can the Kingdom of Heaven come about. Notice the emphasis on moral perfectionism, often a hallmark of new religious movements.

We dwell in ignorance of history, uncertain about its origin, the direction in which it is heading, and its final destination. Concerning eschatology, or the doctrine of the "Last Days," many Christians believe literally what is written in the Bible. . . . One pertinent question for Christians is whether these events will take place literally or whether the verses are symbolic, as are many parts of the Bible. To address this issue, we should first understand such fundamental matters as the purpose of God's creation, the meaning of the human Fall, and the goal of the providence of restoration.

[1.1] We have discussed how God's purpose in creating human beings was to rejoice with them. Thus, our purpose of existence is to bring joy to God. What must we do to bring joy to God and fully manifest our original value? Created beings other than humans are

endowed with the innate nature to grow to maturity naturally and become object partners which bring God joy. Human beings, on the other hand, can become true and authentic object partners who bring joy to God only through their free will and free actions. . . .

The relationship between God and a person who has attained individual perfection can be compared to that between the mind and the body. The body is the dwelling place of the mind and moves according to the mind's direction. Likewise, God abides within the mind of a fully mature person. Such a person becomes a temple of God and leads his life in harmony with His Will. . . . Living in oneness with God, he acquires a divine nature. Thus, it is impossible for him to commit sin or to fall. A person who has perfected his individual character embodies total goodness and fulfills the purpose of creation.

Divine Principle 1.3, Introduction.

If a person embodying total goodness could fall, this would lead to the illogical conclusion that goodness contains the seed of its own destruction. Moreover, if human beings, who were created by the all-powerful God, could fall even after becoming perfect, we would have reason to doubt the omnipotence of God. God is the absolute and eternal Subject. To give Him true joy, His object partner must necessarily also be eternal and absolute. For these reasons, a person who has perfected his individual character can never fall. Had Adam and Eve reached perfection, being thereafter unsusceptible to sin, they would have borne good children and founded a sinless family and society in complete concordance with God's blessings. They would have founded the Kingdom of Heaven, which consists of one great family with the same parents.....

Regardless of the purity of the people of this society, if they were living in primitive circumstances like cavemen, this could not be considered the Kingdom of Heaven which both God and human beings desire. God gave us the mandate to have dominion over all things. Hence, to realize the ideal of creation, people of perfected character should advance science, harness the natural world, and create an extremely pleasant social and living environment. This will be the Kingdom of Heaven on earth. Once people have attained full maturity and enjoyed life in God's earthly Kingdom, then when they shed their physical bodies and pass into the spirit world, they will form the Kingdom of Heaven in heaven. Accordingly, God's primary purpose of creation is to build the Kingdom of Heaven on earth.

Salvation Through the Second Messiah, the True Parent

This short reading presents the essence of the Unification teaching of salvation, achievable by following the Second Messiah, the True Parent who will begin a new, perfect human family that will usher in the Kingdom of Heaven.

The *providence of restoration* refers to God's work to restore human beings to our original, unfallen state so that we may fulfill the purpose of creation. As discussed in Part I, human beings fell from the top of the growth stage and have been held under Satan's dominion ever since. To restore human beings, God works to cut off Satan's influence. Yet, as was explained in Christology, we must have the original sin removed before we can sever Satan's bonds and be restored to the state before the Fall. This is possible only when we are born anew through the Messiah,

the True Parent. To explain further: we first need to go through a course to separate Satan from ourselves. We do this in order to restore ourselves in form to the spiritual level which Adam and Eve had reached before the Fall—the top of the growth stage. On this foundation, we are to receive the Messiah and be reborn, and thereby be fully restored to the original state of human beings before the Fall. Finally, by following the Messiah, we should continue our growth to maturity where we can fulfill the purpose of creation.

Divine Principle 2, Introduction.

The Advent of the Second Messiah as a Korean

In Unification thought, which now explicitly identifies Sun Myung Moon as the Second Messiah, this Messiah "returns" by being born as a human. He finishes the work that Jesus began and founds the Kingdom of Heaven on earth by means of propagating a "True Family." The first part of this reading defends Moon's knowledge of the end times against traditional Christian teaching that it is hidden from human knowledge. The second part advances the idea that when the Second Messiah comes, he will come from Korea.

Jesus clearly foretold his return. Yet he added that no one knew of the day and hour of his return, not the angels, not even himself (*Matthew* 24:36). Hence, it has been commonly thought unwise to speculate about the date, place, and manner of the Second Advent. Nevertheless, we can deduce from the words of Jesus, "But of that day and hour no one knows...but the Father only," and the verse, "Surely the Lord God does nothing, without revealing his secret to his servants the prophets" (*Amos* 3:7) that God, who knows the day and hour, will surely reveal all secrets about the Second Advent to His prophets before He carries out His work....

[2.6.3.2] As Jesus explained through the parable of the vineyard, when the Jewish people, like the tenants in the parable who killed the son of their master, led Jesus to the cross, they lost their providential mission. Which nation, then, will inherit the work of God and bear its fruits? The Bible suggests that this nation is in the East.

The Book of Revelation describes the opening of a scroll sealed with seven seals... (*Revelation* 5:1–5). The Lion of the tribe of Judah signifies Christ; it is he who will open the seven seals in the Last Days. "After six of the seals are opened: Then I saw another angel ascend from the rising of the sun, with the seal of the living God, and he called with a loud voice ...saying, 'Do not harm the earth or the sea or the trees, till we have sealed the servants of our God upon their foreheads.' And I heard the number of the sealed, a hundred and forty-four thousand" (*Revelation* 7:2–4). This indicates that the seal of the living God will be placed on the foreheads of the 144,000 in the East, where the sun rises. These chosen ones will accompany the Lamb at his return. We can thus infer that the nation which will inherit the work of God and bear its fruit for the sake of the Second Advent is in the East. There Christ will be born and received by the 144,000 elect of God. Which among the nations of the East is chosen to receive the Lord?

[3.3] Since ancient times, the nations in the East have traditionally been considered to be the three nations of Korea, Japan, and China. Among them, Japan throughout its history has worshipped the sun goddess Amaterasu-omi-kami. Japan entered the period of the Second Advent as a fascist nation and severely persecuted Korean Christians. China at the time of the Second Advent was a hotbed of communism and would become a communist nation. Thus, both nations belonged to Satan's side. Korea, then, is the nation in the East where Christ will return.

Divine Principle 2.6, Introduction; 2.6.3.2–3.

GLOSSARY

Book of Mormon the main scripture of the Church of Jesus Christ of Latter-day Saints; it relates the story of the coming of ancient Israelites to the Americas and the creation of golden plates of sacred writings.

Divine Principle the main scripture of the Unification Church, written by Sun Myung Moon.

Doctrine and Covenants the third canonical writing of the Church of Jesus Christ of Latter-day Saints; it contains revelations on doctrine and "official declarations" on ending polygamy and admitting blacks to the priesthood.

Holy Writings the scriptures of Baha'i, written by the Bab, Baha'u'llah, Abdu'l-Baha, and Shogi Effendi.

new religious movements religious groups that arose since the nineteenth century and now have sufficient size, longevity, and cultural impact to merit academic study.

Pearl of Great Price the second canonical writing of the Church of Jesus Christ of Latter-day Saints; it is a selection of Joseph Smith's testimony and his translations of sacred writings.

Science and Health with Key to the Scriptures the scripture of the Christian Science Church, written by Mary Baker Eddy. "Science and Health" explains the principles of healing; "Key to the Scriptures" interprets several biblical passages in Christian Science terms.

QUESTIONS FOR STUDY AND DISCUSSION

1. How adequate is the term *new religious movement* in your view? What are its strengths and weaknesses?

2. What are the main similarities and differences between Baha'i scriptures and the *Qur'an*? In what sense are the Baha'i *Holy Writings* a successor to the *Qur'an*?

3. Critique this statement: "The *Book of Mormon* is, among all world scriptures, the most American."

4. The Church of Jesus Christ of Latter-day Saints has given the *Book of Mormon* an unofficial subtitle: "Another Testament of Jesus Christ."

What do you think was the church's reason for doing so? What might this subtitle be intended to imply about the *New Testament*?

5. Discuss the origin and growth of the Christian Science scripture from "Science and Health" to its supplement by "Key to the Scriptures" and the testimonial section "Fruitage."

6. Discuss the main teachings of the *Divine Principle*. How is it based on, and how does it depart from, the teachings of mainstream Christianity? Would you say that the Unification Church is a Christian church? Why or why not?

SCRIPTURES IN FILM

Perhaps because of their controversial nature, the stories of new religious movements are not often captured in feature films. One exception is the Latter-day Saint church, which has its own motion-picture operation (nicknamed "Mollywood"). The *Book of Mormon Movie* (vol. 1 of 2; 2004, rated PG), directed by Gary Rogers, tells roughly the first half of the *Book of Mormon*. The portrayal of this book is selective but literal. Viewers accustomed to typical Hollywood production values may be disappointed in the cinematic quality of this film, but it is worthwhile watching as an example of Mormons explaining their scriptures through the medium of film. Volume 2 of the *Book of Mormon Movie* is in production as this book is published and is scheduled for release in 2007.

SUGGESTIONS FOR FURTHER READING

Scholarship on scripture in new religious movements is slim because academic inquiry into the nature and use of their scriptures has hardly begun. For primary sources on new religious movements, many of which deal with scriptures, see especially Dereck Daschke and W. Michael Ashcroft, *New Religious Movements: A Documentary Reader* (New York: New York University Press, 2005).

On the *Book of Mormon,* see Terryl L. Givens, *By the Hand of Mormon: The American Scripture That Launched a New World Religion* (New York: Oxford University Press, 2002). Therefore, students of religion should concentrate on the scriptures themselves. Published editions of these scriptures are listed in the footnotes in this chapter, and access to most of these scriptures is available on the World Wide Web by way of the Wadsworth website accompanying this book.

COMPANION WEBSITE

Visit the *Anthology of World Scriptures* companion website at **www.thomsonedu.com** for learning tools such as map explorations, flashcards of glossary terms, learning objectives, chapter practice quizzes, links to other websites for learning and research, and chapter summaries in PowerPoint® format.

INDEX

(Note: Boldface entries indicate pages where subjects are defined in a glossary section.)